Welcome to the exciting 1st edition of
Forensic Science:
From the Crime Scene to the Crime Lab

FORENSIC SCIENCE
From the Crime Scene to the Crime Lab

Richard Saferstein

Less Science...
More Crime Scene,
More Crime Lab

Richard Saferstein has carefully adapted his classic
Criminalistics text to create a comprehensive, yet more
straightforward
and student-friendly text **for Forensic Science students.**
Forensic Science: From the Crime Scene to the Crime Lab
sets out to teach an introduction to crime scene procedures
and crime lab procedures.

Less Science...
More Crime Scene,
More Crime Lab

Table of Contents

Chapter Openers

A stunning visual element starts off each chapter, bringing the topic to life.

Dimensional Illustrations

Full-color art program helps students better understand key forensics concepts.

Open & Accessible Design

Every design detail has been carefully thought out—even the text font and open space.

Learning Tools

Learning Objectives

This feature highlights the key concepts of the chapter.

Learning Objectives

After studying this chapter you should be able to:

- Review the common types of physical evidence encountered at crime scenes
- Explain the difference between the identification and comparison of physical evidence
- Define and contrast individual and class characteristics of physical evidence
- Appreciate the value of class evidence as it relates to a criminal investigation
- List and explain the function of national databases available to forensic scientists
- Explain the purpose physical evidence plays in reconstructing the events surrounding the commission of a crime

Key Terms

Forensic-specific vocabulary is explained in the margins.

Root The root and other surrounding cells within the hair follicle provide the tools necessary to produce hair and continue its growth. Human head hair grows in three developmental stages, and the shape and size of the hair root is determined by the hair's current growth phase. The three phases of hair growth are the anagen, catagen, and telogen phases.

In the anagen phase (the initial growth phase), which may last up to six years, the root is attached to the follicle for continued growth, giving the root bulb a flame-shaped appearance (Figure 12–6[a]). When pulled from the root, some hairs in the anagen phase have a follicular tag. With the advent of DNA analysis, this follicular tag is important for individualizing hair.

Hair continues to grow, but at a decreasing rate, during the catagen phase, which can last anywhere from two to three weeks. In the catagen phase, roots typically take on an elongated appearance (Figure 12–6 [b]) as the root bulb shrinks and is pushed out of the hair follicle. Once hair growth ends, the telogen phase begins and the root takes on a club-shaped appearance (Figure 12-6[c]). Over two to six months, the hair is pushed out of the follicle, causing the hair to be naturally shed.

Identification and Comparison of Hair

Most often the prime purpose for examining hair evidence in a crime laboratory is to establish whether the hair is human or animal in origin, or to determine whether human hair retrieved at a crime scene compares with hair from a particular individual. A careful microscopic examination of hair reveals morphological features that can distinguish human hair from

anagen phase
The initial growth phase during which the hair follicle actively produces hair.

catagen phase
A transition stage between the anagen and telogen phases of hair growth.

telogen phase
The final growth phase in which hair naturally falls out of the skin.

follicular tag
A translucent piece of tissue surrounding the hair's shaft near the root that contains the richest source of DNA associated with hair.

WebExtras

With a click of the mouse, the power of the Web brings forensic principles to life.

WebExtra 2.1
Making a Photographic Record of the Crime Scene
www.prenhall.com/hsforensics

Forensics at Work

Liquid Explosives

Of the hundreds of types of explosives, most are solid. Only about a dozen are liquid. But some of those liquid explosives can be readily purchased and others can be made from hundreds of different kinds of chemicals that are not difficult to blow up ten international planes to obtain. A memo issued by federal security officials about the plot, highlighted a type of liquid explosive based on peroxide.

The most common peroxide explosive is triacetone triperoxide, or TATP, which is made from two liquids: acetone, the primary ingredient of most nail polish removers, and hydrogen peroxide, commonly used in diluted form as an antiseptic. TATP, which can be used as a detonator or a primary explosive, has been used in Qaeda-related bomb plots and by Palestinian suicide bombers.

TATP itself is a white powder made up of crystals that form when acetone and hydrogen peroxide are mixed together, usually with a catalyst added to speed the chemical reactions. But there is no need to wait for the crystals. Acetone and peroxide form an "exceedingly reactive mixture" that can be easily detonated by an electrical spark, said Neal Langerman, president of Advanced Chemical Safety, a consulting company in San Diego.

Acetone is easy to obtain; hydrogen peroxide is somewhat more difficult to obtain. The hydrogen peroxide solution sold in pharmacies is too dilute—only 3 percent—to be used in an explosive. Stronger hydrogen peroxide of 30 percent concentration can be ordered from chemical supply companies, but concentrations strong enough to generate a powerful explosion—about 70 percent—are not readily available, Dr. Langerman said.

Liquids and gels discarded by airline passengers before boarding.

"Forensics at Work" Boxes

Forensic applications provide students with examples from the real world.

Forensic Brief

Death by Radiation Poisoning

In November 2006, Alexander V. Litvinenko lay at death's doorstep in a London hospital. He was in excruciating pain and had symptoms that included hair loss, an inability to make blood cells, and gastrointestinal distress. His organs slowly failed as he lingered for three weeks before dying. British investigators soon confirmed that Litvinenko died from the intake of polonium 210, a radioactive element, in what appeared to be its first use as a murder weapon.

Litvinenko's death almost immediately set off an international uproar. Litvinenko, a former KBG operative, became a vocal critic of the Russian spy agency FSB, the domestic successor to the KGB. In 2000, he fled to London, where he was granted asylum. Litvinenko continued to voice his criticisms of the Russian spy agency and also became highly critical of Russia's President Vladimir Putin. Just before his death, Litvinenko intimated that the Prime Minister of Italy was a KGB operative.

Suspicions immediately fell onto Andrei Lugovoi and Dmitri Kovtun, business associates of Mr. Litvinenko. Lugovoi was himself a former KGB officer. On the day he fell ill, Litvinenko met Lugovoi and Kovtun at the Pine Bar of the Millennium Hotel in London. At the meeting, Mr. Litvinenko drank tea out of a teapot later found to be highly radioactive. British officials have accused Lugovoi of poisoning Litvinenko. The precise nature of the evidence against him has not been made clear, though investigators have linked him and Mr. Kovtun to a trail of polonium 210 radioactivity stretching from hotel rooms, restaurant and bars, and offices in London to Hamburg, Germany, and to British Airways planes that had flown to Moscow. Each man has denied killing Mr. Litvinenko.

Polonium 210 is highly radioactive and very toxic. By weight, it is about 250 million times as toxic as cyanide, so a particle the size of a few grains of sand could be fatal. It emits a radioactive ray known as an alpha particle. Because this form of radiation cannot penetrate the skin, polonium 210 can only be effective as a poison if it is swallowed, breathed in, or injected. The particles disperse through the body and

 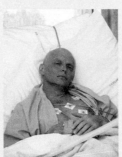

Alexander Litvinenko, former KGB agent, before and after he became sick. *Courtesy*

(Continued)

"Forensic Brief" Boxes

Linked to the chapter material, these boxes provide students with quick and pertinent facts about forensic cases.

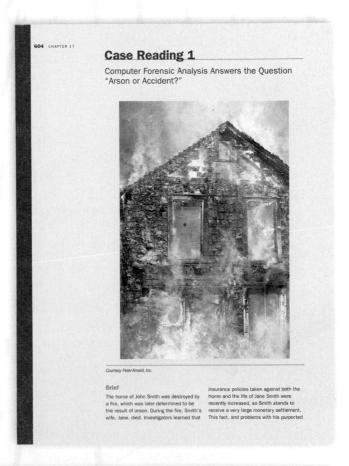

604 CHAPTER 17

Case Reading 1

Computer Forensic Analysis Answers the Question "Arson or Accident?"

Courtesy Peter Arnold, Inc.

Brief

The home of John Smith was destroyed by a fire, which was later determined to be the result of arson. During the fire, Smith's wife, Jane, died. Investigators learned that insurance policies taken against both the home and the life of Jane Smith were recently increased, so Smith stands to receive a very large monetary settlement. This fact, and problems with his purported

Case Readings

End-of-chapter in-depth cases that further explore the world of forensic science.

Engaging Forensic Cases

Each chapter begins with a gripping forensic case, showing students how that chapter relates to the real world.

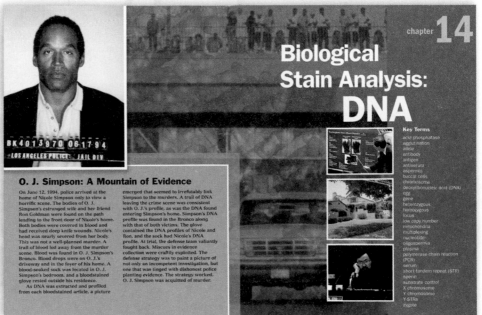

O. J. Simpson: A Mountain of Evidence

On June 12, 1994, police arrived at the home of Nicole Simpson only to view a horrific scene. The bodies of O. J. Simpson's estranged wife and her friend Ron Goldman were found on the path leading to the front door of Nicole's home. Both bodies were covered in blood and had received deep knife wounds. Nicole's head was nearly severed from her body. This was not a well-planned murder. A trail of blood led away from the murder scene. Blood was found in O. J.'s Bronco. Blood drops were on O. J.'s driveway and in the foyer of his home. A blood-soaked sock was located in O. J. Simpson's bedroom, and a bloodstained glove rested outside his residence.

As DNA was extracted and profiled from each bloodstained article, a picture emerged that seemed to irrefutably link Simpson to the murders. A trail of DNA leaving the crime scene was consistent with O. J.'s profile, as was the DNA found entering Simpson's home. Simpson's DNA profile was found in the Bronco along with that of both victims. The glove contained the DNA profiles of Nicole and Ron, and the sock had Nicole's DNA profile. At trial, the defense team valiantly fought back. Miscues in evidence collection were craftily exploited. The defense strategy was to paint a picture of not only an incompetent investigation, but one that was tinged with dishonest police planting evidence. The strategy worked. O. J. Simpson was acquitted of murder.

chapter **14**

Biological Stain Analysis: DNA

Key Terms

acid phosphatase
agglutination
allele
antibody
antigen
antiserum
aspermia
buccal cells
chromosome
deoxyribonucleic acid (DNA)
egg
gene
heterozygous
homozygous
locus
low copy number
mitochondria
multiplexing
nucleotide
oligospermia
plasma
polymerase chain reaction (PCR)
serum
short tandem repeat (STR)
sperm
substrate control
X chromosome
Y chromosome
Y-STRs
zygote

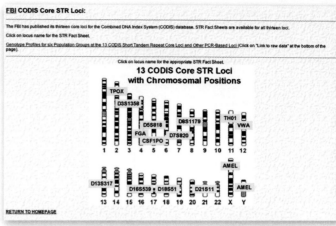

WebExtras

Interactive activities and in-depth information are just a click away. Hand-picked by the author, WebExtras deliver bonus Internet-related information.

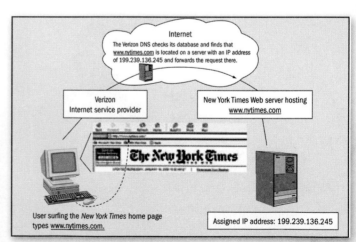

Computer Forensics

Chapter 18 shows students how computers are playing an increasingly significant role in criminal activity and the collection of forensic evidence.

Forensic Science and the Internet

There is a full chapter on the role the Web plays in modern forensic science.

Student Supplements

BASIC LABORATORY EXERCISES FOR FORENSIC SCIENCE

RICHARD SAFERSTEIN

Basic Laboratory Exercises for Forensic Science

0-13-196143-8

The Basic Laboratory Exercises workbook brings the real world of forensic science into the classroom with hands-on activities from fingerprinting, to blood stain analysis, to forensic entomology, to forensic anthropology.

Companion Website

www.prenhall.com/saferstein

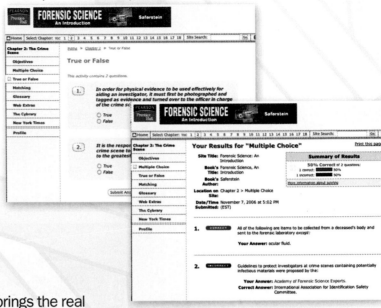

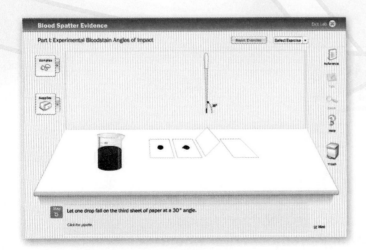

Virtual Forensic Science Labs

0-53-650267-6

- 13 Virtual Forensic Science Labs
- Interactive lab environment—no need for lab buildings or lab equipment!
- Student access labs via purchased access cards

DNA EVIDENCE CD

0-13-114469-3

Utilizing video clips and fully searchable crime scene environments, the CD-ROM asks students to make choices about how they would identify, handle, and preserve DNA evidence at each crime scene.

Instructor Supplements
(All available for online download)

Online Instructor's Manual

(download only)

Online PowerPoints

(download only)

Online TestGen

(download only)

www.pearsonhighered.com/irc

To access supplementary materials online, instructors need to request an instructor access code. Go to **www.pearsonhighered.com/irc**, where you can register for an instructor access code. Within 48 hours after registering you will receive a confirming e-mail including an instructor access code. Once you have received your code, go the site and log on for full instructions on downloading the materials you wish to use.

FORENSIC SCIENCE

From the Crime Scene to the Crime Lab

RICHARD SAFERSTEIN, Ph.D.

Forensic Science Consultant, Mt. Laurel, New Jersey

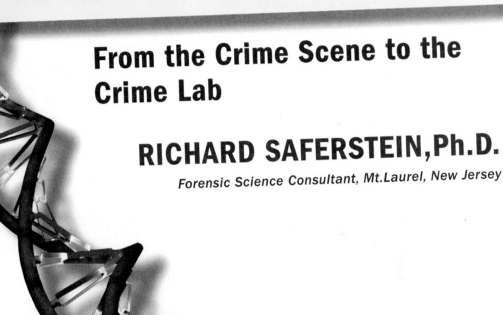

PEARSON

Prentice
Hall

Upper Saddle River, New Jersey
Columbus, Ohio

Library of Congress Cataloging-in-Publication Data
Saferstein, Richard
  Forensic science : from the crime scene to the crime lab / Richard Saferstein.
    p. cm.
  Includes bibliographical references and index.
  ISBN 0-13-515849-4 (alk. paper)
  1. Criminal investigation.   2. Crime scene searches.   3. Forensic sciences.   4. Evidence, Criminal.   I. Title.

HV8073.S214 2009
363.25—dc22   2007048119

Editor in Chief: Vernon R. Anthony
Editor: Tim Peyton
Editorial Assistant: Alicia Kelly
Production Coordination: Linda Zuk, WordCraft LLC
Project Manager: Stephen C. Robb
Senior Operations Supervisor: Pat Tonneman
Interior Design: Pronk and Associates
Art Director: Diane Ernsberger
Cover Designer: Jeff Vanik
Cover Photos: (lab technician) © Jim Craigmyle/CORBIS. All rights reserved.
  (crime sence) Courtesy Sirchie Finger Print Laboratories, Inc., Youngsville, NC, www.sirchie.com
Director, Image Resource Center: Melinda Patelli
Manager, Rights and Permissions: Zina Arabia
Manager, Visual Research: Beth Brenzel
Manager, Cover Visual Research & Permissions: Karen Sanatar
Image Permission Coordinator: Annette Linder
Director of Marketing: David Gesell
Marketing Manager: Adam Kloza
Marketing Assistant: Alicia Dysert
Copyeditor: Patsy Fortney

This book was set in Versailles by S4 Carlisle Publishing Services. It was printed and bound by Quebecor/World
Color. The cover was printed by Phoenix Color Corp.

Pearson Education Ltd., London
Pearson Education Singapore Pte. Ltd.
Pearson Education Canada, Inc.
Pearson Education—Japan

Pearson Education Australia Pty. Limited
Pearson Education North Asia Ltd., Hong Kong
Pearson Educación de Mexico, S.A. de C.V.
Pearson Education Malaysia Pte. Ltd.

10 9 8 7 6 5 4 3 2
ISBN-13:   978-0-13-515849-4
ISBN-10:   0-13-515849-4

To Mom
(1917)

and

Zave
(2007)

CONTENTS

Chapter 9

Bloodstain Pattern Analysis   251

Chapter 10

Drugs   279

Chapter 11

Forensic Toxicology   329

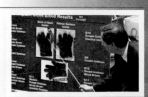

Chapter 15

Forensic Aspects of Fire Investigation   501

Chapter 16

Forensic Investigation of Explosions   527

Chapter 17

Document Examination 551

Chapter 18

Computer Forensics 577

Chapter 19

Forensic Science and the Internet 609

PREFACE

When one sets out to write a textbook on the current state of forensic science, the first thing that comes to mind is all the sophisticated high-tech devices at the disposal of the forensic analyst. A textbook devoted to this topic can quickly overwhelm the student who has little or no prior coursework in the basic sciences and who is averse to correcting this deficiency. Although a study of forensic science must include coverage of some basic scientific principles, the coverage must be presented in a fashion that will not "turn off" the student. *Forensic Science: From the Crime Scene to the Crime Lab* is designed to accomplish this objective by presenting the science of forensics in a straightforward and student-friendly format.

Topics are arranged to integrate scientific methodology with actual forensic applications. Discussions of the scientific topics are focused on explaining state-of-the-art technology without delving into extraneous theories that may bore or overwhelm the nonscience student. Only the most relevant scientific and technological concepts are presented, so as not to water down the subject with superfluous and frivolous discussions that, in the end, have no real significance or meaning to current practices in the field of forensic science.

The reader is offered the option of delving into the more difficult technical aspects of the book by reading the Closer Analysis features in the chapters. This option can be bypassed without detracting from a basic comprehension of the subject of forensic science.

Forensic science begins at the crime scene. All of the modern technologies found in today's crime laboratory are rendered impotent if appropriate evidence is not identified, documented, and properly collected at the crime scene. To this end, *Forensic Science: From the Crime Scene to the Crime Lab* devotes its initial chapters to the role of the crime-scene investigator at the crime scene. Common items of physical evidence are identified. In-depth discussions of both digital and film crime-scene photography are presented, and recognized procedures for conducting the crime-scene search are emphasized. The philosophy underlying the appropriate undertaking of a crime-scene reconstruction is detailed as exemplified by blood pattern interpretation.

It is my belief that an interactive learning environment that includes the Internet will motivate readers and encourage them to be active participants in the learning process. The text is accompanied by a Companion Website (**www.prenhall.com/saferstein**) that provides additional exercises, information, and WebExtras. The latter serve to expand the coverage of the book through video presentations and graphic displays keyed to enhancing readers' understanding of the subject's more difficult concepts.

One of the constants of forensic science is how frequently its applications become front-page news. Whether the story is sniper shootings or the tragic consequences of the terrorist attacks of 9/11, forensic science is at the forefront of the public response. In order to merge theory with practice, a good number of actual forensic case histories are included in the text. These cases are intended to capture the interest of the reader and to move forensic science from the domain of the abstract into the real world of criminal investigation.

At the end of each chapter is a chapter summary of the major points of the chapter. The summary is followed by review questions and Application and Critical Thinking exercises designed to enhance the reader's learning experience. Finally, Web resources are suggested for the readers who wish to pursue the chapter's subjects in more detail.

Acknowledgments

I am most appreciative of the contribution that Detective Sergeant Andrew (Drew) Donofrio of New Jersey's Bergen County Prosecutor's Office made to this book. I was fortunate to find in Drew a contributor who not only possesses extraordinary skill, knowledge, and hands-on experience with computer forensics, but who is able to combine those attributes with sophisticated communication skills.

Likewise, I was very fortunate to engage the services of Michelle Tetreault as my research assistant during the preparation of *Forensic Science: From the Crime Scene to the Crime Lab*. Michelle is an extraordinarily gifted student out of Cedar Crest College in Allentown, Pennsylvania. She was instrumental in helping me write and organize a number of the chapters in this text. Her skills and tenacity in carrying out her tasks are acknowledged and greatly appreciated.

Many people provided assistance and advice in the preparation of this book. Many faculty members, colleagues, and friends have read and commented on various portions of the text. I would like to acknowledge the contributions of Anita Wonder, Robert J. Phillips, Norman H. Reeves, Jeffrey C. Kercheval, Robert Thompson, Roger Ely, Jose R. Almirall, Darlene Brezinski, Gavin Edmondstone, Michael Malone, John Haley, and Chuck LeVine.

I would also like to acknowledge my editor, Tim Peyton, for supporting and encouraging all of my authorship endeavors on behalf of Pearson Education. As always, I'm appreciative of the talent and skills that my project editor, Linda Zuk, brings to the task of converting a manuscript into a finished product.

I thank the following reviewers for their insights and suggestions: Sherry Brown, York College of Pennsylvania; Larry Pressley, NMS Labs; Jerry Rose, Northwest Arkansas Community College; Jo Ann Short, Northern Virginia Community College; David Spencer, Texas State University; Michael Ullenmeyer, Santa Barbara Police Department; and Jeffrey Zack, Fayetteville Technical College.

Finally, I am grateful to those law enforcement agencies, government entities, private individuals, and equipment manufacturers cited in the text for their photographs and illustrations.

ABOUT THE AUTHOR

Richard Saferstein, Ph.D., retired in 1991 after serving 21 years as the Chief Forensic Scientist of the New Jersey State Police Laboratory, one of the largest crime laboratories in the United States. He currently acts as a consultant for attorneys and the media in the area of forensic science. During the O. J. Simpson criminal trial, Dr. Saferstein provided extensive commentary on forensic aspects of the case for the *Rivera Live* show, the E! television network, ABC radio, and various radio talk shows. Dr. Saferstein holds degrees from the City College of New York and earned his doctorate degree in chemistry in 1970 from the City University of New York. From 1972 to 1991, he taught an introductory forensic science course in the criminal justice programs at The College of New Jersey and Ocean County College. These teaching experiences played an influential role in Dr. Saferstein's authorship in 1977 of the widely used introductory textbook *Criminalistics: An Introduction to Forensic Science,* currently in its ninth edition. Dr. Saferstein's basic philosophy in writing *Forensic Science: From the Crime Scene to the Crime Lab* is to make forensic science understandable and meaningful to the nonscience reader while giving the reader an appreciation for the scientific principles that underlie the subject.

Dr. Saferstein has authored or co-authored more than 44 technical papers covering a variety of forensic topics. He authored *Basic Laboratory Exercises for Forensic Science* (Prentice Hall, 2007) and co-authored *Lab Manual for Criminalistics* (Prentice Hall 2007). He has also edited the widely used professional reference books *Forensic Science Handbook*, Volume 1, 2nd edition (Prentice Hall, 2002), *Forensic Science Handbook,* Volume 2, 2nd edition (Prentice Hall 2005), and *Forensic Science Handbook,* Volume 3 (Prentice Hall, 2009). Dr. Saferstein is a member of the American Chemical Society, the American Academy of Forensic Sciences, the Canadian Society of Forensic Scientists, the International Association for Identification, the Mid-Atlantic Association of Forensic Scientists, the Northeastern Association of Forensic Scientists, and the Society of Forensic Toxicologists.

In 2006, Dr. Saferstein received the American Academy of Forensic Sciences Paul L. Kirk award for distinguished service and contributions to the field of criminalistics.

FORENSIC SCIENCE

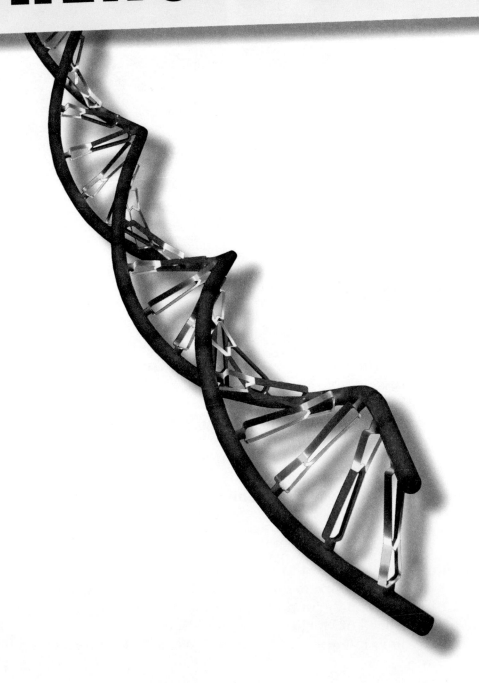

Ted Bundy, Serial Killer

The name Ted Bundy is synonymous with the term *serial killer*. This handsome, gregarious, and worldly onetime law student is believed to be responsible for forty murders between 1964 and 1978. His reign of terror stretched from the Pacific Northwest down to California and into Utah, Idaho, and Colorado, finally ending in Florida. His victims were typically young women, usually murdered with a blunt instrument or by strangulation, and sexually assaulted before and after death.

First convicted in Utah in 1976 on a charge of kidnapping, Bundy managed to escape after his extradition to Colorado on a murder charge. Ultimately, Bundy found his way to the Tallahassee area of Florida. There he unleashed mayhem, killing two women at a Florida State University sorority house and then murdering a 12-year-old girl three weeks later. Fortunately, future victims were spared when Bundy was arrested while driving a stolen vehicle. As police investigated the sorority murders, they noted that one victim, who had been beaten over the head with a log, raped, and strangled, also had bite marks on her left buttock and breast.

Supremely confident that he could beat the sorority murder charges, the arrogant Bundy insisted on acting as his own attorney. His unfounded optimism was shattered in the courtroom when a forensic odontologist matched the bite mark on the victim's buttock to Bundy's front teeth. Bundy was ultimately executed in 1989.

chapter 1

Introduction

Donna Gail Manson   Susan Elaine Rancourt

Key Terms

expert witness

Locard's exchange principle

scientific method

Learning Objectives

After studying this chapter, you should be able to:

- Define forensic science and list the major disciplines it encompasses.

- Recognize the major contributors to the development of forensic science.

- Account for the rapid growth of forensic laboratories in the past forty years.

- Describe the services of a typical comprehensive crime laboratory in the criminal justice system.

- Compare and contrast the *Frye* and *Daubert* decisions relating to the admissibility of scientific evidence in the courtroom.

- Explain the role and responsibilities of the expert witness.

- List the specialized forensic services, aside from the crime laboratory, that are generally available to law enforcement personnel.

Definition and Scope of Forensic Science

Forensic science in its broadest definition is the application of science to law. As our society has grown more complex, it has become more dependent on rules of law to regulate the activities of its members. Forensic science applies the knowledge and technology of science to the definition and enforcement of such laws.

Each year, as government finds it increasingly necessary to regulate the activities that most intimately influence our daily lives, science merges more closely with civil and criminal law. Consider, for example, the laws and agencies that regulate the quality of our food, the nature and potency of drugs, the extent of automobile emissions, the kind of fuel oil we burn, the purity of our drinking water, and the pesticides we use on our crops and plants. It would be difficult to conceive of any food and drug regulation or environmental protection act that could be effectively monitored and enforced without the assistance of scientific technology and the skill of the scientific community.

Laws are continually being broadened and revised to counter the alarming increase in crime rates. In response to public concern, law enforcement agencies have expanded their patrol and investigative functions, hoping to stem the rising tide of crime. At the same time they are looking more to the scientific community for advice and technical support for their efforts. Can the technology that put astronauts on the moon, split the atom, and eradicated most dreaded diseases be enlisted in this critical battle?

Unfortunately, science cannot offer final and authoritative solutions to problems that stem from a maze of social and psychological factors. However, as the content of this book attests, science occupies an important and unique role in the criminal justice system—a role that relates to the scientist's ability to supply accurate and objective information that reflects the events that have occurred at a crime scene. A good deal of work remains to be done if the full potential of science as applied to criminal investigations is to be realized.

Considering the vast array of civil and criminal laws that regulate society, forensic science, in its broadest sense, has become so comprehensive

FIGURE 1–1   A scene from *CSI*, a forensic science television show. *Courtesy Picture Desk, Inc./ Kobal Collection*

a subject as to make a meaningful introductory textbook treatment of its role and techniques difficult, if not overwhelming. For this reason, we must narrow the scope of the subject. Fortunately, common usage provides us with such a limited definition: **Forensic science is the application of science to the criminal and civil laws that are enforced by police agencies in a criminal justice system.** *Forensic science* is an umbrella term encompassing a myriad of professions that bring skills to bear to aid law enforcement officials in conducting their investigations.

The diversity of professions practicing forensic science is illustrated by the ten sections of the American Academy of Forensic Science, the largest forensic science organization in the world:

1. Criminalistics

2. Engineering Science

3. General

4. Jurisprudence

5. Odontology

6. Pathology/Biology

7. Physical Anthropology

8. Psychiatry and Behavioral Science

9. Questioned Documents

10. Toxicology

Even this list of professions is not exclusive. It does not encompass skills such as fingerprint examination, firearm and tool mark examination, computer and digital data analysis, and photography.

Obviously, any intent to author a book covering all of the major activities of forensic science as they apply to the enforcement of criminal and civil laws by police agencies would be a major undertaking. Thus, this book will restrict itself to discussions of the subjects of chemistry, biology, physics, geology, and computer technology, which are useful for determining the evidential value of crime-scene and related evidence. Forensic pathology, psychology, anthropology, and odontology encompass important and relevant areas of knowledge and practice in law enforcement, each being an integral part of the total forensic science service that is provided to any up-to-date criminal justice system. However, except for brief discussions, along with pointing the reader to relevent websites, these subjects go beyond the intended scope of this book, and the reader is referred elsewhere for discussions of their applications and techniques.[1] Instead, we will attempt to focus on the services of what has popularly become known as the crime laboratory, where the principles and techniques of the physical and natural sciences are practiced and applied to the analysis of crime-scene evidence.

For many, the term *criminalistics* seems more descriptive than *forensic science* for describing the services of a crime laboratory. Regardless of title—criminalist or forensic scientist—the trend of events has made the scientist in the crime laboratory an active participant in the criminal justice system.

History and Development of Forensic Science

Forensic science owes its origins first to the individuals who developed the principles and techniques needed to identify or compare physical evidence, and second to those who recognized the need to merge these principles into a coherent discipline that could be practically applied to a criminal justice system.

The roots of forensic science reach back many centuries, and history records a number of instances in which individuals used close observation of evidence and applied basic scientific principles to solve crimes. Not until relatively recently, however, did forensic science take on the more careful and systematic approach that characterizes the modern discipline.

Early Developments

One of the earliest records of applying forensics to solve criminal cases comes from third-century China. A manuscript titled *Yi Yu Ji* ("A Collection of Criminal Cases") reports how a coroner solved a case in which a woman was suspected of murdering her husband and burning the body, then claiming that he died in an accidental fire. Noticing that the husband's corpse had no ashes in its mouth, the coroner performed an experiment to test the woman's story. He burned two pigs—one alive and one dead—and then checked for ashes inside the mouth of each. He found ashes in the mouth of the pig that was alive before it was burned, but none in the mouth of the pig that was dead beforehand. The coroner thus concluded that the husband, too, was dead before his body was burned. Confronted with this evidence, the woman admitted her guilt. The Chinese were also among the first to recognize the potential of fingerprints as a means of identification.

Although cases such as that of the Chinese coroner are noteworthy, this kind of scientific approach to criminal investigation was for many years the exception rather than the rule. Limited knowledge of anatomy and pathology hampered the development of forensic science until the late seventeeth and early eighteenth centuries. For example, the first recorded notes about fingerprint characteristics were prepared in 1686 by Marcello Malpighi, a professor of anatomy at the University of Bologna in Italy. Malpighi, however, did not acknowledge the value of fingerprints as a method of identification. The first scientific paper about the nature of fingerprints did not appear until more than a century later, but that work also did not recognize their potential as a form of identification.

Initial Scientific Advances

As physicians gained a greater understanding of the workings of the body, the first scientific treatises on forensic science began to appear, such as the 1798 work "A Treatise on Forensic Medicine and Public Health" by the French physician François-Emanuel Fodéré. Breakthroughs in chemistry at this time also helped forensic science take significant strides forward. In 1775, the Swedish chemist Carl Wilhelm Scheele devised the first successful test for detecting the poison arsenic in corpses. By 1806, the German chemist Valentin Ross had discovered a more precise method for detecting small amounts of arsenic in the walls of a victim's stomach. The most significant early figure in this area was Mathieu Orfila, a Spaniard who is considered the father of forensic toxicology. In 1814, Orfila published the first scientific treatise on the detection of poisons and their effects on animals. This treatise established forensic toxicology as a legitimate scientific endeavor.

FIGURE 1–2 **Mathieu Orfila.** *Courtesy The Granga Collection, New York*

The mid-1800s saw a spate of advances in several scientific disciplines that furthered the field of forensic science. In 1828, William Nichol invented the polarizing microscope. Eleven years later, Henri-Louis Bayard formulated the first procedures for microscopic detection of sperm. Other developments during this time included the first microcrystalline test for hemoglobin (1853) and the first presumptive test for blood (1863). Such tests soon found practical applications in criminal trials. Toxicological evidence at trial was first used in 1839, when a Scottish chemist named James Marsh testified on the detection of arsenic in a victim's body. During the 1850s and 1860s, the new science of photography was also used in forensics, recording images of prisoners and crime scenes.

Late-Nineteenth-Century Progress

By the late nineteenth century, public officials were beginning to apply knowledge from virtually all scientific disciplines to the study of crime. Anthropology and morphology (the study of the structure of living organisms) were applied to the first system of personal identification, devised by the French scientist Alphonse Bertillon in 1879. Bertillon's system, which he dubbed *anthropometry,* was a systematic procedure that involved taking a series of body measurements as a means of distinguishing one individual from another. For nearly two decades, this system was considered the most accurate method of personal identification, before being replaced by fingerprinting in the early 1900s. Bertillon's early efforts earned him the distinction of being known as the father of criminal identification.

Bertillon's anthropometry, however, would soon be supplanted by the more reliable method of identification by fingerprinting. Two years before the publication of Bertillon's system, the U.S. microscopist Thomas Taylor suggested that fingerprints could be used as a means of identification, but his ideas were not immediately followed up. Three years later, the Scottish physician Henry Faulds made a similar assertion in a paper published in the journal *Nature.* However, the Englishman Francis Henry Galton undertook the first definitive study of fingerprints and developed a methodology of classifying them for filing. In 1892, Galton published a book titled *Finger Prints,* which contained the first statistical proof supporting the uniqueness of his method of personal identification. His work went on to describe the basic principles that form the present system of identification by fingerprints.

The first treatise describing the application of scientific disciplines to the field of criminal investigation was written by Hans Gross in 1893. Gross, a public prosecutor and judge in Graz, Austria, spent many years studying and developing principles of criminal investigation. In his classic book, *Handbuch für Untersuchungsrichter als System der Kriminalistik* (later published in English under the title *Criminal Investigation*), he detailed the assistance that investigators could expect from the fields of microscopy, chemistry, physics, mineralogy, zoology, botany, anthropometry, and fingerprinting. He later introduced the forensic journal *Archiv für Kriminal Anthropologie und Kriminalistik,* which still reports improved methods of scientific crime detection.

Ironically, the best-known figure in nineteenth-century forensics was not a real person, but a fictional character, the legendary detective Sherlock Holmes. Many people today believe that Holmes's creator, Sir Arthur Conan Doyle, had a considerable influence on popularizing scientific crime-detection methods. In adventures with his partner and biographer,

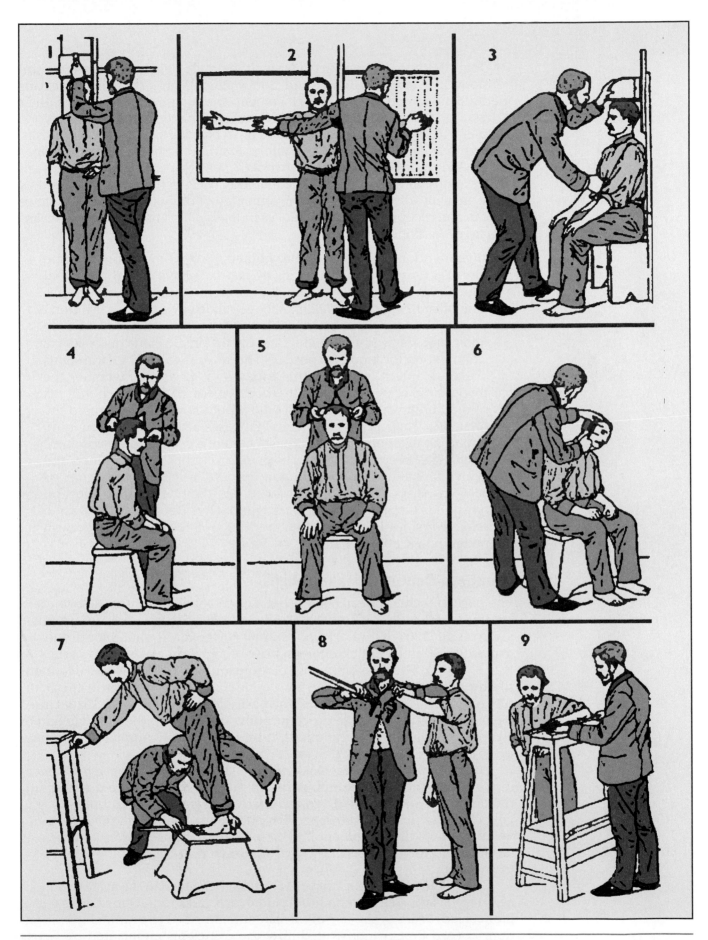

FIGURE 1–3 Bertillon's system of bodily measurements as used for the identification of an individual. *Courtesy Sirchie Finger Print Laboratories, Inc., Youngsville, N.C., www.sirchie.com*

Dr. John Watson, Holmes first applied the newly developing principles of serology (the study of blood and bodily fluids), fingerprinting, firearms identification, and questioned-document examination long before their value was recognized and accepted by real-life criminal investigators. Holmes's feats excited the imagination of an emerging generation of forensic scientists and criminal investigators. Even in the first Sherlock Holmes novel, *A Study in Scarlet,* published in 1887, we find examples of Doyle's uncanny ability to describe scientific methods of detection years before they were actually discovered and implemented. For instance, here Holmes probes and recognizes the potential usefulness of forensic serology to criminal investigation:

> "I've found it. I've found it," he shouted to my companion, running towards us with a test tube in his hand. "I have found a reagent which is precipitated by hemoglobin and by nothing else. . . . Why, man, it is the most practical medico-legal discovery for years. Don't you see that it gives us an infallible test for blood stains? . . . The old guaiacum test was very clumsy and uncertain. So is the microscopic examination for blood corpuscles. The latter is valueless if the stains are a few hours old. Now, this appears to act as well whether the blood is old or new. Had this test been invented, there are hundreds of men now walking the earth who would long ago have paid the penalty of their crimes. . . . Criminal cases are continually hinging upon that one point. A man is suspected of a crime months perhaps after it has been committed. His linen or clothes are examined and brownish stains discovered upon them. Are they blood stains, or rust stains, or fruit stains, or what are they? That is a question which has puzzled many an expert, and why? Because there was no reliable test. Now we have the Sherlock Holmes test, and there will no longer be any difficulty."

Twentieth-Century Breakthroughs

The pace of technological change quickened considerably in the twentieth century, and with it the rate of advancement in the field of forensic science. In 1901, Dr. Karl Landsteiner discovered that blood can be grouped into different categories, now recognized as the blood types A, B, AB, and O. The possibility that blood grouping could be useful in identifying an individual intrigued Dr. Leone Lattes, a professor at the Institute of Forensic Medicine at the University of Turin in Italy. In 1915, Lattes devised a relatively simple procedure for determining the blood group of a dried bloodstain, a technique that he immediately applied to criminal investigations.

At around the same time, Albert S. Osborn was conducting pioneering work in document examination. In 1910, Osborn wrote the first significant text in this field, *Questioned Documents.* This book is still considered a primary reference for document examiners. Osborn's development of the fundamental principles of document examination was responsible for the acceptance of documents as scientific evidence by the courts.

One of the most important contributors to the field in the early twentieth century was the Frenchman Edmond Locard. Although Hans Gross was a pioneer advocate of the use of the scientific method in criminal investigation, Locard first demonstrated how the principles enunciated by Gross could be incorporated within a workable crime laboratory. Locard's formal

FIGURE 1–4 **Sir Arthur Conan Doyle's legendary detective Sherlock Holmes applied many of the principles of modern forensic science long before they were adopted widely by police.** *© Paul C. Chauncey/CORBIS. All rights reserved.*

education was in both medicine and law. In 1910, he persuaded the Lyons police department to give him two attic rooms and two assistants to start a police laboratory. During Locard's first years of work, the only available instruments were a microscope and a rudimentary spectrometer. However, his enthusiasm quickly overcame the technical and monetary deficiencies he encountered. From these modest beginnings, Locard's research and accomplishments became known throughout the world by forensic scientists and criminal investigators. Eventually he became the founder and director of the Institute of Criminalistics at the University of Lyons; this quickly developed into a leading international center for study and research in forensic science.

Locard asserted that when two objects come into contact with each other, a cross-transfer of materials occurs (**Locard's exchange principle**). He strongly believed that every criminal can be connected to a crime by dust particles carried from the crime scene. This concept was reinforced by a series of successful and well-publicized investigations. In one case, presented with counterfeit coins and the names of three suspects, Locard urged the police to bring the suspects' clothing to his laboratory. On careful examination, he located small metallic particles in all the garments. Chemical analysis revealed that the particles and coins were composed of exactly the same metallic elements. Confronted with this evidence, the suspects were arrested and soon confessed to the crime. After World War I, Locard's successes served as an impetus for the formation of police laboratories in Vienna, Berlin, Sweden, Finland, and Holland.

Locard's exchange principle
Whenever two objects come into contact with one another, materials are exchanged between them.

FIGURE 1–5 **Edmond Locard.** *Courtesy Collection of Roger-Viollet, The Image Works*

The microscope came into widespread use in forensic science during the twentieth century, and its applications grew dramatically. Perhaps the leading figure in the field of microscopy was Dr. Walter C. McCrone. During his lifetime, McCrone became the world's preeminent microscopist. Through his books, journal publications, and research institute, he was a tireless advocate for applying microscopy to analytical problems, particularly forensic science cases. McCrone's exceptional communication skills made him a much-sought-after instructor, and he educated thousands of forensic scientists throughout the world in the application of microscopic techniques. Dr. McCrone used microscopy, often in conjunction with other analytical methodologies, to examine evidence in thousands of criminal and civil cases throughout a long and illustrious career.

Another trailblazer in forensic applications of microscopy was U.S. Army Colonel Calvin Goddard, who refined the techniques of firearms examination by using the comparison microscope. Goddard's work allowed investigators to determine whether a particular gun has fired a bullet by comparing the bullet with one that has been test-fired from the suspect's weapon. His expertise established the comparison microscope as the indispensable tool of the modern firearms examiner.

Modern Scientific Advances

Since the mid-twentieth century, a revolution in computer technology has made possible a quantum leap forward in human knowledge. The resulting explosion of scientific advances has dramatically impacted the field of forensic science by introducing a wide array of sophisticated techniques for analyzing evidence related to a crime. Procedures such as chromatography, spectrophotometry, and electrophoresis (all discussed in later chapters) allow the modern forensic scientist to determine with astounding accuracy the identity of a suspect substance, and to connect even tiny fragments of evidence to a particular person and place.

The most significant modern advance in forensic science undoubtedly has been the discovery and refinement of DNA typing in the late twentieth and early twenty-first centuries. Sir Alec Jeffreys developed the first DNA profiling test in 1984, and two years later he applied it for the first time to solve a crime by identifying Colin Pitchfork as the murderer of two young English girls. The same case also marked the first time DNA profiling established the innocence of a criminal suspect. Made possible by scientific breakthroughs in the 1950s and 1960s, DNA typing offers law enforcement officials a powerful tool for establishing the precise identity of a suspect, even when only a small amount of physical evidence is available. Combined with the modern analytical tools mentioned earlier, DNA typing has revolutionized the practice of forensic science.

Another significant recent development in forensics is the establishment of computerized databases on physical evidence such as fingerprints, markings on bullets and shell casings, and DNA. These databases have proven to be invaluable, enabling law enforcement officials to compare evidence found at crime scenes to records of thousands of pieces of similar information. This has significantly reduced the time required to analyze evidence and increased the accuracy of the work done by police and forensic investigators.

FIGURE 1–6 Sir Alec Jeffreys. *Courtesy Homer Sykes, Alamy Images Royalty Free*

Although this brief narrative is by no means a complete summary of historical advances in forensics, it provides an idea of the progress made in the field by dedicated scientists and law enforcement personnel. Even Sherlock Holmes probably couldn't have imagined the lengths to which science today is applied in the service of criminal investigation.

Key Points

- Forensic science is the application of science to criminal and civil laws that are enforced by police agencies in a criminal justice system.

- The first system of personal identification was called anthropometry. It distinguished one individual from another based on a series of body measurements.

- Forensic science owes its origins to individuals such as Bertillon, Galton, Lattes, Goddard, Osborn, and Locard, who developed the principles and techniques needed to identify or compare physical evidence.

- Locard's exchange principle states that when two objects come into contact with each other, a cross-transfer of materials occurs that can connect a criminal suspect to his or her victim.

Crime Laboratories

The steady advance of forensic science technologies during the twentieth century led to the establishment of the first facilities specifically dedicated to forensic analysis of criminal evidence. These crime laboratories are now the centers for both forensic investigation of ongoing criminal cases and research into new techniques and procedures to aid investigators in the future.

History of Crime Labs in the United States

The oldest forensic laboratory in the United States is that of the Los Angeles Police Department, created in 1923 by August Vollmer, a police chief from Berkeley, California. In the 1930s, Vollmer headed the first U.S. university institute for criminology and criminalistics at the University of California at Berkeley. However, this institute lacked any official status in the university until 1948, when a school of criminology was formed. The famous criminalist Paul Kirk was selected to head its criminalistics department. Many graduates of this school have gone on to develop forensic laboratories in other parts of the state and country.

In 1932, the Federal Bureau of Investigation (FBI), under the directorship of J. Edgar Hoover, organized a national laboratory that offered forensic services to all law enforcement agencies in the country. During its formative stages, Hoover consulted extensively with business executives, manufacturers, and scientists, whose knowledge and experience guided the new facility through its infancy. The FBI Laboratory is now the world's largest forensic laboratory, performing more than one million examinations every year. Its accomplishments have earned it worldwide recognition, and its structure and organization have served as a model for forensic laboratories formed at the state and local levels in the United States as well as in other countries. Furthermore, the opening of the FBI's Forensic Science Research and Training Center in 1981 gave the United States, for the

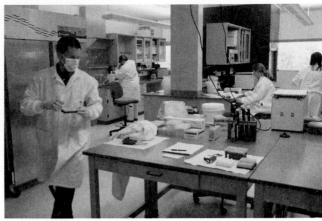

(a)   (b)

FIGURE 1–7 **(a) Exterior and (b) interior views of the FBI crime laboratory in Quantico, Virginia.** *Courtesy AP Wide World Photos*

first time, a facility dedicated to conducting research to develop new and reliable scientific methods that can be applied to forensic science. This facility is also used to train crime laboratory personnel in the latest forensic science techniques and methods.

Despite the existence of the FBI Laboratory, the United States has no national system of forensic laboratories. Instead, many local law enforcement jurisdictions—city, county, and state—around the country each operate their own independent crime labs. California, for example, has numerous federal, state, county, and city crime laboratories, many of which operate independently. However, in 1972 the California Department of Justice created a network of integrated state-operated crime laboratories consisting of regional and satellite facilities. An informal exchange of information and expertise occurs within California's criminalist community through a regional professional society, the California Association of Criminalists. This organization was the forerunner of a number of regional organizations that have developed throughout the United States to foster cooperation among the nation's growing community of criminalists.

Organization of a Crime Laboratory

The development of crime laboratories in the United States has been characterized by rapid growth accompanied by a lack of national and regional planning and coordination. Approximately 350 public crime laboratories operate at various levels of government—federal, state, county, and municipal. The size and diversity of crime laboratories make it impossible to select any one model that best describes a typical crime laboratory. Although most of these facilities function as part of a police department, others operate under the direction of the prosecutor's or district attorney's office; some work with the laboratories of the medical examiner or coroner. Far fewer are affiliated with universities or exist as independent agencies in government. Laboratory staff sizes range from one person to more than 100, and their services may be diverse or specialized, depending on the responsibilities of the agency that houses the laboratory.

The Growth of Crime Laboratories

Crime laboratories have mostly been organized by agencies that either foresaw their potential application to criminal investigation or were pressed by the increasing demands of casework. Several reasons explain the unparalleled growth of crime laboratories during the past forty years. Supreme Court decisions in the 1960s compelled police to place greater emphasis on securing scientifically evaluated evidence. The requirement to advise criminal suspects of their constitutional rights and their right of immediate access to counsel has all but eliminated confessions as a routine investigative tool. Successful prosecution of criminal cases requires a thorough and professional police investigation, frequently incorporating the skills of forensic science experts. Modern technology has provided forensic scientists with many new skills and techniques to meet the challenges accompanying their increased participation in the criminal justice system.

Coinciding with changing judicial requirements has been the staggering increase in crime rates in the United States over the past forty years. This factor alone would probably have accounted for the increased use of crime laboratory services by police agencies, but only a small percentage of police investigations generate evidence requiring scientific examination. There is, however, one important exception to this observation: drug-related arrests. All illicit-drug seizures must be sent to a forensic laboratory for confirmatory chemical analysis before the case can be adjudicated. Since the mid-1960s, drug abuse has accelerated to nearly uncontrollable levels and has resulted in crime laboratories being inundated with drug specimens.

A more recent impetus leading to the growth and maturation of crime laboratories has been the advent of DNA profiling. Since the early 1990s, this technology has progressed to the point at which traces of bloodstains, semen stains, hair, and saliva residues left behind on stamps, cups, bite marks, and so on, have made possible the individualization or near-individualization of biological evidence. To meet the demands of DNA technology, crime labs have expanded staff and in many cases modernized their physical plants. Although drug cases still far outnumber DNA cases, the labor-intensive demands and sophisticated technology requirements of the latter have affected the structure of the forensic laboratory as has no other technology in the past fifty years. Likewise, DNA profiling has become the dominant factor in explaining how the general public perceives the workings and capabilities of the modern crime laboratory.

In coming years an estimated ten thousand forensic scientists will be added to the rolls of both public and private forensic laboratories to process crime-scene evidence for DNA and to acquire DNA profiles, as mandated by state laws, from the hundreds of thousands of individuals convicted of crimes. This will more than double the number of scientists currently employed by forensic laboratories in the United States. These DNA profiles are continually added to state and national DNA data banks, which have proven to be invaluable investigative resources for law enforcement. The United States has a substantial backlog of samples requiring DNA analysis. Approximately 200,000 to 300,000 convicted-offender samples and more than 540,000 evidentiary samples, for which no suspect has been located, remain to be analyzed nationwide.

Crime Laboratories in the United States   Historically, a federal system of government, combined with a desire to retain local control, has produced a variety of independent laboratories in the United States, precluding the creation of a national system. Crime laboratories to a large extent mirror the fragmented law enforcement structure that exists on the national, state, and local levels. The federal government has no single law enforcement or investigative agency with unlimited jurisdiction.

Four major federal crime laboratories have been created to help investigate and enforce criminal laws that extend beyond the jurisdictional boundaries of state and local forces. The FBI (Department of Justice) maintains the largest crime laboratory in the world. An ultramodern facility housing the FBI's forensic science services is located in Quantico, Virginia. Its expertise and technology support its broad investigative powers. The Drug Enforcement Administration laboratories (Department of Justice) analyze drugs seized in violation of federal laws regulating the production, sale, and transportation of drugs. The laboratories of the Bureau of Alcohol, Tobacco, Firearms and Explosives (Department of Justice) analyze alcoholic beverages and documents relating to alcohol and firearm excise tax law enforcement and examine weapons, explosive devices, and related evidence to enforce the Gun Control Act of 1968 and the Organized Crime Control Act of 1970. The U.S. Postal Inspection Service maintains laboratories concerned with criminal investigations relating to the postal service. Each of these federal facilities offers its expertise to any local agency that requests assistance in relevant investigative matters.

Most state governments maintain a crime laboratory to service state and local law enforcement agencies that do not have ready access to a laboratory. Some states, such as Alabama, California, Illinois, Michigan, New Jersey, Texas, Washington, Oregon, Virginia, and Florida, have developed a comprehensive statewide system of regional or satellite laboratories. These operate under the direction of a central facility and provide forensic services to most areas of the state. The concept of a regional laboratory operating as part of a statewide system has increased the accessibility of many local law enforcement agencies to a crime laboratory, while minimizing duplication of services and ensuring maximum interlaboratory cooperation through the sharing of expertise and equipment.

Local laboratories provide services to county and municipal agencies. Generally, these facilities operate independently of the state crime laboratory and are financed directly by local government. However, as costs have risen, some counties have combined resources and created multicounty laboratories to service their jurisdictions. Many of the larger cities in the United States maintain their own crime laboratories, usually under the direction of the local police department. Frequently, high population and high crime rates combine to make a municipal facility, such as that of New York City, the largest crime laboratory in the state.

Crime Laboratories Abroad Like the United States, most countries in the world have created and now maintain forensic facilities. In contrast to the American system of independent local laboratories, Great Britain has developed a national system of regional laboratories under the direction of the government's Home Office. England and Wales are serviced by six regional laboratories, including the Metropolitan Police Laboratory (established in 1935), which services London. In the early 1990s, the British Home Office reorganized the country's forensic laboratories into the Forensic Science Service and instituted a system in which police agencies are charged a fee for services rendered by the laboratory. The fees are based on "products," or a set of examinations that are packaged together and designed to be suitable for particular types of physical evidence.

The fee-for-service concept has encouraged the creation of a number of private laboratories that provide services to both police and criminal defense attorneys. One such laboratory, Forensic Alliance, has two facilities employing more than 100 forensic scientists.

In Canada, forensic services are provided by three government-funded institutes: (1) six Royal Canadian Mounted Police regional laboratories, (2) the Centre of Forensic Sciences in Toronto, and (3) the Institute of Legal Medicine and Police Science in Montreal. Altogether, more than 100 countries throughout the world have at least one laboratory facility offering forensic science services.

Services of the Crime Laboratory

Bearing in mind the independent development of crime laboratories in the United States, the wide variation in total services offered in different communities is not surprising. There are many reasons for this, including (1) variations in local laws, (2) the different capabilities and functions of the organization to which a laboratory is attached, and (3) budgetary and staffing limitations.

In recent years, many local crime laboratories have been created solely to process drug specimens. Often these facilities were staffed with few personnel and operated under limited budgets. Although many have expanded their forensic services, some still primarily perform drug analyses. However, even among crime laboratories providing services beyond drug identification, the diversity and quality of services rendered varies significantly. For the purposes of this text, I have arbitrarily designated the following units as those that should constitute a "full-service" crime laboratory.

Basic Services Provided by Full-Service Crime Laboratories

Physical Science Unit The physical science unit applies principles and techniques of chemistry, physics, and geology to the identification and comparison of crime-scene evidence. It is staffed by criminalists who have the expertise to use chemical tests and modern analytical instrumentation to examine items as diverse as drugs, glass, paint, explosives, and soil. In a laboratory that has a staff large enough to permit specialization, the responsibilities of this unit may be further subdivided into drug identification, soil and mineral analyses, and examination of a variety of trace physical evidence.

Biology Unit The biology unit is staffed with biologists and biochemists who identify and perform DNA profiling on dried bloodstains and other body fluids, compare hairs and fibers, and identify and compare botanical materials such as wood and plants.

Firearms Unit The firearms unit examines firearms, discharged bullets, cartridge cases, shotgun shells, and ammunition of all types. Garments and other objects are also examined to detect firearms discharge residues and to approximate the distance from a target at which a weapon was fired. The basic principles of firearms examination are also applied here to the comparison of marks made by tools.

Document Examination Unit The document examination unit studies the handwriting and typewriting on questioned documents to ascertain

FIGURE 1–8   A forensic scientist performing DNA analysis. *Courtesy Mauro Fermariello, Photo Researchers, Inc.*

FIGURE 1–9   A forensic analyst examining a firearm. *Courtesy Mediacolors, Alamy Images*

authenticity and/or source. Related responsibilities include analyzing paper and ink and examining indented writings (the term usually applied to the partially visible depressions appearing on a sheet of paper underneath the one on which the visible writing appears), obliterations, erasures, and burned or charred documents.

Photography Unit A complete photographic laboratory examines and records physical evidence. Its procedures may require the use of highly specialized photographic techniques, such as digital imaging, infrared, ultraviolet, and X-ray photography, to make invisible information visible to the naked eye. This unit also prepares photographic exhibits for courtroom presentation.

Optional Services Provided by Full-Service Crime Laboratories

Toxicology Unit The toxicology group examines body fluids and organs to determine the presence or absence of drugs and poisons. Frequently, such functions are shared with or may be the sole responsibility of a separate laboratory facility placed under the direction of the medical examiner's or coroner's office. In most jurisdictions, field instruments such as the Intoxilyzer are used to determine the alcoholic consumption of individuals. Often the toxicology section also trains operators and maintains and services these instruments.

Latent Fingerprint Unit The latent fingerprint unit processes and examines evidence for latent fingerprints when they are submitted in conjunction with other laboratory examinations.

Polygraph Unit The polygraph, or lie detector, has come to be recognized as an essential tool of the criminal investigator rather than the forensic scientist. However, during the formative years of polygraph technology, many police agencies incorporated this unit into the laboratory's administrative structure, where it sometimes remains today. In any case, its functions are handled by people trained in the techniques of criminal investigation and interrogation.

FIGURE 1–10 An individual undergoing a polygraph test. *Courtesy Woodfin Camp & Associates*

Voiceprint Analysis Unit   In cases involving telephoned threats or tape-recorded messages, investigators may require the skills of the voiceprint analysis unit to tie the voice to a particular suspect. To this end, a good deal of casework has been performed with the sound spectrograph, an instrument that transforms speech into a visual graphic display called a *voiceprint*. The validity of this technique as a means of personal identification rests on the premise that the sound patterns produced in speech are unique to the individual and that the voiceprint displays this uniqueness.

Crime-Scene Investigation Unit   The concept of incorporating crime-scene evidence collection into the total forensic science service is slowly gaining recognition in the United States. This unit dispatches specially trained personnel (civilian and/or police) to the crime scene to collect and preserve physical evidence that will later be processed at the crime laboratory.

Whatever the organizational structure of a forensic science laboratory may be, specialization must not impede the overall coordination of services demanded by today's criminal investigator. Laboratory administrators need to keep open the lines of communication between analysts (civilian and uniformed), crime-scene investigators, and police personnel. Inevitably, forensic investigations require the skills of many individuals. One notoriously high-profile investigation illustrates this process—the search for the source of the anthrax letters mailed shortly after September 11, 2001. Figure 1–11 shows one of the letters and illustrates the multitude of skills required in the investigation—skills possessed by forensic chemists and biologists, fingerprint examiners, and forensic document examiners.

WebExtra 1.1

Take a Virtual Tour of a Forensic Laboratory
www.prenhall.com/saferstein

Other Forensic Science Services

Even though this textbook is devoted to describing the services normally provided by a crime laboratory, the field of forensic science is by no means limited to the areas covered in this book. A number of specialized forensic science services outside the crime laboratory are routinely available to law enforcement personnel. These services are important aids to a criminal investigation and require the involvement of individuals who have highly specialized skills.

Three specialized forensic services—forensic pathology, forensic anthropology, and forensic entomology—are frequently employed at a murder scene and will be discussed at greater length when we examine crime-scene procedures in Chapter 2. Other services, such as those discussed next, are used in a wide variety of criminal investigations.

Forensic Psychiatry   Forensic psychiatry is a specialized area that examines the relationship between human behavior and legal proceedings. Forensic psychiatrists are retained for both civil and criminal litigations. In civil cases, they typically perform tasks such as determining whether an individual is competent to make decisions about preparing a will, settling property, or refusing medical treatment. In criminal cases, forensic psychologists evaluate behavioral disorders and determine whether defendants are competent to stand trial. Forensic psychiatrists also examine behavior patterns of criminals as an aid in developing a suspect's behavioral profile.

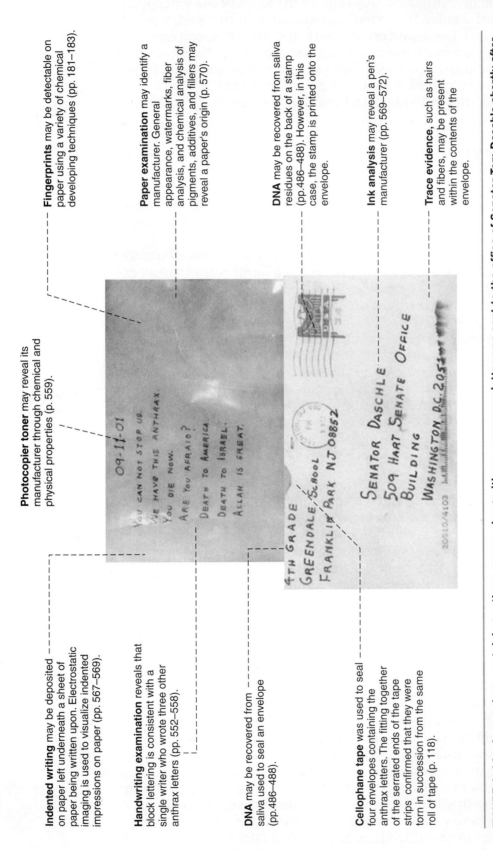

Indented writing may be deposited on paper left underneath a sheet of paper being written upon. Electrostatic imaging is used to visualize indented impressions on paper (pp. 567–569).

Handwriting examination reveals that block lettering is consistent with a single writer who wrote three other anthrax letters (pp. 552–558).

DNA may be recovered from saliva used to seal an envelope (pp.486–488).

Cellophane tape was used to seal four envelopes containing the anthrax letters. The fitting together of the serrated ends of the tape strips confirmed that they were torn in succession from the same roll of tape (p. 118).

Photocopier toner may reveal its manufacturer through chemical and physical properties (p. 559).

Fingerprints may be detectable on paper using a variety of chemical developing techniques (pp. 181–183).

Paper examination may identify a manufacturer. General appearance, watermarks, fiber analysis, and chemical analysis of pigments, additives, and fillers may reveal a paper's origin (p. 570).

DNA may be recovered from saliva residues on the back of a stamp (pp.486–488). However, in this case, the stamp is printed onto the envelope.

Ink analysis may reveal a pen's manufacturer (pp. 569–572).

Trace evidence, such as hairs and fibers, may be present within the contents of the envelope.

FIGURE 1–11   An envelope containing anthrax spores along with an anonymous letter was sent to the office of Senator Tom Daschle shortly after the terrorist attacks of September 11, 2001. A variety of forensic skills was used to examine the envelope and letter. Also, bar codes placed on the front and back of the envelope by mail-sorting machines contain address information and information about where the envelope was first processed. *Courtesy Getty Images, Inc.–Liaison*

Forensic Odontology Practitioners of forensic odontology help identify victims based on dental evidence when the body is left in an unrecognizable state. Teeth are composed of enamel, the hardest substance in the body. Because of enamel's resilience, the teeth outlast tissues and organs as decomposition begins. The characteristics of teeth, their alignment, and the overall structure of the mouth provide individual evidence for identifying a specific person. With the use of dental records such as X-rays and dental casts or even a photograph of the person's smile, a set of dental remains can be compared to a suspected victim. Another application of forensic odontology to criminal investigations is bite mark analysis. Bite marks are sometimes left on the victim in assault cases. A forensic odontologist can compare the marks left on a victim and the tooth structure of the suspect.

WebExtra 1.2
Explore Forensic Dentistry
www.prenhall.com/saferstein

Forensic Engineering Forensic engineers are concerned with failure analysis, accident reconstruction, and causes and origins of fires or explosions. Forensic engineers answer questions such as these: How did an accident or structural failure occur? Were the parties involved responsible? If so, how were they responsible? Accident scenes are examined, photographs are reviewed, and any mechanical objects involved are inspected.

Forensic Computer and Digital Analysis Forensic computer science is a new and fast-growing field that involves identifying, collecting, preserving, and examining information derived from computers and other digital devices, such as cell phones. Law enforcement aspects of this work normally involve recovering deleted or overwritten data from a computer's hard drive and tracking hacking activities within a compromised system. This field of forensic computer analysis will be addressed in detail in Chapters 18 and 19.

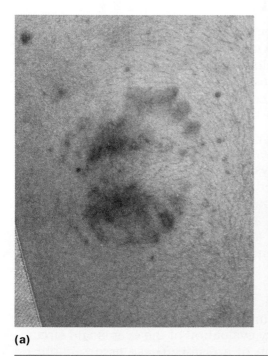
(a)

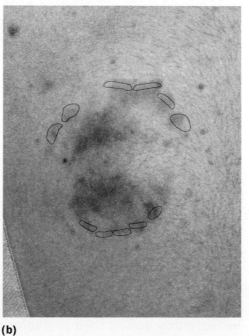
(b)

FIGURE 1–12 **(a) A bite mark on a victim's body. (b) Comparison to a suspect's teeth.**
Courtesy David Sweet, DMD, Ph.D., DABFO BOLD Forensic Laboratory, Vancouver, B.C., Canada

Key Points

- The development of crime laboratories in the United States has been characterized by rapid growth accompanied by a lack of national and regional planning and coordination.

- Four major reasons for the increase in the number of crime laboratories in the United States since the 1960s are as follows: (1) The fact that the requirement to advise criminal suspects of their constitutional rights and their right of immediate access to counsel has all but eliminated confessions as a routine investigative tool; (2) the staggering increase in crime rates in the United States; (3) the fact that all illicit-drug seizures must be sent to a forensic laboratory for confirmatory chemical analysis before the case can be adjudicated in court; and (4) the advent of DNA profiling.

- The technical support provided by crime laboratories can be assigned to five basic services: the physical science unit, the biology unit, the firearms unit, the document examination unit, and the photography unit.

- Some crime laboratories offer optional services such as toxicology, fingerprint analysis, polygraph administration, voiceprint analysis, and crime-scene investigation.

- Special forensic science services available to the law enforcement community include forensic pathology, forensic anthropology, forensic entomology, forensic psychiatry, forensic odontology, forensic engineering, and forensic computer and digital analysis.

Functions of the Forensic Scientist

Although a forensic scientist relies primarily on scientific knowledge and skill, only half of the job is performed in the laboratory. The other half takes place in the courtroom, where the ultimate significance of the evidence is determined. The forensic scientist must not only analyze physical evidence but also persuade a jury to accept the conclusions derived from that analysis.

Analyzing Physical Evidence

First and foremost, the forensic scientist must be skilled in applying the principles and techniques of the physical and natural sciences to analyze the many types of physical evidence that may be recovered during a criminal investigation. Of the three major avenues available to police investigators for assistance in solving a crime—confessions, eyewitness accounts by victims or witnesses, and the evaluation of physical evidence retrieved from the crime scene—only physical evidence is free of inherent error or bias.

Criminal cases are replete with examples of individuals who were incorrectly charged with and convicted of committing a crime because of faulty memories or lapses in judgment. For example, investigators may be led astray during their preliminary evaluation of the events and circumstances surrounding the commission of a crime. These errors might be compounded by misleading eyewitness statements and inappropriate confessions. These same concerns don't apply to physical evidence.

What about physical evidence allows investigators to sort out facts as they are and not what one wishes they were? The hallmark of physical evidence is that it must undergo scientific inquiry. Science derives its integrity from adherence to strict guidelines that ensure the careful and systematic collection, organization, and analysis of information—a process known as the **scientific method.** The underlying principles of the scientific method provide a safety net to ensure that the outcome of an investigation is not tainted by human emotion or compromised by distorting, belittling, or ignoring contrary evidence.

scientific method
A process that uses strict guidelines to ensure careful and systematic collection, organization, and analysis of information.

The scientific method begins by formulating a question worthy of investigation, such as who committed a particular crime. The investigator next formulates a hypothesis, a reasonable explanation proposed to answer the question. What follows is the basic foundation of scientific inquiry—the testing of the hypothesis through experimentation. The testing process must be thorough and recognized by other scientists as valid. Scientists and investigators must accept the experimental findings even when they wish they were different. Finally, when the hypothesis is validated by experimentation, it becomes suitable as scientific evidence, appropriate for use in a criminal investigation and ultimately available for admission in a court of law.

Determining Admissibility of Evidence   In rejecting the scientific validity of the lie detector (polygraph), the District of Columbia Circuit Court in 1923 set forth what has since become a standard guideline for determining the judicial admissibility of scientific examinations. In *Frye* v. *United States*,[2] the court ruled that in order to be admitted as evidence at trial, the questioned procedure, technique, or principles must be "generally accepted" by a meaningful segment of the relevant scientific community. In practice, this approach requires the proponent of a scientific test to present to the court a collection of experts who can testify that the scientific issue before the court is generally accepted by the relevant members of the scientific community. Furthermore, in determining whether a novel technique meets criteria associated with "general acceptance," courts have frequently taken note of books and papers written on the subject, as well as prior judicial decisions relating to the reliability and general acceptance of the technique. In recent years many observers have questioned whether this approach is sufficiently flexible to deal with new scientific issues that may not have gained widespread support within the scientific community.

The Federal Rules of Evidence offer an alternative to the *Frye* standard, one that some courts believe espouses a more flexible standard for admitting scientific evidence. Part of the Federal Rules of Evidence governs the admissibility of all evidence, including expert testimony, in federal courts, and many states have adopted codes similar to those of the Federal Rules. Specifically, Rule 702 of the Federal Rules of Evidence sets a different standard from "general acceptance" for admissibility of expert testimony. Under this standard, a witness "qualified as an expert by knowledge, skill, experience, training, or education" may offer expert testimony on a scientific or technical matter if "(1) the testimony is based upon sufficient facts or data, (2) the testimony is the product of reliable principles and methods, and (3) the witness has applied the principles and methods reliably to the facts of the case."

In a landmark ruling in the 1993 case of *Daubert* v. *Merrell Dow Pharmaceuticals, Inc.*,[3] the U.S. Supreme Court asserted that "general acceptance," or the *Frye* standard, is not an absolute prerequisite to the admissibility of scientific evidence under the Federal Rules of Evidence. According to the Court, the Rules of Evidence—especially Rule 702—assign to the trial judge the task of ensuring that an expert's testimony rests on a reliable foundation and is relevant to the case. Although this ruling applies only to federal courts, many state courts are expected to use this decision as a guideline in setting standards for the admissibility of scientific evidence.

Judging Scientific Evidence In *Daubert,* the Court advocates that trial judges assume the ultimate responsibility for acting as a "gatekeeper" in judging the admissibility and reliability of scientific evidence presented in their courts. The Court offered some guidelines as to how a judge can gauge the veracity of scientific evidence, emphasizing that the inquiry should be flexible. Suggested areas of inquiry include the following:

1. Whether the scientific technique or theory can be (and has been) tested

2. Whether the technique or theory has been subject to peer review and publication

3. The technique's potential rate of error

4. The existence and maintenance of standards controlling the technique's operation

5. Whether the scientific theory or method has attracted widespread acceptance within a relevant scientific community

Some legal experts have expressed concern that abandoning *Frye's* general-acceptance test will result in the introduction of absurd and irrational pseudoscientific claims in the courtroom. The Supreme Court rejected these concerns, pointing out the inherent strengths of the American judicial process in identifying unreliable evidence:

> In this regard the respondent seems to us to be overly pessimistic about the capabilities of the jury and of the adversary system generally. Vigorous cross-examination, presentation of contrary evidence, and careful instruction on the burden of proof are the traditional and appropriate means of attacking shaky but admissible evidence.

In a 1999 decision, *Kumho Tire Co., Ltd.* v. *Carmichael,*[4] the Court unanimously ruled that the "gatekeeping" role of the trial judge applied not only to scientific testimony, but to all expert testimony:

> We conclude that *Daubert's* general holding—setting forth the trial judge's general "gatekeeping" obligation—applies not only to testimony based on "scientific" knowledge, but also to testimony based on "technical" and "other specialized" knowledge. . . . We also conclude that a trial court may consider one or more of the more specific factors that *Daubert* mentioned when doing so will help determine that testimony's reliability. But, as the Court stated in *Daubert,* the test of reliability is "flexible," and *Daubert's* list of specific factors neither necessarily nor exclusively applies to all experts in every case.

The case of *Coppolino* v. *State*[5] (examined more closely in the following case study) exemplifies the flexibility and wide discretion that the *Daubert* ruling, twenty-five years later, apparently gave to trial judges in matters of scientific inquiry. The issue in question was whether the results of a new procedure that have not been widely accepted in the scientific community are necessarily inadmissible as evidence. The court rejected this argument, recognizing that researchers must devise new scientific tests to solve the special problems that continually arise in the forensic laboratory.

Case Study

Dr. Coppolino's Deadly House Calls

A frantic late-night telephone call to Dr. Juliette Karow brought her to the Longport Key, Florida, home of Drs. Carl and Carmela Coppolino. Carl had called for Dr. Karow's help because he believed Carmela was dying. He said she had complained of chest pains earlier in the evening, and he was certain she had suffered a heart attack. Dr. Karow arrived to find Carmela beyond help.

Although Dr. Karow felt that the scene in the room appeared staged and her own observations of Carmela's body did not support Carl's claim of heart trouble, she agreed to sign 32-year-old Carmela's death certificate. Dr. Karow cited "coronary occlusion" as the cause of death, but reported the death to the local police department. The investigating officer was satisfied that Dr. Karow had correctly listed the cause of death, so he did not apply the law that required that an autopsy be performed. The medical examiner could not order an autopsy without a request from the police or the district attorney, which was not forthcoming. Thus, Carmela Coppolino's body, unexamined by anyone, was buried in her family's plot in her home state of New Jersey.

A little more than a month later, Carl married a moneyed socialite, Mary Gibson. News of Carl's marriage infuriated Marjorie Farber, a former New Jersey neighbor of Dr. Coppolino who had been a having an affair with the good doctor. Soon Marjorie had an interesting story to recount to investigators. Her husband's death two years before, although ruled to be from natural causes, had actually been murder! Carl, an anesthesiologist, had given Marjorie a syringe containing some medication and told her to inject her husband, William, while he was sleeping. Ultimately, Marjorie claimed, she was unable to inject the full dose and called

Carl, who finished the job by suffocating William with a pillow.

In a cruel and ironic twist, Carl called his wife, Carmela, to sign William Farber's death certificate. She listed the cause of death, at Carl's insistence, as coronary artery disease. This type of death is common, especially in men in their fifties. Such deaths are rarely questioned, and the Department of Health accepted the certificate without any inquiry.

Marjorie Farber's astonishing story was supported in part by Carl's recent increase in his wife's life insurance. Carmela's $65,000 policy, along with his new wife's fortune, would keep Dr. Coppolino in high society for the rest of his life. Based on this information, authorities in New Jersey and Florida now obtained exhumation orders for both William Farber and Carmela Coppolino. After examination of both bodies, Dr. Coppolino was charged with the murders of William and Carmela.

Officials decided to try Dr. Coppolino first in New Jersey for the murder of William Farber. Coppolino was represented by the famous defense attorney F. Lee Bailey. The Farber autopsy did not reveal any evidence of poisoning, but seemed to show strong evidence of strangulation. The absence of toxicological findings left the jury to deliberate the conflicting medical expert testimony versus the sensational story told by a scorned and embittered woman. In the end, Bailey secured an acquittal for his client.

The Florida trial presented another chance to bring Carl Coppolino to justice. Florida officials called on the experienced New York City medical examiner Dr. Milton Halpern and his colleague, toxicologist Dr. Charles Umberger, to determine how Carl Coppolino had killed his wife. Recalling Dr. Coppolino's career as an

(Continued)

Case Study

Dr. Coppolino's Deadly House Calls (Continued)

anesthesiologist, Halpern theorized that Coppolino had exploited his access to the many potent drugs used during surgery to commit these murders, specifically an injectable paralytic agent called succinylcholine chloride.

After having Carmela's body exhumed, Halpern examined her body with a magnifying glass in search of an injection site. He found that Carmela had been injected in her left buttock shortly before her death. Dr. Umberger's mission as the toxicologist in this case was to prove the administration of succinylcholine chloride by chemical analysis of Carmela's tissues.

This presented a serious problem because succinylcholine was purported to be untraceable in human tissue. The drug breaks down in the body to succinic acid and choline, both of which are naturally occurring chemicals in the human body. The chemical method necessary to make this determination did not exist at the time of the murder.

Ultimately, Dr. Umberger developed a completely novel procedure for detecting succinylcholine chloride. He isolated elevated levels of succinic acid in Carmela's brain, which proved that she had received a large dose of the paralytic drug shortly before her death. This evidence, along with the finding of the same drug residues in the injection site on her buttock, was presented in the Florida murder trial of Carl Coppolino, who was convicted of second-degree murder.

On appeal, the defense raised an interesting point of law. Can a defendant be convicted of murder based on a series of tests that were specifically devised for this case? Tests that indirectly showed that Carmela had been injected with succinylcholine chloride had never before been used in a criminal trial. The court ruled that the novelty of a scientific method does not preclude its significance to a criminal prosecution. Just because an otherwise valid method was developed specifically for this trial and had not yet been proven in court did not mean that the murderer should be allowed to get away with the perfect crime. The conviction of Dr. Coppolino was upheld.

The *Coppolino* ruling acknowledged that even well-established scientific procedures were once new and unproven, and noted the court's duty to protect the public when weighing the admissibility of a new test. In the words of the concurring opinion, "Society need not tolerate homicide until there develops a body of medical literature about some particular lethal agent." The court emphasized, however, that although these tests may be new and unique, they are admissible only if they are based on scientifically valid principles and techniques.

Providing Expert Testimony

expert witness
An individual whom the court determines to possess knowledge relevant to the trial that is not expected of the average layperson.

Because the results of their work may ultimately be a factor in determining a person's guilt or innocence, forensic scientists may be required to testify about their methods and conclusions at a trial or hearing. Trial courts have broad discretion in accepting an individual as an **expert witness** on any particular subject. Generally, if a witness can establish to the satisfaction of a trial judge that he or she possesses a particular skill or has knowledge in a trade or profession that will aid the court in determining the truth of the matter at issue, that individual will be accepted as an expert witness. Depending on the subject area in question, the court will usually consider knowledge acquired through experience, training, education, or a combination as sufficient grounds for qualification as an expert witness.

In court, an expert witness may be asked questions intended to demonstrate his or her ability and competence pertaining to the matter at hand. Competency may be established by having the witness cite educational degrees, participation in special courses, membership in professional societies, and any professional articles or books published. Also important is the number of years of occupational experience the witness has in areas related to the matter before the court.

Unfortunately, few schools confer degrees in forensic science. Most chemists, biologists, geologists, and physicists prepare themselves for careers in forensic science by combining training under an experienced examiner with independent study. Of course, formal education in the physical sciences provides a firm foundation for learning and understanding the principles and techniques of forensic science. Nevertheless, for the most part, courts must rely on training and years of experience as a measurement of the knowledge and ability of the expert.

Before the judge rules on the witness's qualifications, the opposing attorney may cross-examine the witness and point out weaknesses in background and knowledge. Most courts are reluctant to disqualify an individual as an expert even when presented with someone whose background is only remotely associated with the issue at hand. The question of what credentials are suitable for qualification as an expert is ambiguous and highly subjective and one that the courts wisely try to avoid.

The weight that a judge or jury assigns to "expert" testimony in subsequent deliberations is, however, quite another matter. Undoubtedly, education and experience have considerable bearing on the value assigned to the expert's opinions. Just as important may be his or her demeanor and ability to explain scientific data and conclusions clearly, concisely, and logically to a judge and jury composed of nonscientists. The problem of sorting out the strengths and weaknesses of expert testimony falls to prosecution and defense counsel.

The ordinary or lay witness must testify on events or observations that arise from personal knowledge. This testimony must be factual and, with few exceptions, cannot contain the personal opinions of the witness. On the other hand, the expert witness is called on to evaluate evidence when the court lacks the expertise to do so. This expert then expresses an opinion as to the significance of the findings. The views expressed are accepted only as representing the expert's opinion and may later be accepted or ignored in jury deliberations (see Figure 1–13).

The expert cannot render any view with absolute certainty. At best, he or she may only be able to offer an opinion based on a reasonable scientific certainty derived from training and experience. Obviously, the expert is expected to defend vigorously the techniques and conclusions of the analysis, but at the same time must not be reluctant to discuss impartially any findings that could minimize the significance of the analysis. The forensic scientist should not be an advocate of one party's cause, but only an advocate of truth. An adversary system of justice must give the prosecutor and defense ample opportunity to offer expert opinions and to argue the merits of such testimony. Ultimately, the duty of the judge or jury is to weigh the pros and cons of all the information presented in deciding guilt or innocence.

WebExtra 1.3

Watch a Forensic Expert Witness Testify—I
www.prenhall.com/saferstein

WebExtra 1.4

Watch a Forensic Expert Witness Testify—II
www.prenhall.com/saferstein

FIGURE 1–13 **An expert witness testifying in court.** *Courtesy Jeff Siner, Corbis/Sygma*

Furnishing Training in the Proper Recognition, Collection, and Preservation of Physical Evidence

The competence of a laboratory staff and the sophistication of its analytical equipment have little or no value if relevant evidence cannot be properly recognized, collected, and preserved at the site of a crime. For this reason, the forensic staff must have responsibilities that will influence the conduct of the crime-scene investigation.

The most direct and effective response to this problem has been to dispatch specially trained evidence-collection technicians to the crime scene. A growing number of crime laboratories and the police agencies they service keep trained "evidence technicians" on 24-hour call to help criminal investigators retrieve evidence. These technicians are trained by the laboratory staff to recognize and gather pertinent physical evidence at the crime scene. They are assigned to the laboratory full-time for continued exposure to forensic techniques and procedures. They have at their disposal all the proper tools and supplies for proper collection and packaging of evidence for future scientific examination.

Unfortunately, many police forces still have not adopted this approach. Often a patrol officer or detective collects the evidence. The individual's effectiveness in this role depends on the extent of his or her training and working relationship with the laboratory. For maximum use of the skills of the crime laboratory, training of the crime-scene investigator must go beyond superficial classroom lectures to involve extensive personal contact with the forensic scientist. Each must become aware of the other's problems, techniques, and limitations.

The training of police officers in evidence collection and their familiarization with the capabilities of a crime laboratory should not be restricted to

FIGURE 1–14 Representative evidence-collection guides prepared by various governmental agencies.

a select group of personnel on the force. Every officer engaged in fieldwork, whether it be traffic, patrol, investigation, or juvenile control, often must process evidence for laboratory examination. Obviously, it would be difficult and time consuming to give everyone the in-depth training and attention that a qualified criminal investigator requires. However, familiarity with crime laboratory services and capabilities can be gained through periodic lectures, laboratory tours, and dissemination of manuals prepared by the laboratory staff that outline the proper methods for collecting and submitting physical evidence to the laboratory (see Figure 1–14).

A brief outline describing the proper collection and packaging of common types of physical evidence is found in Appendix I. The procedures and information summarized in this appendix are discussed in greater detail in forthcoming chapters.

Key Points

- A forensic scientist must be skilled in applying the principles and techniques of the physical and natural sciences to analyzing evidence that may be recovered during a criminal investigation.

- The cases *Frye* v. *United States* and *Daubert* v. *Merrell Dow Pharmaceuticals, Inc.* set guidelines for determining the admissibility of scientific evidence into the courtroom.

- An expert witness evaluates evidence based on specialized training and experience.

- Forensic scientists participate in training law enforcement personnel in the proper recognition, collection, and preservation of physical evidence.

Chapter Summary

In its broadest definition, forensic science is the application of science to criminal and civil laws. This book emphasizes the application of science to the criminal and civil laws that are enforced by police agencies in a criminal justice system. Forensic science owes its origins to a wide variety of individuals who developed the principles and techniques needed to identify or compare physical evidence.

The development of crime laboratories in the United States has been characterized by rapid growth accompanied by a lack of national and regional planning and coordination. Approximately 350 public crime laboratories operate at various levels of government—federal, state, county, and municipal.

The technical support provided by crime laboratories can be assigned to five basic services. The physical science unit uses the principles of chemistry, physics, and geology to identify and compare physical evidence. The biology unit uses knowledge of biological sciences to investigate blood samples, body fluids, hair, and fiber samples. The firearms unit investigates discharged bullets, cartridge cases, shotgun shells, and ammunition. The document examination unit performs handwriting analysis and other questioned-document examination. Finally, the photography unit uses specialized photographic techniques to record and examine physical evidence.

Some crime laboratories offer the optional services of toxicology, fingerprint analysis, polygraph administration, voiceprint analysis, and crime-scene investigation. Several special forensic science services are available to the law enforcement community to augment the services of the crime laboratory. These services include forensic pathology, forensic anthropology, forensic entomology, forensic psychiatry, forensic odontology, forensic engineering, and forensic computer and digital analysis.

A forensic scientist must be skilled in applying the principles and techniques of the physical and natural sciences to analyze the many types of evidence that may be recovered during a criminal investigation. A forensic scientist may also provide expert court testimony. An expert witness evaluates evidence based on specialized training and experience and expresses an opinion as to the significance of the findings. Also, forensic scientists participate in training law enforcement personnel in the proper recognition, collection, and preservation of physical evidence.

The *Frye* v. *United States* decision set guidelines for determining the admissibility of scientific evidence into the courtroom. To meet the *Frye* standard, the evidence in question must be "generally accepted" by the scientific community. However, in the 1993 case of *Daubert* v. *Merrell Dow Pharmaceuticals, Inc.,* the U.S. Supreme Court asserted that the *Frye* standard is not an absolute prerequisite to the admissibility of scientific evidence. Trial judges were said to be ultimately responsible as "gatekeepers" for the admissibility and validity of scientific evidence presented in their courts.

Review Questions

1. The application of science to law describes _____.

2. The Spaniard _____ published the first writings about the detection of poisons and the effects of poisons on animals, and he is considered the father of forensic toxicology.

3. A system of personal identification using a series of body measurements was first devised by _____, and he called it _____.

4. The fictional exploits of _____ excited the imagination of an emerging generation of forensic scientists and criminal investigators.

5. One of the first functional crime laboratories was formed in Lyons, France, in 1910 under the direction of _____, who developed _____, a theory stating that there is mutual transfer of material when two objects make contact with each other.

6. The application of science to criminal investigation was advocated by the Austrian magistrate _____.

7. True or False: The important advancement in the fields of blood typing and document examination were made in the early part of the twentieth century. ____

8. The Italian scientist _____ devised the first workable procedure for typing dried bloodstains.

9. Early efforts at applying scientific principles to document examination are associated with. _____

10. The first DNA profiling test was developed by _____ in 1984, and it was first used in 1986 to identify the murderer of two young English girls.

11. True or False: Computerized databases exist for fingerprints, bullets, cartridge cases, and DNA. _____

12. The first forensic laboratory in the United States was created in 1923 by the _____ Police Department.

13. Although no national system of forensic laboratories exists in the United States, the state of _____ is an excellent example of a geographical area in the United States that has created a system of integrated regional and satellite laboratories.

14. A decentralized system of crime laboratories currently exists in the United States under the auspices of various governmental agencies at the _____, _____, _____, and _____ levels of government.

15. In contrast to the United States, Britain's crime laboratory system is characterized by a national system of _____ laboratories.

16. Four important federal agencies offering forensic services are _____, _____, _____, and _____.

17. The application of chemistry, physics, and geology to the identification and comparison of crime-scene evidence is the function of the _____ unit of a crime laboratory.

18. The examination of blood, hairs, fibers, and botanical materials is conducted in the _____ unit of a crime laboratory.

19. The examination of bullets, cartridge cases, shotgun shells, and ammunition of all types is the responsibility of the _____ unit.

20. The study of handwriting and typewriting on questioned documents is carried out by the _____ unit to ascertain authenticity and/or source.

21. The examination of body fluids and organs for drugs and poisons is a function of the _____ unit.

22. The _____ unit dispatches trained personnel to the scene of a crime to retrieve evidence for laboratory examination.

23. True or False: Special forensic science services available to the law enforcement community include forensic pathology, forensic anthropology, and forensic astronomy. _____

24. The "general acceptance" principle, which serves as a criterion for the judicial admissibility of scientific evidence, was set forth in the case of _____.

25. In the case of _____, the Supreme Court ruled that in assessing the admissibility of new and unique scientific tests the trial judge did not have to rely solely on the concept of "general acceptance."

26. True or False: The U.S. Supreme Court decision in *Kumho Tire Co., Ltd.* v. *Carmichael* restricted the "gatekeeping" role of a trial judge only to scientific testimony. _____

27. A Florida case that exemplifies the flexibility and wide discretion that the trial judge has in matters of scientific inquiry is _____.

28. A(n) _____ is a person who can demonstrate a particular skill or has knowledge in a trade or profession that will help the court determine the truth of the matter at issue.

29. True or False: The expert witness' courtroom demeanor may play an important role in deciding what weight the court will assign to his or her testimony._____

30. True or False: The testimony of an expert witness incorporates his or her personal opinion relating to a matter he or she has either studied or examined. _____

31. The ability of the investigator to recognize and collect crime-scene evidence properly depends on the amount of _____ received from the crime laboratory.

Application and Critical Thinking

1. Most crime labs in the United States are funded and operated by the government and provide services free to police and prosecutors. Great Britain, however, uses a quasi-governmental agency that charges fees for its services and keeps any profits it makes. Suggest potential strengths and weaknesses of each system.

2. Police investigating an apparent suicide collect the following items at the scene: a note purportedly written by the victim, a revolver bearing very faint fingerprints, and traces of skin and blood under the victim's fingernails. What units of the crime laboratory will examine each piece of evidence?

3. List at least three advantages of having an evidence-collection unit process a crime scene instead of a patrol officer or detective.

4. What legal issue was raised on appeal by the defense in Carl Coppolino's Florida murder trial? What court ruling is most relevant to the decision to reject the appeal? Explain your answer.

Web Resources

Admissibility of Scientific Evidence under *Daubert* (A brief comparison and discussion of the *Frye* and *Daubert* tests)
www.apsu.edu/oconnort/3210/3210lect01a.htm

History of Forensic Science
www.crimezzz.net/forensic_history/index.htm

Timeline of the History of Autopsies and Death Investigation
www.hbo.com/autopsy/swf/timeline/timeline.html

Endnotes

1. Two excellent references are André A. Moenssens, Fred E. Inbau, James Starrs, and Carol E. Henderson, *Scientific Evidence in Civil and Criminal Cases,* 4th ed. (Mineola, N.Y.: Foundation Press, 1995); and Werner U. Spitz, ed., *Medicolegal Investigation of Death,* 3rd ed. (Springfield, Ill.: Charles C. Thomas, 1993).

2. 293 Fed. 1013 (D.C. Cir. 1923).

3. 509 U.S. 579 (1993).

4. 526 U.S 137 (1999).

5. 223 So. 2d 68 (Fla. App. 1968), *app. dismissed,* 234 So. 2d (Fla. 1969), *cert. denied,* 399 U.S. 927 (1970).

JonBenet Ramsey: Who Did It?

Patsy and John Ramsey were in the upper crust of Boulder, Colorado, society. In the span of five short years, John had built his computer company into a billion-dollar corporation. In addition to financial success, the Ramseys also had a beautiful 6-year-old daughter, JonBenet.

Just after five a.m. on December 26, 1996, Patsy Ramsey awoke and walked downstairs to her kitchen. At the foot of the staircase, she found a two-and-a-half-page note saying that JonBenet had been kidnapped. The note contained a ransom demand of $118,000. When the police arrived to investigate, it was quite apparent to all that JonBenet was missing.

In retrospect, some serious mistakes were made in securing the crime scene—the Ramsey household. Initially, the police conducted a cursory search of the house, but failed to find JonBenet. The house was not sealed off; in fact, four friends along with the Ramsey pastor were let into the home and allowed to move about at will. John was permitted to leave the premises unattended for one and a half hours. One hour after his return, John and two of his friends searched the house again. This time John went down into the basement, where he discovered JonBenet's body. He removed a white blanket from JonBenet and carried her upstairs, placing the body on the living room floor.

The murder of JonBenet Ramsey remains as baffling a mystery today as it was on its first day. Ample physical evidence supports the theory that the crime was committed by an outsider, as well as the competing theory that JonBenet was murdered by someone who resided in the Ramsey household. Perhaps better care at securing and processing the crime scene could have resolved some of the crime's outstanding questions.

chapter 2

Securing and Searching the Crime Scene

Key Terms

command center

grid search

line/strip search

primary scene

quadrant/zone search

secondary scene

spiral search

walk-through

wheel/ray search

Learning Objectives

After studying this chapter, you should be able to:

- Discuss the responsibilities of the first police officer who arrives at the crime scene.

- Comprehend the role of the lead investigator in coordinating the crime-scene search.

- Describe the conditions at the crime scene that should be given particular notice.

- Understand the various search patterns investigators can use to systematically search the crime scene for evidence.

- Appreciate the necessity of documenting all initial observations and evidence collected.

Forensic science begins at the crime scene. To be useful to investigators, evidence at a crime scene must be preserved and recorded in its original condition as much as possible. Failure to protect a crime scene properly may result in the destruction or altering of evidence, or hinder the search for the perpetrator by misleading investigators about the facts of the incident.

Securing the Crime Scene

The first officer arriving on the scene of a crime is responsible for taking steps to preserve and protect the area to the greatest extent possible. The officer should not let his or her guard down; the scene should always be treated as though the crime were still occurring until it is proven otherwise. The officer must rely on his or her training to deal with any violent or hazardous circumstances. Special note should be taken of any vehicles or people leaving the scene.

Of course, first priority should be given to obtaining medical assistance for individuals in need of it. If medical assistance is needed, the officer should direct medical workers to approach the body by an indirect route to minimize the possibility of disturbing evidence. This pathway should later be used by investigative personnel for the same reason. The first responding officer must quickly evaluate the victim's condition before the victim is taken to a medical facility. The officer must also record any statements made by the victim and instruct the emergency medical personnel to record any statements the victim makes on the way to the hospital. This information should later be included in notes.

The officer should call for any backup or investigative personnel required and, as soon as possible, detain all potential suspects or witnesses still at the scene. The officer must identify all individuals at the scene, including bystanders and medical personnel. At the same time, he or she should exclude all unauthorized personnel from the scene. This includes family and friends of the victim, who should be shown as much compassion as possible.

The first responder is responsible for establishing the boundaries of the scene to be protected. The boundaries should encompass the center of the scene where the crime occurred, any paths of entry or exit, and any areas where evidence may have been discarded or moved. For indoor scenes this may include anything from a single room to an entire house and yard. The center of the crime scene is usually apparent, and a sufficient area

FIGURE 2–1   The first investigators to arrive must secure the crime scene and establish a perimeter. This perimeter may be delineated by crime-scene tape, ropes, or barricades.
Courtesy Sirchie Finger Print Laboratories, Inc., Youngsville, N.C., www.sirchie.com

around this spot should be closed off. The boundaries of an outdoor crime scene are more difficult to determine and can span miles, especially if a vehicle is involved. The officer should initially denote the boundaries of the scene using crime-scene tape, ropes, or traffic cones (see Figure 2–1). As additional officers arrive, investigators should immediately take measures to isolate the area around the taped-off section. Police barricades, along with the strategic positioning of guards, will prevent unauthorized access to the area. Only investigative personnel assigned to the scene should be admitted. The responding officers must keep an accurate log of who enters and exits the scene and the time they do so.

Sometimes the exclusion of unauthorized personnel proves to be more difficult than expected. Crimes of violence are especially susceptible to attention by higher-level police officials and members of the media, as well as by emotionally charged neighbors and curiosity seekers. Every individual who enters the scene has the potential to destroy physical evidence, even if by unintentional carelessness. To exercise proper control over the crime scene, the officer charged with the responsibility for protecting it must have the authority to exclude everyone, including fellow police officers not directly involved in processing the site or in conducting the investigation. Seasoned criminal investigators are always prepared to relate horror stories about crime scenes where physical evidence was rendered totally valueless by hordes of people who, for one reason or another, trampled through the site. Securing and isolating the crime scene are critical steps in an investigation, the accomplishment of which is the mark of a trained and professional crime-scene investigative team. It is also important to park the crime-scene vehicle where is will not destroy evidence but also where it will be secure and easily accessible.

It is worth noting that personnel should *never* do anything while at the crime scene—including smoking, eating, drinking, or littering—that might alter the scene. No aspects of the scene, including a body at a death scene, should be moved or disturbed unless they pose a serious threat to investigating officers or bystanders. This means that no one should open or close faucets or flush toilets at the scene. Also, officers should avoid altering temperature conditions at the scene by adjusting windows, doors, or the heat or air-conditioning.

Key Points

- The first officer arriving on the scene of a crime has the responsibility to preserve and protect the area to the greatest extent possible.

- First priority should be given to obtaining medical assistance for individuals in need of it.

- Steps must be taken by the first responder to exclude all unauthorized personnel from the scene and keep an accurate log of who enters and exits the scene and the time they do so.

Surveying the Crime Scene

Once the scene has been secured, a lead investigator with the help of others will start the process of evaluating the area. The lead investigator will immediately proceed to gain an overview of the situation and develop a strategy for the systematic examination and documentation of the entire crime scene.

The Walk-Through

walk-through
The initial survey of the crime scene carried out by the lead investigator to gain an overview of the scene in order to formulate a plan for processing the scene.

The initial survey of the scene is typically called the **walk-through**. First, the perpetrator's path of entry and exit should be established. The investigators should then follow an indirect path to the center of the scene, possibly one already established by the first responding officer to allow for medical attention. Some investigators attempt to follow the path of the suspect, but this may destroy possible evidence.

Logic dictates that obvious items of crime-scene evidence will first come to the attention of the crime-scene investigator. The investigator must document and photograph these items. Any fragile evidence may be secured by the investigator or tagged for the search team. The investigators should remember that the crime scene is three-dimensional; evidence may be found on the walls or ceilings as well as on the floor and other surfaces. It may also be practical to have one or two individuals canvas the area outside the barricaded scene.

The investigator should ask the following questions:

- Is the scene indoors or outdoons?

- What is the location (street address if applicable) of the scene?

- What are the weather or temperature conditions?

- What type of building and neighborhood is the scene located in?

- Was there any odor detected upon arrival of the first responder?

- Are doors and windows open or closed, locked or unlocked?

- Given the states of windows and doors, what are possible points of entry and exit?

- Is anything damaged, out of place, or missing? Are there objects that do not appear to belong there?

- Does an object's condition suggest that a struggle took place?

- Are lights or electrical appliances on or off?

- Is food present? Is it in the middle of being prepared, partially eaten, etc.?

- Does this scene appear to involve violence?

- What are the contents of any ashtrays and trash cans at the crime site? Are there tooth marks or lipstick on cigarette butts?

- What is the state of the bathroom? Are towels wet or dry? Is the toilet seat up or down?

- Are there any places where the suspect could have easily and quickly hidden a weapon?

- Is a vehicle nearby? If so, is the engine hot or cold?

Investigators should take particular note of aspects of the scene that suggest the timing of the incident. For example, if today's newspaper is on the table, it suggests that the incident occurred after the paper was delivered. The investigator's notes should include answers to basic questions and descriptions of everything observed at the scene. These simple observations may prove significant in the later investigation.

The presence or absence of certain evidence can offer key clues to the investigator. For example, objects that appear out of place, such as a child's toy in the house of a couple without children or relatives with children, may be very important. It is also important to observe whether objects that should be at the scene, such as a television or computer, are missing or displaced.

The presence or absence of evidence may also suggest whether the scene is a primary or secondary scene. A **primary scene** is one at which the original incident occurred. The **secondary scene** is a location that became part of the crime by activities after the initial incident, such as using a car to transport a body. If a victim suffered severe injury involving heavy loss of blood, but little or no blood is present where the body is found, this is likely to be a secondary scene.

Assigning Tasks

Investigators must establish a center of operations or **command center** at the scene. Here, members of the investigative team receive their assignments, store their equipment, and meet to discuss aspects of the case. The command center must be located outside the taped-off boundary of the scene and contain the basic equipment needed to photograph, sketch, process, and collect evidence. An equipped crime-scene vehicle usually serves the purpose well. If multiple scenes are involved, the command center should also be a center for communicating with investigators at the other scenes.

At the command center, the lead investigator assigns tasks after the initial walk-through. Basic tasks include locating possible evidence, assessing the evidence, processing evidence (e.g., dusting for fingerprints and casting footprints or tire impressions), and photographing and sketching the scene. The tasks should be carried out in that exact order to properly process the scene. The number of personnel assigned to each task depends

primary scene
A crime scene at which the original criminal act was perpetrated.

secondary scene
A crime scene separate from the primary scene that became part of the crime by its involvement in activities after the initial criminal act was perpetrated.

command center
A secure site outside the boundaries of a crime scene where equipment is stored, tasks are assigned, and communication occurs.

on the scene and the discretion of the lead investigator. In some cases, a single crime-scene investigator might be required to handle all these tasks.

Key Points

- The lead investigator is responsible for developing a strategy for the systematic examination and documentation of the entire crime scene.

- The lead investigator must gain an overview of the general setting of the scene. Of particular importance are objects that do not appear to belong or aspects of the scene that may suggest a timing of the incident.

- The presence or absence of evidence may also suggest whether the scene is a primary or secondary scene.

- At the command center, members of the investigative team receive their assignments, store their equipment, congregate to talk about aspects of the case, and communicate with personnel at other crime scenes.

Searching the Crime Scene

There are many methods for searching the scene in a logical fashion to locate evidence. How one carries out a crime-scene search depends on the locale and size of the area, as well as on the actions of the suspect(s) and victim(s) at the scene. When possible, it is advisable to have one person supervising and coordinating the collection of evidence. Without proper control, the search may be conducted in an atmosphere of confusion with needless duplication of effort. The areas searched must include all probable points of entry and exit used by the criminals. The search team may want to use a simple flashlight to illuminate surfaces at an oblique angle to visualize latent (hidden) fingerprints, handprints, footwear imprints, and other residues.

Types of Search Patterns

line/strip search
A search method used by one or two investigators who walk in straight lines across the crime scene.

Line/Strip Search Pattern   In the **line/strip search pattern**, one or two investigators start at the boundary at one end of the scene and walk straight across to the other side. They then move a little farther along the border and walk straight back to the other side (see Figure 2–2[a]). This method is best used in scenes where the boundaries are well established because the boundaries dictate the beginning and end of the search lines. If the boundary is incorrectly chosen, important evidence may remain undiscovered outside the search area.

grid search
A search method employed by two or more people who perform overlapping line searches forming a grid.

Grid Search Pattern   The **grid search pattern** employs two people performing line searches that originate from adjacent corners and form perpendicular lines (see Figure 2–2[b]). This method is very thorough, but the boundaries must be well established.

spiral search
A search method in which the investigator moves in an inward spiral from the boundary to the center of the scene or in an outward spiral from the center to the boundary of a scene.

Spiral Search Pattern   The **spiral search pattern** usually employs one person. The investigator moves either in an inward spiral from the boundary to the center of the scene or in an outward spiral from the center to the boundary (see Figure 2–2[c]). The inward spiral method is helpful because the searcher is moving from an area light with evidence to an area where more evidence will most likely be found. Either spiral approach facilitates

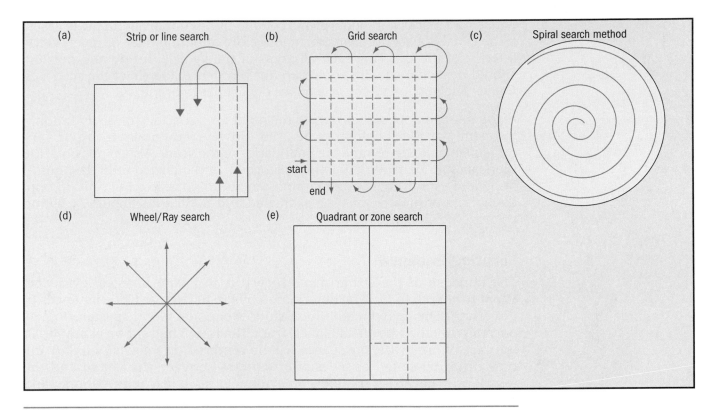

FIGURE 2–2 **(a) Line/strip search pattern; (b) grid search pattern; (c) spiral search pattern; (d) wheel/ray search pattern; (e) quadrant/zone search pattern.**

the location of footprints leading away from the scene in any direction. However, it is often difficult for a searcher to complete a perfect spiral, and evidence could be missed.

Wheel/Ray Search Pattern The **wheel/ray search pattern** employs several people moving from the boundary straight toward the center of the scene (inward) or from the center straight to the boundary (outward). This method is not preferred because the areas between the "rays" are not searched (see Figure 2–2[d]).

Quadrant/Zone Search Pattern The **quadrant/zone search pattern** involves dividing the scene into zones or quadrants, and team members are assigned to search each section. Each of these sections can be subdivided into smaller sections for smaller teams to search thoroughly (see Figure 2–2[e]). This method is best suited for scenes that cover a large area.

Vehicle Searches If the scene includes a vehicle, the vehicle search must be carefully planned and systematically carried out. The nature of the case determines how detailed the search must be. At all times investigators must be careful to avoid contact with surfaces that may contain fingerprints such as a steering wheel or door handle. In hit-and-run cases, the outside and undercarriage of the car must be examined with care. In this case the vehicle itself is the "weapon." Particular attention is paid to looking for any evidence resulting from a cross-transfer of evidence between the car and the victim; this includes blood, tissue, hair, fibers, and fabric impressions. Traces of paint or broken glass may be located on the victim or roadway. In vehicle burglary or theft, the search focuses on the place of

wheel/ray search pattern
A search method employed by several people who move from the boundary straight toward the center of the scene (inward) or from the center straight to the boundary (outward).

quadrant/zone search
A search method in which the crime scene is divided into smaller sections (zones or quadrants) and team members are assigned to search each section. Each of these sections can be subdivided into smaller sections for smaller teams to search thoroughly.

entry. Tool marks and fingerprints commonly are important in these cases. If the car was used for transportation, more attention may be given to the interior of the car. However, all areas of the vehicle, inside and outside, should be searched with equal care for physical evidence at the scene, or the vehicle may be towed to a police department garage.

Night Searches   Searches during the night are especially difficult. Indoors frequently artificial lights can be used. However, outdoors it can be very difficult even to determine the boundaries of the scene. When possible, the scene should be taped off, left undisturbed, and guarded until daylight. If impending weather or other circumstances do not allow for waiting until daylight, a perimeter must be estimated and floodlights should be set up prior to the search.

Locating Evidence

The purpose of the crime-scene search is to locate physical evidence. What to search for will be determined by the particular circumstances of the crime. This may include footprints, weapons, blood spatter, objects possibly touched by the suspect, trace fibers, or hairs. For example, in the case of homicide, the search will be centered on the weapon and any type of evidence left as a result of contact between the victim and the assailant. The cross-transfer of evidence, such as hairs, fibers, and blood, between individuals involved in the crime is particularly useful for linking suspects to the crime site and for corroborating events that transpired during the commission of the crime. Special attention should be paid to the body and the area surrounding it. During the investigation of a burglary, officers should attempt to locate tool marks at the point of entry. In most crimes, a thorough and systematic search for latent fingerprints is required. When an investigator finds an object of possible evidentiary value, he or she should record its location in notes, sketches, and photographs and then mark its location with an evidence marker (see Figure 2–3).

The search ends when the team or lead investigator determines that all pertinent evidence has been located to the best of the team's ability. When this determination is made, the team carries out a final survey of the scene. This should include a visual overview of all parts of the scene. Investigators should take an inventory of all evidence collected so nothing is lost or left behind. The team members should be sure to retrieve all equipment. They should also verify that any threats to health or safety at the scene have been or will be dealt with properly. Once all of these measures have been taken, the scene can be released to the proper authorities.

Obviously, the skill of crime-scene investigators at recognizing evidence and searching relevant locations is paramount to successfully processing the crime scene. Although training imparts general knowledge for conducting a proper crime-scene investigation, ultimately the investigator must rely on the experience gained from numerous investigations to formulate a successful strategy for recovering relevant physical evidence at crime scenes. If the investigator cannot recognize physical evidence or cannot properly preserve it for laboratory examination, no amount of sophisticated laboratory instrumentation or technical expertise can salvage the situation.

The know-how for conducting a proper crime-scene search for physical evidence is not beyond the grasp of any police department, regardless of its size. With proper training, police agencies can ensure competent

FIGURE 2–3 **Numbered evidence markers are used to show the location of (1) a firearm, (2) a beverage can, and (3) another beverage can at a crime scene.** *Courtesy Sirchie Finger Print Laboratories, Inc., Youngsville, N.C., www.sirchie.com*

performance at crime scenes. In many jurisdictions, police agencies have delegated this task to a specialized team of technicians known as crime-scene investigators.

Key Points

- How one carries out a crime-scene search will depend on the locale and size of the area, as well as on the actions of the suspect(s) and victim(s) at the scene.

- The purpose of the crime-scene search is to locate physical evidence. The particular circumstances of the crime determine what to search for first.

- When evidence is found, the location is documented in notes, photographs, and sketches.

- When the search is deemed complete, the investigating team conducts a final survey that includes a visual overview of all parts of the scene, an inventory of all evidence collected, the retrieval of all equipment, and the neutralization of all health or safety threats. Once all of these measures have been taken, the scene can be released to the proper authorities.

WebExtra 2.1

Search for clues at the scene of a murder. Once you've located the relevant evidence, you will need to collect the evidence for laboratory testing.

Virtual Crime Scene

www.prenhall.com/saferstein

Chapter Summary

Forensic science begins at the crime scene. The crime scene is dynamic, and conditions can change in a short amount of time. It is clearly important that the original conditions of the scene be preserved by securing the crime scene. This includes barring all persons not directly involved with the processing of the crime scene. Failure to protect a crime scene properly may result in the destruction or altering of evidence, or hinder the search for the perpetrator by misleading investigators about the facts of the incident.

The role of the first responding police officer is to obtain medical assistance for victims, detain witnesses and suspects, secure the boundaries of the scene, begin keeping a log of personnel arrivals and departures, and take notes on the original condition of the crime scene. All of these things must be done before the crime-scene investigation team arrives. The first responder may then accompany the lead investigator on the walk-through.

The lead investigator must complete the walk-through to prepare a plan for the processing of the scene. At the command center, the lead investigator assigns tasks to the rest of the team and begins the crime-scene search. The search method employed by the search team depends greatly on the location and layout of the crime scene.

Once objects of evidence have been located, they must be tagged for documentation and eventual collection. Once investigators have determined that all physical evidence has been located, documented, and collected, a final survey of the scene takes place. When the processing is complete, the scene is turned over to the appropriate authorities.

Review Questions

1. True or False: Failure to protect a crime scene properly may result in the destruction or altering of evidence. _____

2. The _____ arriving on the scene of a crime is responsible for taking steps to preserve and protect the area to the greatest extent possible, and he or she must rely on his or her training to deal with any violent or hazardous circumstances.

3. At a crime scene, first priority should be given to obtaining _____ for individuals in need of it and attempting to minimize the disturbance of evidence.

4. All unauthorized personnel must be _____ from crime scenes.

5. True or False: The boundaries of the crime scene, denoted by crime-scene tape, rope, or traffic cones, should only encompass the center of the scene where the crime occurred. _____

6. Even though all unauthorized personnel are not admitted to the scene, a very accurate _____ must be kept of those who do enter and exit the scene and the time they do so.

7. True or False: The lead investigator immediately proceeds to gain an overview of the situation and develop a strategy for the systematic examination of the crime scene during the final survey. _____

8. A _____ crime scene is one at which the original incident occurred such as a beating or rape. A _____ crime scene became part of the crime as a result of activities that occurred after the initial incident.

9. The investigative team receives assignments, stores equipment, and congregates to talk about aspects of the case at the _____.

10. A detailed search of the crime scene must be conducted in a(n) _____ fashion.

11. The crime-scene search is undertaken to locate _____.

12. True or False: The search patterns that may be used to search a crime scene for evidence include the line pattern, grid pattern, polar coordinate pattern, and spiral pattern. _____

13. When carrying out vehicle searches, investigators must be careful to avoid contact with surfaces that may contain _____ such as steering wheels or door handles.

14. True or False: During nighttime, outdoor scenes should be taped off, left undisturbed, and guarded until daylight. _____

15. True or False: The search is concluded when the district attorney determines that all pertinent evidence has been located to the best of the team's ability. _____

16. Once a _____ of the scene has been carried out, the scene can be released to the proper authorities.

17. True or False: If the investigator does not recognize physical evidence or does not properly preserve it for laboratory examination, sophisticated laboratory instrumentation or technical expertise can salvage the situation and attain the desired results. _____

Application and Critical Thinking

1. You are the first officer at the scene of an outdoor assault. You find the victim bleeding but conscious, with two of the victim's friends and several onlookers standing nearby. You call for backup and quickly glance around but see no one fleeing the scene. Describe the steps you would take while you wait for backup to arrive.

2. What kind of search pattern(s) would investigators be most likely to employ in each of the following situations:
   a. Two people searching a small area with well-defined boundaries
   b. Several people searching a large area
   c. A single person searching a large area

3. Officer Bill Walter arrives at the scene of an apparent murder: a body bearing several gunshot wounds lies on the floor of a small, un-air-conditioned house in late July. A pungent odor almost overwhelms him when he enters the house, so he opens a window to allow him to breathe so he can investigate the scene. While airing out the house, he secures the scene and interviews bystanders. When he inspects the scene, he discovers very little blood in the room and little evidence of a struggle. What mistake did Officer Walter make in his investigation? What conclusion did he draw about the scene from his observations?

Case Analysis

Investigators looking into the kidnapping and murder of DEA special agent Enrique Camarena and DEA source Alfredo Zavala faced several hurdles that threatened to derail their efforts to collect evidence in the case. These hurdles almost prevented forensics experts from determining the facts of the case and threatened to undermine the investigation of the crime. However, despite these obstacles, use of standard forensic techniques eventually enabled investigators to solve the case.

1. What were the main challenges facing investigators who were collecting evidence in the case? Give specific examples of these challenges.

2. Explain how investigators used reference samples to determine that the victims had been held at the residence located at 881 Lope De Vega.

3. Explain how investigators used soil evidence to determine that the victims' bodies had been buried and later moved to the site where they were discovered.

Web Resources

Crime and Clues (Articles on crime-scene protection, processing, and reconstruction)
www.crimeandclues.com/crimescene.htm

Crime-Scene Investigation (Guidelines and articles on response, evidence collection, photography, and other topics)
www.crime-scene-investigator.net

Crime Scene Investigation: A Reference for Law Enforcement Training
www.ojp.usdoj.gov/nij/pubs-sum/200160.htm

Crime-Scene Investigations (Links to articles written by Hayden B. Baldwin, former M/Sgt with the Illinois State Police)
www.feinc.net/cs-inv-p.htm

Case Reading

The Enrique Camarena Case: A Forensic Nightmare

Michael P. Malone
Special Agent, Laboratory Division
Federal Bureau of Investigation,
Washington, D.C.

On February 7, 1985, U.S. Drug Enforcement Agency (DEA) Special Agent (SA) Enrique Camarena was abducted near the U.S. Consulate in Guadalajara, Mexico. A short time later, Capt. Alfredo Zavala, a DEA source, was also abducted from a car near the Guadalajara Airport. These two abductions would trigger a series of events leading to one of the largest investigations ever conducted by the DEA and would result in one of the most extensive cases ever received by the FBI Laboratory.

Throughout this lengthy investigation, unusual forensic problems arose that required unusual solutions. Eventually, numerous suspects were arrested, both in the United States and Mexico, which culminated in an 8-week trial held in U.S. District Court in Los Angeles, CA.

The Abduction

On February 7, 1985, SA Camarena left the DEA Resident Office to meet his wife for lunch. On this day, a witness observed a man being forced into the rear seat of a light-colored compact car in front of the Camelot Restaurant and provided descriptions of several of the assailants. After some initial reluctance, Primer Comandante Pavon-Reyes of the Mexican Federal Judicial Police (MFJP) was put in charge of the investigation, and Mexican investigators were assigned to the case. Two known drug traffickers, Rafael Caro-Quintero and Ernesto Fonseca, were quickly developed as suspects. A short time later at the Guadalajara Airport, as

Caro-Quintero and his men attempted to flee by private jet, a confrontation developed between Caro-Quintero's men, the MFJP, and DEA agents. After some discussion, Caro-Quintero and his men were permitted to board and leave. It was later learned that a 6-figure bribe had been paid to Pavon-Reyes to allow this departure.

The Investigation

During February 1985, searches of several residences and ranches throughout Mexico proved fruitless, despite the efforts of the DEA task force assigned to investigate this matter and the tremendous pressure being applied by the U.S. Government to accelerate the investigation. High-level U.S. Government officials, as well as their Mexican counterparts, were becoming directly involved in the case. It is believed

Undated photo of Enrique Camarena.
Courtesy AP Wide World Photos

Reprinted from *FBI Law Enforcement Bulletin*, September 1989.

that because of this "heat," the Mexican drug traffickers and certain Mexican law enforcement officials fabricated a plan. According to the plan, the MFJP would receive an anonymous letter indicating that SA Camarena and Captain Zavala were being held at the Bravo drug gang's ranch in La Angostura, Michoacan, approximately 60 miles southeast of Guadalajara. The MFJP was supposed to raid the ranch, eliminate the drug gang, and eventually discover the bodies of SA Camarena and Captain Zavala buried on the ranch. The DEA would then be notified and the case would be closed. Thus, the Bravo gang would provide an easy scapegoat.

During early March, MFJP officers raided the Bravo ranch before the DEA agents arrived. In the resulting shootout, all of the gang members, as well as one MFJP officer, were killed. However, due to a mix-up, the bodies of SA Camarena and Captain Zavala were not buried on the Bravo ranch in time to be discovered as planned. The individuals paid to do this job simply left them by the side of a road near the ranch. It was later learned that certain Mexican law enforcement officials were paid a large sum of money to formulate and carry out this plan in order to obstruct and prematurely conclude the investigation.

Shortly after this shootout, a passerby found two partially decomposed bodies, wrapped in plastic bags, along a road near the Bravo ranch. The bodies were removed and transported to a local morgue where they were autopsied. The DEA was then advised of the discovery of the bodies and their subsequent removal to another morgue in Guadalajara, where a second autopsy was performed.

On March 7, 1985, the FBI dispatched a forensic team to Guadalajara. They immediately proceeded to the morgue to identify the bodies and to process any evidence which might be present. After much bureaucratic delay from the local officials, they were finally allowed to proceed. The bodies were identified only

as cadavers number 1 and number 2. It was apparent that each body had been autopsied and that both were in an advanced state of decomposition. Cadaver number 1 was quickly identified by the fingerprint expert as that of SA Camarena. Mexican officials would not allow the second body to be identified at this time; however, it was later identified through dental records as Captain Zavala.

The FBI forensic team requested permission to process the clothing, cordage, and burial sheet found with the bodies, but the request was denied. However, they were allowed to cut small, "known" samples from these items and obtain hair samples from both bodies. Soil samples were also removed from the bodies and the clothing items.

A forensic pathologist from the Armed Forces Institute of Pathology was allowed to examine the body of SA Camarena. He concluded that SA Camarena's death was caused by blunt-force injuries. In addition, SA Camarena had a hole in his skull caused by a rod-like instrument. SA Camarena's body was then released to the American officials and immediately flown to the United States.

The next day, both FBI and DEA personnel proceeded to the Bravo ranch where the bodies were initially found. Because this site had been a completely uncontrolled crime scene, contaminated by both police personnel and onlookers, only a limited crime-scene search was conducted. It was immediately noted that there was no grave site in the area and that the color of the soil where the bodies had been deposited differed from the soil that had been removed from the bodies. Therefore, "known" soil samples from the drop site were taken to compare with soil removed from the victims. It was also noted that there were no significant body fluids at the "burial" site. This led the forensic team to conclude that the bodies had been buried elsewhere, exhumed, and transported to this site.

The MFJP officials were later confronted with the evidence that the bodies had been relocated to the Michoacan area. This was one of the factors which led to a new, unilateral MFJP investigation. As a result, several suspects, including State Judicial Police Officers, were arrested and interrogated concerning the kidnapping of SA Camarena. Primer Comandante Pavon-Reyes was fired, and arrest warrants were issued for a number of international drug traffickers, including Rafael Caro-Quintero and Ernesto Fonseca.

In late March 1985, DEA Agents located a black Mercury Gran Marquis which they believed was used in the kidnapping or transportation of SA Camarena. The vehicle had been stored in a garage in Guadalajara, and a brick wall had been constructed at the entrance to conceal it. The vehicle was traced to a Ford dealership owned by Caro-Quintero. Under the watchful eye of the MFJP at the Guadalajara Airport, the FBI forensic team processed the vehicle for any hair, fiber, blood, and/or fingerprint evidence it might contain.

During April 1985, the MFJP informed the DEA that they believed they had located the residence where SA Camarena and Captain Zavala had been held. The FBI forensic team was immediately dispatched to Guadalajara; however, they were not allowed to proceed to the residence, located at 881 Lope De Vega, until an MFJP forensic team had processed the residence and had removed all of the obvious evidence. The DEA was also informed that since the abduction of SA Camarena, all of the interior walls had been painted, the entire residence had recently been cleaned, and a group of MFJP officers were presently occupying, and thereby contaminating, the residence.

On the first day after the arrival of the FBI forensic team, they surveyed and began a crime scene search of the residence and surrounding grounds. (See Figure 1.) The residence consists of a large, two-story structure with a swimming pool, covered patio, aviary, and tennis court surrounded by a common wall. The most logical place to hold a prisoner at this location would be in the small outbuilding located to the rear of the main residence. This outbuilding, designated as the "guest house," consisted of a small room, carpeted by a beige rug, with an adjoining bathroom. The entire room and bathroom were processed for hairs, fibers, and latent fingerprints. The single door into this room was made of steel and reinforced by iron bars. It was ultimately determined by means of testimony and forensic evidence that several individuals interrogated and tortured SA Camarena in this room. In addition, a locked bedroom, located on the second floor of the main house, was also processed, and the bed linens were removed from a single bed. Known carpet samples were taken from every room in the residence.

A beige VW Atlantic, which fit the general description of the smaller vehicle noted by the person who witnessed SA Camarena's abduction, was parked under a carport at the rear of the residence. The VW Atlantic was also processed for hairs, fibers, and fingerprints.

On the second day, a thorough grounds search was conducted. As FBI forensic team members were walking around the tennis court, they caught a glimpse of something blue in one of the drains. Upon closer inspection, it appeared to be a folded license plate, at the bottom of the drain. However, a heavy iron grate covered the drain and prevented the plate's immediate retrieval.

When one of the FBI Agents returned to the main house to ask the MFJP officers for a crowbar, they became extremely curious and followed the Agent as he returned, empty handed, to the tennis court. By this time, a second Agent had managed to remove the grate by using a heavy-wire coat hanger. The license plate was retrieved, unfolded and photographed. The MFJP officers, all of whom were now at the tennis court, became upset at this

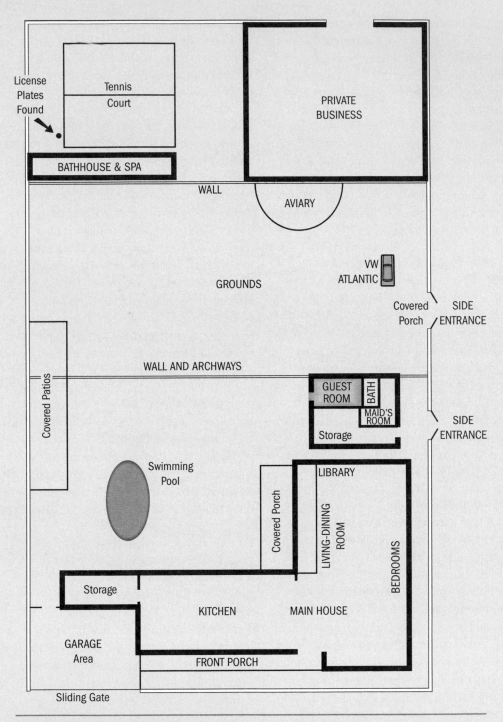

FIGURE 1 **A diagram of the 881 Lope De Vega grounds. Camarena was held prisoner in the guest house.**

discovery, and one of them immediately contacted his superior at MFJP headquarters, who ordered them to secure the license plate until the Assistant Primer Comandante arrived on the scene. After his arrival approximately 20 minutes later, he seized the license plate and would not allow the Americans to conduct any further searches.

However, by this time, five very large plastic bags of evidence had been recovered and were placed in the rear of a DEA truck. The evidence was quickly transported to the DEA vault in the U.S. Consulate.

After negotiations between the United States and Mexico, the MFJP did allow a second, final search of the residence. On June 24, 1985, a forensic team returned and processed the four remaining rooms on the first floor of the main house.

By this point in the investigation, an associate of Rafael Caro-Quintero had been arrested and interrogated by the MFJP. He stated that the bodies of two Americans, Albert Radelat and John Walker, who had been abducted and killed by Mexican drug traffickers, were buried on the south side of La Primavera Park, a large, primitive park west of Guadalajara. The bodies of Radelat and Walker were located and recovered. Soil samples taken from the surface of an area near their graves were similar in most respects to the soil recovered earlier from the bodies of SA Camarena and Captain Zavala.

In September 1985, DEA personnel went to La Primavera Park and sampled an area approximately 2 feet below the surface near the same site. This sample matched the soil samples from SA Camarena and Captain Zavala almost grain for grain, indicating that this site was almost certainly their burial site before they were relocated to the Bravo ranch.

Later that fall, after further negotiations between the U.S. and the Mexican governments, permission was finally granted for an FBI forensic team to process the evidence seized by the MFJP forensic team from 881 Lope De Vega the previous April. The evidence consisted of small samples the MFJP had taken of SA Camarena's burial sheet, a piece of rope used to bind SA Camarena, a portion of a pillowcase removed from bedroom number 3, a piece of unsoiled rope removed from the covered patio, and a laboratory report prepared by the MFJP Crime Laboratory.

The remainder of the evidence had been destroyed for "health reasons."

In January 1986, a drug trafficker named Rene Verdugo, who was considered to be a high-ranking member of the Caro-Quintero gang, was apprehended and taken to San Diego, where he was arrested by the DEA. He was then transported to Washington, D.C., where hair samples were taken. He refused to testify before a federal grand jury investigating the Camarena case. Later that year, DEA personnel obtained hair samples in Mexico City from Sergio Espino-Verdin, a former federal comandante, who is believed to have been SA Camarena's primary interrogator during his ordeal at 881 Lope De Vega.

The Trial

In July 1988, the main trial of the murder, interrogation, and abduction of SA Camarena began in U.S. District Court in Los Angeles, CA. The forensic evidence presented in this trial identified 881 Lope De Vega as the site where SA Camarena had been held. The evidence also strongly associated two Mexican citizens, Rene Verdugo and Sergio Espino-Verdin, with the "guest house" at 881 Lope De Vega. Several types of forensic evidence were used to associate SA Camarena with 881 Lope De Vega: forcibly removed head hairs, found in the "guest house" and bedroom number 4, in the VW Atlantic and in the Mercury Gran Marquis, and two types of polyester rug fibers, a dark, rose-colored fiber and a light-colored fiber. [See Figures 2 and 3.] Fabric evidence was also presented, which demonstrated the similarities of color, composition, construction, and design between SA Camarena's burial sheet and the two pillowcases recovered from bedrooms number 3 and 5.

Based on this evidence associating SA Camarena and 881 Lope De Vega, the FBI Laboratory examiner was able to testify that SA Camarena was at this residence, as well as in the VW Atlantic and the

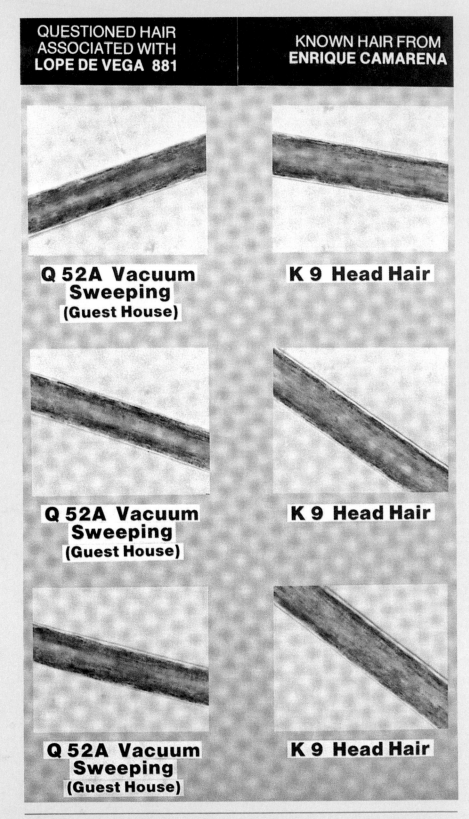

FIGURE 2   A trial chart showing hair comparisons between known Camarena hairs and hairs recovered from 881 Lope De Vega.

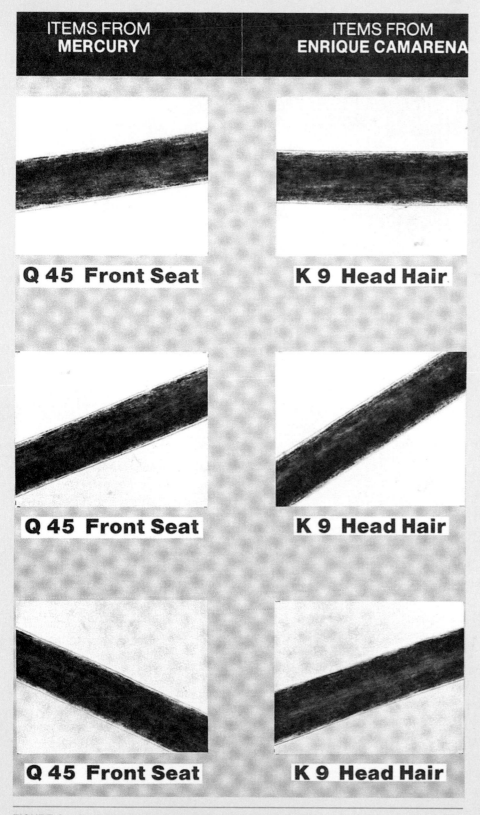

ITEMS FROM **MERCURY**

ITEMS FROM **ENRIQUE CAMARENA**

Q 45 Front Seat

K 9 Head Hair

Q 45 Front Seat

K 9 Head Hair

Q 45 Front Seat

K 9 Head Hair

FIGURE 3 A trial chart showing hair comparisons between known Camarena hairs and hairs recovered from the Mercury Gran Marquis.

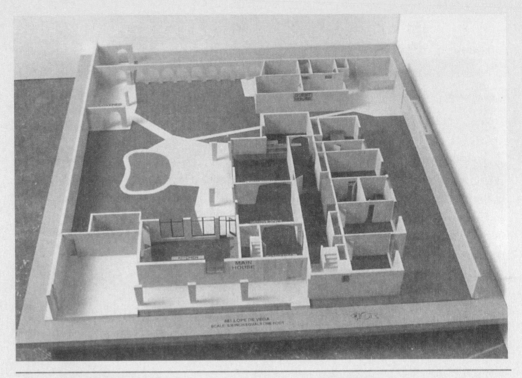

FIGURE 4 A model of 881 Lope De Vega prepared as a trial exhibit.

Mercury Gran Marquis, and that he had been in a position such that his head hairs were forcibly removed. Captain Alfredo Zavala was also found to be associated with the "guest house" at 881 Lope De Vega. Light-colored nylon rug fibers, found on samples of his clothing taken at the second autopsy, matched the fibers from the "guest house" carpet.

A detailed model of the residence at 881 Lope De Vega was prepared by the Special Projects Section of the FBI Laboratory for the trial. [See Figure 4.] Over 20 trial charts were also prepared to explain the various types of forensic evidence. These charts proved invaluable in clarifying the complicated techniques and characteristics used in the examination of the hair, fiber, fabric, and cordage evidence. [See Figure 5.]

Conclusion

The forensic pitfalls and problems in this case (i.e., destruction of evidence, contamination of crime scenes) were eventually resolved. In some cases, certain routine procedures had to be ignored or unconventional methods employed. However, in many instances, detailed trial testimony overcame the limitations of certain evidence, and eventually, almost all of the evidence introduced at the trial made a tremendous impact on the outcome of this proceeding. After an 8-week trial, conducted under tight security and involving hundreds of witnesses, all of the defendants were found guilty, convicted on all counts, and are currently serving lengthy sentences.

CATEGORIES OF FORENSIC EVIDENCE
IN CAMARENA CASE

LOCATION	TYPE OF EVIDENCE					
	Hair	Carpet Fibers	Fabric Match	Cordage Match	Tape Match	Misc.
Mercury	Camarena Head Hair					Blood on Floor Mat
VW Atlantic	Camarena Head Hair					Blood on Tissue
Guest House	Camarena Head Hair	Zavala Clothes Nylon				
Bedroom #3		Camarena Blindfold Polyester	Pillow Case Camarena Burial Sheet			
Bedroom #4	Camarena Head Hair	Camarena Blindfold & Burial Sheet Polyester				
Bedroom #5			Pillow Case Camarena Burial Sheet			
Tennis Court						License Plate VW/Merc.
Camarena Burial Sheet	Camarena Head Hair	Bedroom #4 Polyester	Pillow Case Bedrooms #3 and #5			Soil La Primavera
Source — Blindfold/ Rope	Camarena Head Hair	Bedrooms #3 and #4 Polyester			Camarena Blindfold Tape	
Camarena Burial Cordage				Burial Rope from Covered Patio		
Zavala Clothing	Zavala Head Hair	Guest House Nylon				Soil La Primavera

FIGURE 5 **A trial chart used to show the association of Camarena and Zavala with various locations.**

The Lindbergh Baby Case

On the evening of March 1, 1932, a kidnapper crept up his homemade ladder and stole the baby of Charles and Anne Lindbergh directly from the second-floor nursery of their house in Hopewell, New Jersey. The only evidence of his coming was a ransom note, the ladder, a chisel, and the tragic absence of the infant. A couple of months later, although the $50,000 ransom had been paid, the baby turned up dead in the woods a mile away. There was no additional sign of the killer. Fortunately, when finally studied by wood technologist Arthur Koehler, the abandoned ladder yielded some important investigative clues (see the case reading on page 000).

By studying the types of wood used and the cutter marks on the wood, Koehler ascertained where the materials might have come from and what specific equipment was used to create them. Koehler traced the wood from a South Carolina mill to a lumberyard in the Bronx, New York. Unfortunately, the trail went cold, as the lumberyard did not keep sales records of purchases. The break in the case came in 1934, when Bruno Richard Hauptmann paid for gasoline with a bill that matched a serial number on the ransom money. Koehler showed that microscopic markings on the wood were made by a tool in Hauptmann's possession. A ladder rail recovered from the homemade ladder had characteristics consistent with wood present in Hauptmann's attic. Ultimately, handwriting analysis of the ransom note clearly showed it to be written by Hauptmann.

Recording the Crime Scene

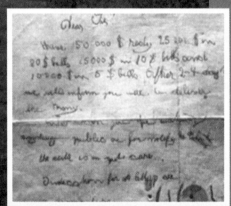

Learning Objectives

After studying this chapter, you should be able to:

- Explain the steps to be taken to fully record the crime scene.

- Describe the proper format and content of crime-scene notes.

- Understand the basic features of film and digital cameras in order to produce examination-quality photographs.

- Describe the process and importance of creating a rough and finished crime-scene sketch.

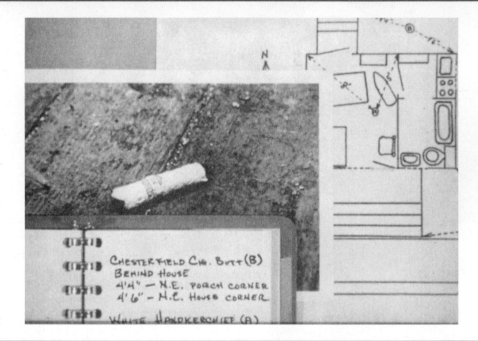

FIGURE 3–1 **The finding of an evidential cigarette butt at the crime scene requires photographing it, making a sketch showing its relation to the crime scene, and recording the find in notes.** *Courtesy Police Science Services, Niles, Ill.*

Investigators have only a limited amount of time to work a crime site in its untouched state. They must not lose the opportunity to permanently record the scene in its original condition. Such records not only will prove useful during the subsequent investigation, but also are required for presentation at a trial in order to document the condition of the crime scene and the location of physical evidence. Notes, photographs, and sketches are the three methods for crime-scene recording (see Figure 3–1).

Notes

The note-taking process begins with the call to a crime-scene investigator to report to a scene. The notes should start by identifying the person who contacted the investigator, the time of the contact, and any preliminary information disclosed, including the case number. When the lead investigator arrives, the note-taker should record the date and time of arrival, who is present, and the identities of any other personnel who are being contacted. If additional personnel are contacted, their names, titles, and times of arrival should be recorded.

A crime scene should be off-limits to any people who are not directly involved with the processing. Investigators must keep very precise records of personnel movements in and out of the scene, beginning with the movements of the first responding officer. It is also important to record the tasks assigned to each member of a team, as well as the beginning and ending times for the processing of the scene.

Before the scene is sketched, photographed, or searched, the lead investigator carries out the initial walk-through. During this walk-through, the investigator should take notes on many aspects of the crime scene in its original condition. Notes taken by an investigator should be uniform in layout for all cases. The notes should be in ink (preferably black or blue) and written in a bound notebook. Most important, notes should be written at the time of the crime-scene investigation, and not left to memory to record at a later time. At this time, the investigator may need to interview the first responding officer. The officer should supply information on any known events that occurred at the crime scene that the officer or others witnessed. When the walk-through is complete, the lead investigator assigns specific tasks or areas to members of the crime-scene team. The notes should also record these assignments, as well as the times at which each task was started and completed.

Once a search for evidence has taken place, the team members mark the location of all evidence. The investigator should note if any evidence was disturbed by emergency medical personnel, a suspect, or investigative personnel. Before the team collects items of evidence, the investigator must fully describe each item in his or her notes. The person who collects a piece of evidence should note who found it, where it was located, how it was packaged, who packaged it, and when it was packaged. The notes should also mention whether the evidence underwent any field tests or processing.

If a victim is present at a homicide scene, the investigator should observe and record the state of the body before the medical examiner or coroner moves it. The notes should describe the victim's appearance and record the position of the body and any visible wounds or blood spatter. The investigator should make note of any identifying features or marks on the body, such as tattoos. He or she should also make a list of objects found on the body, such as a wallet or jewelry, before collecting those items. Moving the body may reveal previously unseen injuries and physical evidence that the investigator should record. The notes should indicate when the medical examiner or coroner moved the body and whether the victim was moved or affected in some way by emergency medical procedures. Any preliminary identification of a victim or suspect should be recorded.

Tape recording notes at a scene can be advantageous because detailed notes can be taped much faster than they can be written. This may also leave hands free to carry out other tasks while recording the notes. Audiotapes have the added security feature of preventing erasure or taping over if the security tab on the tape is in place. However, care must be taken to avoid embarrassing conversation on tapes that will be used as evidence in a trial. Some investigators may use digital voice recorders to record their notes. These recordings are easily uploaded to a computer, but they must be copied to a disk to produce a hard copy. Another method of recording notes is by narrating a videotape of the crime scene. This has the advantage of combining note taking with photography. However, at some point the tape must be transcribed into a written document.

The note taker must keep in mind that this written record may be the only source of information for refreshing his or her memory months, perhaps years, after a crime has been processed. The notes must be sufficiently detailed to anticipate this need.

Key Points

- Because investigators have only a limited amount of time to work a crime site in its untouched state, the opportunity must not be lost.

- Crime-scene notes should include contact information, personnel information and movements, task assignments, observations of the victim and scene, and information about the evidence before and after it is processed.

- Recording notes on tape or digital voice recorders is advantageous, but investigators should take care to speak clearly and avoid including side conversations.

Photography

All jurisdictions commonly accept photographs of crime scenes as visual evidence in criminal investigations. Investigators should therefore understand the procedures and principles of good crime-scene photography in order to best illustrate aspects of the scene. The goal of photography at crime scenes is to produce examination-quality photographs. This means that everyone involved in the case, from the investigators to the judge and jury, must be able to interpret the photographs easily.

Crime-scene photographs can show the layout of the scene, the position of evidence to be collected, and the relation of objects at the scene to one another. Photographs taken from many angles can show possible lines of sight of victims, suspects, or witnesses. Photography is also important for documenting biological evidence in its original condition, because this kind of evidence is often altered during testing. Photographs cannot stand alone, however; they are complementary to notes and sketches.

Film and Digital Photography

digital photography
The use of electronic means to capture light and save an image on a microchip.

Currently there are two methods or approaches to crime-scene photography: film and **digital photography**. The differences between the two relate to the ways they convert light into images.

Film Photographic film consists of a sheet of light-reactive silver halide grains and comes in several varieties. Print film produces a negative image that is developed to produce a positive image. Slide film, by contrast, produces positive images on transparent slides used for presentation. A special type of infrared film produces images when exposed to infrared light.

Film also comes in a variety of sizes. The most common film size for still photography in modern times is 135, commonly known as *35 mm*. The image area on this type of film is 24 × 36 mm. The next size up is known as *medium format* or *120 film*. The 120 film is 60 mm wide and the image can be 45 or 60 mm in length. Medium or large prints can be made on sheet film instead of rolled film. Sheet film commonly measures 4 × 5 inches.

film speed
The rate at which the silver halide grains of a given film react to light.

Film speed determines how sharp or grainy a photograph appears. The film speed is the rate at which the film reacts with light. High-speed films contain larger grains of silver that react more quickly with light, making them ideal for scenes in which light is at a minimum. High-speed films, however, produce grainier pictures than lower-speed films. Lower-speed films produce sharper photographs, but they require more light to react with the smaller grains. Film speed is measured by two different scales. The International Standardization Organization (ISO) scale is simply arithmetic: 200 ISO speed film simply has twice the speed of 100 ISO speed film. The German Institution for Standardization (DIN) uses a logarithmic scale in which a three-unit increase is equal to twice the speed. Thus, DIN 28 film is twice the speed of DIN 25 film.

Other film types may be used for unique circumstances. Polaroid film prints an instant photograph that can ensure that the setting will produce an acceptable crime-scene photograph. A Polaroid can also serve as a quick record of evidence that might be not be available for a second try if the pictures do not turn out right. Examples of this are impressions in soil or snow and fingerprints developed at the crime scene.

Infrared film records only images that reflect infrared light. Because some inks reflect infrared light, this type of film is frequently used in questioned-document examination to view text that has been crossed out or altered. It is also useful for locating gravesites in aerial photography, visualizing gunshot residue on dark fabrics, and viewing underlying patterns in bite and bruise marks. Many cameras have separate settings for infrared film. Infrared film should not be stored for long periods of time because it will deteriorate.

Digital Image Recording   A digital photograph is made when a light-sensitive microchip inside the camera is exposed to light coming from an object or scene. A digital camera captures light on each of millions of tiny picture elements, called pixels. The light is recorded on each pixel as a specific electric charge using a charged coupled device (CCD) or complementary metal oxide semi-conductor (CMOS). The camera reads this charge number as image information, then stores the image as a file on a memory card.

The number of pixels that capture light is directly related to the resolution of the picture. Resolution is defined as the minimum distance that must separate two objects in order for them to be viewed as distinct objects. The lower the distance needed, the greater the resolution of the photograph is said to be. Photographs with increasingly good resolution show more and more detail and sharpness. The greater the number of pixels featured on the digital camera, the better the resolution will be.

Because the number of pixels on a digital camera is in the millions, the number is usually referred to in terms of megapixels. A camera that has four million pixels is a four-megapixel camera. A standard four-megapixel camera can create a clear image up to an 8×10-inch print. As the number of megapixels increases, the clarity increases, allowing photographers to create bigger prints. Crime-scene photographers usually use cameras that feature as many as ten megapixels.

megapixel
One million pixels; used to describe a digital camera in terms of sensor resolution (i.e., four megapixels equals four million pixels).

Photographic Equipment and Principles

Whether they employ film or digital methods, photographers must master the same basic methods and use many of the same kinds of specialized equipment. The cameras, lenses, flashes, and filters used in digital and film photography perform the same functions and operate on the same set of principles.

FIGURE 3–2 An example of a digital single lens reflex camera (DSLR). *Courtesy Sony Electronics Inc.*

single lens reflex (SLR or DSLR) camera
A type of camera that uses the same lens for viewing and for taking the picture. The image seen in the viewfinder or on the LCD monitor is how the photo will turn out.

Cameras The most commonly used camera for film crime-scene photography is the **single lens reflex camera** or SLR. The digital version of this camera is called a digital single lens reflex, or DSLR (see Figure 3–2). Although digital imaging technology is becoming dominant in all aspects of photography, many jurisdictions still advocate the use of film or a combination of film and digital.

Although the general public is more familiar with digital "point and shoot" cameras, the SLR and DSLR cameras are required for photographing a crime scene. Both kinds of SLR cameras allow for the use of a wide range of lenses, flashes, and filters. Further, SLR and DSLR cameras give photographers the option of manually selecting f-stop, shutter speed, and other variables associated with photography. These settings are discussed in further detail in the following sections. DSLRs also have the advantage of having a large imaging microchip that produces higher-quality images and prints than the traditional "point and shoot" digital cameras can produce.

Lenses The lens of the camera is the mechanism that bends light to focus an image on the film or digital microchip. In general, the thicker the lens, the greater its ability to bend light. Each lens has a specific focal length, which is the distance between the lens and the image projected on the film or microchip. As the thickness and bending ability of the lens increases, the focal length decreases because the lens can bend light onto a surface closer to it. Photographers generally use lenses with long focal lengths to capture more details of objects far from the camera. The kind of lens one uses, therefore, has a great impact on the quality of the photograph.

Normal Lens The normal lens has a 50 to 55 mm focal length. It can be used for most photographs that need to be taken at a crime scene because it can show as much area as half a wall. It can also take satisfactory photographs of pieces of evidence at standard distances.

Telephoto Lens   The telephoto lens is like a telescope attachment for the camera, magnifying the image. This lens has a focal length of 100 mm or greater. This means that a 200 mm telephoto lens, for example, produces an image that is a four times the magnification of the normal 50 mm lens.

Wide-Angle Lens   A photographer who needs to capture a wider area uses a wide-angle lens with a focal length less than 50 mm. The typical focal length of the wide-angle lens is 35 mm, and it can show much more area in one photograph than can a normal lens. For example, this lens is useful in photographing wide objects such as the facade of a building; it captures more detail to the left and right of the center of the structure than does a normal lens.

Macro Lens   When very close photographs and good detail are required, the photographer might use a macro lens. The macro lens has a focal length less than 50 mm with a 1:1 or 1:2 magnification ratio. It is especially useful for close-ups of fiber or tool mark evidence.

Multipurpose Lens   A multipurpose lens, commonly called a zoom lens, can also be used for crime-scene photography. These lenses have a range of focal length usually from 28 to 80 mm. This type of lens allows the photographer to take normal, wide-angle, and telephoto photographs without changing lenses.

Most DSLR cameras have a fixed normal or multipurpose lens, typically in the range of 14 to 55 mm and accept a variety of other lenses. Some digital cameras have specific settings to mimic the effects of special lenses. For example, the macro setting on a digital camera, usually represented by a flower symbol, offers the attributes of a macro lens by making the foreground appear larger and the background appear smaller.

Aperture and Shutter Speed   The amount of light gathered by the camera is regulated by the aperture and shutter speed of the camera. The camera aperture is the diameter of the opening of the mechanism, called the *diaphragm,* which allows in light. On film or digital cameras, one adjusts the aperture by setting the f-number, which is equal to the focal length divided by the aperture. Thus, the f-number and aperture are inversely related. The lower the f-number setting, the wider the aperture and the more light it allows in. Standard f-number settings have come to be known as f-stops, ranging along a continuum of possible aperture sizes. For example, the lowest f-number (1.0) is arbitrarily designated as f-stop zero (f-0). Each f-stop represents a twofold difference in the amount of light entering the camera. Because f-stop and aperture are inversely related, f-2 thus would have a larger aperture than f-22. Some film and digital cameras, called *aperture priority cameras,* allow the user to control the f-stop manually, but not the shutter speed.

The shutter of a camera is the mechanism that controls the exposure of the film or microchip to light. The shutter speed is the length of time that the film or microchip is exposed to light. This is measured in fractions of a second by factors of 1/2 (i.e., 1/2, 1/4, 1/8, etc.). A film camera that allows the user to manually change the shutter speed shows only the bottom number. On these cameras, the optimal setting is usually marked in red.

DSLR cameras have a wide range of options for adjusting f-stop and shutter speed. The green "auto" mode automatically selects an appropriate f-stop and shutter speed for the conditions. Alternately, digital cameras may have a setting known as "sports mode" to capture subjects in motion

aperture
The size of the diaphragm opening through which light enters the camera.

f-stop
A setting on a camera that controls the aperture diameter to determine the amount of light transmitted the lens.

shutter speed
The length of time that the film or microchip is exposed to light.

by using a higher (faster) shutter speed. This setting is usually represented by a symbol of a figure running or a foot kicking a ball. A digital camera's "night mode," denoted by a moon or star, is set for a lower (slower) shutter speed. This allows the shutter to be open longer to gather as much light as possible to create the image. SLR and DSLR cameras allow the user to change shutter speed by adjusting a control knob on the camera. Also, the photographer can operate the camera in a fully manual mode.

depth of field
The range of in the foreground and background of a photographic subject that are also relatively in focus.

Depth of Field   An important trait of a photograph is the depth of field shown in the photograph. This is the amount of area in the foreground and background of an object in focus that is also relatively in focus. This is especially important for photographs of an entire scene and of three-dimensional objects. The smaller the aperture is, the greater the depth of field will be. It is important to remember that the aperture is measured on a camera by the f-stop number, which is inversely related to the aperture diameter. This means that higher f-stops will yield higher depths of field. The "landscape mode" on a digital camera (generally represented by a mountain symbol) automatically selects higher f-stops to improve the depth of field when the background and foreground are important, such as in scenery photographs. The "portrait mode" of a digital camera, on the other hand, selects lower f-stops to decrease the depth of field and make the subject stand out clearly against a blurred background.

color temperature
The measure of the "degree of whiteness" of a light source as compared to a hypothetical source of perfect white light.

Illumination   Illumination refers to the light falling on the object in a photograph. An important photographic aspect of light is its color temperature. This is the measurement of the difference in hue between a light source and a theoretical source of perfect white light. On the color temperature scale, a "hot" light source has a bluer hue, whereas a "cold" light source has a red-orange hue. Different light sources exhibit different color temperatures. Similarly, sunlight will exhibit varying color temperatures during different times of the day and different weather conditions.

Film cameras will detect or even exaggerate the color of the light source, making the scene appear different on film than it appears to the naked eye. Specific film should be purchased for use under certain light conditions. For example, tungsten film is best suited for use under incandescent indoor lighting, whereas daylight film is better for use under sunlight. Most digital cameras have automatic "white balance" settings that allow them to automatically compensate for color temperatures that deviate from white. Some digital cameras feature additional white balance modes for specific light sources, including incandescent lighting, fluorescent lighting, direct sunlight, and overcast sunlight.

Manipulating illumination   A photographer must be able to recognize and manipulate the amount of light and the angle of illumination in a photograph. Light meters are devices that allow photographers to measure the amount of light in a shot. An incident light meter in a film camera measures the amount of light being projected onto a photographic subject regardless of whether the surface is reflective (white) or nonreflective (black). A reflective light meter in a film camera measures the amount of light reflected off photographic subjects. For a picture that is neither too dark nor too light, a surface that reflects 18 percent of the light (gray colored) is recommended. Film photographers can also manipulate the angle of illumination by using a movable light source such as a flash on a stretchable cord. Sometimes direct light at 90 degrees to the subject is acceptable. However, in the case of three-dimensional objects that need to display depth, light from oblique angles (commonly 30 degrees or 60 degrees) can be used to cause shadows that show depth. This technique is especially helpful for illuminating footwear and tire impressions.

Most digital cameras also have light meters, but the user may have to choose a function from the menu to activate the light meter. Digital cameras designed for the casual user rely on preprogrammed settings and computer technology to determine the optimal settings (such as shutter speed and f-stop) for each photograph taken. In place of manual f-stop operation, a digital camera may use exposure compensation that the user can adjust to capture an extremely bright or dark image. Most digital cameras offer values ranging from –2, –1, 0, 1, and 2. The "0" setting refers to the starting point—that is, the conditions the camera's auto focus feature determines to be optimal. Adjusting toward negative numbers will reduce the exposure, thereby darkening a bright (overexposed) shot.

To compensate for backlighting, a camera may have a center-weighted or spot metering setting. Center-weighted metering directs the camera to determine the optimal settings based on the light conditions present in the center of the field. Spot metering directs the camera to calculate the best settings for the light conditions at the spot on the center of the viewfinder. The default setting, called matrix or evaluative metering, is based on the average light intensity across the entire field of view. Some manufacturers have preprogrammed settings named for specific light conditions and composition. Some of the more expensive digital cameras show a graph of the light present in the photograph to help suggest exposure settings.

Flashes   The electronic strobe flash is the most commonly used source of artificial illumination in photography. This type of flash is usually mounted on the top or front of a camera. A flash unit is an electronic flash that is not mounted to the camera. It is either separately operated or connected to the camera by a cord. In either case, the user must time the flash with the correct shutter speed for flash photography (usually 1/60). The flash unit, also called a slave flash, is very important to crime-scene photography because it can illuminate dark areas or create lighting at various angles to show greater detail.

A flash can produce both direct reflective lighting and oblique lighting, depending on the photographer's needs, Direct reflective lighting occurs when the flash is attached or placed at 90 degrees to the plane of view. It provides high contrast, but may show light reflectance in the photograph. Direct lighting is aimed 45 degrees to the plane of view to minimize reflectance. Oblique lighting places the flash at an angle to the plane of view lower than 45 degrees to show greater detail by creating a shadowing effect. Regardless of what kind of flash is used, it may be necessary to manually increase or decrease the flash power. For example, decreasing the flash power can help avoid overexposing a close subject.

Most commercially available digital cameras have mounted electronic strobe flashes. This integrated flash can illuminate subjects up to only ten feet away. At one time, this meant that film photography had an advantage in its ability to accommodate flash unit light sources. However, an adapter called a hot shoe now allows digital cameras to use a flash unit or non-mounted flash. Digital cameras also have a feature called "fill flash." This narrows the range of the flash to concentrate illumination on only a dark, backlit subject or object to bring out detail. However, the detail of the background may suffer.

Because mounted flashes on either film or digital cameras illuminate only a specific distance, a photographer may have to use reflectors to direct light to illuminate specific objects.

FIGURE 3–3 **A tripod used for crime-scene photography should have adjustable legs that are sturdy to ensure 90-degree photographs.** *Courtesy Sirchie Finger Print Laboratories, Inc., Youngsville, N.C., www.sirchie.com*

Filters The use of filters in photography can help enhance specific elements of a picture or show elements of the picture not usually visible. Filters allow only specific wavelengths (colors) of light to reach the film.

The most common types of filters are barrier and bypass filters. *Barrier filters* block one specific wavelength (color) of light from reaching the film or microchip, making areas of that color appear lighter in the photograph. This is helpful when a fingerprint or other feature on a piece of evidence is difficult to see against a specific color. A *bypass filter* allows only a small range of wavelengths of light to reach the film or microchip and blocks all others. Ultraviolet photography uses a bypass filter that allows only ultraviolet light to reach black-and-white film. Objects that fluoresce, or glow, under ultraviolet light—such as semen, components of some fibers, and fluorescent fingerprint powder—appear more readily using this technique. It is also sometimes used when photographing wounds to show greater contrast.

By using a filter of a complementary color, a photographer can make certain areas of an object appear darker. A red filter, for example, will darken blue/green areas, and an orange/yellow filter will darken blue/violet areas. A polarizer filter may be used to eliminate reflections from windows and water and to eliminate glare. A photographer may also employ a filter when the light source used at the scene is a laser.

Tripods The use of a tripod can improve the quality of a photograph by eliminating the possibility of blurred photos resulting from unsteady hands. Any photograph taken at a shutter speed less than 60 (1/60 second) must be taken from a tripod. A tripod with independently adjustable legs is a superior choice because it is suitable for uneven terrain. The tripod should also have a bubble level to ensure 90-degree images of evidence (see Figure 3–3).

Key Points

- Film is made of a sheet of light-reactive silver halide grains. The light-capturing ability of the grains is called film speed, and higher-speed films have bigger grains in order to capture light faster. This means that higher-speed films create grainier photographs.

- Digital cameras feature a light-sensitive microchip that captures light on each of millions of tiny picture elements, called pixels. The light is recorded on each pixel as a specific charge that will later be electronically translated to an image. The number of pixels on a camera is measured in the millions as megapixels and directly affects an image's resolution.

- SLR and DSLR cameras allow for the use of a wide range of lenses including normal lenses, telephoto lenses, wide-angle lenses, macro lenses, and multipurpose lenses. The kind of lens used affects the appearance of the image.

- The aperture and shutter speed regulate the amount of light gathered by the camera. These settings can be manually adjusted on SLR and DSLR cameras.

- The f-stop determines depth of field, or the amount of area in the foreground and background that is in focus. The higher the f-stop, the smaller the aperture and the greater the depth of field. Landscape and portrait settings on a digital camera adjust for higher and lower f-stops, respectively.

- The color temperature of the light source used makes a photographic image appear orange or blue. Many digital cameras combat this with "white balance" capability. Exposure compensation and electronic flashes can be used to capture images of dark or light subjects. Flash units, or slave flashes, are helpful to provide oblique or versatile illumination.

- Filters are used with SLR or DSLR cameras and are designed to block a certain range of light (barrier filters) or allow in only a certain range of light (bypass filters). Filters can be used to show greater detail in photographs by adjusting the appearance of specific colors.

- Tripods can greatly improve photograph quality by preventing blurriness caused by the movement of the photographer's hand. They also ensure 90-degree close-up photographs of evidence.

Crime-Scene Photography

The first picture on each roll of film taken at the crime scene should show the **photography log**. The top of the photography log should include the case number, type of scene, date, location of scene, description of the camera and lenses being used, film type and speed (if applicable), and the photographer's name and title. The log should also contain a table in which each photograph will be logged. Each photograph's log should show the date and time the photograph was taken, the location of the picture, the f-stop and

photography log
The form on which the investigator records the details of each photograph taken at a crime scene.

shutter speed settings, the lighting used and the lighting angle (if applicable), the angle of the camera, and a description of the subject of the picture. Because this log will be important in recognizing photographs later in the investigation, it should be included in the case file. A pair of investigators may work best with one person taking the pictures and the other filling in the photo log and placing a ruler or measuring scale in each photograph as a point of reference for size.

Some digital cameras produce an electronic photography log. This log must be submitted along with notes, a written photography log, and the testimony of the investigator for the digital photographs to be considered for admissibility.

Procedures and Techniques

The most important prerequisite for photographing a crime scene is that it be in an unaltered condition. Except for injured parties, objects must not be moved until they have been photographed from all necessary angles. If objects are removed, positions changed, or items added, the photographs may not be admissible as evidence at a trial. In that case, their intended value will be lost. The crime-scene report should note whether evidence was removed or moved prior to photography. Evidence should not be reintroduced into the scene in order to take photographs.

Each crime scene should be photographed as completely as possible in a logical succession. This means that the crime scene should include the area in which the crime actually took place and all adjacent areas where important acts occurred immediately before or after the commission of the crime. The photographer commonly will work from the perimeter to the center of a scene. The sequence used must be kept consistent for all crime scenes. This will show the overall scene first, then work down to individual pieces of evidence that jurors in the trial can easily relate back to the larger scene (see Figure 3–4).

In addition to original film photos, investigators may make additional prints or slides to use in court. All printed photos should be signed, dated, and labeled on the back after they are inspected. If negatives from print film are not kept in evidence storage, they should be stored in a locked location, perhaps in a case folder.

Photographing a crime scene requires specific equipment:

- Camera (film or digital)
- Variety of lenses or a multipurpose lens
- Electronic flash with connector cord
- Tripod
- Film of different types and exposures as needed
- Documentation and labeling materials
- Scale or ruler
- Flashlight
- Batteries or battery charger
- Photography log

Overview Photographs The first pictures the photographer takes should be overview photographs of the entire scene and surrounding area, including

(a)

(b)

(c)

FIGURE 3–4 **This sequence of crime-scene photographs shows the proper progression of photographing the scene. (a) The sequence begins with an overview photograph of the entry to the victim's bedroom showing evidence markers in place. (b) The medium-range photograph shows the evidence marker next to the door denoting a cartridge case. (c) The close-up photograph shows the cartridge in detail with a scale in the photograph.**

points of exit and entry. These photographs should be taken from the outside borders of the scene and from various angles. If the crime took place indoors, the entire room should be photographed to show each wall area. Rooms adjacent to the actual crime site must be similarly photographed. If the crime scene includes a body, photographs must show the body's position and location relative to the entire scene. When taking overview photographs, the crime-scene photographer should include at least one object in multiple overview photographs to help visually piece the scene together. This object is called a "visual tag." Although one should avoid having individuals present in photographs, it may be helpful to photograph witnesses in the locations from which they viewed the crime. This can help the jury determine what a witness could or could not have seen from these locations. One may also wish to photograph the sight lines of suspects and victims. If a camera boom is available, the photographer should take pictures from overhead.

Medium-Range Photographs The next set of pictures should be medium-range photographs that show the layout of smaller significant areas of the crime scene. Medium-range pictures should be taken with evidence markers in place to show the spatial relationships between and among pieces of evidence in greater detail than the overview photographs. A key medium-range photograph standard to all crime scenes is one that includes the "center" of the scene. In violent crimes, this usually includes the site where the victim was found and the surrounding area.

Close-Up Photographs Close-up photographs, taken last, show greater detail of individual objects or evidence. The pictures must be taken at a 90-degree angle to the object, with and without evidence markers and scales. Scales should be placed as close to the evidence as possible without affecting it in any way. After the 90-degree photographs have been taken, photographs from other angles may be taken. For three-dimensional objects, oblique lighting may be needed. It is also important to *bracket* close-up photographs. This means that the same photograph should be taken at varying f-stops and shutter speeds to ensure the best detail possible. Filters may also be important for close-up photographs. The most important close-up photographs are those depicting injuries and weapons lying near a body. After the body is removed from the scene, the surface beneath the body should be photographed.

To summarize, the four minimum photographs required at a crime scene are an overview photograph, a medium-range photograph, a close-up photograph, and a close-up photograph with a scale. These photographs create an adequate visual record of the position and appearance of an item of evidence at a crime scene.

Photographs at Night Photography at night can be very challenging. It is best to wait until morning, but there are a few methods to use if this is not possible. Fire departments or police commonly bring floodlights to outdoor crime scenes at night. Photographers often use reflectors to focus flash illumination on both indoor and outdoor scenes. A technique called "painting with light" allows photographers to illuminate long distances at night. This involves mounting a camera on a tripod and locking the shutter open in complete darkness. The photographer then proceeds around the crime scene, firing off a flash to illuminate all areas of the crime scene, usually about three or four flashes in total. The shutter is then closed to capture the image.

Special Photography In addition to general photography, specific types of photography may be needed for various crime scenes. Photographers use a wide variety of film speeds, film types, and filters to make the best visual record possible.

Indoor scenes Typically, the earliest photographs of an indoor crime scene are overview photographs of the exterior of the building that locate the scene and any evidence present on the exterior. The next photographs should be of the entrance itself, followed by photographs of the scene as viewed from the entrance. The photographer then moves around the interior of the scene in a clockwise or counterclockwise direction, taking photographs from each corner and possibly the middle of each wall to provide a complete 360-degree view of the scene. Medium-range photographs must then be taken of each wall, the floor, the ceiling, and the relative locations of groups of evidence from different angles. The crime-scene photographer should also be conscious of other rooms that may contain evidence and photograph them thoroughly as well. Close-up photographs should be taken of all located evidence (with and without scales) and injuries on a victim. Investigators should give special attention to locating and photographing any footwear impression into or out of an indoor scene.

Outdoor scenes At outdoor crime scenes, especially those involving vehicles, the earliest photographs may be of the street signs closest to the scene. Overview photographs are then taken from the defined borders of the scene. Investigators note the positions of these pictures on the photography log using global positioning device coordinates or by measuring the distance to the position from the nearest roadways. Medium-range photographs are taken of groups of evidence or zones of a large scene. Close-up photographs must be taken correctly because evidence at an outdoor scene rarely remains undisturbed for very long. If a vehicle is included in the scene or *is* the scene, overview photographs should be taken of the front and left side and then the back and right side. This angle will minimize glare to clearly show the license plate. If the vehicle was stolen or burglarized, pictures should show where on the vehicle the culprit gained access. Aerial photography may be required for large outdoor scenes or to show the relation of multiple scenes. It may also be useful to show weather conditions and traffic patterns near an outdoor site.

Arson photography   Overview photographs of an arson scene should show the relative location of the scene with the aid of street signs if possible. The arson scene also requires specific medium-range and close-up photographs of the likely point of entry, point of origin, and any areas of fire activity. Close-up photographs are also required for all located evidence. Photographers may use special lighting techniques or filters to show the dark-colored arson debris against dark-colored backgrounds. Because perpetrators of arson crimes frequently return to the scene, it may be especially important to photograph the crowd outside an arson scene.

Sexual assault victim photography   In cases involving sexual assault, once again overview photographs should be taken of the scene and surrounding area. Medium-range photographs of the position of the victim in relation to the scene may be important. Medium-range and close-up photographs should be taken of any wounds the victim may have sustained. These may include cuts, bruises, or blunt force trauma wounds. However, given the nature of the crime and probable locations of wounds on the victim's body, it is important that photographing be respectful. It is also important to photograph the clothing the victim was wearing during the attack.

Impression photography   If tire or footwear impressions are found at a crime scene, overview and medium-range photographs should be taken to show the relative position and direction of the impressions. Close-up photographs of tire and footwear impressions must be taken before the impression is cast. A tripod must be used to ensure that the film is arranged 90 degrees to the plane of view (see Figure 3–5). Oblique lighting and bracketing should be used to provide the best detail and maximum contrast through shadowing. A scale must be included in the photograph so that a 1:1 ratio print can later be created for comparison to exemplar tires or footwear (see Figure 3–6). It may also be wise to include an identifying tag in the photograph to indicate where the impression was found and which part of the impression is represented in the photograph. A tire impression must be photographed using an overlapping photograph sequence, and a minimum of 8 feet of the tire impression should be photographed.

Bloodstain photography   Overview and medium-range photographs should show the orientation and location of bloodstain evidence. Close-up photographs should be taken of each pertinent stain or group of stains. The photographs must be taken at 90 degrees to the stain. If analysis of a spatter pattern is done at the scene, photographs should be taken of the drawn area of convergence and area of origin. Bloodstains detected

FIGURE 3–5   A tripod and scale are used to take a close-up photograph of a tire impression marked with an evidence marker at 90 degrees. *Courtesy Sirchie Finger Print Laboratories, Inc., Youngsville, N.C., www.sirchie.com*

FIGURE 3–6   This tire impression photograph includes a scale so a 1:1 image can later be produced. *Courtesy Sirchie Finger Print Laboratories, Inc., Youngsville, N.C., www.sirchie.com*

with luminol (see Chapter 9) must be photographed in complete darkness. The shutter is locked open for approximately 30 seconds at an f-stop of 1.4.

Latent fingerprint photography Close-up photographs of latent (hidden) fingerprints must show the ridge details of the fingerprints for possible identification of the source. Any developed prints should be photographed before they are lifted. Photographs can be taken by a special latent fingerprint camera, which is designed to create a 1:1 photograph of evidence (see Figure 3–7) or by a standard film or digital camera fitted with an adapter. Commonly, black-and-white film photography is used to show greater contrast. An item label should be included in the photograph to identify the location of the fingerprint. The picture must be taken at 90 degrees using a high f-stop and oblique lighting for maximum detail. A fingerprint should be photographed using SLR color print film or a standard digital camera with a scale included in the photograph. If the pattern is enhanced with a blood reagent, photographs should be taken as the pattern develops.

Use of Digital Photography

Digital photography of crime scenes has many advantages. Investigators can observe images immediately after taking them to ensure that important photographs are clear and show the best possible detail. Also, the resolution available on many modern digital cameras can exceed six megapixels, whereas the maximum resolution offered by an SLR camera is equivalent to about five megapixels. As technology advances, digital photography provides other advantages over traditional film. For example, photographers can stitch together electronically individual images of a crime scene captured with a digital camera to reveal a nearly three-dimensional panoramic view of the crime scene (see Figure 3–8). With the aid of a computer, any area of the scene captured digitally can be enhanced and examined in fine detail.

WebExtra 3.1
Making a Photographic Record of the Crime Scene
www.prenhall.com/saferstein

(a) (b)

FIGURE 3–7 **(a) A specialized camera is used to photograph latent fingerprints on a cereal box (b) and creates a 1:1 photograph.** *Courtesy Sirchie Finger Print Laboratories, Inc., Youngsville, N.C., www.sirchie.com*

FIGURE 3–8 Individual images (top) are shown before being electronically stitched together into a single panoramic image (bottom). Individual photographs should be taken with about a 30 percent overlap. *Courtesy Imaging Forensics, Fountain Valley, Calif., www.imagingforensics.com*

The very nature of digital images, however, opens digital photography to important criticisms within forensic science casework. Because the photographs are digital, they can be easily manipulated by using computer software. This manipulation goes beyond traditional photograph enhancement such as adjusting brightness and contrast or color balancing. Computer software also allows a person to crop a photo, remove repeating patterns such as window screens, superimpose images, and alter photos significantly in many other ways. Because the primary function of crime-scene photography is to provide an accurate depiction, this is a major concern.

The crime-scene photographer using digital photography also has to be conscious of the kind of file format in which the crime-scene images are saved. Digital images are preserved by either lossy or lossless compression. Lossy compression condenses files by discarding some image information. The information lost during this compression is irretrievable. Lossless compression condenses files without discarding information so no important image information is lost. For this reason, all digital crime-scene photographs should be saved by lossless compression.

To ensure that their digital images are admissible, many jurisdictions have developed or are developing standard operating procedures (SOPs) for the use of digital photography. Sometimes admissibility requires a detailed and accurate photography log kept by the crime-scene photographer to be submitted along with the testimony of the photographer as to the accuracy of the photographs. The goal is to set guidelines for determining the circumstances under which digital photography may be used

lossless compression
A compression method for digital files that decreases the file size without discarding digital data.

and to establish and enforce strict protocols for image security and chain of custody. For example, digital photographs should be copied only to writable disks. They should never be placed on rewritable disks that can be altered or erased. If an image is to be enhanced in some way, the new image must be saved separately, not written over the original image.

The digital era promises new and elegant approaches to document the crime scene. Cameras such as that shown in Figure 3–9 are capable of taking dozens of digital images while scanning the crime scene. Photographic and laser data from multiple scan locations are combined to produce 3D models of the scene in full color that can be viewed from any vantage point, measured, and used for analysis and courtroom presentations.

Video Documentation

The use of videotape at crime scenes is becoming increasingly popular because the cost of this equipment is decreasing. Videotaping of crime scenes is even required in some jurisdictions as a preliminary "tour" of the scene.

The same principles used in crime-scene photographs apply to videotaping. As with conventional photography, videotaping should include the entire scene and the immediate surrounding area. Long shots as well as close-ups should be taken in a slow and systematic manner. The way the investigator moves through the scene should be logical and should illustrate potential paths of entry, exit, and movement. Furthermore, it is desirable to have one crime-scene investigator narrate the events and scenes being taped while another does the actual shooting. Only the narrator's voice should be heard, and no personnel should be in the shots.

Videotaping can have advantages over still photography in certain situations. For example, modern video cameras allow the user to play back the tape of a scene and check it for completeness. Video also is usually very

WebExtra 3.2
Creating a 3D model of a crime scene with the ability to measure relevant areas of the scene.
www.prenhall.com/saferstein

FIGURE 3–9 A computer-controlled scanner has both a high-resolution, professional digital camera and a long-range laser rangefinder. The tripod-mounted device rotates a full 360 degrees, taking dozens of photographs and measuring millions of individual points. Photographic and laser data from multiple scan locations are combined to produce 3D models of the scene. *Courtesy 3rd Tech, Inc., Durham, N.C. 27713, www.deltasphere.com*

helpful in arson cases where still photographs have trouble showing detail, and where determining the path of the fire is very important. In addition, many video cameras can also take still photographs, or stills can be created from the tape on a computer. Video essentially combines notes and photography. Some cameras even have a "night vision" feature, which is similar to infrared photography.

There are also disadvantages to videotaping crime scenes. The camera will always shake, although some cameras have a stabilization feature. Also, zooming and panning can be very sloppy; these techniques should be used only occasionally and should be done very slowly. Extra noise due to wind or other investigators can obscure narration or may be inappropriate and damaging. Because of the "on the spot" nature of the narration, investigators may stumble over words, which can be confusing when a video is used in court. To avoid this, some investigators record the video with the sound off and dub notes over it later. Still images taken from videotape are usually of much poorer quality than those taken by film or digital camera. Videotapes also begin deteriorating from the first time they are played back, and they deteriorate during storage in about five years. Videotape is also sensitive, and it can be affected by high temperatures, humidity, and magnetic fields. The advent of digital video cameras is alleviating these problems.

Although videotaping can capture the sounds and scenes of the crime site with relative ease, the technique cannot at this time be used in place of still photography. The still photograph remains unsurpassed in the definition of detail it provides to the human eye.

Key Points

- Film and digital photography are both used widely for documenting crime scenes.

- The crime scene should be recorded with a minimum of four photographs: an overview photograph, a medium-range photograph, a close-up photograph, and a close-up photograph with a scale.

- Special techniques and considerations are needed when photographing indoor scenes, outdoor scenes, night scenes, arson scenes, sexual assault victims, impression evidence, bloodstain evidence, and latent fingerprint evidence.

- Although many digital cameras have far surpassed the common film camera in resolution and ease of use, admissibility issues may still exist in the use of digital images during legal proceedings.

- Video documentation is helpful for showing possible paths and for including note narration with photography. However, still pictures are still required for detail and especially for close-up views of evidence.

Sketching the Crime Scene

Once the crime-scene investigator has taken sufficient notes and photographs, he or she sketches the scene. The sketch serves many important functions in the legal investigation of a crime. If done correctly, a sketch can clearly show the layout of an indoor or outdoor crime scene and the relationship in space of all the items and features significant to the investigation. Sketches are especially important to illustrate the location of collected evidence. A sketch can clarify objects and features already described in notes or shown in photographs. Sketches can also show measurements over long distances and the topography of outdoor scenes. Possible paths of entry, exit, and movement through the scene may be speculated from a good sketch. The state of the scene illustrated by the sketch may help to demonstrate whether a witness's testimony is feasible. To be effective, a sketch must be clear enough to be used in reconstruction by other investigative personnel and to illustrate aspects of the crime scene to a jury.

The Rough Sketch

The investigator may have neither the skill nor the time to make a polished sketch of the scene. However, this is not required during the early phase of the investigation. What is necessary is a **rough sketch** containing an accurate depiction of the dimensions of the scene and showing the location of all objects having a bearing on the case. It shows all recovered items of physical evidence, as well as other important features of the crime scene (see Figure 3–10).

Following are tools required to create the sketch (see Figure 3–11).

rough sketch
The rudimentary first sketch created at the crime scene with care for accuracy in depicting dimensions and locations but no concern for aesthetic appearance.

- Graph paper or drawing paper

- Two measuring tapes

- Clipboard or drawing surface

- Pencils

- Straight edge ruler

- Erasers

- Compass or global positioning device

- Optional tools including drawing compasses, protractors (half or full circle), architect scales, French curves, drafting triangles, and rolling measuring devices

All sketches must include the following features:

- The *title block* contains the case number, the agency number (if applicable), the name and title of the artist, the location of the scene, and the date and time at which the sketch was created. It may also state the victim's name, the names of any suspects, or the type of crime. The title block should appear in the lower right corner of the sketch paper.

- The *legend* should contain the key to the identity and dimensions of objects or evidence and may be represented by symbols, letters, or numbers.

- The *compass* should show an arrow to denote north in relation to the scene.

- The *body* of the sketch contains the drawing itself and all dimensions and objects located within it.

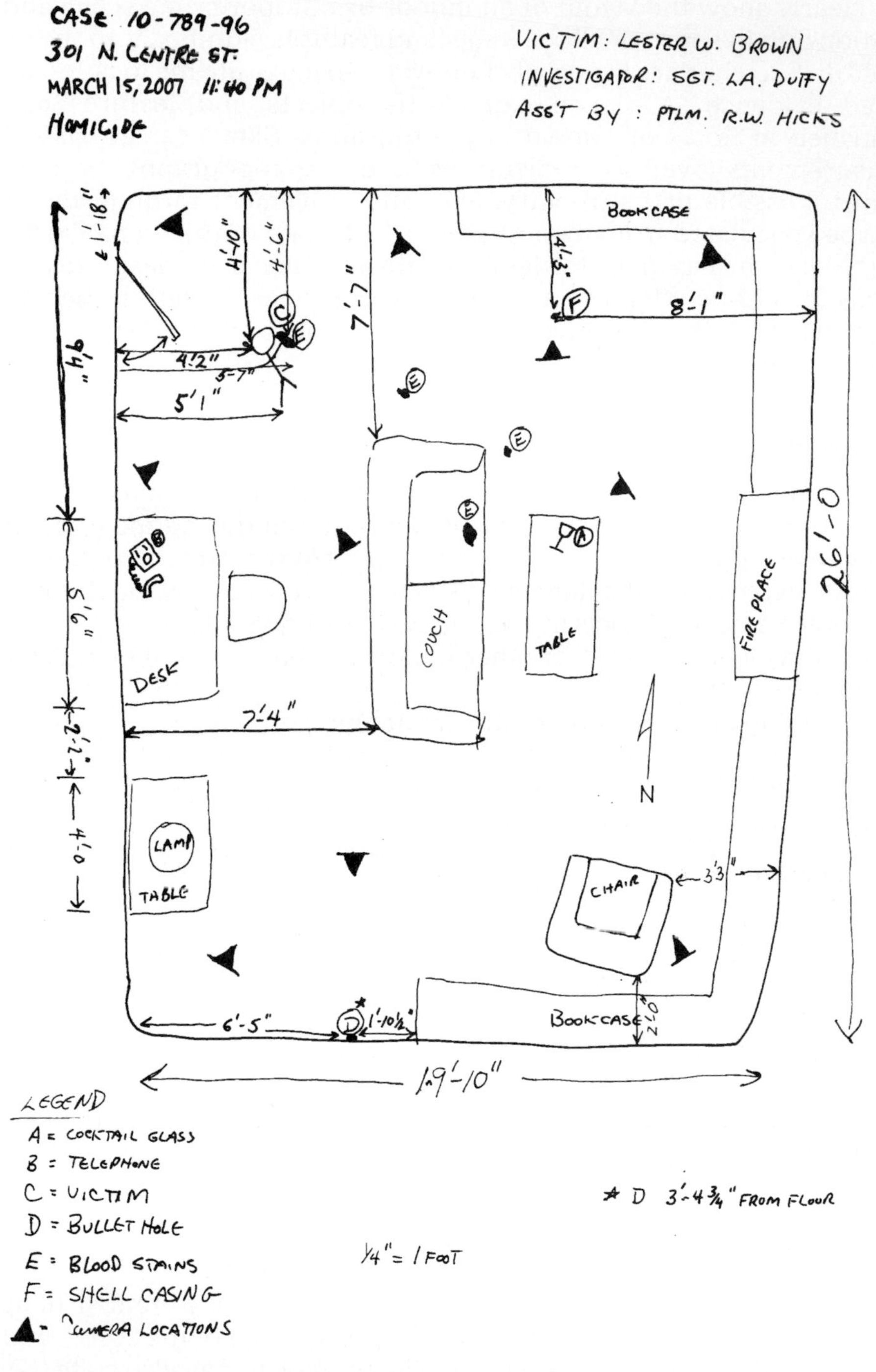

FIGURE 3–10 A rough sketch of a crime scene. *Courtesy Sirchie Finger Print Laboratories, Inc., Youngsville, N.C., www.sirchie.com*

Creating the Sketch

1. Define the boundaries of the sketch. These may be walls for an indoor sketch. Make sure that the area within these boundaries includes all the pertinent objects and evidence.

2. Establish known points from which to measure the locations of objects and evidence. These points should be fixed. This can be walls or doors in indoor scenes. Trees, telephone poles, street signs, or natural features (e.g., boulders) can be used for outdoor scenes.

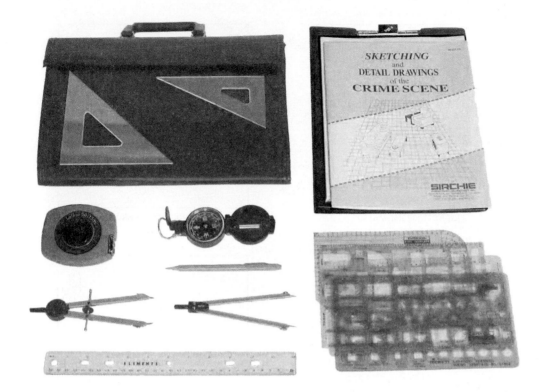

FIGURE 3–11 A basic kit for sketching the crime scene. *Courtesy Sirchie Finger Print Laboratories, Inc., Youngsville, N.C., www.sirchie.com*

3. The walls or boundaries should be drawn in first, leaving as much room as possible for the contents. If walls are used, their dimensions should be recorded.

4. Measurements should be taken from the fixed points to pieces of evidence first. There are three methods of measurement from the two points of reference.
    - The *rectangular* method measures two distances to an object that make a right angle with each other and two fixed, flat surfaces. These surfaces are usually walls (see Figure 3–12a).

    - The *triangulation* method measures the distance of the object from two fixed points of known distance from each other. This forms a triangle. In an indoor scene these points are usually the corners of a room (see Figure 3–12b).

    - The *baseline* method is especially useful for outdoor scenes. First, two fixed objects on opposite sides of the scene are located (designated A and B). A line is then made between them and measured. Each object or piece of evidence has a line drawn from it to the baseline to make a 90-degree angle with the baseline. The distance of the line from the object to the baseline is then measured, along with its point of intersection with the baseline (see Figure 3–12c).

    - The *polar coordinates* method uses only one reference point. The sketch shows the distance and angle at which an object is located in the scene relative to the reference point (see Figure 3–12d).

Distances shown on the sketch must be accurate and not the result of a guess or estimate. For this reason, all measurements should be made with a tape measure and confirmed by two people. The simplest way to show the

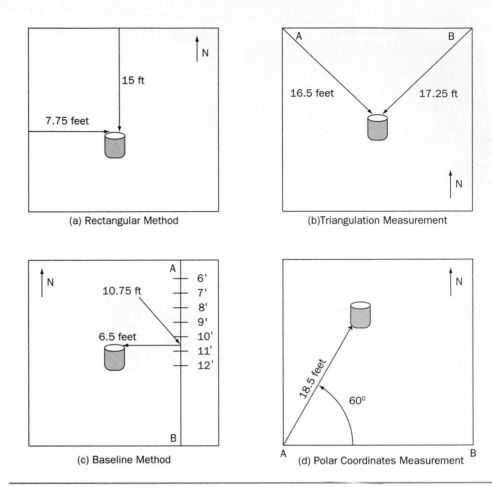

FIGURE 3–12 **(a) The rectangular measurement method; (b) the triangulation measurement method; (c) the baseline measurement method; (d) and the polar coordinates measurement method.**

location of an item in a sketch is to assign it a number or letter. A legend will then correlate the letter to the item's description and dimensions. Symbols for objects should be consistent. Commonly, items of evidence are assigned numbers (possibly correlating to their evidence marker number), and nonevidentiary objects are assigned letters. The distances and dimensions of objects not considered evidence are measured, recorded, and drawn last. Distances between objects can also be measured and drawn. It is very important that units of measure are kept the same throughout the sketch. Usually inches and feet are used in the United States because those measurements are easily understood by the investigative personnel and the jury.

The Finished Sketch

finished sketch
The perfected final sketch that is constructed with care and concern for aesthetic appearance and is drawn to scale.

Unlike the rough sketch, the **finished sketch** is constructed with care and concern for aesthetic appearance. The finished sketch must be drawn to scale. The legend should contain the scale (e.g., 1/2" = 1'). When the finished sketch is completed, it must reflect information contained within the rough sketch to be admissible evidence in a courtroom. An indoor overview sketch shows the floors of one or more rooms, doors and windows, and any evidence or objects on the floor (see Figures 3–13 and 3–14). An outdoor overview sketch is like an aerial view of a small or large outdoor scene. A final sketch can be done by an investigator or a hired professional. It can be done by hand in pen or by computer (see Figure 3–15).

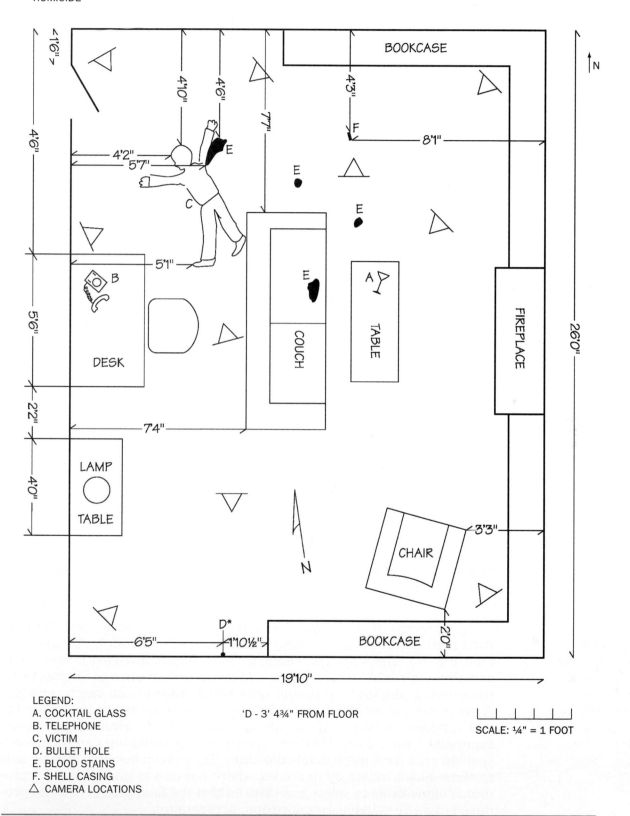

CASE 10-789-90
301 N. CENTRE ST.
March 15, 2007 11: 40 PM
HOMICIDE

VICTIM: LESTER W. BROWN
INVESTIGATOR: SGT. L.A. DUFFY
ASS'T BY: PTLM. R.W. HICKS

BOOKCASE

N

4'1'6"

4'10"

4'6"

7'7"

4'3"

F

8'1"

4'6"

4'2"

5'7"

E

E

C

E

E

5'1"

B

E

COUCH

A

TABLE

FIREPLACE

26'0"

DESK

5'6"

74"

2'2"

LAMP

4'0"

TABLE

CHAIR

3'3"

2'0"

N

D*

BOOKCASE

6'5"

1'10½"

19'10"

LEGEND:
A. COCKTAIL GLASS
B. TELEPHONE
C. VICTIM
D. BULLET HOLE
E. BLOOD STAINS
F. SHELL CASING
△ CAMERA LOCATIONS

'D - 3' 4¾" FROM FLOOR

SCALE: ¼" = 1 FOOT

FIGURE 3–13 An overview finished sketch of a room interior. *Courtesy Sirchie Finger Print Laboratories, Inc., Youngsville, N.C., www.sirchie.com*

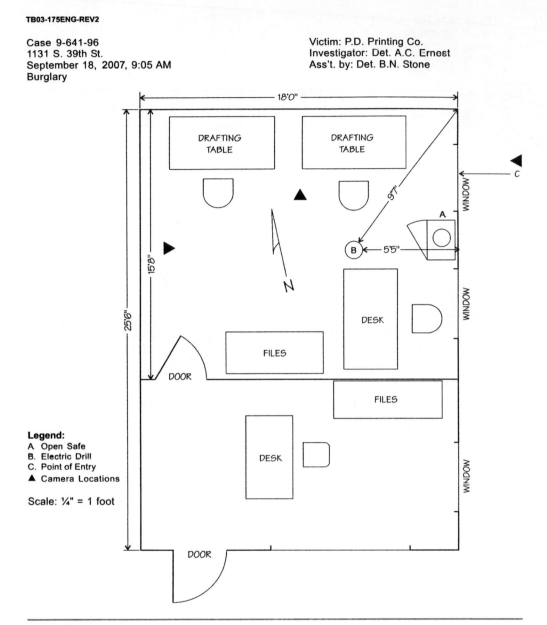

TB03-175ENG-REV2

Case 9-641-96
1131 S. 39th St.
September 18, 2007, 9:05 AM
Burglary

Victim: P.D. Printing Co.
Investigator: Det. A.C. Ernest
Ass't. by: Det. B.N. Stone

DRAFTING TABLE

DRAFTING TABLE

WINDOW

C

A

B

5'5"

9'7"

N

DESK

WINDOW

FILES

DOOR

FILES

DESK

WINDOW

DOOR

18'0"

15'8"

25'6"

Legend:
A Open Safe
B. Electric Drill
C. Point of Entry
▲ Camera Locations

Scale: ¼" = 1 foot

FIGURE 3–14   An overview finished sketch of an office scene. *Courtesy Sirchie Finger Print Laboratories, Inc., Youngsville, N.C., www.sirchie.com*

computer-aided drafting (CAD)
The process of creating scaled drawing using specially designed computer software.

The process of **computer-aided drafting (CAD)** has become the standard method for reconstructing crime scenes from rough sketches (see Figure 3–16). The software, ranging from simple, low-cost programs to complex, expensive ones, contains predrawn objects such as intersections, roadways, buildings, and rooms, onto which information can be entered. A generous symbol library provides a variety of images that can be used to add intricate details such as blood spatters to a crime-scene sketch. Equipped with a zoom function, computerized sketching can focus on a specific area for a more detailed picture. These sketches may also be able to show bullet trajectory in scenes where a gun was involved. CAD programs allow users to select scale size so that the final product can be produced in a size suitable for courtroom presentation.

Three-dimensional CAD sketches can also be created. These sketches show the nature of the crime scene from many angles. This can be helpful in reconstruction and in the trial setting. Some can also be animated to

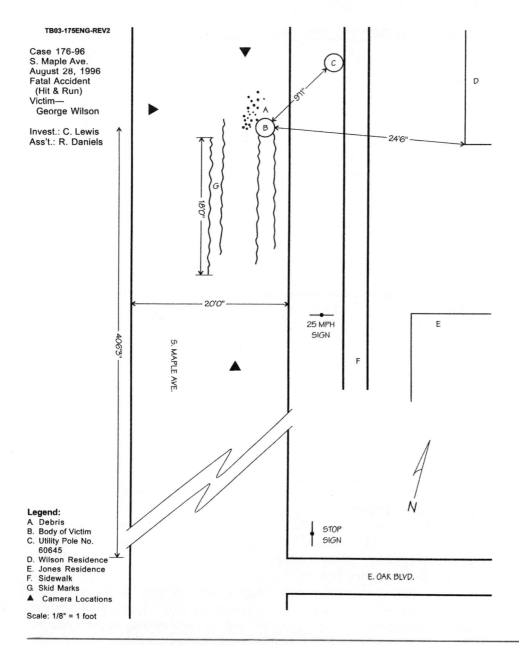

TB03-175ENG-REV2

Case 176-96
S. Maple Ave.
August 28, 1996
Fatal Accident
   (Hit & Run)
Victim—
   George Wilson

Invest.: C. Lewis
Ass't.: R. Daniels

C

D

A

9'11"

B

24'6"

G

180"

20'0"

406'3"

S. MAPLE AVE.

25 MPH
SIGN

E

F

N

Legend:
A. Debris
B. Body of Victim
C. Utility Pole No.
   60645
D. Wilson Residence
E. Jones Residence
F. Sidewalk
G. Skid Marks
▲ Camera Locations

Scale: 1/8" = 1 foot

STOP
SIGN

E. OAK BLVD.

FIGURE 3–15   A finished sketch of an outdoor crime scene. *Courtesy Sirchie Finger Print Laboratories, Inc., Youngsville, N.C., www.sirchie.com*

show the events suggested in the reconstruction and how they would lead to the final state of the scene.

Key Points

- The crime scene sketch plays an important role in the legal investigation of a crime by clearly showing possible points of entry or exit, evidence locations, and the general layout of the crime scene. It will also refresh memories about the case after time has passed.

- The rough sketch is made at the scene to show basic measurements of the scene and spatial relationships between items.

- The finished sketch is created from the rough sketch with care and concern for appearance. It must include a scale, and it may be created using a computer-aided drafting program.

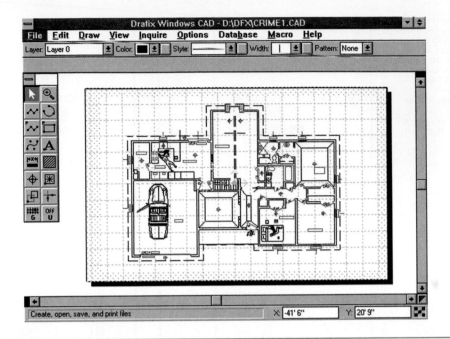

FIGURE 3–16 **Construction of a crime-scene diagram with the aid of a computer-aided drafting program.** *Courtesy Sirchie Finger Print Laboratories, Inc., Youngsville, N.C., www.sirchie.com*

Chapter Summary

Because investigators have only a limited amount of time to work a crime site in its untouched state, the opportunity must not be lost. Notes, photographs, and sketches are the three methods for crime-scene recording.

The note-taking process begins with the call to a crime-scene investigator to report to a scene. Once the notes are started, the general format should include contact information, personnel information and movements, task assignments, observations of the victim and scene, and information about the evidence before and after it is processed in black or blue pen. Some investigators prefer recording notes on tape or digital voice recorders. If the investigator is experienced in this area, clear and thorough notes may be recorded and later transcribed. However, the notes must be recorded carefully, and side conversations should be avoided.

Photography of crime scenes is commonly accepted in all jurisdictions as visual evidence in a criminal investigation. This documentation method is unmatched in its ability to show overview and details of the crime scene. Crime-scene photographs can show the layout of the scene, position of evidence to be collected, and relation of objects to one another in the scene. Photographs taken from many angles can show possible lines of sight of victims, suspects, or witnesses.

The forensic photographer must understand the interaction of lenses, aperture, shutter speed, illumination, recording mediums, filters, and tripods to produce examination-quality photographs. Photographs must be easily interpreted by everyone involved in the case from the investigators to the judge and jury. The increasing use of digital photography has necessitated the adoption of protocols to ensure image security and prevent their alteration by computer software. Video documentation can be used at a crime scene, but only in conjunction with still photographs, which show greater detail.

The crime-scene sketch serves many important functions in the legal investigation of a crime. If the sketch is done correctly, it can clearly show the layout of an indoor or outdoor crime scene and the relationship in space of all the items and features significant to the investigation, especially collected and uncollected evidence. The rough sketch at the scene is usually hand-drawn to show positions and spatial relationships. The finished sketch is a scaled version of the rough sketch. Finished sketches can be carefully made by hand or by using a computer-aided drafting program.

Review Questions

1. Three methods for recording the crime scene are _____ _____, _____, and _____.

2. True or False: The note-taking process begins with the call to a crime-scene investigator to report to a scene. _____

3. The crime-scene notes should include a precise record of personnel movements in and out of the scene starting with the _____.

4. True or False: Crime-scene notes should be written from memory back at the laboratory. _____

5. Before evidence is collected, it must be fully described in the investigator's _____.

6. True or False: When an injured or deceased victim is present at the scene, the state of the body before being moved should be observed but not recorded. _____

7. True or False: The value of crime-scene photographs lies in their ability to show the layout of the scene, position of witnesses, and relation of people to one another in the scene. _____

8. The most commonly used camera for crime-scene photography is the _____ camera, which can be film or digital.

9. True or False: The lens of the camera is the mechanism for bending light to focus the image on the film or digital microchip, and the kind of lens is determined by the lens's focal length. _____

10. The camera _____ is the measure of the diameter of the opening of the the diaphragm, and it is adjusted on a film or digital camera by adjusting the f-stop.

11. The _____, measured in fractions of a second, is the length of time the film or microchip is exposed to light.

12. The _____ of a photograph is the amount of area in the foreground and background of an object in focus that is also relatively in focus.

13. True or False: On the color temperature scale, a "hot" light source has a red-orange hue, whereas a "cold" light source has a blue hue. _____

14. The _____, is the most commonly used type of flash in photography. This type of flash is usually on the top or front of a camera.

15. True or False: Film may be either color print film (producing a negative to be developed), color slide film (producing transparent positives on slides for presentations), black-and-white film, or infrared film. _____

16. High-speed films produce grainier photographs because of the (large, small) size of the film grains.

17. A digital camera captures light on a light-sensitive _____.

18. True or False: Crime-scene photographers generally use simple "point and shoot" digital cameras. _____

19. A _____ filter blocks one wavelength of light from the subject and allows all others to reach the film or microchip.

20. The _____, filled out by the crime-scene photographer, should include the case and scene information and the parameters of each photograph.

21. The most important prerequisite for photographing a crime scene is to have it in a(n) _____ condition.

22. True or False: Each crime scene should be photographed as completely as possible in a logical sequence that includes the area in which the crime actually took place and all adjacent areas where important acts occurred. _____

23. The succession of photographs taken at a crime scene is _____ photographs first, _____ photographs second, and _____ photographs last.

24. True or False: Overview photographs should include only points of entry and points of exit. _____

25. To show the greatest detail of individual objects or evidence, close-up photographs must be taken at an angle of _____ and with and without evidence markers and scales.

26. A technique called _____ may be used to illuminate long distances in total darkness in night photography.

27. True or False: In indoor or outdoor scenes the crime-scene photographer moves around the boundary of the scene in a clockwise or counterclockwise direction, taking photographs from many vantage points and angles to provide a complete 360-degree view of the scene. _____

28. In _____ cases it may be especially important to photograph the crowd outside the scene because perpetrators of these crimes frequently return to the scene.

29. True or False: Victims of violent crimes may have wounds that should be photographed, but this should be done respectfully. _____

30. True or False: Close-up photographs of tire and footwear impressions at a crime scene must be taken after the impression is cast. _____

31. True or False: The traditional film cameras available on the market produce photographs with greater resolution than digital cameras do. _____

32. To ensure that their digital images will be admissible, many jurisdictions have developed or are developing _____ for the use of digital photography

to avoid the possibility of enhancement or doctoring of crime-scene photographs.

33. The process of _____ _____ the crime scene essentially combines notes and photography.

34. An investigator need only draw a(n) _____ sketch at the crime scene to show its dimensions and pertinent objects.

35. When creating a rough sketch, measurements should be taken from the fixed points to pieces of evidence by using either the _____, _____, _____, or _____ methods.

36. True or False: The distances and dimensions shown on the sketch can be a guess or estimate, and the use of a tape measure is not required. _____

37. Unlike the rough sketch, the _____ is constructed with care and concern for aesthetic appearance and must be drawn to scale.

38. _____ programs provide an extensive symbol library and may create a three-dimensional sketch.

Application and Critical Thinking

1. What type of lens would a photographer most likely use to create each of the following photos?
   a) An extreme close-up photo of a fiber found at a crime scene
   b) A medium-range shot of part of a wall
   c) A photo showing the entire length of a wall

2. What kind of filter would a photographer most likely use for the following shots?
   a) A photo of a fingerprint imaged with a fluorescent powder
   b) A photo in which the investigator wishes to highlight an area of a particular color
   c) A piece of evidence that is difficult to see against a specific background color

3. What kind of film would a photographer most likely use for the following shots?
   a) A photo of gunshot residue on a dark fabric
   b) An indoor shot under incandescent lighting
   c) A photo showing very fine details

Web Resources

Crime and Clues (Articles on crime-scene protection, processing, and reconstruction)
www.crimeandclues.com/crimescene.htm

Crime-Scene Investigation (Guidelines and articles on response, evidence collection, photography, and other topics)
www.crime-scene-investigator.net

Crime Scene Investigation: A Reference for Law Enforcement Training
www.ojp.usdoj.gov/nij/pubs-sum/200160.htm

Overview of Crime-Scene Photography
www.rcmp-learning.org/docs/ecdd1004.htm

VideoJug (Links to videos about digital photography)
www.videojug.com/search?keywords=Digital+Camera

Murder and the Horse Chestnut Tree

Roger Severs was the son of a wealthy English couple, Eileen and Derek Severs, who were reported missing in 1983. Police investigators were greeted at the Severs home by Roger, who at first explained that his parents had decided to spend some time in London. Suspicion of foul play quickly arose when investigators located traces of blood in the residence. More blood was found in Derek's car and signs of blood spatter were on the garage door. Curiously, a number of green fibers were located throughout the house, as well as in the trunk of Derek's car.

A thorough geological examination of soil and vegetation caked onto Severs's car wheel rims seemed to indicate that the car had been in a location at the edge of a wooded area. Closer examination of the debris also revealed the presence of horse chestnut pollen. Horse chestnut is an exceptionally rare tree in the region of the Severs residence.

Using land maps, a geologist located possible areas where horse chestnut pollen might be found. In one of the locations, investigators found a shallow grave that contained the bludgeoned bodies of the elder Severses. Not surprisingly, they were wrapped in a green blanket. A jury rejected Roger's defense of diminished capacity and found him guilty of murder.

chapter 4

Collection of Crime-Scene Evidence

Key Terms

buccal swab

chain of custody

contamination

physical evidence

standard/reference sample

substrate control

Learning Objectives

After studying this chapter, you should be able to:

- Define physical evidence.

- Review the common types of physical evidence encountered at crime scenes.

- Describe proper techniques for handling evidence to avoid damage or contamination.

- Understand collecting and packaging procedures for common types of physical evidence.

- Define and understand the concept of chain of custody.

- Discuss the implications of the *Mincey* and *Tyler* cases.

physical evidence
Any object that can establish that a crime has been committed or can link a crime and its victim or perpetrator.

As automobiles run on gasoline, crime laboratories "run" on **physical evidence**. Physical evidence includes any and all objects that can establish that a crime has been committed or that can provide a link between a crime and its victim or perpetrator.

However, for physical evidence to aid the investigator, its presence first must be recognized at the crime scene. If investigators gathered all the natural and commercial objects within a reasonable distance so that the scientist could uncover significant clues from them, the deluge of material into the crime laboratory would quickly immobilize the facility. This is why it is important for investigators to get it right the first time. The collection of evidence must be thorough enough to include as many pertinent clues as possible, but selective enough not to bog down the laboratory. Physical evidence achieves its value in criminal investigations only when the investigator collects it selectively and with a thorough knowledge of the crime laboratory's techniques, capabilities, and limitations.

Common Types of Physical Evidence

It would be impossible to list all the objects that could conceivably be important to a crime; every crime scene obviously has to be treated on an individual basis, having its own peculiar history, circumstances, and problems. It is practical, however, to list items whose scientific examination is likely to yield significant results in ascertaining the nature and circumstances of a crime. The investigator who is thoroughly familiar with the recognition, collection, and analysis of these items, as well as with laboratory procedures and capabilities, can make logical decisions when faced with uncommon and unexpected circumstances at the crime scene. Just as important, a qualified evidence collector cannot rely on collection procedures memorized from a pamphlet but must be able to make innovative, on-the-spot decisions at the crime scene.

Blood, Semen, and Saliva All suspected blood, semen, or saliva—liquid or dried, animal or human—presents in a form that suggests a relation to the offense or people involved in a crime. This category includes blood or semen dried onto fabrics or other objects, as well as cigarette butts that may contain saliva residues. These substances are subjected to serological and biochemical analysis to determine identity and possible origin.

Documents Any handwriting and typewriting submitted so that authenticity or source can be determined. Related items include paper, ink, indented writings, obliterations, and burned or charred documents.

Drugs   Any substance in violation of laws regulating the sale, manufacture, distribution, and use of drugs.

Explosives   Any device containing an explosive charge, as well as all objects removed from the scene of an explosion that are suspected to contain the residues of an explosive.

Fibers   Any natural or synthetic fiber whose transfer may be useful in establishing a relationship between objects and/or people.

Fingerprints   All prints of this nature, hidden (latent) and visible.

Firearms and Ammunition   Any firearm, as well as discharged or intact ammunition, suspected of being involved in a criminal offense.

Glass   Any glass particle or fragment that may have been transferred to a person or object involved in a crime. This category includes windowpanes containing holes made by a bullet or other projectile.

Hair   Any animal or human hair present that could link a person with a crime.

Impressions   Tire markings, shoe prints, depressions in soft soils, and all other forms of tracks. Glove and other fabric impressions, as well as bite marks in skin or foodstuffs, are also included.

Organs and Physiological Fluids   Body organs and fluids are submitted for analysis to detect the possible existence of drugs and poisons. This category includes blood to be analyzed for the presence of alcohol and other drugs.

Paint   Any paint, liquid or dried, that may have been transferred from the surface of one object to another during the commission of a crime. A common example is the transfer of paint from one vehicle to another during an automobile collision.

Petroleum Products   Any petroleum product removed from a suspect or recovered from a crime scene. The most common examples are gasoline residues removed from the scene of an arson, or grease and oil stains whose presence may suggest involvement in a crime.

Plastic Bags   A disposable polyethylene bag such as a garbage bag may be evidential in a homicide or drug case. Examinations are conducted to associate a bag with a similar bag in the possession of a suspect.

Plastic, Rubber, and Other Polymers   Remnants of these manufactured materials recovered at crime scenes may be linked to objects recovered in the possession of a criminal suspect.

Powder Residues   Any item suspected of containing powder residues resulting from the discharge of a firearm.

Serial Numbers   This category includes all stolen property submitted to the laboratory for the restoration of erased identification numbers.

Soil and Minerals   All items containing soil or minerals that could link a person or object to a particular location. Common examples are soil imbedded in shoes and insulation found on garments.

Tool Marks   This category includes any object suspected of containing the impression of another object that served as a tool in a crime. For example, a screwdriver or crowbar could produce tool marks by being impressed into or scraped along a wall.

Vehicle Lights   The examination of vehicle headlights and taillights is normally conducted to determine whether a light was on or off at the time of impact.

Wood and Other Vegetative Matter Any fragments of wood, sawdust, shavings, or vegetative matter discovered on clothing, shoes, or tools that could link a person or object to a crime location.

Evidence-Collection Tools

The well-prepared evidence collector arrives at a crime scene with a large assortment of packaging materials and tools ready to encounter any type of situation. These tools are usually kept in an evidence-collection kit (see Figure 4–1).

- Notebook
- Pen (black or blue ink)
- Ruler
- Chalk or crayons
- Magnifying glass
- Flashlight
- Disposable forceps and similar tools may have to be used to pick up small items
- Scalpels or razor blades
- Swabs and medicine droppers for presumptive testing
- Gauze or sterile cloth
- Unbreakable plastic pill bottles with pressure lids

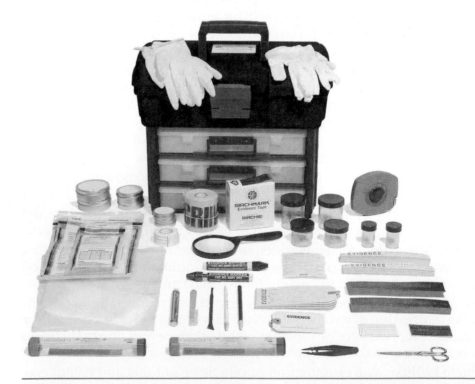

FIGURE 4–1 A typical evidence-collection kit. *Courtesy Sirchie Finger Print Laboratories, Inc., Youngsville, N.C., www.sirchie.com*

- Evidence sealing tape

- Evidence tags (indoor) or flags (outdoor) (see Figure 4–2)

- Various size paper bags, boxes, and manila envelopes

- Paper for wrapping or "druggist folds"

- Alternate light source (see Figure 4–3)

- Lifting tape for hair or trace evidence

- Vacuum collector with filters

- Fingerprint powders, brushes, and lifters

- Disposable gloves, face masks, and shoe covers

Mobile Crime Laboratories

In recent years, many police departments have gone to the expense of purchasing and equipping "mobile crime laboratories" for their evidence technicians. However, the term *mobile crime laboratory* is a misnomer. These vehicles carry the necessary supplies to protect the crime scene; photograph, collect, and package physical evidence; and perform latent print development. They are not designed to carry out the functions of a chemical laboratory. *Crime-scene search vehicle* would be a more appropriate but perhaps less dramatic name for such a vehicle (see Figure 4–4).

FIGURE 4–2   Evidence flags are used for outdoor crime scenes. *Courtesy Sirchie Finger Print Laboratories, Inc., Youngsville, N.C., www.sirchie.com*

FIGURE 4–3 An example of an alternate light source in use. This can be used to visually enhance many types of evidence. *Courtesy Sirchie Finger Print Laboratories, Inc., Youngsville, N.C., www.sirchie.com*

Procedures for Collecting and Packaging Physical Evidence

Physical evidence can be anything from massive objects to microscopic traces. Often, many items of evidence are obvious in their presence, but others may be detected only through examination in the crime laboratory. For example, minute traces of blood may be discovered on garments only after a thorough search in the laboratory, or the presence of hairs and fibers may be revealed in vacuum sweepings or on garments only after close laboratory scrutiny. For this reason, investigators should collect possible carriers of trace evidence in addition to more discernible items. This may include vacuum sweepings, fingernail scrapings, clothing, and vehicles.

The investigator should vacuum critical areas of the crime scene and submit the sweepings to the laboratory for analysis. The sweepings from different areas must be collected and packaged separately. A portable vacuum cleaner equipped with a special filter attachment is suitable for this purpose (see Figure 4–5). Fingernail scrapings from individuals who were in contact with other individuals may contain minute fragments of evidence capable of providing a link between assailant and victim. The investigator should scrape the undersurface of each nail with a dull object such as a toothpick to avoid cutting the skin. These scrapings will be subjected to microscopic examination in the laboratory. All clothing from the victim and

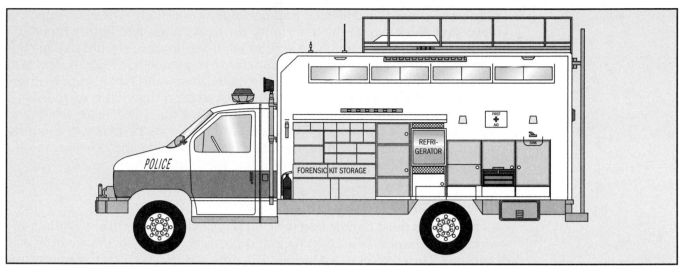

(a)

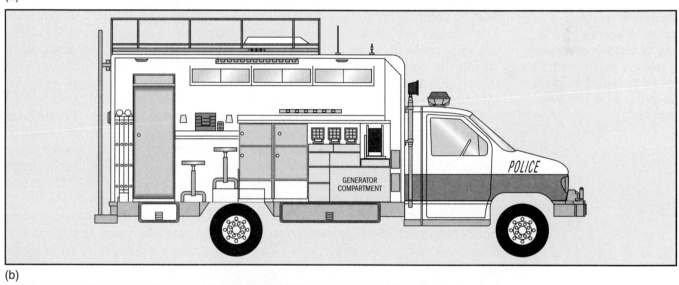

(b)

FIGURE 4–4 **An inside view of a mobile crime-scene van: (a) driver's side and (b) passenger's side.** *Courtesy Sirchie Finger Print Laboratories, Inc., Youngsville, N.C., www.sirchie.com*

FIGURE 4–5 **A vacuum sweeper attachment, constructed of clear plastic in two pieces that are joined by a threaded joint. A metal screen is mounted in one half to support a filter paper to collect debris. The unit attaches to the hose of the vacuum sweeper. After a designated area of the crime scene is vacuumed, the filter paper is removed and retained for laboratory examination.** *Courtesy Sirchie Finger Print Laboratories, Inc., Youngsville, N.C., www.sirchie.com*

suspect(s) should be collected and packaged separately. These objects will be further examined at the laboratory for trace, fiber, and hair evidence.

When a vehicle is involved in a crime, investigators should pay particular attention to signs of a cross-transfer of evidence between the car and the victim—this includes blood, tissue, hair, fibers, and fabric impressions. Traces of paint or broken glass may be located on the victim or roadway. The entire car should be processed for fingerprints. In cases in which the car was used for transportation, more attention may be given to the interior of the car. However, all areas of the vehicle, inside and outside, should be searched with equal care for physical evidence.

Handling Evidence

contamination
The transfer of extraneous matter between the collector and the evidence or multiple pieces of evidence, producing tainted evidence that cannot be used in the subsequent investigation.

Investigators must handle and process physical evidence in a way that prevents any change from taking place between the time the evidence is removed from the crime scene and the time it is received by the crime laboratory. Changes can arise through contamination, breakage, evaporation, accidental scratching or bending, or improper or careless packaging. The use of latex gloves or disposable forceps when touching evidence often can prevent such problems. Any equipment that is not disposable should be cleaned and/or sanitized between collecting each piece of evidence. Evidence should remain unmoved until investigators have documented its location and appearance in notes, sketches, and photographs.

Evidence best maintains its integrity when kept in its original condition as found at the crime site. Whenever possible, one should submit evidence to the laboratory intact. The investigator normally should not remove blood, hairs, fibers, soil particles, and other types of trace evidence from garments, weapons, or other articles that bear them. Instead, he or she should send the entire object to the laboratory for processing.

Of course, if evidence is adhering to an object in a precarious manner, good judgment dictates removing and packaging the item. Investigators must use common sense when handling evidence adhering to a large structure, such as a door, wall, or floor; they should remove the specimen with a forceps or other appropriate tool. In the case of a bloodstain, the investigator may either scrape the stain off the surface, transfer the stain to a moistened swab, or cut out the area of the object bearing the stain.

Packaging Evidence

The well-prepared evidence collector arrives at a crime scene with a large assortment of packaging materials and tools, ready to encounter any type of situation. Forceps and similar tools may be used to pick up small items. Unbreakable plastic pill bottles with pressure lids are excellent containers for hairs, glass, fibers, and various other kinds of small or trace evidence. Alternatively, manila envelopes, screw-cap glass vials, sealable plastic bags, or metal pillboxes are adequate containers for most trace evidence encountered at crime sites (see Figure 4–6). Charred debris recovered from the scene of a suspicious fire must be sealed in an airtight container to prevent the evaporation of volatile petroleum residues. New paint cans or tightly sealed jars are recommended in such situations (see Figure 4–7).

Ordinary mailing envelopes should not be used as evidence containers because powders and fine particles will leak out of their corners. Instead, small amounts of trace evidence can be conveniently packaged in a carefully folded paper, using what is known as a "druggist fold" (see Figure 4–8).

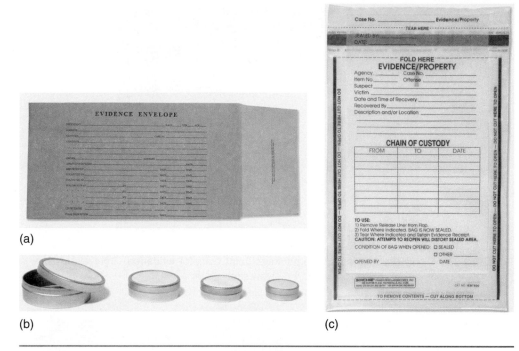

FIGURE 4–6 **(a) A manila evidence envelope, (b) metal pillboxes, and (c) a sealable plastic evidence bag.** *Courtesy Sirchie Finger Print Laboratories, Inc., Youngsville, N.C., www.sirchie.com*

FIGURE 4–7 **Airtight metal cans used to package arson evidence.** *Courtesy Sirchie Finger Print Laboratories, Inc., Youngsville, N.C., www.sirchie.com*

This consists of folding one end of the paper over one-third, then folding the other end (one-third) over that, and repeating the process from the other two sides. After folding the paper in this manner, one should tuck the outside two edges into each other to produce a closed container that keeps the specimen from falling out.

Each different item or similar items collected at different locations should be placed in separate containers. Packaging evidence separately prevents damage through contact and prevents cross-contamination.

Biological Materials Use only disposable tools to collect biological materials for packaging. If biological materials such as blood are stored in airtight containers, the accumulation of moisture may encourage the growth of mold, which can destroy their evidential value. In these instances, wrapping

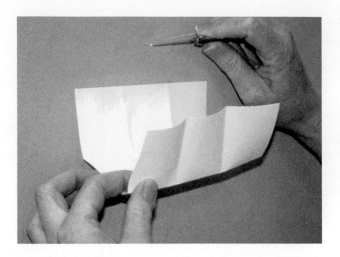

FIGURE 4–8   A druggist fold is used to package paint transfer evidence. *Courtesy Sirchie Finger Print Laboratories, Inc., Youngsville, N.C., www.sirchie.com*

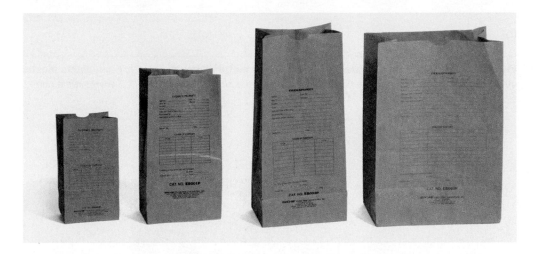

FIGURE 4–9   Paper bags and manila envelopes are recommended evidence containers for biological evidence and especially for objects suspected of containing blood and semen stains. Each object should be packaged in a separate bag or envelope. *Courtesy Sirchie Finger Print Laboratories, Inc., Youngsville, N.C., www.sirchie.com*

paper, manila envelopes, or paper bags are recommended packaging materials (see Figure 4–9). As a matter of routine, all items possibly containing biological fluid evidence should be air-dried and placed individually in separate paper bags to ensure a constant circulation of air through them. This will prevent the formation of mold and mildew. Paper packaging is easily written on, but seals may not be sturdy.

The evidence collector must handle all body fluids and biologically stained materials with a minimum of personal contact. All body fluids must be assumed to be infectious, so investigators must wear disposable latex gloves while handling the evidence. Latex gloves also significantly reduce the possibility that the evidence collector will contaminate the evidence. Investigators should change gloves frequently during the evidence-collection phase of the investigation. Safety considerations and avoidance of contamination also dictate that evidence collectors wear face masks and shoe covers.

DNA Evidence   The advent of DNA analysis is one of the most significant recent advances in crime-scene investigation. This technique is valuable in its ability to identify suspects by detecting and analyzing minute quantities of DNA deposited on evidence as a result of contact with saliva, sweat, or skin cells. The search for evidence should include any and all objects with which the suspect or victim may have come into bodily contact. Likely sources of DNA evidence include stamps and envelopes licked with saliva, a cup or can that has touched a person's lips, chewing gum, the sweatband of a hat, or a bedsheet containing dead skin cells.

One key concern during the collection of a DNA-containing specimen is contamination. Contamination can occur by introducing foreign DNA through coughing or sneezing onto evidence during the collection process. Transfer of DNA can also occur when items of evidence are incorrectly placed in contact with each other during packaging. To prevent contamination, the evidence collector must wear a face mask and use disposable latex gloves and disposable forceps. The evidence collector may also consider wearing coveralls and shoe covers as an extra precaution to avoid contaminating DNA evidence.

Blood has great evidential value when the investigator can demonstrate a transfer between a victim and a suspect. For this reason, all clothing from both the victim and suspect should be collected and sent to the laboratory for examination, even when the presence of blood on a garment does not appear obvious to the investigator. Laboratory search procedures are far more revealing and sensitive than any that can be conducted at the crime scene.

A detailed description of the proper collection and packaging of various types of physical evidence will be discussed in forthcoming chapters; additionally, most of this information is summarized in the evidence guide found in Appendix I.

Maintaining the Chain of Custody

Whenever evidence is presented in court as an exhibit, the investigator must establish continuity of possession, or the **chain of custody**. This means that he or she must account for every person who handled or examined the evidence. Failure to substantiate the evidence's chain of custody may lead to serious questions regarding the authenticity and integrity of the evidence and the examinations of it. Adhering to standard procedures in recording the location of evidence, marking it for identification, and properly completing evidence submission forms for laboratory analysis are the best guarantee that the evidence will withstand inquiries about what happened to it from the time it was found to its presentation in court.

Once an investigator selects an evidence container, he or she must mark it for identification. All packaged evidence must be sealed with evidence tape at the opening and labeled (see Figure 4–10). The investigator who packaged the evidence must write his or her initials and the date on the evidence tape seal. Anyone who removes the evidence for further testing or observation at a later time should try to avoid breaking the orginal seal if possible so that the information on the seal will not be lost. The person who reseals the packaging should record his or her initials and the date on the new seal. Evidence containers often have a preprinted identification form that the evidence collector fills out. Otherwise, the collector must attach an evidence tag to the container (see Figure 4–11).

A minimum record of the evidence to demonstrate chain of custody would show the collector's initials, the location of the evidence, and the date of collection. Transfer of evidence to another individual, or delivery to the laboratory, must be recorded in notes and other appropriate forms (see Figure 4–12). In fact, every individual who possesses the evidence must maintain a written record of its acquisition and disposition. Frequently, all

chain of custody
A list of all people who came into possession of an item of evidence.

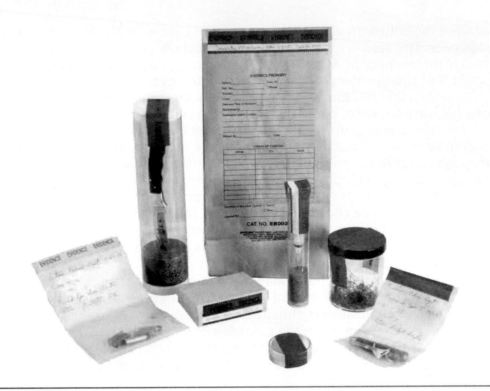

FIGURE 4–10   Proper evidence tape seals on evidence in various packages. *Courtesy Sirchie Finger Print Laboratories, Inc., Youngsville, N.C., www.sirchie.com*

FIGURE 4–11   Examples of evidence tags that may be attached directly to the evidence. *Courtesy Sirchie Finger Print Laboratories, Inc., Youngsville, N.C., www.sirchie.com*

of the individuals involved in the collection and transportation of the evidence are requested to testify in court. Thus, to avoid confusion and to retain complete control of the evidence at all times, the chain of custody should be kept to a minimum.

Failure to substantiate the evidence's chain of custody may lead to serious questions regarding the authenticity and integrity of the evidence and the examinations rendered upon it. Adhering to standard procedures in recording the location of evidence, marking it for identification, and properly completing evidence submission forms for laboratory analysis is the best way to guarantee that the evidence will withstand inquiries

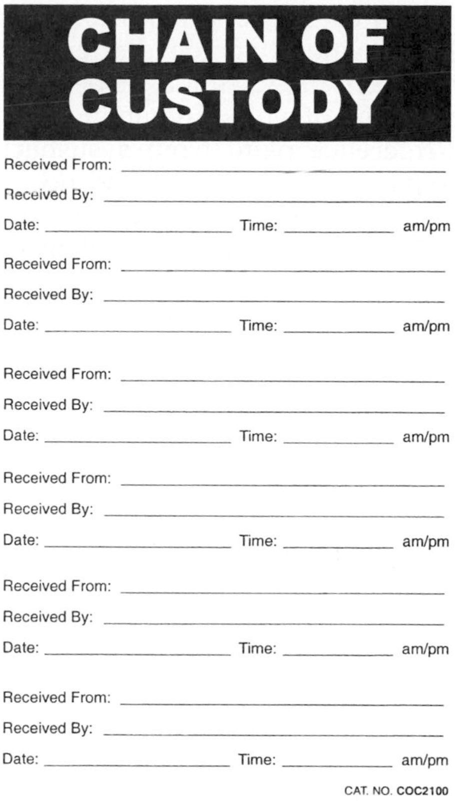

CHAIN OF CUSTODY

Received From: _____

Received By: _____

Date: _____ Time: _____ am/pm

Received From: _____

Received By: _____

Date: _____ Time: _____ am/pm

Received From: _____

Received By: _____

Date: _____ Time: _____ am/pm

Received From: _____

Received By: _____

Date: _____ Time: _____ am/pm

Received From: _____

Received By: _____

Date: _____ Time: _____ am/pm

Received From: _____

Received By: _____

Date: _____ Time: _____ am/pm

CAT. NO. **COC2100**

FIGURE 4–12   A chain of custody form is used to record the name of every person who handled or examined the collected evidence. *Courtesy Sirchie Finger Print Laboratories, Inc., Youngsville, N.C., www.sirchie.com*

FIGURE 4–13   An example of a secure evidence locker. *Courtesy Sirchie Finger Print Laboratories, Inc., Youngsville, N.C., www.sirchie.com*

about what happened to it from the time of its finding to its presentation in court. If a delay occurs between the time evidence is collected and the time it is submitted to the forensic laboratory, the investigator must store the evidence in a secured area with limited access by police personnel (see Figure 4–13).

Obtaining Standard/Reference Samples

To examine evidence, whether soil, blood, glass, hair, or fibers, the forensic scientist must often compare it with a sample of similar material whose origin is known. This is known as a **standard/reference sample**. Although most investigators have little difficulty recognizing and collecting relevant

standard/reference sample
Physical evidence whose origin is known, such as blood or hair from a suspect, that can be compared to crime-scene evidence.

crime-scene evidence, few seem aware of the necessity and importance of providing the crime lab with a thorough sampling of standard/reference materials. Such materials may be obtained from the victim, a suspect, or other known sources. For instance, investigation of a hit-and-run incident might require the removal of standard/reference paint from a suspect vehicle. This will permit its comparison to paint recovered at the scene.

The presence of standard/reference samples greatly facilitates the work of the forensic scientist. For example, hair found at a crime scene will be of optimum value only when compared to standard/reference hairs removed from the suspect and victim. Likewise, bloodstained evidence must be accompanied by a whole-blood or buccal swab standard/reference sample obtained from all relevant crime-scene participants. The quality and quantity of standard/reference specimens often determine the evidential value of crime-scene evidence, and so must be treated with equal care.

Some types of evidence must also be accompanied by substrate controls. These are materials close to areas where physical evidence has been deposited. For example, an arson investigator who suspects that a surface has been exposed to an accelerant, such as gasoline, should collect a piece of the same surface material that he or she believes was *not* exposed to the accelerant. At the laboratory, forensic scientists will first test the substrate control to see whether the surface itself will interfere with the procedures used to detect and identify accelerants. Another common example of a substrate control is a material containing a bloodstain. Unstained areas close to the stain may be sampled to determine whether this material can interfere with the interpretation of laboratory results. Thorough collection and proper packaging of standard/reference specimens and substrate controls are marks of a skilled investigator.

buccal swab
A swab of the inner portion of the cheek; performed to collect cells for use in determining the DNA profile of an individual.

substrate controls
Surface material close to areas where physical evidence has been deposited.

FIGURE 4–14 Evidence that has been correctly packaged and labeled can be sent through the mail. *Courtesy Sirchie Finger Print Laboratories, Inc., Youngsville, N.C., www.sirchie.com*

Submitting Evidence

Evidence is usually submitted to the laboratory either personally or by mail. Although most evidence can be shipped by mail, postal regulations restrict the shipment of certain chemicals and live ammunition and prohibit the mailing of explosives. In such situations, one should consult the laboratory to determine the disposition of these substances. One must also exercise care when packaging evidence in order to prevent breakage or other accidental destruction during transit to the laboratory (see Figure 4–14). If the evidence is delivered personally, the deliverer should be familiar with the case to facilitate any discussions with laboratory personnel concerning specific aspects of the case.

Most laboratories require that an evidence-submission form accompany all evidence submitted (see Figure 4–15). The information on this form enables the laboratory analyst to make an intelligent and complete examination of the evidence. Providing a brief description of the case history is particularly important. This information allows the examiner to analyze the specimens in a logical sequence and make the proper comparisons; it also facilitates the search for trace quantities of evidence.

The submission form should specify the particular kind of examination requested for each type of evidence. However, the analyst is not bound to adhere strictly to the specific tests requested by the investigator. The discovery of new evidence may dictate changes in the tests required, or the analyst may find the initial requests incomplete or not totally relevant to the case. The evidence-submission form should also include a list of items submitted for examination. Each item must be packaged separately and assigned a number or letter, with all items listed in an orderly and logical sequence.

Once evidence is received, it will undergo the requested tests and examinations. When a piece of evidence has been fully examined and tested, it must be submitted to long-term storage. The storage area and containers should be secure to prevent tampering and maintain the chain of custody.

Key Points

- Physical evidence includes any and all objects that can establish that a crime has been committed or can link the crime and its victim or perpetrator.

- Many items of evidence may be detected only through examination at the crime laboratory. For this reason, it is important to collect possible carriers of trace evidence, such as clothing, vacuum sweepings, and fingernail scrapings, in addition to more discernable items.

- Each item of physical evidence collected at a crime scene must be placed in a separate appropriate container to prevent damage through contact or cross-contamination.

- Investigators must maintain the chain of custody, a record for denoting the location of the evidence.

- Proper standard/reference samples must be collected at the crime scene and from appropriate subjects for comparison purposes in the laboratory. Substrate controls must also be collected.

- Typically, an evidence submission form accompanies all evidence submitted to the crime laboratory. The form lists all items submitted for examination.

CRIME: Homicide; Aggravated Sexual Assault					COUNTY OF: Mercer			
VICTIM: Jane Doe (v)	Age 25	Sex F	Race C	SUSPECT: John Doe(s)		Age 30	Sex M	Race C

SUBMITTING AGENCY: (Address)
Trenton P.D. Central Evidence 225 N. Clinton Avenue, Trenton, N.J. 08609

FORWARD REPLIES TO: Capt. John Smith, Chief of Detectives	(Name) Same as above	(Address)	Telephone Number: 609 555-5555

INVESTIGATED BY:
Detective John Jones

DELIVERED BY: (Signature of Person Delivering Evidence)

BRIEF HISTORY OF CASE: (Include Date and Location, if Applicable)
On March 1st, 2001 the victim was found dead in her bedroom. Victim was partially clothed and autopsy revealed that victim was stabbed numerous times and medical examiner stated that there was evidence of sexual assault. Victim was last seen drinking with suspect at a local tavern. Suspect was arrested and item # 23, a folding knife, was found in his pocket.

* Note* Suspect is HIV+

EXAMINATION REQUESTED ON SPECIMENS LISTED BELOW:

Examine items 2, 5, 8-11, 13-15, 18 and 19 for seminal material and compare to controls #'s 12 and 26. Examine #1, 2, 4, 7,13, 14, 15, 18, 20, 21, 22 and 23 for trace evidence transfer. Examine #3 for saliva from suspect. Examine #6 for skin, blood and trace evidence. Examine #'s 20-23 for transfer blood evidence and compare to control #'s 12 and 26.

Item #	* Code	LIST OF SPECIMENS *SOURCE OF EVIDENCE CODE (V-Victim, S-Suspect, SC-Scene)
1	V	Debris collection
2	V	Clothing, white panties
3	V	Dried Secretions/bite marks
4	V	Head Hair Combings
5	V	Oral Specimens
6	V	Fingernail Specimens
7	V	Pubic Hair Combings
8	V	External Genital Specimen
9	V	Vaginal Specimens
10	V	Cervical Specimens

(Right margin checkboxes, LABORATORY USE ONLY): DRUG ☐ TRACE ☐ BIO/CHEM ☐ TOX ☐ ABC ☐ EQUINE ☐ BALLISTICS ☐

FOR ADDITIONAL INFORMATION USE FORM 631A AND ATTACH

Page 1 of 2 pages

FIGURE 4-15 An example of a properly completed evidence-submission form. *Courtesy New Jersey State Police*

Ensuring Crime-Scene Safety

The increasing spread of AIDS and hepatitis B has sensitized the law enforcement community to the potential health hazards at crime scenes. Law enforcement officers have an extremely small chance of contracting AIDS or hepatitis at the crime scene. Both diseases are normally transmitted by the exchange of body fluids, such as blood, semen, and vaginal and cervical secretions; intravenous drug needles and syringes; and the transfusion of infected blood products. However, the presence of blood and semen at crime scenes presents the investigator with biological specimens of unknown origin; investigators have no way of gauging what health hazards they may contain. Therefore, investigators must use caution and protect themselves at all times.

Fortunately, inoculation can easily prevent hepatitis B infection in most people. Furthermore, the federal Occupational Safety and Health Administration (OSHA) requires that law enforcement agencies offer hepatitis B vaccinations to all officers who may have contact with body fluids while on the job, at no expense to the officer.

The International Association for Identification's Safety Committee has proposed the following guidelines to protect investigators at crime scenes containing potentially infectious materials:

1. Forensic and crime-scene personnel may encounter potentially infectious materials, such as in the case of a homicide, in which blood or body fluids may be localized to the area of the body or dispersed throughout the crime scene. At such scenes, it is recommended that personnel wear a minimum of latex gloves (double gloved) and protective (Tyvek-type) shoe covers. In cases of large contamination areas, liquid repellent coveralls (Tyvek or Kleengard suits) are recommended along with the gloves and shoe covers.

2. The use of a particle mask/respirator, goggles, or face shield is recommended in addition to the protective items listed in item 1 when potentially infectious dust or mist may be encountered at the crime scene. This includes the collection of dried bloodstains by scraping; the collection, folding, and preservation of garments that may be contaminated with blood or body fluids, especially if they are in a dried state; and the application of aerosol chemicals to bloodstains or prints for their detection and/or enhancement.

3. When processing and collecting evidence at a crime scene, personnel should be alert to sharp objects, knives, hypodermic syringes, razor blades, and similar items. In the event that such sharp objects are encountered and must be recovered as evidence, the items should be placed in an appropriate container and properly labeled. When conventional latent-print powder techniques are used in or around areas contaminated with blood, a specific brush should be designated so that it can be subsequently decontaminated or appropriately disposed of after processing is complete. If latents are developed in or around blood-contaminated areas, they should be photographed, or lifted and placed in a sealed plastic bag. The sealed bag then should be affixed with an appropriate biohazard label.

   Evidence collected for transport should be packaged to maintain its integrity and to prevent contamination of personnel or personal items. Evidence contaminated with wet blood should first be placed in a paper bag and then temporarily stored in a red biohazard plastic bag for immediate transport to an appropriate drying facility.

4. When potentially infectious materials are present at a crime scene, personnel should maintain a red biohazard plastic bag for the disposal of contaminated gloves, clothing, masks, pencils, wrapping paper, and so on. On departure from the scene, the biohazard bag must be taped shut and transported to an approved biohazardous waste pickup site.

5. Note taking should be done while wearing uncontaminated gloves to avoid contamination of pens, pencils, notebook, paper, and so on. Pens or markers used to mark and package contaminated evidence should be designated for proper disposal in a red biohazard bag before investigators leave the crime scene.

6. If individual protective equipment becomes soiled or torn, it must be removed immediately. Personnel must then disinfect/decontaminate the potentially contaminated body areas using a recommended solution, such as a 10 percent bleach solution, or an antimicrobial soap or towelette. After cleansing, the area must be covered with clean, replacement protective equipment. On departure from the scene, this procedure should be repeated on any body area where contamination could have occurred.

7. Eating, drinking, smoking, and application of makeup are prohibited at the immediate crime scene.

8. All nondisposable items, such as lab coats, towels, and personal clothing, that may be contaminated with potentially infectious material should be placed in a yellow plastic bag labeled "Infectious Linen" and laundered, at the expense of the employer, by a qualified laundry service. Personal clothing that may have been contaminated should never be taken home for cleaning.

Key Points

- Law enforcement officers have an extremely small chance of contracting AIDS or hepatitis at the crime scene, but bodily fluids must always be treated as though they were infectious.

- It is recommended that personnel always wear double-gloved latex gloves and possibly Tyvek-type shoe covers, a particle mask/respirator, goggles, or face shields when potentially infectious material is present. Gloves should be changed often, and all contaminated protective gear should be removed and disposed of in biohazard bags. Nondisposable items should be laundered.

- When processing and collecting evidence at a crime scene, personnel should be alert to sharp objects, knives, hypodermic syringes, razor blades, and similar items.

- Eating, drinking, smoking, and applying makeup are prohibited at the immediate crime scene.

Legal Considerations at the Crime Scene

In police work, there is perhaps no experience more exasperating or demoralizing than to watch valuable evidence excluded from use against the accused because of legal considerations. This situation most often arises from what is deemed an "unreasonable" search and seizure of evidence. Therefore, the removal of any evidence from a person or from the scene of a crime must be done in conformity with Fourth Amendment privileges: "The right of the people to be secure in their persons, houses, papers, and effects, against unreasonable searches and seizures, shall not be violated, and no warrants shall issue, but upon probable cause, supported by oath or affirmation, and particularly describing the place to be searched, and the persons or things to be seized."

Since the 1960s, the Supreme Court of the United States has been particularly concerned with defining the circumstances under which the police can search for evidence in the absence of a court-approved search warrant. The court has made a number of allowances to justify a warrantless search: (1) the existence of emergency circumstances, (2) the need to prevent the immediate loss or destruction of evidence, (3) a search of a person and property within the immediate control of the person provided it is made incident to a lawful arrest, and (4) a search made by consent of the parties involved. In cases other than these, police must be particularly cautious about processing a crime scene without a search warrant. In 1978, the Supreme Court addressed this very issue and in so doing set forth guidelines for investigators to follow in determining the propriety of conducting a warrantless search at a crime scene. Significantly, the two cases decided on this issue related to homicide and arson crime scenes, both of which are normally subjected to the most intensive forms of physical evidence searches by police.

In the case of *Mincey* v. *Arizona,*[1] the Court dealt with the legality of a four-day search at a homicide scene. The case involved a police raid on the home of Rufus Mincey, who had been suspected of dealing drugs. Under the pretext of buying drugs, an undercover police officer forced entry into Mincey's apartment and was killed in a scuffle that ensued. Without a search warrant, the police spent four days searching the apartment, recovering, among other things, bullets, drugs, and drug paraphernalia. These items were subsequently introduced as evidence at the trial. Mincey was convicted and on appeal contended that the evidence gathered from his apartment, without a warrant and without his consent, was illegally seized. The Court unanimously upheld Mincey's position, stating:

> We do not question the right of the police to respond to emergency situations. Numerous state and federal cases have recognized that the Fourth Amendment does not bar police officers from making warrantless entries and searches when they reasonably believe that a person within is in need of immediate aid. Similarly, when the police come upon the scene of a homicide they may make a prompt warrantless search of the area to see if there are other victims or if a killer is still on the premises. . . . Except for the fact that the offense under investigation was a homicide, there were no exigent circumstances in this case. . . . There was no indication that evidence would be lost, destroyed or removed during the time required to obtain a search warrant. Indeed, the police guard at the apartment minimized that possibility. And there is no suggestion that a search warrant could not easily and conveniently have been obtained. We decline to hold that the seriousness of the offense under investigation itself creates exigent circumstances of the kind that under the Fourth Amendment justify a warrantless search.

In *Michigan* v. *Tyler,*[2] fire destroyed a business establishment leased by Loren Tyler and a business partner. The fire was finally extinguished in the early hours of the morning; smoke, steam, and darkness, however, prevented fire and police officials from thoroughly examining the scene for evidence of arson. Officials then left the building unattended until eight a.m.

of that day, when they returned and began an inspection of the burned premises. During the morning, searchers recovered and removed assorted items of evidence from the building. On three other occasions—four days, seven days, and twenty-five days after the fire—investigators reentered the premises and removed additional items of evidence with neither a warrant nor consent. The evidence seized was used to convict Tyler and his partner of conspiracy to burn real property and related offenses. The Supreme Court upheld the reversal of the conviction, holding the initial morning search to be proper but contending that evidence obtained from subsequent reentries to the scene was inadmissible: "We hold that an entry to fight a fire requires no warrant, and that once in the building, officials may remain there for a reasonable time to investigate the cause of a blaze. Thereafter, additional entries to investigate the cause of the fire must be made pursuant to the warrant procedures."

The message from the Supreme Court is clear: When time and circumstances permit, obtain a search warrant before investigating and retrieving physical evidence at the crime scene.

Key Points

- The removal of any evidence from a person or from the scene of a crime must be done in accordance with proper search and seizure procedure.

- Warrantless searches are allowed in situations including (1) the existence of emergency circumstances, (2) the need to prevent the immediate loss or destruction of evidence, (3) a search of a person and property within the immediate control of the person provided it is made incident to a lawful arrest, and (4) a search made by consent of the parties involved.

Chapter Summary

Physical evidence includes any and all objects that can establish that a crime has been committed or can provide a link between a crime and its victim or perpetrator. The collection of evidence must be thorough enough to include as much pertinent clues as possible, but selective enough not to bog down the laboratory. Physical evidence can be anything from massive objects to microscopic traces. Many kinds of objects may become evidence when they are affected by the events of a crime.

Many items of evidence are clearly visible, but others may be detected only through examination at the crime laboratory. For this reason, it is important to collect possible carriers of trace evidence, such as clothing, vacuum sweepings, and fingernail scrapings, in additional to more discernable items. Each item of physical evidence collected at different locations at a crime scene must be placed in a separate appropriate container depending on the characteristics of the evidence. This will prevent damage through contact or cross-contamination.

During the collection of evidence, the chain of custody, a record for denoting the location of the evidence, must be maintained. In addition, proper standard/reference samples, such as hairs, blood, and fibers, must bc collected at the crime scene and from appropriate subjects for comparison purposes in the laboratory. Substrate controls must also be collected.

For personal and professional protection, safety and legal considerations must be taken into account during the collection of evidence at a crime scene. All personnel must wear protective clothing and gear in accordance with the health hazards present. The officers who remove any evidence from a person or from the scene of a crime must do so in accordance with appropriate search and seizure protocols.

Review Questions

1. The term _____ encompasses all objects that can establish whether a crime has been committed or can link a crime and its victim or perpetrator.

2. True or False: The well-prepared evidence collector arrives at a crime scene with a large assortment of packaging materials and tools ready to encounter any type of situation. _____

3. The _____ purchased by some police departments for evidence collection carry the necessary supplies to protect the crime scene; photograph, collect, and package physical evidence; and perform latent-print development.

4. Because some items of evidence may be detected only through examination in the crime laboratory, it is important to collect all potential _____ of physical evidence.

5. True or False: Critical areas of the crime scene should be vacuumed and the sweepings submitted to the laboratory for analysis. _____

6. Individuals may have hand contact with other individuals during the commission of a crime so _____ scrapings should be collected because they may contain minute fragments of evidence capable of providing a link between assailant and victim.

7. True or False: The problems of contamination can often be avoided through the use of latex gloves or disposable forceps when touching evidence. _____

8. True or False: Whenever possible, trace evidence is to be removed from the object that bears it. _____

9. Each item collected at the crime scene must be placed in a(n) _____ container.

10. True or False: Unbreakable plastic pill bottles, manila envelopes, screw-cap glass vials, sealable plastic bags, and metal pillboxes with pressure lids are excellent containers for blood or arson evidence. _____

11. True or False: An ordinary mailing envelope is considered a good general-purpose evidence container. _____

12. True or False: Charred debris recovered from the scene of an arson is best placed in a porous container. _____

13. Small amounts of trace evidence can also be conveniently packaged in a(n) _____, a carefully folded paper packet.

14. Only _____ tools should be used to collect biological materials for packaging.

15. Packaging material for biological evidence, including bloodstained evidence, should be made of _____ to ensure a constant circulation of air through them.

16. _____ of DNA-containing evidence can easily occur by coughing or sneezing onto a stain during the collection process or contact caused by improper packaging.

17. As a matter of routine, all moist biological stains are to be _____ before packaging.

18. The possibility of future legal proceedings requires that a(n) _____ be established with respect to the possession and location of all physical evidence.

19. True or False: The investigator who packaged the evidence must write his or her initials and the date on the evidence tape seal, and the evidence should be opened at a different location on the packaging for further testing. _____

20. Most physical evidence collected at the crime site will require the accompanying submission of _____ material for comparison purposes.

21. Blood evidence should be accompanied by known controls in the form of whole blood or _____ from victims or suspects.

22. Uncontaminated areas close to where bloodstains were deposited are called _____ and should be collected from the crime scene.

23. True or False: Evidence is usually submitted to the laboratory either personally or by mail depending on by the distance the submitting agency must travel to the laboratory and the urgency of the case. _____

24. A(n) _____ form accompanies all evidence submitted and delineates the examination requested for each item of evidence.

25. Although the chance of law enforcement officers contracting AIDS or hepatitis at the crime scene is low, bodily fluids must always be treated as though they were _____.

26. At the crime scene, latex gloves should be changed often, and all contaminated protective gear should be removed and disposed of in _____ bags.

27. True or False: The removal of any evidence from a person must be done in accordance with proper search and seizure procedure, but it is not required for removal of crime scene evidence. _____

28. In the case of *Mincey* v. *Arizona*, the Supreme Court restricted the practice of conducting a(n) _____ search at a homicide scene.

29. In the case of *Michigan* v. *Tyler*, the Supreme Court dealt with search and seizure procedures at a(n) _____ scene.

Application and Critical Thinking

1. Officer Martin Guajardo is the first responder at an apparent homicide scene. After securing the area, interviewing the sole witness, and calling for backup, he begins to search for evidence. He makes note of a bloody knife lying next to the body. A small scrap of bloody cloth is clinging precariously to the knife. Because it is a very windy day, Officer Guajardo removes the scrap of fabric and seals it in a plastic bag. A few moments later, a crime-scene team, including a photographer, arrives to take over the investigation. What mistakes, if any, did Officer Guajardo make prior to the arrival of the crime-scene team?

2. During his search of a homicide scene, investigator David Gurney collects evidence that includes a bloody shirt. After the crime-scene team has completely processed the scene, Investigator Gurney packages the shirt in a paper bag, seals the bag, and labels it to indicate the contents. He then delivers the shirt to the laboratory with an evidence-submission form. There, a forensic scientist breaks the seal, removes the shirt, and performs a series of tests on it. He replaces the shirt, discards the old seal, and places a new seal on the package containing his initials and the date at which it was resealed. What mistakes, if any, were made in handling the shirt?

3. That important elements are missing from the following crime-scene sketch?

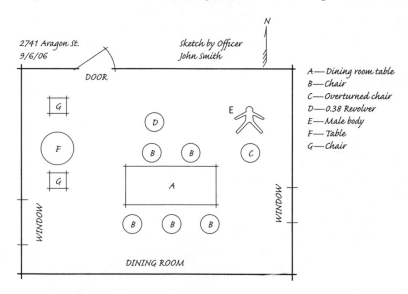

Web Resources

Crime and Clues (Articles on crime-scene protection, processing, and reconstruction)
www.crimeandclues.com/crimescene.htm

Crime-Scene Investigation (Guidelines and articles on response, evidence collection, photography, and other topics)
www.crime-scene-investigator.net

Crime Scene Investigation: A Reference for Law Enforcement Training
www.ojp.usdoj.gov/nij/pubs-sum/200160.htm

Endnotes

1. 437 U.S. 385 (1978).
2. 436 U.S. 499 (1978).

What Killed Napoleon?

Napoleon I, emperor of France, was sent into exile on the remote island of St. Helena by the British after his defeat at the Battle of Waterloo in 1815. St. Helena was hot, unsanitary, and rampant with disease. There, Napoleon was confined to a large reconstructed agricultural building known as Longwood House. Boredom and unhealthy living conditions gradually took their toll on Napoleon's mental and physical state. He began suffering from severe abdominal pains and experienced swelling of the ankles and general weakness of his limbs. From the fall of 1820, Napoleon's health began to deteriorate rapidly until death arrived on May 5, 1821. An autopsy concluded the cause of death to be stomach cancer.

It was inevitable that dying under British control, as Napoleon did, would bring with it numerous conspiratorial theories to account for his death. One of the most fascinating inquiries was conducted by a Swedish dentist, Sven Forshufvud, who systematically correlated the clinical symptoms of Napoleon's last days to those of arsenic poisoning. For Forshufvud, the key to unlocking the cause of Napoleon's death rested with Napoleon's hair. Forshufvud arranged to have Napoleon's hair measured for arsenic content by neutron activation analysis and found it consistent with arsenic poisoning. Nevertheless, the cause of Napoleon's demise is still a matter for debate and speculation. Other Napoleon hairs collected in 1805 and 1814 have also shown high concentrations of arsenic giving rise to the speculation that Napoleon was innocently exposed to arsenic. Even hair collected from Napoleon's three sisters show significant levels of arsenic. Some question whether Napoleon even had clinical symptoms associated with arsenic poisoning. In truth, forensic science may never be able to answer the question—what killed Napoleon?

chapter 5

Physical Evidence

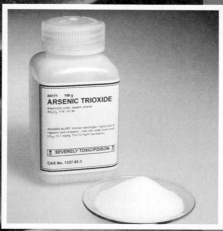

Key Terms

algor mortis

autopsy

class characteristics

comparison

forensic anthropology

forensic entomology

forensic pathologist

identification

individual characteristics

livor mortis

postmortem interval (PMI)

product rule

rigor mortis

Examination of Physical Evidence

Physical evidence is usually examined by a forensic scientist for identification or comparison.

Identification

identification
The process of determining a substance's physical or chemical identity.

Identification has as its purpose the determination of the physical or chemical identity of a substance with as near absolute certainty as existing analytical techniques will permit. For example, the crime laboratory is frequently asked to identify the chemical composition of preparations that may contain illicit drugs such as heroin, cocaine, or barbiturates. It may be asked to identify gasoline in residues recovered from the debris of a fire, or it may have to identify the nature of explosive residues—for example, dynamite or TNT. Also, the identification of blood, semen, hair, or wood would, as a matter of routine, include a determination of species origin. For example, did a bloodstain originate from a human as opposed to a dog or cat? Each of these requests requires the analysis and ultimate identification of a specific physical or chemical substance to the exclusion of all other possible substances.

The process of identification first requires the adoption of testing procedures that give characteristic results for specific standard materials. Once these test results have been established, they may be permanently recorded and used repeatedly to prove the identity of suspect materials. For example, to ascertain that a particular suspect powder is heroin, the test results on the powder must be identical to those that have been previously obtained from a known heroin sample.

Second, identification requires that the number and type of tests needed to identify a substance be sufficient to exclude all other substances. This means that the examiner must devise a specific analytical scheme that will eliminate all but one substance from consideration. Hence, if the examiner concludes that a white powder contains heroin, the test results must have been comprehensive enough to have excluded all other drugs—or, for that matter, all other substances—from consideration.

Simple rules cannot be devised for defining what constitutes a thorough and foolproof analytical scheme. Each type of evidence obviously requires a unique test, and each test has a different degree of specificity. Thus, one substance could conceivably be identified by one test, whereas another may require the combination of five or six different tests to arrive at an identification. In a science in which the practitioner has little or no control over the quality and quantity of the specimens received, a standard series of tests cannot encompass all possible problems and pitfalls. So the forensic scientist must determine at what point the analysis can be concluded and the criteria for positive identification satisfied; for this, he or she must rely on knowledge gained through education and experience. Ultimately, the conclusion will have to be substantiated beyond any reasonable doubt in a court of law.

Comparison

A comparison analysis subjects a suspect specimen and a standard/reference specimen to the same tests and examinations for the ultimate purpose of determining whether they have a common origin. For example, the forensic scientist may place a suspect at a particular location by noting the similarities of a hair found at the crime scene to hairs removed from the suspect's head (Figure 5–1). Or a paint chip found on a hit-and-run victim's garment may be compared with paint removed from a vehicle suspected of being involved in the incident.

comparison
The process of ascertaining whether two or more objects have a common origin.

The forensic comparison is actually a two-step procedure. First, combinations of select properties are chosen from the suspect and the standard/reference specimen for comparison. The question of which and how many properties are selected obviously depends on the type of materials being examined. (This subject will receive a good deal of discussion in forthcoming chapters.) The overriding consideration must be the ultimate evidential value of the conclusion.

This brings us to the second objective. Once the examination has been completed, the forensic scientist must draw a conclusion about the origins

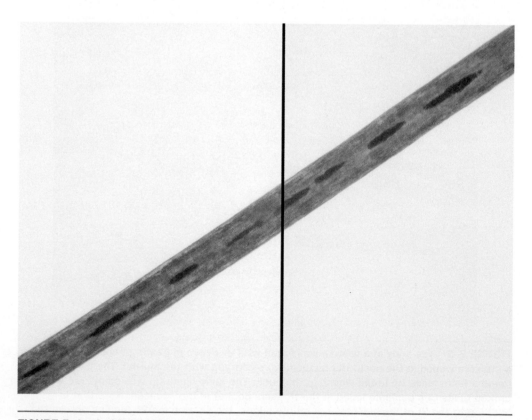

FIGURE 5–1 A side-by-side comparison of hairs. *Courtesy Chris Palenik, Microtrace, Elgin, IL., www.microtracescientific.com*

of the specimens. Do they or do they not come from the same source? Certainly if one or more of the properties selected for comparison do not agree, the analyst will conclude that the specimens are not the same and hence could not have originated from the same source. Suppose, on the other hand, that all the properties do compare and the specimens, as far as the examiner can determine, are indistinguishable. Does it logically follow that they came from the same source? Not necessarily so.

To comprehend the evidential value of a comparison, one must appreciate the role that probability has in ascertaining the origins of two or more specimens. Simply defined, *probability* is the frequency of occurrence of an event. If a coin is flipped a hundred times, in theory we can expect heads to come up fifty times. Hence, the probability of the event (heads) occurring is fifty in one hundred. In other words, probability defines the odds that a certain event will occur.

Individual Characteristics   Evidence that can be associated with a common source with an extremely high degree of probability is said to possess **individual characteristics**. Examples of such associations are the matching ridge characteristics of two fingerprints, the comparison of random striations (markings) on bullets or tool marks, the comparison of irregular and random wear patterns in tire or footwear impressions, the comparison of handwriting characteristics, the fitting together of the irregular edges of broken objects in the manner of a jigsaw puzzle (see Figure 5–2), or matching sequentially made plastic bags by striation marks running across the bags (see Figure 5–3).

individual characteristics
Properties of evidence that can be attributed to a common source with an extremely high degree of certainty.

FIGURE 5–2 The body of a woman was found with evidence of beating about the head and a stablike wound in the neck. Her husband was charged with the murder. The pathologist found a knife blade tip in the wound in the neck. The knife blade tip was compared with the broken blade of a penknife found in the trousers pocket of the accused. Note that in addition to the fit of the indentations on the edges, the scratch marks running across the blade tip correspond in detail to those on the broken blade. *Courtesy Centre of Forensic Sciences, Toronto, Canada*

FIGURE 5–3 The bound body of a young woman was recovered from a river. Her head was covered with a black polyethylene trash bag (shown on the right). Among the items recovered from one of several suspects was a black polyethylene trash bag (shown on the left). A side-by-side comparison of the two bags' extrusion marks and pigment bands showed them to be consecutively manufactured. This information allowed investigators to focus their attention on one suspect, who ultimately was convicted of the homicide. *Courtesy George W. Neighbor, New Jersey State Police*

In all of these cases, it is not possible to state with mathematical exactness the probability that the specimens are of common origin; it can only be concluded that this probability is so high as to defy mathematical calculations or human comprehension. Furthermore, the conclusion of common origin must be substantiated by the practical experience of the examiner. For example, the French scientist Victor Balthazard mathematically determined that the probability of two individuals having the same fingerprints is one out of 1×10^{60}, or 1 followed by sixty zeros. This probability is so small as to exclude the possibility of any two individuals having the same fingerprints. This contention is also supported by the experience of fingerprint examiners who, after classifying millions of prints over the past hundred years, have never found any two to be exactly alike.

Class Characteristics   One disappointment awaiting the investigator unfamiliar with the limitations of forensic science is the frequent inability of the laboratory to relate physical evidence to a common origin with a high degree of certainty. Evidence is said to possess **class characteristics** when it can be associated only with a group and not with a single source. Here again, probability is a determining factor. For example, if we compare two single-layer automobile paint chips of a similar color, their chance of originating from the same car is not nearly as great as when we compare two paint chips with seven similar layers of paint, not all of which were part of the car's original color. The former will have class characteristics and could be associated at best only with one car model (which may number in the thousands), whereas the latter may be judged to have individual characteristics and to have a high probability of originating from one specific car.

Blood offers another good example of evidence that can have class characteristics. For example, suppose that two blood specimens are compared and both are found to be of human origin, type A. The frequency of occurrence in the population of type A blood is 26 percent—hardly offering a basis for establishing the common origin of the stains. However, if other blood factors are also determined and are found to compare, the probability that the two bloods originated from a common source increases. Thus, if one uses a series of blood factors that occur independently of each other, then one can apply the **product rule** to calculate the overall frequency of occurrence of the blood in a population. In this case, the product rule states that multiplying together the frequency of each factor present in a blood

class characteristics
Properties of evidence that can be associated only with a group and not with a single source.

product rule
A formula for determining how frequently a certain combination of characteristics occurs in a population. The product rule states that one must first determine the probability of each characteristic occurring separately, then multiply together the frequencies of all independently occurring characteristics. The result is the overall frequency of occurrence for that particular combination of characteristics.

sample will determine how common blood containing that combination of factors is in the general population.

For example, in the O. J. Simpson murder case, a bloodstain located at the crime scene was found to contain a number of factors that compared to O. J.'s blood:

Blood Factors	Frequency
A	26%
EsD	85%
PGM 2+2−	2%

The product of all the frequencies shown in the table determines the probability that any one individual possesses such a combination of blood factors. In this instance, applying the product rule, $0.26 \times 0.85 \times 0.02$ equals 0.0044. Thus, only 0.44 percent, or less than 1 in 200 people, would be expected to have this particular combination of blood factors. These bloodstain factors did not match either of the two victims, Nicole Brown Simpson or Ronald Goldman, thus eliminating them as possible sources of the blood. Although the forensic scientist has still not individualized the bloodstains to one person (in this case, O. J. Simpson), data have been provided that will permit investigators and the courts to better assess the evidential value of the crime-scene stain.

As we will learn in Chapter 9, the product rule is used to determine the frequency of occurrence of DNA profiles typically determined from blood and other biological materials. Importantly, modern DNA technology provides enough factors to allow an analyst to individualize blood, semen, and other biological materials to a single person.

Key Points

- Two methods used by forensic scientists when examining physical evidence are identification and comparison.

- Identification is the process of determining a substance's chemical or physical identity to the exclusion of all other substances (e.g., drugs, explosives, petroleum products, blood, semen, and hair species).

- A comparison analysis determines whether a suspect specimen and a standard/reference specimen have a common origin.

- Evidence that can be associated with a common source with an extremely high degree of probability is said to possess individual characteristics.

- Evidence associated with only a group is said to have class characteristics.

- The overall frequency of occurrence of an event can be obtained by multiplying the frequencies of all independently occurring instances related to that event. This is known as the product rule.

Significance of Physical Evidence

One of the current weaknesses of forensic science is the inability of the examiner to assign exact or even approximate probability values to the comparison of most class physical evidence. For example, what is the probability that a nylon fiber originated from a particular sweater, or that a hair came from a particular person's head, or that a paint chip came from a car suspected to have been involved in a hit-and-run accident? Very few statistical data are available from which to derive this information, and in a society that is increasingly dependent on mass-produced products, the gathering of such data is becoming an increasingly elusive goal.

One of the primary endeavors of forensic scientists must be to create and update statistical databases for evaluating the significance of class physical evidence. Of course, when such information—for example, the population frequency of blood factors—is available, it is used; but for the most part, the forensic scientist must rely on personal experience when interpreting the significance of class physical evidence.

People who are unfamiliar with the realities of modern criminalistics are often disappointed to learn that most items of physical evidence retrieved at crime scenes cannot be linked definitively to a single person or object. Although investigators always try to uncover physical evidence with individual characteristics—such as fingerprints, tool marks, and bullets—the chances of finding class physical evidence are far greater. To deny or belittle the value of such evidence is to reject the potential role that criminalistics can play in a criminal investigation.

In practice, criminal cases are fashioned for the courtroom around a collection of diverse elements, each pointing to the guilt or involvement of a party in a criminal act. Often, most of the evidence gathered is subjective, prone to human error and bias. The believability of eyewitness accounts, confessions, and informant testimony can all be disputed, maligned, and subjected to severe attack and skepticism in the courtroom. Under these circumstances, errors in human judgment are often magnified to detract from the credibility of the witness.

Assessing the Value of Evidence

The value of class physical evidence lies in its ability to corroborate events with data in a manner that is, as nearly as possible, free of human error and bias. It is the thread that binds together other investigative findings that are more dependent on human judgments and, therefore, more prone to human failings. The fact that scientists have not yet learned to individualize many kinds of physical evidence means that criminal investigators should not abdicate or falter in their pursuit of all investigative leads. However, the ability of scientists to achieve a high degree of success in evaluating class physical evidence means that criminal investigators can pursue their work with a much greater chance of success.

Admittedly, defining the significance of an item of class evidence in exact mathematical terms is usually a difficult if not impossible goal. Although class evidence is by its very nature not unique, meaningful items of physical evidence, such as those listed at the beginning of this chapter, are extremely diverse in our environment. Select, for example, a colored fiber from an article of clothing and try to locate that exact color on the clothing of random individuals you meet, or select a car color and try to match it to that of other cars you see on local streets. Furthermore, keep in mind that a forensic comparison goes beyond a mere color comparison and involves examining and comparing a variety of chemical and/or physical properties (Figure 5–4). The chances are low of encountering two indistinguishable items of physical evidence at a crime scene that actually originated from different sources. Obviously, given these circumstances, only objects that

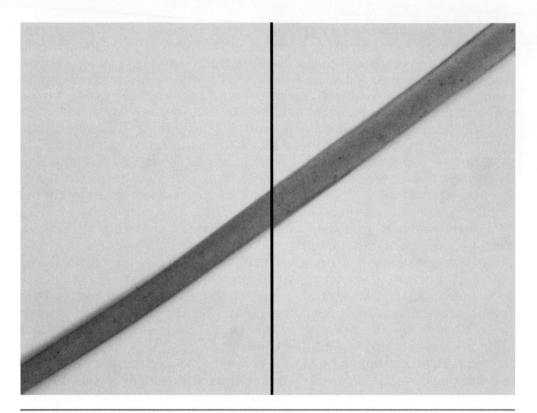

FIGURE 5–4   A side-by-side comparison of fibers. *Courtesy Chris Palenik, Microtrace, Elgin, Ill., www.microtracescientific.com*

exhibit significant diversity are appropriate for classification as physical evidence.

In the same way, when one is dealing with more than one type of class evidence, their collective presence may lead to an extremely high certainty that they originated from the same source. As the number of objects linking an individual to a crime increases, the probability of involvement increases dramatically. A classic example of this situation can be found in the evidence presented at the trial of Wayne Williams (see the case reading at the end of Chapter 12). Williams was charged with the murders of two individuals in the Atlanta, Georgia, metropolitan area; he was also linked to the murders of ten other boys and young men. An essential element of the state's case involved the association of Williams with the victims through a variety of fiber evidence. Actually, twenty-eight types of fibers linked Williams to the murder victims, evidence that the forensic examiner characterized as "overwhelming."

Cautions and Limitations in Dealing with Physical Evidence

In further evaluating the contribution of physical evidence, one cannot overlook one important reality in the courtroom: The weight or significance accorded physical evidence is a determination left entirely to the trier of fact, usually a jury of laypeople. Given the high esteem in which scientists are generally held by society and the infallible image of forensic science created by books and television, scientifically evaluated evidence often takes on an aura of special reliability and trustworthiness in the courtroom. Often, physical evidence, whether individual or class, is accorded great weight during jury deliberations and becomes a primary factor in reinforcing or overcoming lingering doubts about guilt or innocence. In fact, a number of jurists have already cautioned against giving carte blanche approval to admitting scientific testimony without first considering its relevance to the case. Given the potential weight of scientific evidence, failure to take proper safeguards may unfairly prejudice a case against the accused.

Physical evidence may also serve to exclude or exonerate a person from suspicion. For instance, if type A blood is linked to the suspect, all individuals who have types B, AB, and O blood can be eliminated from consideration. Because it is not possible to assess at the crime scene what value, if any, the scientist will find in the evidence collected, or what significance such findings will ultimately have to a jury, the thorough collection and scientific evaluation of physical evidence must become a routine part of all criminal investigations.

Just when an item of physical evidence crosses the line that distinguishes class from individual is difficult to determine and is often the source of heated debate and honest disagreement among forensic scientists. How many striations are necessary to individualize a mark to a single tool and no other? How many color layers individualize a paint chip to a single car? How many ridge characteristics individualize a fingerprint, and how many handwriting characteristics tie a person to a signature? These questions defy simple answers. The task of the forensic scientist is to find as many characteristics as possible to compare one substance with another. The significance attached to the findings is decided by the quality and composition of the evidence, the case history, and the examiner's experience. Ultimately, the conclusion can range from mere speculation to near certainty.

There are practical limits to the properties and characteristics the forensic scientist can select for comparison. Carried to the extreme, no two things in this world are alike in every detail. Modern analytical techniques have become so sophisticated and sensitive that the criminalist must define the limits of natural variation among materials when interpreting the data gathered from a comparative analysis. For example, we will learn in Chapter 13 that two properties, density and refractive index, are best suited for comparing two pieces of glass. But the latest techniques that have been developed to measure these properties are so sensitive that they can even distinguish glass originating from a single pane of glass. Certainly this goes beyond the desires of a criminalist trying to determine only whether two glass particles originated from the same window. Similarly, if the surface of a paint chip is magnified 1,600 times with a powerful scanning electron microscope, it is apparent that the fine details that are revealed could not be duplicated in any other paint chip. Under these circumstances, no two paint chips, even those coming from the same surface, could ever compare in the true sense of the word. Therefore, practicality dictates that such examinations be conducted at a less revealing, but more meaningful, magnification (see Figure 5–5).

Distinguishing evidential variations from natural variations is not always an easy task. Learning how to use the microscope and all the other modern instruments in a crime laboratory properly is one thing; gaining the proficiency needed to interpret the observations and data is another. As new crime laboratories are created and others expand to meet the requirements of the law enforcement community, many individuals are starting new careers in forensic science. They must be cautioned that merely reading relevant textbooks and journals is no substitute for experience in this most practical of sciences.

FIGURE 5–5 (a) A two-layer paint chip magnified 244 times with a scanning electron microscope. (b) The same paint chip viewed at a magnification of 1,600 times. *Courtesy Jeff Albright*

(a)

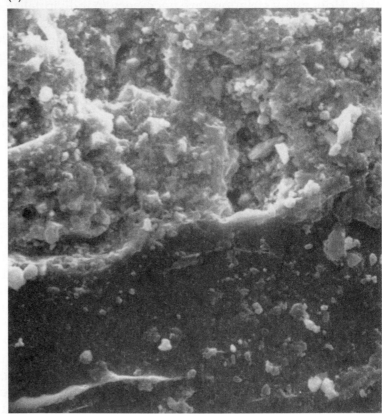

(b)

Key Points

- The value of class physical evidence lies in its ability to corroborate events with data in a manner that is, as nearly as possible, free of human error and bias.

- As the number of objects linking an individual to a crime scene increases, so does the likelihood of that individual's involvement with the crime.

- A person may be exonerated or excluded from suspicion if physical evidence collected at a crime scene is found to be different from standard/reference samples collected from that subject.

Forensic Databases

In a criminal investigation, the ultimate contribution a criminalist can make is to link a suspect to a crime through comparative analysis. This comparison defines the unique role of the criminalist in a criminal investigation. Of course, a one-on-one comparison requires a suspect. Little or nothing of evidential value can be accomplished if crime-scene investigators acquire fingerprints, hairs, fibers, paint, blood, and semen without the ability to link these items to a suspect. In this respect, computer technology has dramatically altered the role of the crime laboratory in the investigative process.

No longer is the crime laboratory a passive bystander waiting for investigators to uncover clues about who may have committed a crime. Today, the crime laboratory is on the forefront of the investigation seeking to identify perpetrators. This dramatic enhancement of the role of forensic science in criminal investigation has come about through the creation of computerized databases that not only link all fifty states, but also tie together police agencies throughout the world.

Fingerprint Databases

The premier model of all forensic database systems is the *Integrated Automated Fingerprint Identification System* (IAFIS), a national fingerprint and criminal history system maintained by the FBI and launched in 1999. IAFIS contains fingerprints and corresponding criminal history information for nearly 50 million subjects (or 500 million fingerprint images), which are submitted voluntarily to the FBI by state, local, and federal law enforcement agencies.

A crime-scene fingerprint or latent fingerprint is a dramatic find for the criminal investigator. Once the quality of the print has been deemed suitable for the IAFIS search, the latent-print examiner creates a digital image of the print with either a digital camera or a scanner. Next, the examiner, with the aid of a coder, marks points on the print to guide the computerized search. The print is then electronically submitted to IAFIS and within minutes the search is completed against all fingerprint images in IAFIS; the examiner may receive a list of potential candidates and their corresponding fingerprints for comparison and verification (see Figure 5–6).

Many countries throughout the world have created *national automated fingerprint identification systems* that are comparable to the FBI's model. For example, a computerized fingerprint database containing nearly nine million ten-print records connects the Home Office and forty-three police forces throughout England and Wales.

DNA Databases

In 1998, the FBI's *Combined DNA Index System* (CODIS) became fully operational. CODIS enables federal, state, and local crime laboratories to electronically exchange and compare DNA profiles, thereby linking crimes to each other and to convicted offenders. All fifty states have enacted legislation to establish a data bank containing DNA profiles of individuals

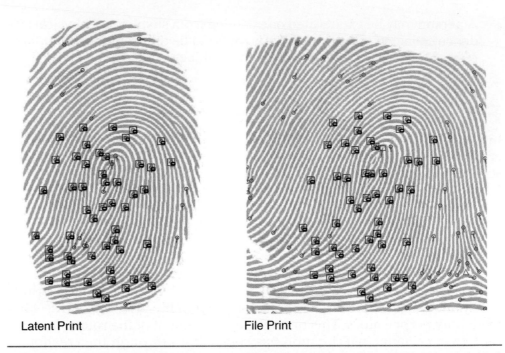

Latent Print   File Print

FIGURE 5–6 **The computerized search of a fingerprint database first requires that selected ridge characteristics be designated by a coder. The positions of these ridge characteristics serve as a basis for comparing the print against file fingerprints.** *Courtesy Sirchie Finger Print Laboratories, Inc., Youngsville, N.C., www.sirchie.com*

Forensic Brief

In 1975, police found Gerald Wallace's body on his living room couch. He had been savagely beaten, his hands bound with an electric cord. Detectives searched his ransacked house, cataloging every piece of evidence they could find. None of it led to the murderer. They had no witnesses. Sixteen years after the fact, a lone fingerprint, lifted from a cigarette pack found in Wallace's house and kept for sixteen years in the police files, was entered into the Pennsylvania State Police AFIS database. Within minutes, it hit a match. That print, police say, gave investigators the identity of a man who had been at the house the night of the murder. Police talked to him. He led them to other witnesses, who led them to the man police ultimately charged with the murder of Gerald Wallace.

convicted of felony sexual offenses (and other crimes, depending on each state's statute).

CODIS creates investigative leads from two sources: the *forensic index* and the *offender index*. The forensic index currently contains about 110,000 profiles from unsolved crime-scene evidence. Based on a match, police in multiple jurisdictions can identify serial crimes, allowing coordination of investigations and sharing of leads developed independently. The offender index contains the profiles of nearly three million convicted or arrested individuals. (Unfortunately, hundreds of thousands of samples are backlogged, still awaiting DNA analysis and entry into the offender index.) Law enforcement agencies search this index against DNA profiles recovered from biological evidence found at unsolved crime scenes. This approach has been tremendously successful in identifying perpetrators because most crimes involving biological evidence are committed by repeat offenders.

Forensic Brief

Fort Collins, Colorado, and Philadelphia, Pennsylvania, are separated by nearly 1,800 miles, but in 2001 they were tragically linked though DNA. Troy Graves left the Philadelphia area in 1999, joined the Air Force, and settled down with his wife in Colorado. A frenzied string of eight sexual assaults around the Colorado University campus set off a manhunt that ultimately resulted in the arrest of Graves. However, his DNA profile inextricably identified him as Philadelphia's notorious "Center City rapist." This assailant attacked four women in 1997 and brutally murdered Shannon Schieber, a Wharton School graduate student, in 1998. His last known attack in Philadelphia was the rape of an 18-year-old student in August 1999, shortly before he left the city. In 2002, Graves was returned to Philadelphia, where he was sentenced to life in prison without parole.

Several countries throughout the world have initiated national DNA data banks. The United Kingdom's *National DNA Database*, established in 1995, was the world's first national database. Currently it holds more than four million profiles, and DNA can be taken for entry into the database from anyone arrested for an offense likely to involve a prison term. In a typical month, matches are found linking suspects to 26 murders; 57 rapes and other sexual offenses; and 3,000 motor vehicle, property and drug crimes.

Other Databases

The *National Integrated Ballistics Information Network* (NIBIN) maintained by the Bureau of Alcohol, Tobacco, Firearms and Explosives, allows firearms analysts to acquire, digitize, and compare markings made by a firearm on bullets and cartridge casings recovered from crime scenes. The NIBIN program currently has 236 sites that are electronically joined to sixteen multistate regions.

The heart of NIBIN is the *Integrated Ballistic Identification System* (IBIS), comprising a microscope and a computer unit that can capture an image of a bullet or cartridge casing. The images are then forwarded to a regional server, where they are stored and correlated against other images in the regional database. IBIS does not positively match bullets or casings fired from the same weapon; this must be done by a firearms examiner. IBIS does, however, facilitate the work of the firearms examiner by producing a short list of candidates for the examiner to manually compare. Nearly 900,000 pieces of crime-scene evidence have been entered in NIBIN, and more than 10,000 "hits" have been recorded, many of them yielding investigative information not obtainable by other means.

The *International Forensic Automotive Paint Data Query* (PDQ) database contains chemical and color information pertaining to original automotive paints. This database, developed and maintained by the Forensic Laboratory Services of the Royal Canadian Mounted Police (RCMP), contains information about the make, model, year, and assembly plant on more than 13,000 vehicles, with a library of more than 50,000 layers of paint. Contributors to the PDQ include the RCMP and forensic laboratories in Ontario and Quebec, as well as forty U.S. forensic laboratories and police agencies in twenty-one other countries. Accredited users of PDQ are required to submit sixty new automotive paint samples per year for addition to the database. The PDQ database has found its greatest utility in the investigation

Forensic Brief

After a series of armed robberies in which suspects fired shots, the sheriff's office of Broward County, Florida, entered the cartridge casings from the crime scenes into NIBIN. Through NIBIN, four of the armed robberies were linked to the same .40-caliber handgun. A short time later, sheriff's deputies noticed suspicious activity around a local business. When they attempted to interview the suspects, the suspects fled in a vehicle. During the chase, the suspects attempted to dispose of a handgun; deputies recovered the gun after making the arrests. The gun was test-fired and the resulting evidence entered into NIBIN, which indicated a possible link between this handgun and the four previous armed robberies. Firearms examiners confirmed the link by examining the original evidence. The suspects were arrested and charged with four prior armed robbery offenses.

Forensic Brief

A 53-year-old man was walking his dog in the early morning hours. He was struck and killed by an unknown vehicle and later found lying in the roadway. No witnesses were present and the police had no leads regarding the suspect vehicle. A gold metallic painted plastic fragment recovered from the scene and the victim's clothing were submitted to the Virginia Department of Forensic Science for analysis.

The victim's clothing was scraped and several minute gold metallic paint particles were recovered. The majority of these particles contained only topcoats, while one very minute particle contained two primer layers and a very limited amount of colorcoat. The color of the primer surfacer layer is similar to that typically associated with some Fords. Subsequent spectral searches in the PDQ database indicated that the paint most likely originated from a 1990 or newer Ford.

The most discriminating aspect of this paint was the unusual looking gold metallic topcoat color. A search of automotive repaint books yielded only one color that closely matched the paint recovered in this case. The color, Aztec Gold Metallic, was determined to have been used only on 1997 Ford Mustangs.

The results of the examination were relayed via telephone to the investigating detective. The investigating detective quickly determined that only 11,000 1997 Ford Mustangs were produced in Aztec Gold Metallic. Only two of these vehicles were registered, and had been previously stopped, in the jurisdiction of the offense. Ninety minutes after the make/model/year information was relayed to the investigator, he called back to say he had located a suspect vehicle. Molding from the vehicle and known paint samples were submitted for comparison. Subsequent laboratory comparisons showed that the painted plastic piece recovered from the scene was physically fitted together with the molding and the paint recovered from the victim's clothing was consistent with paint samples taken from the suspect vehicle.

Source: Brenda Christy, Virginia Department of Forensic Science.

of hit-and-runs by providing police with possible make, model, and year information to aid in the search for the unknown vehicle.

The previously described databases are maintained and controlled by government agencies. There is one exception: a commercially available computer retrieval system for comparing and identifying crime-scene shoe prints known as *SICAR (shoeprint image capture and retrieval)*.[1] SICAR's pattern-coding system enables an analyst to create a simple description of a shoe print by assigning codes to individual pattern features (see Figure 5–7). Shoe print images can be entered into SICAR by either a scanner or a digital camera. This product has a comprehensive shoe sole database that includes more than three hundred manufacturers of shoes with more than eight thousand sole patterns, providing investigators with a means for linking a crime-scene footwear impression to a particular shoe manufacturer.

Key Points

- The creation of computerized databases for fingerprints, criminal histories, DNA profiles, markings on bullets and cartridges, automotive paints, and shoe prints has dramatically enhanced the role of forensic science in criminal investigation.

- IAFIS is the Integrated Automated Fingerprint Identification System, a national fingerprint and criminal history database maintained by the FBI. IAFIS allows criminal investigators to compare fingerprints at a crime scene to an index of 500 million known prints. CODIS is the FBI's Combined DNA Index System. It enables federal, state, and local crime laboratories to electronically exchange and compare DNA profiles, linking crimes to each other and to convicted offenders.

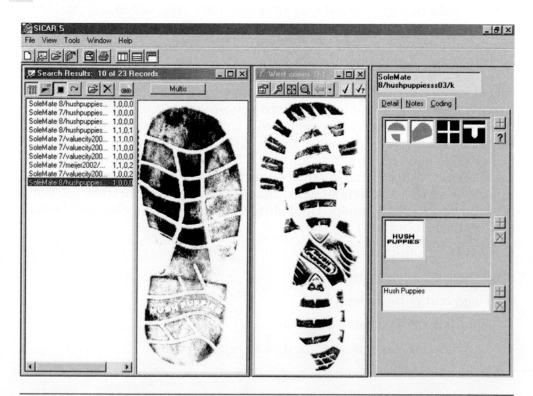

FIGURE 5–7 **The crime-scene footwear print on the right is being searched against eight thousand sole patterns to determine its make and model.** *Courtesy Foster & Freeman Limited, Worcestershire, U.K., www.fosterfreeman.co.uk*

The Murder Scene: Death and Autopsies

Unfortunately, the most important piece of evidence at many crime scenes is the dead body of a victim. When foul play is suspected, a victim's corpse is subjected to the same kind of intense physical analysis as any other piece of evidence. This task falls primarily to a forensic pathologist, often aided by the skills of specialists including forensic anthropologists and forensic entomologists. In its broadest sense, forensic pathology involves the study of medicine as it relates to the application of the law, particularly criminal law. In practice, this most often involves the investigation of sudden, unnatural, unexplained, or violent deaths.

Role of the Forensic Pathologist

Typically, forensic pathologists, in their role as medical examiners or coroners, must answer several basic questions: Who is the victim? What injuries are present? When did the injuries occur? Why and how were the injuries produced? The primary role of the medical examiner is to determine the cause of death. If a cause cannot be found through observation, an autopsy is normally performed to establish the cause of death. The manner in which death occurred is classified into five categories: natural, homicide, suicide, accident, or undetermined, based on the circumstances surrounding the incident.

Frequently, a medical examiner must perform an autopsy if a death is deemed suspicious or unexplained. The cause of death may not always be what it seems at first glance. For example, a decedent with a gunshot wound and a gun in his hand may appear to have committed suicide. However, an autopsy may reveal that the victim actually died of suffocation and the gunshot wound occurred after death to cover up the circumstances surrounding the commission of a crime.

Evidence from the Autopsy   The search for physical evidence must extend beyond the crime scene to the autopsy room of a deceased victim. Here, the medical examiner or coroner will carefully examine the victim to establish a cause and manner of death. As a matter of routine, tissues and organs are retained for pathological and toxicological examination. At the same time, arrangements must be made between the examiner and investigator to secure a variety of items that may be obtainable from the body for laboratory examination. The following are to be collected and sent to the forensic laboratory:

- Victim's clothing
- Fingernail scrapings
- Head and pubic hairs
- Blood (for DNA typing purposes)
- Vaginal, anal, and oral swabs (in sex-related crimes)
- Recovered bullets from the body
- Hand swabs from shooting victims (for gunshot residue analysis).

These pieces of evidence should be properly packaged and labeled like all other evidence. Once the body is buried, efforts at obtaining these items

---

forensic pathologists
Investigative personnel, typically medical examiners or coroners, who investigate the cause and time of death of a victim in a crime.

autopsy
A surgical procedure performed by a pathologist on a dead body to ascertain from the body, organs, and bodily fluids the cause of death.

may prove difficult or futile. Furthermore, a lengthy time delay in obtaining many of these items will diminish or destroy their forensic value.

Estimating Time of Death

After a human body expires, it goes through several stages of decomposition. A medical examiner can often estimate the time of death by evaluating the stage of decomposition in which the victim was found. Immediately following death, the muscles relax and then become rigid. This condition, rigor mortis, manifests itself within the first twenty-four hours and disappears within thirty-six hours.

Another condition occurring in the early stages of decomposition is livor mortis. When the human heart stops pumping, the blood begins to settle in the parts of the body closest to the ground. The skin appears dark blue or purple in these areas. The onset of this condition begins immediately and continues for up to twelve hours after death. The skin does not appear discolored in areas where the body is restricted by either clothing or an object pressing against the body. This information can be useful in determining whether the victim's position was changed after death.

Other physical and chemical changes within the body also help approximate the time of death. Algor mortis is the process by which the body temperature continually cools after death until it reaches the ambient or room temperature. The rate of heat loss is influenced by factors such as the location and size of the body, the victim's clothing, and weather conditions. Because of such factors, this method can only estimate the approximate time period since death. As a general rule, beginning about an hour after death, the body loses heat at a rate of approximately 1 to 1.5°F per hour until the body reaches the environmental temperature.

Another approach helpful for estimating the time of death is to determine potassium levels in the ocular fluid (fluid within the eye, also known as the vitreous humor). After death, cells within the inner surface of the eyeball release potassium into the ocular fluid. By analyzing the amount of potassium present at various intervals after death, the forensic pathologist can determine the rate at which potassium is released into the vitreous humor and use it to approximate the time of death. During the autopsy, other factors may indicate the time period in which death occurred. For example, the amount of food in the stomach can help estimate when a person's last meal was eaten. This information can be valuable when investigating a death.

Forensic Anthropology: Skeletal Detectives

Forensic anthropology is concerned primarily with the identification and examination of human skeletal remains. Bones are remarkably durable and undergo an extremely slow breakdown process that lasts decades or even centuries. Because of their resistance to rapid decomposition, skeletal remains can reveal a multitude of individual characteristics. An examination of bones may reveal the sex, approximate age, race, and skeletal injury of the person. For example, a female's bone structure differs from a male's, especially within the pelvic area because of a woman's childbearing capabilities.

This area of expertise is not limited just to identification, however. A forensic anthropologist may also help create facial reconstructions to identify skeletal remains. With the help of this technique, a composite of the victim can be drawn and advertised in an attempt to identify the victim. Forensic anthropologists are also helpful in identifying victims of a

---

WebExtra 5.1

See how an autopsy is performed
www.prenhall.com/saferstein

rigor mortis
A medical condition that occurs after death and results in the stiffening of muscle mass; the rigidity of the body begins within twenty-four hours of death and disappears within thirty-six hours of death.

livor mortis
A medical condition that occurs after death and results in the settling of blood in areas of the body closest to the ground.

algor mortis
A process that occurs after death in which the body temperature continually cools until it reaches the ambient or room temperature.

forensic anthropology
The use of anthropological knowledge of humans and skeletal structure to examine and identify human skeletal remains.

WebExtra 5.2

Explore Forensic Anthropology
www.prenhall.com/saferstein

mass disaster such as a plane crash. When such a tragedy occurs, forensic anthropologists can help identify victims through the collection of bone fragments. The definite identification of remains can be made only through the analysis of the decedent's DNA profile, fingerprints, or medical records. The remains may still contain some soft tissue material upon discovery. The soft tissue cells may be able to yield a DNA profile for identification purposes. Sometimes the tissue of the hand is still present although dried out. It may be possible to rehydrate the tissue to recover fingerprints. However, usually the identification of the remains will depend on medical records, especially dental records.

Thorough documentation is required throughout the processes of recovery and examination. All the information that has been mentioned that can be obtained from these processes may be recorded in a forensic anthropology report for further use in the investigation.

The sites where human remains are found must be treated as crime scenes (see Figure 5–8). These sites are usually located by civilians who then contact law enforcement personnel. Such a scene should be secured as soon as possible to prevent any further alteration of the scene. The scene should then be searched to locate all bones if they are scattered or other aspects of evidence such as footwear impressions or discarded items. Some tools can be very useful in the search for evidence at a "tomb" site. They include aerial photography, metal detectors, ground-penetrating radar, infrared photography, apparatuses that detect the gases produced by biological decomposition, or so-called "cadaver dogs," which detect the odors caused by biological decomposition. All of the items found must be tagged, photographed, sketched, and documented in notes. Once all bones or evidence is found, a scene sketch should be made to show the exact location of each item (preferably using global positioning system coordinates) and the spatial relationship of all evidence.

FIGURE 5–8 A crime-scene site showing a pelvis partly buried in sand and a femur lying across a pistol. *Courtesy Paul Sledzik*

Case Study

Identifying a Serial Killer's Victims

The worst serial killer in America calmly admitted his guilt as he led investigators to a crawl space under his house. There, John Wayne Gacy had buried twenty-eight young men, after brutally raping and murdering them in cold blood. Because no identification was found with the bodies, the police were forced to examine missing-person reports for leads. However, these boys and men were so alike in age, race, and stature that police were unable to make individual identifications for most of the victims. Clyde Snow, the world-renowned forensic anthropologist from Oklahoma, was asked to help the investigators make these difficult identifications.

Snow began by making a thirty-five-point examination of each skull for comparison to known individuals. By examining each skeleton, he made sure each bone was correctly attributed to an individual. This was crucial to later efforts because some of the victims had been buried on top of older graves, mingling their remains. Once Snow was sure all the bones were sorted properly, he began his in-depth study. Long bones such as the femur (thigh bone) were used to estimate each individual's height. This helped narrow the search when attempting to match the victims with the descriptions of missing people.

After narrowing the possibilities to missing people fitting the general description, investigators consulted potential victims' hospital and dental records. Evidence of injury, illness, surgery, or other unique skeletal defects were used to make identifications. Snow also pointed out

features that gave clues to the victim's behavior and medical history. For example, he discovered that one of Gacy's victims had an old fracture of his left arm, and that his left scapula (shoulder blade) and arm bore the telltale signs of a left-handed individual. These details were matched to a missing-person report, and another young victim was identified.

For the most difficult cases, Snow called in the help of forensic sculptor and facial reconstructionist Betty Pat Gatliff. She used clay and depth markers to put the flesh back on the faces of these forgotten boys in the hope that someone would recognize them after their photographs were released to the media. Her efforts were successful, but investigators found some families unwilling to accept the idea that their loved ones were among Gacy's victims. Even with Gatliff's help, nine of Gacy's victims remain unidentified.

John Wayne Gacy. © Bettmann/CORBIS. All Rights Reserved

Forensic Entomology: Testimony from Insects

The study of insects and their relation to a criminal investigation is known as **forensic entomology.** Such a practice is commonly used to estimate the time of death when the circumstances surrounding the crime are unknown. After decomposition begins, insects such as blowflies are the

forensic entomology
The study of insect matter, growth patterns, and succession of arrival at a crime scene to determine the time to death.

FIGURE 5–9 A scanning electron micrograph of two-hour-old blowfly maggots.
Courtesy Science Photo Library

postmortem interval (PMI)
The length of time that has elapsed since a person has died. If the time is not known, a number of medical or scientific techniques may be used to estimate it.

first to infest the body. Their eggs are laid in the human remains and ultimately hatch into maggots or fly larvae (see Figure 5–9), which consume human organs and tissues. Forensic entomologists can identify the specific insects present in the body and approximate how long a body has been left exposed by examining the stage of development of the fly larvae. This kind of determination is best for a timeline of hours to approximately one month. This is because the blowfly goes through the stages of its life cycle at known time intervals. By determining the oldest stage of fly found on the body, entomologists can approximate the postmortem interval (PMI). The time it takes for a fly to move through each stage depends on the species of fly and the temperature conditions.

These determinations are not always straightforward, however. The time required for stage development is affected by environmental influences such as geographical location, climate, and weather conditions. For example, cold temperatures hinder the development of fly eggs into adult flies. The forensic entomologist must consider these conditions when estimating the PMI. Knowledge of insects, their life cycles, and their habits make entomological evidence an invaluable tool for an investigation (see Figure 5–10).

If resources allow, all entomological, or insect, evidence should be collected by a forensic entomology expert. When this is not possible, collection should be carried out by an investigator with experience in death investigation. The entire body and area where insect evidence was found must be photographed and documented before collection. The temperature of the scene and the center of any "masses" of maggots should also be measured. Specimen samples should be taken from each area on the body where they are found. For all insects and stages, half of the specimens should be sealed in a glass vial with a food source so that the entomologist can observe their further development. The other half of the specimens, except for the newly emerged adult blowflies, should be preserved in a sealed glass vial with alcohol for further testing. The newly emerged adult

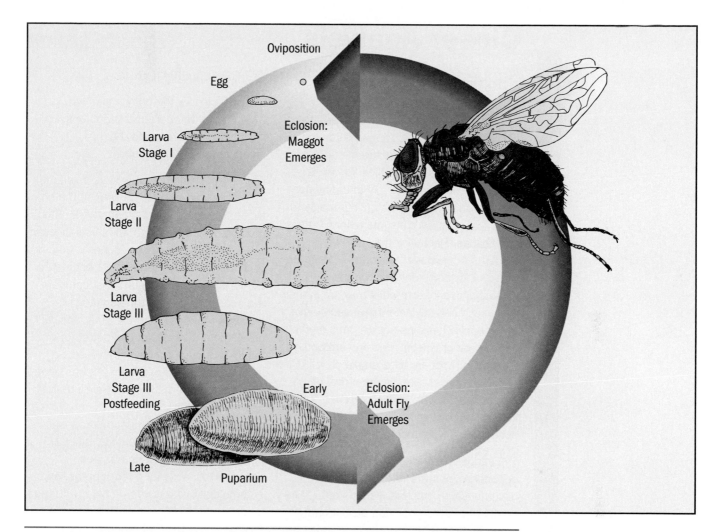

FIGURE 5–10 **The typical blowfly life cycle from egg deposition to adult fly emergence. This cycle is representative of any of one of the nearly ninety species of blowflies in North America.** *Courtesy E.P. Catts, Ph.D., deceased, and Neal H. Haskell, Ph.D., forensic entomology consultant, www.forensic-entomology.com*

flies should instead be dried out for preservation. Soil samples from near (not under) the body should also be collected.

Key Points

- An autopsy is normally performed if a death is suspicious or unexplained.

- Rigor mortis occurs after death and results in the stiffening of body parts in the positions they were in when death occurred. Livor mortis occurs after death and results in the settling of blood in areas of the body closest to the ground. Algor mortis refers to postmortem changes that cause a body to lose heat.

- Forensic anthropology is concerned primarily with the identification and examination of human skeltal remains.

- Forensic entomology is the study of the development of insect larvae in or the sucession of insects on a body to estimate the time of death.

Closer Analysis

Sequence of Arrival of Entomological Evidence

After death, *necrophagous insects*, or insects that feed on dead tissue, are the first to infest the body. The most common and important of these is the metallic greenbottle or bluebottle flies known as blowflies. Their eggs are laid in the human remains and ultimately hatch into maggots, or fly larvae, which consume human organs and tissues. Flesh flies may also be present at this stage. Meanwhile, *predator insects* may arrive and prey on the necrophagous insects while they are in their weak stages. Next, *omnivore insects* arrive at the body. These insects will feed on the body, on other insects, and on surrounding vegetation. Ants are an example of omnivore insects. Last is the arrival of *indigenous insects*, whose presence on or near the body is coincidental as they move about their environment.

The sequence of arrival of these groups is dependent mostly on the body's natural decomposition process. Various by-products of decomposition attract one group and repel others over time. However, the kinds of insects found on a body are also affected by the body's location, weather and temperature conditions, indigenous species, and the characteristics of the body.

The known sequence of arrival of various insect groups can help determine the time that has elapsed since death (PMI). This method of determining PMI is usually used when months have elapsed since the time of death. To make an accurate estimate, the forensic entomologist must compare the species found on the body to experimental data from the geographical area. The entomologist looks first for what earlier groups are missing. This sets a minimum PMI. For example, if it has been shown experimentally in that area that all necrophagous insects leave the body after about three months and no necrophagous insects are found on the body, it can be deduced that the person has been deceased for at least three months. An entomologist who is very familiar with the insect patterns of an area may be able to further define the PMI range by noting which groups have not yet arrived.

Chapter Summary

Physical evidence is usually examined by a forensic scientist for identification or comparison. The object of identification is to determine the physical or chemical identity with as near absolute certainty as existing analytical techniques will permit. Identification first requires the adoption of testing procedures that give characteristic results for specific standard/reference materials. Once this is done, the examiner uses an appropriate number of tests to identify a substance and exclude all other substances from consideration. The identification process is normally used in crime laboratories to identify drugs, explosives, and petroleum products. Also, evidence such as blood, semen, and hair is routinely identified in a crime laboratory. Normally these identifications include a determination of species origin (such as human blood or rabbit hair).

A comparative analysis has the important role of determining whether a suspect specimen and a standard/reference specimen have a common origin. Both the standard/reference and the suspect specimen are subject to the same tests. Evidence that can be associated with a common source with an extremely high degree of probability is said to possess individual characteristics. Evidence associated only with a group is said to have class characteristics. Nevertheless, the high diversity of class evidence in our environment makes their comparison very significant in the context of a criminal investigation. As the number of objects linking an individual to a crime scene increases, so does the likelihood of that individual's involvement with the crime. Importantly, a person may be exonerated or excluded from suspicion if physical evidence collected at a crime scene is found to be different from standard/reference samples collected from that subject.

A dramatic enhancement of the role of forensic science in criminal investigation has come about through the creation of computerized databases. The Integrated Automated Fingerprint Identification System (IAFIS), a national fingerprint and criminal history system, is maintained by the FBI. The FBI's Combined DNA Index System (CODIS) enables federal, state, and local crime laboratories to electronically exchange and compare DNA profiles, thereby linking crimes to each other and to convicted offenders. The National Integrated Ballistics Information Network (NIBIN), maintained by the Bureau of Alcohol, Tobacco, Firearms and Explosives, allows firearms analysts to acquire, digitize, and compare markings made by a firearm on bullets and cartridge casings recovered from crime scenes. The International Forensic Automotive Paint Data Query (PDQ) database contains chemical and color information pertaining to original automotive paints. SICAR (shoeprint image capture and retrieval) has a comprehensive shoe sole database.

Several special forensic science services are available to the law enforcement community to augment the services of the crime laboratory in a death investigation. The services of a forensic pathologist, forensic anthropologist, or forensic entomologist may be required in the investigation of a sudden, unnatural, unexplained, or violent death.

Review Questions

1. The process of _____ determines a substance's physical or chemical identity with as near absolute certainty as existing analytical techniques will permit.

2. The number and type of tests needed to identify a substance must be sufficient to _____ all other substances from consideration.

3. A(n) _____ analysis subjects a suspect and a standard/reference specimen to the same tests and examination for the ultimate purpose of determining whether they have a common origin.

4. _____ is the frequency of occurrence of an event.

5. Evidence that can be traced to a common source with an extremely high degree of probability is said to possess _____ characteristics.

6. Evidence associated with a group and not to a single source is said to possess _____ characteristics.

7. True or False: One of the major deficiencies of forensic science is the inability of the examiner to assign exact or approximate probability values to the comparison of most class physical evidence. _____

8. Although databases are consistently updated to assist in the assignment of probabilities to class evidence, for the most part forensic scientists must rely on _____ when interpreting the significance of class physical evidence.

9. The believability of _____ accounts, confessions, and informant testimony can all be disputed, maligned, and subjected to severe attack and skepticism in the courtroom.

10. The value of class physical evidence lies in its ability to _____ events with data in a manner that is, as nearly as possible, free of human error and bias.

11. The _____ accorded physical evidence during a trial is left entirely to the trier of fact.

12. True or False: Given the potential weight of scientific evidence in a trial setting, failure to take proper safeguards may unfairly prejudice a case against the suspect. _____

13. True or False: Physical evidence cannot be used to exclude or exonerate a person from suspicion of committing a crime. _____

14. True or False: The distinction between individual and class evidence is always easy to make. _____

15. Modern analytical techniques have become so sensitive that the forensic examiner must be aware of the _____ among materials when interpreting the significance of comparative data.

16. Students studying forensic science must be cautioned that merely reading relevant textbooks and journals is no substitute for _____ in this most practical of sciences.

17. True or False: A fingerprint can be positively identified through the IAFIS database. _____

18. A database applicable to DNA profiling is the FBI's _____.

19. _____ involves the study of medicine as it relates to the application of the law, most often pertaining to the investigation of sudden, unnatural, unexplained, or violent deaths.

20. The cause of death, whether natural, homicide, suicide, accident, or undetermined, is normally determined by performing an _____ and investigating the circumstances surrounding the death.

21. In cooperation with the medical examiner or coroner, evidence retrieved from a deceased victim to be submitted to the crime laboratory should include _____, _____, _____, _____, _____, _____, and _____.

22. In determining time of death, _____ occurs after death and results in the stiffening of body parts in the position they are in when death occurs, _____ occurs after death and results in the settling of blood in areas of the body closest to the ground, and _____ refers to postmortem changes that cause a body to lose heat.

23. Another approach for estimating the time of death is to determine potassium levels in the _____ fluid.

24. The field of _____ takes advantage of the durable nature of bones over long periods of time to examine and identify human skeletal remains through a multitude of individual characteristics.

25. The female bone structure differs from the male structure within the _____ area because of a woman's childbearing capabilities.

26. A forensic anthropologist may also help create a(n)_____ of the decedent from which a composite drawing of the victim can be drawn and advertised in an attempt to identify the victim.

27. True or False: The definite identification of remains cannot be made through the analysis of the decedent's DNA profile, fingerprints, or medical records. _____

28. True or False: A site where human remains are found must be treated as a crime scene, and the site and surrounding area should be secured, searched, and carefully processed. _____

29. Once all bones or evidence is found at a "tomb" site, a _____ should be made to show the exact location of each item.

30. The study of insects and their relation to a criminal investigation, known as _____, is commonly used to estimate the time of death when the circumstances surrounding the crime are unknown.

31. By determining the oldest stage of fly found on the body and taking environmental factors into consideration, entomologists can approximate the _____ interval.

32. The entomological evidence collected at a scene should include samples from every area where insects are found and _____ measurements.

33. True or False: Another method of determining PMI is observing the schedule of arrival of various insect species on the body. _____

Application and Critical Thinking

1. Arrange the following tasks in order from the one that would require the least extensive testing procedure to the one that would require the most extensive. Explain your answer.
   a) Determining whether an unknown substance contains an illicit drug
   b) Determining the composition of an unknown substance
   c) Determining whether an unknown substance contains heroin

2. The following are three possible combinations of DNA characteristics that might be found in an individual's genetic profile. Using the probability rule, rank each of these combinations from most common to least common. The number after each characteristic indicates its percentage distribution in the population.
   a) FGA 24,24 (3.6%), TH01 6,8 (8.1%), and D16S539 11, 12 (8.9%)
   b) vWA 14,19 (6.2%), D21S11 30,30 (3.9%), and D13S317 12,12 (8.5%)
   c) CSF1PO 9,10 (11.2%), D18S51 14,17 (2.8%), and D8S1179 17,18 (6.7%)

3. For each of the following pieces of evidence, indicate whether the item is more likely to possess class or individual characteristics and explain your answers:
   a) An impression from a new automobile tire
   b) A fingerprint
   c) A spent bullet cartridge

   d) A mass-produced synthetic fiber
   e) Pieces of a shredded document
   f) Commercial potting soil
   g) Skin and hair scrapings
   h) Fragments of a multilayer custom automobile paint

4. Which of the forensic databases described in the text contain information that relates primarily to evidence exhibiting class characteristics? Which ones contain information that relates primarily to evidence exhibiting individual characteristics? Explain your answers.

5. An investigator at a murder scene notes signs of a prolonged struggle between the attacker and victim. Name at least three types of physical evidence for which the investigator would likely collect standard/reference samples and explain why he or she would collect them.

6. Rigor mortis, livor mortis, and algor mortis are all used to help determine time of death. However, each method has its limitations. For each method, describe at least one condition that would render that method unsuitable or inaccurate for determining time of death.

7. What kind of forensic expert would most likely be asked to help identify human remains in each of the following conditions?
   a. a body that has been decomposing for a day or two
   b. fragmentary remains of a few arm bones and part of a jaw
   c. a skeleton that is missing the skull

Case Analysis

In the 1930s, the Lindbergh kidnapping case became the latest "trial of the century," marked by sensationalism and continuous media coverage. The key piece of evidence was a homemade ladder left at the scene by the kidnapper. Forensic investigation of the ladder by Arthur Koehler, a wood technologist with the U.S. Forest Products Laboratory, eventually tied the accused kidnapper, Bruno Hauptmann, to the ladder and helped secure his conviction for the crime.

1. What aspects of the ladder rail did Koehler note that helped him determine the source of the wood used to make it? How did Koehler interpret each of these pieces of information to arrive at his conclusions?

2. How did Koehler determine that a belt-driven planer had been used to finish the wood? How did this information help pinpoint where the wood was purchased?

3. The wood used to make the rails was very common and used widely throughout the United States. Why did Koehler believe it was milled in the general area where the kidnapping occurred? How did this information help the investigation?

4. What additional discoveries allowed Koehler to link the wood used in the ladder to Bruno Hauptmann?

Web Resources

An Introduction to Criminalistics and Physical Evidence (An article providing a brief introduction to concepts and principles of physical evidence)
www.apsu.edu/oconnort/3210/3210lect02.htm

Autopsy (A step-by-step description of an autopsy written by a pathologist, with additional links to articles and videos about autopsies)
www.pathguy.com/autopsy.htm

CODIS Database Homepage
www.fbi.gov/hq/lab/codis/index1.htm

Death Investigation (Links to articles about death investigation, forensic
anthropology and archaeology, and forensic entomology)
www.crimeandclues.com/deathinvestigation.htm

Death Investigation: A Guide for the Scene Investigator
www.ncjrs.gov/pdffiles/167568.pdf

Forensic Anthropology (Articles, essays, and links to topics in forensic anthropology)
http://library.med.utah.edu/kw/osteo/forensics/index.html

Forensic Entomology (A Guide to the Science of Entomology)
www.forensic-entomology.com

Houck, M.M., "Statistics and Trace Evidence: The Tyranny of Numbers," *Forensic
Science Communications*, 1, no. 3 (1999)
www.fbi.gov/hq/lab/fsc/backissu/oct1999/houck.htm

IAFIS Home Page (The FBI website for the Integrated Automated Fingerprint
Identification System; describes the functions and organization of IAFIS and the
fingerprint identification services it provides)
www.fbi.gov/hq/cjisd/iafis.htm

NIBIN Database Homepage
www.nibin.gov/

Royal Canadian Mounted Police Homepage
www.rcmp-grc.gc.ca//factsheets/fact_pdq_e.htm

Endnotes

1. Foster & Freeman Limited, Worcestershire, U.K., www.fosterfreeman.co.uk.

Case Reading

Microscopic Trace Evidence: The Overlooked Clue
Arthur Koehler, Wood Detective

Skip Palenik
Walter C McCrone Associates Inc.

. . . Arthur Koehler . . . wood technologist and chief of the division of silvicultural relations at the U.S. Forest Products Laboratory in Madison, Wisconsin, . . . was born on June 4, 1885, in Mishicot, Wisconsin. His father was a carpenter and young Koehler grew up on a farm with a love of both wood and fine tools. This love naturally led him into forestry and he received a B.S. degree in the subject from the University of Michigan in 1911. . . . Upon graduation he went to work for the U.S. Forest Service in Washington, D.C., and three years later obtained a post at the U.S. Forest Products Laboratory where he served in various capacities until his retirement.

Although his primary responsibilities lay in wood identification and the correlation of microscopic wood structure and end use, Koehler also began to build a reputation as a wood detective after his success in obtaining evidence from wood fragments which were submitted to the laboratory in several cases of local importance. . . . The case which thrust Koehler into the limelight of international publicity, however, was the Lindbergh kidnapping case in which he, by the most painstaking work, traced the kidnap ladder back to the lumberyard from which its constituent parts had been purchased.

Sometime between the hours of 8 and 10 p.m. on the night of March 1, 1932, a kidnapper climbed into the nursery of the newly completed home of Charles and Anne Lindbergh in Hopewell, New Jersey, and abducted their infant son. The only clues left behind were a few indistinct muddy footprints, a ransom note in the

nursery, a homemade ladder and a chisel found a short distance from the house. Scarcely two months later, on May 12, the dead body of the child was found, half buried in the woods, about a mile from the Lindbergh home. One of the most intensive manhunts in U.S. history ensued, but failed to uncover any trace of the kidnapper or the ransom money which had been paid.[1]

Shortly after the news of the kidnapping broke in the press Koehler wrote a letter to Colonel Lindbergh offering his services to help with the investigation of the ladder. He never received a reply (which was not surprising considering the flood of mail which arrived at the Lindbergh home in the weeks following the kidnapping). He was not entirely surprised though when his boss, Carlyle P. Winslow, placed before him some slivers of the ladder with the request that the wood be accurately identified.[2] This Koehler did, noting in his report the presence of golden brown, white and black wool fibers which he speculated might be from clothing worn by the kidnapper. That was the last he heard about the ladder for almost a year. During this time it was carried around the country (carefully wrapped in a wool blanket) to various experts including specialists at the National Bureau of Standards.[3] However, after a year of investigation the authorities were no closer to arresting a suspect than they were the day after the crime.

It was almost a year after the kidnapping when Koehler was asked by the head of the U.S. Forest Service, Major Robert Y. Stuart, to travel to Trenton to give the ladder an in-depth examination. Discussions between Colonel Norman Schwarzkopf, who headed the New Jersey State Police (and the kidnap investigation), and Major Stuart had convinced Colonel

Schwarzkopf that the ladder might still yield clues about its maker if Koehler were given a chance to examine it thoroughly. Schwarzkopf wasn't too certain about Koehler's ability ("Wasn't he the one who identified the blanket fibers on the wood we sent him?" he asked) but felt he had nothing to lose.

For the first time, Koehler saw the ladder (Figure 1). He was immediately struck by the fact that, although it was cleverly contrived, it was shamefully constructed. Instead of rungs it had cleats, which had been carelessly mortised with a dull chisel. A dull hand plane had been used needlessly in some places and a handsaw had been drawn carelessly across some of the boards.

Alone for four days, Koehler studied the ladder in the police training school in Wilburtha. He then returned to the Forest Products Laboratory with the ladder and closed himself up in a private laboratory with the best optical equipment available.[4] He began by completely dissecting the ladder into its component parts. Each piece was numbered. The cleats were labeled 1 (bottom) through 11 (top). The rails were numbered starting from 12 (bottom left) to 17 (right-hand top). . . . Each mark was noted and indexed. After probing with microscopes, calipers and a variety of lighting and photographic techniques, the ladder slowly began to give up its secrets.

The sheer number of observations, facts and deductions about the origin of the ladder (and its producer) made by Koehler are truly staggering. We are concerned here only with those facts and observations which (1) allowed the parts to be traced and (2) described the carpenter and the previous environment of the ladder. The results were presented not

FIGURE 1 The ladder used in the kidnapping of the Lindbergh baby.
© CORBIS. All rights reserved.

as the subject of a single report but of daily letters to the director of the laboratory. As certain aspects were revealed they were pursued until the object could be traced no further. The most pertinent observations and deductions are listed and described below.

1. Microscopical examination showed four types of wood were used (Table 1). North Carolina pine is a trade name for wood from the

Table 1	Woods Used in Kidnap Ladder
Cleats	
1–10	**Ponderosa Pine** Thirteen 6-inch boards ripped lengthwise into strips 2¾ inches wide to make cleats.
11	**Douglas Fir** Grain matched bottom of rail 15.
Side Rails	
12, 13	**North Carolina Pine** Second growth. Cut from one board originally 14 feet long. Dressed to 3¾ inches in width. Both dressed on same planer.
14, 15	**Douglas Fir** Dressed on two different planers.
16	**North Carolina Pine** Narrowed from a wider board as indicated by handsaw and hand-planer marks on edges.
17	**Douglas Fir** Dressed on different planers than 14 and 15.
Dowel Pins	
All	**Birch**

southern yellow pine group which grows in commercial stands in the Southern U.S. along the Gulf of Mexico and along the Eastern Seaboard up into New Jersey and southern New York.[5] Douglas fir and ponderosa pine grow in the Western U.S. and birch is found throughout the country.[6]

2. Rails 12 and 13 showed faint marks which gave information about the planer in the mill where the wood was dressed. . . . Figure 2 shows the operation of a mill planer in diagrammatic form. Defects in the cutters allowed the number of knives in the cutters to be determined by counting cutter marks between defect marks. Eight cutter heads dressed the wide surface and six heads the edges. . . .

The lumber went through the planer at a rate of 0.93 inches per complete revolution of the top and bottom cutter heads and 0.86 inches per revolution of the cutter heads that dressed the edges. This was determined by the distance of identical cuts made by a defective

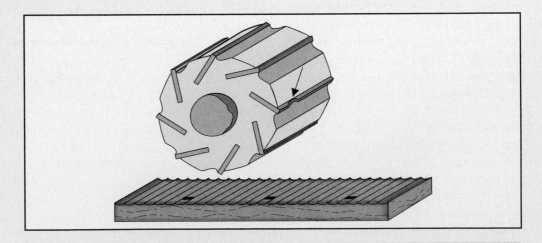

FIGURE 2 Detail of a cutter head illustrating how a defect allowed the number of knives to be determined.

knife on each surface. . . .[7] Using the fact that the cutters in mill planers are usually driven at 3600 revolutions per minute it was possible to calculate the speed at which the wood passed into the planer as 258 feet per minute for the edge and 279 feet per minute for the board surfaces. The difference in the speed of the horizontal and vertical heads indicated that the planer was belt driven.

3. Rail 16 had four nail holes made by old fashioned square cut 8-penny nails. The holes had no connection with the construction of the ladder and therefore indicated prior use. The nail holes were clean and free from rust indicating inside use. This was confirmed by the general appearance of the rail which, although sapwood, showed no sign of exposure to the weather for any length of time since it was bright and unchecked. Therefore, it must have been nailed down indoors. Since it was low-grade lumber it would not have been used for finish purposes, but for rough construction. The spacing of the nails at 16 and 32-inches was considered significant and the suggestion was made that the rail came from the interior of a barn, garage or attic.

After an initial, futile attempt to trace the birch dowels, Koehler set out to try and trace the North Carolina rails (numbers 12 and 13). Although North Carolina pine grew in a large region it would not be profitable to ship it far, and since the ladder had turned up in New Jersey he felt certain that it had been milled somewhere in the Atlantic States. Using the Southern Lumberman's Directory, a list of 1598 planing mills from Alabama to New York was compiled. A confidential letter from Colonel Schwarzkopf and a two-page description written by Koehler were sent off to all of the mills on the list.

Of all the letters sent, only 25 mills reported having planers which matched the specifications outlined in the letter. Two were immediately excluded since they didn't dress lumber of the requisite size. Samples of 1- × 4-inch wood were requested from each of the remaining 23 mills. A sample received from the M. G. and J. J. Dorn mill of McCormick, South Carolina, showed exactly the marks Koehler was looking for.

A visit to the mill showed that the particular spacing was due to a pulley which had been purchased in September of 1929. The records of the mill showed that forty-six carloads of 1 × 4 had been shipped north of the Potomac River in the time between the purchases of the pulley and the kidnapping. . . . After personally visiting the final destination of each of the shipments, Koehler and Detective Bornmann finally arrived at a Bronx firm, the National Lumber and Millwork Company. Although the entire shipment had long before been sold, the foreman remembered that some storage bins had been built from some of the wood. The wood matched that from the ladder perfectly (Figures 3 and 4). Examination of wood from shipments before and after the Bronx carload showed that the belt on the planer had been changed and the knife sharpened. This meant that this shipment was the only one from which the two particular rails from the attic could have come. Whoever built the ladder had purchased part of the wood here! Koehler was unprepared for the foreman's answer to his request to see the sales records. They had none. They had started selling cash and carry sometime before the Dorn shipment arrived and had no records.

FIGURE 3   Comparison of knife marks from mill planer on edges of 1- × 4-inch pine from two shipments from the Dorn mill and a ladder rail.

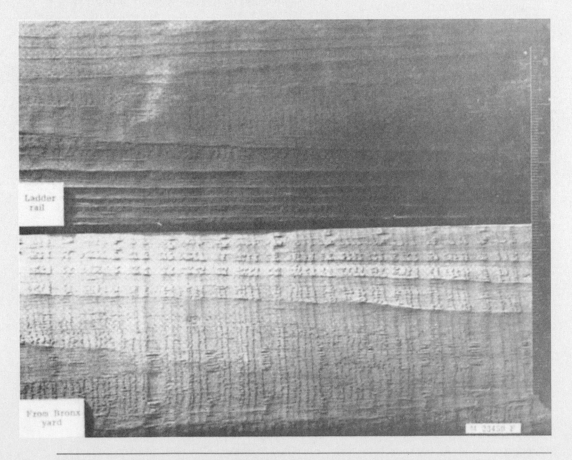

FIGURE 4   Comparison of knife marks on upper surface of ladder rail and North Carolina pine board located in shipment to the National Lumber and Millwork Company.

Although he had failed to come up with the carpenter's name, the authorities at least now knew the region where the kidnapper lived and bought his wood for the ladder.

Koehler went back to his laboratory and, undaunted, started tracing the Douglas fir rails. At the time a suspect was arrested, he had succeeded in tracing one of the boards to a mill in Bend, Oregon, and another to Spokane, Washington. With the arrest of Richard Hauptmann on

September 19, 1934, . . . his role in the case changed from an investigative to a comparative one. In Hauptmann's garage a variety of tools were found whose markings could be compared with those from the ladder. Comparative micrographs of marks made with Hauptmann's plane and plane marks on the ladder showed that his plane was used to plane the cleats (Figure 5). Finally, one of the investigators searching the attic of the suspect's home found that a board had been sawed out of the floor

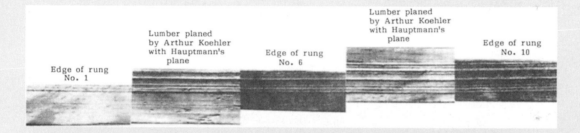

FIGURE 5   **Comparison of defect marks in Hauptmann's hand-plane with marks on cleats (runs) from the ladder.**

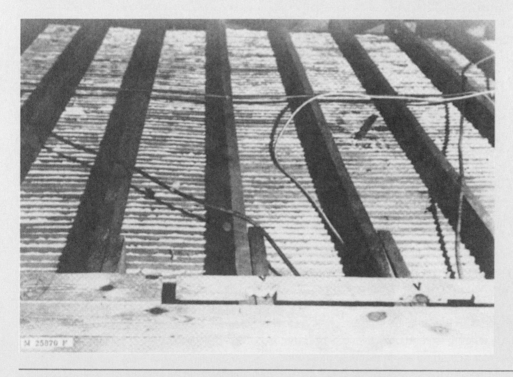

FIGURE 6   **Rail 16 fitted into its original position in Hauptmann's attic.**

FIGURE 7   Composite photograph by Koehler showing comparison of end grain (growth rings) in board from attic and rail 16.

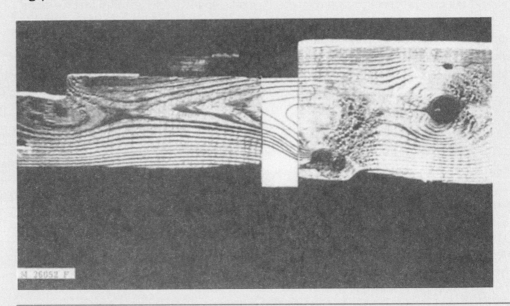

FIGURE 8   Construction by Koehler showing probable grain pattern of missing piece between attic board and rail 16.

(Figure 6). Koehler's examination showed that the nail holes in the floor joists and the ladder rail (No. 16) aligned perfectly. A detailed analysis of the grain and wood itself showed that rail 16 and the section of board remaining in the attic were originally all one piece (Figure 7 and Figure 8).

Richard Bruno Hauptmann was convicted and sentenced to death in a sensational trial. Although, in retrospect, there may have been many errors and a good deal of prejudice in the trial itself, the professionalism and objectiveness of Arthur Koehler still stand as an example of science at its best in the service of the law. . . .

Endnotes

1. Waller, George. *Kidnap: The Story of the Lindbergh Case*. Dial Press, New York, 1961.

2. Koehler, Arthur. "Who Made That Ladder?" as told to Boyden Sparkes. *The Saturday Evening Post*, 297, p. 10, April 20, 1935.

3. Saylor, Charles Proffer. "Optical Microscopy as Used in Unorthodox Ways," *SPIE*, 104, Multi-disciplinary Microscopy, 31–33, 1977.

4. Koehler, Arthur. *The Saturday Evening Post*, 297, p. 84, April 20, 1935.

5. Isenberg, Irving. *Pulpwoods of the United States and Canada*. Institute of Paper Chemistry, Appleton, Wisc., pp. 19–22, 1951.

6. Christensen, Donna. *Wood Technology and the Lindbergh Kidnap Case*. Report, May 1971.

7. Koehler, Arthur. "Techniques Used in Tracing the Lindbergh Kidnapping Ladder," *Am. J. Police Science*, 27, 5 (1937).

Acknowledgment

The author gratefully acknowledges the invaluable assistance of Dr. Regis Miller and Donna Christensen of the Forest Products Laboratory in Madison, Wisconsin, for making available documents and photographs which were necessary to this article. Additional thanks are due Jame Gerakaris of McCrone Associates for preparing the drawings of the ladder and mill planer.

REYNOLDS
RUSSELL
PATTERSON
LEWIS

ERSON BLVD.

GUINYARD
CALLAWAY

DALLAS
POLICE
54018
23 63

The Assassination of President Kennedy

Ever since President John F. Kennedy was killed in 1963, questions have lingered about whether Lee Harvey Oswald was part of a conspiracy to assassinate the president, or a lone assassin. The Warren Commission, the official government body appointed to investigate the shooting, concluded that Oswald acted alone. However, over the years, eyewitness accounts and acoustical data interpreted by some experts have been used to contend that a second shooter fired at the president from a region in front of the limousine (the so-called grassy knoll).

In arriving at its conclusions, the Warren Commission reconstructed the crime as follows: From a hidden position on the sixth floor of the Texas School Book Depository building where he worked, Oswald fired three shots from behind the president. Two bullets struck the president, with one bullet missing the president's limousine. One bullet hit the president in the back, exited his throat, and went on to strike Texas Governor John Connally, who was sitting in a jump seat in front of the president. In a sixth-floor room at the Texas School Book

Depository, police found a rifle with Oswald's palm print on it. They also found three spent cartridge cases.

In 1977, the U.S. House of Representatives Select Committee on Assassinations requested that the bullet taken from Connally's stretcher—along with bullet fragments recovered from the car and various wound areas—be examined for trace element levels. Investigators compared the antimony and silver content of the bullet and bullet fragments recovered after the assassination and concluded that all of the fragments probably came from two bullets.

In 2003, ABC TV broadcast the results of a ten-year 3-D computer animation study of the events of November 22, 1963. The animation graphically showed that the bullet wounds were completely consistent with Kennedy's and Governor Connally's positions at the time of shooting, and that by following the bullet's trajectory backward they could be found to have originated from a narrow cone including only a few windows of the sixth floor of the School Book Depository.

chapter 6

Crime-Scene Reconstruction

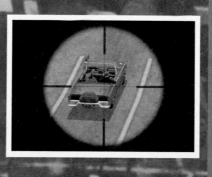

Key Terms

circumstantial evidence

crime-scene reconstruction

deductive reasoning

direct physical evidence

event timeline

falsifiability

inductive reasoning

objectivity

reenactment

testimonial evidence

Learning Objectives

After studying this chapter, you should be able to:

- Define *crime-scene reconstruction*.

- Discuss the ways investigators maintain objectivity during reconstruction.

- Understand the processes of deductive reasoning, inductive reasoning, and falsifiability and how these processes are used in reconstruction.

- Describe the limitations and fallacies involved in the reconstruction of crime scenes.

- Explain the role physical evidence, testimonial evidence, and reenactments play in reconstructing the events surrounding the commission of a crime.

- Describe the utility of an event timeline in a crime scene reconstruction.

Fundamentals of Crime-Scene Reconstruction

Previous discussions dealing with the processes of identification and comparison have stressed laboratory work routinely performed by forensic scientists. However, there is another dimension to the role that forensic scientists play during the course of a criminal investigation: participating in a team effort to reconstruct events that occurred prior to, during, and subsequent to the commission of a crime.

Reconstructing the circumstances of a crime scene entails a collaborative effort that includes experienced law enforcement personnel, medical examiners, and criminalists. All of these professionals contribute unique perspectives to develop the crime-scene reconstruction. Was more than one person involved? How was the victim killed? Were actions taken to cover up what took place? To answer these questions, all personnel involved with the investigation must pay careful attention and think logically.

Crime-scene reconstruction is the method used to support a likely sequence of events at a crime scene by observing and evaluating physical evidence and statements made by individuals involved with the incident. The evidence may also include information obtained from reenactments. Therefore, reconstructions have the best chance of being accurate when investigators use proper documentation and collection methods for all types of evidence.

crime-scene reconstruction
The method used to support a likely sequence of events at a crime scene by the observation and evaluation of physical evidence and statements made by individuals involved with the incident.

objectivity
A manner of professional detachment practiced by individuals to avoid letting personal beliefs or biases affect the conclusions reached through observations.

Striving for Objectivity

One of the most important features of a logical and systematic inquiry is objectivity. **Objectivity** is the professional detachment practiced by individuals to avoid letting personal beliefs or biases affect the conclusions reached through observations. Even trained scientists come to their jobs with some expectations or biases. These can have a negative effect on the process of reconstruction by leading to the incorrect analysis or interpretation of the information provided by the evidence. For that reason, all data and evidence must be continually reevaluated throughout the process of crime-scene reconstruction. It may also be wise to have several individuals analyze the evidence and present independent interpretations.

Investigators should approach each case free of previous theories or expectations. For example, if a person is found dead from a gunshot wound to the temple and he is holding a gun, the investigator should not assume this death was a suicide. Surmising that the death is a suicide may cause the investigator to create a "self-fulfilling prophecy" by considering only information that supports the theory in the reconstruction. Crime-scene reconstruction personnel should never try to *prove* any theory or hypothesis. Instead, they should use the processes of deductive reasoning, inductive reasoning, and falsifiability to create a logical reconstruction of crime-scene events.

Deductive Reasoning Deductive reasoning is the process of drawing a conclusion based on known facts or premises. Using deductive reasoning allows an investigator to come to a definitive conclusion. For example, if an investigator finds a fingerprint from the victim on a table, then the victim *definitely* touched the table with whatever finger the print came from. This conclusion makes no assumptions about how, when, or why the victim touched the table, but it establishes a concrete event.

deductive reasoning
The process of drawing a conclusion based on known facts or premises.

Inductive Reasoning When using inductive reasoning, one attempts to draw a conclusion based on premises one does not know are correct. This process leads to a conclusion that is probable, but not definitive. For example, if a large amount of a victim's blood is found at a crime scene, then the victim *probably* was present and injured at the crime scene. It is also possible that the victim was injured somewhere else and large amounts of her blood were transported to the scene, but this scenario is not *probable*. One must be careful using conclusions drawn from inductive reasoning, and never confuse them with conclusions drawn from deductive reasoning.

inductive reasoning
The process of drawing a conclusion from premises one does not know are correct.

Falsifiability It is very easy for an investigator to locate and include evidence that supports a theory. To avoid bringing about a self-fulfilling prophecy, investigators should seek to test the falsifiability of theories. This means that they should seek to *disprove* a theory. Those involved in reconstructing the crime scene must always be aware of all *plausible alternatives* that could have led to the state of any piece of evidence. They must keep an open mind to avoid narrowing their view to one or a few possibilities and potentially excluding more plausible scenarios. Once they have identified all possibilities, the investigators should set about prioritizing their reconstruction theories. They may do this by examining each alternative explanation and determining how consistent it is with the physical evidence, eyewitness accounts, and general dynamics of the crime scene.

falsifiability
The ability of a theory to be disproved by being tested against known information.

The crime-scene reconstruction typically produces the *most probable* conclusion. However, being mindful of plausible alternate explanations will help provide other leads if an aspect of a reconstruction theory does not appear to fit all the facts of the case. No evidence or data should ever be excluded. A crime-scene reconstruction theory must be supported by *all* interpreted evidence or it cannot be accepted.

Limitations to Reconstruction

Crime-scene investigators apply systematic reasoning to bolster their reconstructions, but certain fallacies of reasoning can undermine their conclusions. Each inquiry must be accompanied by skepticism and knowledge of fallacies that can impede a search for the truth.

Bifurcation The fallacy of bifurcation exists when investigators or attorneys try to apply a simple "yes or no" answer to a complex question. Not all information gained from the crime scene leads to a clear-cut solution or conclusion, and asking for a simple answer to a complex question may be an attempt to cloud the truth.

Generalization   Generalizing about aspects of evidence can be both helpful and harmful to an investigation. Generalizations about the shape of bloodstains can help determine the direction and approximate angle of deposition of a droplet. This is helpful to the investigation and reconstruction. However, generalizations about the kind of force that creates a pattern may send the investigation in the wrong direction. For example, fine droplets called high-velocity spatter are usually found when a victim suffers a gunshot wound. However, some beatings can also produce fine droplets that look like high-velocity spatter. If an investigator generalizes that high-velocity spatter always comes from gunshot wounds, this may divert the investigation toward looking for a weapon that doesn't exist.

False Linkage   False linkage occurs when an investigator assumes a link between two or more objects of evidence that may start the investigation down the wrong path. For example, suppose that investigators find footwear impressions at a crime scene in a high-traffic area of a park. The investigators may assume the impressions are linked to the perpetrator when in truth they may belong to an unrelated person who walked there earlier in the day.

The biggest limitation associated with reconstruction is that investigators can only use what is left behind to theorize what occurred in the past. The information available to make these theories is often much less than needed to create a full timeline of events. The reconstruction team can only strive to make optimum use of all the available evidence, witness statements, and appropriate investigative leads to define what events occurred at specific moments and the order in which they happened. Reconstruction also relies on information from toxicology tests, DNA typing, autopsies, interrogations, and many other sources. However, the results of these tests and processes may take quite a bit of time. This means that the reconstructing team may not receive all relevant information for days, weeks, or months after the incident. It is important to remember that crime-scene reconstruction does not provide instant gratification for all the effort it requires.

Key Points

- Because crime-scene reconstruction supports a likely sequence of events at a crime scene with physical evidence, testimony, and reenactments, proper documentation and collection methods must be used for all types of evidence.

- Investigative personnel may bring some expectations or biases to the reconstruction process, and these can have a negative effect on the process. It is, therefore, very important for personnel to practice objectivity, or professional distance.

- The processes of deductive reasoning, inductive reasoning, and falsifiability are very important to the reconstruction process, but they must be differentiated and used properly.

- Investigators must be aware that the fallacies of bifurcation, generalization, and false linkage can impede a search for the truth. Avoiding these fallacies will help investigators maintain objectivity throughout the reconstruction.

Requirements for Crime-Scene Reconstruction

Personnel Involved in Reconstruction

Because investigators consider many types of evidence when reconstructing a crime scene, reconstruction is a team effort that involves various professionals putting together many pieces of a puzzle. The team as a whole works to answer the typical "who, what, where, when, why, and how" of a crime scene. Often, reconstruction requires the involvement of a medical examiner and at least one criminalist. For example, an investigator might call upon a trained medical examiner to determine whether a body has been moved after death by evaluating the livor distribution within the body. A criminalist or trained crime-scene investigator can also bring special skills to the reconstruction of events that occurred during the commission of a crime.

For example, a criminalist using a laser beam to plot the approximate trajectory of a bullet can help determine the probable position of the shooter relative to that of the victim (see Figure 6–1). Other skills that a criminalist or expert may employ during a crime-scene reconstruction analysis include blood spatter analysis (discussed more fully in Chapter 9), determining the direction of impact of projectiles penetrating glass objects (discussed in Chapter 13), locating gunshot residues deposited on victims' clothing for the purpose of estimating the distance of a shooter from a target (discussed in Chapter 8), and searching for primer residues deposited on the hands of a suspect shooter (discussed in Chapter 8).

Gathering Evidence and Data from the Crime Scene

Physical evidence left behind at a crime scene plays a crucial role in reconstructing the sequence of events surrounding the crime. Although the evidence alone may not describe everything that happened, it can support or contradict accounts given by witnesses and/or suspects. Information obtained

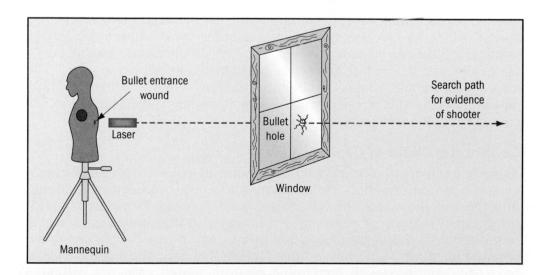

FIGURE 6–1   A laser beam is used to determine the search area for the position of a shooter who has fired a bullet through a window and wounded a victim. The bullet path is determined by lining up the victim's bullet wound with the bullet hole in the glass pane.

from physical evidence can also generate leads and confirm the reconstruction of a crime to a jury. The collection, documentation, and interpretation of physical evidence is the foundation of a reconstruction. Reconstruction supports a likely sequence of events by the observation and evaluation of physical evidence, as well as statements made by witnesses and input from those involved with the investigation of the incident. Analysis of all available data will help to create a workable model for reconstruction.

direct physical evidence
An item of evidence from which an indisputable fact or detail of the events at the crime scene can be concluded.

Direct Physical Evidence   Information from direct physical evidence provides a definite conclusion or direction. The analysis of direct physical evidence employs deductive reasoning to state a fact that can be understood by everyone. For example, if a transfer bloodstain on the clothing of a homicide victim has a DNA type consistent with that of the suspect, the victim must have had contact with the suspect after the suspect was injured and began bleeding. However, this assumes no prior contact or relationship existed between the victim and the suspect.

circumstantial evidence
An item of evidence that suggests the occurrence of one of several possible events at the crime scene.

Circumstantial Evidence   Information from circumstantial evidence provides a lead but no definite conclusion. With the use of inductive reasoning, an investigator can identify many possible causes for the state of the evidence. For example, the presence of semen in the DNA analysis of a female victim can be consistent with either forcible rape or consensual sex. Individual hair or fiber evidence found at the scene is considered highly circumstantial. It may suggest that an individual was present during the commission of the crime, but there are also other probable explanations as to how it got there. Circumstantial evidence, when examined in the context of a crime scene, has only a few possible explanations; however, one of these may be more probable than the others.

testimonial evidence
Informational evidence gained from statements from witnesses, suspects, and others who have some knowledge of the crime scene.

Testimonial Evidence   An investigator should carefully scrutinize eyewitness testimony about what occurred at a crime scene. Eyewitness accounts, also called testimonial evidence, are sometimes highly subjective and heavily biased. Unfortunately, people lie or misinterpret the facts. Fortunately, physical evidence does not lie. Therefore, crime-scene reconstruction should only include testimonial evidence that is corroborated by aspects of physical evidence.

reenactment
The process by which investigators attempt to recreate the circumstances surrounding a particular event at the crime scene in order to observe the result and gain information.

Reenactments   Some events at the crime scene lend themselves to a reenactment by live personnel, mannequins, or computer-generated models. Individuals used in live reenactments should be as close as possible in size and strength to the actual participants at the crime scene. The information gained from reenactments can show whether a theory of how an event occurred is physically possible and whether physical evidence is consistent with that theory.

Confirming Chain of Custody

As mentioned previously, a great deal of time may pass before all pertinent evidence and information can be gathered in order to begin reconstruction. Once all the evidence has been gathered, investigators must establish the chain of custody of items and the integrity of testimonial evidence. A missing link in the chain of custody of an item means that it was unaccounted for during a period of time. During this time, the evidence could have been tampered with, contaminated, or damaged. Evidence without a confirmed chain of custody cannot and should not be included in reconstruction. If there is any question as to the legality or authenticity of testimonial evidence, it should be excluded from reconstruction.

Key Points

- Crime-scene reconstruction is a team effort that requires the expertise of various professionals depending on the kind of case.

- Information gathered from direct physical evidence provides a definite conclusion or direction, whereas circumstantial evidence provides a lead but no definite conclusion for reconstructing the crime.

- Testimonial evidence from eyewitnesses is sometimes highly subjective and heavily biased and must be used in reconstruction only if it is corroborated by physical evidence.

- Reenactments of events at a crime scene can be carried out by live personnel, mannequins, or computer-generated models.

- Evidence used in a crime-scene reconstruction must have a complete and valid chain of custody.

Assessment of Evidence and Information to Form Theories

One of the pitfalls of crime-scene reconstruction is generalizing the assessment and processing of evidence. Different categories or types of crime-scene evidence must be studied with very specific techniques and considerations during the investigation. The kinds of evidence that may be found at a crime scene are highly diverse. In forthcoming chapters, we will discuss the reconstructive properties of specific groups of crime-scene evidence.

Assessment of Evidence

Each item of evidence should first be analyzed and tested separately from all other evidence. To maintain objectivity and avoid the fallacy of false linkage, items of evidence should not be linked or grouped together during the initial phase of the investigation. Once all possible information has been recovered from each item, this information can be coupled with that from other items of evidence. It is important at this step to observe whether separate items of evidence make sense together or verify an event. For example, suppose an investigator finds that a trail of blood leading down the back stairs of a house stops abruptly at a patch of dirt. This might seem unusual, but would make perfect sense if tire impressions were found in the dirt at the location where the trail stops. The investigator seeks to use evidence to link the crime scene, victims, suspects, and witnesses. These links provide the foundation for theories about specific events at the crime scene. Missing links may help to suggest what further data need to be recovered from available evidence or witnesses.

Studying the pattern formed by cartridges ejected from a firearm provides an excellent illustration of the process and difficulty of gaining information from a specific type of evidence. The location of a cartridge casing at a crime scene may suggest the position of the shooter, but the investigator must take into consideration the type of firearm used, the type of ammunition used, the position of the gun with respect to the shooter's body, the height of the firearm from the ground, and the terrain and layout of the scene. Investigators study the effect of these conditions through reenactments that must be as authentic as possible. The reenactment should involve the same firearm and ammunition used in the crime. Even the amount of lubrication of the firearm may affect cartridge ejection characteristics. The firing position of the firearm—whether sideways, upright, or otherwise—can affect where a cartridge will fall.

As with many kinds of evidence, investigators must take substrate conditions into consideration with cartridge case ejection. The type and topography of the surface onto which the cartridge falls may also affect its position. For example, a cartridge may travel farther after landing on an angled surface or a hard surface, such as concrete, than it would after landing on a level or soft surface. Cartridge cases may also contain trace evidence of damage if they contacted an intermediate surface before landing. A matching mark on the surface the cartridge impacted may also help to determine the shooter's position.

The cartridge itself can provide clues about the firearm that ejected it. The cartridge may bear marks on the base from the breechblock, firing pin, and ejector mechanism of the gun. The shaft of the cartridge may show chambering marks, gouge marks, and drag marks imparted by the firing chamber of the firearm. The collection of marks, their position, and any striations (fine grooves) within the marks will likely be unique to one firearm. Cartridge cases represent only one example of many types of evidentiary items that may be found at a crime scene. However, this example clearly demonstrates that a complex set of techniques and considerations are involved in studying each piece of evidence.

The example of cartridge case ejection patterns also raises the specter that a reconstruction can fail. That is, the movement of the shooter, the number of shooters, and the number of bullets discharged will produce multiple cartridge cases in various locations, introducing complexities into the analysis. These complexities may not be as easy to resolve as they would in a single cartridge case reconstruction. When such complexities arise, some investigators fall into the trap of reading too much into evidence that may not provide resolution. The fact is, reconstruction may not be able to answer all of the questions. The complexities of the analysis may overwhelm the reconstruction team and prevent them from coming up with plausible answers.

Forming Theories for Reconstruction

The final steps of crime-scene reconstruction require the reconstruction team to bring together all the evidence and information to form plausible theories and a plausible sequence of individual events. Theories can suggest how a group of linked items was created by individual events at a crime scene.

Often the beginning and end of the sequence of events at a crime scene are obvious to the investigators. For example, a tool mark or a footwear impression can mark the site of forced entry into a house, beginning the sequence of events at the crime scene. Footwear impressions or tire impressions leading away from the house may show the exit of the suspect from the crime scene and thus the end of the sequence of events. However, the sequence or timeline of the remaining events may be much more difficult to determine. Sometimes the evidence that signifies the start or end of events provides clues to the missing events in the middle. For example, suppose an investigator finds bloody footwear imprints exiting a crime

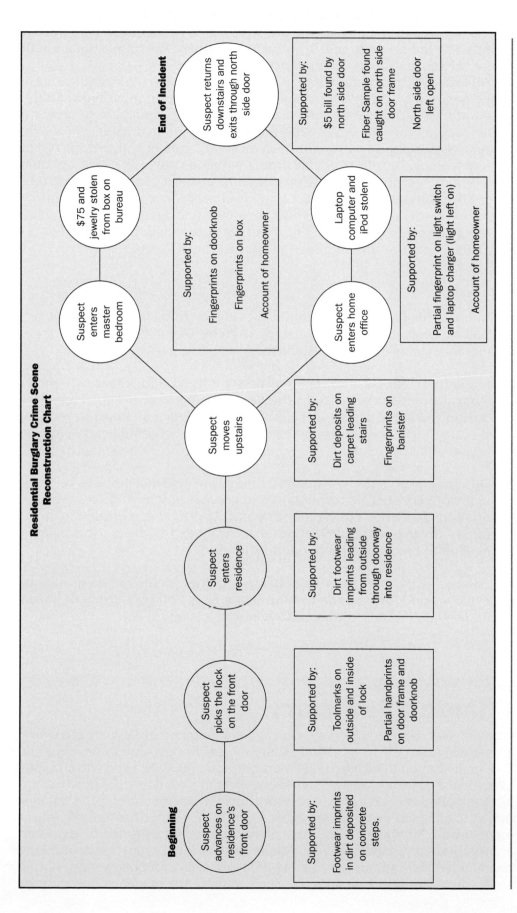

FIGURE 6–2 An example of an event timeline chart for a residential burglary. At one point two possible sequences of events are shown. Each event contains a list of evidence that supports the event's occurrence and sequence.

scene. Logic dictates that blood was present at the crime scene, and that it somehow became deposited on the shoes of an individual who subsequently left the crime scene. These clues can provide suggestions about where the reconstruction should focus its attention.

All available information and evidence must fit into the overall picture. When creating a crime-scene reconstruction, the team must focus on the issues at hand and use the information that is not in dispute to create a framework in which to explore those events that are in dispute.

An **event timeline** will define each event or "moment" that occurred at a crime scene in various probable orders within a known or estimated time frame. Some reconstruction teams develop an event timeline chart (see Figure 6–2). Investigators should chart each sequence and include information on evidence to illustrate how each event occurred and the timeline in which the events occurred. Once the various orders have been identified, each sequence should be tested against the evidence.

event timeline
The end product of crime-scene reconstruction that shows the possible sequence of occurrences at the crime scene and the known or estimated time period in which they took place.

Key Points

- In order for physical or testimonial evidence to be used in reconstruction theories, the chain of custody of items and the integrity of testimonial evidence must be established.

- Individual items of evidence are first analyzed and tested separately from all other evidence; items should not be linked or grouped together during the initial phase of the investigation. Once all items have been evaluated this way, they may be coupled with other items of evidence that are clearly linked.

- Different categories or types of crime-scene evidence have to be studied with very specific techniques and considerations during the investigation. The kinds of evidence that may be found at a crime scene are highly diverse, and knowledge of techniques for processing each is needed to recover all pertinent information.

- The reconstruction team must bring together all the linked groups of evidence and information to form theories as to how a group of linked items was created by individual events at a crime scene.

Chapter Summary

Crime-scene reconstruction supports a likely sequence of events at a crime scene with the aid of physical evidence, testimony, and reenactments. Proper documentation and collection methods must be used for all types of evidence collected at the crime scene. Proper procedures of note taking, photography, and sketching are important for documenting physical evidence to be used in reconstruction. Legal procedures for gaining statements and testimonies must be strictly adhered to in order to generate admissible testimonial evidence. All data and evidence must be continually reevaluated throughout the process of crime-scene reconstruction. It may also be wise to have several individuals analyze the evidence and present their own interpretations. Investigators should never try to prove any theory, or they will risk creating a self-fulfilling prophecy.

Deductive reasoning allows definite conclusions to be drawn from information, whereas inductive reasoning only suggests a number of alternative conclusions. Investigators never try to prove a theory; they should instead test the theory to establish its plausibility against the evidence.

Information for reconstruction can be gained from direct physical evidence, circumstantial evidence, testimonial evidence, and reenactments. Direct physical evidence will provide a definite conclusion or "fact" about an aspect of evidence at a crime scene. Circumstantial evidence may suggest a variety of conclusions, some of which are more probable than others. Testimonial evidence should be used only when its validity is corroborated by physical evidence in a reconstruction. Reenactments may provide information on the way events unfolded at the crime scene.

Crime-scene reconstruction relies on the combined efforts of medical examiners, criminalists, and law enforcement personnel to recover physical evidence and to sort out the events surrounding the occurrence of a crime. The kinds of evidence recovered at a crime scene are highly diverse. Because each type of evidence is unique, specific techniques and considerations must be used in the processing of each item.

Items of evidence must first be evaluated separately from all other evidence. To maintain objectivity and avoid the fallacy of false cause, items of evidence should not be linked or grouped together during the initial phase of the investigation. Once all possible information has been recovered from each item, this information can be coupled with that of other items of evidence. Theories are then formed to suggest how this group of linked items was created.

Often the beginning and end of the sequence of events at a crime scene are obvious to investigators. Sometimes the evidence that signifies the start or end of events can also give a clue as to the missing events that must fit in the middle. The team must use information or sequences not in dispute to create a framework in which to explore those events that are in dispute to form an event timeline. Once the various orders have been identified, each sequence should be tested against the evidence.

Review Questions

1. _____ is the method used to support a likely sequence of events at a crime scene by the observation and evaluation of physical evidence and statements made by individuals involved with the incident.

2. Reconstructing the circumstances of a crime scene is a team effort that may include the help of law enforcement personnel, medical examiners, and _____.

3. To avoid letting personal beliefs or biases affect the conclusions reached through observations, crime-scene reconstruction teams must practice _____.

4. True or False: Expectations or biases can have a positive effect on the process of reconstruction by leading to correct analysis or interpretation of the information provided by the evidence. _____

5. True or False: Members of the crime-scene reconstruction team should design the examination and theory formation process to prove a theory or hypothesis that they believe to be true. _____

6. _____ reasoning is in use when a given fact or finding leads to a conclusion that is probable but not definitive. _____ reasoning is in use when a given fact or finding leads to a definitive conclusion.

7. Inductive reasoning is used to analyze _____ that provides a lead but no definite conclusion.

8. Another way to avoid bias is to test the _____ of all theories of how a crime occurred and all plausible alternatives against the evidence.

9. The inherent fallacy of _____ exists when investigators or attorneys try to apply a simple "yes or no" question to a complex answer.

10. True or False: Generalizing about aspects of evidence is always helpful to an investigation. _____

11. When a link is prematurely assumed between two or more objects of evidence, this is the fallacy of _____.

12. True or False: The biggest limitation to crime-scene reconstruction is the fact that what is left behind at a crime scene is often much less than needed to create a full timeline of events to theorize what occurred in the past. _____

13. _____ left behind at the crime scene is helpful in reconstruction to support or contradict accounts given by witnesses and/or suspects.

14. The analysis of _____ employs deductive reasoning and provides a definite conclusion or direction.

15. Eyewitness accounts, called _____, are sometimes highly subjective and heavily biased due to the fact that people may lie or misinterpret the facts.

16. The recreation of events at a crime scene, called a _____, may be performed by live personnel, mannequins, or computer-generated models.

17. For an item of physical evidence to be used in a reconstruction, it must have a confirmed and intact _____.

18. True or False: Each item of evidence should first be analyzed and tested separately from all other evidence to avoid false linkage of evidence. _____

19. True or False: The kinds of evidence that may be found at a crime scene are few, and similar categories or types of crime-scene evidence have to be studied with similar techniques and considerations. _____

20. Once all evidence has been evaluated, the reconstruction team must bring together all the evidence and information to form plausible _____.

21. True or False: The beginning and end of the sequence of events at a crime scene are usually obvious to the investigators and may suggest what events occurred in between. _____

22. A(n) _____ created for the reconstruction defines each event that occurred at a crime scene in various probable orders within a known or estimated time frame.

Application and Critical Thinking

1. Which logical fallacy is described in each of the following situations?
   a) An investigator finds a body wrapped in a bloody sheet and assumes that all the blood came from the victim.
   b) An officer investigating a hit-and-run accident spots a car with a dented bumper near the scene and assumes it was involved.
   c) The district attorney asks an investigator whether highly suggestive circumstantial evidence leads to a particular conclusion.

2. While investigating a murder scene, police gather evidence that includes a dead body riddled with stab wounds, fingerprints on a bloody knife found near the body, and a ticket stub from a theater several miles away from the scene. Investigators determine that the knife belonged to the victim, but matched the prints on the knife to an acquaintance of the victim. When questioned, the acquaintance claims he was at the movies at the time of the murder—the same movie shown on the stub found at the scene. What direct physical evidence connects the acquaintance to the crime scene? What circumstantial evidence connects him to the scene? What can you conclude about the acquaintance's involvement solely from direct physical evidence and deductive reasoning? What might you conclude considering circumstantial evidence and inductive reasoning as well?

Web Resources

An Introduction to Crime Scene Reconstruction: With a Primer on Logical Reasoning (An article providing a brief introduction to concepts and principles of crime-scene reconstruction)
www.apsu.edu/oconnort/3210/3210lect02a.htm

Evidence Dynamics: Locard's Exchange Principle & Crime Reconstruction (An online article from the *Journal of Behavioral Profiling* discussing crime-scene reconstruction and the integrity of physical evidence)
www.profiling.org/journal/vol1_no1/jbp_ed_january2000_1-1.html

Mock Crime-Scene Evidence Files and Theory Postings
www.crimescene.com

Why Crime Scene Reconstruction Does Not Answer the Why? Question
www.crimeandclues.com/why.htm

James Earl Ray: Conspirator or Lone Gunman?

Since his arrest in 1968 for the assassination of Dr. Martin Luther King, Jr., endless speculation has swirled around the motives and connections of James Earl Ray. Ray was a career criminal who was serving time for armed robbery when he escaped from the Missouri State Prison almost one year before the assassination. On April 3, 1968, Ray arrived in Memphis, Tennessee. The next day he rented a room at Bessie Brewer's Rooming House, across the street from the Lorraine Motel where Dr. King was staying.

At 6:00 p.m., Dr. King left his second-story motel room and stepped onto the balcony. As King turned toward his room, a shot rang out, striking the civil rights activist. Nothing could be done to revive him, and Dr. King was pronounced dead at 7:05 p.m. As the assailant ran on foot

from Bessie Brewer's, he left a blanket-covered package in front of a nearby building and then drove off in a white Mustang. The package contained a high-powered rifle equipped with a scope, a radio, some clothes, a pair of binoculars, a couple of beer cans, and a receipt for the binoculars. Almost a week after the shooting, the white Mustang was found abandoned in Atlanta, Georgia.

Fingerprints later identified as James Earl Ray's were found in the Mustang, on the rifle, on the binoculars, and on a beer can. In 1969, Ray entered a guilty plea in return for a sentence of ninety-nine years. While a variety of conspiracy theories surround this crime, the indisputable fact is that a fingerprint put the rifle that killed Martin Luther King, Jr., in the hands of James Earl Ray.

chapter 7

Fingerprints

Key Terms

anthropometry

arch

digital imaging

fluoresce

iodine fuming

latent fingerprint

livescan

loop

ninhydrin

Physical Developer

pixel

plastic print

portrait parlé

ridge characteristics
(minutiae)

sublimation

Super Glue fuming

visible print

whorl

portrait parlé
A verbal description of a perpetrator's physical characteristics and dress provided by an eyewitness.

anthropometry
A system of identification of individuals by measurement of parts of the body, developed by Alphonse Bertillon.

History of Fingerprinting

Since the beginnings of criminal investigation, police have sought an infallible means of human identification. The first systematic attempt at personal identification was devised and introduced by a French police expert, Alphonse Bertillon, in 1883. The Bertillon system relied on a detailed description (portrait parlé) of the subject, combined with full-length and profile photographs and a system of precise body measurements known as anthropometry.

The use of anthropometry as a method of identification rested on the premise that the dimensions of the human bone system remained fixed from age 20 until death. Skeleton sizes were thought to be so extremely diverse that no two individuals could have exactly the same measurements. Bertillon recommended routine taking of eleven measurements of the human anatomy, including height, reach, width of head, and length of the left foot.

For two decades, this system was considered the most accurate method of identification. But in the early years of the twentieth century, police began to appreciate and accept a system of identification based on the classification of finger ridge patterns known as *fingerprints*. Today, the fingerprint is the pillar of modern criminal identification.

Early Use of Fingerprints

The Chinese used fingerprints to sign legal documents as far back as three thousand years ago. Whether this practice was performed for ceremonial custom or as a means of personal identity remains a point of conjecture lost to history. In any case, the examples of fingerprinting in ancient history are ambiguous, and the few that exist did not contribute to the development of fingerprinting techniques as we know them today.

Several years before Bertillon began work on his system, William Herschel, an English civil servant stationed in India, started requiring natives to sign contracts with the imprint of their right hand, which was pressed against a stamp pad for the purpose. The motives for Herschel's requirement remain unclear; he may have envisioned fingerprinting as a means of personal identification or just as a form of the Hindu custom that a trace of bodily contact was more binding than a signature on a contract. In any case, he did not publish anything about his activities until after a Scottish physician, Henry Fauld, working in a hospital in Japan, published his views on the potential application of fingerprinting to personal identification.

In 1880, Fauld suggested that skin ridge patterns could be important for the identification of criminals. He told about a thief who left his fingerprint on a whitewashed wall, and how in comparing these prints with those of a suspect, he found that they were quite different. A few days later another suspect was found whose fingerprints compared with those on the wall. When confronted with this evidence, the individual confessed to the crime.

Fauld was convinced that fingerprints furnished infallible proof of identification. He even offered to set up at his own expense a fingerprint bureau at Scotland Yard to test the practicality of the method. But his offer was rejected in favor of the Bertillon system. This decision was reversed less than two decades later.

Early Classification of Fingerprints

The extensive research into fingerprinting conducted by another Englishman, Francis Galton, provided the needed impetus that made police agencies aware of its potential application. In 1892, Galton published his classic textbook *Finger Prints,* the first book of its kind on the subject. In his book, Galton discussed the anatomy of fingerprints and suggested methods for recording them. He also proposed assigning fingerprints to three pattern types—loops, arches, and whorls. Most important, the book demonstrated that no two prints are identical and that an individual's prints remain unchanged from year to year. At Galton's insistence, the British government adopted fingerprinting as a supplement to the Bertillon system.

The next step in the development of fingerprint technology was the creation of classification systems capable of filing thousands of prints in a logical and searchable sequence. Dr. Juan Vucetich, an Argentinian police officer fascinated by Galton's work, devised a workable concept in 1891. His classification system has been refined over the years and is still widely used today in most Spanish-speaking countries. In 1897, another classification system was proposed by an Englishman, Sir Edward Richard Henry. Four years later, Henry's system was adopted by Scotland Yard. Today, most English-speaking countries, including the United States, use some version of Henry's classification system to file fingerprints.

Adoption of Fingerprinting

Early in the twentieth century, Bertillon's measurement system began to fall into disfavor. Its results were highly susceptible to error, particularly when the measurements were taken by people who were not thoroughly trained. The method was dealt its most severe and notable setback in 1903 when a convict, Will West, arrived at Fort Leavenworth prison. A routine check of the prison files startlingly revealed that a William West, already in the prison, could not be distinguished from the new prisoner by body measurements or even by photographs. In fact, the two men looked just like twins, and their measurements were practically the same. Subsequently, fingerprints of the prisoners clearly distinguished them.

In the United States, the first systematic and official use of fingerprints for personal identification was adopted by the New York City Civil Service Commission in 1901. The method was used for certifying all civil service applications. Several American police officials received instruction in fingerprint identification at the 1904 World's Fair in St. Louis from representatives of Scotland Yard. After the fair and the Will West incident, fingerprinting began to be used in earnest in all major cities of the United States.

In 1924, the fingerprint records of the Bureau of Investigation and Leavenworth were merged to form the nucleus of the identification records of the new Federal Bureau of Investigation. The FBI has the largest collection of fingerprints in the world. By the beginning of World War I, England and practically all of Europe had adopted fingerprinting as their primary method of identifying criminals.

Fundamental Principles of Fingerprints

Since Galton's time, and as a result of his efforts, fingerprints have become an integral part of policing and forensic science. The principal reason for this is that fingerprints constitute a unique and unchanging means of personal identification. In fact, fingerprint analysts have formulated three basic principles of fingerprints that encompass these notions of the uniqueness and stability of fingerprint identification.

First Principle: A Fingerprint Is an Individual Characteristic; No Two Fingers Have Yet Been Found to Possess Identical Ridge Characteristics

The acceptance of fingerprint evidence by the courts has always been predicated on the assumption that no two individuals have identical fingerprints. Early fingerprint experts consistently referred to Galton's calculation, showing the possible existence of 64 billion different fingerprints, to support this contention. Later, researchers questioned the validity of Galton's figures and attempted to devise mathematical models to better approximate this value. However, no matter what mathematical model one refers to, the conclusions are always the same: The probability for the existence of two identical fingerprint patterns in the world's population is extremely small.

Not only is this principle supported by theoretical calculations, but just as important, it is verified by the millions of individuals who have had their prints classified during the past 110 years—no two have ever been found to be identical. The FBI has nearly 50 million fingerprint records in its computer database and has yet to find an identical image belonging to two different people.

ridge characteristics (minutiae)
Ridge endings, bifurcations, enclosures, and other ridge details, which must match in two fingerprints to establish their common origin.

The individuality of a fingerprint is not determined by its general shape or pattern but by a careful study of its ridge characteristics (also known as minutiae). The identity, number, and relative location of characteristics such as those illustrated in Figure 7–1 impart individuality to a fingerprint. If two prints are to match, they must reveal characteristics that not only are identical but also have the same relative location to one another in a print. In a judicial proceeding, a point-by-point comparison must be demonstrated by the expert, using charts similar to the one shown in Figure 7–2, in order to prove the identity of an individual.

An expert can easily compare the characteristics of the complete fingerprint; the average fingerprint has as many as 150 individual ridge characteristics. However, most prints recovered at crime scenes are partial impressions, showing only a segment of the entire print. Under these circumstances, the expert can compare only a small number of ridge characteristics from the recovered print to a known recorded print.

For years, experts have debated how many ridge comparisons are necessary to identify two fingerprints as the same. Numbers that range from

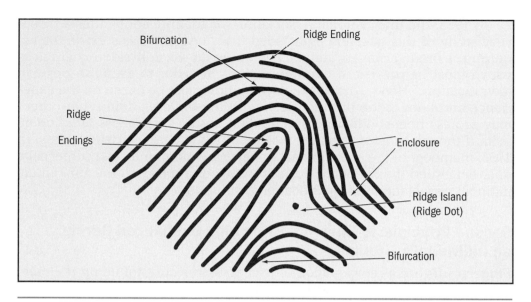

FIGURE 7–1 **Fingerprint ridge characteristics.** *Courtesy Sirchie Finger Print Laboratories, Inc., Youngsville, N.C., www.sirchie.com*

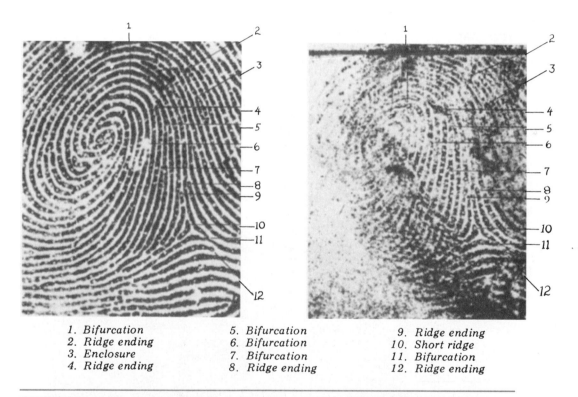

1. *Bifurcation*	5. *Bifurcation*	9. *Ridge ending*
2. *Ridge ending*	6. *Bifurcation*	10. *Short ridge*
3. *Enclosure*	7. *Bifurcation*	11. *Bifurcation*
4. *Ridge ending*	8. *Ridge ending*	12. *Ridge ending*

FIGURE 7–2 **A fingerprint exhibit illustrating the matching ridge characteristics between the crime-scene print and an inked impression of one of the suspect's fingers.** *Courtesy New Jersey State Police*

eight to sixteen have been suggested as being sufficient to meet the criteria of individuality. However, the difficulty in establishing such a minimum is that no comprehensive statistical study has ever determined the frequency of occurrence of different ridge characteristics and their relative locations. Until such a study is undertaken and completed, no meaningful guidelines can be established for defining the uniqueness of a fingerprint.

In 1973, the International Association for Identification, after a three-year study of this question, concluded that "no valid basis exists for requiring a predetermined minimum number of friction ridge characters which must be present in two impressions in order to establish positive identification." Hence, the final determination must be based on the experience and knowledge of the expert, with the understanding that others may profess honest differences of opinion on the uniqueness of a fingerprint if the question of minimal number of ridge characteristics exists. In 1995, members of the international fingerprint community at a conference in Israel issued the Ne'urim Declaration, which supported the 1973 International Association for Identification resolution.

Second Principle: A Fingerprint Remains Unchanged During an Individual's Lifetime

Fingerprints are a reproduction of friction skin ridges found on the palm side of the fingers and thumbs. Similar friction skin can also be found on the surface of the palms and soles of the feet. Apparently, these skin surfaces have been designed by nature to provide our bodies with a firmer grasp and a resistance to slippage. A visual inspection of friction skin reveals a series of lines corresponding to hills (ridges) and valleys (grooves). The shape and form of the skin ridges are what one sees as the black lines of an inked fingerprint impression.

Actually, skin is composed of layers of cells. Those nearest the surface make up the outer portion of the skin known as the *epidermis,* and the inner skin is known as the *dermis.* A cross-section of skin (see Figure 7–3) reveals a boundary of cells separating the epidermis and dermis. The shape of this boundary, made up of *dermal papillae,* determines the form and pattern of the ridges on the surface of the skin. Once the dermal papillae develop in the human fetus, the ridge patterns remain unchanged throughout life except to enlarge during growth.

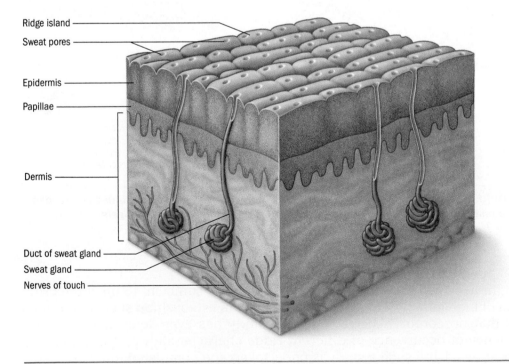

Ridge island
Sweat pores
Epidermis
Papillae
Dermis
Duct of sweat gland
Sweat gland
Nerves of touch

FIGURE 7–3   Cross-section of human skin.

Each skin ridge is populated by a single row of pores that are the openings for ducts leading from the sweat glands. Through these pores, perspiration is discharged and deposited on the surface of the skin. Once the finger touches a surface, perspiration, along with oils that may have been picked up by touching the hairy portions of the body, is transferred onto that surface, thereby leaving an impression of the finger's ridge pattern (a fingerprint). Prints deposited in this manner are invisible to the eye and are commonly referred to as latent fingerprints.

Although it is impossible to change one's fingerprints, some criminals have tried to obscure them. If an injury reaches deeply enough into the skin and damages the dermal papillae, a permanent scar forms. However, for this to happen, such a wound would have to penetrate 1 to 2 millimeters beneath the skin's surface. Indeed, efforts at intentionally scarring the skin can only be self-defeating, for it is totally impossible to obliterate all of the ridge characteristics on the hand, and the presence of permanent scars merely provides new characteristics for identification.

Perhaps the most publicized attempt at obliteration was that of the notorious gangster John Dillinger, who tried to destroy his own fingerprints by applying a corrosive acid to them. Prints taken at the morgue after he was shot to death, compared with fingerprints recorded at the time of a previous arrest, proved that his efforts had been fruitless (see Figure 7–4).

Third Principle: Fingerprints Have General Ridge Patterns That Permit Them to Be Systematically Classified

All fingerprints are divided into three classes on the basis of their general pattern: loops, whorls, and arches. Sixty to 65 percent of the population have loops, 30 to 35 percent have whorls, and about 5 percent have arches. These three classes form the basis for all ten-finger classification systems presently in use.

A loop must have one or more ridges entering from one side of the print, recurving, and exiting from the same side. If the loop opens toward the little finger, it is called an *ulnar loop;* if it opens toward the thumb, it is a *radial loop*. The pattern area of the loop is surrounded by two diverging ridges known as *type lines*. The ridge point at or nearest the

latent fingerprint
A fingerprint made by the deposit of oils and/or perspiration; it is invisible to the naked eye.

loop
A class of fingerprints characterized by ridge lines that enter from one side of the pattern and curve around to exit from the same side of the pattern.

whorl
A class of fingerprints that includes ridge patterns that are generally rounded or circular and have two deltas.

arch
A class of fingerprints characterized by ridge lines that enter the print from one side and flow out the other side.

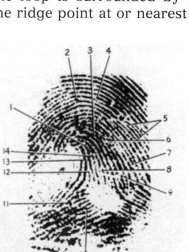

FIGURE 7–4 **The right index finger impression of John Dillinger, before scarification on the left and afterward on the right. Comparison is proved by the fourteen matching ridge characteristics.** *Courtesy American Institute of Applied Science, Youngsville, N.C.*

type-line divergence and located at or directly in front of the point of divergence is known as the *delta*. To many, a fingerprint delta resembles the silt formation that builds up as a river flows into the entrance of a lake—hence, the analogy to the geological formation known as a delta. All loops must have one delta. The *core,* as the name suggests, is the approximate center of the pattern. A typical loop pattern is illustrated in Figure 7–5.

Whorls are actually divided into four distinct groups, as shown in Figure 7–6: plain, central pocket loop, double loop, and accidental. All whorl patterns must have type lines and at least two deltas. A plain whorl and a central pocket loop have at least one ridge that makes a complete circuit. This ridge may be in the form of a spiral, oval, or any variant of a circle. If an imaginary line drawn between the two deltas contained within these two patterns touches any one of the spiral ridges, the pattern is a plain whorl. If no such ridge is touched, the pattern is a central pocket loop.

As the name implies, the double loop is made up of two loops combined into one fingerprint. Any whorl classified as an accidental either contains two or more patterns (not including the plain arch) or is a pattern not covered by other categories. Hence, an accidental may consist of a combination loop and plain whorl or loop and tented arch.

Arches, the least common of the three general patterns, are subdivided into two distinct groups: plain arches and tented arches, as shown in Figure 7–7. The plain arch is the simplest of all fingerprint patterns; it is formed by ridges entering from one side of the print and exiting on the opposite side. Generally, these ridges tend to rise in the center of the pattern, forming a wavelike pattern. The tented arch is similar to the plain arch except that instead of rising smoothly at the center, there is a sharp upthrust or spike, or the ridges meet at an angle that is less than 90 degrees.[1] Arches do not have type lines, deltas, or cores.

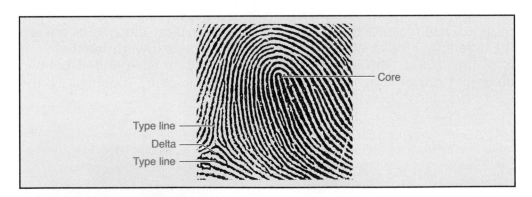

FIGURE 7–5 Loop pattern.

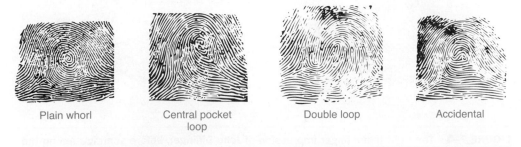

| Plain whorl | Central pocket loop | Double loop | Accidental |

FIGURE 7–6 Whorl patterns.

Plain   Tented

FIGURE 7–7   Arch patterns.

Key Points

- Fingerprints are a reproduction of friction skin ridges found on the palm side of the fingers and thumbs.

- The basic principles underlying the use of fingerprints in criminal investigations are as follows: (1) A fingerprint is an individual characteristic because no two fingers have yet been found to possess identical ridge characteristics; (2) a fingerprint remains unchanged during an individual's lifetime; and (3) fingerprints have general ridge patterns that permit them to be systematically classified.

- All fingerprints are divided into three classes on the basis of their general pattern: loops, whorls, and arches.

- The individuality of a fingerprint is determined not by its general shape or pattern, but by a careful study of its ridge characteristics. The expert must demonstrate a point-by-point comparison in order to prove the identity of an individual.

- When the finger touches a surface, perspiration and oils are transferred onto that surface, leaving a fingerprint. Prints deposited in this manner are invisible to the eye and are commonly referred to as latent or invisible fingerprints.

Classification of Fingerprints

The original Henry system, as adopted by Scotland Yard in 1901, converted ridge patterns on all ten fingers into a series of letters and numbers arranged in the form of a fraction. However, the system as it was originally designed could accommodate files of up to only 100,000 sets of prints. Thus, as collections grew in size, it became necessary to expand the capacity of the classification system. In the United States, the FBI, faced with the problem of filing ever-increasing numbers of prints, expanded its classification capacity by modifying the original Henry system and adding additional extensions. These modifications are collectively known as the *FBI system* and are used by most agencies in the United States today. Although we will not discuss all of the divisions of the FBI system, a description of just one part, the primary classification, will provide an interesting insight into the process of fingerprint classification.

The primary classification is part of the original Henry system and provides the first classification step in the FBI system. Using this classification alone, all of the fingerprint cards in the world could be divided into 1,024 groups. The first step in obtaining the primary classification is to pair up fingers, placing one finger in the numerator of a fraction, the other in the denominator. The fingers are paired in the following sequence:

$$\frac{\text{R. Index}}{\text{R. Thumb}} \quad \frac{\text{R. Ring}}{\text{R. Middle}} \quad \frac{\text{L. Thumb}}{\text{R. Little}} \quad \frac{\text{L. Middle}}{\text{L. Index}} \quad \frac{\text{L. Little}}{\text{L. Ring}}$$

The presence or absence of the whorl pattern is the basis for the determination of the primary classification. If a whorl pattern is found on any finger of the first pair, it is assigned a value of 16; on the second pair, a value of 8; on the third pair, a value of 4; on the fourth pair, a value of 2; and on the last pair, a value of 1. Any finger with an arch or loop pattern is assigned a value of 0. Approximately 25 percent of the population falls into the 1/1 category; that is, all their fingers have either loops or arches.

After values for all ten fingers are obtained in this manner, they are totaled, and 1 is added to both the numerator and denominator. The fraction thus obtained is the primary classification. For example, if the right index and right middle fingers are whorls and all the others are loops, the primary classification is

$$\frac{16 + 0 + 0 + 0 + 0 + 1}{0 + 8 + 0 + 0 + 0 + 1} = \frac{17}{8}$$

A fingerprint classification system cannot in itself unequivocally identify an individual; it merely provides the fingerprint examiner with a number of candidates, all of whom have an indistinguishable set of prints in the system's file. The identification must always be made by a final visual comparison of the suspect print's and file print's ridge characteristics; only these features can impart individuality to a fingerprint. Although ridge patterns impart class characteristics to the print, the type and position of ridge characteristics give it its individual character.

Key Points

- The primary classification is the first step in classifying fingerprints under the FBI system. The presence or absence of the whorl pattern is the basis for the determination of the primary classification.

Automated Fingerprint Identification Systems

The Henry system and its subclassifications have proven to be a cumbersome system for storing, retrieving, and searching for fingerprints, particularly as fingerprint collections grow in size. Nevertheless, until the emergence of fingerprint computer technology, this manual approach was the only viable method for maintaining fingerprint collections. Since 1970, technological advances have made possible the classification and retrieval of fingerprints by computers. Automated fingerprint identification systems (AFISs) have proliferated throughout the law enforcement community.

In 1999, the FBI initiated full operation of the Integrated Automated Fingerprint Identification System (IAFIS), the largest AFIS in the United States, which links state AFIS computers with the FBI database. This database contains nearly 50 million fingerprint records. However, an AFIS can come

FIGURE 7–8 An AFIS system designed for use by local law enforcement agencies. *Courtesy AFIX Technologies Inc., Pittsburg, KS 66762. www.afix.net*

in all sizes ranging from the FBI's to independent systems operated by cities, counties, and other agencies of local government (see Figure 7–8). Unfortunately, these local systems often cannot be linked to the state's AFIS system because of differences in software configurations.

How AFIS Works

The heart of AFIS technology is the ability of a computer to scan and digitally encode fingerprints so that they can be subject to high-speed computer processing. The AFIS uses automatic scanning devices that convert the image of a fingerprint into digital minutiae that contain data showing ridges at their points of termination (ridge endings) and the branching of ridges into two ridges (bifurcations). The relative position and orientation of the minutiae are also determined, allowing the computer to store each fingerprint in the form of a digitally recorded geometric pattern.

The computer's search algorithm determines the degree of correlation between the location and relationship of the minutiae for both the search and file prints. In this manner, a computer can make thousands of fingerprint comparisons in a second. For example, a set of ten fingerprints can be searched against a file of 500,000 ten-finger prints (ten-prints) in about eight-tenths of a second. During the search for a match, the computer uses a scoring system that assigns prints to each of the criteria set by an operator. When the search is complete, the computer produces a list of file prints that have the closest correlation to the search prints. All of the selected prints are then examined by a fingerprint expert, who makes the final verification of the print's identity. Thus, the AFIS makes no final decisions on the identity of a fingerprint, leaving this function to the eyes of a trained examiner.

The speed and accuracy of ten-print processing by AFISs have made possible the search of single latent crime-scene fingerprints against an entire file's print collection. Before AFIS, police were usually restricted to comparing crime-scene fingerprints against those of known suspects. The impact of the AFIS on no-suspect cases has been dramatic. In its first year of operation, San Francisco's AFIS computer conducted 5,514 latent fingerprint searches and achieved 1,001 identifications—a hit rate of 18 percent. This compares to the previous year's average of 8 percent for manual latent-print searches.

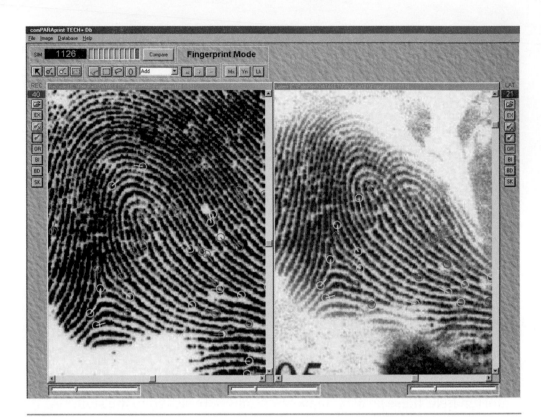

FIGURE 7–9 **A side-by-side comparison of a latent print against a file fingerprint is conducted in seconds and their similarity rating (SIM) is displayed on the upper-left portion of the screen.** *Courtesy Sirchie Finger Print Laboratories, Inc., Youngsville, N.C., www.sirchie.com*

As an example of how an AFIS computer operates, one system has been designed to automatically filter out imperfections in a latent print, enhance its image, and create a graphic representation of the fingerprint's ridge endings and bifurcations and their directions. The print is then computer searched against file prints. The image of the latent print and a matching file print are then displayed side by side on a high-resolution video monitor as shown in Figure 7–9. The matching latent and file prints are then verified and charted by a fingerprint examiner at a video workstation.

The stereotypical image of a booking officer rolling inked fingers onto a standard ten-print card for ultimate transmission to a database has, for the most part, been replaced with digital-capture devices (**livescan**) that eliminate ink and paper (see Figure 7–10). The livescan captures the image on each finger and the palms as they are lightly pressed against a glass platen. These livescan images can then be sent to the AFIS database electronically, so that within minutes the booking agency can enter the fingerprint record into the AFIS database and search the database for previous entries of the same individual.

livescan
An inkless device that captures digital images of fingerprints and palm prints and electronically transmits them to an AFIS.

Considerations with AFIS

AFIS has fundamentally changed the way criminal investigators operate, allowing them to spend less time developing suspect lists and more time investigating the suspects generated by the computer. However, investigators must be cautioned against overreliance on a computer. Sometimes a latent print does not make a hit because of the poor quality of the file print. To avoid these potential problems, investigators must still print all known suspects in a case and manually search these prints against the crime-scene prints.

Forensic Brief

The Night Stalker

Richard Ramirez committed his first murder in June 1984. His victim was a 79-year-old woman who was stabbed repeatedly and sexually assaulted, and then had her throat slashed. It would be eight months before Ramirez murdered again. In the spring, Ramirez began a murderous rampage that resulted in thirteen additional killings and five rapes.

His modus operandi was to enter a home through an open window, shoot the male residents, and savagely rape his female victims. He scribed a pentagram on the wall of one of his victims and the words "Jack the Knife," and was reported by another to force her to "swear to Satan" during the assault. His identity still unknown, the news media dubbed him the "Night Stalker." As the body count continued to rise, public hysteria and a media frenzy prevailed.

The break in the case came when the license plate of what seemed to be a suspicious car relating to a sighting of the Night Stalker was reported to the police. The police determined that the car had been stolen and eventually located it, abandoned in a parking lot. After processing the car for prints, police found one usable partial fingerprint. This fingerprint was entered into the Los Angeles Police Department's brand-new AFIS computerized fingerprint system.

Without AFIS, it would have taken a single technician, manually searching

Richard Ramirez, the Night Stalker.
© *Bettmann/CORBIS. All Rights Reserved.*

Los Angeles' 1.7 million print cards, sixty-seven years to come up with the perpetrator's prints. Thanks to AFIS, it took only a few seconds to locate and identify them. The Night Stalker was identified as Richard Ramirez, who had been fingerprinted following a traffic violation some years before. Police searching the home of one of his friends found the gun used to commit the murders, and jewelry belonging to his victims was found in the possession of Ramirez's sister. Ramirez was convicted of murder and sentenced to death in 1989. He remains on death row.

AFIS computers are available from several suppliers. Each system scans fingerprint images and detects and records information about minutiae (ridge endings and bifurcations); however, they do not all incorporate the same features, coordinate systems, or units of measure to record fingerprint information. These software incompatibilities often mean that although state systems can communicate with the FBI's IAFIS, they do not communicate with each other directly. Likewise, local and state systems frequently cannot share information with each other. Many of these technical problems will be resolved as more agencies follow transmission standards developed by the National Institute of Standards and Technology and the FBI.

FIGURE 7–10 Livescan technology enables law enforcement personnel to print and compare a subject's fingerprints rapidly, without inking the fingerprints. *Courtesy Printrac International*

Forensic Brief

The Mayfield Affair

On March 11, 2004, a series of ten explosions at four sites occurred on commuter trains traveling to or near the Atocha train station in Madrid, Spain. The death toll from these explosions was nearly 200, with more than 1,500 injured. On the day of the attack, a plastic bag was found in a van previously reported as stolen. The bag contained copper detonators like those used on the train bombs.

On March 17 the FBI received electronic images of latent fingerprints that were recovered from the plastic bag, and a search was initiated on the FBI's IAFIS. A senior fingerprint examiner encoded seven minutiae points from the high-resolution image of one suspect latent fingerprint and initiated an IAFIS search matching the print to Brandon Mayfield. Mayfield's prints were in the FBI's central database because they had been taken when he joined the military, where he served for eight years before being honorably discharged as a second lieutenant.

After a visual comparison of the suspect and file prints, the examiner concluded a "100 percent match." The identification

Forensic Brief

was verified by a retired FBI fingerprint examiner with more than thirty years of experience who was under working contract with the bureau, as well as by a court-appointed independent fingerprint examiner (see figure).

Mayfield, age 37, a Muslim convert, was arrested on May 6 on a material witness warrant. The U.S. Attorney's Office came up with a list of Mayfield's potential ties to Muslim terrorists, which they included in the affidavit they presented to the federal judge who ordered his arrest and detention. The document also said that while no travel records were found for Mayfield, "It is believed that Mayfield may have traveled under a false or fictitious name." On May 24, after the Spaniards had linked the print from the plastic bag to an Algerian national, Mayfield's case was thrown out. The FBI issued him a highly unusual official apology, and his ordeal became a stunning embarrassment to the U.S. government.

As part of its corrective-action process, the FBI formed an international committee of distinguished latent-print examiners and forensic experts. Their task was to review the analysis performed by the FBI Laboratory and make recommendations that would help prevent this type of error in the future. The committee came up with some startling findings and observations (available at www.fbi.gov/hq/lab/fsc/backissu/jan2005/special_report/2005_special_report.htm).

The committee members agreed that "the quality of the images that were used to make the erroneous identification was not a factor. . . . The identification is filled with dissimilarities that were easily observed when a detailed analysis of the latent print was conducted." They further stated, the power of the IAFIS match, coupled with the inherent pressure of working an extremely high-profile case, was thought to have influenced the initial examiner's judgment and subsequent examination. . . . The apparent mind-set of the initial examiner after reviewing the results of the IAFIS search was that a match did exist; therefore, it would be reasonable to assume

(a)

(b)

(a) A questioned print recovered in connection with the Madrid bombing Investigation. (b) A file print of Brandon Mayfield. *(a) Courtesy www.onin.com/fp/problemidents.html/madrid*

(continued)

Forensic Brief

The Mayfield Affair (*continued*)

that the other characteristics must match as well. In the absence of a detailed analysis of the print, it can be a short distance from finding only seven characteristics sufficient for plotting, prior to the automated search, to the position of 12 or 13 matching characteristics once the mind-set of identification has become dominant. . . .

> Once the mind-set occurred with the initial examiner, the subsequent examinations were tainted. . . . Because of the inherent pressure of such a high-profile case, the power of an IAFIS match in conjunction with the similarities in the candidate's print, and the knowledge of the previous examiners' conclusions (especially since the initial examiner was a highly respected supervisor with many years of experience), it was concluded that subsequent examinations were incomplete and inaccurate. To disagree was not an expected response. . . . When the individualization had been made by the examiner, it became increasingly difficult for others in the agency to disagree.

The committee went on to make a number of quality-assurance recommendations to help avoid a recurrence of this type of error.

The Mayfield incident has also been the subject of an investigation by the Office of the Inspector General (OIG), U.S. Department of Justice (www.usdoj.gov/oig/special/s0601/final.pdf). The OIG investigation concluded that a "series of systemic issues" in the FBI Laboratory contributed to the Mayfield misidentification. The report noted that the FBI has made significant procedural modifications to help prevent similar errors in the future, and strongly supported the FBI's decision to develop more objective standards for fingerprint identification. An internal review of the FBI Latent Print Unit conducted in the aftermath of the Mayfield affair has resulted in the implementation of revisions in training, as well as in the decision-making process when determining the comparative value of a latent print, along with more stringent verification policies and procedures.

The impact of the Mayfield affair on fingerprint technology as currently practiced and the weight courts will assign to fingerprint matches remain open questions.

Source: Smrz, M. A., et al., *Journal of Forensic Identification* 56 (2006): 402–434.

Key Points

- The fingerprint database known as AFIS converts the image of a fingerprint into digital minutiae that contain data showing ridges at their points of termination (ridge endings) and their branching into two ridges (bifurcations).

- AFIS makes no final decisions on the identification of a fingerprint, instead leaving this function to a trained examiner.

- Livescan is an inkless device that captures digital images of fingerprints and palm prints and electronically transmits them to an AFIS.

Methods of Detecting Fingerprints

Through common usage, the term *latent fingerprint* has come to be associated with any fingerprint discovered at a crime scene. Sometimes, however, prints found at the scene of a crime are quite visible to the eye, and the word *latent* is a misnomer.

Actually, there are three kinds of crime-scene prints. **Visible prints** are made by fingers touching a surface after the ridges have been in contact with a colored material such as blood, paint, grease, or ink; **plastic prints** are ridge impressions left on a soft material such as putty, wax, soap, or dust; and *latent* or *invisible prints* are impressions caused by the transfer of body perspiration or oils present on finger ridges to the surface of an object.

Locating Fingerprints

Locating visible or plastic prints at the crime scene normally presents little problem to the investigator, because these prints are usually distinct and visible to the eye. Locating latent or invisible prints is obviously much more difficult and requires the use of techniques to make the print visible. Although the investigator can choose from several methods for visualizing a latent print, the choice depends on the type of surface being examined.

Hard and nonabsorbent surfaces (such as glass, mirror, tile, and painted wood) require different development procedures from surfaces that are soft and porous (such as papers, cardboard, and cloth). Prints on the former are preferably developed by the application of a powder or treatment with Super Glue, whereas prints on the latter generally require treatment with one or more chemicals.

Sometimes the most difficult aspect of fingerprint examination is the location of prints. Recent advances in fingerprint technology have led to the development of an ultraviolet image converter for the purpose of detecting latent fingerprints. This device, called the Reflected Ultraviolet Imaging System (RUVIS), can locate prints on most nonabsorbent surfaces without the aid of chemical or powder treatments (see Figure 7–11).

RUVIS detects the print in its natural state by aiming UV light at the surface suspected of containing prints. When the UV light strikes the fingerprint, the light is reflected back to the viewer, differentiating the print from its background surface. The transmitted UV light is then converted into visible light by an image intensifier. Once the print is located in this manner, the crime-scene investigator can develop it in the most appropriate fashion (see Figure 7–12).

Developing Latent Prints

Several techniques are available to the criminalist to develop latent prints on a variety of surfaces. These range from chemical methods such as powders and iodine fuming to the use of laser light.

visible print
A fingerprint made when the finger deposits a visible material such as ink, dirt, or blood onto a surface.

plastic print
A fingerprint impressed in a soft surface.

FIGURE 7–11 A Reflected Ultraviolet Imaging System allows an investigator to directly view surfaces for the presence of untreated latent fingerprints. *Courtesy Sirchie Finger Print Laboratories, Inc., Youngsville, N.C., www.sirchie.com*

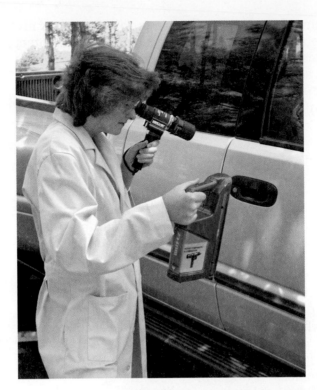

FIGURE 7–12 Using a Reflected Ultraviolet Imaging System with the aid of a UV lamp to search for latent fingerprints. *Courtesy Sirchie Finger Print Laboratories, Inc., Youngsville, N.C., www.sirchie.com*

FIGURE 7–13 Developing a latent fingerprint on a surface by applying a fingerprint powder with a fiberglass brush. *Courtesy Sirchie Finger Print Laboratories, Inc., Youngsville, N.C., www. sirchie.com*

Fingerprint Powders Fingerprint powders are commercially available in a variety of compositions and colors. These powders, when applied lightly to a nonabsorbent surface with a camel's-hair or fiberglass brush, readily adhere to perspiration residues and/or deposits of body oils left on the surface (see Figure 7–13).

Experienced examiners find that gray and black powders are adequate for most latent-print work; the examiner selects the powder that affords the best color contrast with the surface being dusted. Hence, the gray powder, composed of an aluminum dust, is used on dark-colored surfaces. It is also applied to mirrors and metal surfaces that are polished to a mirrorlike finish, because these surfaces photograph as black. The black powder, composed basically of black carbon or charcoal, is applied to white or light-colored surfaces.

Other types of powders are available for developing latent prints. A magnetic-sensitive powder can be spread over a surface with a magnet in the form of a Magna Brush. A Magna Brush does not have any bristles to come in contact with the surface, so there is less chance that the print will be destroyed or damaged. The magnetic-sensitive powder comes in black and gray and is especially useful on such items as finished leather and rough plastics, on which the minute texture of the surface tends to hold particles of ordinary powder. Fluorescent powders are also used to develop latent fingerprints. These powders fluoresce under ultraviolet light. By photographing the fluorescence pattern of the developing print under UV light, it is possible to avoid having the color of the surface obscure the print.

Iodine Fuming   Of the several chemical methods used for visualizing latent prints, iodine fuming is the oldest. Iodine is a solid crystal that, when heated, transforms into a vapor without passing through a liquid phase; such a transformation is called sublimation. Most often, the suspect material is placed in an enclosed cabinet along with iodine crystals (see Figure 7–14). As the crystals are heated, the resultant vapors fill the chamber and combine with constituents of the latent print to make it visible.

Unfortunately, iodine prints are not permanent and begin to fade once the fuming process is stopped. Therefore, the examiner must photograph the prints immediately on development in order to retain a permanent record. Also, iodine-developed prints can be fixed with a 1 percent solution of starch in water, applied by spraying. The print turns blue and lasts for several weeks to several months.

iodine fuming
A technique for visualizing latent fingerprints by exposing them to iodine vapors.

sublimation
A physical change from a solid directly into a gaseous state.

FIGURE 7–14   A heated fuming cabinet. *Courtesy Sirchie Finger Print Laboratories, Inc., Youngsville, N.C., www.sirchie.com*

The reasons latent prints are visualized by iodine vapors are not yet fully understood. Many believe that the iodine fumes combine with fatty oils; however, there is also convincing evidence that the iodine may actually interact with residual water left on a print from perspiration.[2]

ninhydrin
A chemical reagent used to develop latent fingerprints on porous materials by reacting with amino acids in perspiration.

Ninhydrin Another chemical used for visualizing latent prints is ninhydrin. The development of latent prints with ninhydrin depends on its chemical reaction to form a purple-blue color with amino acids present in trace amounts in perspiration. Ninhydrin (triketohydrindene hydrate) is commonly sprayed onto the porous surface from an aerosol can. A solution is prepared by mixing the ninhydrin powder with a suitable solvent, such as acetone or ethyl alcohol; a 0.6 percent solution appears to be effective for most applications.

Generally, prints begin to appear within an hour or two after ninhydrin application; however, weaker prints may be visualized after twenty-four to forty-eight hours. The development can be hastened if the treated specimen is heated in an oven or on a hot plate at a temperature of 80 to 100°C. The ninhydrin method has developed latent prints on paper as old as fifteen years.

Physical Developer
A silver nitrate–based reagent formulated to develop latent fingerprints on porous surfaces.

Physical Developer Physical Developer is a third chemical mixture used for visualizing latent prints. Physical Developer is a silver nitrate–based liquid reagent. This method has gained wide acceptance by fingerprint examiners, who have found it effective for visualizing latent prints that remain undetected by the previously described methods. Also, this technique is very effective for developing latent fingerprints on porous articles that may have been wet at one time.

For most fingerprint examiners, the chemical method of choice is ninhydrin. Its extreme sensitivity and ease of application have all but eliminated the use of iodine for latent-print visualization. However, when ninhydrin fails, development with Physical Developer may provide identifiable results. Application of Physical Developer washes away any traces of proteins from an object's surface; hence, if one wishes to use all of the previously mentioned chemical development methods on the same surface, it is necessary to first fume with iodine, follow this treatment with ninhydrin, and then apply Physical Developer to the object.

Super Glue fuming
A technique for visualizing latent fingerprints on nonporous surfaces by exposing them to cyanoacrylate vapors; named for the commercial product Super Glue.

Super Glue Fuming In the past, chemical treatment for fingerprint development was reserved for porous surfaces such as paper and cardboard. However, since 1982, a chemical technique known as **Super Glue fuming** has gained wide popularity for developing latent prints on nonporous surfaces such as metals, electrical tape, leather, and plastic bags[3] (See Figure 7–15).

Super Glue is approximately 98 to 99 percent cyanoacrylate ester, a chemical that interacts with and visualizes a latent fingerprint. Cyanoacrylate ester fumes can be created when Super Glue is placed on absorbent cotton treated with sodium hydroxide. The fumes can also be created by heating the glue. The fumes and the evidential object are contained within an enclosed chamber for up to six hours. Development occurs when fumes from the glue adhere to the latent print, usually producing a white-appearing latent print. Interestingly, small enclosed areas, such as the interior of an automobile, have been successfully processed for latent prints with fumes from Super Glue.

Through the use of a small handheld wand, cyanoacrylate fuming is now easily done at a crime scene or in a laboratory setting. The wand heats a small cartridge containing cyanoacrylate. Once heated, the cyanoacrylate

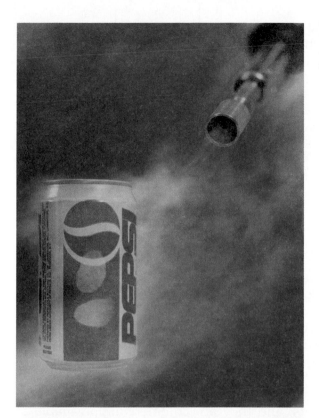

FIGURE 7–15 Super Glue fuming a nonporous metallic surface in the search for latent fingerprints.
Courtesy Sirchie Finger Print Laboratories, Inc., Youngsville, N.C., www.sirchie.com

(a)

(b)

FIGURE 7–16 (a) A handheld fuming wand uses disposable cartridges containing cyanoacrylate. The wand is used to develop prints at the crime scene and (b) in the laboratory. *Courtesy Sirchie Finger Print Laboratories, Inc., Youngsville, N.C., www.sirchie.com*

vaporizes, allowing the operator to direct the fumes onto the suspect area (see Figure 7–16).

Other Techniques for Visualization In recent years, researchers have explored a variety of new processes applicable to the visualization of latent fingerprints. However, for many years progress in this field was minimal. Fingerprint specialists traditionally relied on three chemical techniques—iodine, ninhydrin, and silver nitrate—to reveal a hidden fingerprint. Then, Super Glue fuming extended chemical development to prints deposited on nonporous surfaces.

Another hint of things to come emerged with the discovery that latent fingerprints could be visualized by exposure to laser light. This laser

fluoresce
To emit visible light when exposed to light of a shorter wavelength.

method took advantage of the fact that perspiration contains a variety of components that fluoresce when illuminated by laser light.

The next advancement in latent-fingerprint development occurred with the discovery that fingerprints could be treated with chemicals that would induce fluorescence when exposed to laser illumination. For example, application of zinc chloride after ninhydrin treatment or application of the dye rhodamine 6G after Super Glue fuming caused fluorescence and increased the sensitivity of detection on exposure to laser illumination. The discovery of numerous chemical developers for visualizing fingerprints through fluorescence quickly followed. This knowledge set the stage for the next advance in latent-fingerprint development—the *alternate light source*.

With the advent of chemically induced fluorescence, lasers were no longer needed to induce fingerprints to fluoresce through perspiration residues. High-intensity light sources or alternate light sources have proliferated and all but replaced laser lights (see Figure 7–17). High-intensity quartz halogen or xenon-arc light sources can be focused on a suspect area through a fiber-optic cable. This light can be passed through several filters, giving the user more flexibility in selecting the wavelength of light to be aimed at the latent print. Alternatively, lightweight, portable alternate light sources that use light-emitting diodes (LEDs) are also commercially available (see Figure 7–18).

In most cases, these light sources have proven to be as effective as laser light in developing latent prints, and they are commercially available at costs significantly below those of laser illuminators. Furthermore, these light sources are portable and can be readily taken to any crime scene.

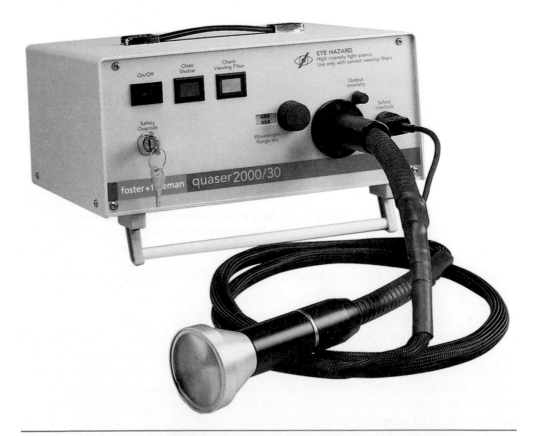

FIGURE 7–17 An alternate light source system incorporating a high-intensity light source.
Courtesy Foster & Freeman Limited, Worcestershire, U.K., www.fosterfreeman.co.uk

FIGURE 7–18 A lightweight handheld alternate light source that uses an LED light source.
Courtesy Foster & Freeman Limited, Worcestershire, U.K., www.fosterfreeman.co.uk

A large number of chemical treatment processes are available to the fingerprint examiner (see Figure 7–19), and the field is in a constant state of flux. Selection of an appropriate procedure is best left to technicians who have developed their skills through casework experience. Newer chemical processes include a substitute for ninhydrin called DFO (1,8-diazafluoren-9-one). This chemical visualizes latent prints on porous materials when exposed to an alternate light source. DFO has been shown to develop 2.5 times more latent prints on paper than ninhydrin. 1,2-indanedione is also emerging as a potential reagent for the development of latent fingerprints on porous surfaces. 1,2-indanedione gives both good initial color and strong fluorescence when reacted with amino acids derived from prints and thus has the potential to provide in one process what ninhydrin and DFO can do in two steps. Dye combinations known as RAM, RAY, and MRM 10 when used in conjunction with Super Glue fuming have been effective in visualizing latent fingerprints by fluorescence. A number of chemical formulas useful for latent-print development are listed in Appendix III.

Studies have demonstrated that common fingerprint-developing agents do not interfere with DNA-testing methods used for characterizing bloodstains.[4] Nonetheless, in cases involving items with material adhering to their surfaces and/or items that will require further laboratory examinations, fingerprint processing should not be performed at the crime scene. Rather, the items should be submitted to the laboratory, where they can be processed for fingerprints in conjunction with other necessary examinations.

Key Points

- Visible prints are made when fingers touch a surface after the ridges have been in contact with a colored material such as blood, paint, grease, or ink.

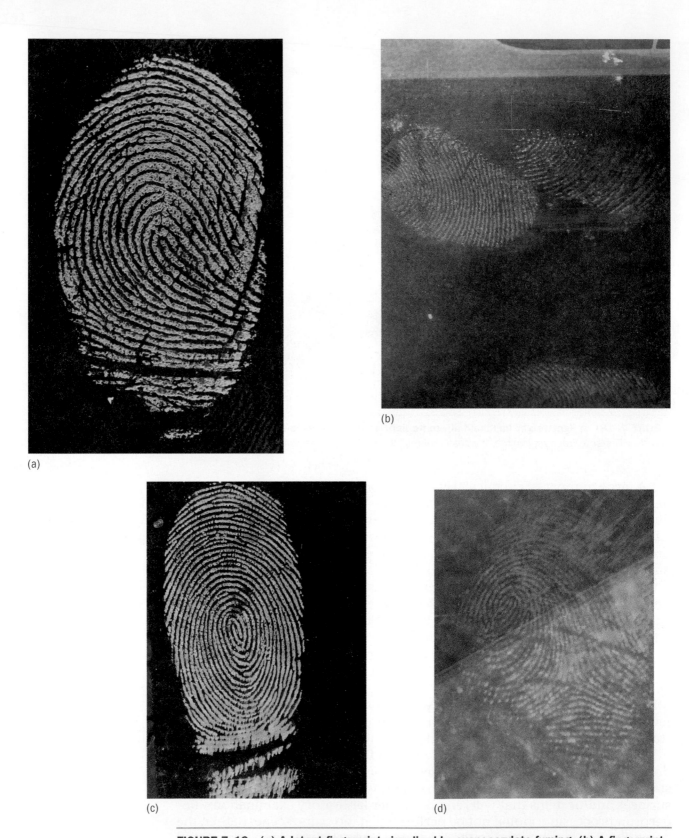

FIGURE 7-19 (a) A latent fingerprint visualized by cyanoacrylate fuming. (b) A fingerprint treated with cyanoacrylate and a blue-green fluorescent dye. (c) A fingerprint treated with cyanoacrylate and rhodamine 6G fluorescent dye. (d) A fingerprint treated with cyanoacrylate and the fluorescent dye combination RAM. *(a) Courtesy North Carolina State Bureau of Investigation, Raleigh, N.C. (b) Courtesy 3M Corp., Austin, Texas*

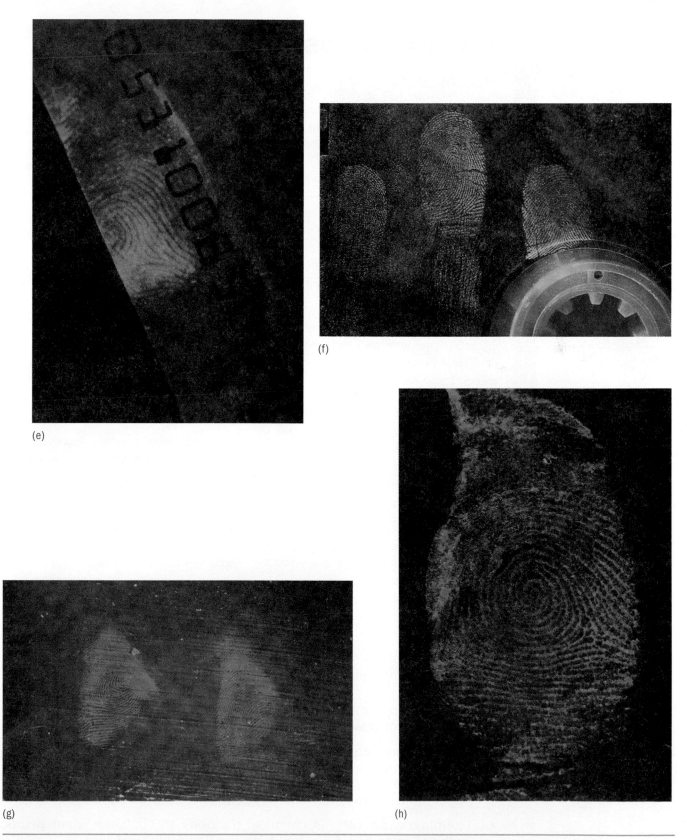

FIGURE 7–19 **(e) A fingerprint visualized by the fluorescent chemical DFO. (f) A fingerprint visualized by Redwop fluorescent fingerprint powder. (g) A bloody fingerprint detected by laser light without any chemical treatment. (h) A bloody fingerprint detected by laser light after spraying with merbromin and hydrogen peroxide.** *(f) Courtesy Melles Griot Inc., Carlsbad, Calif.*

Closer Analysis

Fluorescence

Fluorescence occurs when a substance absorbs light and reemits the light in wavelengths longer than that of the illuminating source. Importantly, substances that emit light or fluoresce are more readily seen either with the naked eye or through photography than are non-light-emitting materials. The high sensitivity of fluorescence serves as the underlying principle of many of the new chemical techniques used to visualize latent fingerprints.

The earliest use of fluorescence to visualize fingerprints came with the direct illumination of a fingerprint with argon–ion lasers. This laser type was chosen because its blue-green light output induced some of the perspiration components of a fingerprint to fluoresce (see figure). The major drawback of this approach is that the perspiration components of a fingerprint are often present in quantities too minute to observe even with the aid of fluorescence.

The fingerprint examiner, wearing safety goggles containing optical filters, visually examines the specimen being exposed to the laser light. The filters absorb the laser light and permit the wavelengths at

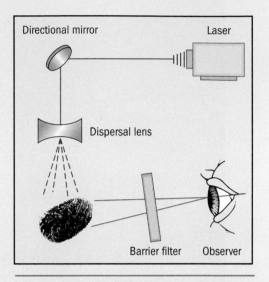

A schematic depicting latent-print detection with the aid of a laser. *Courtesy Federal Bureau of Investigation, Washington, D.C.*

which latent-print residues fluoresce to pass through to the eyes of the wearer. The filter also protects the operator against eye damage from scattered or reflected laser light. Likewise, latent-print residue producing sufficient fluorescence can be photographed by placing this same filter across the lens of the camera. Examination of specimens and photography of the fluorescing latent prints are carried out in a darkened room.

- Plastic prints are ridge impressions left on a soft material, such as putty, wax, soap, or dust.

- Latent prints deposited on hard and nonabsorbent surfaces (such as glass, mirror, tile, and painted wood) are usually developed by the application of a powder, whereas prints on porous surfaces (such as papers and cardboard) generally require treatment with a chemical.

- Examiners use various chemical methods to visualize latent prints, such as iodine fuming, ninhydrin, and Physical Developer.

- Super Glue fuming develops latent prints on nonporous surfaces.

- Latent fingerprints can also be treated with chemicals that induce fluorescence when exposed to a high-intensity light or an alternate light source.

Preservation of Developed Prints

Once the latent print has been visualized, it must be permanently preserved for future comparison and possible use in court as evidence. A photograph must be taken before any further attempts at preservation. Any camera equipped with a close-up lens will do; however, many investigators prefer to use a camera specially designed for fingerprint photography. Such a camera comes equipped with a fixed focus to take photographs on a 1:1 scale when the camera's open eye is held exactly flush against the print's surface (see Figure 7–20). In addition, photographs must be taken to provide an overall view of the print's location with respect to other evidential items at the crime scene.

Once photographs have been secured, one of two procedures is to be followed. If the object is small enough to be transported without destroying the print, it should be preserved in its entirety. The print should be covered with cellophane so it will be protected from damage. On the other hand, prints on large immovable objects that have been developed with a powder can best be preserved by "lifting." The most popular type of lifter is a broad adhesive tape similar to Scotch tape. Fingerprint powder is applied to the print, and the surface containing the print is covered with the adhesive side of the tape. When the tape is pulled up, the powder is transferred to the tape. Then the tape is placed on a properly labeled card that provides a good background contrast with the powder.

A variation of this procedure is the use of an adhesive-backed clear plastic sheet attached to a colored cardboard backing. Before it is applied to the print, a celluloid separator is peeled from the plastic sheet to expose the adhesive lifting surface. The tape is then pressed evenly and firmly over the powdered print and pulled up (see Figure 7–21). The sheet containing

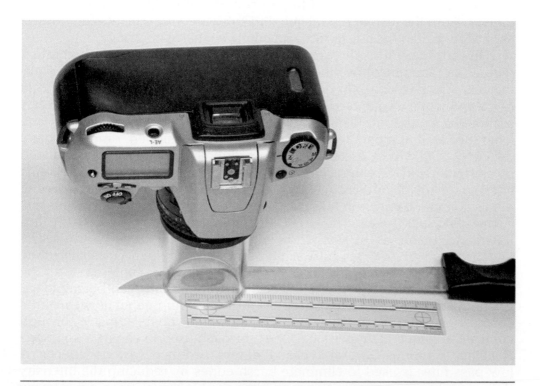

FIGURE 7–20   A camera fitted with an adapter designed to give an approximate 1:1 photograph of a fingerprint. *Courtesy Sirchie Finger Print Laboratories, Inc., Youngsville, N.C., www.sirchie.com*

FIGURE 7–21 **"Lifting" a fingerprint.** *Courtesy Sirchie Finger Print Laboratories, Inc., Youngsville, N.C., www.sirchie.com*

the adhering powder is now pressed against the cardboard backing to provide a permanent record of the fingerprint.

Digital Imaging for Fingerprint Enhancement

When fingerprints are lifted from a crime scene, they are not usually in perfect condition, making the analysis difficult. Computers have advanced technology in most fields, and fingerprint identification has not been left behind. With the help of digital imaging software, fingerprints can now be enhanced for the most accurate and comprehensive analysis.

digital imaging
A process through which a picture is converted into a series of square electronic dots known as pixels.

pixel
A square electronic dot that is used to compose a digital image.

Digital imaging is the process by which a picture is converted into a digital file. The image produced from this digital file is composed of numerous square electronic dots called **pixels**. Images composed of only black and white elements are referred to as *grayscale images*. Each pixel is assigned a number according to its intensity. The grayscale image is made from the set of numbers to which a pixel may be assigned, ranging from 0 (black) to 255 (white). Once an image is digitally stored, it is manipulated by computer software that changes the numerical value of each pixel, thus altering the image as directed by the user. Resolution reveals the degree of detail that can be seen in an image. It is defined in terms of dimensions, such as 800 × 600 pixels. The larger the numbers, the more closely the digital image resembles the real-world image.

The input of pictures into a digital imaging system is usually done through the use of scanners, digital cameras, and video cameras. After the picture is changed to its digital image, several methods can be employed to enhance the image. The overall brightness of an image, as well as the contrast between the image and the background, can be adjusted through contrast-enhancement methods. One approach used to enhance an image is *spatial filtering*. Several types of filters produce various effects. A low-pass filter is used to eliminate harsh edges by reducing the intensity difference between pixels. A second filter, the high-pass filter, operates by modifying a pixel's numerical value to exaggerate its intensity difference from that of its neighbor. The resulting effect increases the contrast of the edges, thus providing a high contrast between the elements and the background. Frequency analysis, also referred to as *frequency Fourier transform* (FFT), is used to identify periodic or repetitive patterns such as lines or dots that interfere with the interpretation of the image. These patterns are diminished or eliminated to enhance the appearance of the image. Interestingly, the spacings between fingerprint ridges are themselves periodic. Therefore, the contribution of the fingerprint can be identified in FFT mode and then enhanced. Likewise, if ridges from overlapping prints are positioned in different directions, their corresponding frequency information is at different locations in FFT mode. The ridges of one latent print can then be enhanced while the ridges of the other are suppressed.

Color interferences can pose a problem when analyzing an image. For example, a latent fingerprint found on paper currency or a check may be difficult to analyze because of the distracting colored background. With the imaging software, the colored background can simply be removed to make the image stand out (see Figure 7–22). If the image itself is a particular color, such as a ninhydrin-developed print, the color can be isolated and enhanced to distinguish it from the background.

Digital imaging software also provides functions in which portions of the image can be examined individually. With a scaling and resizing tool, the user can select a part of an image and resize it for a closer look. This function operates much like a magnifying glass, helping the examiner view fine details of an image.

An important and useful tool, especially for fingerprint identification, is the compare function. This specialized feature places two images side by side and allows the examiner to chart the common features on both images simultaneously (see Figure 7–23). The zoom function is used in conjunction with the compare tool. As the examiner zooms into a portion of one image, the software automatically zooms into the second image for comparison.

Although digital imaging is undoubtedly an effective tool for enhancing and analyzing images, it is only as useful as the images it has to work with. If the details do not exist on the original images, the enhancement

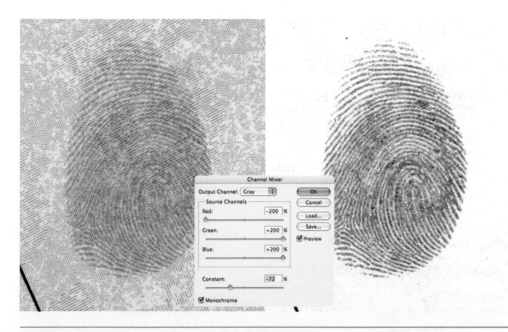

FIGURE 7–22 **A fingerprint being enhanced in Adobe Photoshop. In this example, on the left is the original scan of an inked fingerprint on a check. On the right is the same image after using Adobe Photoshop's Channel Mixer to eliminate the green security background.**
Courtesy Imaging Forensics, Fountain Valley, Calif., www.imagingforensics.com

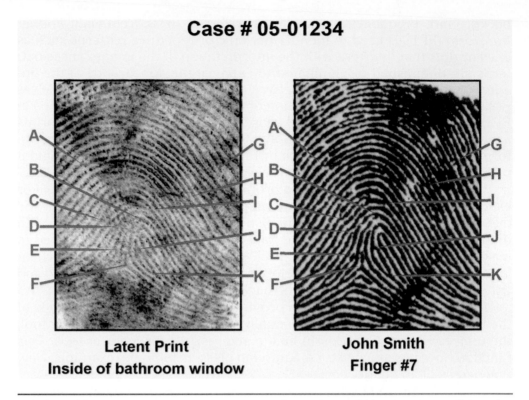

Case # 05-01234

Latent Print

Inside of bathroom window

John Smith

Finger #7

FIGURE 7–23 **Current imaging software allows fingerprint analysts to prepare a fingerprint comparison chart. The fingerprint examiner can compare prints side by side and display important features that are consistent between the fingerprints. The time needed to create a display of this sort digitally is about thirty to sixty minutes.** *Courtesy Imaging Forensics, Fountain Valley, Calif., www.Imagingforensics.com*

procedures are not going to work. The benefits of digital enhancement methods are apparent when weak images are made more distinguishable.

Key Points

- Once a latent print has been visualized, it must be permanently preserved for future comparison and for possible use as court evidence. A photograph must be taken before any further attempts at preservation are made.

- A common method for preserving a print developed with a powder is lifting the print with an adhesive tape.

- Digital imaging is a process through which a picture is converted into a series of square electronic dots known as pixels. Fingerprints can be enhanced with digital imaging.

Chapter Summary

Fingerprints are a reproduction of friction skin ridges found on the palm side of the fingers and thumbs. The basic principles underlying the use of fingerprints in criminal investigations are that (1) a fingerprint is an individual characteristic because no two fingers have yet been found to possess identical ridge characteristics; (2) a fingerprint remains unchanged during an individual's lifetime; and (3) fingerprints have general ridge patterns that permit them to be systematically classified.

All fingerprints are divided into three classes on the basis of their general pattern: loops, whorls, and arches. Fingerprint classification systems are based on knowledge of fingerprint pattern classes. The individuality of a fingerprint is not determined by its general shape or pattern, but by a careful study of its ridge characteristics. The expert must demonstrate a point-by-point comparison in order to prove the identity of an individual. AFIS aids this process by converting the image of a fingerprint into digital minutiae that contain data showing ridges at their points of termination (ridge endings) and their branching into two ridges (bifurcations). A single fingerprint can be searched against the FBI IAFIS digital database of 50 million fingerprint records in a matter of minutes.

Once the finger touches a surface, perspiration, along with oils that may have been picked up by touching the hairy portions of the body, is transferred onto that surface, thereby leaving an impression of the finger's ridge pattern (a fingerprint). Prints deposited in this manner are invisible to the eye and are commonly referred to as latent or invisible fingerprints.

Visible prints are made when fingers touch a surface after the ridges have been in contact with a colored material such as blood, paint, grease, or ink. Plastic prints are ridge impressions left on a soft material, such as putty, wax, soap, or dust.

Latent prints deposited on hard and nonabsorbent surfaces (such as glass, mirror, tile, and painted wood) are preferably developed by application of a powder; prints on porous surfaces (such as paper and cardboard) generally require treatment with a chemical. Examiners use various chemical methods to visualize latent prints, such as iodine fuming, ninhydrin, and Physical Developer. Super Glue fuming develops latent prints on non-porous surfaces, such as metals, electrical tape, leather, and plastic bags. Development occurs when fumes from the glue adhere to the print, usually producing a white latent print.

The high sensitivity of fluorescence serves as the underlying principle of many of the new chemical techniques used to visualize latent fingerprints. Fingerprints are treated with chemicals that induce fluorescence when exposed to a high-intensity light or an alternate light source.

Once the latent print has been visualized, it must be permanently preserved for future comparison and for possible use as court evidence. A photograph must be taken before any further attempts at preservation are made. If the object is small enough to be transported without destroying the print, it should be preserved in its entirety. Prints on large immovable objects that have been developed with a powder are best preserved by "lifting" with a broad adhesive tape.

Review Questions

1. The first systematic attempt at personal identification was devised and introduced by _____.

2. A system of identification relying on precise body measurements is known as _____.

3. The first book written on the subject of fingerprints, called *Finger Prints,* was written in 1892 by _____ and discussed the anatomy of fingerprints and suggested methods for recording them.

4. The fingerprint classification system used in most English-speaking countries was devised by _____.

5. True or False: The first systematic and official use of fingerprints for personal identification in the United States was adopted by the New York City Civil Service Commission. _____

6. The _____ has the largest collection of fingerprints in the world.

7. Galton calculated that approximately _____ different fingerprints could exist, and current figures are similarly high.

8. True or False: The individuality of a fingerprint is determined by its pattern. _____

9. A point-by-point comparison of a fingerprint's _____ must be demonstrated in order to prove identity.

10. _____ are a reproduction of friction skin ridges.

11. The form and pattern of skin ridges are determined by the skin layer called the _____.

12. Fingerprints deposited on a surface when oils and sweat are excreted from pores on the friction ridges are called _____ fingerprints.

13. A permanent scar forms in the skin only when an injury damages the _____.

14. True or False: Fingerprints cannot be changed during a person's lifetime. _____

15. The three general patterns into which fingerprints are divided are _____, _____, and _____.

16. The most common fingerprint pattern is the _____.

17. Approximately 5 percent of the population has the _____ fingerprint pattern.

18. A loop pattern that opens toward the thumb is known as a(n) _____ loop.

19. The pattern area of the loop is enclosed by two diverging ridges known as _____.

20. The ridge point nearest the type-line divergence is known as the _____.

21. True or False: All loops must have two deltas. _____

22. The approximate center of a loop pattern is called the _____.

23. A whorl pattern has _____ deltas and at least _____ ridge(s) that make a complete circuit.

24. If an imaginary line drawn between the two deltas of a whorl pattern touches any of the spiral ridges, the pattern is classified as a _____.

25. The simplest of all fingerprint patterns is the _____.

26. True or False: Arches have type lines, deltas, and cores. _____

27. The presence or absence of the _____ pattern is used as a basis for determining the primary classification in the Henry system.

28. The largest category (25 percent) of the population has a _____ classification in the primary classification meaning all their fingers have loops or arches.

29. True or False: A fingerprint classification system can unequivocally identify an individual. _____

30. True or False: Computerized fingerprint search systems match prints by comparing the positions of bifurcations and ridge endings. _____

31. By determining the degree of correlation between the location and relationship of the _____ for both the search and file fingerprints, a computer can make thousands of fingerprint comparisons in a second.

32. The digital-capture device called _____ has eliminated ink and paper for the collection of exemplar fingerprints.

33. A fingerprint left by a person with soiled or stained fingertips is called a _____.

34. _____ fingerprints are impressions left on a soft material.

35. Fingerprints on hard and nonabsorbent surfaces are best developed by the application of a(n) _____.

36. Fingerprints on porous surfaces are best developed with _____ treatment.

37. _____ vapors chemically combine with fatty oils or residual water to visualize a fingerprint.

38. The chemical _____ visualizes fingerprints by its reaction with amino acids.

39. Chemical treatment with _____ visualizes fingerprints on porous articles that may have been wet at one time.

40. True or False: A latent fingerprint is first treated with Physical Developer followed by ninhydrin. _____

41. A chemical technique known as _____ is used to develop latent prints on nonporous surfaces such as metal and plastic.

42. _____ occurs when a substance absorbs light and reemits the light in wavelengths longer than the illuminating source.

43. High-intensity light sources, known as _____, are effective in developing latent fingerprints.

44. Once a fingerprint has been visualized, it must first be preserved by _____.

45. Fingerprints on large immovable objects that have been developed with a powder can best be preserved by _____ with a broad adhesive tape similar to Scotch tape.

Application and Critical Thinking

1. Classify each of the following prints as loop, whorl, or arch.

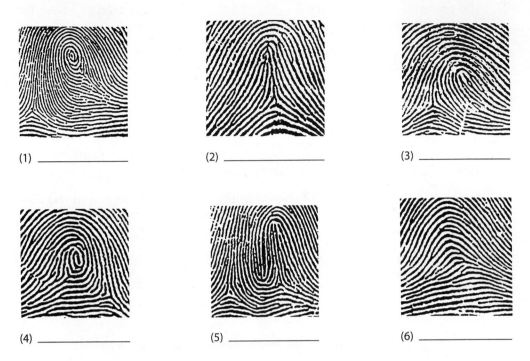

(1) _____   (2) _____   (3) _____

(4) _____   (5) _____   (6) _____

2. Following is a description of the types of prints from the fingers of a criminal suspect. Using the FBI system, determine the primary classification of this individual.

Finger	Right Hand	Left Hand
Thumb	Whorl	Whorl
Index	Loop	Whorl
Middle	Whorl	Arch
Ring	Whorl	Whorl
Little	Arch	Whorl

3. While searching a murder scene, you find the following items that you believe may contain latent fingerprints. Indicate whether prints on each item should be developed using fingerprint powder or chemicals.
   a) A leather sofa
   b) A mirror
   c) A painted wooden knife handle
   d) Blood-soaked newspapers
   e) A revolver

4. Criminalist Frank Mortimer is using digital imaging to enhance latent fingerprints. Indicate which features of digital imaging he would most likely use for each of the following tasks:
   a) Isolating part of a print and enlarging it for closer examination
   b) Increasing the contrast between a print and the background surface on which it is located
   c) Examining two prints that overlap each other

Web Resources

Averbeck, R., "Super Glue to the Rescue"
www.detectoprint.com/article.htm

The Detection and Enhancement of Latent Fingerprints (An Adobe Acrobat article from the 2001 Interpol Forensic Science Symposium)
www.interpol.int/Public/Forensic/IFSS/meeting13/SpecialPresentation.pdf

Fingerprint Patterns (An online article discussing the various types of fingerprint patterns, accompanied by extensive illustrations)
www.policensw.com/info/fingerprints/finger07.html

The Fingerprint System (An online article that traces the history of fingerprinting and discusses the elements of the standard fingerprinting system used by law enforcement)
www.criminaljustice.state.ny.us/ojis/history/fp_sys.htm

Frequently Asked Questions About Fingerprints
www.onin.com/fp/lpfaq.html

The History of Fingerprints (An article that traces the history of the use of fingerprints in crime solving)
www.onin.com/fp/fphistory.html

IAFIS Home Page (The FBI website for the Integrated Automated Fingerprint Identification System; describes the functions and organization of IAFIS and the fingerprint identification services it provides)
www.fbi.gov/hq/cjisd/iafis.htm

Is Fingerprint Identification a "Science"? (An article written by a fingerprinting expert that examines the criteria that validate the science of fingerprinting; also includes a large list of links to identification evidence)
www.forensic-evidence.com/site/ID/ID00004_2.html

Ridges and Furrows (A site that presents information on fingerprinting history, the anatomy of skin, friction ridge identification, latent print development, AFIS, and more)
www.ridgesandfurrows.homestead.com

Taking Legible Fingerprints (Information from the FBI outlining proper procedures for lifting fingerprints)
www.fbi.gov/hq/cjisd/takingfps.html

Endnotes

1. A tented arch is also any pattern that resembles a loop but lacks one of the essential requirements for classification as a loop.
2. J. Almag, Y. Sasson, and A. Anati, "Chemical Reagents for the Development of Latent Fingerprints II: Controlled Addition of Water Vapor to Iodine Fumes—A Solution to the Aging Problem," *Journal of Forensic Sciences* 24 (1979): 431.
3. F. G. Kendall and B. W. Rehn, "Rapid Method of Super Glue Fuming Application for the Development of Latent Fingerprints," *Journal of Forensic Sciences* 28 (1983): 777.
4. C. Roux et al., "A Further Study to Investigate the Effect of Fingerprint Enhancement Techniques on the DNA Analysis of Bloodstains," *Journal of Forensic Identification* 49 (1999): 357; C. J. Frégeau et al., "Fingerprint Enhancement Revisited and the Effects of Blood Enhancement Chemicals on Subsequent Profiler Plus™ Fluorescent Short Tandem Repeat DNA Analysis of Fresh and Aged Bloody Fingerprints," *Journal of Forensic Sciences* 45 (2000): 354; P. Grubwieser et al., "Systematic Study on STR Profiling on Blood and Saliva Traces after Visualization of Fingerprints," *Journal of Forensic Sciences* 48 (2003): 733.

The Beltway Snipers

During a three-week period in October 2002, ten people were killed and three others wounded as two snipers terrorized the region in and around the Baltimore–Washington metropolitan area. The arrest of John Allen Muhammad, 41, and Lee Boyd Malvo, 17, ended the ordeal. The semiautomatic .223-caliber rifle seized from them was ultimately linked by ballistics tests to eight of the ten killings. The car that Muhammad and Malvo were driving had been specially configured with one hole in the trunk through which a rifle barrel could protrude, so that a sniper could shoot from inside a slightly ajar trunk.

The major break in the case came when a friend of Muhammad's called police suggesting that Muhammad and his friend Malvo were the likely snipers. Muhammad's automobile records revealed numerous traffic stops in the Beltway area during the time of the shootings. Another break in the case came when Malvo called a priest to boast of a killing weeks before in Montgomery, Alabama. Investigators traced the claim to a recent liquor store holdup that left one person dead. Fortunately, the perpetrator of this crime left a latent fingerprint at the murder scene. Authorities quickly tracked the print to Malvo, a Jamaican citizen, through his fingerprints on file with the Immigration and Naturalization Service. A description of Muhammad's car was released to the media, leading to tips from alert citizens who noticed the car parked in a rest area with both occupants asleep.

The motive for the shooting spree was believed to be a plot to extort $10 million from local and state governments. Muhammad was sentenced to death, and Malvo is currently serving life imprisonment without parole.

Learning Objectives

After studying this chapter, you should be able to:

- Describe techniques for rifling a barrel.

- Recognize the class and individual characteristics of bullets and cartridge cases.

- Understand the use of the comparison microscope to compare bullets and cartridge cases.

- Explain the concept of the NIBIN database.

- Explain the procedure for determining how far a weapon was fired from a target.

- Identify the laboratory tests for determining whether an individual has fired a weapon.

- Explain the forensic significance of class and individual characteristics to the comparison of tool mark, footwear, and tire impressions.

- List some common field reagents used to enhance bloody footprints.

firearms identification
A discipline primarily concerned with determining whether a bullet or cartridge was fired by a particular weapon.

Just as natural variations in skin ridge patterns and characteristics provide a key to human identification, minute random markings on surfaces can impart individuality to inanimate objects. Structural variations and irregularities caused by scratches, nicks, breaks, and wear permit the criminalist to relate a bullet to a gun; a scratch or abrasion mark to a single tool; or a tire track to a particular automobile. Individualization, so vigorously pursued in all other areas of criminalistics, is frequently attainable in firearms and tool mark examination.

Although a portion of this chapter will be devoted to the comparison of surface features for the purpose of bullet identification, a complete description of the services and capabilities of the modern forensic firearms laboratory cannot be restricted to just this one subject, important as it may be. The high frequency of shooting cases means that the science of firearms identification must extend beyond mere comparison of bullets to include knowledge of the operation of all types of weapons, restoration of obliterated serial numbers on weapons, detection and characterization of gunpowder residues on garments and around wounds, estimation of muzzle-to-target distances, and detection of powder residues on hands. Each of these functions will be covered in this chapter.

Types of Firearms

Generally, firearms can be divided into two categories—handguns and long guns. Handguns, or pistols, consist of firearms that are designed to be held and fired with one hand. The three most common types of handguns are single-shot, revolvers, and semiautomatics. All pistols can be classified as single-action or double-action firearms. Single-action firearms require the hammer to be manually cocked backward before the trigger is pulled in order to fire each time. Double-action firearms cock the hammer when the trigger is pulled and then reload the firing chamber after the round is fired.

Single-shot pistols can fire only one round at a time. Each round must be manually loaded into the chamber before firing.

The revolver features several firing chambers located within a revolving cylinder. As the pistol is fired, the cylinder can rotate clockwise or

Firearms, Tool Marks, and Other Impressions

Key Terms

bore

breechblock

caliber

choke

distance determination

ejector

extractor

firearms identification

gauge

Greiss test

grooves

lands

rifling

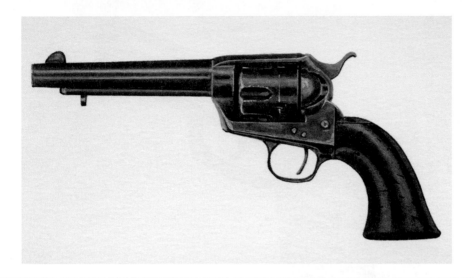

FIGURE 8–1 **A swing-out type of revolver features a cylinder that swings out to the side of the weapon to be loaded.** *Courtesy Dorling Kindersley Media Library*

counterclockwise. Each firing chamber holds one cartridge, which is lined up with the barrel mechanically when the round is fired. The cartridge cases have to be manually ejected to reload the firing chambers. *Swing-out revolvers* feature a cylinder that swings out to the side of the weapon to be loaded (see Figure 8–1). *Break-top revolvers* are hinged so that both the barrel and the cylinder flip downward for loading. *Solid-frame revolvers* have no mechanism to uncover all the firing chambers at once. Instead a small "gate" at the back of the gun allows one chamber to be loaded at a time; the cylinder is then rotated, and the next chamber is loaded with a cartridge.

Semiautomatic pistols feature a removable magazine that is most often contained within the grip of the firearm. Once the magazine is loaded, the hammer is cocked by pulling the slide on the top of the gun rearward and then releasing it to load the first round. The firing of the cartridge generates gases that are used to eject the cartridge case, cock the hammer, and load the next round. A semiautomatic pistol (see Figure 8–2) fires one shot per trigger pull. An automatic firearm, such as a machine gun, fires as long as the trigger is pressed or until the ammunition is depleted.

Long guns are either rifles or shotguns. Rifles and shotguns are designed to be fired while resting on the shoulder. The two principal differences between rifled firearms and shotguns are found in the ammunition and the barrel. Shotgun ammunition, called a shell, contains numerous ball-shaped projectiles, called shot. The barrel of a shotgun is smooth without the grooves and lands found in rifles. A shotgun barrel can also be narrowed toward the muzzle in order to concentrate shot when fired. This narrowing of the barrel is called the *choke* of the shotgun. A shotgun may be single or double barreled. The two barrels of a double-barreled shotgun may be arranged horizontally (side by side) or vertically (one over another). The barrels may also have different choke diameters.

The various types of rifles and shotguns have different reloading mechanisms. The single-shot gun can chamber and fire only one round at a time. Just as with single-shot pistols, the round has to be loaded manually each time. Repeating long guns use a mechanical instrument of some sort to eject spent cartridges, load a new round, and cock the hammer after a round is fired. These include lever-action, pump or slide-action, bolt-action

FIGURE 8–2 A semiautomatic pistol. *Courtesy Dorling Kindersley Media Library*

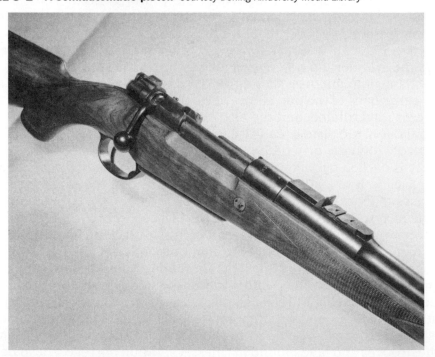

FIGURE 8–3 A bolt-action long gun uses the movement of a bolt mechanism to expel the spent cartridge case, load the next round, and cock the hammer. *Courtesy Getty Images Inc.–Hulton Archive Photos*

(see Figure 8–3), and semiautomatic (see Figure 8–4) long guns referring to the loading mechanism used on each. Semiautomatic rifles use the force of the gas produced during firing to eject the spent cartridge, load a new round, and cock the hammer. Semiautomatic firearms use a disconnector mechanism to fire one shot per trigger pull, whereas fully automatic firearms do not have such a mechanism and fire multiple shots with a single pull of the trigger.

FIGURE 8–4 **A semiautomatic long gun uses the energy from the firing reaction to expel the spent cartridge case, load the next round, and cock the hammer.** *Courtesy Dorling Kindersly Media Library*

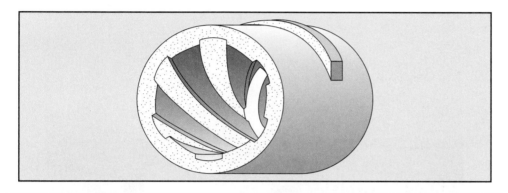

FIGURE 8–5 **The interior view of a gun barrel, showing the presence of lands and grooves.**

Bullet and Cartridge Comparisons

The inner surface of the rifled barrel of a gun leaves its markings on a bullet passing through it. These markings are peculiar to each gun. Hence, if one bullet found at the scene of a crime and another test-fired from a suspect's gun show the same markings, the suspect is linked to the crime. Because these inner surface markings, or striations, are so important for bullet comparison, it is important to know why and how they originate.

The Gun Barrel

The gun barrel is produced from a solid bar of steel that has been hollowed out by drilling. The microscopic drill marks left on the barrel's inner surface are randomly irregular and in themselves impart a uniqueness to each barrel. However, the manufacture of a barrel requires the additional step of impressing its inner surface with spiral **grooves**, a step known as **rifling**. The surfaces of the original **bore** remaining between the grooves are called **lands** (see Figure 8–5).

As a fired bullet travels through a barrel, it engages the rifling grooves. These grooves then guide the bullet through the barrel, giving it a rapid spin. This is done because a spinning bullet does not tumble end over end on leaving the barrel, but remains instead on a true and accurate course.

The diameter of the gun barrel, shown in Figure 8–6, measured between opposite lands, is known as the **caliber** of the weapon. Caliber is normally recorded in hundredths of an inch or in millimeters—for example,

grooves
The cut or low-lying portions between the lands in a rifled bore.

rifling
The spiral grooves formed in the bore of a firearm barrel that impart spin to the projectile when it is fired.

bore
The interior of a firearm barrel.

lands
The raised portion between the grooves in a rifled bore.

caliber
The diameter of the bore of a rifled firearm, usually expressed in hundredths of an inch or millimeters—for example, .22 caliber and 9 millimeter.

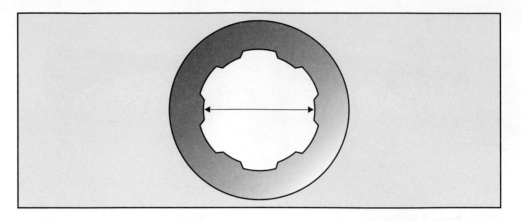

FIGURE 8–6   A cross-section of a barrel with six grooves. The diameter of the bore is the caliber.

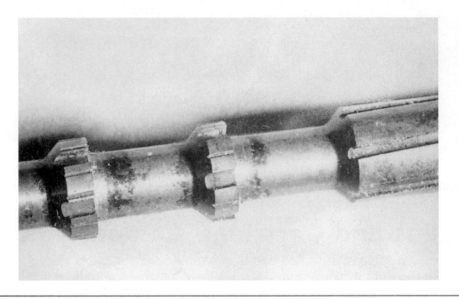

FIGURE 8–7   A segment of a broach cutter. *Courtesy New Jersey State Police*

.22 caliber and 9 millimeter. Actually, the term *caliber,* as it is commonly applied, is not an exact measurement of the barrel's diameter; for example, a .38-caliber weapon might actually have a bore diameter that ranges from 0.345 to 0.365 inch.

Rifling Methods   Before 1940, barrels were rifled by having one or two grooves at a time cut into the surface with steel hook cutters. The cutting tool was rotated as it passed down the barrel, so that the final results were grooves spiraling to either the right or left. However, as the need for increased speed in weapons manufacture became apparent, newer techniques were developed that were far more suitable for the mass production of weapons.

The broach cutter, shown in Figure 8–7, consists of a series of concentric steel rings, with each ring slightly larger than the preceding one. As the broach passes through the barrel, it simultaneously cuts all grooves into the barrel at the required depth. The broach rotates as it passes through the barrel, giving the grooves their desired direction and rate of twist.

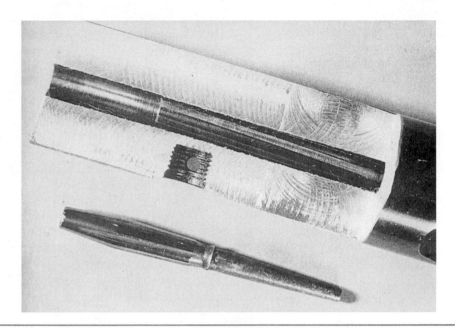

FIGURE 8–8 (*top*) **Cross-section of a .22-caliber rifled barrel.** (*bottom*) **A button used to produce the lands and grooves in the barrel.** *Courtesy New Jersey State Police*

In contrast to the broach, the button process involves no cuttings. A steel plug or "button" impressed with the desired number of grooves is forced under extremely high pressure through the barrel. A single pass of the button down the barrel compresses the metal to create lands and grooves on the barrel walls that are negative forms of those on the button. The button rotates to produce the desired direction and rate of twist (see Figure 8–8).

Like the button process, the mandrel rifling hammer forging process involves no cutting of metal. A mandrel is a rod of hardened steel machined so its form is the reverse impression of the rifling it is intended to produce. The mandrel is inserted into a slightly oversized bore, and the barrel is compressed with hammering or heavy rollers into the mandrel's form.

Every firearms manufacturer chooses a rifling process that is best suited to meet the production standards and requirements of its product. Once the choice is made, however, the class characteristics of the weapon's barrel remain consistent; each has the same number of lands and grooves, with the same approximate width and direction of twist. For example, .32-caliber Smith & Wesson revolvers have five lands and grooves twisting to the right. On the other hand, Colt .32-caliber revolvers exhibit six lands and grooves twisting to the left. Although these class characteristics permit the examiner to distinguish one type or brand name of weapon from another, they do not impart individuality to any one barrel; no class characteristic can do this.

If one could cut a barrel open lengthwise, careful examination of the interior would reveal the existence of fine lines, or *striations,* many running the length of the barrel's lands and grooves. These striations are impressed into the metal as the negatives of minute imperfections found on the rifling cutter's surface, or they are produced by minute chips of steel pushed against the barrel's inner surface by a moving broach cutter. The random distribution and irregularities of these markings are impossible to duplicate exactly in any two barrels. No two rifled barrels, even those manufactured in succession, have identical striation markings. These striations form the individual characteristics of the barrel.

FIGURE 8–9 **A bullet is impressed with the rifling markings of the barrel when it emerges from the weapon.** *Courtesy New Jersey State Police*

WebExtra 8.1

Practice Matching Bullets With the Aid of a 3-D Interactive Illustration
www.prenhall.com/saferstein

Comparing Bullet Markings   As the bullet passes through the barrel, its surface is impressed with the rifled markings of the barrel. The bullet emerges from the barrel carrying the impressions of the bore's interior surface (see Figure 8–9). Because there is no practical way to directly compare the markings on the fired bullet and those within a barrel, the examiner must obtain test bullets fired through the suspect barrel for comparison. To prevent damage to the test bullet's markings and to facilitate the bullet's recovery, test firings are normally made into a recovery box filled with cotton or into a water tank.

The number of lands and grooves, and their direction of twist, are obvious points of comparison during the initial stages of the examination. Any differences in these class characteristics immediately eliminate the possibility that both bullets traveled through the same barrel. A bullet with five lands and grooves could not possibly have been fired from a weapon of like caliber with six lands and grooves, nor could one having a right twist have come through a barrel impressed with a left twist. If both bullets carry the same class characteristics, the analyst must begin to match the striated markings on both bullets. This can be done only with the assistance of the comparison microscope.

Modern firearms identification began with the development and use of the comparison microscope. This instrument is the firearms examiner's most important tool. The test and evidence bullets are mounted on cylindrical adjustable holders beneath the objective lenses of the microscope,

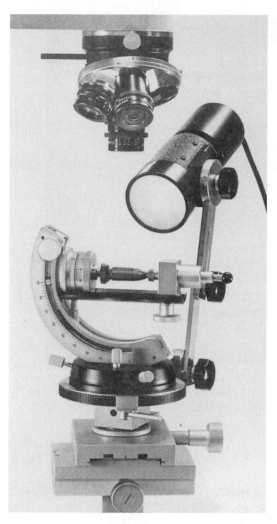

FIGURE 8–10   A bullet holder beneath the objective lens of a comparison microscope. *Courtesy Leica Microsystems, Buffalo, N.Y., www.leica-microsystems.com*

each pointing in the same direction (see Figure 8–10). Both bullets are observed simultaneously within the same field of view, and the examiner rotates one bullet until a well-defined land or groove comes into view.

Once the striation markings are located, the other bullet is rotated until a matching region is found. Not only must the lands and grooves of the test and evidence bullet have identical widths, but the longitudinal striations on each must coincide. When a matching area is located, the two bullets are simultaneously rotated to obtain additional matching areas around the periphery of the bullets. Figure 8–11 shows a typical photomicrograph of a bullet match as viewed under a comparison microscope.

Considerations in Bullet Comparison   Unfortunately, the firearms examiner rarely encounters a perfect match all around the bullet's periphery. The presence of grit and rust can alter the markings on bullets fired through the same barrel. More commonly, recovered evidence bullets become so mutilated and distorted on impact that they yield only a small area with intact markings.

Furthermore, striation markings on a barrel are not permanent structures; they are subject to continuing alteration through wear as succeeding bullets traverse the length of the barrel. Fortunately these changes are usually not dramatic and do not prevent the matching of two bullets fired by the same weapon. As with fingerprint comparison, there are no hard-and-fast rules governing the minimum number of points required for a

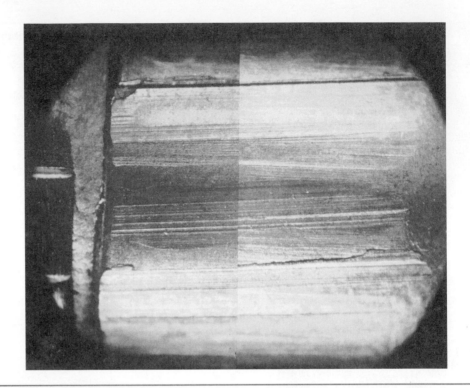

FIGURE 8–11 **A photomicrograph of two bullets through a comparison microscope. The test bullet is on the right; the questioned bullet is on the left.** *Courtesy Philadelphia Police Department Laboratory*

bullet comparison. The final opinion must be based on the judgment, experience, and knowledge of the expert.

Frequently, the firearms examiner receives a spent bullet without an accompanying suspect weapon and is asked to determine the caliber and possible make of the weapon. If a bullet appears not to have lost its metal, its weight may be one factor in determining its caliber. In some instances, the number of lands and grooves, the direction of twist, and the widths of lands and grooves are useful class characteristics for eliminating certain makes of weapons from consideration. For example, a bullet that has five lands and grooves and twists to the right could not have come from a weapon manufactured by Colt, because Colts are not manufactured with these class characteristics.

Sometimes a bullet has rifling marks that set it apart from most other manufactured weapons, as in the case of Marlin rifles. These weapons are rifled by a technique known as *microgrooving* and may have eight to twenty-four grooves impressed into their barrels; few other weapons are manufactured in this fashion. In this respect, the FBI maintains a record known as the General Rifling Characteristics File. This file contains listings of class characteristics, such as land and groove width dimensions, for known weapons. It is periodically updated and distributed to the law enforcement community to help identify rifled weapons from retrieved bullets.

Unlike rifled firearms, a shotgun has a smooth barrel, so projectiles passing through a shotgun barrel are not impressed with any characteristic markings that can later be related back to the weapon. Shotguns generally fire small lead balls or pellets contained within a shotgun shell (see Figure 8–12). A paper or plastic wad pushes the pellets through the barrel on ignition of the cartridge's powder charge. By weighing and measuring

Closer Analysis

The Comparison Microscope

Forensic microscopy often requires a side-by-side comparison of specimens. This kind of examination can best be performed with a comparison microscope, such as the one pictured in the figure.

Basically, the comparison microscope is two compound microscopes combined into one unit. The unique feature of its design is that it uses a bridge incorporating a series of mirrors and lenses to join two independent objective lenses into a single binocular unit. A viewer looking through the eyepiece lenses of the comparison microscope observes a circular field equally divided into two parts by a fine line. The specimen mounted under the left-hand objective appears in the left half of the field, and the specimen under the right-hand objective appears in the right half of the field. It is important to closely match the optical characteristics of the objective lenses to ensure that both specimens are seen at equal magnification and with minimal but identical lens distortions. Comparison microscopes designed to compare opaque objects, such as bullets and cartridges, are equipped with vertical or reflected illumination. Comparison microscopes used to compare hairs or fibers use transmitted illumination.

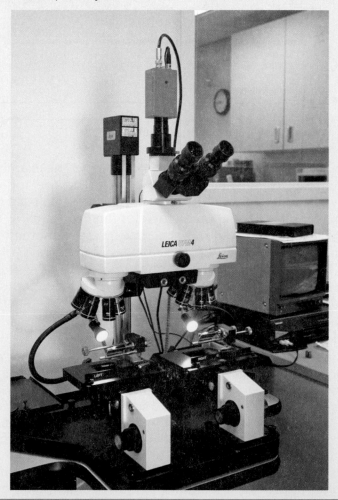

The comparison microscope – two independent objective lenses joined together by an optical bridge. *Courtesy Leica Microsystems*

(continued)

Closer Analysis *(Continued)*

Figure 8–11 shows the striation markings on two bullets that have been placed under the objective lenses of a comparison microscope. Modern firearms examination began with the introduction of the comparison microscope, with its ability to give the firearms examiner a side-by-side magnified view of bullets. Bullets that are fired through the same rifle barrel display comparable rifling markings on their surfaces. Matching the majority of striations present on each bullet justifies a conclusion that both bullets traveled through the same barrel.

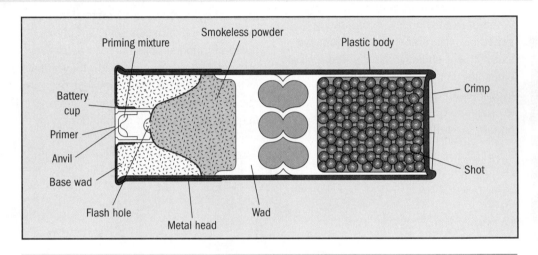

FIGURE 8–12   A cross-section of a loaded shotgun shell.

gauge

The size designation of a shotgun; originally the number of lead balls with the same diameter as the barrel that would make a pound. The only exception is the .410 shotgun, in which bore size is 0.41 inch.

WebExtra 8.2

3-D Shotgun Shell Illustrations
www.prenhall.com/saferstein

breechblock

The rear part of a firearm barrel.

WebExtra 8.3

3-D Revolver Cartridge Illustrations
www.prenhall.com/saferstein

WebExtra 8.4

3-D Pistol Cartridge Illustrations
www.prenhall.com/saferstein

the diameter of the shot recovered at a crime scene, the examiner can usually determine the size of shot used in the shell. The size and shape of the recovered wad may also reveal the gauge of the shotgun used and, in some instances, may indicate the manufacturer of the fired shell.

The diameter of the shotgun barrel is expressed by the term **gauge**.[1] The higher the gauge number, the smaller the barrel's diameter. For example, a 12-gauge shotgun has a bore diameter of 0.730 inch as contrasted to 0.670 inch for a 16-gauge shotgun. The exception to this rule is the .410-gauge shotgun, which refers to a barrel 0.41 inch in diameter.

Cartridge Cases

The act of pulling a trigger releases the weapon's firing pin, causing it to strike the primer, which in turn ignites the powder. The expanding gases generated by the burning gunpowder propel the bullet forward through the barrel, simultaneously pushing the spent cartridge case or shell back with equal force against the **breechblock**. As the bullet is marked by its passage through the barrel, the shell is also impressed with markings by its contact with the metal surfaces of the weapon's firing and loading mechanisms. As with bullets, these markings can be reproduced in test-fired cartridges to provide distinctive points of comparison for individualizing a spent shell to a rifled weapon or shotgun.

The shape of the firing pin is impressed into the relatively soft metal of the primer on the cartridge case, revealing the minute distortions of the firing pin. These imperfections may be sufficiently random to individualize

Case Study

Sacco and Vanzetti

Courtesy Corbis/Bettmann

In 1920, two security guards were viciously gunned down by unidentified assailants. The security guards were transporting shoe factory payroll, nearly $16,000 in cash, at the time of the robbery-murder. Eyewitnesses described the assailants as "Italian-looking," one with a full handlebar moustache. The robbers had used two firearms, leaving behind three different brands of shells.

Two suspects were identified and arrested—Nicola Sacco and his friend, the amply mustachioed Bartolomeo Vanzetti. After denying owning any firearms, each was found to be in possession of a loaded pistol. In fact, Sacco's pistol was .32 caliber, the same caliber as the crime-scene bullets. In Sacco's pockets were found twenty-three bullets matching the brands of the empty shells found at the murder scene.

This case coincided with the "Red Scare," a politically turbulent time in post–World War I America. Citizens feared socialist zealots, and the media played up these emotions. Political maneuvering and the use of the media muddied the waters surrounding the case, and the fact that

both suspects belonged to anarchist political groups that advocated revolutionary violence against the government only incited public animosity toward them. Sympathetic socialist organizations attempted to turn Sacco and Vanzetti into martyrs, calling their prosecution a "witch hunt."

The outcome of the trial ultimately depended on whether the prosecution could prove that Sacco's pistol fired the bullets that killed the two security guards. At trial, the ballistics experts testified that the bullets used were no longer in production and they could not find similar ammunition to use in test firings—aside from the unused cartridges found in Sacco's pockets. A forensics expert for the prosecution concluded that a visual examination showed that the bullets matched, leading the jury to return a verdict of guilty. Sacco and Vanzetti were sentenced to death.

Because of continued public protests, a committee was appointed in 1927 to review the case. Around this time, Calvin Goddard, at the Bureau of Forensic Ballistics in New York, perfected the comparison microscope for use in forensic firearms investigations. With this instrument, two bullets are viewed side by side to compare the striations imparted to a bullet's surface as it travels through the gun's barrel. The committee asked Goddard to examine the bullets in question. A test-fired bullet from Sacco's weapon was matched conclusively by Goddard to one of the crime-scene bullets. The fates of Sacco and Vanzetti were sealed, and they were put to death in 1927.

the pin impression to a single weapon. Similarly, the cartridge case, in its rearward thrust, is impressed with the surface markings of the breech-block. The breechblock, like any machined surface, is populated with random striation markings that become a highly distinctive signature for individualizing its surface.

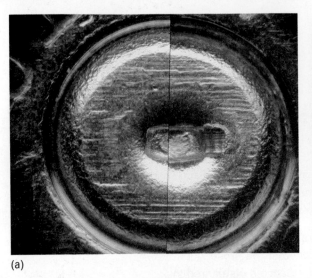 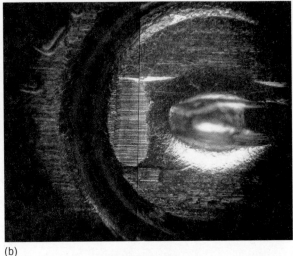

(a)   (b)

FIGURE 8–13   A comparison microscope photomicrograph showing a match between (a) firing pin impressions and (b) the breechblock markings on two shells. *Courtesy Ronald Welsh, Bureau of Forensic Services, Central Valley Laboratory, Ripon, Calif.*

extractor

The mechanism in a firearm that withdraws a cartridge or fired case from the chamber.

ejector

The mechanism in a firearm that throws the cartridge or fired case from the firearm.

WebExtra 8.5

3-D Rifle Cartridge Illustrations
www.prenhall.com/saferstein

WebExtra 8.6

View Animations to Illustrate the Firing Process and the Extraction/Ejection Process of a Semiautomatic Pistol
www.prenhall.com/saferstein

Other distinctive markings that may appear on the shell as a result of metal-to-metal contact are caused by the extractor and ejector mechanism and the magazine or clip, as well as by imperfections on the firing chamber walls. The photomicrographs in Figure 8–13 reveal a comparison of the firing pin and breechblock impressions on evidence and test-fired shells.

Firing pin, breechblock, extractor, and ejector marks may also be impressed onto the surface of the brass portion of shells fired by a shotgun. These impressions provide points for individualizing the shell to a weapon that are just as valuable as cartridge cases discharged from a rifled firearm. Furthermore, in the absence of a suspect weapon, the size and shape of a firing pin impression and/or the position of ejector marks in relationship to extractor and other markings may provide some clue to the type or make of the weapon that fired the questioned shell, or at least eliminate a large number of possibilities.

Key Points

- The manufacture of a gun barrel requires impressing its inner surface with spiral grooves, a step known as rifling. Rifling imparts spin to the projectile when it is fired, which keeps it on an accurate course.

- No two rifled barrels have identical striation markings. These striations form the individual characteristics of the barrel. The inner surface of the barrel of a gun leaves its striation markings on a bullet passing through it.

- The class characteristics of a rifled barrel include the number of lands and grooves and the width and direction of twist.

- The comparison microscope is a firearms examiner's most important tool because it allows two bullets to be compared simultaneously.

- The firing pin, breechblock, and ejector and extractor mechanism also offer a highly distinctive signature for individualization of cartridge cases.

- Unlike handguns, a shotgun is not rifled—it has a smooth barrel. Because of this, shotgun shells are not impressed with any characteristic markings that can be used to compare two shotgun shells to determine whether they were fired from the same weapon.

Automated Firearms Search Systems

The use of firearms, especially semiautomatic weapons, during the commission of a crime has significantly increased throughout the United States. Because of the expense of such firearms, the likelihood that a specific weapon will be used in multiple crimes has risen. The advent of computerized imaging technology has made possible the storage of bullet and cartridge surface characteristics in a manner analogous to the storage of automated fingerprint files. Using this concept, crime laboratories can be networked, allowing them to share information on bullets and cartridges retrieved from several jurisdictions.

Early Systems

The effort to build a national computerized database for firearms evidence in the United States had a rather confusing and inefficient start in the early 1990s. Two major federal law enforcement agencies, the FBI and the Bureau of Alcohol, Tobacco, Firearms and Explosives (ATF), offered the law enforcement community competing and incompatible computerized systems.

The automated search system developed for the FBI was known as *DRUGFIRE*. This system emphasized the examination of unique markings on the cartridge casings expended by the weapon. The specimen was analyzed through a microscope attached to a video camera. The magnification allowed for a close-up view to identify individual characteristics. The image was captured by a video camera, digitized, and stored in a database. Although DRUGFIRE emphasized cartridge-case imagery, the images of highly characteristic bullet striations could also be stored in a like manner for comparisons.

The *Integrated Ballistic Identification System (IBIS)*, developed for the Bureau of Alcohol, Tobacco, Firearms and Explosives, processed digital microscopic images of identifying features found on both expended bullets and cartridge casings. IBIS incorporated two software programs: Bulletproof, a bullet-analyzing module, and Brasscatcher, a cartridge-case-analyzing module. A schematic diagram of Bulletproof's operation is depicted in Figure 8–14.[2]

NIBIN In 1999, members of the FBI and ATF joined forces to introduce the *National Integrated Ballistics Information Network (NIBIN)* program to the discipline of firearms examination. The new unified system incorporates both DRUGFIRE and IBIS technologies available in prior years. ATF has overall responsibility for the system sites, while the FBI is responsible for the communications network.

Agencies using the new NIBIN technology produce database files from bullets and cartridge casings retrieved from crime scenes or test fires from retrieved firearms. More than two hundred law enforcement agencies worldwide have adapted to this technology. The success of the system has been proven with more than 800,000 images compiled; nationwide, law

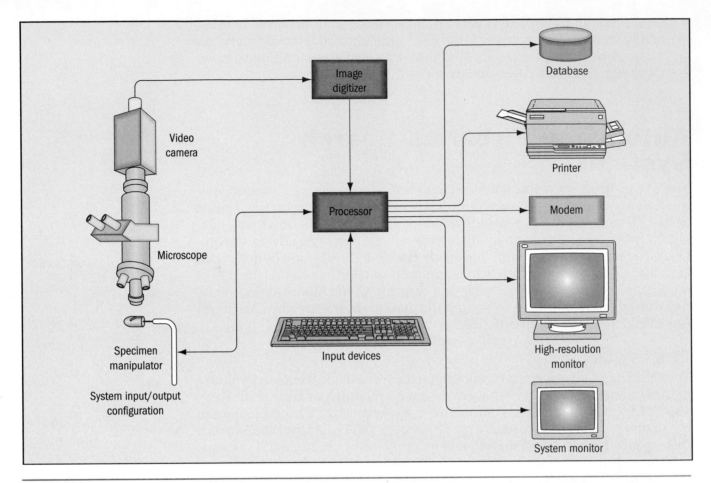

FIGURE 8–14 **Bulletproof configuration. The sample is mounted on the specimen manipulator and illuminated by the light source from a microscope. The image is captured by a video camera and digitized. This digital image is then stored in a database, available for retrieval and comparison. The search for a match includes analyzing the width of land and groove impressions along with both rifling and individual characteristics. The Brasscatcher software uses the same system configuration but emphasizes the analysis of expended cartridge casings rather than the expended bullets.** *Courtesy Forensic Technology (WAI) Inc., Côte St-Luc, Quebec, Canada*

enforcement agencies have connected more than 11,000 bullets and casings to more than one crime (see Figure 8–15).

For example, in a recent case, a Houston security guard was shot and killed during a botched armed robbery. A bullet and .40-caliber Smith & Wesson cartridge casing were recovered and imaged into NIBIN. Earlier that day, a robbery-turned-double-homicide left two store clerks dead. Again, two bullets and two .40-caliber Smith & Wesson cartridge casings were recovered. Once they were processed into NIBIN, a correlation was found between the murder of the security officer and a separate aggravated robbery that occurred two weeks earlier. All three crimes were linked with a firearm believed to be a .40-caliber Smith & Wesson pistol.

Further investigation into the use of a victim's credit card helped police locate two suspects. In the possession of one suspect was a .40-caliber Smith & Wesson pistol. The gun was test-fired and imaged into NIBIN. The casing from the test-fired weapon matched the evidence obtained in the robbery and the aggravated robbery-homicides. A firearms examiner verified the associations by traditional comparisons. Before this computerized technology was developed, it would have taken years, or may have been impossible, to link all of these shootings to a single firearm.

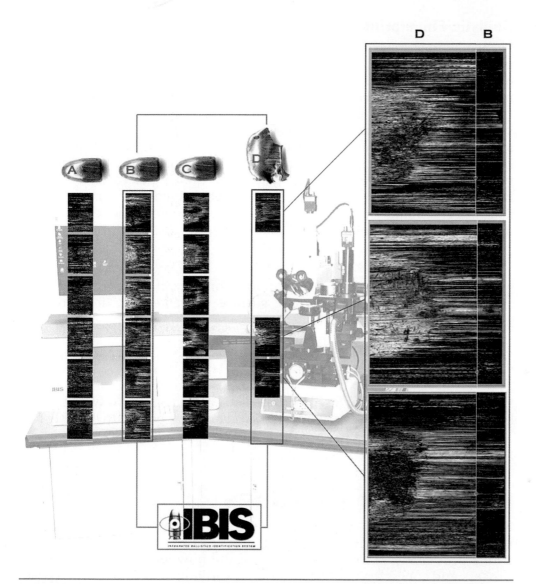

FIGURE 8–15 **Bullets A, B, C, and D were acquired in the IBIS database at different times from different crime scenes. D is a fragmented bullet that had only three land impressions available for acquisition. Upon the entry of bullet D, IBIS found a potential matching candidate in the database: B. On the far right, bullet D is compared to bullet B using the IBIS imaging software. Finally, a forensic firearms examiner using the actual evidence under a conventional comparison microscope will confirm the match between B and D.** *Courtesy Forensic Technology (WAI) Inc., Côte St-Luc, Quebec, Canada*

In another example, the ATF laboratory in Rockville, Maryland, received 1,466 cartridge casings from the Ovcara mass burial site in Bosnia. After processing and imaging profiles for all casings, the examiners determined that eighteen different firearms were used at the site. With the help of NIBIN technology and competent examiners, jurists attempted to convict an individual for war crimes.

NIBIN serves only as a screening tool for firearms evidence. A computerized system does not replace the skills of the firearms examiner. NIBIN can screen hundreds of unsolved firearms cases and may narrow the possibilities to several firearms. However, the final comparison will be made by a forensic examiner through traditional microscopic methods.

Ballistic Fingerprinting

Participating crime laboratories in the United States are building databases of bullet and cartridge cases found at crime scenes and those fired in tests of guns seized from criminals. As these databases come online and prove their usefulness in solving crimes, law enforcement officials and the political community are scrutinizing the feasibility of scaling this concept up to create a system of *ballistic fingerprinting*. This system would entail the capture and storage of appropriate markings on bullets and cartridges test-fired from handguns and rifles before they are sold to the public. Questions regarding who will be responsible for collecting the images and details of how will they be stored are but two of many issues to be determined. The concept of ballistic fingerprinting is an intriguing one for the law enforcement community and promises to be explored and debated intensely in the future.

Key Points

- The advent of computerized imaging technology has made possible the storage of bullet and cartridge surface characteristics in a manner analogous to automated fingerprint files.

- Two automated firearms search systems are DRUGFIRE, developed by the FBI, and IBIS, developed by the ATF.

- NIBIN is the National Integrated Ballistics Information Network, a unified firearms search system that incorporates both DRUGFIRE and IBIS technologies.

Gunpowder Residues

Modern ammunition is propelled toward a target by the expanding gases created by the ignition of smokeless powder or nitrocellulose in a cartridge. Under ideal circumstances, all of the powder is consumed in the process and converted into the rapidly expanding gases. However, in practice the powder is never totally burned. When a firearm is discharged, unburned and partially burned particles of gunpowder in addition to smoke are propelled out of the barrel along with the bullet toward the target. If the muzzle of the weapon is sufficiently close, these products are deposited onto the target. The distribution of gunpowder particles and other discharge residues around the bullet hole permits a distance determination, an assessment of the distance from which a handgun or rifle was fired.

distance determination
The process of determining the distance between the firearm and a target, usually based on the distribution of powder patterns or the spread of a shot pattern.

Distance Determination

In incidents involving gunshot wounds, it is often necessary to determine the distance from which the weapon was fired. For example, in incidents involving a shooting death, the suspect often pleads self-defense as the motive for the attack. Such claims are fertile grounds for distance determinations, because finding the proximity of the people involved is necessary to establish the facts of the incident. Similarly, careful examination of the wounds of suicide victims usually reveals characteristics associated with a very close-range gunshot wound. The absence of such characteristics strongly indicates that the wound was not self-inflicted and signals the possibility of foul play.

The accuracy of a distance determination varies according to the circumstances of the case. When the investigator is unable to recover a suspect weapon, the best the examiner can do is to state whether a shot could have been fired within some distance from the target. More exact opinions are possible only when the examiner has the suspect weapon in hand and knows the type of ammunition used in the shooting.

Handguns and Rifles   The precise distance from which a handgun or rifle has been fired must be determined by carefully comparing the powder residue pattern on the victim's clothing or skin to test patterns made when the suspect weapon is fired at varying distances from a target. A white cloth or a fabric comparable to the victim's clothing may be used as a test target (see Figure 8–16). Because the spread and density of the residue

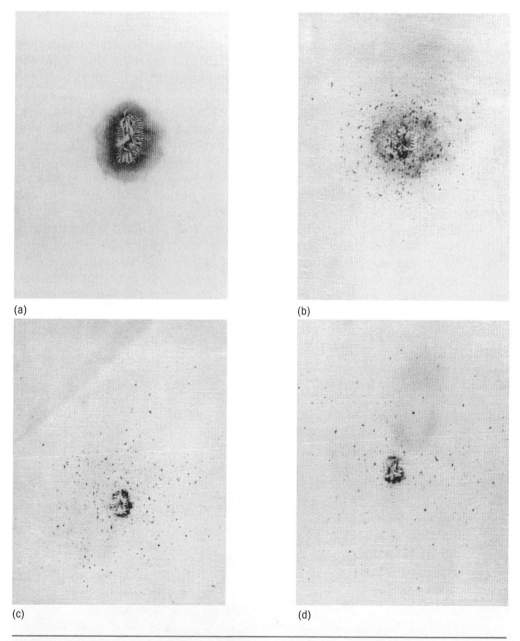

(a)

(b)

(c)

(d)

FIGURE 8–16   **Test powder patterns made with a .38 Special Smith & Wesson revolver fired at the following distances from the target: (a) contact, (b) 6 inches, (c) 12 inches, and (d) 18 inches.** *Courtesy New Jersey State Police*

pattern vary widely among weapons and ammunition, such a comparison is significant only when it is made with the suspect weapon and suspect ammunition, or with ammunition of the same type and make. By comparing the test and evidence patterns, the examiner may find enough similarity in shape and density on which to judge the distance from which the shot was fired.

Without the weapon, the examiner is restricted to looking for recognizable characteristics around the bullet hole. Such findings are at best approximations made as a result of general observations and the examiner's experience. However, some noticeable characteristics should be sought. For instance, when the weapon is held in contact with or less than 1 inch from the target, a heavy concentration of smokelike vaporous lead usually surrounds the bullet entrance hole. Often loose fibers surrounding a contact hole show scorch marks from the flame discharge of the weapon, and some synthetic fibers may show signs of being melted as a result of the heat from the discharge. Furthermore, the blowback of muzzle gases may produce a stellate (star-shape) tear pattern around the hole. Such a hole is invariably surrounded by a rim of a smokelike deposit of vaporous lead (see Figure 8–17).

A halo of vaporous lead (smoke) deposited around a bullet hole normally indicates a discharge 12 to 18 inches or less from the target. The presence of scattered specks of unburned and partially burned powder grains without any accompanying soot can often be observed at distances up to approximately 25 inches. Occasionally, however, scattered gunpowder particles are noted at a firing distance as far out as 36 inches. With ball powder ammunition, this distance may be extended to 8 feet.

Finally, a weapon that has been fired more than 3 feet from a target usually does not deposit any powder residues on the target's surface. In these cases, the only visual indication that the hole was made by a bullet is a dark ring, known as *bullet wipe,* around the perimeter of the entrance hole. Bullet wipe consists of a mixture of carbon, dirt, lubricant, primer residue, and

FIGURE 8–17   A contact shot. *Courtesy New Jersey State Police*

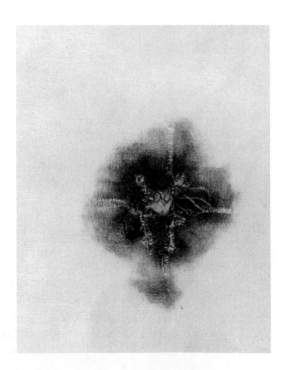

lead wiped off the bullet's surface as it passes through the target. Again, in the absence of a suspect weapon, these observations are general guidelines for estimating target distances. Numerous factors—barrel length, caliber, type of ammunition, and type and condition of the weapon fired—influence the amount of gunpowder residue deposited on a target.

Shotguns The determination of firing distances involving shotguns must also be related to test firings performed with the suspect weapon, using the same type of ammunition known to be used in the crime. In the absence of a weapon, the muzzle-to-target distance can be estimated by measuring the spread of the discharged shot. With close-range shots varying in distance up to 5 feet, the shot charge enters the target as a concentrated mass, producing a hole somewhat larger than the bore of the barrel. As the distance increases, the pellets progressively separate and spread out. Generally speaking, the spread in the pattern made by a 12-gauge shotgun increases 1 inch for each yard of distance. Thus, a 10-inch pattern would be produced at approximately 10 yards. Of course, this is only a rule of thumb; normally, many variables can affect the shot pattern.

Other factors include the barrel length, the size and quantity of the pellets fired, the quantity of powder charge used to propel the pellets, and the choke of the gun under examination. Choke is the degree of constriction placed at the muzzle end of the barrel. The greater the choke, the narrower the shotgun pattern and the faster and farther the pellets will travel.

choke
An interior constriction placed at or near the muzzle end of a shotgun's barrel to control shot dispersion.

Powder Residues on Garments

When garments or other evidence relevant to a shooting are received in the crime laboratory, the surfaces of all items are first examined microscopically for gunpowder residue. These particles may be identifiable by their characteristic colors, sizes, and shapes. However, the absence of visual indications does not preclude the possibility that gunpowder residue is present. Sometimes the lack of color contrast between the powder and garment or the presence of heavily encrusted deposits of blood can obscure the visual detection of gunpowder. Often, an infrared photograph of the suspect area overcomes the problem. Such a photograph may enhance the contrast, thus revealing vaporous lead and powder particles deposited around the hole (see Figure 8–18). In other situations, this may not help, and the analyst must use chemical tests to detect gunpowder residues.

Nitrites are one type of chemical product that results from the incomplete combustion of smokeless (nitrocellulose) powder. One test method for locating powder residues involves transferring particles embedded on the target surface to chemically treated gelatin-coated photographic paper. This procedure is known as the Greiss test. The examiner presses the photographic paper onto the target with a hot iron; once the nitrite particles are on the paper, they are made easily visible by chemical treatment.[3] In addition, comparing the developed nitrite pattern to nitrite patterns obtained from test firings at known distances can be useful in determining the shooting distance from the target. A second chemical test is then performed to detect any trace of lead residue around the bullet hole. The questioned surface is sprayed with a solution of sodium rhodizonate, followed by a series of oversprays with acid solutions. This treatment turns lead particles pink, followed by blue-violet.

Greiss test
A chemical test used to examine patterns of gunpowder residues around bullet holes.

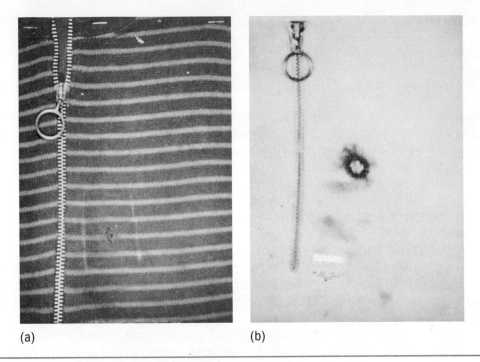

(a)   (b)

FIGURE 8–18   **(a) A shirt bearing a powder stain, photographed under normal light. (b) An infrared photograph of the same shirt.** *Courtesy New Jersey State Police*

Key Points

- The distribution of gunpowder particles and other discharge residues around a bullet hole permits an assessment of the distance from which a handgun or rifle was fired.

- The precise distance from which a handgun or rifle was fired is determined by carefully comparing the powder residue pattern on the victim's clothing to test patterns made when the suspect weapon is fired at varying distances from a target.

- The Greiss test is a chemical test used to examine patterns of gunpowder residues around bullet holes. It tests for the presence of nitrates.

Primer Residues on the Hands

The firing of a weapon not only propels residues toward the target, but also blows gunpowder and primer residues back toward the shooter (see Figure 8–19). As a result, traces of these residues are often deposited on the firing hand of the shooter, and their detection can provide valuable information as to whether an individual has recently fired a weapon.

Detecting Primer Residues

Early efforts at demonstrating powder residues on the hands centered on chemical tests that could detect unburned gunpowder or nitrates. For many years, the *dermal nitrate test* was popular. It required the application of hot paraffin or wax to the suspect's hand with a paintbrush. After drying into a solid crust, the paraffin was removed and tested with diphenylamine. A blue

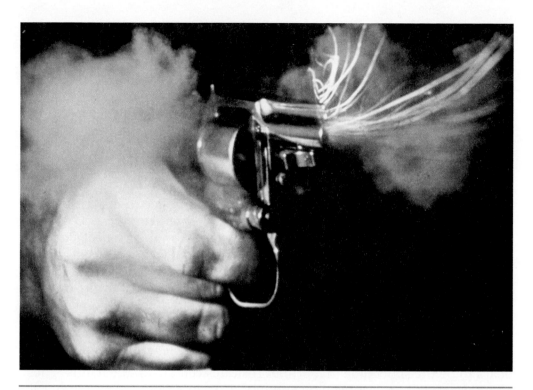

FIGURE 8–19 **When a handgun is fired, gunpowder and primer residues are normally blown back toward the hand of the shooter.** *Courtesy Centre of Forensic Sciences, Toronto, Canada*

color indicated a positive reaction for nitrates. However, the dermal nitrate test has fallen into disfavor with law enforcement agencies, owing mainly to its lack of specificity. Common materials such as fertilizers, cosmetics, urine, and tobacco all give positive reactions that are indistinguishable from that obtained for gunpowder by this test.

Efforts to identify a shooter now center on the detection of primer residues deposited on the hand of a shooter at the time of firing. With the exception of most .22-caliber ammunition, primers currently manufactured contain a blend of lead styphnate, barium nitrate, and antimony sulfide. Residues from these materials are most likely to be deposited on the thumb web and the back of the firing hand of a shooter, because these areas are closest to gases escaping along the side or back of the gun during discharge. In addition, individuals who handle a gun without firing it may have primer residues deposited on the palm of the hand coming in contact with the weapon.

However, with the handling of a used firearm, the passage of time, and the resumption of normal activities following a shooting, gunshot residues from the back of the hand are frequently redistributed to other areas, including the palms. Therefore, it is not unusual to find higher levels of barium and antimony on the palms than on the backs of the hands of known shooters. Another possibility is the deposition of significant levels of barium and antimony on the hands of an individual who is near a firearm when it is discharged.

Tests for Primer Residues

The determination of whether a person has fired or handled a weapon or has been near a discharged firearm is normally made by measuring the presence and possibly the amount of barium and antimony on the relevant portions of the suspect's hands. A variety of materials and techniques are used for removing these residues. The most popular approach, and certainly the most convenient for the field investigator, is to apply an adhesive tape or adhesive to the hand's surface to remove any adhering residue particles.

Swabbing   Another approach is to remove any residues present by swabbing both the firing and nonfiring hands with cotton that has been moistened with 5 percent nitric acid. The front and back of each hand are swabbed separately. All four swabs, along with a moistened control, are then forwarded to the crime laboratory for analysis.

In any case, once the hands are treated for the collection of barium and antimony, the collection medium must be analyzed for the presence of these elements. High barium and antimony levels on the suspect's hand(s) strongly indicate that the person fired or handled a weapon or was near a firearm when it was discharged. Because these elements are normally present in small quantities (less than 10 micrograms) after a firing, only the most sensitive analytical techniques can be used to detect them.

Unfortunately, even though most specimens submitted for this type of analysis have been from individuals strongly suspected of having fired a gun, there has been a low rate of positive findings. The major difficulty appears to be the short time that primer residues remain on the hands. These residues are readily removed by intentional or unintentional washing, rubbing, or wiping of the hands. In fact, one study demonstrated that it is very difficult to detect primer residues on cotton hand swabs taken as soon as two hours after firing a weapon.[4] Hence, some laboratories do not accept cotton hand swabs taken from living people six or more hours after a firing has occurred.

In cases that involve suicide victims, a higher rate of positives for the presence of gunshot residue is obtained when the hand swabbing is conducted before the person's body is moved or when the hands are protected by paper bags.[5] However, hand swabbing or the application of an adhesive cannot be used to detect firings with most .22-caliber rim-fire ammunition. Such ammunition may contain only barium or neither barium nor antimony in its primer composition.

SEM Testing   Most laboratories that can detect gunshot residue require application of an adhesive to the shooter's hands.[6] Microscopic primer and gunpowder particles on the adhesive are then found with a scanning electron microscope (SEM). The characteristic size and shape of these particles distinguishes them from other contaminants on the hands (see Figure 8–20). When the SEM is linked to an X-ray analyzer, an elemental analysis of the particles can be conducted. A finding of a select combination of elements (lead, barium, and antimony) confirms that the particles were indeed primer residue (see Figure 8–21).

The major advantage of the SEM approach for primer residue detection is its enhanced specificity over hand swabbing. The SEM characterizes primer particles by their size and shape as well as by their chemical composition. Unfortunately, the excessive operator time required to find and characterize gunshot residue has deterred this technique's use. The availability of automated particle search and identification systems for use with scanning electron microscopes may overcome this problem. Results of work performed with automated systems show it to be significantly faster than a manual approach for finding gunshot residue particles.[7] Appendix II contains a detailed description of primer residue collection procedures.

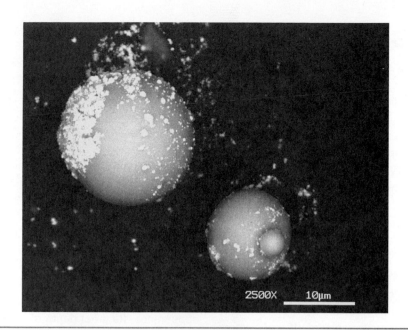

FIGURE 8–20   An SEM view of gunshot residue particles. *Courtesy Jeol USA Inc., Peabody, Mass., www.jeolusa.com*

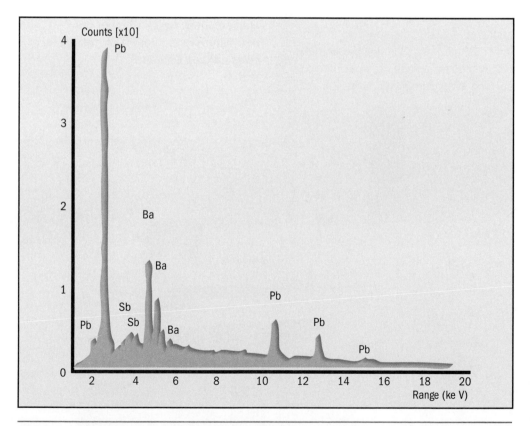

FIGURE 8–21   A spectrum showing the presence of lead, barium, and antimony in gunshot residue. *Courtesy Jeol USA Inc., Peabody, Mass., www.jeolusa.com*

Closer Analysis

The Scanning Electron Microscope (SEM)

The scanning electron microscope (SEM) creates an image by aiming a beam of electrons onto a specimen and studying electron emissions from the specimen on a closed TV circuit (see Figure 1). This is accomplished by directing electrons emitted by a hot tungsten filament with the aid of electromagnetic focusing onto the surface of the specimen. This primary electron beam causes the elements that make up the upper layers of the specimen to emit electrons known as secondary electrons. About 20 to 30 percent of the primary electrons rebound off the surface of the specimen. These electrons are known as *backscattered electrons*. The emitted electrons (both secondary and backscattered) are collected, and the amplified signal is displayed on a cathode-ray or TV tube. By scanning the primary electron beam across the specimen's surface in synchronization with the cathode-ray tube, the SEM converts the emitted electrons into an image of the specimen for display on the cathode-ray tube.

The major attractions of the SEM image are its high magnification, high resolution, and great depth of focus. In its usual mode, the SEM has a magnification that ranges from 10× to 100,000×. Its depth of focus is 300 times better than optical systems at similar magnifications, and the resultant picture is almost stereoscopic in appearance. Its great depth of field and magnification are exemplified by the magnification of cystolithic hair on the marijuana leaf, as shown in Figure 2. An SEM image of a vehicle's headlight filaments may reveal whether the headlights were on or off at the time of a collision (see Figures 3 and 4).

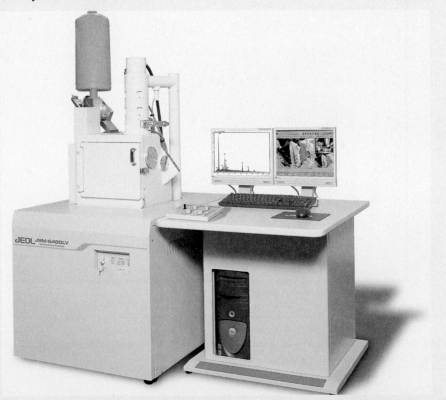

FIGURE 1 A scanning electron microscope. *Courtesy Jeol USA Inc., Peabody, Mass., www.jeolusa.com*

Closer Analysis

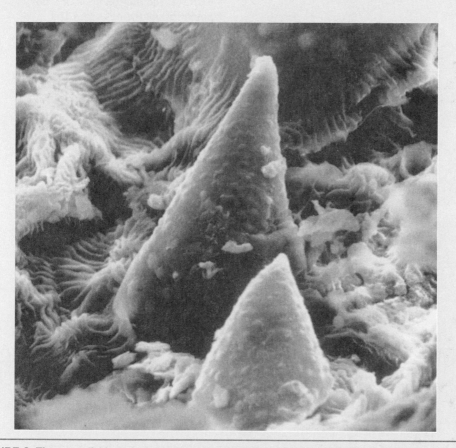

FIGURE 2 The cystolithic hairs of the marijuana leaf, as viewed with a scanning electron microscope (800x). *Courtesy Jeff Albright*

Another facet of scanning electron microscopy has been the use of X-ray production to determine the elemental composition of a specimen. X-rays are generated when the electron beam of the scanning electron microscope strikes a target. When the SEM is coupled to an X-ray analyzer, the emitted X-rays can be sorted according to their energy values and used to build a picture of the elemental distribution in the specimen. Because each element emits X-rays of characteristic energy values, the X-ray analyzer can identify the elements present in a specimen. Furthermore, the elemental concentration can be determined by measuring the intensity of the X-ray emission.

As shown in Figure 5, when a sample of gunshot residue collected off the hands of a suspect shooter is exposed to a beam of electrons from the scanning electron microscope, X-rays are emitted. These X-rays are passed into a detector, where they are converted into electrical signals. These signals are sorted and displayed according to the energies of the emitted X-rays. Through the use of this technique, the elements lead, antimony, and barium, frequently found in most primers, can be rapidly detected and identified.

(Continued)

Closer Analysis

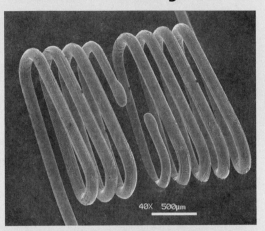

FIGURE 3 **The melted ends of a hot filament break indicate that the headlights were on when an accident occurred.** *Courtesy Jeol USA Inc., Peabody, Mass., www.jeolusa.com*

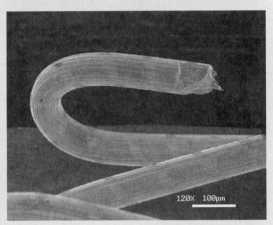

FIGURE 4 **The sharp ends of a cold filament break indicate that the headlights were off when an accident occurred.** *Courtesy Jeol USA Inc., Peabody, Mass., www.jeolusa.com*

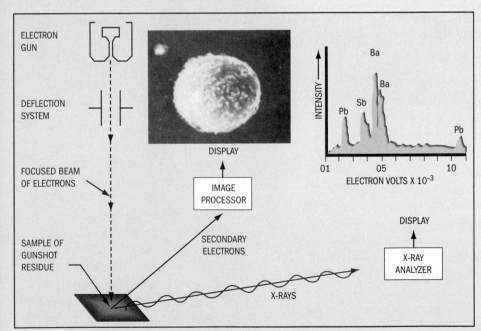

FIGURE 5 **A schematic diagram of a scanning electron microscope displaying the image of a gunshot residue particle. Simultaneously, an X-ray analyzer detects and displays X-ray emissions from the elements lead (Pb), antimony (Sb), and barium (Ba) present in the particle.** *Courtesy Aerospace Corp., El Segundo, Calif.*

Key Points

- Firing a weapon propels residues toward the target and blows gunpowder and primer residues back toward the shooter. Traces of these residues are often deposited on the firing hand of the shooter, providing valuable information as to whether an individual has recently fired a weapon.

- Examiners measure the amount of barium and antimony on the relevant portion of the suspect's hands or characterize the morphology of particles containing these elements to determine whether a person has fired or handled a weapon or was near a discharged firearm.

Serial Number Restoration

Today, many manufactured items, including automobile engine blocks and firearms, are impressed with serial numbers for identification. Increasingly, the criminalist must restore such numbers when they have been removed or obliterated by grinding, rifling, or punching.

Serial numbers are usually stamped on a metal body or frame, or on a plate, with hard steel dies. These dies strike the metal surface with a force that allows each digit to sink into the metal at a prescribed depth. Serial numbers can be restored because the metal crystals in the stamped zone are placed under a permanent strain that extends a short distance beneath the original numbers. When a suitable etching agent is applied, the strained area dissolves faster than the unaltered metal, thus revealing the etched pattern in the form of the original numbers. However, if the zone of strain has been removed, or if the area has been impressed with a different strain pattern, the number usually cannot be restored.

Before any treatment with the etching reagent, the obliterated surface must be thoroughly cleaned of dirt and oil and polished to a mirrorlike finish. The reagent is swabbed onto the surface with a cotton ball. The choice of etching reagent depends on the type of metal surface being worked on. A solution of hydrochloric acid (120 milliliters), copper chloride (90 grams), and water (100 milliliters) generally works well for steel surfaces.

Collection and Preservation of Firearms Evidence

Firearms

The Hollywood technique of picking up a weapon by its barrel with a pencil or stick in order to protect fingerprints must be avoided. This practice only disturbs powder deposits, rust, or dirt lodged in the barrel, and consequently may alter the striation markings on test-fired bullets. If recovery of latent fingerprints is a primary concern, the investigator should hold the weapon by the edge of the trigger guard or by the checkered portion of the grip, which usually does not retain identifiable fingerprints.

The most important consideration in handling a weapon is safety. Before any weapon is sent to the laboratory, all precautions must be taken to prevent an accidental discharge of a loaded weapon in transit. In most cases, it will be necessary to unload the weapon. If this is done, a record should first be made of the weapon's hammer and safety position; likewise, the location of all fired and unfired ammunition in the weapon must be recorded.

When a revolver is recovered, the chamber position in line with the barrel should be indicated by a scratch mark on the cylinder. Each chamber is designated with a number on a diagram, and as each cartridge or casing is removed, it should be marked to correspond to the numbered chambers in the diagram. Knowledge of the cylinder position of a cartridge casing may be useful for later determination of the sequence of events, particularly in shooting cases, when more than one shot was fired. Each round should be placed in a separate box or envelope. If the weapon is an automatic, the magazine must be removed and checked for prints and the chamber then emptied.

As with any other type of physical evidence recovered at a crime scene, firearms evidence must be marked for identification and a chain of custody must be established. Therefore, when a firearm is recovered, an identification tag should be attached to the trigger guard. The tag should be marked to show appropriate identifying data, including the weapon's serial number, make, and model and the investigator's initials. The firearm itself may be further identified by being marked directly with a sharp-pointed scriber in an inconspicuous area of the weapon—for example, the inside of the trigger guard. This practice will avoid any permanent defacement of the weapon.

When a weapon is recovered from an underwater location, no effort should be made to dry or clean it. Instead, the firearm should be transported to the laboratory in a receptacle containing enough of the same water necessary to keep it submerged. This procedure prevents rust from developing during transport.

Ammunition

The protection of class and individual markings on bullets and cartridge cases must be the primary concern of the field investigator. Thus, extreme caution is needed when removing a lodged bullet from a wall or other object. If the bullet's surface is accidentally scratched during this operation, valuable striation markings could be obliterated. It is best to free bullets from their target by carefully breaking away the surrounding support material while avoiding direct contact with the projectile.

Bullets recovered at the crime scene should be scribed with the investigator's initials, on either the base or the nose of the bullet (see Figure 8–22). Again, obliteration of any striation markings on the bullet must be scrupulously avoided. If the bullet is badly deformed and there is no apparent place for identification, it should just be placed in a container that is appropriately marked for identification. In any case, the investigator must protect the bullet by wrapping it in tissue paper before placing it in a pillbox or an envelope for shipment to the crime laboratory.

Minute traces of evidence such as paint and fibers may be adhering to the bullet; the investigator must take care to leave these trace materials intact. Similarly, a fired casing must be identified so as to avoid destroying marks impressed on it from the weapon. The investigator's initials should be placed near the outside or inside mouth of the shell (see Figure 8–23). Discharged shells from shotguns are initialed with ink or indelible pencil on the paper or plastic tube remaining on the shell or on the metal nearest the mouth of the shell. In incidents involving shotguns, any wads recovered should also be packaged and sent to the laboratory. An examination of the size and composition of the wad may

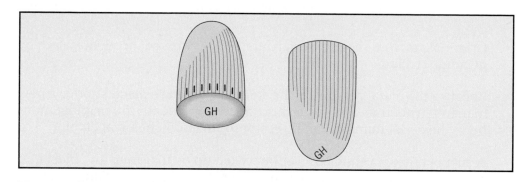

FIGURE 8–22 Discharged evidence bullets should be marked on the base or nose. When there is more than one bullet, a number should accompany the initials. *Never* mark bullets on the side.

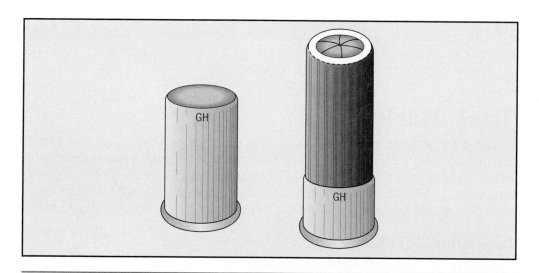

FIGURE 8–23 Discharged evidence shells should be marked on the outside or inside, as close as possible to the mouth of the shell. Discharged shotgun shells should be marked on the brass, close to the paper or plastic. *Never* mark the shells where the firing pin strikes the primer.

reveal information about the type of ammunition used and the gauge of the shotgun.

When semiautomatic or automatic weapons have been fired, the ejection pattern of the casings can help establish the relationship of the suspect to the victim. For this reason, the investigator must note the exact location where a shell casing was recovered.

Gunpowder Deposits

The clothing of a firearms victim must be carefully preserved to prevent damage or disruption to powder residues deposited around a bullet or shell hole. Cutting or tearing of clothing in the area of the holes must be avoided when removing the clothing. All wet clothing should be air-dried out of direct sunlight and then folded carefully so as not to disrupt the area around the bullet hole. Each item should be placed in a separate paper bag.

Key Points

- Criminalists can restore serial numbers removed or obliterated by grinding, rifling, or punching.

- Because the metal crystals in the stamped zone are placed under a permanent strain that extends a short distance beneath the original numbers, the serial number can be restored through chemical etching.

- A suspect firearm should never be picked up by inserting an object into its barrel because this practice may alter the striation markings on test-fired bullets.

- Before unloading a suspect weapon, the weapon's hammer and safety position should be recorded, as well as the location of all fired and unfired ammunition in the weapon.

- The protection of class and individual markings on bullets and cartridge cases is the primary concern of the field investigator when recovering bullets and cartridge casings.

Tool Marks

A *tool mark* is any impression, cut, gouge, or abrasion caused by a tool coming into contact with another object. Most often, tool marks are encountered at burglary scenes that involve forcible entry into a building or safe. Generally, these marks occur as indented impressions into a softer surface or as abrasion marks caused by the tool cutting or sliding against another object.

Comparing Tool Marks

Typically, an indented impression is left on the frame of a door or window as a result of the prying action of a screwdriver or crowbar. Careful examination of these impressions can reveal important class characteristics—that is, the size and shape of the tool. However, they rarely reveal any significant individual characteristics that could permit the examiner to individualize the mark to a single tool. Such characteristics, when they do exist, usually take the form of discernible random nicks and breaks that the tool has acquired through wear and use (Figure 8–24).

Just as the machined surfaces of a firearm are impressed with random striations during its manufacture, the edges of a pry bar, chisel, screwdriver, knife, or cutting tool likewise display a series of microscopic irregularities that look like ridges and valleys. Such markings are left as a result of the machining processes used to cut and finish tools. The shape and pattern of such minute imperfections are further modified by damage and wear during the life of the tool. Considering the variety of patterns that the hills and valleys can assume, it is highly unlikely that any two tools will be identical. Hence, these minute imperfections impart individuality to each tool.

If the edge of a tool is scraped against a softer surface, it may cut a series of striated lines that reflect the pattern of the tool's edge. Markings left in this manner are compared in the laboratory through a comparison microscope with test tool marks made from the suspect tool. The result can be a positive comparison, and hence a definitive association of the tool with the evidence mark, when a sufficient quantity of striations match between the evidence and test markings.

FIGURE 8–24 A comparison of a tool mark with a suspect screwdriver. Note how the presence of nicks and breaks on the tool's edge helps individualize the tool to the mark. *Courtesy New Jersey State Police*

A major problem of tool mark comparisons is the difficulty in duplicating in the laboratory the tool mark left at the crime scene. A thorough comparison requires preparing a series of test marks by applying the suspect tool at various angles and pressures to a soft metal surface (lead is commonly used). This approach gives the examiner ample opportunity to duplicate many of the details of the original evidence marking. A photomicrograph of a typical tool mark comparison is illustrated in Figure 8–25.

Collecting Tool Mark Evidence

Whenever practical, the entire object or the part of the object bearing a tool mark should be submitted to the crime laboratory for examination. When removal of the tool mark is impractical, the only recourse is to photograph the marked area to scale and make a cast of the mark. Liquid silicone casting material is best for reproducing most of the fine details of the mark (see Figure 8–26). However, even under the best conditions, the clarity of many of the tool mark's minute details will be lost or obscured in a photograph or cast. Of course, this will reduce the chance of individualizing the mark to a single tool.

The crime-scene investigator must never attempt to fit the suspect tool into the tool mark. Any contact between the tool and the marked surface may alter the mark and will, at the least, raise serious questions about the integrity of the evidence. The suspect tool and mark must be packaged in separate containers, with every precaution taken to avoid contact between the tool or mark and another hard surface. Failure to protect the tool or mark from damage could result in the destruction of its individual characteristics.

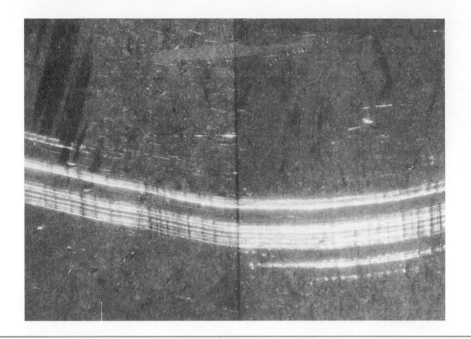

FIGURE 8–25 **A photograph of a tool mark comparison seen under a comparison microscope.** *Courtesy Leica Microsystems, Buffalo, N.Y., www.leica-microsystems.com*

(a)   (b)

FIGURE 8–26 **(a) Casting a tool mark impression with a silicone-based putty. (b) An impression alongside a suspect tool.** *Courtesy Sirchie Finger Print Laboratories, Inc., Youngsville, N.C., www.sirchie.com*

Furthermore, the tool or its impression may contain valuable trace evidence. Chips of paint adhering to the mark or tool provide perhaps the best example of how the transfer of trace physical evidence can occur as a result of using a tool to gain forcible entry into a building. Obviously, the presence of trace evidence greatly enhances the evidential value of the tool or its mark. Such evidence requires special care in handling and packaging to avoid loss or destruction.

Key Points

- The presence of minute imperfections on a tool imparts individuality to that tool. The shape and pattern of such imperfections are further modified by damage and wear during the life of the tool.

- The comparison microscope is used to compare crime-scene tool marks with test impressions made with the suspect tool.

Other Impressions

From time to time, other types of impressions are left at a crime scene. This evidence may take the form of a shoe, tire, or fabric impression. It may be as varied as a shoe impression left on a piece of paper at the scene of a burglary (Figure 8–27), a hit-and-run victim's garment that has come into violent contact with an automobile (Figure 8–28), or the impression of a bloody shoe print left on a floor or carpet at a homicide scene (Figure 8–29).

Preserving Impressions

The primary consideration in collecting impressions at the crime scene is the preservation of the impression or its reproduction for later examination in the crime laboratory. Before any impression is moved or otherwise handled, it must be photographed (a scale should be included in the picture) to show all the observable details of the impression. Several shots should be taken directly over the impression as well as at various angles around the impression. Skillful use of side lighting for illumination will help highlight many ridge details that might otherwise remain obscured.

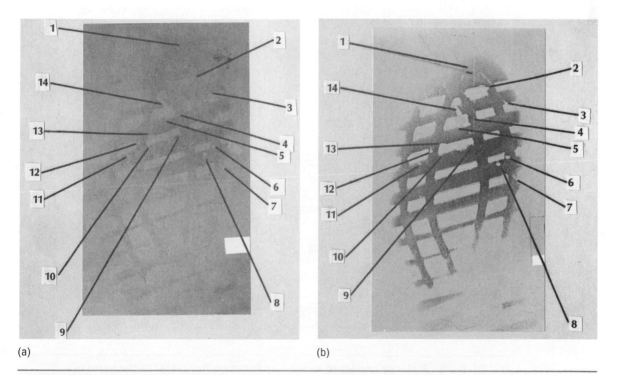

(a) (b)

FIGURE 8–27 **(a) An impression of a shoe found at a crime scene. (b) A test impression made with a suspect shoe. A sufficient number of points of comparison exist to support the conclusion that the suspect shoe left the impression at the crime scene.** *Courtesy New Jersey State Police*

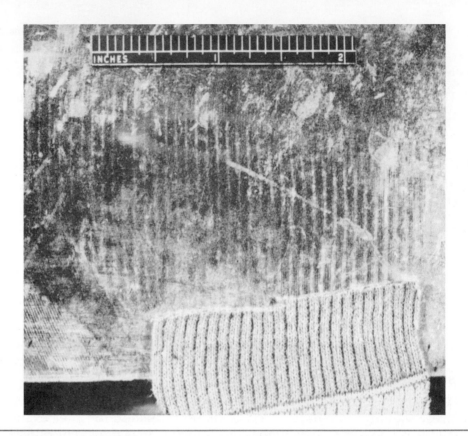

FIGURE 8–28 A small child was found dead at the edge of a rural road near a railroad crossing, the victim of a hit-and-run driver. A local resident was suspected, but he denied any knowledge of the incident. The investigating officer noted what appeared to be a fabric imprint on the bumper of the suspect's automobile. The weave pattern of the clothing of the deceased was compared with the imprint on the bumper and was found to match. When the suspect was confronted with this information, he admitted his guilt. *Courtesy Centre for Forensic Sciences, Toronto. Canada*

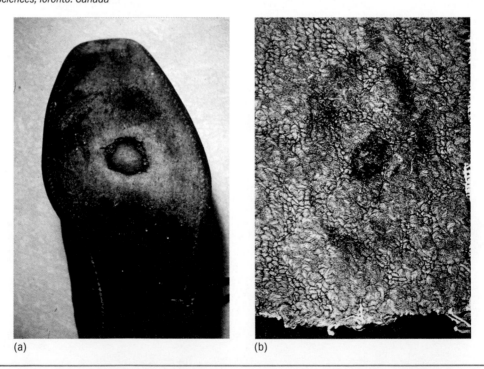

(a)   (b)

FIGURE 8–29 A bloody imprint of a shoe was found on the carpet in the home of a homicide victim. (b) The suspect's shoe, shown in (a), made the impression. Note the distinctive impression of the hole present in the shoe's sole. *Courtesy Dade County Crime Lab, Miami, Fla.*

Photographs should also be taken to show the position of the questioned impression in relation to the overall crime scene.

Although photography is an important first step in preserving an impression, it must be considered merely a backup procedure that is available to the examiner if the impression is damaged before reaching the crime laboratory. Naturally, the examiner prefers to receive the original impression for comparison to the suspect shoe, tire, garment, and so forth. In most cases when the impression is on a readily recoverable item, such as glass, paper, or floor tile, the evidence is easily transported intact to the laboratory.

Lifting Impressions

If an impression is encountered on a surface that cannot be submitted to the laboratory, the investigator may be able to preserve the print in a manner that is analogous to lifting a fingerprint. This is especially true of impressions made in light deposits of dust or dirt. A lifting material large enough to lift the entire impression should be used. Carefully place the lifting material over the entire impression. Use a fingerprint roller to eliminate any air pockets before lifting the impression off the surface.

A more exotic approach to lifting and preserving dust impressions involves the use of a portable electrostatic lifting device.[8] The principle is similar to that of creating an electrostatic charge on a comb and using the comb to lift small pieces of tissue paper. A sheet of mylar film is placed on top of the dust mark, and the film is pressed against the impression with the aid of a roller. The high-voltage electrode of the electrostatic unit is then placed in contact with the film while the unit's earth electrodes are placed against a metal plate (earth plate; see Figure 8–30). A charge difference develops between the mylar film and the surface below the dust mark so that the dust is attached to the lifting film. In this manner, dust prints on chairs, walls, floors, and the like can be transferred to the mylar film. Floor surfaces up to 40 feet long can be covered with a mylar sheet and searched for dust impressions. The electrostatic lifting technique is particularly helpful in recovering barely visible dust prints on colored

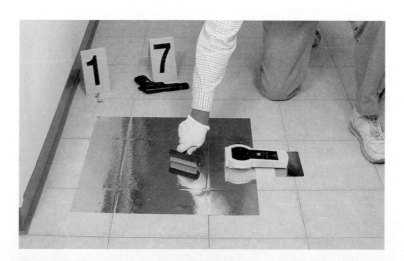

FIGURE 8–30 **Electrostatic lifting of a dust impression off a floor using an electrostatic unit.** *Courtesy Sirchie Finger Print Laboratories, Inc., Youngsville, N.C., www.sirchie.com*

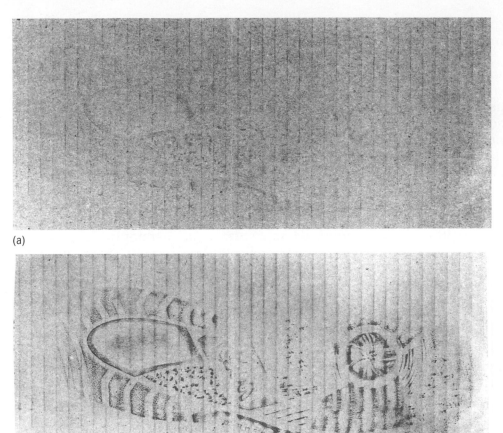

(a)

(b)

FIGURE 8–31 **(a) A dust impression of a shoe print on cardboard before enhancement. (b) A shoe print after chemical enhancement with Bromophenol Blue and exposure to water vapor.** *Courtesy Division of Identification and Forensic Science, Israel Police Headquarters, Jerusalem, Israel*

surfaces. Dust impressions can also be enhanced through chemical development (see Figure 8–31).[9]

Casting Impressions

Shoe and tire marks impressed into soft earth at a crime scene are best preserved by photography and casting.[10] Class I dental stone, a form of gypsum, is widely recommended for making casts of shoe and tire impressions. A series of photographs clearly illustrating the steps in casting an impression may be found at www.sccja.org/csr-cast.htm. The cast should be allowed to air-dry for twenty-four to forty-eight hours before it is shipped to the forensic science laboratory for examination. Figure 8–32 illustrates a cast made from a shoe print in mud. The cast compares to the suspect shoe.

An aerosol product known as Snow Impression Wax is available for casting snow impressions.[11] The recommended procedure is to spray three light coats of the wax at an interval of one to two minutes between layers, and then let it dry for ten minutes. A viscous mixture of Class I dental stone

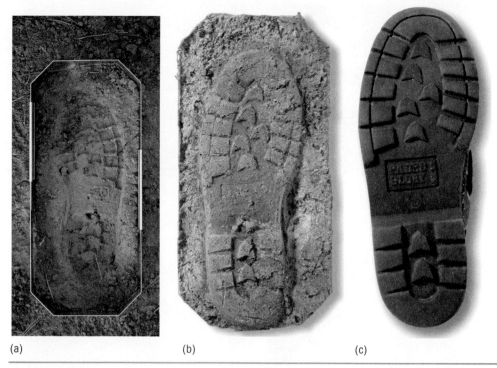

(a)   (b)   (c)

FIGURE 8–32   (a) A shoe impression in mud. (b) A cast of a shoe impression. (c) A shoe suspected of leaving the muddy impression. *Courtesy Sirchie Finger Print Laboratories, Inc., Youngsville, N.C., www.sirchie.com*

is then poured onto the wax-coated impression. After the casting material has hardened, the cast can be removed.

Several chemicals can be used to develop and enhance footwear impressions made with blood. In areas where a bloody footwear impression is very faint or where the subject has tracked through blood leaving a trail of bloody impressions, chemical enhancement can visualize latent or nearly invisible blood impressions (see Figure 8–33). A number of chemical formulas useful for bloody footwear impression analysis are listed in Appendix IV.

Several blood enhancement chemicals have been examined for their impact on STR DNA typing. None of the chemicals examined had a deleterious effect, on a short-term basis, on the ability to carry out STR DNA typing on the blood.[12]

Comparing Impressions

Whatever the circumstances, the laboratory procedures used to examine any type of impression remain the same. Of course, a comparison is possible only when an item suspected of having made the impression is recovered. Test impressions may be necessary to compare the characteristics of the suspect item with the evidence impression.

The evidential value of the impression is determined by the number of class and individual characteristics that the examiner finds. Agreement with respect to size, shape, or design may permit the conclusion that the impression could have been made by a particular shoe, tire, or garment; however, one cannot entirely exclude other possible sources from having the same class characteristics. More significant is the existence of individual characteristics arising out of wear, cuts, gouges, or other damage. A sufficient

WebExtra 8.7

Casting a Footwear Impression
www.prenhall.com/saferstein

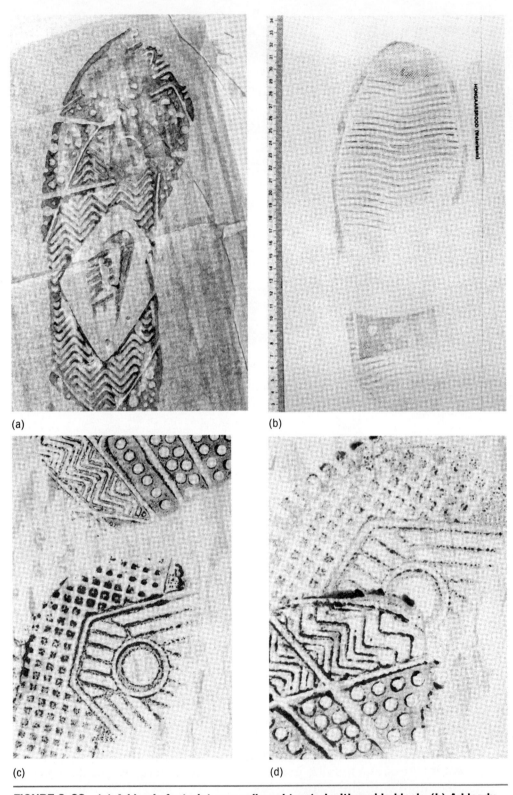

(a)

(b)

(c)

(d)

FIGURE 8–33 **(a) A bloody footprint on cardboard treated with amido black. (b) A bloody footprint treated with Hungarian Red dye. (c) A bloody footprint visualized with leucocrystal violet. (d) A bloody footprint enhanced with patent blue.** *(a) Courtesy Dwane S. Hilderbrand and David P. Coy, Scottsdale Police Crime Laboratory, Scottsdale, Ariz. (b) Courtesy ODV Inc., South Paris, Maine. (c–d) Courtesy William Bodziak, FBI Laboratory*

Closer Analysis

Casting Footwear and Tire Impressions

Footwear and tire impressions may be found at any type of crime scene and can provide a primary means to identify or exclude a suspect. The preferred method of collection for this type of evidence is casting the impression—that is, making a mold and preserving it for analysis in the lab. When a footwear or tire impression is found in dirt at the crime scene, the casting process is as follows:

Materials

Ruler

One small can of aerosol hair spray

1-gallon zip-top bag

Paint stirrer or large, long-handled spoon

Carton of dental stone

Water

Camera

Plastic or metal casting frame (optional)

(a)

(b)

(c)

(d)

(e)

Casting a footwear impression at a crime scene: (a) The impression is hardened using aerosol hair spray. (b) The correct amount of water is added to a known amount of dental stone. (c) The mixture is kneaded by hand until the desired (pancake-batter-like) consistency is reached. (d) The dental stone is poured into the impression using a spoon as a medium to disperse the flow. (e) The impression is filled with dental stone and allowed to dry before removal. *Courtesy Sirchie Finger Print Laboratories, Inc., Youngsville, N.C., www.sirchie.com*

(Continued)

Closer Analysis *(Continued)*

Procedure

1. Retrieve any fragments or debris that is not imbedded within the impression. Photograph the impression before and after retrieving debris; include a ruler in the photograph. A frame may be installed around an impression that is shallow or located on an inclined surface to contain the dental stone.

2. To solidify the soil, a fixative such as hair spray is used (see [a]). Hold the can of hair spray about 18 inches from the soil within the impression. Very lightly, spray an even layer to the impression using a sweeping motion and taking care to avoid any damage to the impression.

3. Allow to stand for ten minutes to allow the hair spray to dry.

4. Add an appropriate amount of water to a premeasured amount of dental stone (see [b]). Add water in increments. The usual amount is about 10 to 12 fluid ounces of water to about 1.5 to 2 pounds of dental stone. If using a zip-top bag, seal the bag and mix by working back and forth with fingers for at least three minutes (see [c]). Mix until a pancake-batter-like consistency is reached.

5. Create an opening in one corner of the bag. Pour the dental stone through the opening onto the ground beside the impression and allow it to carefully run into the impression. Use a paint stirrer, a spoon, or a gloved hand as a medium to disperse the stream so it does not destroy the fine details of the impression (see [d]). Continue pouring until the dental stone completely fills the impression (see [e]). Pour to reach at least 1/2 inch in thickness. If necessary, additional casting material may be poured over the top of the original cast to add thickness.

6. Label the wet plaster surface with the date, initials, and any other information required for evidence labeling.

7. When the cast no longer adheres to the soil and is relatively dry (usually about one hour), remove the cast. If needed, the cast can be dug out from the sides.

8. To dry completely store it for forty-eight hours. If a cast is not allowed to dry long enough, some ridge detail may disappear.

9. Once the cast is dry, rinse any loose soil from it with softly running water. A soft-bristled brush may also be used. Do not scrub or pick off anything. Pat dry with paper towels.

number, or the uniqueness, of such points of comparison support a finding that both the evidence and test impressions originated from only one source.

When a tire tread impression is left at a crime scene, the laboratory can examine the design of the impression and possibly determine the style and/or manufacturer of the tire. This may be particularly helpful to investigators when a suspect tire has not yet been located.

New computer software may help the forensic scientist compare shoe prints. For example, an automated shoe print identification system developed in England, called shoeprint image capture and retrieval (SICAR), incorporates multiple databases to search known and unknown footwear

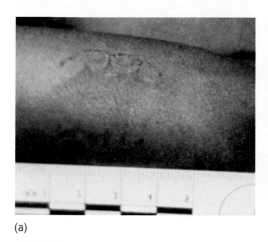
(a)

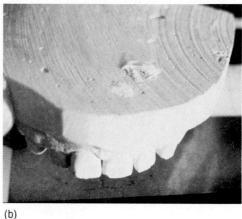
(b)

FIGURE 8–34   (a) A bite mark impression on the victim's forearm. (b) An upper dental model from the teeth of the suspect matches the individual teeth characteristics of the bite marks. *Courtesy Haskin Askin, D.D.S., Chief Forensic Odontologist, City of Philadelphia, Pa.*

files for comparison against footwear specimens. Using the system, an impression from a crime scene can be compared to a reference database to find out what type of shoe caused the imprint. That same impression can also be searched in the suspect and crime databases to reveal whether that shoe print matches the shoes of a person who has been in custody or the shoe prints left behind at another crime scene. When matches are made during the searching process, the images are displayed side by side on the computer screen.

An excellent resource for shoe print and tire impression examiners is a website that has been assembled by the Chesapeake area shoe print and tire track examiners at http://members.aol.com/varfee/mastssite/. The website's goal is to "enable examiners to enhance their footwear or tire track impression examinations by providing references, databases, and links to manufacturers, experts, vendors, trade associations, and professional societies connected to these forensic disciplines."

Human bite mark impressions on skin and foodstuffs have proven to be important items of evidence for convicting defendants in a number of homicide and rape cases in recent years. If a sufficient number of points of similarity between test and suspect marks are present, a forensic odontologist may conclude that a bite mark was made by one particular individual (see Figure 8–34).

Key Points

- Shoe and tire marks impressed into soft earth at a crime scene are best preserved by photography and casting.

- The electrostatic lifting technique is particularly helpful in recovering barely visible dust prints on floor surfaces.

- In areas where a bloody footwear impression is very faint or where the subject has tracked through blood, leaving a trail of bloody impressions, chemical enhancement can visualize latent or nearly invisible blood impressions.

Case Study

The O. J. Simpson Trial: Who Left the Impressions at the Crime Scene?

On the night of June 12, 1994, Nicole Brown—ex-wife of football star O. J. Simpson—and her friend Ron Goldman were brutally murdered on the grounds outside her home in Brentwood, California. O. J. Simpson was arrested for their murders, but professed his innocence. At the crime scene, investigators found bloody shoe impressions along the concrete walkway leading up to the front door of Brown's condominium. These shoe impressions were of extremely high quality and of intricate detail. The news media broadcast countless images of these bloody shoe prints on television, making it obvious to the killer that those shoes would surely link him to the crime.

Famed FBI shoe print examiner William J. Bodziak investigated the footwear evidence from the scene. His first task was to identify the brand of shoe that made the marks. Because the pattern was very clear and distinct, with complete toe-to-heel detail, this seemed a simple task at first. Bodziak compared this pattern to the thousands of sole patterns in the FBI's database. None matched. He then went to his reference collection of books and trade show brochures, again with no success.

Bodziak's experience told him that these were expensive, Italian-made casual dress shoes with a sole made from synthetic material. Using this knowledge, he shopped the high-end stores for a similar tread pattern, but still was unable to identify the shoes. He then drew a composite sketch of the sole and faxed the image to law enforcement agencies and shoe manufacturers and distributors worldwide. The owner of the American distributing company for Bruno Magli shoes was the only one to respond.

Further exhaustive investigation revealed that these were extremely rare shoes. There were two styles of shoe bearing this exact sole design. They were available for only two years, and from a mere forty stores in the United States and Puerto Rico. The Lorenzo style shoe had a bootlike upper that came to the ankle. The Lyon style shoe had the lower, more typical dress shoe cut. The impressions were made by a size 12 shoe, and it was later determined that only 299 pairs of size 12 with this tread pattern were sold in the United States.

Simpson flatly denied ever owning these shoes, adding that he would never wear anything so ugly. However, he was known to wear a size 12, and photographs taken almost nine months before the murders show Simpson wearing a pair of black leather Bruno Magli Lorenzo shoes. These shoes were available in several colors, so this narrows the number of shoes matching Simpson's pair of Lorenzos (this size, color, and style) sold in the United States to twenty-nine pairs.

Proving that Simpson owned a pair of shoes that had the exact pattern found printed in blood at the crime scene was an essential component of the case, but it was not done in time to be used during the criminal prosecution. The photographs of Simpson in his Bruno Magli shoes were released after the culmination of the criminal trial, so the jury never heard the direct evidence that Simpson owned these shoes. However, this proved to be an important link uniting Simpson with the crime scene in the civil trial. Although O. J. Simpson was acquitted of the murders of Nicole Brown and Ron Goldman in the criminal trial, he was judged responsible for their murders in the civil court case.

Chapter Summary

Structural variations and irregularities caused by scratches, nicks, breaks, and wear permit the criminalist to relate a bullet to a gun; a scratch or abrasion mark to a single tool; or a tire track to a particular automobile.

The manufacture of a rifle barrel requires impressing its inner surface with spiral grooves, a step known as rifling. The surfaces of the original bore remaining between the grooves are called lands. No two rifled barrels, even those manufactured in succession, have identical striation markings. These striations form the individual characteristics of the barrel. The inner surface of the barrel of a gun leaves its striation markings on a bullet passing through it.

The number of lands and grooves and their direction of twist are obvious points of comparison during the initial stages of an examination. Any differences in these class characteristics immediately eliminate the possibility that both bullets traveled through the same barrel. Not only must the lands and grooves of the test and evidence bullet have identical widths, but the longitudinal striations on each must coincide. The firing pin, breechblock, and ejector and extractor mechanism also offer a highly distinctive signature for individualization of cartridge cases.

The comparison microscope is a firearms examiner's most important tool. Two bullets can be observed and compared simultaneously within the same field of view. The advent of computerized imaging technology has made possible the storage of bullet and cartridge surface characteristics in a manner analogous to automated fingerprint files. However, the forensic examiner makes the final comparison through traditional methods.

The distribution of gunpowder particles and other discharge residues around a bullet hole permits an assessment of the distance from which a handgun or rifle was fired. The firing of a weapon not only propels residues toward the target, but also blows gunpowder and primer residues back toward the shooter. As a result, traces of these residues are often deposited on the firing hand of the shooter, and their detection can provide valuable information as to whether an individual has recently fired a weapon. Examiners measure the amount of barium and antimony on the relevant portion of the suspect's hands or characterize the morphology of particles containing these elements to determine whether a person has fired or handled a weapon, or was near a discharged firearm.

Increasingly, the criminalist must restore a serial number that has been obliterated by grinding, rifling, or punching. Restoration of serial numbers is possible through chemical etching because the metal crystals in the stamped zone are placed under a permanent strain that extends a short distance beneath the original numbers.

A tool mark is any impression, cut, gouge, or abrasion caused by a tool coming into contact with another object. Any minute imperfections on a tool impart individuality to that tool. The shape and pattern of such imperfections are further modified by damage and wear during the life of the tool. The comparison microscope is used to compare crime-scene tool marks with test impressions made with the suspect tool.

Shoe and tire marks impressed into soft earth at a crime scene are best preserved by photography and casting. In areas where a bloody footwear impression is very faint or where the subject has tracked through blood, leaving a trail of bloody impressions, chemical enhancement can visualize latent or nearly invisible blood impressions. A sufficient number of points of comparison or the uniqueness of such points support a finding that both the questioned and test impressions originated from only one source.

Review Questions

1. Firearms can be divided into two categories: _____ and _____ guns.

2. Handguns, or pistols, are firearms that are designed to be held and fired with one hand, and the most common types of handguns are _____ , _____ , and _____ .

3. The _____ features several firing chambers, each holding one cartridge, located within a revolving cylinder that lines the chamber up with the barrel mechanically when the round is fired.

4. A cartridge for a shotgun, called a shell, contains numerous ball-shaped projectiles, called _____ .

5. A shotgun barrel is not rifled and can also be narrowed toward the muzzle in order to concentrate shot when fired. The degree of narrowing of the barrel is called the _____ of the shotgun.

6. The _____ is the original part of the bore left after rifling grooves are formed.

7. The diameter of the gun barrel is known as its _____ .

8. True or False: The number of lands and grooves is a class characteristic of a barrel. _____

9. The _____ characteristics of a rifled barrel are formed by striations impressed into the barrel's surface.

10. The most important instrument for comparing bullets is the _____ .

11. To make a match between a test bullet and a recovered bullet, the lands and grooves of the test and evidence bullet must have identical widths, and the longitudinal _____ on each must coincide.

12. True or False: It is always possible to determine the make of a weapon by examining a bullet it fired. _____

13. A shotgun has a _____ barrel.

14. The diameter of a shotgun barrel is expressed by the term _____ .

15. True or False: Shotgun pellets can be individualized to a single weapon. _____

16. True or False: A cartridge case can be individualized to a single weapon. _____

17. The automated firearms search system developed by the FBI and ATF as a unified system incorporating both DRUGFIRE and IBIS technologies available in prior years is known as _____.

18. True or False: The distribution of gunpowder particles and other discharge residues around a bullet hole permits an approximate determination of the distance from which the gun was fired. _____

19. True or False: Without the benefit of a weapon, an examiner can make an exact determination of firing distance. _____

20. A halo of vaporous lead (smoke) deposited around a bullet hole normally indicates a discharge _____ to _____ inches from the target.

21. If a firearms has been fired more than 3 feet from a target, usually no residue is deposited, but a dark ring, known as _____ is observed.

22. As a rule of thumb, the spread in the pattern made by a 12-gauge shotgun increases 1 inch for every _____ of distance from the target.

23. A(n) _____ photograph may help visualize gunpowder deposits around a target.

24. True or False: One test method for locating powder residues involves transferring particles embedded on the target surface to chemically treated photographic paper. _____

25. Current methods for identifying a shooter rely on the detection of _____ residues on the hands.

26. Determining whether an individual has fired a weapon is done by measuring the elements _____ and _____ present on the hands.

27. True or False: Firings with all types of ammunition can be detected by hand swabbings with nitric acid. _____

28. Microscopic primer and gunpowder particles on the adhesives applied to a suspected shooter's hand can be detected with a _____.

29. True or False: Restoration of serial numbers is possible because in the stamped zone the metal is placed under a permanent strain that extends beneath the original numbers. _____

30. True or False: It is proper to insert a pencil into the barrel when picking up a crime-scene gun. _____

31. Recovered bullets are initialed on either the _____ or _____ of the bullet.

32. True or False: Because minute traces of evidence such as paint and fibers may be adhering to a recovered bullet, the investigator must take care to remove these trace materials immediately. _____

33. True or False: Cartridge cases are best marked at the base of the shell. _____

34. The clothing of the victim of a shooting must be handled so as to prevent disruption of _____ around bullet holes.

35. A(n) _____ is any impression caused by a tool coming into contact with another object.

36. Tool marks compare only when a sufficient number of _____ match between the evidence and test markings.

37. Objects bearing tool marks should either be submitted intact to the crime lab, or a _____ should be taken of the tool mark.

38. An imprint may be lifted using lifting sheets or a(n) _____.

39. Shoe and tire marks impressed into soft earth at a crime scene are best preserved by _____ and _____.

40. A wear pattern, cut, gouge, or other damage pattern can impart _____ characteristics to a shoe.

Application and Critical Thinking

1. From each of the following descriptions of bullet holes, estimate the distance from the shooter to the target.
   a. A few widely scattered gunpowder particles with no soot around the entrance hole
   b. A dark ring around the bullet hole, but no soot or gunpowder particles
   c. A halo of soot surrounding the entrance hole along with scattered specks of powder grains
   d. Scorch marks and melted fibers surrounding the entrance hole

2. You are investigating a shooting involving a 12-gauge shotgun with a moderately high choke. The spread of the pattern made by the pellets measures 12 inches. In your opinion, which of the following is probably closest to the distance from the target to the shooter? Explain your answer and explain why the other answers are likely to be incorrect.
   a. 18 yards
   b. 12 yards
   c. 6 yards
   d. 30 yards

3. Criminalist Ben Baldanza is collecting evidence from the scene of a shooting. After locating the revolver suspected of firing the shots, Ben picks the gun up by the grip, unloads it, and places the ammunition in an envelope. He then attaches an identification tag to the grip. Searching the scene, Ben finds a bullet lodged in the wall. He uses pliers to grab the bullet and pull it from the wall, then inscribes the bullet with his initials and places it in an envelope. What mistakes, if any, did Ben make in collecting this evidence?

4. How would you go about collecting impressions in each of the following situations?
   a. You discover a shoe print in dry dirt.
   b. You discover a tool mark on a windowsill.
   c. You discover tire marks in soft earth.
   d. You discover a shoe print on a loose piece of tile.
   e. You discover a very faint shoe print in dust on a colored linoleum floor.

Web Resources

Ballistics Slide Presentation
www.stfrancis.edu/ns/diab/Forensic1/Ballistics1_files/frame.htm

FirearmsID.com (Contains information about firearms identification, ballistics, distance determination, history of firearms identification, and case studies)
www.firearmsid.com/new_index.htm

Firearms Identification (A comprehensive article about firearms identification and examination, tool mark identification, and the collection and analysis of evidence)
www.fbi.gov/hq/lab/fsc/backissu/april2000/schehl1.htm#FirearmsID

Firearms Identification and Ballistics (An article that covers bullet and cartridge identification, ballistics, gunshot residue analysis, tool marks, and other impressions, and includes a small list of links)
www.apsu.edu/oconnor/3210/3210lect06b.htm

Firearms Tutorial (Covers many aspects of firearms identification including history, ballistics, tissue injury, gunshot residue, and laboratory methods)
http://library.med.utah.edu/WebPath/TUTORIAL/GUNS/GUNINTRO.html

Footwear and Tire Impression Evidence
www.members.aol.com/varfee/mastssite/index.html

Footwear, The Missed Evidence (An article about the collection and interpretation of footprint evidence)
www.crimeandclues.com/footwear.htm

Forensic Dentistry: Issues in Animal and Human Bite Mark Analysis
www.forensic.to/webhome/bitemarks/

Handwriting, Typewriting, Shoeprints, and Tire Treads: FBI Laboratory's Questioned Documents Unit (An FBI article that includes sections on the identification of shoe prints and tire treads)
www.fbi.gov/hq/lab/fsc/backissu/april2001/held.htm

Endnotes

1. Originally, the number of lead balls with the same diameter as the barrel would make a pound. For example, a 20-gauge shotgun has an inside diameter equal to the diameter of a lead ball that weighs 1/20 of a pound.

2. R. E. Tontarski, Jr., and R. M. Thompson, "Automated Firearms Evidence Comparison: A Forensic Tool for Firearms Identification—An Update," *Journal of Forensic Sciences* 43 (1998): 641.

3. P. C. Maiti, "Powder Patterns Around Bullet Holes in Bloodstained Articles," *Journal of the Forensic Science Society* 13 (1973): 197.

4. J. W. Kilty, "Activity After Shooting and Its Effect on the Retention of Primer Residues," *Journal of Forensic Sciences* 20 (1975): 219.

5. G. E. Reed et al., "Analysis of Gunshot Residue Test Results in 112 Suicides," *Journal of Forensic Sciences* 35 (1990): 62.

6. G. M. Woiten et al., "Particle Analysis for the Detection of Gunshot Residue, I: Scanning Electron Microscopy/Energy Dispersive X-Ray Characterization of Hand Deposits From Firing," *Journal of Forensic Sciences* 24 (1979): 409.

7. R. S. White and A. D. Owens, "Automation of Gunshot Residue Detection and Analysis by Scanning Electron Microscopy/Energy Dispersive X-Ray Analysis (SEM/EDX)," *Journal of Forensic Sciences* 32 (1987): 895; W. L. Tillman, "Automated Gunshot Residue Particle Search and Characterization," *Journal of Forensic Sciences* 32 (1987): 62.

8. See R. Milne, "Electrostatic Lifting of Marks at Crime Scenes and the Development of Pathfinder," *Science & Justice* 38 (1998): 135.

9. B. Glattstein, Y. Shor, N. Levin, and A. Zeichner, "pH Indicators as Chemical Reagents for the Enhancement of Footwear Marks," *Journal of Forensic Sciences* 41 (1996): 23.

10. D. S. Hilderbrand and M. Miller, "Casting Materials—Which One to Use?" *Journal of Forensic Identification* 45 (1995): 618.

11. Available from Sirchie Finger Print Laboratories, Inc., Youngsville, N.C.

12. C. J. Frégeau et al., "Fingerprint Enhancement Revisited and the Effects of Blood Enhancement Chemicals on Subsequent Profiler Plus™ Fluorescent Short Tandem Repeat DNA Analysis of Fresh and Aged Bloody Fingerprints," *Journal of Forensic Sciences* 45 (2000): 354.

The Sam Sheppard Case: A Trail of Blood

Convicted in 1954 of bludgeoning his wife to death, Dr. Sam Sheppard achieved celebrity status when the storyline of TV's *The Fugitive* was apparently modeled on his efforts to seek vindication for the crime he professed not to have committed. Dr. Sheppard, a physician, claimed he was dozing on his living room couch when his pregnant wife, Marilyn, was attacked. Sheppard's story was that he quickly ran upstairs to stop the carnage, but was knocked unconscious briefly by the intruder. The suspicion that fell on Dr. Sheppard was fueled by the revelation that he was having an adulterous affair. At trial, the local coroner testified that a pool of blood on Marilyn's pillow contained the impression of a "surgical instrument." After Sheppard had been imprisoned for ten years, the U.S Supreme Court set aside his conviction due to the "massive, pervasive, and prejudicial publicity" that had attended his trial.

In 1966, the second Sheppard trial commenced. This time, the same coroner was forced to back off from his insistence that the bloody outline of a surgical instrument was present on Marilyn's pillow. However, a medical technician from the coroner's office now testified that blood on Dr. Sheppard's watch was from blood spatter, indicating that Dr. Sheppard was wearing the watch in the presence of the battering of his wife. The defense countered with the expert testimony of eminent criminalist Dr. Paul Kirk. Dr. Kirk concluded that blood spatter marks in the bedroom showed the killer to be left-handed. Dr. Sheppard was right-handed.

Dr. Kirk further testified that Sheppard stained his watch while attempting to obtain a pulse reading. After less than twelve hours of deliberation, the jury failed to convict Sheppard. But the ordeal had taken its toll. Four years later Sheppard died, a victim of drug and alcohol abuse.

chapter 9

Bloodstain Pattern Analysis

Key Terms

angle of impact

area of convergence

area of origin

arterial spray

back spatter

cast-off

expired blood pattern

flows

forward spatter

high-velocity spatter

impact spatter

low-velocity spatter

medium-velocity spatter

satellite spatter

skeletonization

trail pattern

transfer pattern

void

Learning Objectives

After studying this chapter, you should be able to:

- Discuss the information that can be gained from bloodstain pattern analysis about the events involved in a violent crime.

- Explain how surface texture, directionality, and angle of impact affect the shape of individual bloodstains.

- Calculate the angle of impact of a bloodstain using its dimensions.

- Describe the classifications of low-, medium-, and high-velocity impact spatter and appreciate how these classifications should be used.

- Discuss the methods to determine the area of convergence and area of origin for impact spatter patterns.

- Understand how various blood pattern types are created and which features of each pattern can be used to aid in reconstructing events at a crime scene.

- Describe the methods for documenting bloodstain patterns at a crime scene.

General Features of Bloodstain Formation

Crimes involving violent contact between individuals are frequently accompanied by bleeding and resultant bloodstain patterns. Crime-scene analysts have come to appreciate that bloodstain patterns deposited on floors, walls, ceilings, bedding, and other relevant objects can provide valuable insights into events that occurred during the commission of a violent crime. The information one is likely to uncover as a result of blood-stain pattern interpretation includes the following:

- The direction from which blood originated

- The angle at which a blood droplet struck a surface

- The location or position of a victim at the time a bloody wound was inflicted

- The movement of a bleeding individual at the crime scene

- The minimum number of blows that struck a bleeding victim

- The approximate location of an individual delivering blows that produced a bloodstain pattern

The crime-scene investigator must not overlook the fact that the location, distribution, and appearance of bloodstains and spatters may be useful for interpreting and reconstructing the events that accompanied the bleeding. A thorough analysis of the significance of the position and shape of blood patterns with respect to their origin and trajectory is exceedingly complex and requires the services of an examiner who is experienced in such determinations. Most important, the interpretation of bloodstain patterns necessitates a carefully planned control experiment using surface materials comparable to those found at the crime scene. This chapter presents the basic principles and common deductions behind bloodstain pattern analysis to give the reader general knowledge to use at the crime scene.

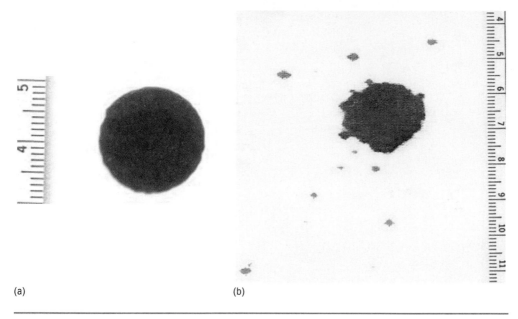

(a)   (b)

FIGURE 9–1 **(a) A bloodstain from a single drop of blood that struck a glass surface after falling 24 inches. (b) A bloodstain from a single drop of blood that struck a cotton muslin sheet after falling 24 inches.** *Courtesy A.Y. Wonder*

Surface Texture

Surface texture is of paramount importance in the interpretation of bloodstain patterns; comparisons between standards and unknowns are valid only when identical surfaces are used. In general, harder and nonporous surfaces (such as glass or smooth tile) result in less spatter. Rough surfaces, such as carpeting or wood, usually result in irregularly shaped stains with serrated edges, possibly with satellite spatter (see Figure 9–1).

Direction and Angle of Impact

An investigator may discern the direction of travel of blood striking an object by studying the stain's shape. The pointed end of a bloodstain always faces its direction of travel. In Figure 9–2, the bloodstain pattern was produced by several droplets of blood that were traveling from left to right before striking a flat, level surface.

It is possible to determine the impact angle of blood on a flat surface by measuring the degree of circular distortion of the stain. A drop deposited at an angle of impact of about 90 degrees (directly vertical to the surface) will be approximately circular in shape with no tail or buildup of blood. However, as the angle of impact deviates from 90 degrees, the stain becomes elongated in shape. Buildup of blood will show up in the larger angles, whereas longer and longer tails will appear as the angle of impact becomes smaller (see Figure 9–3).

Key Points

- Individual bloodstains can convey to the bloodstain analyst the directionality and angle of impact of the blood when it impacted a surface. Bloodstain patterns may convey to the analyst the location of victims (bleeding) or suspects (causing the bleeding), the movement of bleeding individuals, and the number of blows delivered.

satellite spatter
Small droplets of blood that are distributed around the perimeter of a drop or pool of blood and were produced as a result of the blood impacting the target surface.

angle of impact
The acute angle formed between the path of a blood drop and the surface that it contacts.

WebExtra 9.1
See How Bloodstain Spatter Patterns Are Formed
www.prenhall.com/saferstein

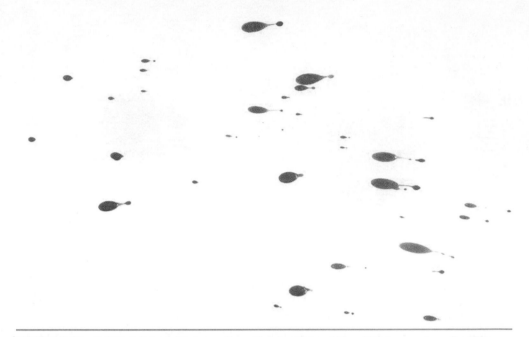

FIGURE 9–2 A bloodstain pattern produced by droplets of blood that were traveling from left to right. *Courtesy A.Y. Wonder*

FIGURE 9–3 The higher pattern is of a single drop of human blood that fell 24 inches and struck hard, smooth cardboard at 50 degrees. On this drop the collection of blood shows the direction. The lower pattern is of a single drop of human blood that fell 24 inches and struck hard, smooth cardboard at 15 degrees. On this drop the tail shows the direction. *Courtesy A.Y. Wonder*

• Surface texture is of paramount importance in the interpretation of bloodstain patterns; rounder drops generally are produced on smooth, nonporous surfaces, whereas rough surfaces result in irregular-edged drops. However, correlations between standards and unknowns are valid only when identical surfaces are used.

Closer Analysis

Determining the Angle of Impact of Bloodstains

The distorted or disrupted edge of an elongated stain indicates the direction of travel of the blood drop. One may establish the location or origin of bloodshed by determining the directionality of the stain and the angle at which blood came into contact with the landing surface. To determine the angle of impact, calculate the stain's length-to-width ratio and apply the formula

$$\text{Sin } A = \frac{\text{width of blood stain}}{\text{length of blood stain}}$$

where A = the angle of impact.

Example: The width of a stain is 11 mm and the length is 22 mm.

Then, Sin A = $\dfrac{11 \text{ mm}}{22 \text{ mm}}$ = (11 mm ÷ 22 mm)

$$= 0.50$$

A scientific calculator having the trigonometric function will calculate that a sine of 0.50 is equal to a 30-degree angle.

Note: There is a 5-degree error factor with this formula. This means that calculations are good to plus or minus 5 degrees of the actual value of the angle of impact. The measurements for length and width should be made with a ruler, micrometer, or photographic loupe.

- The direction of travel of blood striking an object may be discerned by the stain's shape. The pointed end of a bloodstain always faces its direction of travel.

- The angle of impact of an individual bloodstain can be approximated by the degree of distortion or lengthening of the bloodstain, or it can be more effectively estimated using the width-to-length ratio of the stain.

Impact Bloodstain Spatter Patterns

The most common type of bloodstain pattern found at a crime scene is impact spatter. This pattern occurs when an object impacts a source of blood. The spatter projected outward and away from the source is called forward spatter. Back spatter, sometimes called blow-back spatter, consists of the blood projected backward from the source, potentially being deposited on the object or person creating the impact. Impact spatter patterns consist of many droplets radiating in direct lines from the origin of blood to the target (see Figure 9–4).

Investigators have derived a common classification system of impact spatter from the velocity of a blood droplet. In general, as the force of the impact on the source of blood increases, so does the velocity of the blood droplets emanating from the source. It is also generally true that as both the force and velocity of impact increase, the diameter of the resulting blood droplets decreases.

Classifying Impact Spatter

Low-Velocity Spatter An impact pattern consisting of large separate or compounded drops with diameters of 3 millimeters or more is known as

impact spatter
A bloodstain pattern produced when an object makes forceful contact with a source of blood, projecting droplets of blood outward from the source.

forward spatter
Blood that travels away from the source in the same direction as the force that caused the spatter.

back spatter
Blood directed back toward the source of the force that caused the spatter.

FIGURE 9–4 Impact spatter produced by a beating with a baseball bat. The arrows shows the blood droplets' linear direction of travel from the origin of impact for each of numerous blows. *Courtesy A.Y. Wonder*

low-velocity spatter
An impact spatter pattern created by a force traveling at 5 feet per second or less and producing droplets with diameters greater than 3 millimeters.

medium-velocity spatter
An impact spatter pattern created by a force traveling at 5 to 25 feet per second and producing droplets with diameters between 1 and 3 millimeters.

high-velocity spatter
An impact spatter pattern created by a force traveling at 100 feet per second or faster and producing droplets with diameters less than 1 millimeter.

low-velocity spatter. This kind of spatter is normally produced by minimal force or by an object dropping into and splashing blood from a blood pool. Typically, the drops hit the surface at a speed of less than 5 feet per second.

Medium-Velocity Spatter A pattern consisting of small drops with diameters from 1 to 3 millimeters is classified as medium-velocity spatter. This type of impact spatter is normally associated with blunt force trauma to an individual. Drops of medium-velocity spatter hit the surface at 5 to 25 feet per second.

High-Velocity Spatter Very fine droplets with diameters of less than 1 millimeter are classified as high-velocity spatter. Here the drops hit the surface at 100 feet per second or faster. Gunshot exit wounds or explosions commonly produce this type of spatter. However, because the droplets are very small, they may not travel far; they may fall to the floor or ground where investigative personnel could overlook them.

Using droplet size to classify impact patterns by velocity is a useful tool for giving investigators insight into the general nature of a crime, However, the velocity at which blood strikes a surface by itself cannot illuminate the specific events that produced the spatter pattern. For example, beatings can produce high-velocity spatter or patterns that look more like low-velocity spatter. In general, one should use velocity categories very cautiously and for descriptive purposes only in evaluating impact spatter patterns.

As we will learn, blood spatter patterns can arise from a number of distinctly different sources. Illustrations of patterns emanating from impact (above), cast-off (on page 262), and arterial spray (on page 263) are shown in Figure 9–5.

Origin of Impact Patterns

Impact spatter patterns can offer investigators clues that help determine the origin of the blood source and the position of the victim at the time of the impact.

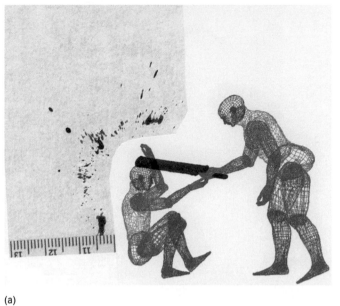

(a)

(b)

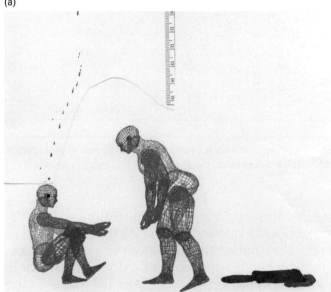

(c)

FIGURE 9–5 **(a) The action associated with producing impact spatter. (b) The action associated with producing cast-off spatter. (c) The action associated with producing arterial spray spatter.** *Courtesy of A.Y. Wonder*

Area of Convergence   The area of convergence is the point on a two-dimensional plane from which the drops originated. This can be established by drawing straight lines through the long axis of several individual bloodstains, following the line of their tails. The intersection of these lines is the area of convergence, and the approximate point of origin will be on a line straight out from this area. Figure 9–6 illustrates how to draw lines to find an area of convergence.

An object hitting a source of blood numerous times will never produce exactly the same pattern each time. One can therefore determine the number of impacts by drawing the area of convergence for groups of stains from separate impacts.

Area of Origin   It may also be important to determine the area of origin of a bloodstain pattern, the area in a three-dimensional space from which the blood was projected. This will show the position of the victim or suspect in space when the stain-producing event took place. The distribution of the droplets in an impact pattern gives a general idea of the distance from the

area of convergence
The area on a two-dimensional plane where lines traced through the long axis of several individual bloodstains meet. This approximates the two-dimensional place from which the bloodstains were projected.

area of origin
The location in three-dimensional space that blood that produced a bloodstain originated from. The location of the area of convergence and the angle of impact for each bloodstain is used to approximate this area.

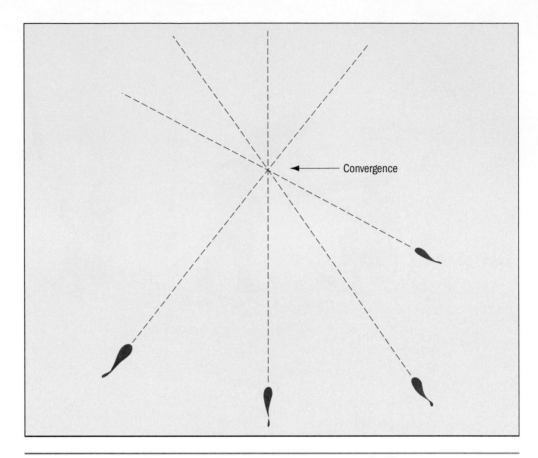

FIGURE 9–6 An illustration of stain convergence on a two-dimensional plane. Convergence represents the area from which the stains emanated. *Courtesy Judith Bunker, J.L. Bunker & Assoc., Ocoee, Fla.*

blood source to the bloodstained surface. Impact patterns produced at a distance close to the surface will appear as clustered stains. As the distance from the surface increases, so do the distribution and distance between droplets.

A common method for determining the area of origin at the crime scene is called the *string method*. Figure 9–7 illustrates the steps in the string method:

1. Find the area of convergence for the stain pattern.

2. Place a pole or stand as an axis coming from the area of convergence.

3. Attach one end of a string next to each droplet. Place a protractor next to each droplet and lift the string until it lines up with the determined angle of impact of the drop. Keeping the string in line with the angle, attach the other end of the string to the axis pole.

4. View the area of origin of the droplets where the strings appear to meet. Secure the strings at this area.

This method produces an approximation of the area of origin with an error of 2 feet.

Key Points

- An impact spatter pattern occurs when an object impacts a source of blood. This produces forward spatter projected forward from the source and back spatter projected backward from the source.

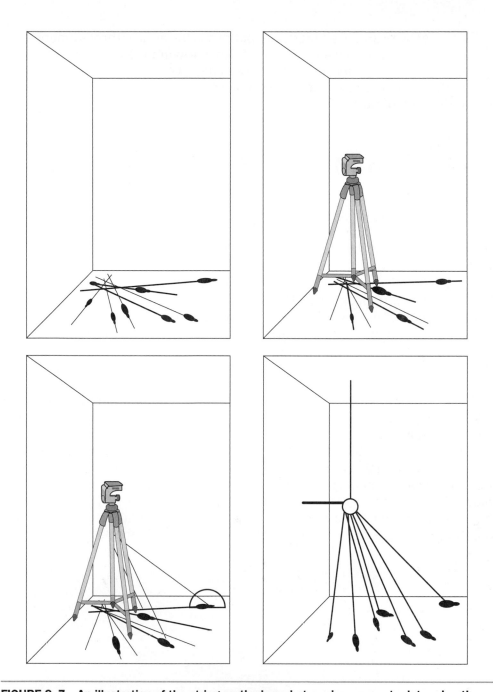

FIGURE 9–7 An illustration of the string method used at a crime scene to determine the area of origin of blood spatter. *Source: Bloodstain Pattern Evidence* by Anita Y. Wonder, p. 47. Copyright Elsevier, 2007.

- Impact spatter patterns can be classified as low-velocity (>3 mm drops), medium-velocity (1–3 mm drops), or high-velocity (<1 mm drops) for descriptive purposes. These categories should not be used to assume what kind of force created the pattern.

- The area of convergence is the point on a two-dimensional plane from which the drops of an impact spatter pattern originated. This area can be estimated by drawing straight lines through the long axis of several individual bloodstains, following the line of their tails.

- The area of origin of a bloodstain pattern is the area in three-dimensional space where blood was projected from, showing the position of the victim or suspect when the stain-producing event took place. The string method is commonly used at a crime scene to approximate the position of the area of origin.

More Bloodstain Spatter Patterns
Gunshot Spatter

A shooting may leave a distinct gunshot spatter pattern. This may be characterized by both forward spatter from an exit wound and back spatter from an entrance wound. However, the gunshot produces only back spatter if the bullet does not exit the body. If the victim is close enough to a vertical surface when suffering a gunshot wound, the blood will be expelled both forward and backward. This will leave a pattern of very fine droplets characteristic of high-velocity spatter (see Figure 9–8).

The location of injury, the size of the wound created, and the distance between the victim and the muzzle of the weapon all affect the amount of back spatter that occurs. Finding high-velocity spatter containing the victim's blood on a suspect can help investigators place the suspect in the vicinity when the gun was discharged. Back spatter created by a firearm discharge generally contains fewer and slightly larger stains than does forward spatter.

Depending on the distance from the victim that the gun was discharged, some back spatter may strike the gunman and enter the gun muzzle. This is called the *drawback effect*. Blood within the muzzle of a gun can place the weapon in the vicinity of the gunshot wound. The presence of blow-back spatter on a weapon's muzzle is consistent with the weapon being close to the victim at the time of firing. (see Figure 9–9).

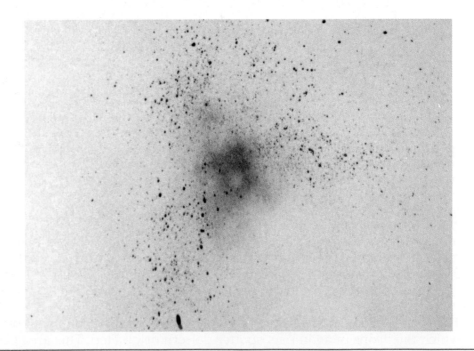

FIGURE 9–8   The high-velocity spatter from the cone-shaped deposit of gunshot spatter.
Courtesy A.Y. Wonder

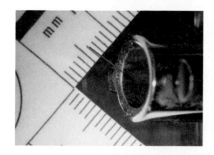

FIGURE 9–9 **Back spatter bloodstains entering the muzzle of a weapon discharged in close proximity to a victim.** *Courtesy of Ralph R. Ristenbatt III and Robert Shaler.*

Forensic Brief

Stephen Scher banged on the door of a cabin in the woods outside Montrose, Pennsylvania. According to Scher, his friend, Marty Dillon, had just shot himself while chasing after a porcupine. The two had been skeet shooting at Scher's cabin, enjoying a friendly sporting weekend, when Dillon spotted a porcupine and took off out of sight. Scher heard a single shot and waited to hear his friend's voice. After a few moments, he chased after Dillon and found him lying on the ground near a tree stump, bleeding from a wound in his chest. Scher administered CPR after locating his dying friend, but he was unable to save Dillon, who later died from his injuries. Police found that Dillon's untied boot had been the cause of his shotgun wound. They determined he had tripped while running with his loaded gun and shot himself. The grief-stricken Scher aroused no suspicion, so the shooting was ruled an accident.

Shortly thereafter, Scher moved from the area, divorced his wife, and married Dillon's widow. This was too suspicious to be ignored; police reopened the case and decided to reconstruct the crime scene. The reconstruction provided investigators with several pieces of blood evidence that pointed to Scher as Dillon's murderer.

Police noticed that Scher's boots bore the unmistakable spray of high-velocity impact blood spatter, evidence that he was standing within an arm's length of Dillon when Dillon was shot. This pattern of bloodstains cannot be created while administering CPR, as Scher claimed had happened. The spatter pattern also clearly refuted Scher's claim that he did not witness the incident. In addition, the tree stump near Dillon's body bore the same type of blood spatter, in a pattern that indicated Dillon was *seated on the stump* and not running when he was shot. Finally, Dillon's ears were free of the high-velocity blood spatter that covered his face, but blood was on his hearing protectors found nearby. This is a clear indication that he was wearing his hearing protectors when he was shot and they were removed before investigators arrived. This and other evidence resulted in Scher's conviction for the murder of his long-time friend, Marty Dillon.

Cast-off Spatter

A **cast-off** pattern is created when a blood-covered object flings blood in an arc onto a nearby surface. This kind of pattern commonly occurs when a person pulls a bloody fist or weapon back between delivering blows to a victim (see Figure 9–5 [b]). The bloodstain tails will point in the direction that the object was moving.

The appearance of the arc produced by a bloody object may help suggest the kind of object that produced the pattern. The sizes of the drops are

cast-off
A bloodstain pattern that is created when blood is flung from a blood-bearing object in motion onto a surface.

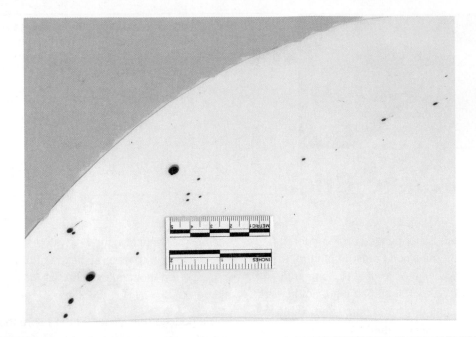

FIGURE 9–10 The castoff pattern created from one backward and one forward motion of an overhand swing. The larger drops are away from the victim because they're made when the weapon holds the greatest amount of blood. The smaller spatters are directed toward the victim. *Source: Bloodstain Pattern Evidence* by Anita Y. Wonder, p. 295. Copyright Elsevier, 2007.

directly related to the size of the point from which they were propelled. Drops propelled from a small or pointed surface will be smaller and the pattern more linear; drops propelled from a large or blunt surface will be larger and the pattern wider. The volume of blood deposited on an object from the source also affects the size and number of droplets in the cast-off pattern. The less blood on the object, the smaller the stains produced. The pattern may also suggest whether the blow that caused the pattern was directed from right to left or left to right. The pattern will point in the direction of the backward thrust, which will be opposite the direction of the blow. This could suggest which hand the assailant used to deliver the blows.

Cast-off patterns may also show the *minimum* number of blows delivered to a victim. Each blow should be marked by an upward-and-downward or forward-and-backward arc pattern (see Figure 9–10). By counting and pairing the patterns, one can estimate the minimum number of blows. An investigator should take into consideration that the first blow would only cause blood to pool to the area; it would not produce a cast-off pattern. Also, some blows may not come into contact with blood and, so, will not produce a pattern. The medical examiner is in the best position to estimate the number of blows a victim received.

Arterial Spray Spatter

arterial spray
A characteristic bloodstain pattern containing spurts that resulted from blood exiting under pressure from an arterial injury.

Arterial spray spatter is created when a victim suffers an injury to a main artery or the heart. The pressure of the continuing pumping of blood causes blood to spurt out of the injured area (see Figure 9–5 [c]). Commonly, the pattern shows large spurted stains for each time the heart pumps. Some radial spikes, satellite spatter, or flow patterns may be evident because of the large volume of blood being expelled with each spurt. Drops may also be seen on the surface in fairly uniform size and shape and in parallel arrangement (see Figure 9–11).

FIGURE 9–11 **Arterial spray spatter found at a crime scene where a victim suffered injury to an artery.** *Courtesy Norman H. Reeves*, Bloodstain Pattern Analysis, *Tucson, AZ, www.bloody1.com*

The lineup of the stains shows the victim's movement. Any vertical arcs or waves in the line show fluctuations in blood pressure. The site of the initial injury to the artery can be found where the pattern begins with the biggest spurt. Arterial patterns can also be differentiated because the oxygenated blood spurting from the artery tends to be a brighter red color than blood expelled from impact wounds.

Expirated Blood Patterns

A pattern created by blood that is expelled from the mouth or nose from an internal injury is called an expirated blood pattern. If the blood that creates such a pattern is under great pressure, it produces very fine high-velocity spatter. Expirated blood at very low velocities produces a stain cluster with irregular edges (see Figure 9–12). The presence of bubbles of oxygen in the drying drops can differentiate a pattern created by expirated blood from other types of bloodstains. Expirated blood also may be lighter in color when compared to impact spatter as a result of dilution by saliva. The presence of expirated blood gives an important clue as to the injuries suffered and the events that took place at a crime scene.

expirated blood pattern
A pattern created by blood that is expelled out of the nose, mouth, or respiratory system as a result of air pressure and/or airflow.

Void Patterns

A void is created when an object blocks the deposition of blood spatter onto a target surface or object (see Figure 9–13). The spatter is deposited onto the object or person instead. The blank space on the surface or object may give a clue as to the size and shape of the missing object or person. Once the object or person is found, the missing piece of the pattern should fit in, much like a puzzle piece, with the rest of the pattern. Voids may be applicable for establishing the body position of the victim or assailant at the time of the incident.

void
An area within a deposited spatter pattern that is clear of spatter, caused by an object or person blocking the area at the time of the spatter's deposition.

Key Points

- Gunshot spatter can consist of both forward spatter from an exit wound and back spatter from an entrance wound; however, only back spatter will be produced if the bullet does not exit the body.

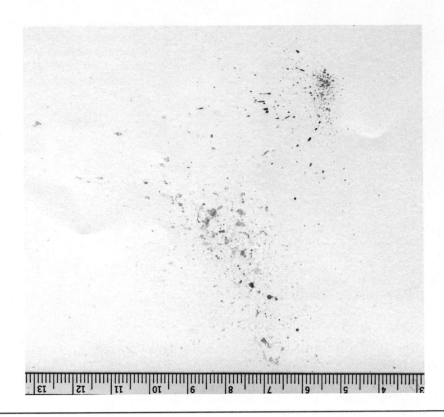

FIGURE 9–12 **An example of expirated blood expelled with two wheezes from the mouth**
Courtesy A.Y. Wonder

FIGURE 9–13 **A void pattern is found behind the door where the surface of the door blocked the deposition of spatter on that area. This void, and the presence of spatter on the door, shows that the door was open when the spatter was deposited.** *Courtesy Norman H. Reeves,* Bloodstain Pattern Analysis, *Tucson, AZ, www.bloody1.com*

- A cast-off pattern is created when a blood-covered object flings blood in an arc onto a nearby surface. This kind of pattern commonly occurs when a person pulls a bloody fist or weapon back between delivering blows to a victim.

- The characteristic arterial spray spatter is created when a victim suffers an injury to a main artery or the heart and the pressure of the continuing pumping of blood projects blood out of the injured area in spurts, which are apparent in the pattern.

- Expired blood is expelled from the mouth or nose and may appear as very fine high-velocity spatter or large low-velocity bloodstain clusters. This kind of pattern may contain bubbles of oxygen or be mixed with saliva.

- A void pattern features an area free of spatter where an object (or person) blocks the deposition of blood spatter onto a target surface or object. Because the spatter is deposited onto the object or person instead, the shape of the void may give a clue as to the size and shape of the missing object or person.

Other Bloodstain Patterns

Not all bloodstains at a crime scene appear as spatter patterns. The circumstances of the crime often create other types of stains that can be useful to investigators.

Contact/Transfer Patterns

When an object with blood on it touches one that does not have blood on it, this produces a contact or transfer pattern. Examples of transfers with features include fingerprints (see Figure 9–14), handprints, footprints, footwear prints, tool prints, and fabric prints in blood. These may provide further leads by offering individual characteristics.

transfer pattern
A bloodstain pattern created when a surface that carries wet blood comes in contact with a second surface. Recognizable imprints of all or a portion of the original surface or the direction of movement may be observed.

The size and general shape of a tool may be seen in a simple transfer. This can lead to narrowing the possible tools by class characteristics. A transfer that shows a very individualistic feature may help point to the tool that made the pattern.

Simple transfer patterns are produced when the object makes contact with the surface and the object is removed without any movement. Other transfers may be caused by movement of the bloody object across a surface. Generally, the pattern will lighten and "feather" as the pattern moves away from the initial contact point. The direction of separate bloody transfers, such as footwear prints in blood, may show the movement of the suspect, victim, or others through the crime scene after the blood was present. The first transfer pattern will be dark and heavy with blood, whereas subsequent transfers will be increasingly lighter in color. As the transfers get lighter, less and less of the transferring object's surface will deposit visible traces of blood. Bloody shoe imprints may also suggest whether the wearer was running or walking. Running typically produces imprints with more space between them and more satellite or drop patterns between each imprint.

FIGURE 9–14 A transfer pattern consisting of bloody fingerprints with apparent ridge detail. *Courtesy Lawrence A. Presley, Arcadia University*

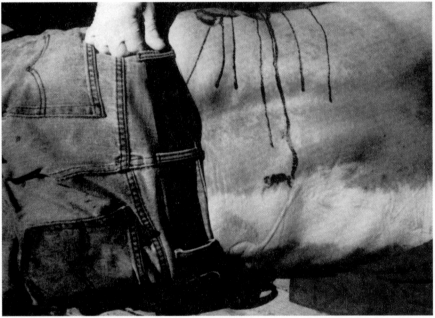

FIGURE 9–15 The flow pattern suggests that the victim was upright and then fell while blood flowed. The assailant claimed the victim was stabbed while sleeping. *Source: Bloodstain Pattern Evidence by Anita Y. Wonder, p. 98. Copyright Elsevier, 2007.*

Flows

flow pattern
A bloodstain pattern formed by the movement of small or large amounts of blood as a result of gravity's pull.

Patterns made by drops or large amounts of blood flowing by the pull of gravity are called **flows**. Flows may be formed by single drops or large volumes of blood. "Active" flows are formed by blood coming from an actively bleeding wound. "Passive" flows originate with blood deposited on a surface such as from an arterial spurt. Clotting of the blood's solid parts may occur when a flow extends onto an absorbent surface.

The flow direction may show movements of objects or bodies while the flow was still in progress or after the blood had dried. Figure 9-15 illustrates a situation in which movement of the surface while the flow was still in progress led to a specific pattern.

Interruption of a flow pattern may be helpful in assessing the sequence and passage of time between the flow and its interruption. If a flow found on an object or body does not appear consistent with the direction of gravity, one may surmise that the object or body was moved after the blood had dried.

Pools   A pool of blood occurs when blood collects in a level (not sloped) and undisturbed place. Blood that pools on an absorbent surface may be absorbed throughout the surface and diffuse, creating a pattern larger than the original pool. This often occurs to pools on beds or sofas.

The approximate drying time of a pool of blood is related to the environmental condition of the scene. By experimentation, an analyst may be able to reasonably estimate the drying times of stains of different sizes. Small and large pools of blood can aid in reconstruction by providing an estimation of the amount of time that elapsed since the blood was deposited. Considering the drying time of a blood pool can yield information about the timing of events that accompanied the incident.

The edges of a stain will dry to the surface, producing a phenomenon called skeletonization (see Figure 9–16). This usually occurs within 50 seconds of deposition of droplets, and longer for larger volumes of blood. If the central area of the pooled bloodstain is altered by wiping, the skeletonized perimeter will be left intact. This can be used to interpret whether movement or activity occurred shortly after the pool was deposited, or whether the perimeter had time to skeletonize before the movement occurred. This may be important for classifying the source of the original stain.

Trail Patterns

A trail pattern is a series of drops that are separate from other patterns, formed by blood dripping off an object or injury. The stains form a kind of line or path usually made by the suspect after injuring or killing the victim. It may simply show movement, lead to a discarded weapon, or provide

skeletonization
The process by which the edges of a stain dry to the surface in a specific period of time (dependent on environmental and surface conditions). Skeletonization will remain apparent even after the rest of the bloodstain has been disturbed from its original position.

trail pattern
A pattern of bloodstains formed by the dripping of blood off a moving surface or person in a recognizable pathway separate from other patterns.

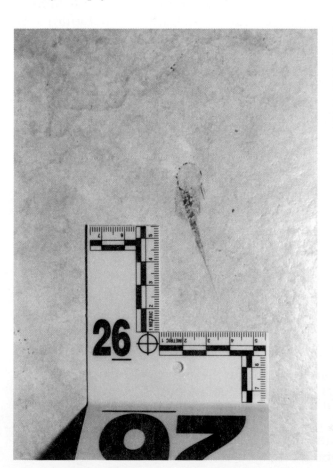

FIGURE 9–16   Skeletonization is shown in a bloodstain that was disturbed after the edges had time to skeletonize.
Courtesy Norman H. Reeves, Bloodstain Pattern Analysis, *Tucson, AZ, www.bloody1.com*

FIGURE 9–17 **A trail pattern leads away from the center of the mixed bloodstain pattern.** *Courtesy Norman H. Reeves, Bloodstain Pattern Analysis, Tucson, AZ, www.bloody1.com*

identification of the suspect by his or her own blood. Investigators often see this type of pattern in stabbings during which the suspect cuts himself or herself as a result of the force necessary to stab the victim. Figure 9–17 shows a trail pattern away from the center of action at a crime scene.

The shape of the stains in a trail pattern can help investigators determine the direction and speed at which a person was moving. The tails of the drops in a trail pattern point in the direction the person was moving. More circular stains are found where the person was moving slowly enough to not form tails. This information may be helpful in reconstruction.

Key Points

- Transfer patterns are created when an object with blood on it makes simple contact with a surface or moves along a surface. The direction of movement may be shown by a feathering of the pattern.

- Flows may originate from a single drop or a large amount of blood. Because the direction of the flow is caused by gravity, the direction of a pattern may suggest the original position of the surface when the flow was formed.

- A pool is formed where large amounts of blood collect. The pool may be absorbed into the surface of deposition over time.

- The presence of skeletonization of the perimeter of a bloodstain suggests that the stain was disturbed after the edges had had sufficient time to skeletonize.

- A trail pattern is separate from other patterns, and it is formed by single blood droplets dripping off an object or injury.

Case Study

An elderly male was found lying dead on his living room floor. He had been beaten about the face and head, then stabbed in the chest and robbed. The reconstruction of bloodstains found on the interior front door and the adjacent wall documented that the victim was beaten about the face with a fist and struck on the back of the head with his cane. A three-dimensional diagram and photograph illustrating the evidential bloodstain patterns is shown in Figure 1(a) and (b).

A detail photograph of bloodstains next to the interior door is shown in Figure 2.

(a)

(b)

FIGURE 1 **(a) A three-dimensional diagram illustrating bloodstain patterns that were located, documented, and reconstructed. (b) A crime-scene photograph of bloodstained areas.** *(a) Courtesy Judith Bunker, J.L. Bunker & Assoc., Ocoee, Fla. (b) Courtesy Sarasota County (Fla.) Sheriff's Department*

(continued)

Case Study

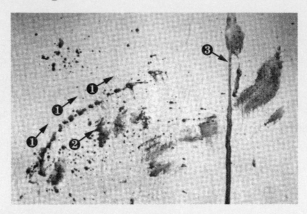

FIGURE 2 **Positions of impact spatter from blows that were inflicted on the victim's face.**
Courtesy Judith Bunker, J.L. Bunker & Assoc., Ocoee, Fla.

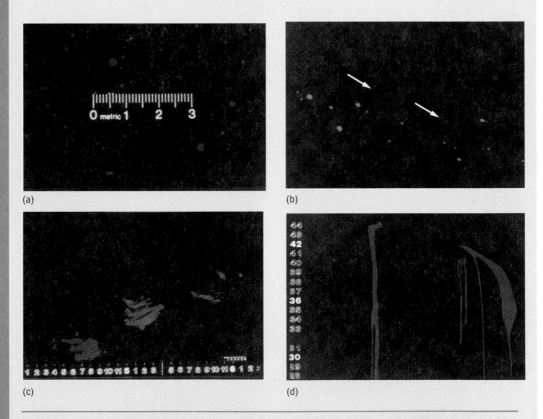

FIGURE 3 **(a) A laboratory test pattern showing an impact spatter. The size and shape of the stains demonstrate a forceful impact 90 degrees to the target. (b)A laboratory test pattern illustrating a cast-off pattern directed left to right from an overhead swing. (c) A laboratory test pattern showing a repetitive transfer impression pattern produced by a bloodstained hand moving left to right across the target. (d) A laboratory test pattern illustrating vertical flow patterns. The left pattern represents a stationary source; the right pattern was produced by left-to-right motion.** *Courtesy Judith Bunker, J.L. Bunker & Assoc., Ocoee, Fla.*

Case Study

Arrow 1 in Figure 2 points to the cast-off pattern directed left to right as blood was flung from the perpetrator's fist while inflicting blows. Arrow 2 in Figure 2 points to three transfer impression patterns directed left to right as the perpetrator's bloodstained hand contacted the wall as the fist blows were being inflicted on the victim. Arrow 3 in Figure 2 points to blood flow from the victim's wounds as he slumped against the wall.

Figure 3 contains a series of laboratory test patterns created to evaluate the patterns contained within Figure 2.

Figure 4 shows how the origin of individual impact spatter patterns located on the wall and door and emanating from the bleeding victim can be documented by the determination of separate areas of convergence.

A suspect was apprehended three days later, and he was found to have an acute fracture of the right hand. When he was confronted with the bloodstain evidence, the suspect admitted striking the victim, first with his fist, then with a cane, and finally stabbing him with a kitchen knife. The suspect pleaded guilty to three first-degree felonies.

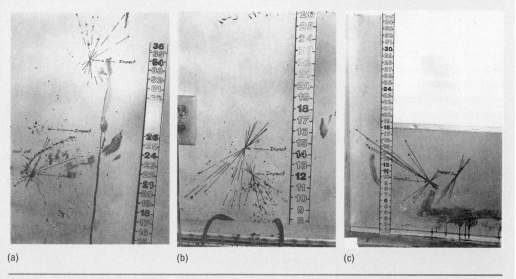

(a) (b) (c)

FIGURE 4 **(a) A convergence of impact spatter patterns associated with beating with a fist. (b) The convergence of impact spatter associated with the victim falling to the floor while bleeding from the nose. (c) The convergence of impact spatter associated with the victim while face down at the door, being struck with a cane.** *Courtesy Judith Bunker, J.L. Bunker & Assoc., Ocoee, Fla.*

Documenting Bloodstain Pattern Evidence

Blood spatter patterns of any kind can provide a great deal of information about the events that took place at a crime scene. For this reason, investigators should note, study, and photograph each pattern and drop. This must be done to accurately record the location of specific patterns and to distinguish the stains from which laboratory samples were taken. The photographs and sketches can also point out specific stains used in determining the direction of force, angle of impact, and area of origin.

Just as in general crime-scene photography, the investigator should create photographs and sketches of the overall pattern to show the orientation of the pattern to the scene. The medium-range documentation

FIGURE 9–18 The grid method may be used for photographing bloodstain pattern evidence. *Source: R.R. Ogle, Jr., Crime Scene Investigation & Reconstruction, 2nd ed., Prentice-Hall, Upper Saddle River, NJ, 2007.*

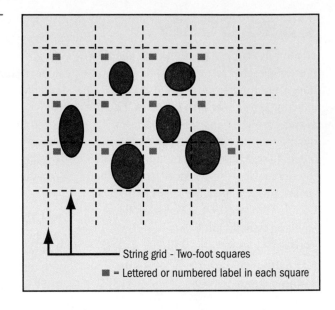

String grid - Two-foot squares

■ = Lettered or numbered label in each square

FIGURE 9–19 The perimeter ruler method may be used for photographing bloodstain pattern evidence. *R.R. Ogle, Jr., Crime Scene Investigation & Resconstruction, 2nd ed., Prentice-Hall, Upper Saddle River, NJ, 2007.*

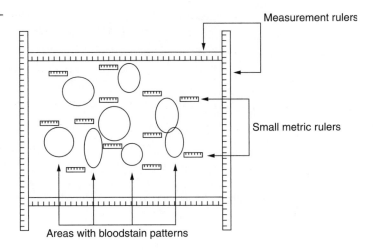

Measurement rulers

Small metric rulers

Areas with bloodstain patterns

should include pictures and sketches of the whole pattern and the relationships between individual stains within the pattern. The close-up photographs and sketches should show the dimensions of each individual stain. Close-up photographs should be taken with a scale of some kind apparent in the photograph.

Two common methods of documenting bloodstain patterns place attention on the scale of the patterns. The *grid method* involves setting up a grid of squares of known dimensions over the entire pattern using string and stakes (see Figure 9–18). All overall, medium-range, and close-up photographs are taken with and without the grid. The second method, called the *perimeter ruler method*, involves setting up a rectangular border of rulers around the pattern and then placing a small ruler next to each stain. In this method, the large rulers show scale in the overall and medium-range photos, whereas the small rulers show scale in the close-up photographs (see Figure 9–19). Some investigation teams use tags in close-up photographs to show evidence numbers or other details.

An area-of-origin determination should be calculated whenever possible. All measurements of stains and calculations of angle of impact and point of origin should be recorded in crime-scene notes. Especially important stains can be roughly sketched within the notes.

Only some jurisdictions have a specialist on staff to decipher patterns either at the scene or from photographs at the lab. Therefore, it is important that all personnel be familiar with patterns to properly record and document them for use in reconstruction.

Key Points

- Photographs and sketches should first be created of the overall bloodstain pattern to show the orientation of the pattern to the scene.

- Medium-range and close-up photographs may use the grid method or perimeter ruler method to show the orientation and relative size of the pattern and individual stains.

Chapter Summary

The location, distribution, and appearance of bloodstains and spatters may be useful for interpreting and reconstructing the events that produced the bleeding. An investigator or bloodstain pattern analyst can decipher from individual bloodstains the directionality and angle of impact of the blood when it impacted the surface of deposition. In addition, bloodstain patterns, consisting of many individual bloodstains, may convey to the analyst the location of victims or suspects, the movement of bleeding individuals, and the number of blows delivered.

Surface texture and an individual stain's shape, size, and location must be considered when determining the direction and angle of impact of the bloodstain. Surface texture can greatly affect the shape of a bloodstain. The directionality of an individual bloodstain may be shown by the stain's tail or the accumulation of blood because the tail or accumulation appears on the side opposite the force. The angle of impact of a bloodstain can be approximated by the shape of the bloodstain, or it can be more effectively estimated using the width-to-length ratio of the stain.

An impact spatter pattern occurs when an object impacts a source of blood producing forward spatter projected forward from the source and back spatter projected backward from the source. Patterns created by impact spatter can be classified as low-velocity (>3 mm drops), medium-velocity (1–3 mm drops), or high-velocity (< 1 mm drops). These classification are for descriptive purposes only and should not be used to determine the kind of force that produced the pattern. The area of convergence of an impact spatter pattern is the area the individual stains emanated from on a two-dimensional plane. The area of origin of a bloodstain pattern in three-dimensional space may represent the position of the victim or suspect when the stain-producing event took place.

Gunshot spatter consists of very fine spatter originating from both forward spatter from an exit wound and back spatter from an entrance wound, or only back spatter if the bullet did not exit the body. Blood cast off from an object, typically a weapon or fist between delivering blows to a victim, may form an arc pattern on a nearby surface. The features of the pattern can suggest the kind of object that created it and the minimum number of blows delivered by the object. The characteristic spurts present in an arterial spray spatter are created by the continuing pumping of blood from an arterial injury. Expirated blood expelled from the mouth or nose may at first appear to be fine high-velocity or large low-velocity impact spatter. It may feature bubbles of oxygen in the drying drops or possibly be mixed with saliva. A void, where an object (or person) blocks the deposition of blood spatter onto a target surface or object, may give a clue as to the size and shape of the missing object or person.

Transfer patterns, created when an object with blood on it makes simple contact with a surface, may reveal the shape or texture characteristics of the object. Because the direction of flows originating from either a single drop or a large amount of blood is caused by gravity, the direction of a pattern may suggest the original position of the surface when the flow was formed. A trail pattern shows a path of droplets separate from other patterns; it is formed by single blood droplets dripping off an object or injury. The presence of skeletonization of the perimeter of a bloodstain suggests that the stain was disturbed after the edges had had sufficient time to skeletonize.

The precise appearance and location of each bloodstain at a crime scene is important. Therefore, each bloodstain pattern located at a crime scene must be properly documented in notes, photographs, and sketches. Medium-range and close-up photographs should be recorded using either the grid method or perimeter ruler method to show the orientation and relative size of the pattern and individual stains.

Review Questions

1. Violent contact between individuals at a crime scene frequently produces bleeding and results in the formation of _____.

2. The proper interpretation of bloodstain patterns necessitates carefully planned _____ using surface materials comparable to those found at the crime scene.

3. Bloodstain patterns may convey to the analyst the location and movements of _____ or _____ during the commission of a crime.

4. True or False: Harder and less porous surfaces result in less spatter, whereas rough surfaces result in stains with more spatter and serrated edges. _____

5. True or False: Generally, bloodstain diameter (increases, decreases) with height. _____

6. The _____ and _____ of blood striking an object may be discerned by the stain's shape.

7. True or False: A drop of blood that strikes a surface at an angle of impact of approximately 90 degrees will be close to (elliptical, circular) in shape. _____

8. The angle of impact of an individual bloodstain can be estimated using the ratio of _____ divided by _____.

9. _____ is the most common type of blood spatter found at a crime scene, and is produced when an object forcefully contacts a source of blood.

10. True or False: Forward spatter consists of the blood projected backward from the source, and back spatter is projected outward and away from the source. _____

11. The classification system of impact spatter is based on the size of droplets resulting from the velocity of the blood droplets produced, and patterns can be classified as _____, _____, or _____ impact spatter.

12. True or False: The velocity classification system is a good way to classify impact patterns and to determine the kind of force that produced them. _____

13. The _____ is the point on a two-dimensional plane from which the drops originated.

14. The _____ of a bloodstain pattern in a three-dimensional space illustrates the position of the victim or suspect when the stain-producing event took place.

15. The _____ method is used at the crime scene to determine the area of origin.

16. A _____ is created by contact between a bloody object and a surface.

17. Movement of a bloody object across a surface, (lightens, darkens) as the pattern moves away from the point of contact.

18. True or False: Footwear transfer patterns created by an individual who was running typically show imprints with more space between them as compared to those of an individual who was walking. _____

19. True or False: The direction of a flow pattern may show movements of objects or bodies while the flow was still in progress or after the blood had dried. _____

20. The approximate drying time of a(n) _____ of blood determined by experimentation is related to the environmental condition of the scene and may suggest how much time has elapsed since its deposition.

21. The edges of a bloodstain will generally _____ within 50 seconds of deposition and be left intact even if the central area of a bloodstain is altered by a wiping motion.

22. A(n) _____ pattern commonly originates from repeated strikes from weapons or fists and is characterized by an arc pattern of separate drops showing directionality.

23. True or False: Characteristics of a cast-off pattern arc cannot give clues as to the kind of object that was used to produce the pattern. _____

24. When an injury is suffered to an artery, the pressure of the continuing pumping of blood projects blood out of the injured area in spurts creating a pattern known as _____.

25. If a _____ pattern is found at a scene, it may show movement, lead to a discarded weapon, or provide identification of the suspect by his or her own blood.

26. A bloodstain pattern created by _____ features bubbles of oxygen in the drying drops and may be lighter in color when compared to impact spatter.

27. The shape and size of the blank space, or _____, created when an object blocks the deposition of spatter onto a surface and is then removed may give a clue as to the size and shape of the missing object or person.

28. True or False: Each bloodstain pattern found at a crime scene should be noted, studied, and photographed. _____

29. When documenting bloodstain patterns, the _____ involves setting up a grid of squares of known dimensions over the entire pattern and taking overview, medium-range, and close-up photographs with and without the grid.

30. The _____ method of bloodstain documentation involves setting up a border of rulers around the pattern and then placing a small ruler next to each stain to show relative position and size in photographs.

31. True or False: The pointed end of a bloodstain always faces toward its direction of travel. _____

Application and Critical Thinking

1. After looking at the bloodstains in the figure, answer the following questions:
   a. Which three drops struck the surface closest to a 90-degree angle? Explain your answer.
   b. Which three drops struck the surface farthest from a 90-degree angle? Explain your answer.
   c. In what direction were drops 2 and 7 traveling when they struck the surface? Explain your answer.

2. Investigator Priscilla Wright arrives at a murder scene and finds the body of a victim who suffered a gunshot wound, but sees no blood spatter on the wall or floor behind it. What should she conclude from this observation?

3. Investigator Terry Martin arrives at an assault scene and finds a cast-off pattern consisting of tiny droplets of blood in a very linear arc pattern on a wall near the victim. What does this tell him about the weapon used in the crime?

Web Resources

Bloodstains as Investigative Evidence (A discussion of the characteristics of blood; the shape, persistence, and age of bloodstains; procedures for processing blood evidence; and lab analysis of blood evidence)
www.pimall.com/nais/nl/n.bloodstains.html

Bloodstain Pattern Analysis Tutorial (An illustrated guide to bloodstain analysis; includes example of different types of bloodstains, blood spatter patterns and directionality, and impact angle determination)
www.bloodspatter.com/BPATutorial.htm

Forensic Serology
http://faculty.ncwc.edu/toconnor/425/425lect13.htm

International Association of Bloodstain Pattern Analysts (Links to articles from the IABPA's newsletter)
www.iabpa.org/newslett.htm

Pablo Escobar, Drug Lord

In 1989, *Forbes* magazine listed Pablo Escobar as the seventh richest man in the world. Escobar began his climb to wealth as a teenage car thief in the streets of Medellin, Colombia, and eventually moved into the cocaine-smuggling business. At the peak of his power in the mid-1980s, he was shipping as much as eleven tons of cocaine per flight in jetliners to the United States. Law enforcement officials estimate that the Medellin cartel controlled 80 percent of the world's cocaine market and was taking in about $25 billion annually.

Escobar ruthlessly ruled by the gun: murdering, assassinating, and kidnapping. He was responsible for killing three presidential candidates in Colombia, as well as the storming of the Colombian Supreme Court, which resulted in the murder of half the justices. All the while, Escobar curried favor with the Colombian general public by cultivating a Robin Hood image and distributing money to the poor.

In 1991, hoping to avoid extradition to the United States, Escobar turned himself in to the Colombian government and agreed to be sent to prison. However, the prison compound could easily be mistaken for a country club. There he continued his high-flying lifestyle, trafficking by telephone and even murdering a few associates. When the Colombian government attempted to move Escobar to another jail, he escaped, again fearing extradition to the United States.

Pressured by the U.S. government, Colombia organized a task force dedicated to apprehending Escobar. The manhunt for Escobar ended on December 2, 1993, when he was cornered on the roof of one of his hideouts. A shootout ensued and Escobar was fatally wounded by a bullet behind his ear.

chapter 10

Drugs

Key Terms

anabolic steroids

analgesic

chromatography

confirmation

depressant

dispersion

electromagnetic spectrum

frequency

hallucinogen

infrared

ion

microcrystalline test

narcotic

physical dependence

psychological dependence

refraction

screening test

spectrophotometry

stimulant

ultraviolet

visible light

wavelength

X-ray

Learning Objectives

After studying this chapter, you should be able to:

- Compare and contrast psychological and physical dependence.

- Name and classify the commonly abused drugs.

- Describe the laboratory tests normally used to perform a routine drug identification analysis.

- Describe and explain the process of chromatography.

- Explain the difference between thin-layer chromatography and gas chromatography.

- Describe the utility of ultraviolet and infrared spectroscopy for the identification of organic compounds.

- Describe the concept and utility of mass spectrometry for identification analysis.

- Understand the proper collection and preservation of drug evidence.

A *drug* can be defined as a natural or synthetic substance that is used to produce physiological or psychological effects in humans or other animals. However, criminalists are concerned primarily with a small number of drugs—many of them illicit—that are commonly used for their intoxicating effects. These include marijuana, the most widely used illicit drug in the United States, and alcohol, which is consumed regularly by 90 million Americans. Drug abuse has grown from a problem generally associated with members of the lower end of the socioeconomic ladder to one that cuts across all social and ethnic classes of society. Today, approximately 23 million people in the United States use illicit drugs.

Because of the epidemic proportions of illegal drug use, more than 75 percent of the evidence evaluated by crime laboratories in the United States is drug related (see Figure 10–1). The deluge of drug specimens has forced the expansion of existing crime laboratories and the creation of new ones. For many concerned forensic scientists, the crime laboratory's preoccupation with drug evidence represents a serious distraction from time that could be devoted to evaluating evidence related to homicides and other types of serious crimes. However, the increasing caseloads associated with drug evidence have justified the expansion of forensic laboratory services. This expansion has increased the overall analytical capabilities of crime laboratories.

Drug Dependence

In assessing the potential danger of drugs, society has become particularly conscious of their effects on human behavior. In fact, the first drugs to be regulated by law in the early years of the twentieth century were those deemed to have "habit-forming" properties. The early laws were aimed primarily at controlling opium and its derivatives, cocaine, and later marijuana. The ability of a drug to induce dependence after repeated use is submerged in a complex array of physiological and social factors.

Dependence on drugs exists in numerous patterns and in all degrees of intensity, depending on the nature of the drug, the route of administration, the dose, the frequency of administration, and the individual's rate of

FIGURE 10–1 A drug bust.
Courtesy Syracuse Newspapers/ The Image Works

metabolism. Furthermore, nondrug factors play an equally crucial role in determining the behavioral patterns associated with drug use. The personal characteristics of the user, his or her expectations about the drug experience, society's attitudes toward and possible responses to the drug, and the setting in which the drug is used are all major determinants of drug dependence.

The questions of how to define and measure a drug's influence on the individual and its danger to society are difficult to assess. The nature and significance of drug dependence must be considered from two over-lapping points of view: the interaction of the drug with the individual, and the drug's impact on society. It will be useful to approach the problem from two distinctly different aspects of human behavior—**psychological dependence** and **physical dependence**.

Psychological Dependence

The common denominator that characterizes all types of repeated drug use is the creation of a psychological dependence for continued use of the drug. It is important to discard the unrealistic image that all drug users are hopeless "addicts" who are social dropouts. Most users present quite a normal appearance and remain both socially and economically integrated in the life of the community.

physical dependence
The conditioned use of a drug caused by underlying emotional needs.

psychological dependence
The physiological need for a drug brought about by its regular use and characterized by withdrawal sickness when administration of the drug is abruptly stopped.

FIGURE 10–2 Young people drinking. *Courtesy Daytona Beach New-Journal/Jim Tiller*

The reasons some people abstain from drugs while others become moderately or heavily involved are difficult if not impossible to delineate. Psychological needs arise from numerous personal and social factors that inevitably stem from the individual's desire to create a sense of well-being and to escape from reality. In some cases, the individual may seek relief from personal problems or stressful situations, or may be trying to sustain a physical and emotional state that permits an improved level of performance. Whatever the reasons, the underlying psychological needs and the desire to fulfill them create a conditioned pattern of drug abuse (see Figure 10–2).

The intensity of the psychological dependence associated with a drug's use is difficult to define and largely depends on the nature of the drug used. For drugs such as alcohol, heroin, amphetamines, barbiturates, and cocaine, continued use will likely result in a high degree of involvement. Other drugs, such as marijuana and codeine, appear to have a considerably lower potential for the development of psychological dependence. However, this does not imply that repeated abuse of drugs deemed to have a low potential for psychological dependence is safe or will always produce low psychological dependence. We have no precise way to measure or predict the impact of drug abuse on the individual. Even if a system could be devised for controlling the many possible variables affecting a user's response, the unpredictability of the human personality would still have to be considered.

Our general knowledge of alcohol consumption should warn us of the fallacy of generalizing when attempting to describe the danger of drug abuse. Obviously, not all alcohol drinkers are psychologically addicted to the drug; most are "social" drinkers who drink in reasonable amounts and on an irregular basis. Many people have progressed beyond this stage and consider alcohol a necessary crutch for dealing with life's stresses and anxieties. However, a wide range of behavioral patterns exists among alcohol abusers, and to a large extent the determination of the degree of psychological dependence must be made on an individual basis. Likewise, it would be fallacious to generalize that all users of marijuana can at worst develop a low degree of dependence on the drug. A wide range of factors also influences marijuana's effect, and heavy users of the drug expose themselves to the danger of developing a high degree of psychological dependence.

Physical Dependence

Although emotional well-being is the primary motive leading to repeated and intensive use of a drug, certain drugs, taken in sufficient dose and frequency, can produce physiological changes that encourage their continued use. Once the user abstains from such a drug, severe physical illness follows. The desire to avoid this *withdrawal sickness*, or *abstinence syndrome*, ultimately causes physical dependence, or addiction. Hence, for the addict who is accustomed to receiving large doses of heroin, the thought of abstaining and encountering body chills, vomiting, stomach cramps, convulsions, insomnia, pain, and hallucinations is a powerful inducement for continued drug use.

Interestingly, some of the more widely abused drugs have little or no potential for creating physical dependence. Drugs such as marijuana, LSD, and cocaine create strong anxieties when their repeated use is discontinued; however, no medical evidence attributes these discomforts to physiological reactions that accompany withdrawal sickness. On the other hand, use of alcohol, heroin, and barbiturates can result in the development of physical dependence.

Physical dependence develops only when the drug user adheres to a regular schedule of drug intake; that is, the interval between doses must be short enough so that the effects of the drug never wear off completely. For example, the interval between injections of heroin for the drug addict probably does not exceed six to eight hours. Beyond this time the addict begins to experience the uncomfortable symptoms of withdrawal. Many users of heroin avoid taking the drug on a regular basis for fear of becoming physically addicted to its use. Similarly, the risk of developing physical dependence on alcohol becomes greatest when the consumption is characterized by a continuing pattern of daily use in large quantities.

Table 10–1 categorizes some of the more commonly abused drugs according to their effects on the body and summarizes their tendency to produce psychological dependence and to induce physical dependence with repeated use.

Societal Aspects of Drug Use

The social impact of drug dependence is directly related to the extent to which the user has become preoccupied with the drug. Here, the most important element is the extent to which drug use has become interwoven in the fabric of the user's life. The more frequently the drug satisfies the person's need, the greater the likelihood that he or she will become preoccupied with its use, with a consequent neglect of individual and social responsibilities. Personal health, economic relationships, and family obligations may all suffer as the drug-seeking behavior increases in frequency and intensity and dominates the individual's life. The extreme of drug dependence may lead to behavior that has serious implications for the public's safety, health, and welfare.

Drug dependence in its broadest sense involves much of the world's population. As a result, a complex array of individual, social, cultural, legal, and medical factors ultimately influence society's decision to prohibit or impose strict controls on a drug's distribution and use. Invariably, society must weigh the beneficial aspects of the drug against the ultimate harm its abuse will do to the individual and to society as a whole. Obviously, many forms of drug dependence do not carry sufficient adverse social consequences to warrant their prohibition, as illustrated by the widespread use of such drug-containing substances as tobacco and coffee. Although the

Table 10–1 The Potential of Some Commonly Abused Drugs to Produce Dependence with Regular Use

Drug	Psychological Dependence	Physical Dependence
Narcotics		
Morphine	High	Yes
Heroin	High	Yes
Methadone	High	Yes
Codeine	Low	Yes
Depressants		
Barbiturates (short-acting)	High	Yes
Barbiturates (long-acting)	Low	Yes
Alcohol	High	Yes
Methaqualone (Quaalude)	High	Yes
Meprobamate (Miltown, Equanil)	Moderate	Yes
Diazepam (Valium)	Moderate	Yes
Chlordiazepoxide (Librium)	Moderate	Yes
Stimulants		
Amphetamines	High	?
Cocaine	High	No
Caffeine	Low	No
Nicotine	High	Yes
Hallucinogens		
Marijuana	Low	No
LSD	Low	No
Phencyclidine (PCP)	High	No

heavy and prolonged use of these drugs may eventually damage body organs and injure an individual's health, there is no evidence that they result in antisocial behavior, even with prolonged or excessive use. Hence, society is willing to accept the widespread use of these substances.

We are certainly all aware of the disastrous failure in the United States to prohibit the use of alcohol during the 1920s and the current debate on whether marijuana should be legalized. Each of these issues emphasizes the delicate balance between individual desires and needs and society's concern with the consequences of drug abuse; moreover, this balance is continuously subject to change and reevaluation.

Key Points

- A drug is a natural or synthetic substance that is used to produce physiological or psychological effects in humans or other animals.

- Nondrug factors that play a part in drug dependence include the personal characteristics of the user, his or her expectations about the drug experience, society's attitudes toward and possible responses to the drug, and the setting in which the drug is used.

- Physical dependence is defined as the physiological need for a drug that has been brought about by its regular use. Psychological dependence is the conditioned use of a drug caused by underlying emotional needs.

Types of Drugs

Narcotic Drugs

The term narcotic is derived from the Greek word *narkotikos*, meaning "numbness" or "deadening." Although pharmacologists classify narcotic drugs as substances that relieve pain and produce sleep, the term *narcotic* has become popularly associated with any drug that is socially unacceptable. As a consequence of this incorrect usage, many drugs are improperly called narcotics.

This confusion has produced legal definitions that differ from the pharmacological actions of many drugs. For example, until the early 1970s, most drug laws in the United States incorrectly designated marijuana as a narcotic. Even today, federal law classifies cocaine as a narcotic drug, although pharmacologically, cocaine is actually a powerful central nervous system stimulant, possessing properties opposite those normally associated with the depressant effects of a narcotic.

Opiates   Medical professionals apply the term *opiate* to most of the drugs properly classified as narcotics. Opiates behave pharmacologically like morphine, a painkiller derived from opium—a gummy, milky juice exuded through a cut made in the unripe pod of the Asian poppy *(Papaver somniferum)*. Although morphine is readily extracted from opium, the most commonly used opium-based drug is heroin, which is produced by reacting morphine with acetic anhydride or acetyl chloride (see Figure 10–3). Heroin's high solubility in water makes its street preparation for intravenous administration rather simple, for only by injection are heroin's effects felt almost instantaneously and with maximum sensitivity. To prepare the drug for injection, the addict frequently dissolves it in a small

narcotic
A drug that induces sleep and depresses vital body functions such as blood pressure, pulse rate, and breathing rate.

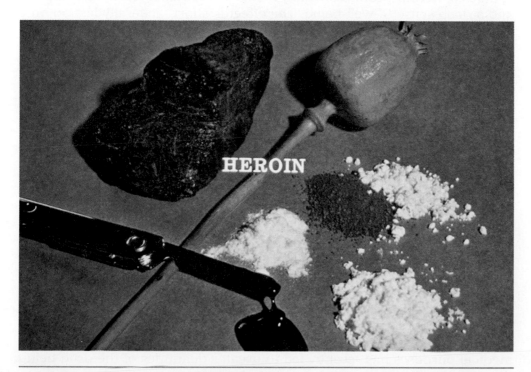

FIGURE 10–3   The opium poppy and its derivatives. Shown are the poppy plant, crude and smoking opium, codeine, heroin, and morphine. *Courtesy Drug Enforcement Administration, Washington, D.C.*

FIGURE 10–4 Heroin paraphernalia. *Courtesy Drug Enforcement Administration, Washington, D.C.*

analgesic
A substance that lessens or
eliminates pain.

quantity of water in a spoon. The process can be speeded up by heating the spoon over a candle or several matches. The solution is then drawn into a syringe or eyedropper for injection under the skin (see Figure 10–4).

Heroin and other narcotic drugs are analgesics—that is, they relieve pain by depressing the central nervous system. Besides being a powerful analgesic, heroin produces a "high" that is accompanied by drowsiness and a deep sense of well-being. The effect is short, generally lasting only three to four hours. Regular use of heroin—or any other narcotic drug— invariably leads to physical dependence, with all its dire consequences.

Codeine is also present in opium, but it is usually prepared synthetically from morphine. It is commonly used as a cough suppressant in prescription cough syrup. Codeine, only one-sixth as strong as morphine, is not an attractive street drug for addicts.

Synthetic Opiates A number of narcotic drugs are not naturally derived from opium. However, because they have similar physiological effects on the body as the opium narcotics, they are also commonly referred to as opiates.

Methadone is perhaps the best known synthetic opiate. In the 1960s, scientists discovered that a person who received periodic doses of methadone would not get high if he or she then took heroin or morphine. Although methadone is pharmacologically related to heroin, its administration appears to eliminate the addict's desire for heroin, with minimal side effects. These discoveries led to the establishment of controversial methadone maintenance programs in which heroin addicts receive methadone to reduce or prevent future heroin use. Physicians increasingly prescribe methadone for pain relief. Unfortunately, the wide availability of methadone for legitimate medical purposes has recently led to greater quantities of the drug being diverted into the illicit market.

In 1995, the U.S. Food and Drug Administration (FDA) approved for use the painkilling drug *OxyContin*. The active ingredient in OxyContin

Closer Analysis

What's in That Bag?

The content of a typical heroin bag is an excellent example of the uncertainty attached to buying illicit drugs. For many years into the 1960s and early 1970s, the average bag contained 15 to 20 percent heroin. Currently, the average purity of heroin obtained in the illicit U.S. market is approximately 35 percent. The addict rarely knows or cares what comprises the other 65 percent or so of the material.

Traditionally, quinine has been the most common diluent of heroin. Like heroin, it has a bitter taste and was probably originally used to obscure the actual potency of a heroin preparation from those who wished to taste-test the material before buying it. Other diluents commonly added to heroin are starch, lactose, procaine (Novocain), and mannitol.

is oxycodone, a synthetic drug closely related to morphine and heroin in its chemical structure. OxyContin is an analgesic narcotic that has effects similar to those of heroin. It is prescribed to a million patients for treatment of chronic pain with doctors writing close to seven million OxyContin prescriptions each year. The drug is compounded with a time-release formulation that the manufacturer initially believed would reduce the risk of abuse and addiction. This has not turned out to be the case. It is estimated that close to a quarter of a million individuals abuse the drug.

Because it is a legal drug that is diverted from legitimate sources, Oxy-Contin is obtained very differently from illegal drugs. Pharmacy robberies, forged prescriptions, and theft of the drug from patients with a legitimate prescription are ways abusers access OxyContin. Some abusers visit numerous doctors and receive prescriptions even though their medical condition may not warrant it.

Hallucinogens

Hallucinogens are drugs that can cause marked alterations in normal thought processes, perceptions, and moods. Perhaps the most popular and controversial member of this class of drugs is marijuana.

hallucinogen
A substance that induces changes in normal thought processes, perceptions, and moods.

Marijuana   Marijuana is the popular name of the plant *Cannabis sativa*, a weed that grows wild under most climatic conditions. The *Cannabis* plant contains a chemical known as *tetrahydrocannabinol*, or THC, which produces the psychoactive effects experienced by users. The THC content of *Cannabis* varies in different parts of the plant. The greatest concentration is usually found in a sticky resin produced by the plant, known as *hashish*. Declining concentrations are typically found in the flowers and leaves, respectively. Little THC is found in the stem, roots, or seeds of the plant. The potency and resulting effect of the drug fluctuate, depending on the relative proportion of these plant parts in the marijuana mixture consumed by the user. The most common method of administration is by smoking either the dried flowers and leaves, or various preparations of hashish (see Figure 10–5). Marijuana is also occasionally taken orally, typically baked in sweets such as brownies or cookies.

Any study of marijuana's effect on humans must consider the potency of the marijuana preparation. An interesting insight into the relationship

FIGURE 10–5 Several rolled marijuana cigarettes lie on a pile of crushed, dried marijuana leaves next to a tobacco cigarette. *Courtesy Drug Enforcement Administration, Washington, D.C.*

between dosage level and marijuana's pharmacological effect was presented in the first report of the National Commission on Marijuana and Drug Abuse:

> At low, usual "social" doses the user may experience an increased sense of well-being; initial restlessness and hilarity followed by a dreamy, carefree state of relaxation; alteration of sensory perceptions including expansion of space and time; a more vivid sense of touch, sight, smell, taste and sound; a feeling of hunger, especially a craving for sweets; and subtle changes in thought formation and expression. To an unknowing observer, an individual in this state of consciousness would not appear noticeably different from his normal state.
>
> At higher, moderate doses these same reactions are intensified but the changes in the individual would still be scarcely noticeable to an observer. At very high doses, psychotomimetic phenomena may be experienced. These include distortion of body image, loss of personal identity, sensory and mental illusions, fantasies and hallucinations.[1]

Marijuana easily qualifies as the most widely used illicit drug in the United States. For instance, more than 43 million Americans have tried marijuana, according to the latest surveys, and almost half that number may be regular users. In addition to its widespread illegal use, accumulating evidence suggests that marijuana has potential medical uses. Two promising areas of research are marijuana's reduction of excessive eye pressure in glaucoma and the lessening of nausea caused by powerful anticancer drugs. Marijuana may also be useful as a muscle relaxant.

Closer Analysis

Marijuana and Hashish

Marijuana is a weed that grows wild under most climatic conditions. The plant grows to a height of 5 to 15 feet and is characterized by an odd number of leaflets on each leaf. Normally each leaf contains five to nine leaflets, all with serrated or saw-tooth edges.

The potency of marijuana depends on its form. Marijuana in the form of loose vegetation has an average THC content of about 3 to 4.5 percent. The more potent sinsemilla form averages about 6 to 12 percent in THC content. Sinsemilla is made from the unfertilized flowering tops of the female *Cannabis* plants, acquired by removing all male plants from the growing field at the first sign of their appearance. Production of sinsemilla requires a great deal of attention and care, and the plant is therefore cultivated on small plots.

Blocks of hashish in front of leaves and flowering tops of the marijuana plant.
Courtesy James King-Holmes, Photo Researchers, Inc.

The marijuana leaf. *Courtesy Drug Enforcement Administration, Washington, D.C.*

Hashish preparations average about 2 to 8 percent THC. On the illicit drug market, hashish (see photo above) usually appears in the form of compressed vegetation containing a high percentage of resin. A particularly potent form of hashish is known as *liquid hashish* or *hashish oil*. Hashish in this form is normally a viscous substance, dark green with a tarry consistency. Liquid hashish is produced by efficiently extracting the THC-rich resin from the marijuana plant with an appropriate solvent, such as alcohol. Liquid hashish typically varies between 8 and 22 percent in THC content. Because of its extraordinary potency, one drop of the material can produce a "high."

No current evidence suggests that experimental or intermittent use causes physical or psychological harm. Marijuana does not cause physical dependence. However, the risk of harm lies instead in heavy, long-term use, particularly of the more potent preparations. Heavy users can develop a strong psychological dependence on the drug. Some effects of marijuana use include increased heart rate, dry mouth, reddened eyes, impaired motor skills and concentration, and frequently hunger and an increased desire for sweets.

Other Hallucinogens   A substantial number of other substances with widely varying chemical compositions are also used recreationally because of their hallucinogenic properties. These include both naturally occurring substances such as mescaline and psilocybin and synthetically created drugs including lysergic acid diethylamide (LSD) and phencyclidine (PCP).

LSD is synthesized from lysergic acid, a substance derived from ergot, which is a type of fungus that attacks certain grasses and grains. The drug appears in a variety of forms—as a pill, added to a cube of sugar, or absorbed onto a small piece of paper—and is taken orally. Its hallucinogenic effects were first described by the Swiss chemist Albert Hofmann after he accidentally ingested some of the material in his laboratory in 1943. LSD produces marked changes in mood, leading to laughing or crying at the slightest provocation. Feelings of anxiety and tension almost always accompany LSD use. LSD is very potent; as little as 25 micrograms

Closer Analysis

A Brief History of Marijuana

Marijuana and its related products have been in use legally and illegally for almost three thousand years. The first reference to medical use of marijuana is in a pharmacy book written about 2737 B.C. by the Chinese emperor Shen Nung, who recommended it for "female weakness, gout, rheumatism, malaria, beriberi, constipation and absent-mindedness." In China, at that time and even today, the marijuana or hemp plant was also a major source of fiber for rope production. Marijuana's mood-altering powers probably did not receive wide attention until about 500 B.C., when it became an integral part of Hindu culture in India. After A.D. 500, marijuana began creeping westward, and references to it began to appear in Persian and Arabian literature.

The plant was probably brought to Europe by Napoleon's soldiers when they returned from Egypt in the early nineteenth century. In Europe, the drug excited the interest of many physicians, who foresaw its application for treating a wide range of ailments. At this time, it also found some use as a painkiller and mild sedative. In later years, these applications were either forgotten or ignored.

Marijuana was first introduced into the United States around 1920. The weed was smuggled by Mexican laborers across the border into Texas. American soldiers also brought the plant in from the ports of Havana, Tampico, and Veracruz. Although its use was confined to a small segment of the population, its popularity quickly spread from the border and Gulf states into most major U.S. cities. By 1937, forty-six states and the federal government had laws prohibiting the use or possession of marijuana. Under most of these laws, marijuana was subject to the same rigorous penalties applicable to morphine, heroin, and cocaine and was often erroneously designated a narcotic.

is enough to start vivid visual hallucinations that can last for about twelve hours. Although physical dependence does not develop with continued use, the individual user may be prone to flashbacks and psychotic reactions even after use is discontinued.

Abuse of the hallucinogen phencyclidine, commonly called PCP, has recently grown to alarming proportions. Because this drug can be synthesized by simple chemical processes, it is manufactured surreptitiously for the illicit market in so-called clandestine laboratories (see Figure 10–6). These laboratories range from large, sophisticated operations to small labs located in garages or bathrooms. Small-time operators normally have little or no training in chemistry and employ "cookbook" methods to synthesize the drug. Some of the more knowledgeable and experienced operators have been able to achieve clandestine production levels that approach a commercial level of operation.

Phencyclidine is often mixed with other drugs, such as LSD or amphetamines, and is sold as a powder ("angel dust"), capsule, or tablet, or as a liquid sprayed on plant leaves. The drug is smoked, ingested, or sniffed. Following oral intake of moderate doses (1 to 6 milligrams), the user first experiences feelings of strength and invulnerability, along with a dreamy sense of detachment. However, the user soon becomes unresponsive, confused, and agitated. Depression, irritability, feelings of isolation, audio and visual hallucinations, and sometimes paranoia accompany PCP use. Severe depression, tendencies toward violence, and suicide accompany long-term daily use of the drug. In some cases, the PCP user experiences sudden schizophrenic behavior days after the drug has been taken.

Depressants

Depressants are drugs that slow down, or depress, the central nervous system. Several types of drugs fall under this category, including the most widely used drug in the United States—alcohol.

FIGURE 10–6 A scene from a clandestine drug laboratory. *Courtesy Drug Enforcement Administration, Washington, D.C.*

depressant

A substance that slows down, or depresses, the functions of the central nervous system.

Alcohol (Ethyl Alcohol) Many people overlook the fact that alcohol is a drug; however, it exerts a powerful **depressant** action on the central nervous system. When alcohol enters the bloodstream, it quickly travels to the brain, where it suppresses the brain's control of thought processes and muscle coordination. Low doses of alcohol tend to inhibit the mental processes of judgment, memory, and concentration. The drinker's personality becomes expansive, and he or she exudes confidence. When taken in moderate doses, alcohol reduces coordination substantially, inhibits orderly thought processes and speech patterns, and slows reaction times. Under these conditions, the ability to walk or drive becomes noticeably impaired. Higher doses of alcohol may cause the user to become highly irritable and emotional; displays of anger and crying are not uncommon. Extremely high doses may cause an individual to lapse into unconsciousness or even a comatose state that may precede a fatal depression of circulatory and respiratory functions. The behavioral patterns of alcohol intoxication vary and depend partly on such factors as the social setting, the amount consumed, and the personal expectation of the individual with regard to alcohol.

In the United States, the alcohol industry annually produces more than one billion gallons of spirits, wine, and beer for which 90 million consumers pay nearly $40 billion. Unquestionably, these and other statistics support the fact that alcohol is the most widely used and abused drug (see Figure 10–7).

Barbiturates Barbiturates are derivatives of barbituric acid, a substance first synthesized by a German chemist, Adolf Von Bayer, more than a hundred years ago. They are commonly referred to as "downers" because they relax the user, create a feeling of well-being, and produce sleep. Like alcohol, barbiturates suppress the vital functions of the central nervous system. Twenty-five barbiturate derivatives are currently used in medical practice in the United States; however, five—amobarbital, secobarbital, phenobarbital, pentobarbital, and butabarbital—tend to be used for most medical applications.

Normally, barbiturate users take these drugs orally. The average sedative dose is about 10 to 70 milligrams. When taken in this fashion, the drug

FIGURE 10–7 Rows of alcohol bottles behind a bar. *Courtesy Jeremy Liebman/Stone/Getty Images*

enters the blood through the walls of the small intestine. Some barbiturates, such as phenobarbital, are classified as long-acting barbiturates. They are absorbed into the bloodstream more slowly than others and therefore produce less pronounced effects than faster-acting barbiturates. The slow action of phenobarbital accounts for its low incidence of abuse. Apparently, barbiturate abusers prefer the faster-acting varieties—secobarbital, pentobarbital, and amobarbital.

Since the early 1970s, a nonbarbiturate depressant, methaqualone (Quaalude), has appeared on the illicit-drug scene. Methaqualone is a powerful sedative and muscle relaxant that possesses many of the depressant properties of barbiturates. When taken in prescribed amounts, barbiturates are relatively safe, but in instances of extensive and prolonged use, physical dependence can develop.

Antipsychotic and Antianxiety Drugs   Although antipsychotic and antianxiety drugs can be considered depressants, they differ from barbiturates in the extent of their actions on the central nervous system. Generally, these drugs produce a relaxing tranquility without impairing high-thinking faculties or inducing sleep. Antipsychotics such as reserpine and chlorpromazine have been used to reduce the anxieties and tensions of mental patients. Antianxiety drugs are commonly prescribed to deal with the everyday tensions of many healthy people. These drugs include meprobamate (Miltown), chlordiazepoxide (Librium), and diazepam (Valium).

In the past thirty-five years, the use of these drugs—particularly antianxiety drugs—has grown dramatically. Medical evidence shows that these drugs produce psychological and physical dependence with repeated and high levels of usage. For this reason, the widespread prescribing of antianxiety drugs to overcome the pressures and tensions of life has worried many who fear the creation of a legalized drug culture.

"Huffing"   Since the early 1960s, "huffing," the practice of sniffing materials containing volatile solvents (airplane glue or model cement, for example), has grown in popularity. Another dimension has recently been added to the problem with the increasing number of incidents involving the sniffing of aerosol gas propellants such as freon. All materials abused by huffing contain volatile or gaseous substances that are primarily central nervous system depressants. Although toluene (a solvent used in airplane glue) seems to be the most popular solvent to sniff, others can produce comparable physiological effects. These chemicals include naphtha, methyl ethyl ketone (antifreeze), gasoline, and trichloroethylene (dry-cleaning solvent).

The usual immediate effects of huffing are a feeling of exhilaration and euphoria combined with slurred speech, impaired judgment, and double vision. Finally, the user may experience drowsiness and stupor, with these depressant effects slowly wearing off as the user returns to a normal state. Most experts believe that users become physiologically dependent on the effects achieved by huffing. However, little evidence suggests that solvent inhalation is addictive. But huffers expose themselves to the danger of liver, heart, and brain damage from the chemicals they have inhaled. Even worse, sniffing of some solvents, particularly halogenated hydrocarbons such as freon and related gases, is accompanied by a significant risk of death.

Stimulants

The term **stimulants** refers to a range of drugs that stimulate, or speed up, the central nervous system.

stimulant
A substance that speeds up, or stimulates, the activity of the central nervous system.

Amphetamines Amphetamines are a group of synthetic stimulants that share a similar chemical structure and are commonly referred to in the terminology of the drug culture as "uppers" or "speed." They are typically taken either orally or via intravenous injection and provide a feeling of well-being and increased alertness that is followed by a decrease in fatigue and a loss of appetite. However, these apparent benefits of the drug are accompanied by restlessness and instability or apprehension, and once the stimulant effect wears off, depression may set in.

In the United States, the most serious form of amphetamine abuse stems from intravenous injection of amphetamine or its chemical derivative, methamphetamine (see Figure 10–8). The desire for a more intense amphetamine experience is the primary motive for this route of administration. The initial sensation of a "flash" or "rush," followed by an intense feeling of pleasure, constitutes the principal appeal of the intravenous route for the user. During a "speed binge," the individual may inject amphetamines every two to three hours. Users have reported experiencing a euphoria that produces hyperactivity, with a feeling of clarity of vision as well as hallucinations. As the effect of the amphetamines wears off, the individual lapses into a period of exhaustion and may sleep continuously for one or two days. Following this, the user often experiences a prolonged period of severe depression, lasting from days to weeks.

A smokable form of methamphetamine known as "ice" is reportedly in heavy demand in some areas of the United States. Ice is prepared by slowly evaporating a methamphetamine solution to produce large, crystal-clear "rocks." Like crack cocaine (discussed next), ice is smoked and produces effects similar to those of crack cocaine, but the effects last longer. Once the effects of ice wear off, users often become depressed and may sleep for days. Chronic users exhibit violent destructive behavior and acute psychosis similar to paranoid schizophrenia. Repeated use of amphetamines leads to a strong psychological dependence, which encourages their continued administration.

FIGURE 10–8 Granular amphetamine beside a razor blade. *Courtesy Cordelia Mollo, Photo Researchers, Inc.*

Cocaine Between 1884 and 1887, pioneering psychologist Sigmund Freud created something of a sensation in European medical circles by describing his experiments with a new drug. He reported a substance of seemingly limitless potential as a source of "exhilaration and lasting euphoria" that permitted "intensive mental or physical work [to be] performed without fatigue. . . . It is as though the need for food and sleep was completely banished."

The object of Freud's enthusiasm was cocaine, a stimulant extracted from the leaves of *Erythroxylon coca*, a plant grown in the Andes mountains of South America as well as in tropical Asia (see Figure 10–9). Most commonly, cocaine is sniffed or "snorted" and is absorbed into the body through the mucous membranes of the nose, although it is sometimes injected. Cocaine is a powerful stimulant to the central nervous system, and its effects resemble those caused by amphetamines—namely, increased alertness and vigor, accompanied by suppression of hunger, fatigue, and boredom. Cocaine produces a feeling of euphoria by stimulating a pleasure center in the base of the brain, in an area connected to nerves that are responsible for emotions. It stimulates this pleasure center to a far greater degree than it would ever normally be stimulated. Some regular users of cocaine report accompanying feelings of restlessness, irritability, and anxiety. Cocaine used chronically or at high doses can have toxic effects. Cocaine-related deaths result from cardiac arrest or seizures followed by respiratory arrest.

A particularly potent form of cocaine known as "crack" can be produced by mixing cocaine with baking soda and water and then heating the resulting solution. This material is then dried and broken into tiny chunks that dealers sell as crack "rocks" that are sufficiently volatile to be smoked. The faster the cocaine level rises in the brain, the greater the euphoria, and the surest way to obtain a fast rise in the brain's cocaine level is to smoke crack. Inhaling the cocaine vapor delivers the drug to the brain in less than fifteen seconds—about as fast as injecting it and much faster than snorting it. The dark side of crack, however, is that the euphoria fades quickly as cocaine levels drop, leaving the user feeling depressed, anxious, and pleasureless. The

coca leaves and cocaine

FIGURE 10–9 Coca leaves and illicit forms of cocaine. *Courtesy Drug Enforcement Administration, Washington, D.C.*

desire to return to a euphoric feeling is so intense that crack users quickly develop a habit for the drug that is almost impossible to overcome. Only a small percentage of crack abusers are ever cured of this drug habit.

In the United States, cocaine abuse is on the rise. Many people are apparently using cocaine to improve their ability to work and to keep going when tired. Although there is no evidence of physical dependency accompanying cocaine's repeated use, abstention from cocaine after prolonged use brings on severe bouts of mental depression, which produce a very strong compulsion to resume using the drug. In fact, laboratory experiments with animals have demonstrated that of all the commonly abused drugs, cocaine produces the strongest psychological compulsions for continued use.

The United States spends millions of dollars annually in attempting to control cultivation of the coca leaf in various South American countries and to prevent cocaine trafficking into the United States. Three-quarters of the cocaine smuggled into the United States is refined in clandestine laboratories in Colombia. The profits are astronomical. Peruvian farmers may be paid $200 for enough coca leaves to make one pound of cocaine. The refined cocaine is worth $1,000 when it leaves Colombia and sells at retail in the United States for up to $20,000.

Club Drugs

The term *club drugs* refers to synthetic drugs that are often used at nightclubs, bars, and raves (all-night dance parties). Substances that are used as club drugs include, but are not limited to, MDMA (Ecstasy; see Figure 10–10), GHB (gamma hydroxybutyrate), Rohypnol ("Roofies"), ketamine, and methamphetamine. These drugs have become popular at the dance scene as a way to stimulate the rave experience. A high incidence of use has been found among teens and young adults.

GHB and Rohypnol are central nervous system depressants that are often connected with drug-facilitated sexual assault, rape, and robbery. Effects

FIGURE 10–10 **Ecstasy, a popular club drug.** *Courtesy Rusty Kennedy, AP World Photos*

accompanying the use of GHB include dizziness, sedation, headache, and nausea. Recreational users have reported euphoria, relaxation, disinhibition, and increased libido (sex drive). Rohypnol causes muscle relaxation, loss of consciousness, and an inability to remember what happened during the hours after ingesting the drug. This is particularly a concern in a sexual assault because victims are physically unable to resist the attack. Unsuspecting victims become drowsy or dizzy. Effects are even stronger when the drug is combined with alcohol because the user experiences memory loss, blackouts, and disinhibition. Drugs such as Rohypnol and GHB are odorless, colorless, and tasteless, and thus remain undetected when slipped into a drink.

Methylenedioxymethamphetamine, also known as MDMA or Ecstasy, is a synthetic, mind-altering drug that exhibits many hallucinogenic and amphetamine-like effects. Ecstasy was originally patented as an appetite suppressant and was later discovered to induce feelings of happiness and relaxation. Recreational drug users find that Ecstasy enhances self-awareness and decreases inhibitions. However, seizures, muscle breakdown, stroke, kidney failure, and cardiovascular system failure often accompany chronic abuse of Ecstasy. In addition, chronic use of Ecstasy leads to serious damage to the areas of the brain responsible for thought and memory. Ecstasy increases heart rate and blood pressure; produces muscle tension, teeth grinding, and nausea; and causes psychological difficulties such as confusion, severe anxiety, and paranoia. The drug can cause significant increases in body temperature from the combination of the drug's stimulant effect with the often hot, crowded atmosphere of a rave club.

Ketamine is primarily used in veterinary medicine as an animal anesthetic. When used by humans, the drug can cause euphoria and feelings of unreality accompanied by visual hallucinations. Ketamine can also cause impaired motor function, high blood pressure, amnesia, and mild respiratory depression.

Anabolic Steroids

Anabolic steroids are synthetic compounds that are chemically related to the male sex hormone testosterone. Testosterone has two effects on the body. It promotes the development of secondary male characteristics (androgenic effects), and it accelerates muscle growth (anabolic effects). Efforts to promote muscle growth and to minimize the hormone's androgenic effects have led to the synthesis of numerous anabolic steroids. However, a steroid free of the accompanying harmful side effects of an androgen drug has not yet been developed.

Incidence of steroid abuse first received widespread public attention when both amateur and professional athletes were discovered using these substances to enhance their performance. Interestingly, current research on male athletes given anabolic steroids has generally found little or, at best, marginal evidence of enhanced strength or performance. Although the full extent of anabolic steroid abuse by the general public is not fully known, the U.S. government is sufficiently concerned to regulate the availability of these drugs to the general population and to severely punish individuals for illegal possession and distribution of anabolic steroids. In 1991, anabolic steroids were classified as controlled dangerous substances, and the Drug Enforcement Administration was given enforcement power to prevent their illegal use and distribution.

Anabolic steroids are usually taken by individuals who are unfamiliar with the harmful medical side effects. Liver cancer and other liver malfunctions have been linked to steroid use. These drugs also cause masculinizing

anabolic steroids
Synthetic compounds, chemically related to the male sex hormone testosterone, that are used to promote muscle growth.

effects in females, infertility, and diminished sex drive in males. For teenagers, anabolic steroids result in the premature halting of bone growth. Anabolic steroids can also cause unpredictable effects on mood and personality, leading to unprovoked acts of anger and destructive behavior. Depression is also a frequent side effect of anabolic steroid abuse.

Key Points

- Narcotic drugs are analgesics, meaning that they relieve pain by depressing the central nervous system.

- The most common source for narcotic drugs is opium. Morphine is extracted from opium and used to synthesize heroin.

- Opiates are not derived from opium or morphine, but they have the same physiological effects on the body. Examples of opiates are methadone and OxyContin (oxycodone).

- Hallucinogens cause marked changes in normal thought processes, perceptions, and moods. Marijuana is the most well-known drug in this class. Other hallucinogens include LSD, mescaline, PCP, psilocybin, and MDMA (Ecstasy).

- Depressants decrease the activity of the central nervous system, calm irritability and excitability, and produce sleep. Depressants include alcohol (ethanol), barbiturates, tranquilizers, and various substances that can be sniffed, such as airplane glue and model cement.

- Stimulants increase the activity of the central nervous system and are taken to increase alertness and activity. Stimulants include amphetamines, sometimes known as "uppers" or "speed," and cocaine, which in its freebase form is known as *crack*.

- Club drugs are synthetic drugs that are used at nightclubs, bars, and raves (all-night dance parties). Some club drugs act as stimulants; others have depressant effects.

- Anabolic steroids are synthetic compounds that are chemically related to the male sex hormone testosterone. Anabolic steroids are often abused by individuals who are interested in accelerating muscle growth.

Drug-Control Laws

The provisions of drug laws are of particular interest to the criminalist, for they may impose specific analytical requirements on drug analysis. For example, the severity of a penalty associated with the manufacture, distribution, possession, and use of a drug may depend on the weight of the drug or its concentration in a mixture. In such cases, the chemist's report must contain all information that is needed to properly charge a suspect under the provisions of the existing law.

The provisions of any drug-control law are an outgrowth of national and local law enforcement requirements and customs, as well as the result of moral and political philosophies. These factors have produced a wide

Closer Analysis

Controlled Substances Act

The federal Controlled Substances Act establishes five schedules of classification for controlled dangerous substances on the basis of a drug's potential for abuse, potential for physical and psychological dependence, and medical value. This classification system is extremely flexible in that the U.S. attorney general has the authority to add, delete, or reschedule a drug as more information becomes available.

Schedule I. Schedule I drugs have a high potential for abuse, have no currently accepted medical use in the United States, and/or lack accepted safety for use in treatment under medical supervision. Drugs controlled under this schedule include heroin, marijuana, methaqualone, and LSD.

Schedule II. Schedule II drugs have a high potential for abuse, a currently accepted medical use or a medical use with severe restrictions, and a potential for severe psychological or physical dependence. Schedule II drugs include opium and its derivatives not listed in schedule I, cocaine, methadone, phencyclidine (PCP), most amphetamine preparations, and most barbiturate preparations containing amobarbital, secobarbital, and pentobarbital. Dronabinol, the synthetic equivalent of the active ingredient in marijuana, has been placed in schedule II in recognition of its growing medical uses in treating glaucoma and chemotherapy patients.

Schedule III. Schedule III drugs have less potential for abuse than those in schedules I and II, a currently accepted medical use in the United States, and a potential for low or moderate physical dependence or high psychological dependence. Schedule III controls, among other substances, all barbiturate preparations (except phenobarbital) not covered under schedule II and certain codeine preparations. Anabolic steroids were added to this schedule in 1991.

Schedule IV. Schedule IV drugs have a low potential for abuse relative to schedule III drugs and have a current medical use in the United States; their abuse may lead to limited dependence relative to schedule III drugs. Drugs controlled in this schedule include propoxyphene (Darvon), phenobarbital, and tranquilizers such as meprobamate (Miltown), diazepam (Valium), and chlordiazepoxide (Librium).

Schedule V. Schedule V drugs must show low abuse potential, have medical use in the United States, and have less potential for producing dependence than schedule IV drugs. Schedule V controls certain opiate drug mixtures that contain nonnarcotic medicinal ingredients.

Controlled dangerous substances listed in schedules I and II are subject to manufacturing quotas set by the attorney general. For example, eight billion doses of amphetamines were manufactured in the United States in 1971. In 1972, production quotas were established reducing amphetamine production approximately 80 percent below 1971 levels.

The criminal penalties for the unauthorized manufacture, sale, or possession of controlled dangerous substances are related to the schedules as well. The most severe penalties are associated with drugs listed in schedules I and II. For example, for drugs included in schedules I and II, a first offense is punishable by up to twenty years in prison and/or a fine of up to $1 million for an individual or up to $5 million for other than individuals. The table summarizes the control mechanisms

(continued)

Closer Analysis (Continued)

Control Mechanisms of the Controlled Substances Act

Schedule	Registration	Record Keeping	Manufacturing Quotas	Distribution Restrictions	Dispensing Limits
I	Required	Separate	Yes	Order forms	Research use only
II	Required	Separate	Yes	Order forms	Rx: written; no refills
III	Required	Readily retrievable	No, but some drugs limited by schedule II quotas	Records required	Rx: written or oral; with medical authorization refills up to 5 times in 6 months
IV	Required	Readily retrievable	No, but some drugs limited by schedule II quotas	Records required	Rx: written or oral; with medical authorization refills up to 5 times in 6 months
V	Required	Readily retrievable	No, but some drugs limited by schedule II quotas	Records required	Over-the-counter (Rx drugs limited to MD's order) refills up to 5 times

Source: Drug Enforcement Administration, Washington, D.C.

and penalties for each schedule of the Controlled Substances Act.

The Controlled Substances Act also stipulates that an offense involving a controlled substance analog, a chemical substance substantially similar in chemical structure to a controlled substance, triggers penalties as if it were a controlled substance listed in schedule i. This section is designed to combat the proliferation of so-called *designer drugs*—substances that are chemically related to some controlled drugs and are pharmacologically very potent. These substances are manufactured by skilled individuals in clandestine laboratories, with the knowledge that their products will not be covered by the schedules of the Controlled Substances Act. For instance, fentanyl is a powerful narcotic that is commercially marketed for medical use

and is also listed as a controlled dangerous substance. This drug is about one hundred times as potent as morphine. A number of substances chemically related to fentanyl have been synthesized by underground chemists and sold on the street. The first such substance encountered was sold under the street name China White. These drugs have been responsible for more than a hundred overdose deaths in California and nearly twenty deaths in western Pennsylvania. As designer drugs, such as China White, are identified and linked to drug abuse, they are placed in appropriate schedules.

The Controlled Substances Act also reflects an effort to decrease the prevalence of clandestine drug laboratories designed to manufacture controlled substances. The act regulates the

Closer Analysis

Import–Export		Security	Manufacturer/Distributor Reports to Drug Enforcement Administration	Criminal Penalties for Individual Trafficking (First Offense)
Narcotic	Nonnarcotic			
Permit	Permit	Vault/safe	Yes	0–20 years/$1 million
Permit	Permit	Vault/safe	Yes	0–20 years/$1 million
Permit	Declaration	Secure storage area	Yes, narcotic; no, nonnarcotic	0–5 years/$250,000
Permit	Declaration	Secure storage area	Manufacturer only; narcotic; no, nonnarcotic	0–3 years/$250,000
Permit to import; declaration to export	Declaration	Secure storage area	Manufacturer only, narcotic; no, nonnarcotic	0–1 year/$100,000

manufacture and distribution of precursors, the chemical compounds used by clandestine drug laboratories to synthesize abused drugs. Targeted precursor chemicals are listed in the definition section of the Controlled Substances Act. Severe penalties are provided for a person who possesses a listed precursor chemical with the intent to manufacture a controlled substance or who possesses or distributes a listed chemical knowing, or having reasonable cause to believe, that the listed chemical will be used to manufacture a controlled substance. In addition, precursors to PCP, amphetamines, and methamphetamines are enumerated specifically in schedule II, making them subject to regulation in the same manner as other schedule II substances.

spectrum of national and local drug-control laws. Although their detailed discussion is beyond the intended scope of this book, a brief description of the U.S. federal law known as the Controlled Substances Act will illustrate a legal drug classification system that has been created to prevent and control drug abuse. Many states have modeled their own drug-control laws after this act, an important step in establishing uniform drug-control laws throughout the United States.

Collection and Preservation of Drug Evidence

Preparation of drug evidence for submission to the crime laboratory is normally relatively simple, accomplished with minimal precautions in the field. The field investigator must ensure that the evidence is properly packaged and labeled for delivery to the laboratory. Considering the countless forms and varieties of drug evidence seized, it is not practical to prescribe any single packaging procedure for fulfilling these requirements. Generally, common sense is the best guide in such situations, keeping in mind that the package must prevent loss and/or cross-contamination of the contents. Often, the original container in which the drug was seized will suffice to meet these requirements. Specimens suspected of containing volatile solvents, such as those involved in glue-sniffing cases, must be packaged in an airtight container to prevent evaporation of the solvent. All packages must be marked with sufficient information to ensure identification by the officer in future legal proceedings and to establish the chain of custody.

To aid the drug analyst, the investigator should supply any background information that may relate to a drug's identity. Analysis time can be markedly reduced when the chemist has this information. For the same reason, the results of drug-screening tests used in the field must also be transmitted to the laboratory. However, although these tests may indicate the presence of a drug and may help the officer establish probable cause to search and arrest a suspect, they do not offer conclusive evidence of a drug's identity.

Key Points

- Federal law establishes five schedules of classification for controlled dangerous substances on the basis of a drug's potential for abuse, potential for physical and psychological dependence, and medical value.

- The packaging of drug evidence must prevent loss and/or cross-contamination of the contents, and often the original container in which the drug was seized is used. Specimens suspected of containing volatile solvents must be packaged in an airtight container to prevent evaporation.

- The investigator may help in the identification of the drug by supplying any background information that may relate to the drug's identity to the drug analyst.

Forensic Drug Analysis

One only has to look into the evidence vaults of crime laboratories to appreciate the assortment of drug specimens that confront the criminalist. The presence of a huge array of powders, tablets, capsules, vegetable matter, liquids, pipes, cigarettes, cookers, and syringes is testimony to the vitality and sophistication of the illicit-drug market. If outward appearance is not evidence enough of the difficult analytical chore facing the forensic chemist, consider the complexity of the drug preparations themselves. Usually these contain active drug ingredients of unknown origin and identity, as well as additives—for example, sugar, starch, and quinine—that dilute their potency and stretch their value on the illicit-drug market.

Do not forget that illicit-drug dealers are not hampered by government regulations that ensure the quality and consistency of a product.

When a forensic chemist picks up a drug specimen for analysis, he or she can expect to find just about anything, so all contingencies must be prepared for. The analysis must leave no room for error, because its results will have a direct bearing on the process of determining the guilt or innocence of a defendant. There is no middle ground in drug identification—either the specimen is a specific drug or it is not—and once a positive conclusion is drawn, the chemist must be prepared to support and defend the validity of the results in a court of law.

Screening and Confirmation

The challenge or difficulty of forensic drug identification comes in selecting analytical procedures that will ensure a specific identification of a drug. Presented with a substance of unknown origin and composition, the forensic chemist must develop a plan of action that will ultimately yield the drug's identity. This plan, or scheme of analysis, is divided into two phases.

First, faced with the prospect that the unknown substance may be any one of a thousand or more commonly encountered drugs, the analyst must employ **screening tests** to reduce these possibilities to a small and manageable number. This objective is often accomplished by subjecting the material to a series of color tests that produce characteristic colors for the more commonly encountered illicit drugs. Even if these tests produce negative results, their value lies in having excluded certain drugs from further consideration.

screening test
A preliminary test used to reduce the number of possible identities of an unknown substance.

Once the number of possibilities has been reduced substantially, the second phase of the analysis must be devoted to pinpointing and confirming the drug's identity. In an era in which crime laboratories receive voluminous quantities of drug evidence, it is impractical to subject a drug to all the chemical and instrumental tests available. Indeed, it is more realistic to look on these techniques as constituting a large analytical arsenal. The chemist, aided by training and experience, must choose tests that will most conveniently identify a particular drug.

Forensic chemists often use a specific test to identify a drug substance to the exclusion of all other known chemical substances. A single test that identifies a substance is known as a **confirmation**. The analytical scheme sometimes consists of a series of nonspecific or presumptive tests. Each test in itself is insufficient to prove the drug's identity; however, the proper analytical scheme encompasses a combination of test results that characterize one and only one chemical substance—the drug under investigation. Furthermore, experimental evidence must confirm that the probability of any other substance responding in an identical manner to the scheme selected is so small as to be beyond any reasonable scientific certainty.

confirmation
A single test that specifically identifies a substance.

Another consideration in selecting an analytical technique is the need for either a *qualitative* or a *quantitative* determination. The former relates just to the identity of the material, whereas the latter refers to the percentage combination of the components of a mixture. Hence, a qualitative identification of a powder may reveal the presence of heroin and quinine, whereas a quantitative analysis may conclude the presence of 10 percent heroin and 90 percent quinine.

Obviously, a qualitative identification must precede any attempt at quantitation, for little value is served by attempting to quantitate a material without first determining its identity. Essentially, a qualitative analysis of a material requires the determination of numerous properties using a

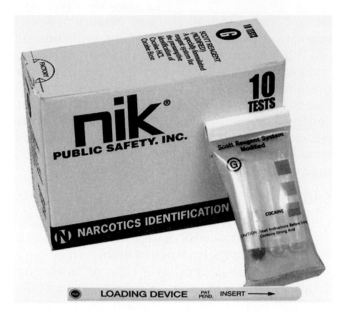

FIGURE 10-11 A field color test kit for cocaine. The suspect drug is placed in the plastic pouch. Tubes containing chemicals are broken open, and the color of the chemical reaction is observed. *Courtesy Tri-Tech, Inc., Southport, N.C., www.tritechusa.com*

variety of analytical techniques. On the other hand, a quantitative measurement is usually accomplished by precise measurement of a single property of the material.

Forensic chemists normally rely on several tests for a routine drug-identification scheme: color tests, microcrystalline tests, chromatography, spectrophotometry, and mass spectrometry.

Color Tests

Many drugs yield characteristic colors when brought into contact with specific chemical reagents. Not only do these tests provide a useful indicator of a drug's presence, but they are also used by investigators in the field to examine materials suspected of containing a drug (see Figure 10–11).[2] However, color tests are useful for screening purposes only and are never taken as conclusive identification of unknown drugs.

Five primary color test reagents are as follows:

1. *Marquis.* The reagent turns purple in the presence of heroin and morphine and most opium derivatives. Marquis also becomes orange-brown when mixed with amphetamines and methamphetamines.

2. *Dillie-Koppanyi.* This is a valuable screening test for barbiturates, in whose presence the reagent turns violet-blue in color.

3. *Duquenois-Levine.* This is a valuable color test for marijuana, performed by adding a series of chemical solutions to the suspect vegetation. A positive result is shown by a purple color when chloroform is added.

4. *Van Urk.* The reagent turns blue-purple in the presence of LSD. However, owing to the extremely small quantities of LSD in illicit preparations, this test is difficult to conduct under field conditions.

5. *Scott Test.* This is a color test for cocaine. A powder containing cocaine turns a cobalt thiocyanate solution blue. Upon the addition of hydrochloric acid, the blue color is transformed to a clear pink color. Upon the addition of chloroform, if cocaine is present, the blue color reappears in the chloroform layer.

Microcrystalline Tests

A technique considerably more specific than color tests is the micro-crystalline test. A drop of a chemical reagent is added to a small quantity of the drug on a microscopic slide. After a short time, a chemical reaction ensues, producing a crystalline precipitate. The size and shape of the crystals, examined under a compound microscope, reveal the identity of the drug. Crystal tests for cocaine and methamphetamine are illustrated in Figure 10–12.

Over the years, analysts have developed hundreds of crystal tests to characterize the most commonly abused drugs. These tests are rapid and often do not require the isolation of a drug from its diluents; however, because diluents can sometimes alter or modify the shape of the crystal, the examiner must develop experience in interpreting the results of the test.

Most color and crystal tests are largely empirical—that is, scientists do not fully understand why they produce the results they do. From the forensic chemist's point of view, this is not important. When the tests are properly chosen and used in proper combination, they reveal characteristics that identify the substance as a certain drug to the exclusion of all others.

microcrystalline test
A test that identifies a specific substance based on the color and shape of crystals formed when the substance is mixed with specific reagents.

Key Points

• Analysts use screening tests to determine the identity of drugs present in a sample. These tests reduce the number of possible drugs to a small and manageable number.

• A series of color tests produce characteristic colors for the more commonly encountered illicit drugs. In a microcrystalline test, a drop of a chemical reagent added to a small quantity of drug on a microscope slide produces crystals highly characteristic of a drug.

• After preliminary testing, forensic chemists use more specific tests to identify a drug substance to the exclusion of all other known chemical substances.

Chromatography

Chromatography is a means of separating and tentatively identifying the components of a mixture. It is particularly useful for analyzing drug

chromatography
Any of several analytical techniques for separating organic mixtures into their components by attraction to a stationary phase while being propelled by a moving phase.

(a)   (b)

FIGURE 10–12 **(a) A photomicrograph of a cocaine crystal formed in platinum chloride (400×). (b) A photomicrograph of a methamphetamine crystal formed in gold chloride (400×).** *Courtesy David P. Blackburn, San Bernardino County Sheriff's Department, San Bernardino, Calif.*

specimens, which may be diluted with practically any material to increase the quantity of the product available to prospective customers. The task of identifying an illicit-drug preparation would be arduous without the aid of chromatographic methods to first separate the mixture into its components.

Thin-Layer Chromatography   Thin-layer chromatography (TLC) uses a solid stationary phase and a moving liquid phase to separate the constituents of a mixture. Thin-layer chromatography is a powerful tool for solving many of the analytical problems presented to the forensic scientist. The method is both rapid and sensitive; moreover, less than 100 micrograms of suspect material are required for the analysis. In addition, the equipment necessary for TLC work has minimal cost and space requirements. Importantly, numerous samples can be analyzed simultaneously on one thin-layer plate. This technique is principally used to detect and identify components in complex mixtures.

In TLC, the components of a suspect mixture are separated as they travel up a glass or plastic plate, eventually appearing as a series of dark or colored spots on the plate. This action is then compared to a standard sample separation of a specific drug, such as heroin. If both the standard and the suspect substance travel the same distance up the plate, they can tentatively be identified as being produced by the same substance.

A thin-layer plate is prepared by coating a glass plate or plastic backing with a thin film of a granular material, usually silica gel or aluminum oxide. This granular material serves as the solid stationary phase and is usually held in place on the plate with a binding agent such as plaster of paris. If the sample to be analyzed is a solid, it must first be dissolved in a suitable solvent and a few microliters of the solution spotted with a capillary tube onto the granular surface near the lower edge of the plate. A liquid sample may be applied directly to the plate in the same manner. The plate is then placed upright into a closed chamber that contains a selected liquid, with care that the liquid does not touch the sample spot.

The liquid slowly rises up the plate by capillary action. This rising liquid is the moving phase in thin-layer chromatography. As the liquid moves past the sample spot, the components of the sample become distributed between the stationary solid phase and the moving liquid phase. The components with the greatest affinity for the moving phase travel up the plate faster than those that have greater affinity for the stationary phase. When the liquid front has moved a sufficient distance (usually 10 centimeters), the development is complete, and the plate is removed from the chamber and dried (see Figure 10–13). An example of the chromatographic separation of ink is shown in Figure 10–14.

Often the plate is sprayed with a chemical reagent that reacts with the separated substances and causes them to form colored spots. Figure 10-15 shows the chromatogram of a marijuana extract that has been separated into its components by TLC and visualized by having been sprayed with a chemical reagent.

Figure 10–16 shows a sample suspected of containing heroin and quinine that has been chromatographed alongside known heroin and quinine standards. The distance the unknown material migrated up the suspect plate is compared to the distances that heroin and quinine migrated up a standard sample plate. If the distances are the same, a tentative identification can be made. However, such an identification cannot be considered definitive, because numerous other substances can migrate the same distance up the plate when chromatographed under similar conditions. Thus, thin-layer

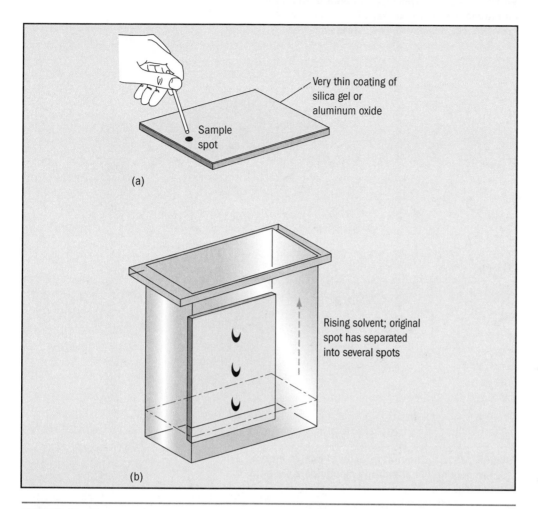

(a)

Very thin coating of
silica gel or
aluminum oxide

Sample
spot

Rising solvent; original
spot has separated
into several spots

(b)

FIGURE 10–13 **(a) In thin-layer chromatography, a liquid sample is spotted onto the granular surface of a gel-coated plate. (b) The plate is placed into a closed chamber that contains a liquid. As the liquid rises up the plate, the components of the sample distribute themselves between the coating and the moving liquid. The mixture is separated, with substances with a greater affinity for the moving liquid traveling up the plate at a faster speed.**

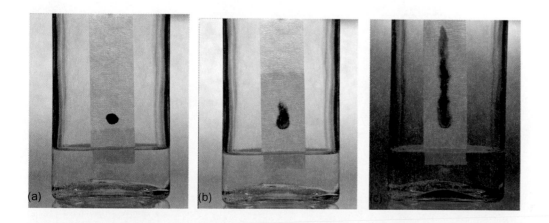

(a)   (b)   (c)

FIGURE 10–14 **(a) In thin-layer chromatography, the liquid phase begins to move up the stationary phase. (b) Liquid moves past the ink spot carrying the ink components up the stationary phase. (c) The moving liquid has separated the ink into its several components.**

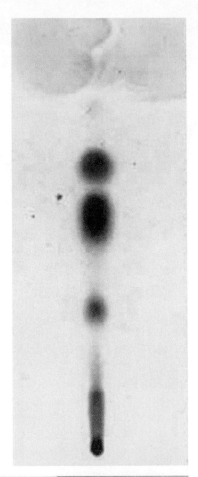

FIGURE 10-15 **A thin-layer chromatogram of a marijuana extract.** *Courtesy Sirchie Fingerprint Laboratories, Youngsville, N.C., www.sirchie.com*

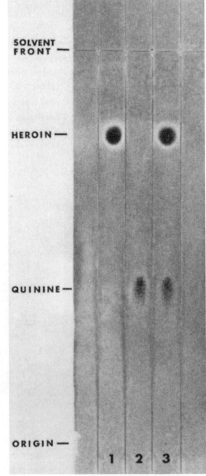

FIGURE 10-16 **Chromatographs of known heroin (1) and quinine (2) standards alongside a suspect sample (3).**

Closer Analysis

The Identification of Marijuana

The enforcement of laws prohibiting the sale and use of marijuana accounts for a high percentage of drug arrests in the United States. Any trial or hearing involving a seizure of marijuana requires identification of the material before the issue of guilt or innocence can be decided.

Unlike most other drugs received by the crime laboratory, marijuana *(Cannabis sativa L.)* possesses botanical features that impart identifiable characteristics. Because most marijuana specimens consist of small leaf fragments, their identification must be partially based on botanical features observed under the microscope by a trained expert. This approach is further augmented with a chemical test that will independently confirm the findings of the botanical examination.

The identification of marijuana by microscopic methods depends largely on observing short hairs shaped like "bear claws" on the upper side of the leaf. These hairs are known as *cystolithic hairs.* Further verification of the identity of marijuana is confirmed by the presence of longer, nonglandular hairs on the opposite side of the leaf.

The Duquenois-Levine color test, described earlier in this chapter, is a highly but not totally specific test for marijuana. However, when used in combination with a botanical examination, the results constitute a specific identification of marijuana. In addition, the analyst may be unable to obtain a microscopic identification of the marijuana leaf, as in the case of hashish or hashish oil. Here, the color test has to be supplemented by another examination, preferably thin-layer chromatography. This method involves separating chemical constituents found in the suspect resin on a thin-layer plate. The separated components are compared on the same plate to those obtained from a known marijuana extract, as shown in Figure 10–15. In this manner, a positive TLC comparison, used in conjunction with the Duquenois-Levine color test, constitutes a specific identification for marijuana.

chromatography alone cannot provide an absolute identification; it must be used in conjunction with other testing procedures to prove absolute identity.

Gas Chromatography (GC)   Gas chromatography (GC) separates mixtures based on their distribution between a stationary liquid phase and a moving gas phase. In gas chromatography, the moving phase is called the *carrier gas,* which flows through a column constructed of glass. The stationary phase is a thin film of liquid within the column, which is known as a *capillary column.*

Capillary columns are composed of glass and are 15 to 60 meters in length. These types of columns are very narrow, ranging from 0.25 to 0.75 millimeter in diameter. Capillary columns can be made narrow because their stationary liquid phase is actually coated as a very thin film directly onto the column's inner wall.

As the carrier gas flows through the capillary column, it carries with it the components of a mixture that have been injected into the column. Components with a greater affinity for the moving gas phase travel through the column more quickly than those with a greater affinity for the stationary liquid phase. Eventually, after the mixture has traversed the length of the column, it emerges separated into its components.

WebExtra 10.1

Watch Animated Depictions of Thin-Layer Chromatography and Gas Chromatography
www.prenhall.com/saferstein

WebExtra 10.2

Watch the Gas Chromatograph at Work
www.prenhall.com/saferstein

spectrophotometry
An analytical method for identifying a substance by its selective absorption of different wavelengths of light.

wavelength
The distance between crests of adjacent waves.

frequency
The number of waves that pass a given point per unit of time.

dispersion
The separation of light into its component wavelengths.

refraction
The bending of a light wave caused by a change in its velocity.

The time required for a component to emerge from the column from the time of its injection into the column is known as the *retention time,* which is a useful identifying characteristic. Figure 10–17(a) shows the chromatogram of two barbiturates; each barbiturate has tentatively been identified by comparing its retention time to those of known barbiturates, shown in Figure 10–17(b). However, because other substances may have comparable retention times under similar chromatographic conditions, gas chromatography cannot be considered an absolute means of identification. Conclusions derived from this technique must be confirmed by other testing procedures.

Gas chromatography is widely used because of its ability to resolve a highly complex mixture into its components, usually within minutes. It has an added advantage in that it is extremely sensitive and can yield quantitative results. Gas chromatography has sufficient sensitivity to detect and quantitate materials at the nanogram (0.000000001 gram or 1×10^{-9} gram) level.[3]

Spectrophotometry

The technique of chromatography is particularly suited for analyzing illicit drugs, because it can separate a drug from other substances that may be present in the drug preparation. However, chromatography has the drawback of not being able to specifically identify the material under investigation. For this reason, other analytical tools are frequently used to identify drugs. These include the technique of **spectrophotometry**, which can identify a substance by exposing it to a specific type of electromagnetic radiation.

Theory of Light   The knowledge of the nature and behavior of light is fundamental to understanding physical properties important to the examination of forensic evidence. One can think of light as a continuous wave. The wave concept depicts light as having the up-and-down motion of a continuous wave, as shown in Figure 10–18. Such a wave can be characterized by two distinct properties: wavelength and frequency. The distance between two consecutive crests (high points) or troughs (low points) of a wave is called the **wavelength**; it is designated by the Greek letter *lambda* (λ) and is typically measured in nanometers (nm), or millionths of a meter. The number of crests (or troughs) passing any one given point in a unit of time is defined as the **frequency** of the wave. Frequency is normally designated by the letter f and is expressed in cycles per second (cps). Frequency and wavelength are inversely proportional to one another, as shown by the relationship expressed in the equation:

$$F = c\lambda$$

In the equation, c represents the speed of light.

Many of us have held a glass prism up toward the sunlight and watched it transform light into the colors of the rainbow. The process of separating light into its component colors is called **dispersion**. Visible light usually travels at a constant velocity of nearly 300 million meters per second. However, on passing through the glass of a prism, each color component of light is slowed to a speed slightly different from those of the others, causing each component to bend at a different angle as it emerges from the prism (see Figure 10–19). This bending of light waves as a result of a change in velocity is called **refraction**.

Closer Analysis

The Gas Chromatograph

A simplified scheme of the gas chromatograph is shown in the figure. The operation of the instrument can be summed up briefly as follows: The carrier gas is fed into the column at a constant rate. The carrier gas is chemically inert and is generally nitrogen or helium. The sample under investigation is injected as a liquid into a heated injection port with a syringe, where it is immediately vaporized and swept into the column by the carrier gas. The column itself is heated in an oven in order to keep the sample in a vapor state as it travels through the column. In the column, the components of the sample travel in the direction of the carrier gas flow at speeds that are determined by their distribution between the stationary and moving phases. If the analyst has selected the proper liquid phase and has made the column long enough, the components of the sample will be completely separated as they emerge from the column.

As each component emerges from the column, it enters a detector. One type of detector uses a flame to ionize the emerging chemical substance, thus generating an electrical signal. The signal is recorded on a strip-chart recorder as a function of time. This written record of the separation is called a chromatogram. A gas chromatogram is a plot of the recorder response (vertical axis) versus time (horizontal axis). A typical chromatogram shows a series of peaks, each of which corresponds to one component of the mixture.

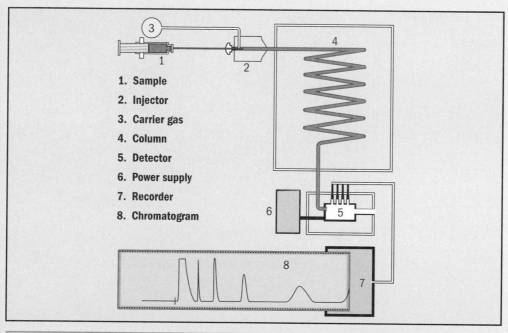

1. **Sample**
2. **Injector**
3. **Carrier gas**
4. **Column**
5. **Detector**
6. **Power supply**
7. **Recorder**
8. **Chromatogram**

Basic gas chromatography. Gas chromatography permits rapid separation of complex mixtures into individual compounds and allows identification and quantitative determination of each compound. As shown, a sample is introduced by a syringe (1) into a heated injection chamber (2). A constant stream of nitrogen gas (3) flows through the injector, carrying the sample into the column (4), which contains a thin film of liquid. The sample is separated in the column, and the carrier gas and separated components emerge from the column and enter the detector (5). Signals developed by the detector activate the recorder (7), which makes a permanent record of the separation by tracing a series of peaks on the chromatograph (8). The time of elution identifies the component present, and the peak area identifies the concentration. *Courtesy Varian, Inc, Palo Alto, Calif.*

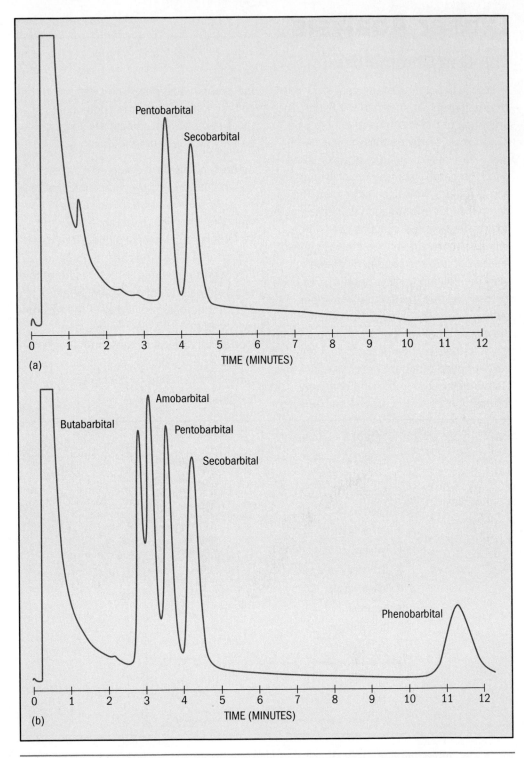

FIGURE 10–17 **(a) An unknown mixture of barbiturates is identified by comparing its retention times to (b), a known mixture of barbiturates.** *Courtesy Varian, Inc., Palo Alto, Calif.*

The observation that a substance has a color is consistent with this description of white light. For example, when light passes through a red glass, the glass absorbs all the component colors of light except red, which passes through or is transmitted by the glass. Likewise, one can determine the color of an opaque object by observing its ability to absorb some of the component colors of light while reflecting others back to the eye. Color is

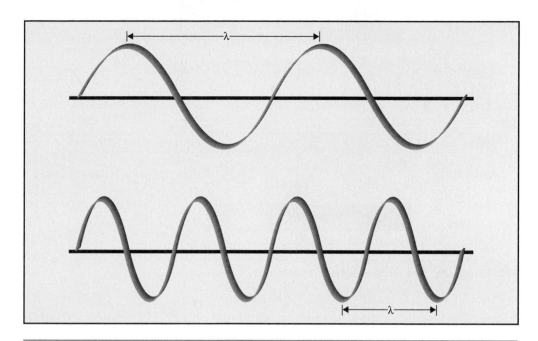

FIGURE 10–18 The frequency of the lower light wave is twice that of the upper wave.

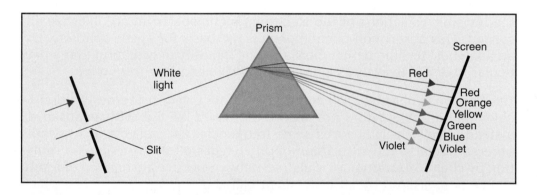

FIGURE 10–19 A representation of the dispersion of light by a glass prism.

thus a visual indication that objects absorb certain portions of **visible light** and transmit or reflect others. Scientists have long recognized this phenomenon and have learned to characterize chemical substances by the type and quantity of light they absorb. This has important applications for the identification and classification of forensic evidence.

Electromagnetic Spectrum Visible light is only a small part of a large family of radiation waves known as the **electromagnetic spectrum** (see Figure 10–20). All electromagnetic waves travel at the speed of light (*c*) and are distinguishable from one another only by their different wavelengths or frequencies. Hence, the only property that distinguishes **X-rays** from radio waves is the different frequencies the two types of waves possess.

Similarly, the range of colors that make up the visible spectrum can be correlated with frequency. For instance, the lowest frequencies of visible light are red; waves with a lower frequency fall into the invisible infrared (IR) region. The highest frequencies of visible light are violet; waves with a

visible light
Colored light ranging from red to violet in the electromagnetic spectrum.

electromagnetic spectrum
The entire range of radiation energy from the most energetic cosmic rays to the least energetic radio waves.

X-ray
A high-energy, short-wavelength form of electromagnetic radiation.

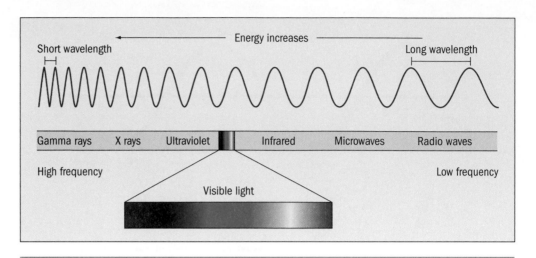

FIGURE 10–20 The electromagnetic spectrum.

higher frequency extend into the invisible ultraviolet (UV) region. No definite boundaries exist between any colors or regions of the electromagnetic spectrum; instead, each region is composed of a continuous range of frequencies, each blending into the other.

Just as a substance can absorb visible light to produce color, many of the invisible radiations of the electromagnetic spectrum are likewise absorbed. This absorption phenomenon is the basis for spectrophotometry, an analytical technique that measures the quantity of radiation that a particular material absorbs as a function of wavelength or frequency.

The Spectrophotometer We have already observed in the description of color that an object does not absorb all the visible light it is exposed to; instead, it selectively absorbs some frequencies and reflects or transmits others. Similarly, the absorption of other types of electromagnetic radiation by chemical substances is also selective. Selective absorption of a substance is measured by an instrument called a *spectrophotometer,* which produces a graph or *absorption spectrum* that depicts the absorption of light as a function of wavelength or frequency.

The spectrophotometer measures and records the absorption spectrum of a chemical. The basic components of a simple spectrophotometer are the same regardless of whether it is designed to measure the absorption of UV, visible, or IR radiation. These components are illustrated diagrammatically in Figure 10–21. They include (1) a radiation source, (2) a monochromator or frequency selector, (3) a sample holder, (4) a detector to convert electromagnetic radiation into an electrical signal, and (5) a recorder to produce a record of the signal.

The absorption of UV, visible, and IR radiation is particularly applicable for obtaining qualitative data pertaining to the identification of drugs.

ultraviolet
Invisible long frequencies of light beyond violet in the visible spectrum.

Ultraviolet and Visible Spectrophotometry Ultraviolet (UV) and visible spectrophotometry measure the absorbance of UV and visible light as a function of wavelength or frequency. For example, the UV absorption spectrum of heroin shows a maximum absorption band at a wavelength of 278 nanometers (see Figure 10–22). This shows that the simplicity of a UV spectrum facilitates its use as a tool for determining a material's probable identity. For instance, a white powder may have a UV spectrum

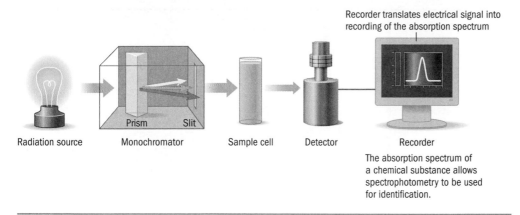

FIGURE 10–21   **The parts of a simple spectrophotometer.**

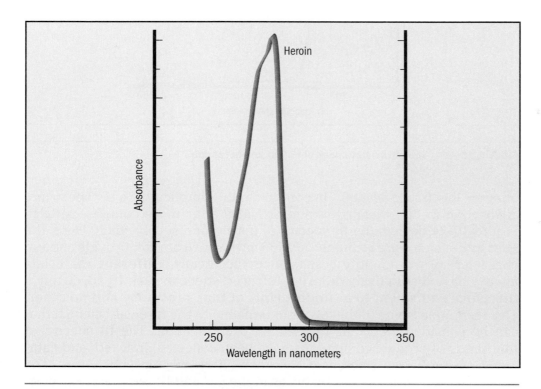

FIGURE 10–22   **The ultraviolet spectrum of heroin.**

comparable to heroin and therefore may be tentatively identified as such. (Fortunately, sugar and starch, common diluents of heroin, do not absorb UV light.)

This technique, however, does not provide a definitive result; other drugs or materials may have a UV absorption spectrum similar to that of heroin. Nevertheless, UV spectrophotometry is often useful in establishing the *probable* identity of a drug. For example, if an unknown substance yields a UV spectrum that resembles that of amphetamine (see Figure 10–23), thousands of substances are immediately eliminated from consideration, and the analyst can begin to identify the material from a relatively small number of possibilities. A comprehensive collection of UV drug spectra provides an index that can rapidly be searched in order to tentatively identify a drug or, failing that, at least to exclude certain drugs from consideration.

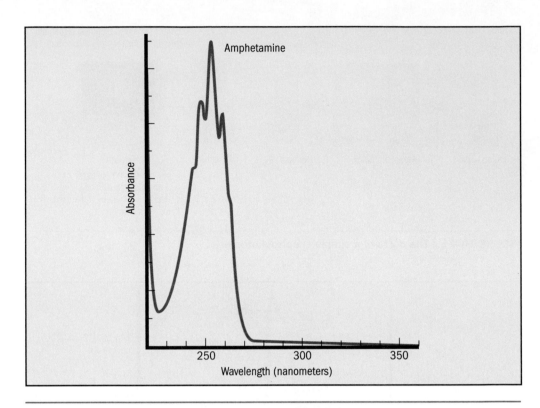

FIGURE 10–23 **The ultraviolet spectrum of an amphetamine.**

Infrared Spectrophotometry In contrast to the simplicity of a UV spectrum, absorption in the **infrared** region provides a far more complex pattern. Figure 10–24 depicts the IR spectra of heroin and secobarbital. Here, the absorption bands are so numerous that each spectrum can provide enough characteristics to identify a substance specifically. **Different materials always have distinctively different infrared spectra; each IR spectrum is therefore equivalent to a "fingerprint" of that substance and no other.** This technique is one of the few tests available to the forensic scientist that can be considered specific in itself for identification. The IR spectra of thousands of organic compounds have been collected, indexed, and cataloged as invaluable references for identifying organic substances. The selective absorption of light by drugs in the UV and IR regions of the electromagnetic spectrum provides a valuable technique for characterizing drugs.

infrared
Invisible short frequencies of light before red in the visible spectrum.

Mass Spectrometry

A previous section discussed the operation of the gas chromatograph. This instrument is one of the most important tools in a crime laboratory. Its ability to separate the components of a complex mixture is unsurpassed. However, gas chromatography has one important drawback—its inability to produce specific identification. A forensic chemist cannot unequivocally state the identification of a substance based solely on a retention time as determined by the gas chromatograph. Fortunately, by coupling the gas chromatograph to a mass spectrometer, forensic chemists have largely overcome this problem.

A mixture's components are first separated on the gas chromatograph. A direct connection between the gas chromatograph column and the mass spectrometer then allows each component to flow into the spectrometer as

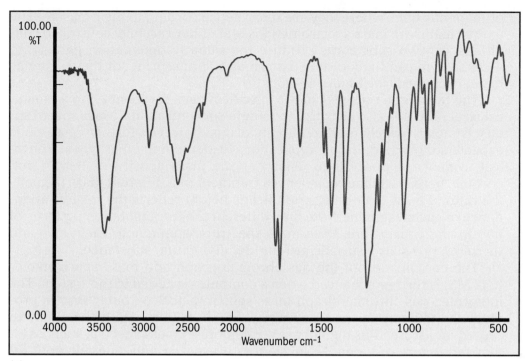

(a)

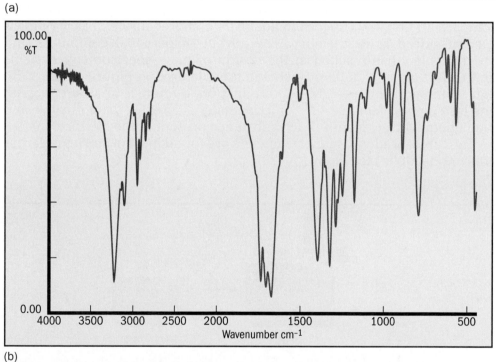

(b)

FIGURE 10-24   (a) The infrared spectrum of heroin. (b) The infrared spectrum of secobarbital.

it emerges from the gas chromatograph. In the mass spectrometer, the material enters a high-vacuum chamber where a beam of high-energy electrons is aimed at the sample molecules. The electrons collide with the molecules, causing them to lose electrons and to acquire a positive charge. These positively charged molecules, or **ions**, are very unstable or are formed with excess energy and almost instantaneously decompose into numerous smaller fragments. The fragments then pass through an electric

ion
An atom or molecule bearing a positive or negative charge.

or magnetic field, where they are separated according to their masses. The unique feature of mass spectrometry is that under carefully controlled conditions, no two substances produce the same fragmentation pattern. In essence, one can think of this pattern as a "fingerprint" of the substance being examined (see Figure 10–25).

The technique thus provides a specific means for identifying a chemical structure. It is also sensitive to minute concentrations. Mass spectrometry is mostly widely used to identify drugs; however, further research is expected to yield significant applications to identifying other types of physical evidence. Figure 10–26 illustrates the mass spectra of heroin and cocaine; here, each line represents a fragment of a different mass (actually the ratio of mass to charge), and the line height reflects the relative abundance of each fragment. Note how different the fragmentation patterns of heroin and cocaine are. Each mass spectrum is unique to each drug and therefore provides a specific test for identifying that substance.

The combination of the gas chromatograph and mass spectrometer (GC/MS) is further enhanced when a computer is added to the system. The integrated gas chromatograph/mass spectrometer/computer system provides the ultimate in speed, accuracy, and sensitivity. With the ability to record and store in its memory several hundred mass spectra, such a system can detect and identify substances present in only one-millionth-of-a-gram quantities. Furthermore, the computer can be programmed to compare an unknown spectrum against a comprehensive library of mass spectra stored in its memory. The advent of personal computers and microcircuitry has resulted in the design of mass spectrometer systems that can fit on small tables. Such a unit is pictured in Figure 10–27. With data obtained from a GC/MS determination, a forensic analyst can, with one instrument, separate the components of a complex drug mixture and then unequivocally identify each substance present in the mixture.

Research-grade mass spectrometers are found in laboratories as larger floor-model units (see Figure 10–28).

WebExtra 10.3

Watch an Animation of a Mass Spectrometer
www.prenhall.com/saferstein

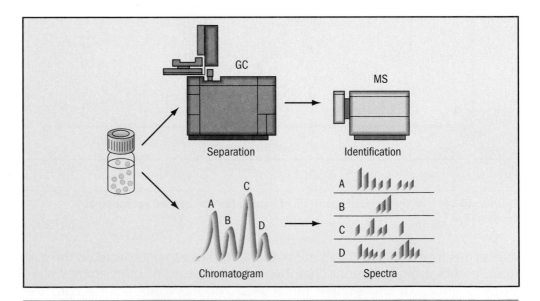

FIGURE 10–25 How GC/MS works. Left to right, the sample is separated into its components by the gas chromatograph, and then the components are ionized and identified by characteristic fragmentation patterns of the spectra produced by the mass spectrometer. *Courtesy Agilent Technologies, Inc., Palo Alto, Calif.*

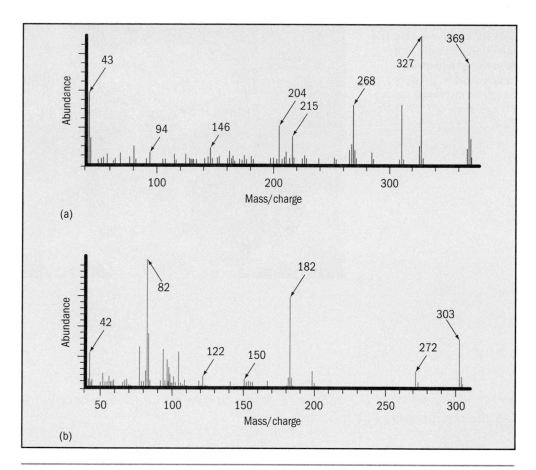

(a)

(b)

FIGURE 10-26 (a) The mass spectrum of heroin. (b) The mass spectrum of cocaine.

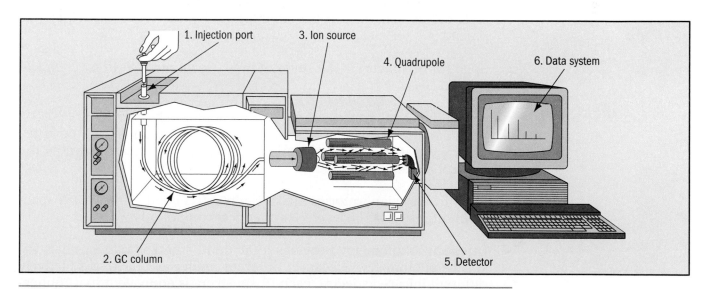

FIGURE 10-27 A tabletop mass spectrometer. (1) The sample is injected into a heated inlet port, and carrier gas sweeps it into the column. (2) The GC column separates the mixture into its components. (3) In the ion source, a filament wire emits electrons that strike the sample molecules, causing them to fragment as they leave the GC column. (4) The quadrupole, consisting of four rods, separates the fragments according to their mass. (5) The detector counts the fragments passing though the quadrupole. The signal is small and must be amplified. (6) The data system is responsible for total control of the entire GC/MS system. It detects and measures the abundance of each fragment and displays the mass spectrum. *Courtesy Agilent Technologies, Inc., Palo Alto, Calif.*

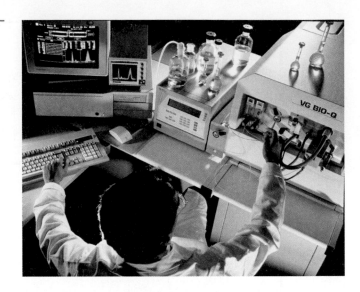

FIGURE 10-28   A scientist injecting a sample into a research-grade mass spectrometer. *Courtesy Geoff/Tompkinson/Science Photo Library*

Key Points

- Chromatography is a means of separating and tentatively identifying the components of a mixture.

- TLC uses a solid stationary phase, usually coated onto a glass plate, and a mobile liquid phase to separate the components of the mixture.

- Gas chromatography (GC) separates mixtures on the basis of their distribution between a stationary liquid phase and a mobile gas phase.

- Spectrophotometry is the study of the absorption of light by chemical substances.

- Dispersion is the process of separating light into its component colors. Each component bends, or refracts, at a different angle as it emerges from the prism. The large family of radiation waves is known as the electromagnetic spectrum.

- Most forensic laboratories use ultraviolet (UV) and infrared (IR) spectrophotometers to characterize chemical compounds.

- IR spectrophotometry provides a far more complex pattern than UV spectrophotometry. Because different materials have distinctively different infrared spectra, each IR spectrum is equivalent to a "fingerprint" of that substance.

- Mass spectrometry characterizes organic molecules by observing their fragmentation pattern after their collision with a beam of high-energy electrons.

- Infrared spectrophotometry and mass spectrophotometry typically are used to specifically identify a drug substance.

Chapter Summary

A drug can be defined as a natural or synthetic substance that is used to produce physiological or psychological effects in humans or other higher-order animals. Narcotic drugs are analgesics, meaning they relieve pain by depressing the central nervous system. Regular use of a narcotic drug leads to physical dependence. The most common source of narcotic drugs is opium. Morphine is readily extracted from opium and is used to synthesize heroin. Opiates, which include methadone and OxyContin (oxycodone), are not derived from opium or morphine, but they have the same physiological effects on the body as do opium narcotics.

Another class of drugs is hallucinogens; marijuana is the most well-known member of this class. Hallucinogens cause marked changes in mood, attitude, thought processes, and perceptions. Marijuana is the most controversial drug in this class because its long-term effects on health are still largely unknown. Other hallucinogens include LSD, mescaline, PCP, psilocybin, and MDMA (Ecstasy).

Depressants are drugs that slow the functioning of the central nervous system. These include alcohol (ethanol), barbiturates, tranquilizers, and various substances that can be sniffed, such as airplane glue and model cement. Stimulants have the opposite effect; they increase the activity of the central nervous system. Stimulants include amphetamines, sometimes known as "uppers" or "speed," and cocaine, which in its freebase form is known as *crack*.

The term *club drugs* refers to synthetic drugs that are used at nightclubs, bars, and raves (all-night dance parties). Substances that are often used as club drugs include, but are not limited to, MDMA (Ecstasy), GHB (gamma hydroxybutyrate), Rohypnol ("Roofies"), ketamine, and methamphetamine.

Anabolic steroids are synthetic compounds that are chemically related to the male sex hormone testosterone. Anabolic steroids are often abused by individuals who want to accelerate muscle growth.

Federal law establishes five schedules of classification for controlled dangerous substances on the basis of a drug's potential for abuse, potential for physical and psychological dependence, and medical value.

Analysts employ screening tests to determine whether a sample contains one or more commonly encountered illicit drugs. These tests include color tests that produce characteristic colors for certain drugs. Once this preliminary analysis is completed, a forensic scientist performs a confirmation test to identify a drug substance to the exclusion of all other known chemical substances.

Light waves are characterized by two distinct properties: wavelength and frequency. Visible light consists of light of all colors; the process of separating light into component colors is called dispersion. Upon passing through the glass of a prism, each color component of light is slowed to a speed slightly different from the others, thus causing each component to bend at a different angle as it emerges from the prism. This bending of light waves as a result of a change in velocity is called refraction. Visible light is part of a large family of radiation waves known as the electromagnetic spectrum. All electromagnetic waves travel at the speed of light

(Continued)

and are distinguishable from one another only by their wavelengths or frequencies.

Chromatography, spectrophotometry, and mass spectrometry are all readily used by forensic scientists to identify drugs of abuse. Chromatography is a means of separating and tentatively identifying the components of a mixture. Gas chromatography (GC) separates mixtures on the basis of their distribution between a stationary liquid phase and a mobile gas phase. Thin-layer chromatography (TLC) uses a solid stationary phase, usually coated onto a glass plate, and a mobile liquid phase to separate the components of the mixture. Spectrophotometry is the study of the absorption of light by chemical substances. Mass spectrometry characterizes organic molecules by observing their fragmentation pattern after their collision with a beam of high-energy electrons. By connecting a gas chromatograph to a mass spectrometer, the forensic scientist can capture a unique "fingerprint" of the substance being examined.

Most forensic laboratories characterize chemical compounds using spectrophotometers that absorb light in the ultraviolet (UV) or infrared (IR) spectra. Absorption in the infrared region provides a far more complex pattern than absorption in the UV spectrum. Different materials always have distinctively different infrared spectra; each IR spectrum is therefore equivalent to a "fingerprint" of that substance.

Review Questions

1. A _____ can be defined as a natural or synthetic substance that is used to produce physiological or psychological effects in humans or other animals.

2. True or False: Underlying emotional factors are the primary motives leading to the repeated use of a drug. _____

3. True or False: Drugs such as alcohol, heroin, amphetamines, barbiturates, and cocaine can lead to a low degree of psychological dependence with repeated use. _____

4. The development of _____ dependence on a drug is shown by withdrawal symptoms such as convulsions when the user stops taking the drug.

5. True or False: Abuse of barbiturates can lead to physical dependency. _____

6. True or False: Repeated use of LSD leads to physical dependency. _____

7. Physical dependency develops only when the drug user adheres to a _____ schedule of drug intake.

8. Narcotic drugs are _____ that have _____ effects on the central nervous system.

9. _____ is a gummy, milky juice exuded through a cut made in the unripe pod of the poppy.

10. _____ is a chemical derivative of morphine made by reacting morphine with acetic anhydride.

11. A legally available drug that is chemically related to heroin and heavily used is _____.

12. True or False: Methadone is classified as a narcotic drug, even though it is not derived from opium or morphine. _____

13. Drugs that cause marked alterations in mood, attitude, thought processes, and perceptions are called _____.

14. _____ is the sticky resin extracted from the marijuana plant.

15. The active ingredient of marijuana largely responsible for its hallucinogenic properties is _____.

16. True or False: The potency of a marijuana preparation depends on the proportion of the various plant parts in the mixture. _____

17. The marijuana preparation with the highest THC content is _____.

18. LSD is a chemical derivative of _____, a chemical obtained from the ergot fungus that grows on certain grasses and grains.

19. The drug phencyclidine is often manufactured for the illicit-drug market in _____ laboratories.

20. True or False: Alcohol depresses the central nervous system. _____

21. _____ are called "downers" because they depress the central nervous system.

22. True or False: Phenobarbital is an example of a long-acting barbiturate. _____

23. _____ is a powerful sedative and muscle relaxant that possesses many of the depressant properties of barbiturates.

24. _____ and _____ drugs are used to relieve anxiety and tension without inducing sleep.

25. True or False: Huffing volatile solvents stimulates the central nervous system. _____

26. _____ are a group of synthetic drugs that stimulate the central nervous system.

27. _____ is extracted from the leaf of the coca plant.

28. Traditionally, cocaine is _____ into the nostrils.

29. True or False: Cocaine is a powerful central nervous system depressant. _____

30. The two drugs usually associated with drug-facilitated sexual assaults are _____ and _____.

31. _____ steroids are designed to promote muscle growth but have harmful side effects.

32. Federal law establishes _____ schedules of classification for the control of dangerous drugs.

33. Drugs that have no accepted medical use are placed in schedule _____.

34. Librium and Valium are listed in schedule _____.

35. True or False: Color tests are used to identify drugs conclusively. _____

36. The _____ color test reagent turns purple in the presence of heroin.

37. The Duquenois-Levine test is a valuable color test for _____.

38. The _____ test is a widely used color test for cocaine.

39. _____ tests tentatively identify drugs by the size and shape of crystals formed when the drug is mixed with specific reagents.

40. A technique that uses a moving liquid phase and a stationary solid phase to separate mixtures is _____.

41. True or False: Thin-layer chromatography yields the positive identification of a material. _____

42. The distance between two successive identical points on a wave is known as _____.

43. The process of separating light into its component colors, is called _____.

44. True or False: Color is a usual indication that substances selectively absorb light. _____

45. Visible light and X-rays are only part of the family of known radiation waves known as the _____.

46. Red light is (higher, lower) in frequency than violet light.

47. The selective absorption of electromagnetic radiation by materials (can, cannot) be used as an aid for identification.

48. The pattern of a(n) _____ and _____ absorption spectrum suggest a probable identity of a drug.

49. A(n) (infrared, ultraviolet) absorption spectrum provides a unique "fingerprint" of a chemical substance.

50. The study of the absorption of light by chemical substances is known as _____, and the instrument used to measure and record this absorption spectrum is the _____.

51. A mixture's components can be separated by the technique of _____, which separates mixtures on the basis of their distribution between a stationary liquid phase and a moving gas phase.

52. The gas chromatograph, in combination with the _____, can separate the components of a drug mixture and then unequivocally identify each substance present in the mixture.

53. The technique of _____ exposes molecules to a beam of high-end electrons in order to fragment them.

54. True or False: A mass spectrum is normally considered a specific means for identifying a chemical substance. _____

Application and Critical Thinking

1. An individual who has been using a drug for an extended period of time suddenly finds himself unable to secure more of the drug. He acts nervous and irritable and is hyperactive. He seems almost desperate to find more of the drug, but experiences no sickness, pain, or other outward physical discomfort. Based on his behavior, what drugs might he possibly have been using? Explain your answer.

2. Following are descriptions of behavior that are characteristic among users of certain classes of drugs. For each description, indicate the class of drug (narcotics, stimulants, and so on) for which the behavior is most characteristic. For each description, also name at least one drug that produces the described effects.
   a) Slurred speech, slow reaction time, impaired judgment, reduced coordination
   b) Intense emotional responses, anxiety, altered sensory perceptions
   c) Alertness, feelings of strength and confidence, rapid speech and movement, decreased appetite
   d) Drowsiness, intense feeling of well-being, relief from pain

3. Following are descriptions of four hypothetical drugs. According to the Controlled Substances Act, under which drug schedule would each substance be classified?
   a) This drug has a high potential for psychological dependence, it currently has accepted medical uses in the United States, and the distributor is not required to report to the U.S. Drug Enforcement Administration.
   b) This drug has medical use in the United States, is not limited by manufacturing quotas, and may be exported without a permit.
   c) This drug must be stored in a vault or safe, requires separate record keeping, and may be distributed with a prescription.
   d) This drug may not be imported or exported without a permit, is subject to manufacturing quotas, and currently has no medical use in the United States.

4. A police officer stops a motorist who is driving erratically and notices a bag of white powder on the front seat of the car that he suspects contains heroin. The officer brings the bag to you, a forensic scientist in the local crime lab. Name one screening test that you might perform to determine the presence of heroin. Assuming the powder tests positive for heroin, what should you do next?

5. The figure on page 326 shows a chromatogram of a known mixture of barbiturates. Based on this figure, answer the following questions:
   a) What barbiturate detected by the chromatogram had the longest retention time?
   b) Which barbiturate had the shortest retention time?
   c) What is the approximate retention time of amobarbital?

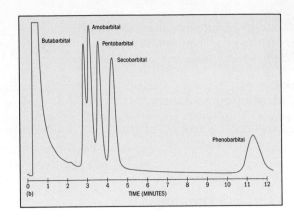

Web Resources

Basic Principles of Spectrophotometry (An online simulation of a spectrophotometer)
www.chm.davidson.edu/ChemistryApplets/spectrophotometry/Spectrophotometry
.html

Chromatography (A simple description of chromatographic processes with diagrams)
http://antoine.frostburg.edu/chem/senese/101/matter/chromatography.shtml

Drugs.com (An extensive database of information about the use and effects of 24,000 different drugs)
www.drugs.com

Drug Schedules (A list of substances classified under each section of the U.S. federal narcotics laws)
www.mspta.com/dre/pdf/Drug_Schedules.pdf

Impaired Driving Factsheet (Statistics compiled by the National Center for Injury Prevention and Control)
www.cdc.gov/ncipc/factsheets/drving.htm

National Institute on Drug Abuse (A division of the National Institutes of Health with links to information about the effects of and studies about legal and illicit drugs)
www.nida.nih.gov/

Neuroscience for Kids (Information about the history, production, use, effects, and detection of the drugs discussed in the text)
http://faculty.washington.edu/chudler/introb.html#drug

StreetDrugs.org (Extensive information about the history and effects of hundreds of legal and illicit drugs)
www.streetdrugs.org/index.htm

Endnotes

1. *Marijuana—A signal of Misunderstanding* (Washington, DC: U.S. Government Printing Office, 1972), p. 56.

2. Field-test color kits for drugs can be purchased from various commercial manufacturers.

3. Powers of 10 are quite useful and simple for handling large or small numbers. The exponent expresses the number of places the decimal point must be moved. If it is positive, the decimal point is moved to the right; if it is negative, the decimal point is moved to the left. Thus, to express 1×10^{-9} as a number, the decimal point is simply moved nine places to the left of 1.

Harold Shipman, Dr. Death

Kathleen Grundy's sudden death in 1998 was shocking news to her daughter, Angela Woodruff. Mrs. Grundy, an 81-year-old widow, was believed to be in good health when her physician, Dr. Harold Shipman, visited her a few hours before her demise. Some hours later, when friends came to her home to check on her whereabouts, they found Mrs. Grundy lying on a sofa fully dressed and dead.

Dr. Shipman pronounced her dead and informed her daughter that an autopsy was not necessary. A few days later, Mrs. Woodruff was surprised to learn that a will had surfaced leaving all of Mrs. Grundy's money to Dr. Shipman. The will was immediately recognized as a forgery and led to the exhumation of Mrs. Grundy's body. A toxicological analysis of the remains revealed a lethal quantity of morphine.

In retrospect, there was good reason to suspect that Dr. Shipman was capable of foul play. In the 1970s, he was asked to leave a medical practice because of a drug abuse problem and charges that he obtained drugs by forgery and deception. However, Dr. Shipman was quickly back to practicing medicine. By 1998, local undertakers became suspicious at the number of his patients who were dying. What is more, they all seemed to be elderly women who were found sitting in a chair or lying fully clothed on a bed. As police investigated, the horror of Dr. Shipman's deeds became apparent. One clinical audit estimated that Dr. Shipman killed at least 236 of his patients over a twenty-four-year period. Most of the deaths were attributed to fatal doses of heroin or morphine. Toxicological analysis on seven exhumed bodies clearly showed significant quantities of morphine. Convicted of murder, Dr. Shipman hanged himself in his jail cell in 2004.

Forensic Toxicology

chapter **11**

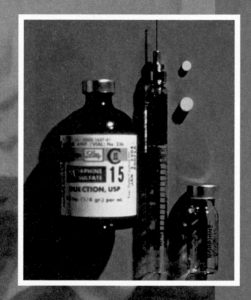

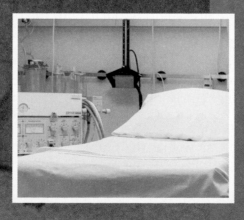

Key Terms

absorption

acid

alveoli

anticoagulant

artery

base

capillary

excretion

fuel cell detector

metabolism

oxidation

pH

preservative

toxicologist

vein

Learning Objectives

After studying this chapter, you should be able to:

- Explain how alcohol is absorbed into the bloodstream, transported throughout the body, and eliminated by oxidation and excretion.

- Understand the process by which alcohol is excreted in the breath via the lungs.

- Understand the concepts of infrared and fuel cell breath-testing devices for alcohol testing.

- Describe commonly employed field sobriety tests to assess alcohol impairment.

- List and contrast laboratory procedures for measuring the concentration of alcohol in the blood.

- Relate the precautions to be taken to properly preserve blood in order to analyze its alcohol content.

- Understand the significance of implied-consent laws and the *Schmerber* v. *California* case to traffic enforcement.

- Describe techniques that forensic toxicologists use to isolate and identify drugs and poisons.

- Appreciate the significance of finding a drug in human tissues and organs to assessing impairment.

- Describe how to coordinate the Drug Recognition Expert program with a forensic toxicology finding.

Role of Forensic Toxicology

toxicologist
An individual charged with the responsibility of detecting and identifying the presence of drugs and poisons in body fluids, tissues, and organs.

Because the uncontrolled use of drugs has become a worldwide problem affecting all segments of society, the role of the toxicologist has taken on new and added significance. Toxicologists detect and identify drugs and poisons in body fluids, tissues, and organs. Their services are required not only in such legal institutions as crime laboratories and medical examiners' offices; they also reach into hospital laboratories—where identifying a drug overdose may represent the difference between life and death—and into various health facilities that monitor the intake of drugs and other toxic substances. Primary examples include performing blood tests on children exposed to leaded paints and analyzing the urine of addicts enrolled in methadone maintenance programs.

The role of the forensic toxicologist is limited to matters that pertain to violations of criminal law. However, responsibility for performing toxicological services in a criminal justice system varies considerably throughout the United States. In systems with a crime laboratory independent of the medical examiner, this responsibility may reside with one or the other or may be shared by both. Some systems, however, take advantage of the expertise of government health department laboratories and assign this role to them. Nevertheless, whatever facility handles this work, its caseload will reflect the prevailing popularity of the drugs that are abused in the community. In most cases, this means that the forensic toxicologist handles numerous requests to determine the presence of alcohol in the body.

All of the statistical and medical evidence shows that ethyl alcohol—a legal, over-the-counter substance—is the most heavily abused drug in Western countries. Forty percent of all traffic deaths in the United States, nearly 17,500 fatalities per year, are alcohol related, along with more than two million injuries each year requiring hospital treatment. This highway death toll, as well as the untold damage to life, limb, and property, shows the dangerous consequences of alcohol abuse. Because of the prevalence of alcohol in the toxicologist's work, we will begin by taking a closer look at how the body processes and responds to alcohol.

Key Points

- Forensic toxicologists detect and identify drugs and poisons in body fluids, tissues, and organs in matters that pertain to violations of criminal laws.

- Ethyl alcohol is the most heavily abused drug in Western countries.

Toxicology of Alcohol

The subject of the analysis of alcohol immediately confronts us with the primary objective of forensic toxicology—detecting and isolating drugs in the body to determine their influence on human behavior. Knowing how the body metabolizes alcohol provides the key to understanding its effects on human behavior. This knowledge has also made possible the development of instruments that measure the presence and concentration of alcohol in individuals suspected of driving under the influence.

Metabolism of Alcohol

All chemicals that enter the body are eventually broken down by chemicals in the body and transformed into other chemicals that are easier to eliminate. This process of transformation, called **metabolism**, consists of three basic steps: absorption, distribution, and elimination.

Absorption and Distribution   Alcohol, or ethyl alcohol, is a colorless liquid normally diluted with water and consumed as a beverage. Alcohol appears in the blood within minutes after it has been consumed and slowly increases in concentration while it is being absorbed from the stomach and the small intestine into the bloodstream. During the **absorption** phase, alcohol slowly enters the body's bloodstream and is carried to all parts of the body. When the absorption period is completed, the alcohol becomes distributed uniformly throughout the watery portions of the body—that is, throughout about two-thirds of the body volume. Fat, bones, and hair are low in water content and therefore contain little alcohol, whereas alcohol concentration in the rest of the body is fairly uniform. After absorption is completed, a maximum alcohol level is reached in the blood, and the postabsorption period begins. Then the alcohol concentration slowly decreases until a zero level is again reached.

Many factors determine the rate at which alcohol is absorbed into the bloodstream, including the total time taken to consume the drink, the alcohol content of the beverage, the amount consumed, and the quantity and type of food present in the stomach at the time of drinking. With so many variables, it is difficult to predict just how long the absorption process will require. For example, beer is absorbed more slowly than an equivalent concentration of alcohol in water, apparently because of the carbohydrates in beer. Also, alcohol consumed on an empty stomach is absorbed faster than an equivalent amount of alcohol taken when there is food in the stomach (see Figure 11–1).

Elimination   As the alcohol is circulated by the bloodstream, the body begins to eliminate it. Alcohol is eliminated through two mechanisms—**oxidation** and **excretion**. Nearly all of the alcohol consumed (95 to 98 percent) is eventually oxidized to carbon dioxide and water. Oxidation

metabolism
The transformation of a chemical in the body to other chemicals for the purpose of facilitating its elimination from the body.

absorption
The passage of substances such as alcohol across the wall of the stomach and small intestine into the bloodstream.

oxidation
The combination of oxygen with other substances to produce new products.

excretion
The elimination of substances such as alcohol from the body in an unchanged state typically in breath and urine.

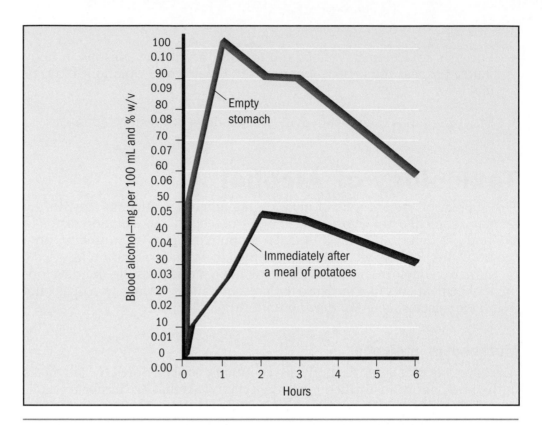

FIGURE 11–1   Blood-alcohol concentrations after ingestion of 2 ounces of pure alcohol mixed in 8 ounces of water (equivalent to about 5 ounces of 80-proof vodka). Courtesy U.S. Department of Transportation, Washington, D.C.

takes place almost entirely in the liver. Here, in the presence of the enzyme alcohol dehydrogenase, the alcohol is converted into acetaldehyde and then to acetic acid. The acetic acid is subsequently oxidized in practically all parts of the body to carbon dioxide and water.

The remaining alcohol is excreted unchanged in the breath, urine, and perspiration. Most significantly, the amount of alcohol exhaled in the breath is in direct proportion to the concentration of alcohol in the blood. This observation has had a tremendous impact on the technology and procedures used for blood-alcohol testing. The development of instruments to reliably measure breath for its alcohol content has made possible the testing of millions of people in a rapid, safe, and convenient manner.

The fate of alcohol in the body is therefore relatively simple—namely, absorption into the bloodstream, distribution throughout the body's water, and finally, elimination by oxidation and excretion. The elimination or "burn-off" rate of alcohol varies in different individuals; 0.015 percent w/v (weight per volume) per hour seems to be an average value once the absorption process is complete.[1] However, this figure is an average that varies by as much as 30 percent among individuals.

Blood-Alcohol Concentration   Logically, the most obvious measure of intoxication would be the amount of liquor a person has consumed. Unfortunately, most arrests are made after the fact, when such information is not available to legal authorities; furthermore, even if these data could be collected, numerous related factors, such as body weight and the rate of alcohol's absorption into the body, are so variable that it would be impossible to prescribe uniform standards that would yield reliable alcohol intoxication levels for all individuals.

Theoretically, for a true determination of the quantity of alcohol impairing an individual's normal body functions, it would be best to remove a portion of brain tissue and analyze it for alcohol content. For obvious reasons, this cannot be done on living subjects. Consequently, toxicologists concentrate on the blood, which provides the medium for circulating alcohol throughout the body, carrying it to all tissues, including the brain. Fortunately, experimental evidence supports this approach and shows blood-alcohol concentration to be directly proportional to the concentration of alcohol in the brain. From the medicolegal point of view, blood-alcohol levels have become the accepted standard for relating alcohol intake to its effect on the body.

The longer the total time required for complete absorption to occur, the lower the peak alcohol concentration in the blood. Depending on a combination of factors, maximum blood-alcohol concentration may not be reached until two or three hours have elapsed from the time of consumption. However, under normal social drinking conditions, it takes anywhere from thirty to ninety minutes from the time of the final drink until the absorption process is completed.

As noted earlier, alcohol becomes concentrated evenly throughout the watery portions of the body. This knowledge can be useful for the toxicologist analyzing a body for the presence of alcohol. If blood is not available, as in some postmortem situations, a medical examiner can select a water-rich organ or fluid—for example, the brain, cerebrospinal fluid, or vitreous humor—to determine the body's alcohol content to a reasonable degree of accuracy.

Alcohol in the Circulatory System

The extent to which an individual may be under the influence of alcohol is usually determined by measuring the quantity of alcohol present in the blood system. Normally, this is accomplished in one of two ways: (1) by analyzing the blood for its alcohol content or (2) by measuring the alcohol content of the breath. In either case, the significance and meaning of the results can better be understood when the movement of alcohol through the circulatory system is studied.

Humans, like all vertebrates, have a closed circulatory system, which consists basically of a heart and numerous arteries, capillaries, and veins. An **artery** is a blood vessel carrying blood away from the heart, and a **vein** is a vessel carrying blood back toward the heart. **Capillaries** are tiny blood vessels that connect the arteries with the veins. The exchange of materials between the blood and the other tissues takes place across the thin walls of the capillaries. A schematic diagram of the circulatory system is shown in Figure 11–2.

Ingestion and Distribution   Let us now trace the movement of alcohol through the human circulatory system. After alcohol is ingested, it moves down the esophagus into the stomach. About 20 percent of the alcohol is absorbed through the stomach walls into the portal vein of the blood system. The remaining alcohol passes into the blood through the walls of the small intestine. Once in the blood, the alcohol is carried to the liver, where enzymes begin to break it down.

As the blood (still carrying the alcohol) leaves the liver, it moves up to the heart. The blood enters the upper right chamber of the heart, called the right

artery
A blood vessel that carries blood away from the heart.

vein
A blood vessel that transports blood toward the heart.

capillary
A tiny blood vessel that receives blood from arteries and carries it to veins, and across whose walls the exchange of materials between the blood and the tissues takes place.

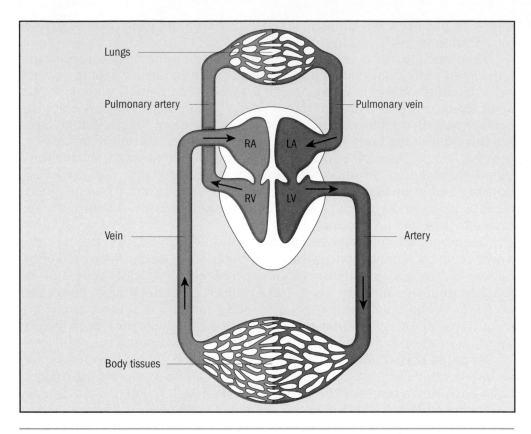

FIGURE 11–2 A simplified diagram of the human circulatory system. Vessels shown in red contain oxygenated blood; vessels shown in gray contain deoxygenated blood.

atrium (or auricle), and is forced into the lower right chamber of the heart, known as the right ventricle. Having returned to the heart from its circulation through the tissues, the blood at this time contains very little oxygen and much carbon dioxide. Consequently, the blood must be pumped up to the lungs, through the pulmonary artery, to be replenished with oxygen.

Aeration   In the lungs, the respiratory system bridges with the circulatory system so that oxygen can enter the blood and carbon dioxide can leave it. As shown in Figure 11–3, the pulmonary artery branches into capillaries lying close to tiny pear-shaped sacs called **alveoli**. The lungs contain about 250 million alveoli, all located at the ends of the bronchial tubes. The bronchial tubes connect to the windpipe (trachea), which leads up to the mouth and nose (see Figure 11–4). At the surface of the alveolar sacs, blood flowing through the capillaries comes in contact with fresh oxygenated air in the sacs.

A rapid exchange now takes place between the fresh air in the sacs and the spent air in the blood. Oxygen passes through the walls of the alveoli into the blood while carbon dioxide is discharged from the blood into the air. If, during this exchange, alcohol or any other volatile substance is in the blood, it too will pass into the alveoli. During breathing, the carbon dioxide and alcohol are expelled through the nose and mouth, and the alveoli are replenished with fresh oxygenated air breathed into the lungs, allowing the process to begin all over again.

The temperature at which the breath leaves the mouth is normally 34°C. At this temperature, the ratio of alcohol in the blood to alcohol in alveolar air is approximately 2,100 to 1. In other words, 1 milliliter of blood contains nearly the same amount of alcohol as 2,100 milliliters of alveolar breath.

alveoli
Small sacs in the lungs through whose walls air and other vapors are exchanged between the breath and the blood.

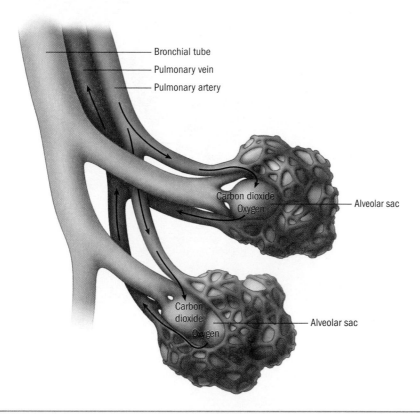

FIGURE 11–3 **Gas exchange in the lungs. Blood flows from the pulmonary artery into vessels that lie close to the walls of the alveoli. Here the blood gives up its carbon dioxide and absorbs oxygen. The oxygenated blood leaves the lungs via the pulmonary vein and returns to the heart.**

Recirculation and Absorption Now let's return to the circulating blood. After emerging from the lungs, the oxygenated blood is rushed back to the upper left chamber of the heart (left atrium) by the pulmonary vein. When the left atrium contracts, it forces the blood through a valve into the left ventricle, which is the lower left chamber of the heart. The left ventricle then pumps the freshly oxygenated blood into the arteries, which carry the blood to all parts of the body. Each of these arteries, in turn, branches into smaller arteries, which eventually connect with the numerous tiny capillaries embedded in the tissues. Here the alcohol moves out of the blood and into the tissues. The blood then runs from the capillaries into tiny veins that fuse to form larger veins. These veins eventually lead back to the heart to complete the circuit.

During absorption, the concentration of alcohol in the arterial blood is considerably higher than the concentration of alcohol in the venous blood. One typical study revealed a subject's arterial blood-alcohol level to be 41 percent higher than the venous level thirty minutes after the last drink.[2] This difference is thought to exist because of the rapid diffusion of alcohol into the body tissues from venous blood during the early phases of absorption. Because the administration of a blood test requires drawing venous blood from the arm, this test is clearly to the advantage of a subject who may still be in the absorption stage. However, once absorption is complete, the alcohol becomes equally distributed throughout the blood system.

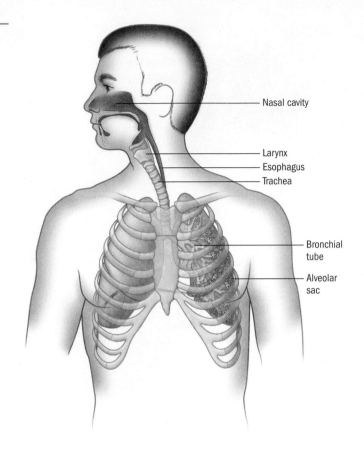

FIGURE 11–4 The respiratory system. The trachea connects the nose and mouth to the bronchial tubes. The bronchial tubes divide into numerous branches that terminate in the alveoli in the lungs.

Nasal cavity

Larynx

Esophagus

Trachea

Bronchial tube

Alveolar sac

Key Points

- Alcohol appears in the blood within minutes after it has been taken by mouth. It slowly increases in concentration while it is being absorbed from the stomach and the small intestine into the bloodstream.

- When all the alcohol has been absorbed, a maximum alcohol level is reached in the blood, and the postabsorption period begins. During postabsorption, the alcohol concentration slowly decreases until a zero level is reached.

- Elimination of alcohol throughout the body is accomplished through oxidation and excretion. Oxidation takes place almost entirely in the liver, whereas alcohol is excreted unchanged in the breath, urine, and perspiration.

- Breath-testing devices operate on the principle that the ratio between the concentration of alcohol in alveolar breath and its concentration in blood is fixed.

Testing for Intoxication

From a practical point of view, the idea of drawing blood from a vein to test motorists suspected of being under the influence of alcohol simply is not convenient. The need to transport the suspect to a location where a medically qualified person can draw blood would be costly and time consuming, considering the hundreds of tests that the average police department must conduct every year. The methods used must be designed to test hundreds of thousands of motorists annually without causing them undue physical harm or unreasonable inconvenience, while providing a reliable diagnosis that can be supported and defended within the framework of the legal system. This means that toxicologists have had to devise rapid and specific procedures for measuring a driver's degree of alcohol intoxication that can be easily administered in the field.

Breath Testing for Alcohol

The most widespread method for rapidly determining alcohol intoxication is breath testing. A breath tester is simply a device for collecting and measuring the alcohol content of alveolar breath. As we saw earlier, alcohol is expelled unchanged in the breath of a person who has been drinking. A breath test measures the alcohol concentration in the pulmonary artery by measuring its concentration in alveolar breath. Thus, breath analysis provides an easily obtainable specimen along with a rapid and accurate result.

Breath-test results obtained during the absorption phase may be higher than results obtained from a simultaneous analysis of venous blood. However, the former are more reflective of the concentration of alcohol reaching the brain and therefore more accurately reflect the effects of alcohol on the subject. Again, once absorption is complete, the difference between a blood test and a breath test should be minimal.

Breath-Test Instruments   The first widely used instrument for measuring the alcohol content of alveolar breath was the *Breathalyzer*, developed in 1954 by R. F. Borkenstein, who was a captain in the Indiana State Police. Starting in the 1970s, the Breathalyzer was phased out and replaced by other instruments for measuring the alcoholic content of alveolar breath. Like the Breathalyzer, they assume that the ratio of alcohol in the blood to alcohol in alveolar breath is 2,100 to 1 at a mouth temperature of 34°C. Unlike the Breathalyzer, modern breath testers are free of chemicals. These devices include infrared light absorption devices (described in the following "Closer Analysis" feature) and **fuel cell detectors**.

Infrared and fuel-cell-based breath testers are microprocessor controlled so that all an operator has to do is press a start button and the instrument automatically moves through a sequence of steps that produce a readout of the subject's test results. These instruments also perform self-diagnostic tests to ascertain whether they are in proper operating condition.

fuel cell detector
A detector in which a chemical reaction involving alcohol produces electricity.

Considerations in Breath Testing   The key to the accuracy of a breath-testing device is to ensure that the unit captures the alcohol in the alveolar (deep-lung) breath of the subject. This is typically accomplished by programming the unit to accept no less than 1.1 to 1.5 liters of breath from the subject. Also, the subject must blow for a minimum time (such as 6 seconds) with a minimum breath flow rate (such as 3 liters per minute).

The breath-test instruments just described feature a *slope detector*, which ensures that the breath sample is alveolar, or deep-lung, breath. As the subject blows into the instrument, the breath-alcohol concentration is continuously monitored. The instrument accepts a breath sample only when consecutive measurements fall within a predetermined rate of change. This approach ensures that the sample measurement is deep-lung breath and closely relates to the true blood-alcohol concentration of the subject being tested.

Closer Analysis

Infrared Light Absorption

(a)   (b)

FIGURE 1   An infrared breath-testing instrument—the BAC Data Master. Courtesy National Patent Analytical Systems, Inc., Mansfield, OH.

In principle, infrared instruments operate no differently from the spectrophotometers described in Chapter 10. An evidential testing instrument that incorporates the principle of infrared light absorption is shown in Figure 1. Any alcohol present in the subject's breath flows into the instrument's breath chamber. As shown in Figure 2, a beam of infrared light is aimed through the chamber. A filter is used to select a wavelength of infrared light at which alcohol will absorb. As the infrared light passes through the chamber, it interacts with the alcohol and causes the light to decrease in intensity. The decrease in light intensity is measured by a photoelectric detector that gives a signal proportional to the concentration of

alcohol present in the breath sample. This information is processed by an electronic microprocessor, and the percent blood-alcohol concentration is displayed on a digital readout. Also, the blood-alcohol level is printed on a card to produce a permanent record of the test result. Most infrared breath testers aim a second infrared beam into the same chamber to check for acetone or other chemical interferences on the breath. If the instrument detects differences in the relative response of the two infrared beams that does not conform to ethyl alcohol, the operator is immediately informed of the presence of an "interferant."

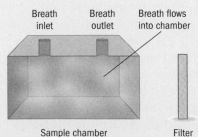
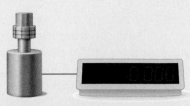

Breath inlet   Breath outlet   Breath flows into chamber

Infrared radiation source   Sample chamber   Filter   Detector

(a)

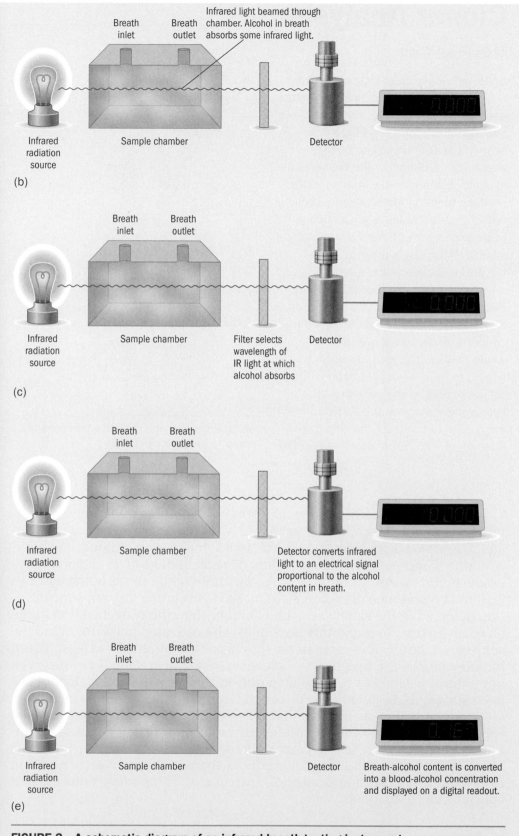

FIGURE 2   A schematic diagram of an infrared breath-testing instrument.

Closer Analysis

The Fuel Cell

A fuel cell converts energy arising from a chemical reaction into electrochemical energy. A typical fuel cell consists of two platinum electrodes separated by an acid- or base-containing porous membrane. A platinum wire connects the electrodes and allows a current to flow between them. In the alcohol fuel cell, one of the electrodes is positioned to come in contact with a subject's breath sample. If alcohol is present in the breath, a reaction at the electrode's surface converts the alcohol to acetic acid. One by-product of this conversion is free electrons, which flow through the connecting wire to the opposite electrode, where they interact with atmospheric oxygen to form water (see figure). The fuel cell also requires the migration of hydrogen ions across the acidic porous membrane to complete the circuit. The strength of the current flow between the two electrodes is proportional to the concentration of alcohol in the breath.

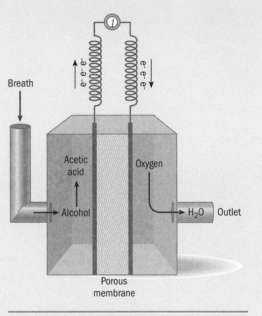

A detector in which chemical reactions are used to produce electricity.

A breath-test operator must take other steps to ensure that the breath-test result truly reflects the actual blood-alcohol concentration of the subject. A major consideration is to avoid measuring "mouth alcohol" resulting from regurgitation, belching, or recent intake of an alcoholic beverage. Also, recent gargling with an alcohol-containing mouthwash can lead to the presence of mouth alcohol. As a result, the alcohol concentration detected in the exhaled breath is higher than the concentration in the alveolar breath. To avoid this possibility, the operator must not allow the subject to take any foreign material into his or her mouth for at least fifteen minutes before the breath test. Likewise, the subject should be observed not to have belched or regurgitated during this period. Mouth alcohol has been shown to dissipate after fifteen to twenty minutes from its inception.

Independent measurement of duplicate breath samples taken within a few minutes of each other is another extremely important check of the integrity of the breath test. Acceptable agreement between the two tests taken minutes apart significantly reduces the possibility of errors arising from the operator, mouth alcohol, instrument component failures, and spurious electric signals.

Field Sobriety Testing

A police officer who suspects that an individual is under the influence of alcohol usually conducts a series of preliminary tests before ordering the suspect to submit to an evidential breath or blood test. These preliminary, or field sobriety, tests are normally performed to ascertain the degree of the suspect's physical impairment and whether an evidential test is justified.

Field sobriety tests usually consist of a series of psychophysical tests and a preliminary breath test (if such devices are authorized and available for use). A portable, handheld, roadside breath tester is shown in Figure 11–5. This device, about the size of a pack of cigarettes, weighs 5 ounces and uses a fuel cell to measure the alcohol content of a breath sample. The fuel cell absorbs the alcohol from the breath sample, oxidizes it, and produces an electrical current proportional to the breath-alcohol content. This instrument can typically perform for three to five years before the fuel cell needs to be replaced. Breath-test results obtained with devices such as those shown in Figure 11–5 must be considered preliminary and nonevidential. They should only establish probable cause for requiring an individual to submit to a more thorough breath or blood test.

Horizontal-gaze nystagmus, walk and turn, and the one-leg stand constitute a series of reliable and effective psychophysical tests. Horizontal-gaze nystagmus is an involuntary jerking of the eye as it moves to the side. A person experiencing nystagmus is usually unaware that the jerking is happening and is unable to stop or control it. The subject being tested is asked to follow a penlight or some other object with his or her eye as far to the side as the eye can go. The more intoxicated the person is, the less the eye has to move toward the side before jerking or nystagmus begins. Usually, when a person's blood-alcohol concentration is in the range of 0.10 percent, the jerking begins before the eyeball has moved 45 degrees to the side (see Figure 11–6). Higher blood-alcohol concentration causes jerking at smaller angles. Also, if the suspect has taken a drug that also causes nystagmus (such as phencyclidine, barbiturates, and other depressants), the nystagmus-onset angle may occur much earlier than would be expected from alcohol alone.

Walk and turn and the one-leg stand are divided-attention tasks, testing the subject's ability to comprehend and execute two or more simple instructions at one time. The ability to understand and simultaneously carry out more than two instructions is significantly affected by increasing blood-alcohol levels. Walk and turn requires the suspect to maintain balance while standing heel-to-toe and at the same time listening to and comprehending the test instructions. During the walking stage, the suspect must walk a straight line, touching heel-to-toe for nine steps, then turn around on the line

(a)

(b)

FIGURE 11–5 **The Alco-Sensor IV.** Courtesy Intoximeters, Inc., St. Louis, Mo.

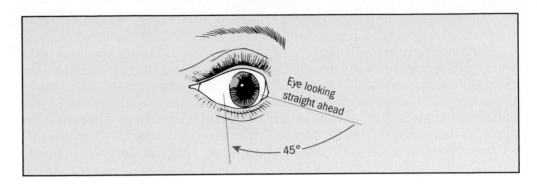

FIGURE 11–6 When a person's blood-alcohol level is in the range of 0.10 percent, jerking of the eye during the horizontal-gaze nystagmus test will begin before the eyeball has moved 45 degrees to the side.

and repeat the process. The one-leg stand requires the suspect to maintain balance while standing with heels together listening to the instructions. During the balancing stage, the suspect must stand on one foot while holding the other foot several inches off the ground for thirty seconds; simultaneously, the suspect must count out loud during the thirty-second time period.

Key Points

- Modern breath testers are free of chemicals. They include infrared light absorption devices and fuel cell detectors.

- The key to the accuracy of a breath-testing device is to ensure that the unit captures the alcohol in the alveolar (deep-lung) breath of the subject.

- Many breath testers collect a set volume of breath and expose it to infrared light. The instrument measures alcohol concentration in breath by measuring the degree of the interaction of the light with alcohol in the collected breath sample.

- Law enforcement officers use field sobriety tests to estimate a motorist's degree of physical impairment by alcohol and to determine whether an evidential test for alcohol is justified.

- The horizontal-gaze nystagmus test, walk and turn, and the one-leg stand are all considered reliable and effective psychophysical tests for alcohol impairment.

Analysis of Blood for Alcohol

Gas chromatography offers the toxicologist the most widely used approach for determining alcohol levels in blood. Under proper gas chromatographic conditions, alcohol can be separated from other volatiles in the blood. By comparing the resultant alcohol peak area to ones obtained with known blood-alcohol standards, the investigator can calculate the alcohol level with a high degree of accuracy (see Figure 11–7).

Another procedure for alcohol analysis involves the oxidation of alcohol to acetaldehyde. This reaction is carried out in the presence of the enzyme alcohol dehydrogenase and the coenzyme nicotin-amide-adenine

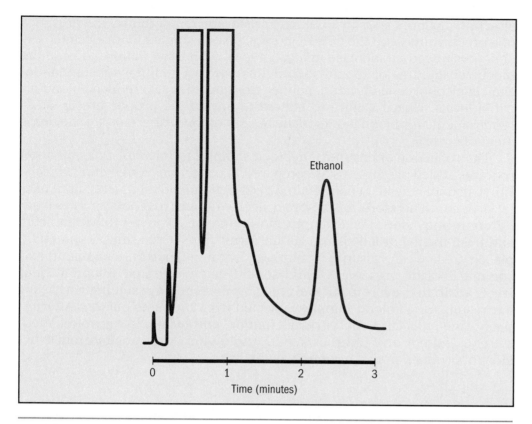

FIGURE 11–7 **A gas chromatogram showing ethyl alcohol (ethanol) in whole blood.** Courtesy Varian Inc., Calif.

dinucleotide (NAD). As the oxidation proceeds, NAD is converted into another chemical species, NADH. The extent of this conversion is measured by a spectrophotometer and is related to alcohol concentration. This approach to blood-alcohol testing is normally associated with instruments used in clinical or hospital settings. On the other hand, forensic laboratories normally use gas chromatography for determining blood-alcohol content.

Collection and Preservation of Blood

Blood must always be drawn under medically accepted conditions by a qualified individual. A nonalcoholic disinfectant should be applied before the suspect's skin is penetrated with a sterile needle or lancet. It is important to negate any argument that an alcoholic disinfectant may have inadvertently contributed to a falsely high blood-alcohol result. Nonalcoholic disinfectants such as aqueous benzalkonium chloride (Zepiran), aqueous mercuric chloride, or povidone-iodine (Betadine) are recommended for this purpose.

Once blood is removed from an individual, it is best preserved sealed in an airtight container after adding an anticoagulant and a preservative. The blood should be stored in a refrigerator until delivery to the toxicology laboratory. The addition of an **anticoagulant**, such as EDTA or potassium oxalate, prevents clotting; a **preservative**, such as sodium fluoride, inhibits the growth of microorganisms capable of destroying alcohol.

One study performed to determine the stability of alcohol in blood removed from living individuals found that the most significant factors

anticoagulant
A substance that prevents coagulation or clotting of the blood.

preservative
A substance that stops the growth of microorganisms in blood.

affecting alcohol's stability in blood are storage temperature, the presence of a preservative, and the time of storage.[3] Not a single blood specimen examined showed an increase in alcohol level with time. Failure to keep the blood refrigerated or to add sodium fluoride resulted in a substantial decline in alcohol concentration. Longer storage times also reduced blood-alcohol levels. Hence, failure to adhere to any of the proper preservation requirements for blood works to the benefit of the suspect and to the detriment of society.

The collection of postmortem blood samples for alcohol determination requires added precautions as compared to collection from living subjects. Ethyl alcohol may be generated in a deceased individual as a result of bacterial action. Therefore, it is best to collect a number of blood samples from different body sites. For example, blood may be removed from the heart and from the femoral (leg) and cubital (arm) veins. Each sample should be placed in a clean, airtight container containing an anticoagulant and sodium fluoride preservative and should be refrigerated. Blood-alcohol levels attributed solely to alcohol consumption should result in nearly similar results for all blood samples collected from the same person. Alternatively, the collection of vitreous humor and urine is recommended. Vitreous humor and urine usually do not suffer from postmortem ethyl alcohol production to any significant extent.

Key Points

- Gas chromatography is the most widely used approach for determining blood-alcohol levels in forensic laboratories.

- An anticoagulant should be added to a blood sample to prevent clotting; a preservative should be added to inhibit the growth of microorganisms capable of destroying alcohol.

Alcohol and the Law

Constitutionally, every state in the United States must establish and administer statutes regulating the operation of motor vehicles. Although such an arrangement might encourage diverse laws defining permissible blood-alcohol levels, this has not been the case. Since the 1930s, both the American Medical Association and the National Safety Council have exerted considerable influence in persuading the states to establish uniform and reasonable blood-alcohol standards.

Blood-Alcohol Laws

The American Medical Association and the National Safety Council initially recommended that a person with a blood-alcohol concentration in excess of 0.15 percent w/v was to be considered under the influence of alcohol.[4] However, continued experimental studies showed a clear correlation between drinking and driving impairment at blood-alcohol levels much below 0.15 percent w/v. These findings eventually led to a lowering of the blood-concentration standard for intoxication from 0.15 percent w/v to its current 0.08 percent w/v.

In 1992, the U.S. Department of Transportation (DOT) recommended that states adopt 0.08 percent blood-alcohol concentration as the legal measure of drunk driving. This recommendation was enacted into federal law in 2000. All fifty states have now established *per se laws,* meaning that any individual meeting or exceeding a defined blood-alcohol level (usually 0.08 percent) shall be deemed intoxicated. No other proof of alcohol impairment is necessary. Starting in 2003, states that had not adopted the 0.08 percent per se level stood to lose part of their federal funds for highway construction. The 0.08 percent level applies only to noncommercial drivers, as the federal government has set the maximum allowable blood-alcohol concentration for commercial truck and bus drivers at 0.04 percent.

Several Western countries have also set 0.08 percent w/v as the blood-alcohol level above which it is an offense to drive a motor vehicle, including Canada, Italy, Switzerland, and the United Kingdom. Finland, France, Germany, Ireland, Japan, the Netherlands, and Norway have a 0.05 percent limit. Australian states have adopted a 0.05 percent blood-alcohol concentration level. Sweden has lowered its blood-alcohol concentration limit to 0.02 percent.

As shown in Figure 11–8, one is about four times as likely to become involved in an automobile accident at the 0.08 percent level as compared to a sober individual. At the 0.15 percent level, the chances are twenty-five times as much for involvement in an automobile accident as compared to a sober driver. The reader can estimate the relationship of blood-alcohol levels to body weight and the quantity of 80-proof liquor consumed by referring to Figure 11–9.

Constitutional Issues

The Fifth Amendment to the U.S. Constitution guarantees all citizens protection against *self-incrimination*—that is, against being forced to make an admission that would prove one's own guilt in a legal matter. Because consenting to a breath test for alcohol might be considered a form of self-incrimination, the National Highway Traffic Safety Administration recommended an *implied-consent law* to prevent a person from refusing to

WebExtra 11.1
Calculate Your Blood-Alcohol Level
www.prenhall.com/Saferstein

WebExtra 11.2
See How Alcohol Affects Your Behavior
www.prenhall.com/Saferstein

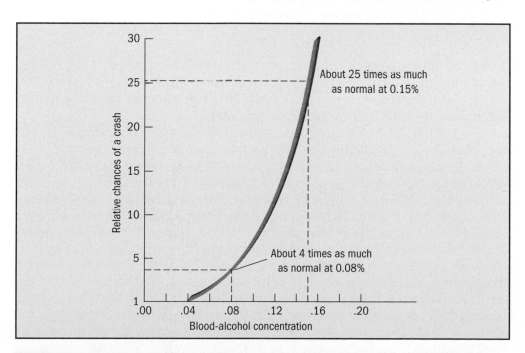

FIGURE 11–8   A diagram of increased driving risk in relation to blood-alcohol concentration.
Courtesy U.S. Department of Transportation, Washington, D.C.

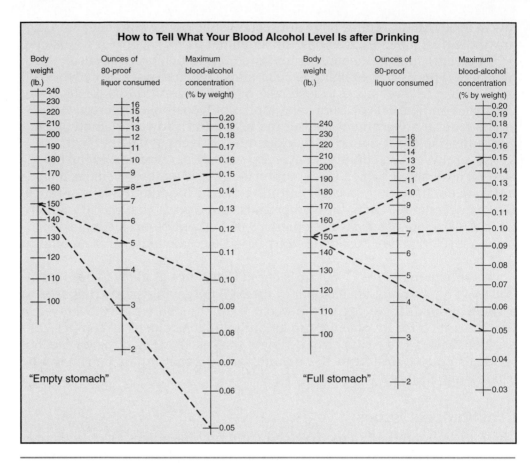

How to Tell What Your Blood Alcohol Level Is after Drinking

(left chart) Body weight (lb.); Ounces of 80-proof liquor consumed; Maximum blood-alcohol concentration (% by weight); "Empty stomach"

(right chart) Body weight (lb.); Ounces of 80-proof liquor consumed; Maximum blood-alcohol concentration (% by weight); "Full stomach"

FIGURE 11–9 To use this diagram, lay a straight edge across your weight and the number of ounces of liquor you've consumed on an empty or full stomach. The point where the edge hits the right-hand column is your maximum blood-alcohol level. The rate of elimination of alcohol from the bloodstream is approximately 0.015 percent per hour. Therefore, to calculate your actual blood-alcohol level, subtract 0.015 from the number indicated in the right-hand column for each hour from the start of drinking.

take a test on those constitutional grounds. This law states that the operator of a motor vehicle on a public highway must either consent to a test for alcohol intoxication, if requested, or lose his or her license for some designated period—usually six months to one year.

The leading case relating to the constitutionality of collecting a blood specimen for alcohol testing, as well as for obtaining other types of physical evidence from a suspect without consent, is *Schmerber* v. *California*.[5] While being treated at a Los Angeles hospital for injuries sustained in an automobile collision, Schmerber was arrested for driving under the influence of alcohol. Despite Schmerber's objections, a physician took a blood sample from him at the direction of the police. Schmerber was convicted of driving while intoxicated, and he subsequently appealed the decision. The case eventually reached the U.S. Supreme Court, where Schmerber argued that his privilege against self-incrimination had been violated by the introduction of the results of the blood test at his trial. The Court ruled against him, reasoning that the Fifth Amendment prohibits only compelling a suspect to give *testimonial* evidence that may prove to be self-incriminating; being compelled to furnish *physical* evidence, such as fingerprints, photographs, measurements, and blood samples, the Court ruled, was not protected by the Fifth Amendment.

The Court also addressed the question of whether the police violated Schmerber's Fourth Amendment protection against unreasonable search and seizure by taking a blood specimen from him without a search warrant. The Court upheld the constitutionality of the blood removal, reasoning in this case that the police were confronted with an emergency situation. By the time police officials would have obtained a warrant, Schmerber's blood-alcohol levels would have declined significantly as a result of natural body elimination processes. In effect, the evidence would have been destroyed. The Court also emphasized that the blood specimen was taken in a medically accepted manner and without unreasonable force. This opinion in no way condones warrantless taking of blood for alcohol or drug testing under all circumstances. The reasonableness of actions a police officer may take to compel an individual to yield evidence can be judged only on a case-by-case basis.

Key Points

- The current legal measure of drunk driving in the United States is a blood-alcohol concentration of 0.08 percent, or 0.08 grams of alcohol per 100 milliliters of blood.

- An implied-consent law states that the operator of a motor vehicle on a public highway must either consent to a test for alcohol intoxication, if requested, or lose his or her license for some designated period—usually six months to one year.

Role of the Toxicologist

Once the forensic toxicologist ventures beyond the analysis of alcohol, he or she encounters an encyclopedic maze of drugs and poisons. Even a cursory discussion of the problems and handicaps imposed on toxicologists is enough to engender a sense of appreciation for their accomplishments and ingenuity.

Challenges Facing the Toxicologist

The toxicologist is presented with body fluids and/or organs and asked to examine them for drugs and poisons. If he or she is fortunate, which is not often, some clue as to the type of toxic substance present may develop from the victim's symptoms, a postmortem pathological examination, an examination of the victim's personal effects, or the nearby presence of empty drug containers or household chemicals. Without such supportive information, the toxicologist must use general screening procedures with the hope of narrowing thousands of possibilities to one.

If this task does not seem monumental, consider that the toxicologist is not dealing with drugs at the concentration levels found in powders and pills. By the time a drug specimen reaches the toxicology laboratory, it has been dissipated and distributed throughout the body. The drug analyst may have gram or milligram quantities of material to work with, but the toxicologist must be satisfied with nanogram or at best microgram amounts, acquired only after careful extraction from body fluids and organs.

Furthermore, the body is an active chemistry laboratory, and no one can appreciate this observation more than a toxicologist. Few substances enter and completely leave the body in the same chemical state. The drug that is injected is not always the substance extracted from the body tissues. Therefore, a thorough understanding of how the body alters or metabolizes the chemical structure of a drug is essential in detecting its presence.

It would, for example, be futile and frustrating to search exhaustively for heroin in the human body. This drug is almost immediately metabolized to morphine on entering the bloodstream. Even with this information, the search may still prove impossible unless the examiner also knows that only a small percentage of morphine is excreted unchanged in urine. For the most part, morphine becomes chemically bonded to body carbohydrates before elimination in urine. Thus, successful detection of morphine requires that its extraction be planned in accordance with a knowledge of its chemical fate in the body.

Last, when and if the toxicologist has surmounted all of these obstacles and has finally detected, identified, and quantitated a drug or poison, he or she must assess the substance's toxicity. Fortunately, there is published information relating to the toxic levels of most drugs. However, even when such data are available, their interpretation must assume that the victim's physiological behavior agrees with that of subjects of previous studies. Such an assumption may not be entirely valid without knowing the subject's case history. No experienced toxicologist would be surprised to find an individual tolerating a toxic level of a drug that would have killed most other people.

Collection and Preservation of Toxicological Evidence

The toxicologist's capabilities depend directly on input from the attending physician, medical examiner, and police investigator. It is a tribute to forensic toxicologists, who must often labor under conditions that do not afford such cooperation, that they can achieve the high level of proficiency that they do.

Generally, with a deceased person, the medical examiner decides what biological specimens must be shipped to the toxicology laboratory for analysis. However, a living person suspected of being under the influence of a drug presents a completely different problem, and few options are available. When possible, both blood and urine are taken from any suspected drug user. The entire urine void (sample) is collected and submitted for toxicological analysis. Preferably, two consecutive voids should be collected in separate specimen containers.

When a licensed physician or registered nurse is available, a sample of blood should also be collected. The amount of blood taken depends on the type of examination to be conducted. Comprehensive toxicological tests for drugs and poisons can conveniently be carried out on a minimum of 10 milliliters of blood. A determination solely for the presence of alcohol will require much less—approximately 5 milliliters of blood. However, many therapeutic drugs, such as tranquilizers and barbiturates, taken in combination with a small, nonintoxicating amount of alcohol, produce behavioral patterns resembling alcohol intoxication. For this reason, the toxicologist must be given enough blood to perform a comprehensive analysis for drugs in cases of low alcohol concentrations (see Figure 11–10).

Techniques Used in Toxicology

For the toxicologist, the upsurge in drug use and abuse has meant that the overwhelming majority of fatal and nonfatal toxic agents are drugs. Not surprisingly, a relatively small number of drugs—namely, those discussed in Chapter 10—comprise nearly all the toxic agents encountered. Of these, alcohol, marijuana, and cocaine account for 90 percent or more of the drugs encountered in a typical toxicology laboratory.

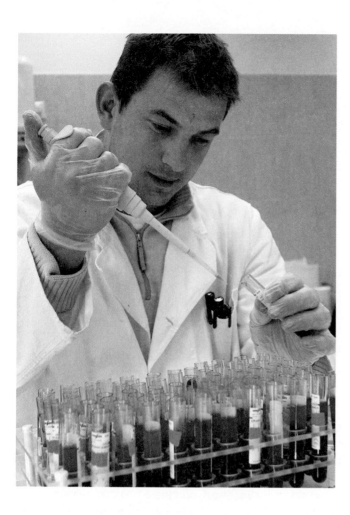

FIGURE 11–10 A scientist analyzing blood samples.
Courtesy Risto Bozovic, AP Wide World Photos

Acids and Bases Like the drug analyst, the toxicologist must devise an analytical scheme to detect, isolate, and identify a toxic substance. The first chore is to remove and isolate drugs and other toxic agents from the biological materials submitted as evidence. Because drugs constitute a large portion of the toxic materials found, a good deal of effort must be devoted to their extraction and detection. Many different procedures are used, and a useful description of them would be too detailed for this text. We can best understand the underlying principle of drug extraction by observing that many drugs fall into the categories of acids and bases.

By controlling the acidity or basicity of a water solution (pH) into which blood, urine, or tissues are dissolved, the toxicologist can control the type of drug that is recovered. For example, acid drugs are easily extracted from an acidified water solution (pH less than 7) with organic solvents such as chloroform. Similarly, basic drugs are readily removed from a basic water solution (pH greater than 7) with organic solvents. This simple approach gives the toxicologist a general technique for extracting and categorizing drugs. Some of the more commonly encountered drugs may be classified as follows:

Acid Drugs	Basic Drugs
Barbiturates	Phencyclidine
Acetylsalicylic acid (aspirin)	Methadone
	Amphetamines
	Cocaine

acid
A compound capable of donating a hydrogen ion (H+) to another compound.

base
A compound capable of accepting a hydrogen ion (H+).

pH
A symbol used to express the basicity or acidity of a substance. A pH of 7 is neutral; lower values are acidic; higher values are basic.

Case Study

Death by Tylenol

Tylenol® on the pharmacy shelf. *Courtesy UPI, Corbis/Bettmann*

In 1982, two firefighters from a Chicago suburb were casually discussing four bizarre deaths that had recently taken place in a neighboring area. As they discussed the circumstances of the deaths, they realized that each of the victims had taken Tylenol. Their suspicions were immediately reported to police investigators. Tragically, before the general public could be alerted, three more victims died after taking poison-laced Tylenol capsules. Seven individuals, all in the Chicago area, were the first victims to die from what has become known as *product tampering*.

A forensic chemical analysis of Tylenol capsules recovered from the victims' residences showed that the capsules were filled with potassium cyanide in a quantity ten thousand times what was needed to kill an average person. It was quickly determined that the cyanide was not introduced into the bottles at the factory. Instead, the perpetrator methodically emptied each of twenty to thirty capsules and then refilled them with potassium cyanide. The tampered capsules were rebottled, carefully repackaged, and placed on the shelves of six different stores. The case of the Tylenol murders remains unsolved, and the $100,000 reward offered by Tylenol's manufacturer remains unclaimed.

Screening and Confirmation   Once the specimen has been extracted and divided into acidic and basic fractions, the toxicologist can identify the drugs present. The strategy for identifying abused drugs entails a two-step approach: *screening* and *confirmation* (see Figure 11–11). A screening test normally gives quick insight into the likelihood that a specimen contains a drug substance. This test allows a toxicologist to examine a large number of specimens within a short period of time for a wide range of drugs. Any positive results from a screening test are tentative at best and must be verified with a confirmation test.

Screening Tests   The three most widely used screening tests are thin-layer chromatography (TLC), gas chromatography (GC), and immunoassay. The techniques of GC and TLC were described in Chapter 10. The third technique, immunoassay, has proven to be a useful screening tool in toxicology laboratories. Its principles are very different from any of the analytical techniques we have discussed so far. Basically, immunoassay is based on specific drug antibody reactions. We will learn about this concept in Chapter 14. The primary advantage of immunoassay is its ability to

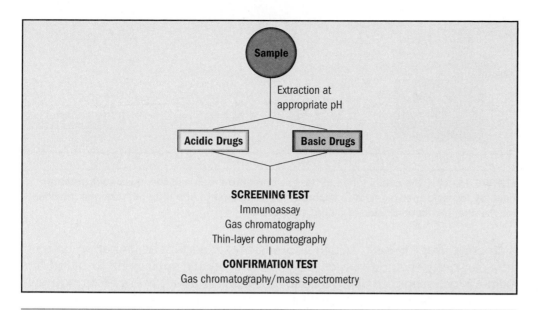

FIGURE 11–11 Biological fluids and tissues are extracted for acidic and basic drugs by controlling the pH of a water solution in which they are dissolved. Once this is accomplished, the toxicologist will analyze for drugs by using screening and confirmation test procedures.

detect small concentrations of drugs in body fluids and organs. In fact, this technique provides the best approach for detecting the low drug levels normally associated with smoking marijuana.

Confirmation Tests A positive screening test may be due to a substance's close chemical structure to an abused drug. For this reason, the toxicologist must follow up any positive screening test with a confirmation test. Because of the potential impact of the results of a drug finding on an individual, only the most conclusive confirmation procedures should be used.

Gas chromatography/mass spectrometry is generally accepted as the confirmation test of choice. As we learned in Chapter 10, the combination of gas chromatography and mass spectrometry provides a one-step confirmation test of unequaled sensitivity and specificity. Figure 11–12 illustrates the process. After being introduced to the gas chromatograph, the sample is separated into its components. When the separated sample component leaves the column of the gas chromatograph, it enters the mass spectrometer, where it is bombarded with high-energy electrons. This bombardment causes the sample to break up into fragments, producing a fragmentation pattern or mass spectrum for each sample. For most compounds, the mass spectrum represents a unique "fingerprint" pattern that can be used for identification.

There is tremendous interest in drug-testing programs conducted not only in criminal matters but for industry and government as well. Urine testing for drugs is becoming common for job applicants and employees in the workplace. Likewise, the U.S. military has an extensive drug urine-testing program for its members. Many urine-testing programs rely on private laboratories to perform the required analyses. In any case, when the test results form the basis for taking action against an individual, both a screening and confirmation test must be incorporated into the testing protocol to ensure the integrity of the laboratory's conclusions.

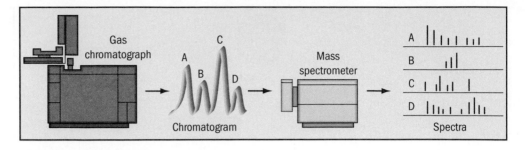

FIGURE 11–12 The combination of the gas chromatograph and the mass spectrometer enables forensic toxicologists to separate the components of a drug mixture and provides for the specific identification of a drug substance.

Detecting Drugs in Hair When a forensic toxicological examination on a living person is required, practicality limits available specimens to blood and urine. Most drugs remain in the bloodstream for about twenty-four hours; in urine, they normally are present up to seventy-two hours. However, it may be necessary to go further back in time to ascertain whether a subject has been abusing a drug. If so, the only viable alternative to blood and urine is head hair.

Hair is nourished by blood flowing through capillaries located close to the hair root. Drugs present in blood diffuse through the capillary walls into the base of the hair and become permanently entrapped in the hair's hardening protein structure. As the hair continues to grow, the drug's location on the hair shaft becomes a historical marker for delineating drug intake. Given that the average human head hair grows at the rate of 1 centimeter per month, analyzing segments of hair for drug content may define the timeline for drug use, dating it back over a period of weeks, months, or even years, depending on the hair's length.

However, caution is required in interpreting the timeline. The chronology of drug intake may be distorted by drugs penetrating the hair's surface as a result of environmental exposure, or drugs may enter the hair's surface through sweat. Nevertheless, drug hair analysis is the only viable approach for measuring long-term abuse of a drug.

Detecting Nondrug Poisons Although forensic toxicologists devote most of their efforts to detecting drugs, they also test for a wide variety of other toxic substances. Some of these are rare elements, not widely or commercially available. Others are so common that virtually everyone is exposed to nontoxic amounts of them every day.

Heavy Metals One group of poisons once commonly encountered in criminal cases of murder are known as *heavy metals*. They include arsenic, bismuth, antimony, mercury, and thallium. These days, however, the forensic toxicologist only occasionally encounters heavy metals because severe environmental protection regulations restrict their availability to the general public. Nevertheless, as the following case study makes clear, their use is by no means only a historical curiosity.

To screen for many of these metals, the investigator may dissolve the suspect body fluid or tissue in a hydrochloric acid solution and insert a copper strip into the solution. This process is known as the Reinsch test. The appearance of a silvery or dark coating on the copper indicates the presence of a heavy metal. Such a finding must be confirmed by analytical techniques suitable for inorganic analysis—namely, emission spectroscopy, or X-ray diffraction.

Case Study

Joann Curley: Caught by a Hair

A vibrant young woman named Joann Curley rushed to the Wilkes-Barre (Pennsylvania) General Hospital. Her husband, Bobby, was having an attack and required immediate medical attention. Bobby was experiencing a burning sensation in his feet, numbness in his hands, a flushed face, and intense sweating. He was diagnosed with Guillain-Barré syndrome, an acute inflammation of the nervous system that accounted for all of Bobby's symptoms. After being discharged, Bobby experienced another bout of debilitating pain and numbness. He was admitted to another hospital, the larger and more capable Hershey Medical Center in Hershey, Pennsylvania. There doctors observed extreme alopecia, or hair loss.

Test results of Bobby's urine showed high levels of the heavy metal thallium in his body. Thallium, a rare and highly toxic metal that was used decades ago in substances such as rat poison and to treat ringworm and gout, was found in sufficient quantities to cause Bobby's sickness. The use of thallium was banned in the United States in 1984. Now, at least, Bobby could be treated. However, before Bobby's doctors could treat him for thallium poisoning, he experienced cardiac arrest and slipped into a coma. Joann Curley made the difficult decision to remove her husband of thirteen months from life support equipment. He died shortly thereafter.

Bobby Curley was an electrician and, for five months before his death, he worked in the chemistry department at nearby Wilkes University. Authorities suspected that Bobby had been accidentally exposed to thallium there among old chemicals and laboratory equipment. The laboratory was searched and several old bottles of powdered thallium salts were discovered in a storage closet. After testing the air and surfaces, these were eliminated as possible sources for exposure. This finding was supported by the discovery that none of Bobby's coworkers had any thallium in their systems. The next most logical route of exposure was in the home; thus, the Curley kitchen was sampled. Of the hundreds of items tested, three thermoses were found to contain traces of thallium. Investigators also learned that Bobby had changed his life insurance to list his wife, Joann, as the beneficiary of his $300,000 policy. Based on this information, police consulted a forensic toxicologist in an effort to glean as much from the physical evidence in Bobby Curley's body as possible. The toxicologist conducted segmental analysis of Bobby's hair, an analytical method based on the predictable rate of hair growth on the human scalp: an average of 1 centimeter per month. Bobby had approximately 5 inches (12.5 centimeters) of hair, which represents almost twelve months of hair growth. Each section tested represented a specific period of time in the final year of Bobby's life.

The hair analysis proved that Bobby Curley was poisoned with thallium long before he began working at Wilkes University. The first few doses were small, which probably barely made him sick at the time. Gradually, over a year or more, Bobby was receiving more doses of thallium until he finally succumbed to a massive dose three or four days before his death. After careful scrutiny of the timeline, investigators concluded that only Joann Curley had access to Bobby during each of these intervals. She also had a motive, in the amount of $300,000. Presented with the timeline and the solid toxicological evidence against her, Joann Curley pleaded guilty to murder. As part of her plea agreement, she provided a forty-page written confession of how she haphazardly dosed Bobby with some rat poison she found in her basement. She admitted that she murdered him for the money she would receive from Bobby's life insurance policy.

Carbon Monoxide Unlike heavy metals, *carbon monoxide* still represents one of the most common poisons encountered in a forensic laboratory. Inhaling the carbon monoxide from automobile exhaust fumes is a relatively common way to commit suicide. The victim typically uses a garden or vacuum cleaner hose to connect the tailpipe with the vehicle's interior, or allows the engine to run in a closed garage. A level of carbon monoxide sufficient to cause death accumulates in five to ten minutes in a closed single-car garage.

When carbon monoxide enters the human body, it is primarily absorbed by the red blood cells, where it combines with hemoglobin to form carboxyhemoglobin. An average red blood cell contains about 280 million molecules of hemoglobin. Oxygen normally combines with hemoglobin, which transports the oxygen throughout the body. However, if a high percentage of the hemoglobin combines with carbon monoxide, not enough is left to carry sufficient oxygen to the tissues, and death by asphyxiation quickly follows.

There are two basic methods for measuring the concentration of carbon monoxide in the blood. Spectrophotometric methods examine the visible spectrum of blood to determine the amount of carboxyhemoglobin relative to oxyhemoglobin or total hemoglobin; or a volume of blood can be treated with a reagent to liberate the carbon monoxide, which is then measured by gas chromatography.

The amount of carbon monoxide in blood is generally expressed as *percent saturation*. This represents the extent to which the available hemoglobin has been converted to carboxyhemoglobin. The transition from normal or occupational levels of carbon monoxide to toxic levels is not sharply defined. It depends, among other things, on the age, health, and general fitness of each individual. In a healthy middle-age individual, a carbon monoxide blood saturation greater than 50 to 60 percent is considered fatal. However, in combination with alcohol or other depressants, fatal levels may be significantly lower. For instance, a carbon monoxide saturation of 35 to 40 percent may prove fatal in the presence of a blood-alcohol concentration of 0.20 percent w/v. Interestingly, chain smokers may have a constant carbon monoxide level of 8 to 10 percent from the carbon monoxide in cigarette smoke.

The level of carbon monoxide in the blood of a victim found dead at the scene of a fire can help ascertain whether foul play has occurred. High levels of carbon monoxide in the blood prove that the victim breathed the combustion products of the fire and was therefore alive when the fire began. By contrast, low levels of carbon monoxide indicate that the victim was likely dead before the fire started, and may have been deliberately placed at the scene in order to destroy the body. Many attempts at covering up a murder by setting fire to a victim's house or car have been uncovered in this manner.

Significance of Toxicological Findings

Once a drug is found and identified, the toxicologist assesses its influence on the behavior of the individual. Interpreting the results of a toxicology finding is one of the toxicologist's most difficult chores. Recall that many countries have designated a specific blood-alcohol level at which an individual is deemed under the influence of alcohol. These levels were established as a result of numerous studies conducted over several years to measure the effects of alcohol levels on driving performance. However, no such legal guidelines are available to the toxicologist who must judge how a drug other than alcohol affects an individual's performance or physical state.

Forensic Brief

Death by Radiation Poisoning

In November 2006, Alexander V. Litvinenko lay at death's doorstep in a London hospital. He was in excruciating pain and had symptoms that included hair loss, an inability to make blood cells, and gastrointestinal distress. His organs slowly failed as he lingered for three weeks before dying. British investigators soon confirmed that Litvinenko died from the intake of polonium 210, a radioactive element, in what appeared to be its first use as a murder weapon.

Litvinenko's death almost immediately set off an international uproar. Litvinenko, a former KBG operative, became a vocal critic of the Russian spy agency FSB, the domestic successor to the KGB. In 2000, he fled to London, where he was granted asylum. Litvinenko continued to voice his criticisms of the Russian spy agency and also became highly critical of Russia's President Vladimir Putin. Just before his death, Litvinenko intimated that the Prime Minister of Italy was a KGB operative.

Suspicions immediately fell onto Andrei Lugovoi and Dmitri Kovtun, business associates of Mr. Litvinenko. Lugovoi was himself a former KGB officer. On the day he fell ill, Litvinenko met Lugovoi and Kovtun at the Pine Bar of the Millennium Hotel in London. At the meeting, Mr. Litvinenko drank tea out of a teapot later found to be highly radioactive. British officials have accused Lugovoi of poisoning Litvinenko. The precise nature of the evidence against him has not been made clear, though investigators have linked him and Mr. Kovtun to a trail of polonium 210 radioactivity stretching from hotel rooms, restaurant and bars, and offices in London to Hamburg, Germany, and to British Airways planes that had flown to Moscow. Each man has denied killing Mr. Litvinenko.

Polonium 210 is highly radioactive and very toxic. By weight, it is about 250 million times as toxic as cyanide, so a particle the size of a few grains of sand could be fatal. It emits a radioactive ray known as an alpha particle. Because this form of radiation cannot penetrate the skin, polonium 210 can only be effective as a poison if it is swallowed, breathed in, or injected. The particles disperse through the body and

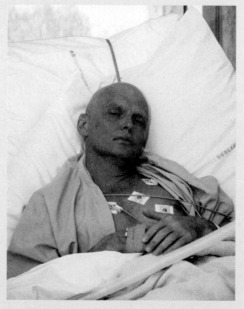

Alexander Litvinenko, former KGB agent, before and after he became sick. *Courtesy AP Wide World Photos (left) and Getty Images, Inc.–Getty News (right)*

(Continued)

Forensic Brief

Death by Radiation Poisoning *(Continued)*

first destroy fast-growing cells such as those in bone marrow, blood, hair, and the digestive tract. That would be consistent with Mr. Litvinenko's symptoms. There is no antidote for polonium poisoning.

Polonium does have industrial uses and is produced by commercial or institutional nuclear reactors. Polonium 210 has been found to be ideal for making antistatic devices that remove dust from film, lenses, as well as the atmosphere of paper and textile plants. Its non-body-penetrating rays produce an electric charge on nearby air. Bits of dust with static attract the charged air, which neutralizes them. Once free of static, the dust is easy to blow or brush away. Manufacturers of such antistatic devices take great pains to make the polonium hard to remove from their products.

For many drugs, blood concentration levels are readily determined and can be used to estimate the pharmacological effects of the drug on the individual. Often, when dealing with a living person, the toxicologist has the added benefit of knowing what a police officer may have observed about an individual's behavior and motor skills. For a deceased person, drug levels in various body organs and tissues provide additional information about the individual's state at the time of death. However, before drawing conclusions about drug-induced behavior, the analyst must consider other factors, including the age, physical condition, and tolerance of the drug user.

With prolonged use of a drug, an individual may become less responsive to a drug's effects and tolerate blood-drug concentrations that would kill a casual drug user. Therefore, knowledge of an individual's history of drug use is important in evaluating drug concentrations. Another consideration is the additive or synergistic effects of the interaction of two or more drugs, which may produce a highly intoxicated or comatose state even though none of the drugs alone is present at high or toxic levels. The combination of alcohol with barbiturates or narcotics is a common example of a potentially lethal drug combination.

The presence of a drug in urine is a poor indicator of how extensively an individual's behavior or state is influenced by the drug. Urine is formed outside the body's circulatory system, and consequently drug levels can build up in it over a relatively long period of time. Some drugs are found in the urine one to three days after they have been taken and long after their effects on the user have disappeared. Nevertheless, the value of this information should not be discounted. Urine drug levels, like blood levels, are best used by law enforcement authorities and the courts to corroborate other investigative and medical findings regarding an individual's condition. Hence, for an individual arrested for suspicion of being under the influence of a drug, a toxicologist's determinations supplement the observations of the arresting officer, including the results of field sobriety tests and a drug influence evaluation (discussed next).

For a deceased person, the medical examiner or coroner must establish a cause of death. However, before a conclusive determination is made, the examining physician depends on the forensic toxicologist to demonstrate the presence or absence of a drug or poison in the tissues or body fluids of the deceased. Only through the combined efforts of the toxicologist and the medical examiner (or coroner) can society be assured that death investigations achieve high professional and legal standards.

Drug Recognition Experts

Although recognizing alcohol-impaired performance is an expertise generally accorded to police officers by the courts, recognizing drug-induced intoxication is much more difficult and generally not part of police training. During the 1970s, the Los Angeles Police Department developed and tested a series of clinical and psychophysical examinations that a trained police officer could use to identify and differentiate among types of drug impairment. This program has evolved into a national program to train police as *drug recognition experts*. Normally, a three- to five-month training program is required to certify an officer as a drug recognition expert (DRE).

The DRE program incorporates standardized methods for examining suspects to determine whether they have taken one or more drugs. The process is systematic and standard; to ensure that each subject has been tested in a routine fashion, each DRE must complete a standard Drug Influence Evaluation form (see Figure 11–13). The entire drug evaluation takes approximately thirty to forty minutes. The components of the twelve-step process are summarized in Table 11–1.

The DRE evaluation process can suggest the presence of the following seven broad categories of drugs:

1. Central nervous system depressants

2. Central nervous system stimulants

3. Hallucinogens

4. Dissociative anesthetics (includes phencyclidine and its analogs)

5. Inhalants

6. Narcotic analgesics

7. Cannabis

The DRE program is not designed to be a substitute for toxicological testing. The toxicologist can often determine that a suspect has a particular drug in his or her body. But the toxicologist often cannot infer with reasonable certainty that the suspect was impaired at a specific time. On the other hand, the DRE can supply credible evidence that the suspect was impaired at a specific time and that the nature of the impairment was consistent with a particular family of drugs. But the DRE program usually cannot determine which specific drug was ingested. Proving drug intoxication requires a coordinated effort and the production of competent data from both the DRE and the forensic toxicologist.

Key Points

- The forensic toxicologist must devise an analytical scheme to detect, isolate, and identify toxic drug substances extracted from biological fluids, tissues, and organs.

- A screening test gives quick insight into the likelihood that a specimen contains a drug substance. Positive results arising from a screening test are tentative at best and must be verified with a confirmation test.

- The most widely used screening tests are thin-layer chromatography, gas chromatography, and immunoassay. Gas chromatography/mass spectrometry is generally accepted as the confirmation test of choice.

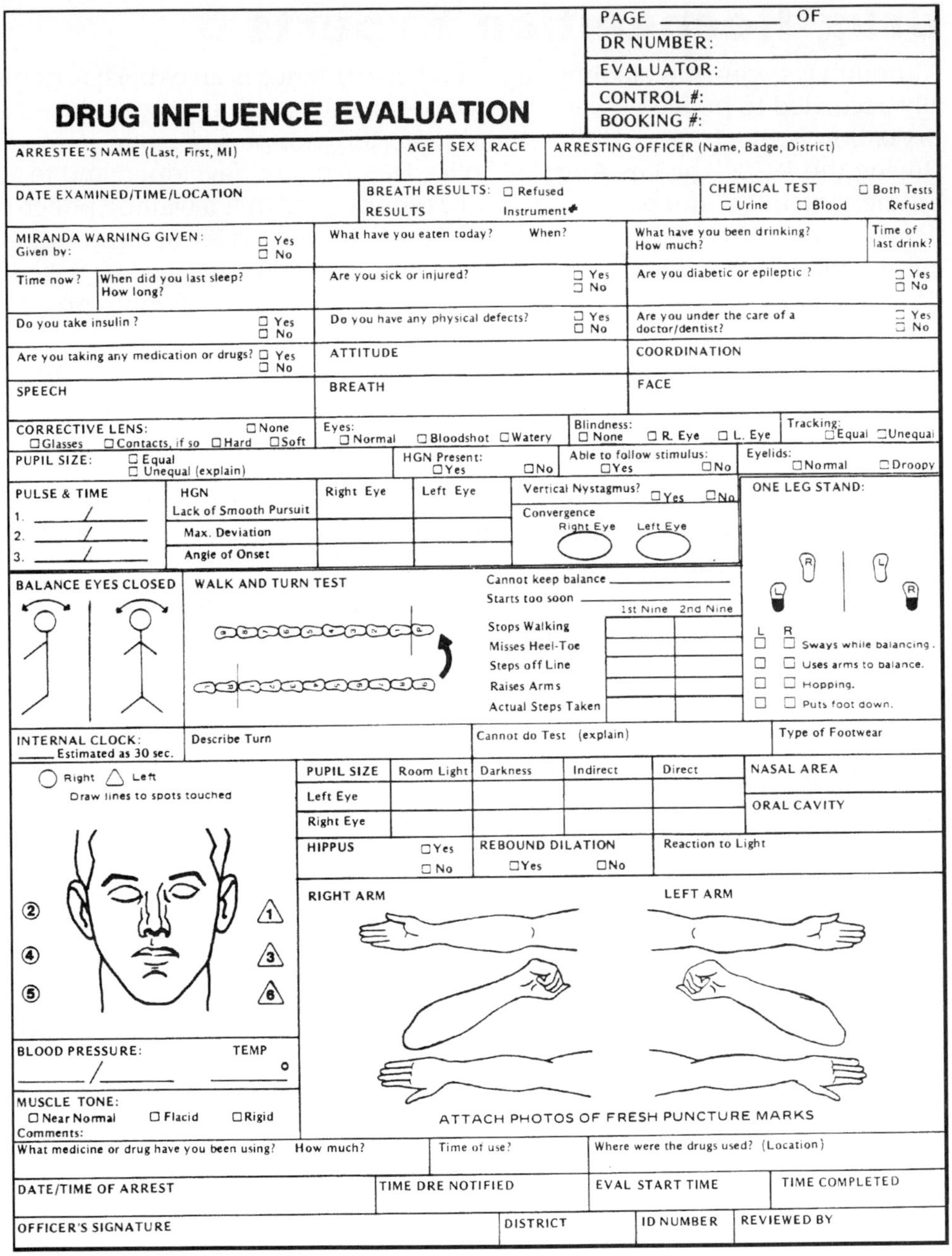

PAGE ______ OF ______
DR NUMBER:
EVALUATOR:
CONTROL #:
BOOKING #:

DRUG INFLUENCE EVALUATION

ARRESTEE'S NAME (Last, First, MI) | AGE | SEX | RACE | ARRESTING OFFICER (Name, Badge, District)

DATE EXAMINED/TIME/LOCATION | BREATH RESULTS: ☐ Refused RESULTS Instrument # | CHEMICAL TEST ☐ Urine ☐ Blood | ☐ Both Tests Refused

MIRANDA WARNING GIVEN: ☐ Yes ☐ No Given by: | What have you eaten today? When? | What have you been drinking? How much? | Time of last drink?

Time now? | When did you last sleep? How long? | Are you sick or injured? ☐ Yes ☐ No | Are you diabetic or epileptic? ☐ Yes ☐ No

Do you take insulin? ☐ Yes ☐ No | Do you have any physical defects? ☐ Yes ☐ No | Are you under the care of a doctor/dentist? ☐ Yes ☐ No

Are you taking any medication or drugs? ☐ Yes ☐ No | ATTITUDE | COORDINATION

SPEECH | BREATH | FACE

CORRECTIVE LENS: ☐ None ☐ Glasses ☐ Contacts, if so ☐ Hard ☐ Soft | Eyes: ☐ Normal ☐ Bloodshot ☐ Watery | Blindness: ☐ None ☐ R. Eye ☐ L. Eye | Tracking: ☐ Equal ☐ Unequal

PUPIL SIZE: ☐ Equal ☐ Unequal (explain) | HGN Present: ☐ Yes ☐ No | Able to follow stimulus: ☐ Yes ☐ No | Eyelids: ☐ Normal ☐ Droopy

PULSE & TIME 1. ___/___ 2. ___/___ 3. ___/___ | HGN: Lack of Smooth Pursuit, Max. Deviation, Angle of Onset | Right Eye | Left Eye | Vertical Nystagmus? ☐ Yes ☐ No | Convergence Right Eye Left Eye | ONE LEG STAND:

BALANCE EYES CLOSED | WALK AND TURN TEST | Cannot keep balance ____ Starts too soon ____ | 1st Nine 2nd Nine: Stops Walking, Misses Heel-Toe, Steps off Line, Raises Arms, Actual Steps Taken | L R ☐ ☐ Sways while balancing. ☐ ☐ Uses arms to balance. ☐ ☐ Hopping. ☐ ☐ Puts foot down.

INTERNAL CLOCK: ____ Estimated as 30 sec. | Describe Turn | Cannot do Test (explain) | Type of Footwear

○ Right △ Left Draw lines to spots touched
② ④ ⑤ △1 △3 △6

PUPIL SIZE | Room Light | Darkness | Indirect | Direct | NASAL AREA
Left Eye | | | | | ORAL CAVITY
Right Eye

HIPPUS ☐ Yes ☐ No | REBOUND DILATION ☐ Yes ☐ No | Reaction to Light

RIGHT ARM | LEFT ARM

BLOOD PRESSURE: ____/____ | TEMP ____°

MUSCLE TONE: ☐ Near Normal ☐ Flacid ☐ Rigid
Comments:

ATTACH PHOTOS OF FRESH PUNCTURE MARKS

What medicine or drug have you been using? How much? | Time of use? | Where were the drugs used? (Location)

DATE/TIME OF ARREST | TIME DRE NOTIFIED | EVAL START TIME | TIME COMPLETED

OFFICER'S SIGNATURE | DISTRICT | ID NUMBER | REVIEWED BY

FIGURE 11–13 Drug Influence Evaluation form.

- Once a drug is extracted and identified, a toxicologist may be required to judge the drug's effect on an individual's natural performance or physical state.
- A three- to five-month training program is required to certify an officer as a drug recognition expert (DRE). This training incorporates standardized methods for examining suspects to determine whether they have taken one or more drugs.

Table 11–1   Components of the Drug Recognition Process

1. *Breath-Alcohol Test.* By obtaining an accurate and immediate measurement of the suspect's blood-alcohol concentration, the drug recognition expert (DRE) can determine whether alcohol may be contributing to the suspect's observable impairment and whether the concentration of alcohol is sufficient to be the sole cause of that impairment.

2. *Interview with the Arresting Officer.* Spending a few minutes with the arresting officer often enables the DRE to determine the most promising areas of investigation.

3. *Preliminary Examination.* This structured series of questions, specific observations, and simple tests provides the first opportunity to examine the suspect closely. It is designed to determine whether the suspect is suffering from an injury or from another condition unrelated to drug consumption. It also affords an opportunity to begin assessing the suspect's appearance and behavior for signs of possible drug influence.

4. *Eye Examination.* Certain categories of drugs induce nystagmus, an involuntary, spasmodic motion of the eyeball. Nystagmus is an indicator of drug-induced impairment. The inability of the eyes to converge toward the bridge of the nose also indicates the possible presence of certain types of drugs.

5. *Divided-Attention Psychophysical Tests.* These tests check balance and physical orientation and include the walk and turn, the one-leg stand, the Romberg balance, and the finger-to-nose.

6. *Vital Signs Examinations.* Precise measurements of blood pressure, pulse rate, and body temperature are taken. Certain drugs elevate these signs; others depress them.

7. *Dark Room Examinations.* The size of the suspect's pupils in room light, near-total darkness, indirect light, and direct light is checked. Some drugs cause the pupils to either dilate or constrict.

8. *Examination for Muscle Rigidity.* Certain categories of drugs cause the muscles to become hypertense and quite rigid. Others may cause the muscles to relax and become flaccid.

9. *Examination for Injection Sites.* Users of certain categories of drugs routinely or occasionally inject their drugs. Evidence of needle use may be found on veins along the neck, arms, and hands.

10. *Suspect's Statements and Other Observations.* The next step is to attempt to interview the suspect concerning the drug or drugs he or she has ingested. Of course, the interview must be conducted in full compliance of the suspect's constitutional rights.

11. *Opinions of the Evaluator.* Using the information obtained in the previous ten steps, the DRE is able to make an informed decision about whether the suspect is impaired by drugs and, if so, what category or combination of categories is the probable cause of the impairment.

12. *Toxicological Examination.* The DRE should obtain a blood or urine sample from the suspect for laboratory analysis in order to secure scientific, admissible evidence to substantiate his or her conclusions.

Chapter Summary

Toxicologists detect and identify drugs and poisons in body fluids, tissues, and organs. A major branch of forensic toxicology deals with the measurement of alcohol in the body for matters that pertain to violations of criminal law.

Alcohol appears in the blood within minutes after it has been taken by mouth and slowly increases in concentration while it is being absorbed from the stomach and the small intestine into the bloodstream. When all the alcohol has been absorbed, a maximum alcohol level is reached in the blood and the postabsorption period begins. Then the alcohol concentration slowly decreases until a zero level is again reached. Alcohol is eliminated from the body through oxidation and excretion. Oxidation takes place almost entirely in the liver, whereas alcohol is excreted unchanged in the breath, urine, and perspiration.

The extent to which an individual is under the influence of alcohol is usually determined by measuring the quantity of alcohol present in the blood or the breath. Breath testers that operate on the principle of infrared light absorption are becoming increasingly popular within the law enforcement community.

Many types of breath testers capture a set volume of breath. The captured breath is exposed to infrared light. The degree of interaction of the light with alcohol in the breath sample allows the instrument to measure blood-alcohol concentration in the breath. These breath-testing devices operate on the principle that the ratio between the concentration of alcohol in deep-lung, or alveolar, breath and its concentration in blood is fixed.

Law enforcement officers typically use field sobriety tests to estimate a motorist's degree of physical impairment by alcohol and whether an evidential test for alcohol is justified. The horizontal-gaze nystagmus test, walk and turn, and the one-leg stand are all reliable and effective psychophysical tests.

Gas chromatography is the most widely used approach for determining alcohol levels in blood. Blood must always be drawn under medically accepted conditions by a qualified individual. A nonalcoholic disinfectant must be applied before the suspect's skin is penetrated with a sterile needle or lancet. Once blood is removed from an individual, it is best preserved sealed in an airtight container after adding an anticoagulant and a preservative.

The forensic toxicologist must devise an analytical scheme to detect, isolate, and identify toxic drug substances. Once the drug has been extracted from appropriate biological fluids, tissues, and organs, the forensic toxicologist can identify the drug substance. The strategy for identifying abused drugs entails a two-step approach: screening and confirmation. A screening test gives quick insight into the likelihood that a specimen contains a drug substance. Positive results from a screening test are tentative at best and must be verified with a confirmation test. The most widely used screening tests are thin-layer chromatography, gas chromatography, and immunoassay. Gas chromatography/mass spectrometry is generally accepted as the confirmation test of choice. Once the drug is extracted and identified, the toxicologist may be required to judge the drug's effect on an individual's natural performance or physical state.

The Drug Recognition Expert program incorporates standardized methods for examining automobile drivers suspected of being under the influence of drugs. But this DRE program usually cannot determine which specific drug was ingested. Hence, reliable data from both the DRE and the forensic toxicologist are required to prove drug intoxication.

Review Questions

1. The _____ studies body fluids, tissues, and organs to detect and identify drugs and poisons.

2. True or False: Toxicologists are employed only by crime laboratories. _____

3. The most heavily abused drug in the Western world is _____.

4. The transformation of chemicals introduced into the body into substances that are easier to eliminate is called _____.

5. Alcohol consumed on an empty stomach is absorbed (faster, slower) than an equivalent amount of alcohol taken when there is food in the stomach.

6. Alcohol is eliminated from the body by _____ and _____.

7. Approximately 98 percent of the ethyl alcohol consumed is oxidized to carbon dioxide and water in the _____.

8. The amount of alcohol exhaled in the _____ is directly proportional to the concentration of alcohol in the blood.

9. Alcohol is eliminated from the blood at an average rate of _____ percent w/v.

10. True or False: The amount of alcohol in the blood is not directly proportional to the concentration of alcohol in the brain. _____

11. True or False: Blood-alcohol levels have become the accepted standard for relating alcohol intake to its effect on the body. _____

12. Under normal drinking conditions, alcohol concentration in the blood peaks in _____ to _____ minutes.

13. A(n) _____ carries blood away from the heart; a(n) _____ carries blood back to the heart.

14. The _____ artery carries deoxygenated blood from the heart to the lungs.

15. Alcohol passes from the blood capillaries into the _____ sacs in the lungs.

16. One milliliter of blood contains the same amount of alcohol as approximately _____ milliliters of alveolar breath.

17. True or False: When alcohol is being absorbed into the blood, the alcohol concentration in venous blood is higher than that in arterial blood. _____

18. True or False: Portable, handheld, roadside breath testers for alcohol provide evidential test results. _____

19. Most modern breath testers use _____ radiation to detect and measure alcohol in the breath.

20. In an alcohol _____, two platinum electrodes are separated by an acid- or base-containing porous membrane, and one of the electrodes is positioned to come in contact with a subject's breath sample.

21. To avoid the possibility of "mouth alcohol" the operator of a breath tester must *not* allow the subject to take any foreign materials into the mouth for _____ to _____ minutes prior to the test.

22. True or False: A series of reliable and effective psychophysical tests are the horizontal-gaze nystagmus, walk and turn, and the one-leg stand. _____

23. Alcohol can be separated from other volatiles in blood and quantitated by the technique of _____.

24. When drawing blood for alcohol testing, the breath test operator must first wipe the suspect's skin that with a _____ disinfectant.

25. True or False: Failure to add a preservative, such as sodium fluoride, to blood removed from a living person may lead to a decline in alcohol concentration. _____

26. Most states have established _____ percent w/v as the impairment limit for blood-alcohol concentration in noncommercial drivers.

27. Studies show that an individual is about _____ times as likely to become involved in an automobile accident at the legal limit for blood alcohol as compared to a sober individual.

28. In the case of _____, the Supreme Court ruled that taking nontestimonial evidence, such as a blood sample, did not violate a suspect's Fifth Amendment rights.

29. Upon entering the body, heroin is changed into _____.

30. The body fluids _____ and _____ are both desirable for the toxicological examination of a living person suspected of being under the influence of a drug.

31. A large number of drugs can be classified chemically as _____ or _____.

32. True or False: Water with a pH value less than 7 is basic. _____

33. Drugs are extracted from body fluids and tissues by carefully controlling the _____ of the medium in which the sample has been dissolved.

34. Both _____ and _____ tests must be incorporated into the drug-testing protocol of a toxicology laboratory to ensure the correctness of the laboratory's conclusions.

35. The most widely used screening tests used by toxicologists are _____, _____, and _____.

36. The preferred method for confirmation testing is a combination of _____ and _____, which creates a unique "fingerprint" pattern that can be used for identification.

37. A toxicologist may be able to detect and identify a long-abused drug or poison because drugs present in blood diffuse through capillary walls into the base of a(n) _____ and become permanently entrapped in its hardening protein structure.

38. The gas _____ combines with hemoglobin in the blood to form carboxyhemoglobin, thus interfering with the transportation of oxygen in the blood.

39. True or False: Blood levels of drugs can alone be used to draw definitive conclusions about the effects of a drug on an individual. _____

40. True or False: The level of a drug present in the urine is by itself a poor indicator of how extensively an individual is affected by a drug. _____

41. Urine and blood-drug levels are best used by law enforcement authorities and the courts to _____ other investigative and medical findings pertaining to an individual's condition.

42. A program to train police as _____ incorporates systematic and standardized methods for examining suspects to determine whether they have taken one or more drugs.

Application and Critical Thinking

1. Answer the following questions about driving risk associated with drinking and blood alcohol concentration:
   a) Randy is just barely legally intoxicated. How much more likely is he to have an accident than someone who is sober?
   b) Marissa, who has been drinking, is fifteen times as likely to have an accident as her sober friend, Christine. What is Marissa's approximate blood-alcohol concentration?
   c) After several drinks, Charles is ten times as likely to have an accident as a sober person. Is he more or less intoxicated than James, whose blood alcohol level is 0.10?
   d) Under the original blood-alcohol standards recommended by the National Highway Traffic Safety Administration, a person considered just barely legally intoxicated was how much more likely to have an accident than a sober individual?

2. Following are descriptions of four individuals who have been drinking. Rank them from highest to lowest blood-alcohol concentration:
   a) John, who weighs 200 pounds and has consumed eight 8-ounce drinks on a full stomach
   b) Frank, who weighs 170 pounds and has consumed four 8-ounce drinks on an empty stomach
   c) Gary, who weighs 240 pounds and has consumed six 8-ounce drinks on an empty stomach
   d) Stephen, who weighs 180 pounds and has consumed six 8-ounce drinks on a full stomach

3. Following are descriptions of four individuals who have been drinking. In which (if any) of the following countries would each be considered legally drunk: the United States, Australia, Sweden?
   a) Bill, who weighs 150 pounds and has consumed three 8-ounce drinks on an empty stomach
   b) Sally, who weighs 110 pounds and has consumed three 8-ounce drinks on a full stomach

    c) Rich, who weighs 200 pounds and has consumed six 8-ounce drinks on an empty stomach

    d) Carrie, who weighs 140 pounds and has consumed four 8-ounce drinks on a full stomach

4. You are a forensic scientist who has been asked to test two blood samples. You know that one sample is suspected of containing barbiturates and the other contains no drugs; however, you cannot tell the two samples apart. Describe how you would use the concept of pH to determine which sample contains barbiturates. Explain your reasoning.

5. You are investigating an arson scene and you find a corpse in the rubble, but you suspect that the victim did not die as a result of the fire. Instead, you suspect that the victim was murdered earlier, and that the blaze was started to cover up the murder. How would you go about determining whether the victim died before the fire?

Web Resources

About Alcohol (A description of the absorption, excretion, metabolism and circulation of alcohol in the body)
www.intox.com/about_alcohol.asp

Alcohol Metabolism (A description of the chemical breakdown of alcohol and the effects of the by-products of alcohol consumption)
www.elmhurst.edu/~chm/vchembook/642alcoholmet.html

Couper, F. J. and B. K. Logan, *Drugs and Human Performance*. Washington, DC: National Highway Traffic Safety Administration, 2004. Available at
www.nhtsa.dot.gov/people/injury/research/job185drugs/technical-page.htm

Drug Recognition Expert (DRE) Program
www.decp.org/experts/

Drugs of Abuse (A report published by the Drug Enforcement Administration)
www.dea.gov/pubs/abuse/index.htm

Forensic Toxicology—A Review
http://faculty.ncwc.edu/toconnor/425/425lect14.htm

Forensic Toxicology Slide Show
www.stfrancis.edu/ns/diab/Forensic1/Toxicology1_files/frame.htm

How Breathalyzers Work (A layperson's guide to understanding how Breathalyzers detect alcohol levels)
http://science.howstuffworks.com/breathalyzer.htm

Impaired Driving Factsheet (Statistics compiled by the National Center for Injury Prevention and Control)
www.cdc.gov/ncipc/factsheets/drving.htm

Endnotes

1. In the United States, laws that define blood-alcohol levels almost exclusively use the unit *percent weight per volume*—% w/v. Hence, 0.015 percent w/v is equivalent to 0.015 gram of alcohol per 100 milliliters of blood, or 15 milligrams of alcohol per 100 milliliters.

2. R. B. Forney et al., "Alcohol Distribution in the Vascular System: Concentrations of Orally Administered Alcohol in Blood from Various Points in the Vascular System and in Rebreathed Air during Absorption," *Quarterly Journal of Studies on Alcohol* 25 (1964): 205.

3. G. A. Brown et al., "The Stability of Ethanol in Stored Blood," *Analytica Chemica Acta* 66 (1973): 271.

4. 0.15 percent w/v is equivalent to 0.15 grams of alcohol per 100 milliliters of blood, or 150 milligrams per 100 milliliters.

5. 384 U.S. 757 (1966).

Jeffrey MacDonald: Fatal Vision

The grisly murder scene that confronted police on February 17, 1970, is one that cannot be wiped from memory. Summoned to the Fort Bragg residence of Captain Jeffrey MacDonald, a physician, police found the bludgeoned body of MacDonald's wife. She had been repeatedly knifed, and her face was smashed to a pulp. MacDonald's two children, ages 2 and 5, had been brutally and repeatedly knifed and battered to death.

Suspicion quickly fell on MacDonald. To the eyes of investigators, the murder scene had a staged appearance. MacDonald described a frantic effort to subdue four intruders who had slashed at him with an ice pick. However, the confrontation left MacDonald with minor wounds and no apparent defensive wounds on his arms. MacDonald then described how he had covered his slashed wife with his blue pajama top. Interestingly, when the body was removed, blue threads were observed under the body. In fact, blue threads

matching the pajama top turned up throughout the house—nineteen in one child's bedroom, including one beneath her fingernail, and two in the other child's bedroom. Eighty-one blue fibers were recovered from the master bedroom, and two were located on a bloodstained piece of wood outside the house.

Later forensic examination showed that the forty-eight ice pick holes in the pajama top were smooth and cylindrical, a sign that the top was stationary when it was slashed. Also, folding the pajama top demonstrated that the forty-eight holes actually could have been made by twenty-one thrusts of an ice pick. This coincided with the number of wounds that MacDonald's wife sustained. As described in the book *Fatal Vision*, which chronicled the murder investigation, when MacDonald was confronted with adulterous conduct, he replied, "You guys are more thorough than I thought." MacDonald is currently serving three consecutive life sentences.

chapter 12

Trace Evidence I:
Hairs and
Fibers

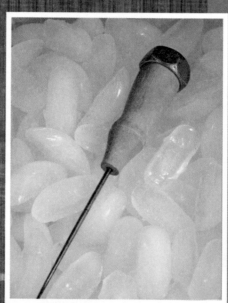

Key Terms

anagen phase

catagen phase

cortex

cuticle

follicular tag

macromolecule

manufactured fibers

medulla

mitochondrial DNA

molecule

monomer

natural fibers

nuclear DNA

polymer

telogen phase

Learning Objectives

After studying this chapter, you should be able to:

- Recognize and understand the cuticle, cortex, and medulla areas of hair.

- List the three phases of hair growth.

- Appreciate the distinction between animal and human hairs.

- List hair features that are useful for microscopic comparisons, of human hairs.

- Explain the proper collection of forensic hair evidence.

- Describe and understand the role of DNA typing in hair comparisons.

- Understand the differences between natural and manufactured fibers.

- List the properties of fibers that are most useful for forensic comparisons.

- Describe the proper collection of fiber evidence.

The trace evidence transferred between individuals and objects during the commission of a crime, if recovered, often corroborates other evidence developed during the course of an investigation. Although in most cases physical evidence cannot by itself positively identify a suspect, laboratory examination may narrow the origin of such evidence to a group that includes the suspect. Using many of the instruments and techniques we have already examined, the crime laboratory has developed a variety of procedures for comparing and tracing the origins of physical evidence. This chapter will focus on the value of hairs and fibers as physical evidence.

Forensic Examination of Hair

Hair is encountered as physical evidence in a wide variety of crimes. However, any review of the forensic aspects of hair examination must start with the observation that it is not yet possible to individualize a human hair to any single head or body through its morphology, or structural characteristics. Over the years, criminalists have tried to isolate the physical and chemical properties of hair that could serve as individual characteristics of identity. Partial success has finally been achieved by isolating and characterizing the DNA present in hair.

The importance of hair as physical evidence cannot be overemphasized. Its removal from the body often denotes physical contact between a victim and perpetrator and hence a crime of a serious or violent nature. When hair is properly collected at the crime scene and submitted to the laboratory along with enough standard/reference samples, it can provide strong corroborative evidence for placing an individual at a crime site. The first step in the forensic examination of hair logically starts with its color and structure, or morphology, and, if warranted, progresses to the more detailed DNA extraction, isolation, and characterization.

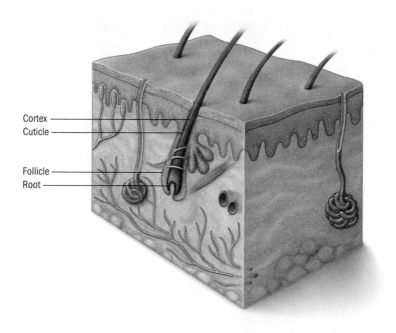

Cortex ———
Cuticle ———

Follicle ———
Root ———

FIGURE 12–1 **A Cross-section of skin showing hair growing out of a tubelike structure called the follicle.**

Morphology of Hair

Hair is an appendage of the skin that grows out of an organ known as the *hair follicle*. The length of a hair extends from its root or bulb embedded in the follicle, continues into the shaft, and terminates at the tip end. The shaft, which is composed of three layers—the cuticle, cortex, and medulla—is most intensely examined by the forensic scientist (see Figure 12–1).

Cuticle   Two features that make hair a good subject for establishing individual identity are its resistance to chemical decomposition and its ability to retain structural features over a long period of time. Much of this resistance and stability is attributed to the cuticle, a scale structure covering the exterior of the hair. The cuticle is formed by overlapping scales that always point toward the tip end of each hair. The scales form from specialized cells that have hardened *(keratinized)* and flattened in progressing from the follicle.

Although the scale pattern is not a useful characteristic for individualizing human hair, the variety of patterns formed by animal hair makes it an important feature for species identification. Figure 12–2 shows the scale patterns of some animal hairs and of a human hair as viewed by the scanning electron microscope. Another method of studying the scale pattern of hair is to make a cast of its surface. This is done by embedding the hair in a soft medium, such as clear nail polish or softened vinyl. When the medium has hardened, the hair is removed, leaving a clear, distinct impression of the hair's cuticle, ideal for examination with a compound microscope.

Cortex   Contained within the protective layer of the cuticle is the cortex, the main body of the hair shaft. The cortex is made up of spindle-shaped cortical cells aligned in a regular array, parallel to the length of the hair. The cortex derives its major forensic importance from the fact that it is embedded with the pigment granules that give hair its color. The color, shape, and distribution of these granules provide important points of comparison among the hairs of different individuals.

cuticle
The scale structure covering the exterior of the hair.

cortex
The main body of the hair shaft.

medulla
A cellular column running through the center of the hair.

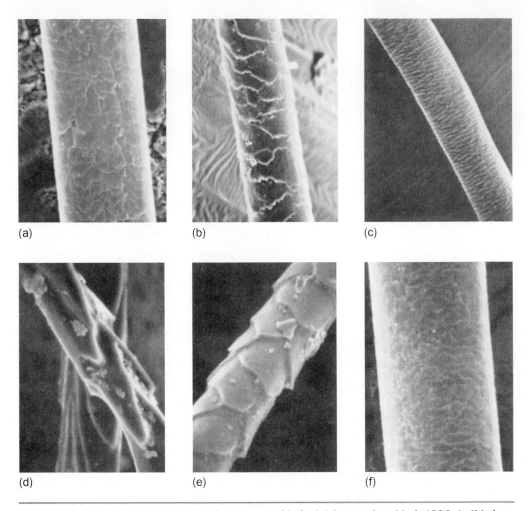

(a)　　　　　　　　(b)　　　　　　　　(c)

(d)　　　　　　　　(e)　　　　　　　　(f)

FIGURE 12–2　Scale patterns of various types of hair: (a) human head hair (600×), (b) dog (1350×), (c) deer (120×), (d) rabbit (300×), (e) cat (2000×), and (f) horse (450×). *Courtesy International Scientific Instruments, Mountain View, Calif., and New Jersey State Police*

The structural features of the cortex are examined microscopically after the hair has been mounted in a liquid medium with a refractive index close to that of the hair. Under these conditions, the amount of light reflected off the hair's surface is minimized, and the amount of light penetrating the hair is optimized.

Medulla　The medulla is a collection of cells that looks like a central canal running through a hair. In many animals, this canal is a predominant feature, occupying more than half of the hair's diameter. The *medullary index* measures the diameter of the medulla relative to the diameter of the hair shaft and is normally expressed as a fraction. For humans, the index is generally less than one-third; for most other animals, the index is one-half or greater.

The presence and appearance of the medulla vary from individual to individual and even among the hairs of a given individual. Not all hairs have medullae, and when they do exist, the degree of medullation can vary. In this respect, medullae may be classified as being either continuous, interrupted, fragmented, or absent (see Figure 12–3). Human head hairs generally exhibit no medullae or have fragmented ones; they rarely show continuous medullation. One noted exception is the Mongoloid race,

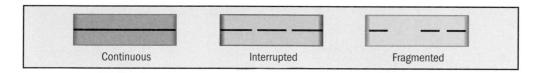

| Continuous | Interrupted | Fragmented |

FIGURE 12–3 Medulla patterns.

whose members usually have head hairs with continuous medullae. Also, most animals have medullae that are either continuous or interrupted.

Another interesting feature of the medulla is its shape. Humans, as well as many animals, have medullae that give a nearly cylindrical appearance. Other animals exhibit medullae that have a patterned shape. For example, the medulla of a cat can best be described as resembling a string of pearls, whereas members of the deer family show a medullary structure consisting of spherical cells occupying the entire hair shaft. Figure 12–4 illustrates medullary sizes and forms for a number of common animal hairs and a human head hair.

A searchable database on CD-ROM of the thirty-five most common animal hairs encountered in forensic casework is commercially available.[1] This database allows an examiner to rapidly search for animal hairs based on scale patterns and/or medulla type using a PC. A typical screen presentation arising from such a data search is shown in Figure 12–5.

Root The root and other surrounding cells within the hair follicle provide the tools necessary to produce hair and continue its growth. Human head hair grows in three developmental stages, and the shape and size of the hair root is determined by the hair's current growth phase. The three phases of hair growth are the anagen, catagen, and telogen phases.

In the anagen phase (the initial growth phase), which may last up to six years, the root is attached to the follicle for continued growth, giving the root bulb a flame-shaped appearance (Figure 12–6[a]). When pulled from the root, some hairs in the anagen phase have a follicular tag. With the advent of DNA analysis, this follicular tag is important for individualizing hair.

Hair continues to grow, but at a decreasing rate, during the catagen phase, which can last anywhere from two to three weeks. In the catagen phase, roots typically take on an elongated appearance (Figure 12–6 [b]) as the root bulb shrinks and is pushed out of the hair follicle. Once hair growth ends, the telogen phase begins and the root takes on a club-shaped appearance (Figure 12–6[c]). Over two to six months, the hair is pushed out of the follicle, causing the hair to be naturally shed.

Identification and Comparison of Hair

Most often the prime purpose for examining hair evidence in a crime laboratory is to establish whether the hair is human or animal in origin, or to determine whether human hair retrieved at a crime scene compares with hair from a particular individual. A careful microscopic examination of hair reveals morphological features that can distinguish human hair from animal hair. The hair of various animals also differs enough in structure that the examiner can often identify the species. Before reaching such a conclusion, however, the examiner must have access to a comprehensive collection of reference standards and the accumulated experience of hundreds of prior hair examinations. Scale structure, medullary index, and medullary shape are particularly important in hair identification.

anagen phase
The initial growth phase during which the hair follicle actively produces hair.

catagen phase
A transition stage between the anagen and telogen phases of hair growth.

telogen phase
The final growth phase in which hair naturally falls out of the skin.

follicular tag
A translucent piece of tissue surrounding the hair's shaft near the root that contains the richest source of DNA associated with hair.

FIGURE 12–4 Medulla patterns for various types of hair: (a) human head hair (400×), (b) dog (400×), (c) deer (500×), (d) rabbit (450×), (e) cat (400×), and (f) mouse (500×).

The most common request when hair is used as forensic evidence is to determine whether hair recovered at the crime scene compares to hair removed from a suspect. In most cases, such a comparison relates to hair obtained from the scalp or pubic area. Ultimately, the evidential value of the comparison depends on the degree of probability with which the examiner can associate the hair in question with a particular individual.

Factors in Comparison of Hair   Although animal hair normally can be distinguished from human hair with little difficulty, human hair comparisons must be undertaken with extreme caution. Hair tends to exhibit variable morphological characteristics, not only from one person to another but also within a single individual. In comparing hair, the criminalist is particularly interested in matching the color, length, and diameter. Other important features are the presence or absence of a medulla and the distribution,

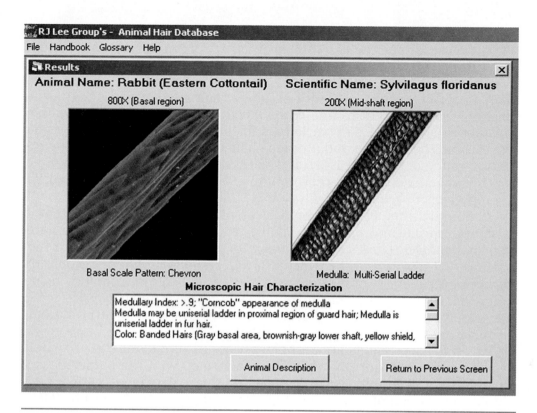

FIGURE 12–5   Information on rabbit hair contained within the *Forensic Animal Hair Atlas.*
Courtesy RJ Lee Group, Inc. Monroeville, Pa.

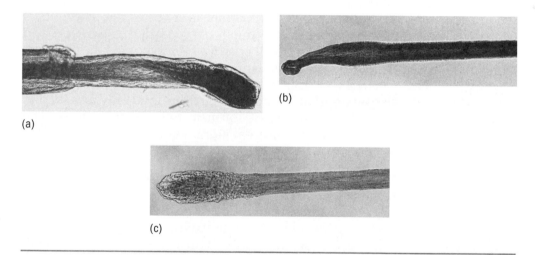

FIGURE 12–6   Hair roots in the (a) anagen phase, (b) catagen phase, and (c) telogen phase
(100×). *Courtesy Charles A. Linch*

shape, and color intensity of the pigment granules in the cortex. A microscopic examination may also distinguish dyed or bleached hair from natural hair. A dyed color is often present in the cuticle as well as throughout
the cortex. Bleaching, on the other hand, tends to remove pigment from
the hair and gives it a yellowish tint.

If hair has grown since it was last bleached or dyed, the natural-end
portion will be quite distinct in color. An estimate of the time since dyeing
or bleaching can be made because hair grows approximately 1 centimeter
per month. Other significant but less frequent features may be observed in

hair. For example, morphological abnormalities may be present due to certain diseases or deficiencies. Also, the presence of fungal and nit infections can further link a hair specimen to a particular individual.

Microscopic Examination of Hair A comparison microscope is an invaluable tool that allows the examiner to view the questioned and known hair together, side by side. Any variations in the microscopic characteristics will thus be readily observed. Because hair from any part of the body exhibits a range of characteristics, it is necessary to have an adequate number of known hairs that are representative of all its features when making a comparison.

Although the microscopic comparison of hairs has long been accepted as an appropriate approach for including and excluding questioned hairs against standard/reference hairs, many forensic scientists have long recognized that this approach is very subjective and is highly dependent on the skills and integrity of the analyst, as well as the hair morphology being examined. However, until the advent of DNA analysis, the forensic science community had no choice but to rely on the microscope to carry out hair comparisons.

Any lingering doubts about the necessity of augmenting microscopic hair examinations with DNA analysis evaporated with the publication of an FBI study describing significant error rates associated with microscopic comparison of hairs.[2] Hair evidence submitted to the FBI for DNA analysis between 1996 and 2000 was examined both microscopically and by DNA analysis. Approximately 11 percent of the hairs (nine out of eighty) in which FBI hair examiners found a positive microscopic match between questioned and standard/reference hairs were found to be nonmatches when they were later subjected to DNA analysis. The course of events is clear; microscopic hair comparisons must be regarded by police and courts as presumptive in nature, and all positive microscopic hair comparisons must be confirmed by DNA determinations.

Questions About Hair Examination A number of questions may be asked to further ascertain the present status of forensic hair examinations. The answers to these questions can be of great significance to the investigator working with hair evidence.

Can the Body Area From Which a Hair Originated Be Determined? Normally it is easy to determine the body area from which a hair came. For example, scalp hairs generally show little diameter variation and have a more uniform distribution of pigment when compared to other body hairs. Pubic hairs are short and curly, with wide variations in shaft diameter, and usually have continuous medullae. Beard hairs are coarse, are normally triangular in cross-section, and have blunt tips acquired from cutting or shaving.

Can the Racial Origin of Hair Be Determined? In many instances, the examiner can distinguish hair originating from members of different races; this is especially true of Caucasian and Negroid head hair. Negroid hairs are normally kinky, containing dense, unevenly distributed pigments. Caucasian hairs are usually straight or wavy, with very fine to coarse pigments that are more evenly distributed when compared to Negroid hair.

Sometimes a cross-sectional examination of hair may help identify race. Cross-sections of hair from Caucasians are oval to round in shape,

Case Study

Central Park Jogger Case Revisited

Battery Park at night. *Courtesy Hans Deumling, Getty Images Inc. Image Bank*

On April 19, 1989, a young woman left her apartment around 9 p.m. to jog in New York's Central Park. Nearly five hours later, she was found comatose lying in a puddle of mud in the park. She had been raped, her skull was fractured, and she had lost 75 percent of her blood. When the woman recovered, she had no memory of what happened to her. The brutality of the crime sent shock waves through the city and seemed to fuel a national perception that crime was running rampant and unchecked through the streets of New York.

Already in custody at the station house of the Central Park Precinct was a group of 14- and 15-year-old boys who had been rounded up leaving the park earlier in the night by police who suspected that they had been involved in a series of random attacks. Over the next two days, four of the teenagers gave videotaped statements, which they later recanted, admitting to participating in the attack. Ultimately, five of the teenagers were charged with the crime. Interestingly, none of the semen collected from the victim could be linked to any of the defendants. However, according to the testimony of a forensic analyst, two head

hairs collected from the clothing of one of the defendants microscopically compared to those of the victim, and a third hair collected from the same defendant's T-shirt microscopically compared to the victim's pubic hair. Besides these three hairs, a fourth hair was found microscopically similar to the victim's. This hair was recovered from the clothing of Steven Lopez, who was originally charged with rape but not prosecuted for the crime.

Hairs were the only pieces of physical evidence offered by the district attorney to directly link any of the teenagers to the crime. The hairs were cited by the district attorney as proof for the jury that the videotaped confessions of the teenagers were reliable. The five defendants were convicted and ultimately served from nine to thirteen years.

In August 1989, more than three months after the jogger attack, New York Police arrested a man named Matias Reyes, who pleaded guilty to murdering a pregnant woman, raping three others, and committing a robbery. Reyes was sentenced to thirty-three years to life for these crimes. In January 2002, Reyes also confessed to the Central Park attack. Follow-up tests revealed that Reyes's DNA compared to semen recovered from the jogger's body and her sock. Other DNA tests showed that the hairs offered into evidence at the original trial did not come from the victim, and so could not be used to link the teenagers to the crime as the district attorney had argued. After an eleven-month reinvestigation of the original charges, a New York State Supreme Court judge dismissed all the convictions against the five teenage suspects in the Central Park jogger case.

whereas cross-sections of Negroid hair are flat to oval in shape. However, all of these observations are general, with many possible exceptions. The criminalist must approach the determination of race from hair with caution and a good deal of experience.

Can the Age and Sex of an Individual Be Determined from a Hair Sample? The age of an individual cannot be learned from a hair examination with any degree of certainty except with infant hair. Infant hairs are fine and short and have fine pigmentation. Although the presence of dye or bleach on the hair may offer some clue to sex, present hairstyles make these characteristics less valuable than they were in the past. The recovery of nuclear DNA either from tissue adhering to hair or from the root structure of the hair will allow a determination of whether the hair originated from a male or female.

Is It Possible to Determine Whether Hair Was Forcibly Removed from the Body? A microscopic examination of the hair root may establish whether the hair fell out or was pulled out of the skin. A hair root with follicular tissue (root sheath cells) adhering to it, as shown in Figure 12–7, indicates a hair that has been pulled out either by a person or by brushing or combing. Hair naturally falling off the body has a bulbous-shaped root free of any adhering tissue.

The absence of sheath cells cannot always be relied on for correctly judging whether hair has been forcibly pulled from the body. In some cases the root of a hair is devoid of any adhering tissue even when it has been pulled from the body. Apparently, an important consideration is how quickly the hair is pulled out of the head. Hairs pulled quickly from the head are much more likely to have sheath cells compared to hairs that have been removed slowly from the scalp.[3]

Are Efforts Being Made to Individualize Human Hair? As we will see in Chapter 14, forensic scientists routinely isolate and characterize individual variations in DNA. Forensic hair examiners can link human hair to a particular individual by characterizing the **nuclear DNA** in the hair root or in follicular tissue adhering to the root (see Figure 12–7). Recall that the follicular tag is the richest source of DNA associated with hair. In the absence of follicular tissue, an examiner must extract DNA from the hair root.

nuclear DNA
DNA that is present in the nucleus of a cell and that is inherited from both parents.

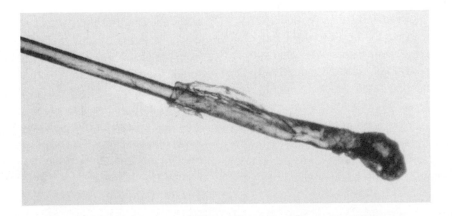

FIGURE 12–7   Forcibly removed head hair, with follicular tissue attached. *Courtesy New Jersey State Police*

The growth phase of hair is a useful predictor of the likelihood of successfully typing DNA in human hair.[4] Examiners have a higher success rate in extracting DNA from hair roots in the anagen phase or from anagen-phase hairs entering the catagen phase of growth. Telogen-phase hairs have an inadequate amount of DNA for typing. Because most hairs are naturally shed and are expected to be in the telogen stage, these observations do not portend well for hairs collected at crime scenes. However, some crime scenes are populated with forcibly removed hairs that are expected to be rich sources for nuclear DNA.

When a questioned hair does not have adhering tissue or a root structure amenable to isolation of nuclear DNA, there is an alternative—**mitochondrial DNA.** Unlike the nuclear DNA described earlier, which is located in the nuclei of practically every cell in the body, mitochondrial DNA is found in cellular material outside the nucleus. Interestingly, unlike nuclear DNA, which is passed down from both parents, mitochondrial DNA is transmitted only from mother to child. Importantly, many more copies of mitochondrial DNA are located in the cells as compared to nuclear DNA. For this reason, the success rate of finding and typing mitochondrial DNA is much greater from samples, such as hair, that have limited quantities of nuclear DNA. Hairs 1 to 2 centimeters long can be subjected to mitochondrial analysis with extremely high odds of success. This subject is discussed in greater detail in Chapter 14.

mitochondrial DNA
DNA present in small structures (mitochondria) outside the nucleus of a cell. Mitochondria supply energy to the cell. This form of DNA is inherited maternally (from the mother).

Can DNA Individualize a Human Hair?   In some cases, the answer is yes. As we will learn in Chapter 14, nuclear DNA produces frequencies of occurrence as low as one in billions or trillions. On the other hand, mitochondrial DNA cannot individualize human hair, but its diversity within the human population often permits the exclusion of a significant portion of a population as potential contributors of a hair sample. Ideally, the combination of a positive microscopic comparison and an association through nuclear or mitochondrial DNA analysis strongly links a questioned hair and standard/reference hairs. However, a word of caution: mitochondrial DNA cannot distinguish microscopically similar hairs from individuals who are maternally related.

Collection and Preservation of Hair Evidence

When questioned hairs are submitted to a forensic laboratory for examination, they must always be accompanied by an adequate number of standard/reference samples from the victim of the crime and from individuals suspected of having deposited hair at the crime scene. We have learned that hair from different parts of the body varies significantly in its physical characteristics. Likewise, hair from any one area of the body can also have a wide range of characteristics. For this reason, the questioned and standard/reference hairs must come from the same area of the body; one cannot, for instance, compare head hair to pubic hair. It is also important that the collection of standard/reference hair be carried out in a way to ensure a representative sampling of hair from any one area of the body.

Forensic hair comparisons generally involve either head hair or pubic hair. Collecting fifty full-length hairs from all areas of the scalp normally ensures a representative sampling of head hair. Likewise, a minimum collection of twenty-four full-length pubic hairs should cover the range of characteristics present in this type of hair. In rape cases, care must first

Forensic Brief

Bill Cosby and his son Ennis Cosby. *Courtesy Andrea Mohin, The New York Times*

The murder of Ennis Cosby, son of entertainer Bill Cosby, at first appeared unsolvable. It was a random act. When his car tire went flat, Ennis pulled off the road and called a friend on his cellular phone to ask for assistance. Shortly thereafter, an assailant demanded money and, when Cosby didn't respond quickly enough, shot him once in the temple. Acting on a tip from a friend of the assailant, police investigators later found a .38-caliber revolver wrapped in a blue cap miles from the crime scene. Mikail Markhasev was arrested and charged with murder.

At trial, the district attorney introduced firearms evidence to show that the recovered gun had fired the bullet aimed at Cosby. However, a single hair also recovered from the hat dramatically linked Markhasev to the crime. Los Angeles Police Department forensic analyst Harry Klann identified six DNA markers from the follicular tissue adhering to the hair root that matched Markhasev's DNA. This particular DNA profile is found in one out of 15,500 members of the general population. Upon hearing all the evidence, the jury deliberated and convicted Markhasev of murder.

be taken to comb the pubic area with a clean comb to remove all loose foreign hair present before the victim is sampled for standard/reference hair. The comb should then be packaged in a separate envelope.

Because a hair may vary in color and other morphological features over its entire length, the entire hair is collected. This requirement is best accomplished by either pulling the hair out of the skin or clipping it at the skin line. During an autopsy, hair samples are routinely collected from a victim of suspicious death. Because the autopsy may occur early in an investigation, the need for hair standard/reference samples may not always be apparent. However, one should never rule out the possible involvement of hair evidence in subsequent investigative findings. Failure to make this simple collection may result in complicated legal problems later.

Key Points

- The hair shaft is composed of three layers called the cuticle, cortex, and medulla and is most intensely examined by the forensic scientist.

- When comparing strands of hair, the criminalist is particularly interested in matching the color, length, and diameter. Other important features for comparing hair are the presence or absence of a medulla and the distribution, shape, and color intensity of pigment granules in the cortex.

- The probability of detecting DNA in hair roots is more likely for hair being examined in its anagen or early growth phase as opposed to its catagen or telogen phases.

- The follicular tag, a translucent piece of tissue surrounding the hair's shaft near the root, is a rich source of DNA associated with hair. Mitochondrial DNA can also be extracted from the hair shaft.

- All positive microscopic hair comparisons must be confirmed by DNA analysis.

Forensic Examination of Fibers

Just as hair left at a crime scene can serve as identification, the same logic can reasonably be extended to the fibers that compose fabrics and garments. Fibers may become important evidence in incidents that involve personal contact—such as homicide, assault, and sexual offenses—in which cross-transfers may occur between the clothing of suspect and victim. Similarly, the force of impact between a hit-and-run victim and a vehicle often leaves fibers, threads, or even whole pieces of clothing adhering to parts of the vehicle. Fibers may also become fixed in screens or glass broken in the course of a breaking-and-entering attempt.

Regardless of where and under what conditions fibers are recovered, their ultimate value as forensic evidence depends on the criminalist's ability to narrow their origin to a limited number of sources or even to a single source. Unfortunately, mass production of garments and fabrics has limited the value of fiber evidence in this respect, and only rarely do fibers recovered at a crime scene provide individual identification with a high degree of certainty.

Types of Fibers

For centuries, humans depended on fibers derived from natural sources such as plants and animals. However, early in the twentieth century, the first manufactured fiber—rayon—became a practical reality, followed in the 1920s by the introduction of cellulose acetate. Since the late 1930s, scientists have produced dozens of new fibers. In fact, the development of fibers, fabrics, finishes, and other textile-processing techniques has made greater advances since 1900 than in the preceding five thousand years of recorded history. Today, such varied items as clothing, carpeting, drapes, wigs, and even artificial turf attest to the predominant role that manufactured fibers have come to play in our culture and environment. When discussing forensic examination of fibers, it is convenient to classify them into two broad groups: *natural* and *manufactured*.

Natural Fibers Natural fibers are wholly derived from animal or plant sources. Natural fibers encountered in crime laboratory examinations come primarily from animals. These include hair coverings from such animals as sheep (wool), goats (mohair, cashmere), camels, llamas, alpacas, and vicuñas. Fur fibers include those obtained from animals such as mink, rabbit, beaver, and muskrat.

The forensic examination of animal fibers uses the same procedures discussed in the previous section for the forensic examination of animal hairs. The identification and comparison of such fibers relies solely on a microscopic examination of color and morphological characteristics.

natural fibers
Fibers derived entirely from animal or plant sources.

Again, a sufficient number of standard/reference specimens must be examined to establish the range of fiber characteristics that make up the suspect fabric.

By far the most prevalent plant fiber is cotton. The wide use of undyed white cotton fibers in clothing and other fabrics has made its evidential value almost meaningless, although the presence of dyed cotton in a combination of colors has, in some cases, enhanced its evidential significance. The microscopic view of cotton fiber shown in Figure 12–8 reveals its most distinguishing feature—a ribbonlike shape with twists at irregular intervals.

manufactured fibers
Fibers derived from either natural or synthetic polymers.

Manufactured Fibers Beginning with the introduction of rayon in 1911 and the development of nylon in 1939, **manufactured fibers** have increasingly replaced natural fibers in garments and fabrics. Such fibers are marketed under hundreds of trade names. To reduce consumer confusion, the U.S. Federal Trade Commission has approved "generic" or family names for the grouping of all manufactured fibers. Many of these generic classes are produced by several manufacturers and are sold under a confusing variety of trade names. For example, in the United States, polyesters are marketed under names that include Dacron, Fortrel, and Kodel. In England, polyesters are called Terylene. Table 12–1 lists major generic fibers, along with common trade names and their characteristics and applications.

The first machine-made fibers were manufactured from raw materials derived from cotton or wood pulp. These materials are processed, and pure cellulose is extracted from them. Depending on the type of fiber desired, the cellulose may be chemically treated and dissolved in an appropriate solvent before it is forced through the small holes of a spinning jet, or spinneret, to produce the fiber. Fibers manufactured from natural raw materials in this manner are classified as *regenerated fibers* and commonly include rayon, acetate, and triacetate, all of which are produced from regenerated cellulose.

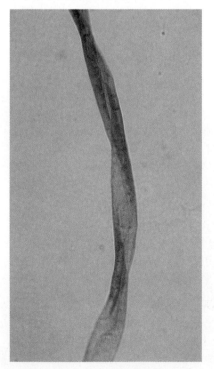

FIGURE 12–8 Photomicrograph of cotton fiber (450×).

Table 12.1 Major Generic Fibers

Major Generic Fiber	Characteristics	Major Domestic and Industrial Uses
Acetate	• Luxurious feel and appearance • Wide range of colors and lusters • Excellent drapability and softness • Relatively fast-drying • Shrink-, moth-, and mildew-resistant	*Apparel:* Blouses, dresses, foundation garments, lingerie, linings, shirts, slacks, sportswear *Fabrics:* Brocade, crepe, double knits, faille, knitted jerseys, lace, satin, taffeta, tricot *Home Furnishings:* Draperies, upholstery *Other:* Cigarette filters, fiberfill for pillows, quilted products
Acrylic	• Soft and warm • Wool-like • Retains shape • Resilient • Quick-drying • Resistant to moths, sunlight, oil, and chemicals	*Apparel:* Dresses, infant wear, knitted garments, skiwear, socks, sportswear, sweaters *Fabrics:* Fleece and pile fabrics, face fabrics in bonded fabrics, simulated furs, jerseys *Home Furnishings:* Blankets, carpets, draperies, upholstery *Other:* Auto tops, awnings, hand-knitting and craft yarns, industrial and geotextile fabrics
Aramid	• Does not melt • Highly flame-resistant • Great strength • Great resistance to stretch • Maintains shape and form at high temperatures	Hot-gas filtration fabrics, protective clothing, military helmets, protective vests, structural composites for aircraft and boats, sailcloth, tires, ropes and cables, mechanical rubber goods, marine and sporting goods
Bicomponent	• Thermal bonding • Self-bulking • Very fine fibers • Unique cross-sections • The functionality of special polymers or additives at reduced cost	Uniform distribution of adhesive; fiber remains a part of structure and adds integrity; customized sheath materials to bond various materials; wide range of bonding temperatures; cleaner, environmentally friendly (no effluent); recyclable; lamination/molding/densification of composites
Lyocell	• Soft, strong, absorbent • Good dyeability • Fibrillates during wet processing to produce special textures	Dresses, slacks, and coats
Melamine	• White and dyeable • Flame resistance and low thermal conductivity • High-heat dimensional stability • Processable on standard textile equipment	*Fire-Blocking Fabrics:* Aircraft seating, fire blockers for upholstered furniture in high-risk occupancies (e.g., to meet California TB 133 requirements) *Protective Clothing:* Firefighters' turnout gear, insulating thermal liners, knit hoods, molten metal splash apparel, heat-resistant gloves *Filter Media:* High-capacity, high-efficiency, high-temperature baghouse air filters
Modacrylic	• Soft • Resilient • Abrasion- and flame-resistant • Quick-drying • Resists acids and alkalies • Retains shape	*Apparel:* Deep-pile coats, trims, linings, simulated fur, wigs and hairpieces *Fabrics:* Fleece fabrics, industrial fabrics, knit-pile fabric backings, nonwoven fabrics *Home Furnishings:* Awnings, blankets, carpets, flame-resistant draperies and curtains, scatter rugs *Other:* Filters, paint rollers, stuffed toys

(continued)

Table 12.1 Major Generic Fibers (*continued*)

Major Generic Fiber	Characteristics	Major Domestic and Industrial Uses
Nylon	<ul><li>Exceptionally strong</li><li>Supple</li><li>Abrasion-resistant</li><li>Lustrous</li><li>Easy to wash</li><li>Resists damage from oil and many chemicals</li><li>Resilient</li><li>Low in moisture absorbency</li></ul>	*Apparel:* Blouses, dresses, foundation garments, hosiery, lingerie and underwear, raincoats, ski and snow apparel, suits, windbreakers *Home Furnishings:* Bedspreads, carpets, draperies, curtains, upholstery *Other:* Air hoses, conveyor and seat belts, parachutes, racket strings, ropes and nets, sleeping bags, tarpaulins, tents, thread, tire cord, geotextiles
Olefin	<ul><li>Unique wicking properties that make it very comfortable</li><li>Abrasion-resistant</li><li>Quick-drying</li><li>Resistant to deterioration from chemicals, mildew, perspiration, rot, and weather</li><li>Sensitive to heat</li><li>Soil-resistant</li><li>Strong; very lightweight</li><li>Excellent colorfastness</li></ul>	*Apparel:* Pantyhose, underwear, knitted sports shirts, men's half-hose, men's knitted sportswear, sweaters *Home Furnishings:* Carpet and carpet backing, slipcovers, upholstery *Other:* Dye nets, filter fabrics, laundry bags, sandbags, geotextiles, automotive interiors, cordage, doll hair, industrial sewing thread
Polyester	<ul><li>Strong</li><li>Resistant to stretching and shrinking</li><li>Resistant to most chemicals</li><li>Quick-drying</li><li>Crisp and resilient when wet or dry</li><li>Wrinkle- and abrasion-resistant</li><li>Retains heat-set pleats and creases</li><li>Easy to wash</li></ul>	*Apparel:* Blouses, shirts, career apparel, children's wear, dresses, half-hose, insulated garments, ties, lingerie and underwear, permanent press garments, slacks, suits *Home Furnishings:* Carpets, curtains, draperies, sheets and pillowcases *Other:* Fiberfill for various products, fire hoses, power belting, ropes and nets, tire cord, sail, V-belts
PBI	<ul><li>Extremely flame-resistant</li><li>Outstanding comfort factor combined with thermal and chemical stability properties</li><li>Will not burn or melt</li><li>Low shrinkage when exposed to flame</li></ul>	Suitable for high-performance protective apparel such as firefighters' turnout coats, astronaut space suits, and applications in which fire resistance is important
Rayon	<ul><li>Highly absorbent</li><li>Soft and comfortable</li><li>Easy to dye</li><li>Versatile</li><li>Good drapability</li></ul>	*Apparel:* Blouses, coats, dresses, jackets, lingerie, linings, millinery, rainwear, slacks, sports shirts, sportswear, suits, ties, work clothes *Home Furnishings:* Bedspreads, blankets, carpets, curtains, draperies, sheets, slipcovers, tablecloths, upholstery *Other:* Industrial products, medical-surgical products, nonwoven products, tire cord
Spandex	<ul><li>Can be stretched 500 percent without breaking</li><li>Can be stretched repeatedly and recover original length</li><li>Lightweight</li><li>Stronger and more durable than rubber</li><li>Resistant to body oils</li></ul>	*Articles* (in which stretch is desired): Athletic apparel, bathing suits, delicate laces, foundation garments, golf jackets, ski pants, slacks, support and surgical hose

Source: American Fiber Manufacturers Assoc. Inc., Washington, D.C., *www.fingersource.com/f-tutor/q-guide.htm.*

Most of the fibers currently manufactured are produced solely from synthetic chemicals and are therefore classified as *synthetic fibers*. These include nylons, polyesters, and acrylics. The creation of synthetic fibers became a reality only when scientists developed a method of synthesizing long-chained molecules called **polymers.**

In 1930, chemists discovered an unusual characteristic of one of the polymers under investigation. When a glass rod in contact with viscous material in a beaker was slowly pulled away, the substance adhered to the rod and formed a fine filament that hardened as soon as it entered the cool air. Furthermore, the cold filaments could be stretched several times their extended length to produce a flexible, strong, and attractive fiber. This first synthetic fiber was improved and then marketed as nylon. Since then, fiber chemists have successfully synthesized new polymers and have developed more efficient methods for manufacturing them. These efforts have produced a multitude of synthetic fibers.

Polymers The polymer is the basic chemical substance of all synthetic fibers. Indeed, an almost unbelievable array of household, industrial, and recreational products is manufactured from polymers; these include plastics, paints, adhesives, and synthetic rubber. Polymers exist in countless forms and varieties and with the proper treatment can be made to assume a variety of chemical and physical properties.

As we have already observed, chemical substances are composed of basic structural units called **molecules.** The molecules of most materials are composed of just a few atoms; for example, water, H_2O, has 2 atoms of hydrogen and 1 atom of oxygen. The heroin molecule, $C_{21}H_{23}O_5N$, contains 21 atoms of carbon, 23 atoms of hydrogen, 5 atoms of oxygen, and 1 atom of nitrogen. Polymers, on the other hand, are formed by linking a large number of molecules, so that a polymer often contains thousands or even millions of atoms. This is why polymers are often referred to as **macromolecules,** or "big" molecules.

Simply, a polymer can be pictured as resembling a long, repeating chain, with each link representing the basic structure of the polymer (see Figure 12–9). The repeating molecular units in the polymer, called **monomers,** are joined end to end, so that thousands link to form a long chain. What makes polymer chemistry so fascinating is the countless possibilities for linking different molecules. By simply varying the chemical structure of the monomers, and by devising numerous ways to weave them together, chemists have created polymers that exhibit different properties. This versatility enables polymer chemists to synthesize glues, plastics, paints, and fibers.

polymer
A substance composed of a large number of atoms that are usually arranged in repeating units.

molecule
Two or more atoms held together by chemical bonds.

macromolecule
A molecule with a high molecular mass.

monomer
The basic unit of structure from which a polymer is constructed.

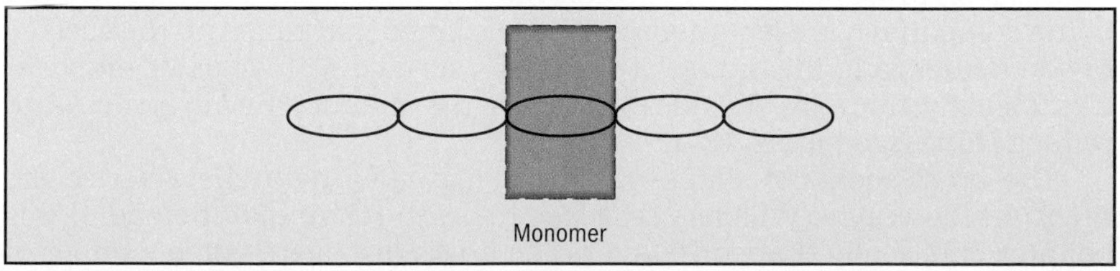

FIGURE 12–9 The chain-link model of a segment of a polymer molecule. The molecule may contain as many as several million monomer units or links.

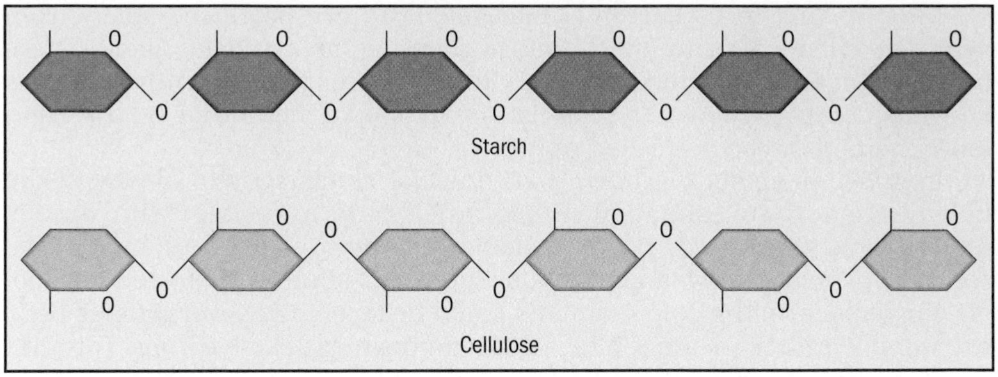

FIGURE 12–10 Starch and cellulose are natural carbohydrate polymers consisting of a large number of repeating units or monomers.

Not all polymers are synthesized in the chemical laboratory; nature has produced polymers that humans have not yet been able to copy. For example, the proteins that form the basic structure of animal hairs, as well as of all living matter, are polymers, composed of thousands of amino acids linked in a highly organized arrangement and sequence. Similarly, cellulose (the basic ingredient of wood and cotton) and starch are both natural polymers built by the combination of several thousand carbohydrate monomers, as shown in Figure 12–10. Hence, the synthesis of manufactured fibers merely represents an extension of chemical principles that nature has used to produce hair and vegetable fibers.

Identification and Comparison of Manufactured Fibers

The evidential value of fibers lies in the criminalist's ability to trace their origin. Obviously, if the examiner is presented with fabrics that can be exactly fitted together at their torn edges, the fabrics must be of common origin. Such a fit is demonstrated in Figure 12–11 for a piece of fabric that was removed from a vehicle suspected of involvement in a hit-and-run fatality. The exact fit with the remains of the victim's trousers directly implicated the car's driver in the incident.

More often, however, the criminalist obtains a limited number of fibers for identification and comparison. Generally, in these situations obtaining a physical match is unlikely, and the examiner must resort to a side-by-side comparison of the standard/reference and crime-scene fibers.

Microscopic Examination of Fibers   The first and most important step in the examination is a microscopic comparison for color and diameter using a comparison microscope. Unless these two characteristics agree, there is little reason to suspect a match. Other morphological features that may aid in the comparison are lengthwise striations (lined markings) on the surface of some fibers and the pitting of the fiber's surface with delustering particles (usually titanium dioxide) added in the manufacturing process to reduce shine (see Figure 12–12).

The cross-sectional shape of a fiber may also help characterize the fiber.[5] In the Wayne Williams case (see the case reading at the end of this chapter), unusually shaped yellow-green fibers discovered on a number of the murder victims were linked to a carpet in the Williams home. This fiber was a key element in proving Williams's guilt. A photomicrograph of this unusually shaped fiber is shown in Figure 12–13.

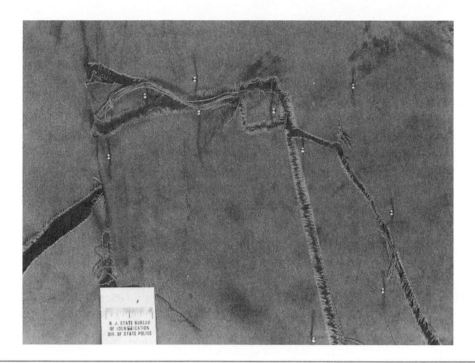

FIGURE 12–11   A piece of fabric found on a suspect hit-and-run vehicle inserted into the torn trousers of the victim. *Courtesy New Jersey State Police*

(a)   (b)

FIGURE 12–12   Photomicrographs of synthetic fibers: (a) cellulose triacetate (450×) and (b) olefin fiber embedded with titanium dioxide particles (450×).

Although two fibers may seem to have the same color when viewed under the microscope, compositional differences may actually exist in the dyes that were applied to them during their manufacture. In fact, most textile fibers are impregnated with a mixture of dyes selected to obtain a desired shade or color. The significance of a fiber comparison is enhanced

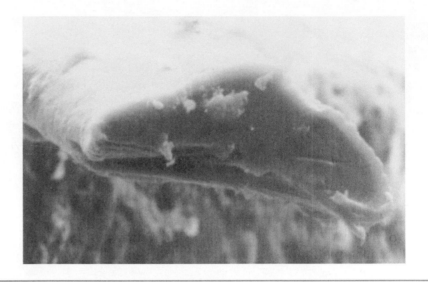

FIGURE 12–13   A scanning electron photomicrograph of the cross-section of a nylon fiber removed from a sheet used to transport the body of a murder victim. The fiber, associated with a carpet in Wayne Williams's home, was manufactured in 1971 in relatively small quantities. *Courtesy Federal Bureau of Investigation, Washington, D.C.*

when the forensic examiner can show that the questioned and standard/reference fibers have the same dye composition.

Analytical Techniques Used in Fiber Examination   In Chapter 10, we saw how a chemist can use selective absorption of light by materials to characterize them. In particular, light in the ultraviolet, visible, and infrared regions of the electromagnetic spectrum is most helpful for this purpose. Unfortunately, in the past, forensic chemists were unable to take full advantage of the capabilities of spectrophotometry for examining trace evidence, because most spectrophotometers are not well suited for examining the very small particles frequently encountered as evidence. Recently, linking the microscope to a computerized spectrophotometer has added a new dimension to its capability. This combination has given rise to a new instrument called the microspectrophotometer. In many respects, this is an ideal marriage from the forensic scientist's viewpoint.

The visible-light microspectrophotometer is a convenient way for analysts to compare the colors of fibers through spectral patterns. This technique is not limited by sample size—a fiber as small as 1 millimeter long or less can be examined by this type of microscope. The examination is nondestructive and is carried out on fibers simply mounted on a microscope slide.

A more detailed analysis of the fiber's dye composition can be obtained through a chromatographic separation of the dye constituents. To accomplish this, small strands of fibers are compared for dye content by first extracting the dye off each fiber with a suitable solvent and then spotting the dye solution onto a thin-layer chromatography plate. The dye components of the questioned and standard/reference fibers are separated on the thin-layer plate and compared side by side for similarity.[6]

Chemical Composition   Before the forensic scientist can reach a conclusion that two or more fibers compare, it must be shown that the fibers in question have the same chemical composition. In this respect, tests are performed to confirm that all of the fibers involved belong to the same broad generic class. Additionally, the comparison will be substantially enhanced

Closer Analysis

The Microspectrophotometer

With the development of the microspectrophotometer, a forensic analyst can view a particle under a microscope while a beam of light is directed at the particle to obtain its absorption spectrum. Depending on the type of light employed, an examiner can acquire either a visible or an infrared (IR) spectral pattern of the substance being viewed under the microscope. The obvious advantage of this approach is to provide added information to characterize trace quantities of evidence. A microspectrophotometer designed to measure the uptake of visible light by materials is shown here.

Visual comparison of color is usually one of the first steps in examining paint, fiber, and ink evidence. Such comparisons are easily obtained using a comparison microscope. A forensic scientist can use the microspectrophotometer to compare the color of materials visually while plotting

an absorption spectrum for each item under examination. This displays the exact wavelengths at which each item absorbs in the visible-light spectrum. Occasionally, colors that appear similar by visual examination show significant differences in their absorption spectra.

Another emerging technique in forensic science is the use of the IR microspectro-photometer to examine fibers and paints. The "fingerprint" IR spectrum (see pages 389–390) is unique for each chemical substance. Therefore, obtaining such a spectrum from either a fiber or a paint chip allows the analyst to better identify and compare the type of chemicals from which these materials are manufactured. With a microspectrophotometer, a forensic analyst can view a substance through the microscope and at the same time have the instrument plot the infrared absorption spectrum for that material.

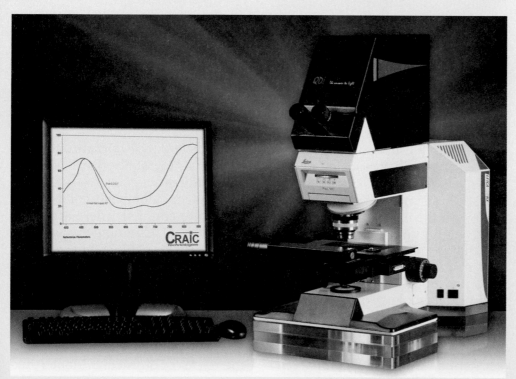

A visible-light microspectrophotometer. *Courtesy Craig Technologies Inc., Altadena, Calif., www. microspectra.com*

if it can be demonstrated that all of the fibers belong to the same subclassification within their generic class. For example, at least four types of nylon are available in commercial and consumer markets, including nylon 6, nylon 6–10, nylon 11, and nylon 6–6. Although all types of nylon have many properties in common, each may differ in physical shape, appearance, and dyeability because of modifications in the basic chemical structure. Similarly, a study of more than two hundred samples of acrylic fibers revealed that they could actually be divided into twenty-four distinguishable groups on the basis of their polymeric structure and microscopic characteristics.[7]

Textile chemists have devised numerous tests for determining the class of a fiber. However, unlike the textile chemist, the criminalist frequently does not have the luxury of having a substantial quantity of fabric to work with and must therefore select tests that will yield the most information with the least amount of material. Only a single fiber may be available for analysis, and often this may amount to no more than a minute strand recovered from a fingernail scraping of a homicide or rape victim.

Infrared Absorption   The polymers that compose a manufactured fiber, just as in any other organic substance, selectively absorb infrared light in a characteristic pattern. Infrared spectrophotometry thus provides a rapid and reliable method for identifying the generic class, and in some cases the subclasses, of fibers. The infrared microspectrophotometer combines a microscope with an infrared spectrophotometer (see page 387). Such a combination makes possible the infrared analysis of a small single-strand fiber while it is being viewed under a microscope.[8]

Significance of Fiber Evidence

Once a fiber match has been determined, the question of the significance of such a finding is bound to be raised. In reality, no analytical technique permits the criminalist to associate a fiber strand definitively to any single garment. Furthermore, except in the most unusual circumstances, no statistical databases are available for determining the probability of a fiber's origin. Considering the mass distribution of synthetic fibers and the constantly changing fashion tastes of our society, it is highly unlikely that such data will be available in the foreseeable future.

Despite these limitations, one should not discount or minimize the significance of a fiber association. An enormous variety of fibers exists in our society. By simply looking at the random individuals we meet every day, we can see how unlikely it is to find two people wearing identically colored fabrics (with the exception of blue denims or white cottons). There are thousands of different-colored fibers in our environment. Combine this with the fact that forensic scientists compare not only the color of fibers but also their size, shape, microscopic appearance, chemical composition, and dye content, and one can now begin to appreciate how unlikely it is to find two indistinguishable colored fibers emanating from randomly selected sources.

Furthermore, the significance of a fiber association increases dramatically when the analyst can link two or more distinctly different fibers to the same object. Likewise, the associative value of fiber evidence is dramatically enhanced if it is accompanied by other types of physical evidence linking a person or object to a crime. As with most class evidence, the significance of a fiber comparison is dictated by the circumstances of the case; by the location, number, and nature of the fibers examined; and, most important, by the judgment of an experienced examiner.

Forensics at Work

Fatal Vision Revisited

Jeffrey MacDonald in 1995 at Sheridan, Oregon, Federal Correctional Institution.
Courtesy AP Wide World Photos

Dr. Jeffrey MacDonald, pictured here, was convicted in 1979 of murdering his wife

and two young daughters. The events surrounding the crime and the subsequent trial were recounted in Joe McGinniss's best-selling book *Fatal Vision*. The focus of MacDonald's defense was that intruders entered his home and committed these violent acts. Eleven years after this conviction, MacDonald's attorneys filed a petition for a new trial, claiming the existence of "critical new" evidence.

The defense asserted that wig fibers found on a hairbrush in the MacDonald residence were evidence that an intruder dressed in a wig entered the MacDonald home on the day of the murder. Subsequent examination of this claim by the FBI Laboratory focused on a blond fall (a type

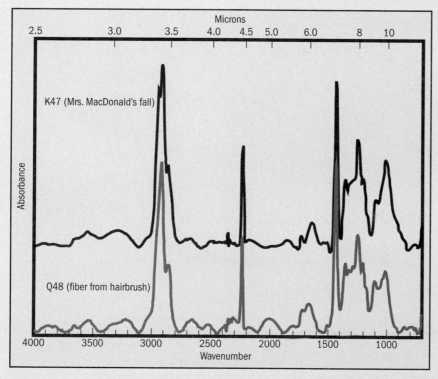

FIGURE 1 A fiber comparison made with an infrared spectrophotometer. The infrared spectrum of a fiber from Mrs. MacDonald's fall compares to a fiber recovered from a hairbrush in the MacDonald home. These fibers were identified as modacrylics, the most common type of synthetic fiber used in the manufacture of human hair goods.
Courtesy SA Michael Malone, FBI Laboratory, Washington, D.C.

Source: B. M. Murtagh and M. P. Malone, "Fatal Vision Revisited," *Police Chief* (June 1993): 15.

(continued)

Forensics at Work

Fatal Vision Revisited *(continued)*

of artificial hair extension) frequently worn by MacDonald's wife. Fibers removed from the fall were shown to clearly match fibers on the hairbrush. The examination included the use of infrared microspectrophotometry to demonstrate that the suspect wig fibers were chemically identical to fibers found in the composition of the MacDonald fall (see Figure 1). Hence, although wig fibers were found at the crime scene, the source of these fibers could be accounted for—they came from Mrs. MacDonald's fall.

Another piece of evidence cited by MacDonald's lawyers was a bluish-black woolen fiber found on the body of Mrs. MacDonald. They claimed that this fiber compared to a bluish-black woolen fiber recovered from the club used to assault her. These wool fibers were central to MacDonald's defense that the "intruders" wore dark-colored clothing. Initial examination showed that the fibers were microscopically indistinguishable. However, the FBI also compared the two wool fibers by visible-light microspectrophotometry. Comparison of their spectra clearly showed that their dye compositions differed, providing no evidence of outside intruders (see Figure 2). Ultimately, the U.S. Supreme Court denied the merits of MacDonald's petition for a new trial.

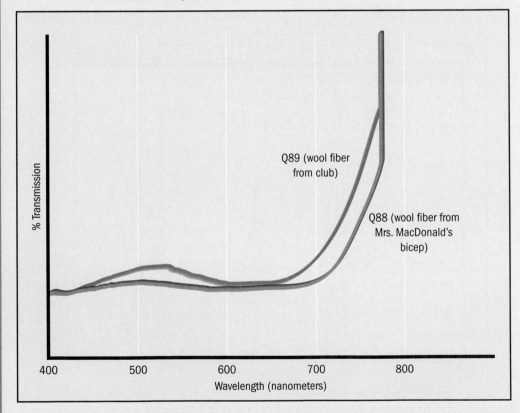

FIGURE 2 **The visible-light spectrum for the woolen fiber recovered from Mrs. MacDonald's body is clearly different from that of the fiber recovered from the club used to assault her.** *Courtesy SA Michael Malone, FBI Laboratory, Washington, D.C.*

Collection and Preservation of Fiber Evidence

As criminal investigators have become more aware of the potential contribution of trace physical evidence to the success of their investigations, they have placed greater emphasis on conducting thorough crime-scene searches for evidence of forensic value. Their skill and determination at carrying out these tasks is tested in the collection of fiber-related evidence. Fiber evidence can be associated with virtually any type of crime. It usually cannot be seen with the naked eye and thus easily can be overlooked by someone not specifically searching for it.

An investigator committed to optimizing the laboratory's chances for locating minute strands of fibers identifies and preserves potential "carriers" of fiber evidence. Relevant articles of clothing should be packaged carefully in paper bags. Each article must be placed in a separate bag to avoid cross-contamination of evidence. Scrupulous care must be taken to prevent articles of clothing from different people or from different locations from coming into contact. Such articles must not even be placed on the same surface prior to packaging. Likewise, carpets, rugs, and bedding are to be folded carefully to protect areas suspected of containing fibers. Car seats should be carefully covered with polyethylene sheets to protect fiber evidence, and knife blades should be covered to protect adhering fibers. If a body is thought to have been wrapped at one time in a blanket or carpet, adhesive tape lifts of exposed body areas may reveal fiber strands.

Occasionally the field investigator may need to remove a fiber from an object, particularly if loosely adhering fibrous material may be lost in transit to the laboratory. These fibers must be removed with a clean forceps and placed in a small sheet of paper, which, after folding and labeling, can be placed inside another container. Again, scrupulous care must be taken to prevent contact between fibers collected from different objects or from different locations.

In the laboratory, the search for fiber evidence on clothing and other relevant objects, as well as in debris, is time consuming and tedious and will test the skill and patience of the examiner. The crime-scene investigator can manage this task by collecting only relevant items for examination, pinpointing areas where a likely transfer of fiber evidence occurred and then ensuring the proper collection and preservation of these materials.

Key Points

- Fibers may be classified into two broad groups: *natural* and *manufactured*.

- Most fibers currently manufactured are produced solely from synthetic chemicals and are therefore classified as *synthetic fibers*. They include nylons, polyesters, and acrylics.

- Microscopic comparisons between questioned and standard/reference fibers are initially undertaken for color and diameter characteristics. Other features that could be important in comparing fibers are striations on the surface of the fiber, the presence of delustering particles, and the cross-sectional shape of the fiber.

- The visible-light microspectrophotometer is a convenient way for analysts to compare the colors of fibers through spectral patterns.

- Infrared microspectrophotometry is a reliable method for identifying the chemical composition of fibers.

- Fiber evidence collected at each location should be placed in separate containers to avoid cross-contamination. Care must be taken to prevent articles of clothing from different people or from different locations from coming into contact with each other.

Case Study

The Telltale Rabbit

On a cold winter's day . . . a female was found in the alleyway of an East Harlem tenement. Close to the body was a California florist flower box and a plastic liner. The victim was identified as a member of a well-known church who had been selling church literature in the buildings that surround the alley in which the body was discovered.

The detectives investigating the case forwarded the flower box, the plastic liner, and the victim's clothing to the forensic science laboratory. On the box and liner were found tan wool fibers, red acrylic fibers, and navy blue wool fibers (all identified by polarized light microscopy). The three types of questioned fibers were compared microscopically with the vicitm's clothing. All three were found to be consistent in all respects to the textile fibers composing the victim's clothing (tan wool overcoat, navy blue wool/polyester blend slacks, and red acrylic sweater), thereby associating the woman with the flower box and liner.

In addition, light blue nylon rug fibers and several brown rabbit hairs were found on the box and liner. Similar light blue nylon rug fibers and rabbit hairs, as well as red nylon rug fibers, were found on the victim's tan wool overcoat. Neither the rabbit hairs nor the nylon rug fibers could be associated with the victim's environment (her clothing or residence). All of this

information was conveyed to the field investigators.

Upon further inquiry in the neighborhood, investigators learned the identity of a man who had, the day after the body was discovered, sold a full-length brown rabbit hair coat to a local man. The investigators obtained the rabbit hair coat from the purchaser. The hair composing the coat was compared microscopically to the questioned rabbit hairs found on the victim's wool coat and the flower box liner. The specimens of questioned rabbit hair were found to be consistent in all physical and microscopic characteristics to the rabbit hair composing the suspect's coat. Armed with this information, the police now had probable cause to obtain a search warrant for the suspect's apartment.

In the suspect's apartment two rugs were found. One was light blue and the other was red, both rugs were composed of nylon fibers. Samples of each rug were collected by the crime-scene unit and forwarded to the forensic science laboratory for comparison with the questioned rug fibers found on the victim's clothing, the flower box, and the plastic liner. The questioned and known rug fibers were found to be consistent in all respects. The presence of light blue nylon rug fibers, red nylon rug fibers, and brown-colored rabbit hairs on the flower box, plastic liner, and woman's clothing enabled the author to make associations between the woman, flower box, and liner found in the alleyway with the suspect and his apartment. . . .

The investigating officers made further inquiries in the neighborhood about the suspect. They located a witness who stated that he saw the suspect carrying a large California flower box a day or two before the body was discovered.

From the evidence, investigators theorized that the woman was killed in the suspect's apartment, placed in the flower box, brought up to the roof of the building in which the defendant resided, and thrown off the building into the alley below. On the basis of all of this evidence, the suspect was arrested, indicted, and tried for second-degree murder. After two trials, at which the author gave extensive testimony (three days) about the trace evidence, the defendant was found guilty of second-degree murder and subsequently sentenced to life imprisonment.

Source: Reprinted in part by permission of the American Society of Testing and Materials from N. Petraco, "Trace Evidence—The Invisible Witness," *Journal of Forensic Sciences* 31 (1986): 321. Copyright 1986.

Chapter Summary

Hair is an appendage of the skin that grows out of an organ known as the hair follicle. The length of a hair extends from its root or bulb embedded in the follicle, continues into a shaft, and terminates at a tip end. The shaft, which is composed of three layers—the cuticle, cortex, and medulla—is most intensely examined by the forensic scientist. The comparison microscope is an indispensable tool for comparing these morphological characteristics.

When comparing strands of hair, the criminalist is particularly interested in matching the color, length, and diameter. A careful microscopic examination of hair reveals morphological features that can distinguish human hair from animal hair. Scale structure, medullary index, and medullary shape are particularly important in hair identification. Other important features for comparing hair are the presence or absence of a medulla and the distribution, shape, and color intensity of pigment granules in the cortex. Microscopic hair examinations tend to be subjective and highly dependent on the skills and integrity of the analyst.

Recent breakthroughs in DNA profiling have extended this technology to the individualization of human hair. The probability of detecting DNA in hair roots is more likely for hair being examined in its anagen or early growth phase as opposed to its catagen or telogen phases. Often when hair is forcibly removed, a follicular tag (a translucent piece of tissue surrounding the hair's shaft near the root) may be present. This is a rich source of DNA associated with hair. Also, mitochondrial DNA can be extracted from the hair shaft. All positive microscopic hair comparisons must be confirmed by DNA analysis.

The quality of fiber evidence depends on the ability of the criminalist to identify the origin of the fiber or at least to narrow the possibilities to a limited number of sources. Microscopic comparisons between questioned and standard/reference fibers are initially undertaken for color and diameter characteristics. Other morphological features that could be important in comparing fibers are striations on the surface of the fiber, the presence of delustering particles, and the cross-sectional shape of the fiber.

The visible-light microspectrophotometer provides a convenient way to compare the colors of fibers through spectral patterns. Infrared spectrophotometry is a rapid and reliable tool for identifying the generic class of fibers.

Review Questions

1. Hair is an appendage of the skin, growing out of an organ known as the _____.

2. The three layers of the hair shaft are the _____, the _____, and the _____.

3. The scale pattern of hair's _____ can be observed by making a cast of its surface in clear nail polish or softened vinyl.

4. The _____ contains the pigment granules that impart color to hair.

5. The central canal running through many hairs is known as the _____.

6. The diameter of the medulla relative to the diameter of the hair shaft is the _____.

7. Human hair generally has a medullary index of less than _____; the hair of most animals has an index of _____ or greater.

8. True or False: Human head hairs generally exhibit no medullae. _____

9. True or False: If a medulla exhibits a pattern, the hair is animal in origin. _____

10. The three stages of hair growth are the _____, _____, and _____ phases.

11. True or False: Individual hairs can show variable morphological characteristics within a single individual. _____

12. True or False: A single hair cannot be individualized to one person by microscopic examination. _____

13. In making hair comparisons, it is best to view the hairs side by side under a(n) _____ microscope.

14. _____ hairs are short and curly, with wide variation in shaft diameter.

15. True or False: It is possible to estimate when hair was last bleached or dyed by microscopic examination. _____

16. True or False: The age and sex of the individual from whom a hair sample has been taken can be determined through an examination of the hair's morphological features. _____

17. True or False: Hair forcibly removed from the body sometimes has follicular tissue adhering to its root. _____

18. Microscopic hair comparisons must be regarded by police and courts as presumptive in nature, and all positive microscopic hair comparisons must be confirmed by _____ typing.

19. A hair root in the _____ or _____ growth phase is a likely candidate for DNA typing.

20. A minimum collection of _____ full-length hairs normally ensures a representative sampling of head hair.

21. A minimum collection of _____ full-length pubic hairs is recommended to cover the range of characteristics present in this region of the body.

22. The ultimate value of fibers as forensic evidence depends on the ability to narrow their _____ to a limited number of sources or even to a single source.

23. _____ fibers are derived totally from animal or plant sources.

24. The most prevalent natural plant fiber is _____.

25. _____ fibers such as rayon, acetate, and triacetate are manufactured from natural raw materials such as cellulose.

26. Fibers manufactured solely from synthetic chemicals are classified as _____.

27. True or False: Polyester was the first synthetic fiber. _____

28. _____ are composed of a large number of atoms arranged in repeating units.

29. The basic unit of the polymer is called the _____.

30. _____ are polymers composed of thousands of amino acids linked in a highly organized arrangement and sequence.

31. True or False: A first step in the forensic examination of fibers is to compare color and diameter. _____

32. The microspectrophotometer employing _____ light is a convenient way for analysts to compare the colors of fibers through spectral patterns.

33. The dye components removed from fibers can be separated and compared by _____ chromatography.

34. The microspectrophotometer employing _____ light provides a rapid and reliable method for identifying the generic class of a single fiber.

35. True or False: Statistical databases are available for determining the probability of a fiber's origin. _____

36. True or False: Normally, fibers possess individual characteristics. _____

37. In order to preserve fiber evidence not originally apparent to the investigator, all _____ of possible fiber evidence should be careful collected and packaged.

Application and Critical Thinking

1. Indicate the phase of growth of each of the following hairs:
   a) The root is club-shaped.
   b) The hair has a follicular tag.
   c) The root bulb is flame-shaped.
   d) The root is elongated.

2. A criminalist studying a dyed sample hair notices that the dyed color ends about 1.5 centimeters from the tip of the hair. Approximately how many weeks before the examination was the hair dyed? Explain your answer.

3. Following are descriptions of several hairs. Based on these descriptions, indicate the likely race of the person from whom the hair originated.
   a) Evenly distributed, fine pigmentation.
   b) Continuous medullation.
   c) Dense, uneven pigmentation.
   d) Wavy with a round cross-section.

4. Criminalist Pete Evett is collecting fiber evidence from a murder scene. He notices fibers on the victim's shirt and trousers, so he places both of these items of clothing in a plastic bag. He also sees fibers on a sheet near the victim, so he balls up the sheet and places it in separate plastic bag. Noticing fibers adhering to the windowsill from which the attacker gained entrance, Pete carefully removes it with his fingers and places it in a regular envelope. What mistakes, if any, did Pete make while collecting this evidence?

Case Analysis

In 1982, the state of Georgia convicted Wayne Williams of murdering several boys and young men in the Atlanta area. The case featured unique uses of fiber evidence that proved crucial to establishing Williams's guilt. The case also highlighted the effectiveness of statistical probability for establishing links between evidence found at multiple crime scenes.

1. In what respects did the use of fiber evidence in the Williams case differ significantly from its use in previous cases?

2. What did investigators hope to learn from their initial examination of fibers found on the bodies of several murder victims found in the Atlanta area from July 1979 to May 1981? What steps did they take to gather this information? What did they learn from their investigations? What was the significance of this information?

3. How could information on the source of the fibers be helpful to investigators? Explain how investigators might use information about the source of a fiber to help them locate the perpetrator.

4. What pieces of information did investigators collect from the West Point Pepperell Corporation that led them to conclude that the fibers found on Nathaniel Cater's body came from the carpeting in Wayne Williams's house? Explain the importance of each of these pieces of information for connecting Williams to Cater's murder.

5. Describe how investigators used the concepts of statistical probability to tie Williams to Nathaniel Cater as well as to his other victims.

Web Resources

Deedrick, D. W., "Hairs, Fibers, Crime, and Evidence" *Forensic Science Communications* 2, no. 3 (2000)
www.fbi.gov/hq/lab/fsc/backissu/july2000/deedrick.htm

Deedrick, D. W., and S. L. Koch, "Microscopy of Hair Part I: A Practical Guide and Manual for Human Hairs," *Forensic Science Communications* 6, no. 1 (2004)
www.fbi.gov/hq/lab/fsc/backissu/jan2004/research/2004_01_research01b.htm

Deedrick, D. W., and S. L. Koch, "Microscopy of Hair Part II: A Practical Guide and Manual for Animal Hairs," *Forensic Science Communications* 6, no. 3 (2004)
www.fbi.gov/hq/lab/fsc/backissu/july2004/research/2004_03_research02.htm

Exline, D. L., "That's Not My Hair," *Forensic Echo* 4, no. 1 (2000)
http://echo.forensicpanel.com/2000/10/13/thatsnot.html

Partin, K. D., A Microscopical Study of Exotic Animal Hair: Part l
www.modernmicroscopy.com/main.asp?article=24&page=1

Trace Evidence (An online article discussing the analysis of hair and fiber evidence based on true crime stories)
www.crimelibrary.com/forensics/trace/

Endnotes

1 J. D. Baker and D. L. Exline, *Forensic Animal Hair Atlas: A Searchable Database on CD-ROM*. RJ Lee Group, Inc., 350 Hochberg Rd., Monroeville, Pa. 15146.

2 M. M. Houk and B. Budowle, "Correlation of Microscopic and Mitochondrial DNA Hair Comparisons," *Journal of Forensic Sciences* 47 (2002): 964.

3 L. A. King, R. Wigmore, and J. M. Twibell, "The Morphology and Occurrence of Human Hair Sheath Cells," *Journal of the Forensic Science Society* 22 (1982): 267.

4 C. A. Linch et al., "Evaluation of the Human Hair Root for DNA Typing Subsequent to Microscopic Comparison," *Journal of Forensic Sciences* 43 (1998): 305.

5 S. Palenki and C. Fitzsimons, "Fiber Cross-Sections: Part I," *Microscope* 38 (1990): 187.

6 D. K. Laing et al., "The Standardisation of Thin-Layer Chromatographic Systems for Comparisons of Fibre Dyes," *Journal of the Forensic Science Society* 30 (1990): 299.

7 M. C. Grieve, "Another Look at the Classification of Acrylic Fibres, Using FTIR Microscopy," *Science & Justice* 35 (1995): 179.

8 M. W. Tungol et al., "Analysis of Single Polymer Fibers by Fourier Transform Infrared Microscopy: The Results of Case Studies," *Journal of Forensic Sciences* 36 (1992): 1027.

Case Reading

Fiber Evidence and the Wayne Williams Trial

Harold A. Deadman
Special Agent, Microscopic
Analysis Unit, Laboratory Division
Federal Bureau of Investigation,
Washington, D.C.

On February 26, 1982, a Fulton County, Ga., Superior Court jury returned a verdict of "guilty as charged" on two counts of murder brought against Wayne Bertram Williams by a Fulton County grand jury in July 1981. Williams had been on trial since December 28, 1981, for the asphyxial murders of Nathaniel Cater and Jimmy Payne in April and May of 1981. During the 8-week trial, evidence linking Williams to those murders and to the murders of 10 other boys or young men was introduced.

An essential part of this case, presented by the Fulton County District Attorney's Office, involved the association of fibrous debris removed from the bodies of 12 murder victims with objects from the everyday environment of Williams.

Fiber evidence has often been an important part of criminal cases, but the Williams trial differed from other cases in several respects. Fiber evidence has not played a significant role in any case involving a large number of murder victims. The victims whose deaths were charged to Williams were 2 of 30 black children and black young men who were reported missing or who had died under suspicious circumstances in the Atlanta area over a 22-month period beginning in July 1979. During the trial, fiber evidence was used to associate Williams with 12 of those victims.

Fiber evidence is often used to corroborate other evidence in a case—it is used to support other testimony and validate other evidence presented at a trial. This was not

Wayne Williams is shown talking to police outside his home. *Courtesy Corbis Bettmann*

Reprinted in part from *FBI Law Enforcement Bulletin,* March and May 1984.

the situation in the Williams trial. Other evidence and other aspects of the trial were important but were used to support and complement the fiber evidence, not the usual order of things. The "hair and fiber matches" between Williams's environment and 11 of the 12 murder victims discussed at the trial were so significant that, in the author's opinion, these victims were positively linked to both the residence and automobiles that were a major part of the world of Wayne Williams.

Another difference between this case and most other cases was the extremely large amount of publicity surrounding both the investigation of the missing and murdered children and the arrest and subsequent trial of Williams. Few other murder trials have received the attention that the Williams case received. . . .

It is often difficult to get an accurate picture from press reports of the physical evidence introduced at a trial and the significance of that evidence. This article will also set forth in some detail the fiber evidence that linked Williams to the murder victims.

By discussing only the fiber evidence introduced at the trial, many other aspects of the case against Williams are being neglected. Additional evidence dealing with Williams's motivations—his character and behavior, his association with several of the victims by eyewitness accounts, and his link to a victim recovered from a river in Atlanta—was also essential to the case. . . .

Development of Williams as a Murder Suspect

Before Wayne Williams became a suspect in the Nathaniel Cater murder case, the Georgia State Crime Laboratory located a number of yellowish-green nylon fibers and some violet acetate fibers on the bodies and clothing of the murder victims whose bodies had been recovered during the period of July 1979 to May 1981. The names of those victims were included on the list of missing and murdered children that was compiled by the Atlanta Task Force (a large group of investigators from law enforcement agencies in the Atlanta area). The yellowish-green nylon fibers were generally similar to each other in appearance and properties and were considered to have originated from a single source. This was also true of the violet acetate fibers. Although there were many other similarities that would link these murders together, the fiber linkage was notable since the possibility existed that a source of these fibers might be located in the future.

Initially, the major concern with these yellowish-green nylon fibers was determining what type of object could have been their source. This information could provide avenues of investigative activity. The fibers were very coarse and had a lobed cross-sectional appearance, tending to indicate that they originated from a carpet or a rug. The lobed cross-sectional shape of these fibers, however, was unique, and initially, the manufacturer of these fibers could not be determined. Photomicrographs of the fibers were prepared for display to contacts within the textile industry. On one occasion, these photomicrographs were distributed among several chemists attending a meeting at the research facilities of a large fiber producer. The chemists concurred that the yellowish-green nylon fiber was very unusual in cross-sectional shape and was consistent with being a carpet fiber, but again, the manufacturer of this fiber could not be determined. Contacts with other textile producers and textile chemists likewise did not result in an identification of the manufacturer.

In February 1981, an Atlanta newspaper article publicized that several different fiber types had been found on two murder victims. Following the publication of this article, bodies recovered from rivers in the Atlanta metropolitan area were either nude or clothed only in undershorts. It appeared possible that the victims were being disposed of in this undressed state and in rivers in order to eliminate fibers from being found on their bodies.[1]

On May 22, 1981, a four-man surveillance team of personnel from the Atlanta Police Department and the Atlanta Office of the FBI was situated under and at both ends of the James Jackson Parkway Bridge over the Chattahoochee River in northwest Atlanta. Around 2 a.m., a loud splash alerted the surveillance team to the presence of an automobile being driven slowly off the bridge. The driver was stopped and identified as Wayne Bertram Williams.

Two days after Williams's presence on the bridge, the nude body of Nathaniel Cater was pulled from the Chattahoochee River, approximately 1 mile downstream from the James Jackson Parkway Bridge. A yellowish-green nylon carpet-type fiber, similar to the nylon fibers discussed above, was recovered from the head hair of Nathaniel Cater. When details of Williams's reason for being on the bridge at 2 a.m. could not be confirmed, search warrants for Williams's home and automobile were obtained and were served on the afternoon of June 3, 1981. During the late evening hours of the same day, the initial associations of fibers from Cater and other murder victims were made with a green carpet in the home of Williams. Associations with a bedspread from Williams's bed and with [Williams's] family dog were also made at that time.

An apparent source of the yellowish-green nylon fibers had been found. It now became important to completely characterize these fibers in order to verify the associations and determine the strength of the associations resulting from the fiber matches. Because of the unusual cross-sectional appearance of the nylon fiber and the difficulty in determining the manufacturer, it was believed that this was a relatively rare fiber type, and therefore, would not be present in large amounts (or in a large number of carpets).

[Williams's] Carpet

Shortly after Williams was developed as a suspect, it was determined the yellowish-green nylon fibers were manufactured by the Wellman Corporation. The next step was to ascertain, if possible, how much carpet like Williams's bedroom carpet had been sold in the Atlanta area—carpet composed of the Wellman fiber and dyed with the same dye formulation as [Williams's] carpet. Names of Wellman Corporation customers who had purchased this fiber type, technical information about the fiber, and data concerning when and how much of this fiber type had been manufactured were obtained.

It was confirmed that the Wellman Corporation had, in fact, manufactured the fiber in Williams's carpet and that no other fiber manufacturer was known to have made a fiber with a similar cross section. It was also determined that fibers having this cross-sectional shape were manufactured and sold during the years

1967 through 1974. Prior to 1967, this company manufactured only a round cross section; after 1974, the unusual trilobal cross section seen in Williams's carpet was modified to a more regular trilobal cross-sectional shape. A list of sales of that fiber type during the period 1967 through 1974 was compiled. . . .

Through numerous contacts with yarn spinners and carpet manufacturers, it was determined that the West Point Pepperell Corporation of Dalton, Ga., had manufactured a line of carpet called "Luxaire," which was constructed in the same manner as [Williams's] carpet. One of the colors offered in the "Luxaire" line was called "English Olive," and this color was the same as that of [Williams's] carpet (both visually and by the use of discriminating chemical and instrumental tests). It was learned that the West Point Pepperell Corporation had manufactured the "Luxaire" line for a five-year period from December 1970 through 1975; however, it had only purchased Wellman 181B fiber for this line during 1970 and 1971. In December 1971, the West Point Pepperell Corporation changed the fiber composition of the "Luxaire" line to a different nylon fiber, one that was dissimilar to the Wellman 181B fiber in appearance. Accordingly, "Luxaire" carpet, like [Williams's] carpet, was only manufactured for a 1-year period. This change of carpet fiber after only 1 year in production was yet another factor that made [Williams's] carpet unusual.

It is interesting to speculate on the course the investigation would have taken if the James Jackson Parkway Bridge had not been covered by the surveillance team. The identification of the manufacturer of the nylon fibers showing up on the bodies could still have occurred and the same list

of purchasers of the Wellman fiber could have been obtained. The same contacts with the yarn and carpet manufacturers could have been made; however, there would not have been an actual carpet sample to display. It is believed that eventually the carpet manufacturer could have been determined. With a sample of carpet supplied by West Point Pepperell— which they had retained in their files for over 10 years—it would have been possible to conduct a house-by-house search of the Atlanta area in an attempt to find a similar carpet. Whether this very difficult task would have been attempted, of course, will never be known. A search of that type, however, would have accurately answered an important question that was discussed at the trial—the question of how many other homes in the Atlanta area had a carpet like [Williams's] carpet. An estimation, to be discussed later, based on sales records provided by the West Point Pepperell Corporation indicated that there was a very low chance (1/7,792) of finding a carpet like Williams's carpet by randomly selecting occupied residences in the Atlanta area.

Only the West Point Pepperell Corporation was found to have manufactured a carpet exactly like [Williams's] carpet. Even though several manufacturers had gone out of business and could not be located, it was believed that, considering the many variables that exist in the manufacture of carpet and the probable uniqueness of each carpet manufacturer's dye formulations, it would be extremely unlikely for two unrelated companies to construct a carpet or dye the carpet fibers in exactly the same way. A large number of other green fibers, visually similar in color to Williams's carpet, were examined. None was found to be consistent with fibers from [Williams's] carpet.

Probability Determinations

To convey the unusual nature of [Williams's] residential carpet, an attempt was made to develop a numerical probability—something never before done in connection with textile materials used as evidence in a criminal trial.[2] The following information was gathered from the West Point Pepperell Corporation:

1. West Point Pepperell reported purchases of Wellman 181B fiber for the "Luxaire" line during a 1-year period. The Wellman 181B fiber was used to manufacture "Luxaire" carpet from December 1970 until December 1971, at which time a new fiber type replaced that Wellman fiber.

2. In 1971, West Point Pepperell sold 5,710 square yards of English Olive "Luxaire" and "Dreamer" carpet to Region C (10 southeastern states which include Georgia). "Dreamer" was a line of carpet similar to "Luxaire" but contained a less dense pile. In order to account for the carpet manufactured during 1971, but sold after that time, all of the "Luxaire" English Olive carpet sold during 1972 to Region C (10,687 square yards) was added to the 1971 sales. Therefore, it was estimated that a total of 16,397 square yards of carpet containing the Wellman 181B fiber and dyed English Olive in color was sold by the West Point Pepperell Corporation to retailers in 10 southeastern states during 1971 and 1972. (In 1979, existing residential carpeted floor space in the United States was estimated at 6.7 billion square yards.)[3]

3. By assuming that this carpet was installed in one room, averaging 12 feet by 15 feet in size, per house, and also assuming that the total sales of carpet were divided equally among the 10 southeastern states, then approximately 82 rooms with this carpet could be found in the state of Georgia.

4. Information from the Atlanta Regional Commission showed that there were 638,995 occupied housing units in the Atlanta metropolitan area in November 1981.[4] Using this figure, the chance of randomly selecting an occupied housing unit in metropolitan Atlanta and finding a house with a room having carpet like Williams's carpet was determined to be 1 chance in 7,792—a very low chance. To the degree that the assumptions used in calculating the above probability number are reasonable, we can be confident in arriving at a valid probability number. . . .

The probability figures illustrate clearly that [Williams's] carpet is, in fact, very uncommon. To enhance the figures even further, it is important to emphasize that these figures are based on the assumption that none of the carpet of concern had been discarded during the past 11 years. In fact, carpet of this type, often used in commercial settings, such as apartment houses, would probably have had a normal life span of only 4 or 5 years. . . .[5]

The Williams Trial

To any experienced forensic fiber examiner, the fiber evidence linking Williams to the murder victims was overwhelming. But regardless of the apparent validity of the fiber findings, it was during the trial that its true weight would be determined. Unless it could be conveyed meaningfully to a jury, its effect would be lost. Because of this, considerable time was spent determining what should be done to convey the full significance of the fiber evidence. Juries are not usually composed of individuals with a scientific background, and therefore, it was necessary to "educate" the jury in what procedures were followed and the significance of the fiber results. In the Williams case, over 40 charts with over 350 photographs were prepared to illustrate exactly what the crime laboratory examiners had observed. . . .

Representatives of the textile fiber industry, including technical representatives from the Wellman and West Point Pepperell Corporations, were involved in educating the jury regarding textile fibers in general and helped lay the foundation for the conclusions of the forensic fiber examiners. The jury also was told about fiber analysis in the crime laboratory.

The trial, as it developed, can be divided into two parts. Initially, testimony was given concerning the murders of Nathaniel Cater and Jimmy Ray Payne, the two victims included in the indictment drawn against Williams in July 1981. Testimony was then given concerning Williams's association with 10 other murder victims.

The fiber matches made between fibers in Williams's environment and fibers from victims Payne and Cater were discussed. The items from Williams's environment that were linked to either or both of the victims are shown in the center of the chart. (See Figure 1.) Not only is Payne linked to Williams's environment by seven items and Cater linked by six items, but both of the victims are linked strongly to each other based on the fiber matches and circumstances surrounding their deaths.

In discussing the significance or strength of an association based on textile fibers, it was emphasized that the more uncommon the fibers, the stronger the association. None of the fiber types from the items in Williams's environment shown in the center of Figure 1 is by definition a "common" fiber type. Several of the fiber types would be termed "uncommon."

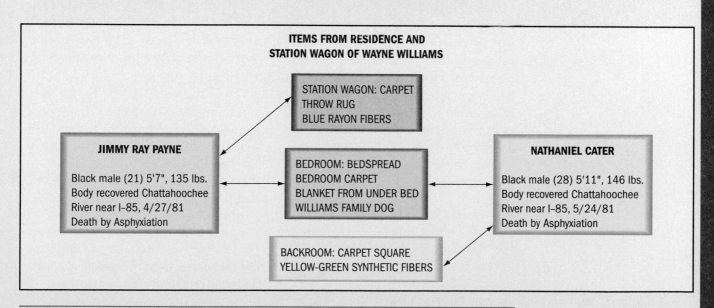

FIGURE 1   Items from the residence and station wagon of Wayne Williams that were found on Jimmy Ray Payne and Nathaniel Cater.

One of the fibers linking the body of Jimmy Ray Payne to the carpet in the 1970 station wagon driven by Williams was a small rayon fiber fragment recovered from Payne's shorts. Data were obtained from the station wagon's manufacturer concerning which automobile models produced prior to 1973 contained carpet made of this fiber type. These data were coupled with additional information from Georgia concerning the number of these models registered in the Atlanta metropolitan area during 1981. This allowed a calculation to be made relating to the probability of randomly selecting an automobile having carpet like that in the 1970 Chevrolet station wagon from the 2,373,512 cars registered in the Atlanta metropolitan area. This probability is 1 chance in 3,828, a very low probability representing a significant association.

Another factor to consider when assessing the significance of fiber evidence is the increased strength of the association when multiple fiber matches become the basis of the association. This is true if different fiber types from more than one object are found and each fiber type either links two people together or links an individual with a particular environment. As the number of different objects increases, the strength of an association increases dramatically. That is, the chance of randomly finding several particular fiber types in a certain location is much smaller than the chance of finding one particular fiber type.

The following example can be used to illustrate the significance of multiple fiber matches linking two items together. If one were to throw a single die one time, the chance or probability of throwing a particular number would be one chance in six. The probability of throwing a second die and getting that same number also would be one chance in six. However, the probability of getting 2 of the same numbers on 2 dice thrown simultaneously is only 1 in every 36 double throws—a much smaller chance than with either of the single throws. This number is a result of the product rule of probability theory. That is, the probability of the joint occurrence of a number of mutually independent events equals the product of the individual probabilities of each of the events (in this example—$\frac{1}{6} \times \frac{1}{6} = \frac{1}{36}$). Since numerous fiber types are in existence, the chance of finding one particular fiber type, other than a common type, in a specific randomly selected location is small. The chance then of finding several fiber types together in a specific location is the product of several small probabilities, resulting in an extremely small chance. . . .

However, no attempt was made to use the product rule and multiply the individual probability numbers together to get an approximation of the probability of finding carpets like Williams's residential carpet and Williams's automobile carpet in the same household. The probability numbers were used only to show that the individual fiber types involved in these associations were very uncommon. . . .[6]

In addition to the two probability numbers already discussed (bedroom and station wagon carpets), each of the other fiber types linking Williams to both Cater and Payne has a probability of being found in a particular location. The chance of finding all of the fiber types indicated on the chart (Figure 1) in one location (seven types on Payne's body and six types on Cater's body) would be extremely small. Although an actual probability number for those findings could not be determined, it is believed that the multiple fiber associations shown on this chart are proof that Williams is linked to the bodies of these two victims, even though each fiber match by itself does not show a positive association with Williams's environment.

Studies have been conducted in England that show that transferred fibers are usually lost rapidly as people go about their daily routine.[7] Therefore, the foreign fibers present on a person are most often from recent surroundings. The fibrous debris found on a murder victim reflects the body's more recent surroundings, especially important if the body was moved after the killing. Accordingly, the victims' bodies in this particular case are not only associated with Williams but are apparently associated with Williams shortly before or after their deaths. It was also pointed out during the trial that the locations of the fibers—on Payne's shorts and in Cater's head hairs and pubic hairs—were not those where one would expect to find fibrous debris transferred from an automobile or a house to victims who had been fully clothed.

Although from these findings it would appear that the victims were in the residence of Williams, there was one other location that contained many of the same fibers as those in the composition of various objects in his residence—Williams's station wagon. The environment of a family automobile might be expected to reflect, to some extent, fibers from objects located within the residence. This was true of the 1970 station wagon. With one exception, all of the fiber types removed from Payne and Cater, consistent with originating from items shown in the center of Figure 1, were present in debris removed by vacuuming the station wagon. The automobile would be the most logical source of the foreign fibers found on both Payne and Cater if they were associated

with Williams shortly before or after their deaths. It should also be pointed out that two objects, the bedspread and the blanket, were portable and could have at one time been present inside the station wagon.

Both Payne and Cater were recovered from the Chattahoochee River. Their bodies had been in the water for several days. Some of the fibers found on these victims were like fibers in the compositions of the bedroom carpet and bedspread except for color intensity. They appeared to have been bleached. By subjecting various known fibers to small amounts of Chattahoochee River water for different periods of time, it was found that bleaching did occur. This was especially true with the carpet and bedspread fibers from Williams's bedroom.

Two crime laboratory examiners testified during the closing stages of the first part of the trial about Williams's association with Payne and Cater. They concluded that it was highly unlikely that any environment other than that present in Wayne Williams's house and car could have resulted in the combination of fibers and hairs found on the victims and that it would be virtually impossible to have matched so many fibers found on Cater and Payne to items in Williams's house and car unless the victims were in contact with or in some way associated with the environment of Wayne Williams.

After testimony was presented concerning the Payne and Cater cases, the Fulton County District Attorney's Office asked the court to be allowed to introduce evidence in the cases of 10 other victims whose murders were similar in many respects. Georgia law allows evidence of another crime to be introduced ". . . if some logical connection can be shown between the two from which it can be said that proof of the one tends to establish the other as relevant to some fact other than general bad character."[8] There need be no conviction for the other crime in order for details about that crime to be admissible.

It was ruled that evidence concerning other murders could be introduced in an attempt to prove a "pattern or scheme" of killing that included the two murders with which Williams was charged. The additional evidence in these cases was to be used to help the jury ". . . decide whether Williams

had committed the two murders with which he is charged."[9]

There were similarities between these additional victims and Payne and Cater. (See Figure 2.) Although some differences can also be seen on this chart, the prosecution considered these differences to fit within the "pattern of killing" of which Payne and Cater were a part. The most important similarities between these additional victims were the fiber matches that linked 9 of the 10 victims to Williams's environment. The fiber findings discussed during the trial and used to associate Williams to the 12 victims were illustrated during the trial. (See Figure 3.)

VICTIM'S NAME	DATE VICTIM MISSING	DAYS MISSING	BODY RECOVERY AREA	CAUSE OF DEATH	AGE	WEIGHT	HEIGHT
EVANS	7/25/79	3	WOODED AREA S.W. ATLANTA	PROBABLE ASPHYXIATION/ STRANGULATION	13	87 LBS.	5'4"
MIDDLEBROOKS	5/18/80	1	NEAR STREET S.E. ATLANTA	BLUNT TRAUMA TO HEAD	14	88 LBS.	4'10"
STEPHENS	10/9/80	1	NEAR STREET S.E. ATLANTA	ASPHYXIATION	10	120 LBS.	5'0"
GETER	1/3/81	33	WOODED AREA FULTON COUNTY	MANUAL STRANGULATION	14	130 LBS.	5'4"
PUE	1/22/81	1	NEAR HIGHWAY ROCKDALE CO.	LIGATURE STRANGULATION	15	105 LBS.	5'5"
BALTAZAR	2/6/81	7	NEAR HIGHWAY DEKALB CO.	LIGATURE STRANGULATION	12	125 LBS.	5'4"
BELL	3/2/81	31	SOUTH RIVER DEKALB CO.	ASPHYXIATION	16	100 LBS.	5'2"
ROGERS	3/30/81	10	NEAR STREET N.W. ATLANTA	ASPHYXIATION/ STRANGULATION	20	110 LBS.	5'3"
PORTER	4/10/81	1	NEAR STREET S.W. ATLANTA	STABBING	28	123 LBS.	5'7"
PAYNE	4/22/81	5	CHATTAHOOCHEE RIVER FULTON COUNTY	ASPHYXIATION	21	135 LBS.	5'7"
BARRETT	5/11/81	1	NEAR STREET DEKALB CO.	LIGATURE STRANGULATION (3 PUNCTURE WOUNDS)	17	125 LBS.	5'4"
CATER	5/21/81	3	CHATTAHOOCHEE RIVER FULTON COUNTY	ASPHYXIATION/ STRANGULATION	28	146 LBS.	5'11"

FIGURE 2   Chart used during the trial to show similarities between Payne and Cater and 10 other murder victims.

NAME OF VICTIM	VIOLET-GREEN BEDSPREAD WILLIAMS' BEDROOM	GREEN CARPET WILLIAMS' BEDROOM	DOG HAIRS WILLIAMS' DOG	YELLOW BLANKET WILLIAMS' BEDROOM	BLUE RAYON FIBERS, DEBRIS FROM WILLIAMS HOME	TRUNK LINER 1978 PLYMOUTH	CARPET 1979 FORD	CARPET 1970 CHEVROLET	ADDITIONAL ITEMS FROM WILLIAMS' HOME, AUTOMOBILES OR PERSON
Alfred Evans	X	X	X			X			
Eric Middlebrooks	X		X				X		YELLOW NYLON — FORD TRUNK LINER
Charles Stephens	X	X	X		X				YELLOW NYLON — WHITE POLYESTER BACKROOM CARPET — FORD TRUNK LINER
Lubie Geter	X	X	X					X	KITCHEN CARPET
Terry Pue	X	X	X						WHITE POLYESTER BACKROOM CARPET
Patrick Baltazar	X	X	X	X				X	YELLOW NYLON GLOVE — JACKET — WHITE POLYESTER — HEAD HAIR PIGMENTED POLYPROPYLENE
Joseph Bell	X				X				
Larry Rogers	X	X	X	X				X	YELLOW NYLON — PORCH BEDSPREAD
John Porter	X	X	X	X	X			X	PORCH BEDSPREAD
Jimmy Payne	X	X	X	X	X			X	BLUE THROW RUG
William Barrett	X	X	X	X	X			X	GLOVE
Nathaniel Cater	X	X	X	X					BACKROOM CARPET — YELLOW-GREEN SYNTHETIC

FIGURE 3 Fiber findings discussed during the trial and used to associate Williams with the 12 victims.

The 12 victims were listed in chronological order based on the dates their bodies were recovered. The time period covered by this chart, approximately 22 months, is from July 1979 until May 1981. During that time period, the Williams family had access to a large number of automobiles, including a number of rental cars. Three of these automobiles are listed at the top of Figure 3. If one or more of the cars was in the possession of the Williams family at the time a victim was found to be missing, the space under that car(s) and after the particular victim's name is shaded.

Four objects (including the dog) from Williams's residence are listed horizontally across the top of Figure 3, along with objects from three of his automobiles. An "X" on the chart indicates an apparent transfer of textile fibers from the listed object to a victim. Other objects from Williams's environment which were linked to various victims by an apparent fiber transfer are listed on the right side of the chart. Fiber types from objects (never actually located) that were matched to fiber types from one or more victims are also listed either at the top or on the right side of the chart. Fourteen specific objects and five fiber types (probably from five other objects) listed on this chart are linked to one or more of the victims. More than 28 different fiber types, along with the dog hairs, were used to link up to 19 objects from Williams's environment to 1 or more of the victims. Of the more than 28 fiber types from Williams's environment, 14 of these originated from a rug or carpet.

The combination of more than 28 different fiber types would not be considered so significant if they were primarily common fiber types. In fact, there is only 1 light green cotton fiber of the 28 that might be considered common. This cotton fiber was blended with acetate fibers in Williams's bedspread. Light green cotton fibers removed from many victims were not considered or compared unless they were physically intermingled with violet acetate fibers which were consistent with originating from the bedspread. It should be noted that a combination of cotton and acetate fibers blended together in a single textile material, as in the bedspread, is in itself uncommon. . . .

The previous discussion concerning the significance of multiple fiber matches can be applied to the associations made in the cases of all the victims except Bell, but especially to the association of Patrick Baltazar to Williams's environment. Fibers and animal hairs consistent with having originated from 10 sources were removed from Baltazar's body. These 10 sources include the uncommon bedroom carpet and station wagon carpet. In addition to the fiber (and animal hair) linkage, two head hairs of Negroid origin were removed from Baltazar's body that were consistent with originating from the scalp area of Williams. Head hair matches were also

very significant in linking Williams to Baltazar's body. In the opinion of the author, the association based upon the hair and fiber analyses is a positive association.

Another important aspect of the fiber linkage between Williams and these victims is the correspondence between the fiber findings and the time periods during which Williams had access to the three automobiles listed on the chart. Nine victims are linked to automobiles used by the Williams family. When Williams did not have access to a particular car, no fibers were recovered that were consistent with having originated from that automobile. Trunk liner fibers of the type used in the trunks of many late-model Ford Motor Company automobiles were also recovered from the bodies of two victims.

One final point should be made concerning Williams's bedroom and station wagon carpets where probability numbers had been determined. Fibers consistent with having originated from both of these "unusual" carpets were recovered from Payne's body. Of the 9 victims who were killed during the time period when Williams had access to the 1970 station wagon, fibers consistent with having originated from both the station wagon carpet and the bedroom carpet were recovered from 6 of these victims.

The apparent bleaching of several fibers removed from the bodies of Payne and Cater was consistent with having been caused by river water. Several fibers similar to those from Payne and Cater were removed from many of the victims whose bodies were recovered on land. Consistent with the bleaching argument, none of the fibers from the victims found on land showed any apparent bleaching. The finding of many of the same fiber types on the remaining victims, who were recovered from many different locations, refutes the possibility that Payne's and Cater's bodies picked up foreign fibers from the river.

The fact that many of the victims were involved with so many of the same fiber types, all of which linked the victims to Williams's environment, is the basis for arguing conclusively against these fibers originating from a source other than Williams's environment.

It is hoped that this article has provided valuable insight concerning the use of fiber evidence in a criminal trial, has provided answers to questions from those in the law enforcement community about textile fiber evidence in general, and has presented convincing arguments to establish Wayne Williams's association with the bodies of the murder victims.

Endnotes

1. Prior to the publication of the February 11, 1981, newspaper article, one victim from the task force list, who was fully clothed, had been recovered from a river in the Atlanta area. In the 2 1/2-month period after publication, the nude or nearly nude bodies of 7 of the 9 victims added to the task force list were recovered from rivers in the Atlanta area.

2. J. Mitchell and D. Holland, "An Unusual Case of Identification of Transferred Fibers," *Journal of the Forensic Science Society,* vol. 19, 1979, p. 23. This article describes a case in which carpet fibers transferred to a murder victim's body in England were traced back to the carpet manufacturer and finally to an automobile owned by the person who eventually confessed to the murder.

3. This information was taken from a study by E. I. du Pont de Nemours & Co. concerned with the existing residential floor space with carpet in the United States. This study was reported in a marketing survey conducted by the Marketing Corporation of America, Westport, Conn.

4. Information regarding the number of housing units in the Atlanta metropolitan area was obtained from a report provided by the Atlanta Regional Commission. The report, dated November 11, 1981, contained population and housing counts for counties, super districts, and census tracts in the Atlanta metropolitan area.

5. Information about carpet similar to Williams's carpet was developed through contacts with carpet manufacturers and carpet salesmen in Georgia. It was determined that this type carpet was often installed in commercial settings, such as apartments, and in those settings, had an average life span of 4 to 5 years.

6. Joseph L. Peterson, ed., *Forensic Science* (New York: AMS Press, 1975), pp. 181–225. This collection of articles, dealing with various aspects of forensic science, contains five papers concerned with using statistics to interpret the meaning of physical evidence. It is a good discussion of probability theory and reviews cases where probability theory has been used in trial situations.

7. C. A. Pounds and K. W. Smalldon, "The Transfer of Fibers between Clothing Materials During Simulated Contacts and Their Persistence During Wear," *Journal of the Forensic Science Society,* vol. 15, 1975, pp. 29–37.

8. *Encyclopedia of Georgia Law,* vol. 11A (The Harrison Company, 1979), p. 70.

9. *The Atlanta Constitution,* "Williams Jury Told of Other Slayings," Sec. 1 = A, 1/26/82, p. 25.

Green River Killer

This case takes its name from the Green River, which flows through Washington State and empties into Puget Sound in Seattle. Within a six-month span in 1982, the bodies of six females were discovered in or near the river. The majority of the victims were known prostitutes who were strangled and apparently raped. As police focused their attention on an area known as Sea-Tac Strip, a haven for prostitutes, girls mysteriously disappeared with increasing frequency. By the end of 1986, the body count in the Seattle region rose to 40, all of whom were believed to have been murdered by the Green River Killer.

As the investigation pressed on into 1987, the police renewed their interest in one suspect, Gary Ridgway, a local truck painter. Ridgway had been known to frequent the Sea-Tac Strip. Interestingly, in 1984 Ridgway actually had passed a lie detector test. Now with a search warrant in hand, police searched Ridgway's residence and also obtained hair and saliva samples from him. Again, insufficient evidence caused Ridgway to be released from custody.

With the exception of one killing in 1998, the murder spree stopped in 1990, and the case remained dormant for nearly ten years. However, the advent of DNA testing brought renewed vigor to the investigation. In 2001, semen samples collected from three early victims of the Green River Killer were compared to saliva that had been collected from Ridgway in 1987. The DNA profiles matched, and the police had their man. An added forensic link to Ridgway was made by the location of minute amounts of spray paint on the clothing of six victims that compared to paints collected from Ridgway's workplace. Ridgway ultimately avoided the death penalty by confessing to the murders of forty-eight women.

chapter 13

Trace Evidence II: Paint, Glass and Soil

Key Terms

Becke line

concentric fractures

density

intensive property

laminated glass

mineral

pyrolysis

radial fractures

refractive index

tempered glass

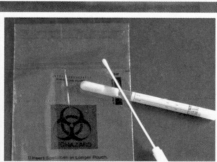

Forensic Examination of Paint

Our environment contains millions of objects whose surfaces are painted. Thus paint, in one form or another, is one of the most prevalent types of physical evidence received by the crime laboratory.

Paint as physical evidence is perhaps most frequently encountered in hit-and-run and burglary cases. For example, a chip of dried paint or a paint smear may be transferred to the clothing of a hit-and-run victim on impact with an automobile, or paint smears could be transferred onto a tool during a burglary. Obviously, in many situations a transfer of paint from one surface to another could impart an object with an identifiable forensic characteristic.

In most circumstances, the criminalist must compare two or more paints to establish their common origin. For example, such a comparison may associate an individual or a vehicle with the crime site. However, the criminalist need not be confined to comparisons alone. Crime laboratories often help identify the color, make, and model of an automobile by examining small quantities of paint recovered at an accident scene. Such requests, normally made in hit-and-run cases, can lead to the apprehension of the responsible vehicle.

Composition of Paint

Paint is composed of a binder and pigments, as well as other additives, all dissolved or dispersed in a suitable solvent. Pigments impart color and hiding (or opacity) to paint and are usually mixtures of various inorganic and organic compounds added to the paint by the manufacturer. The binder is a polymeric substance that provides the support medium for the pigments and additives. After paint has been applied to a surface, the solvent evaporates, leaving behind a hard polymeric binder and any pigments that are suspended in it.

One of the most common types of paint examined in the crime laboratory is finishes from automobiles. Manufacturers apply a variety of coatings to the body of an automobile; this adds significant diversity to automobile paint and contributes to the forensic significance of automobile paint comparisons. The automotive finishing system for steel usually consists of at least four organic coatings:

Electrocoat Primer The first layer applied to the steel body of a car is the electrocoat primer. The primer, consisting of epoxy-based resins, is electroplated onto the steel body of the automobile to provide corrosion resistance.

The resulting coating is uniform in appearance and thickness. The color of these primers ranges from black to gray.

Primer Surfacer   Originally responsible for corrosion control, the surfacer usually follows the electrocoat layer and is applied before the basecoat. Primer surfacers are epoxy-modified polyesters or urethanes. The function of this layer is to completely smooth out and hide any seams or imperfections, because the basecoat will be applied on this surface. This layer is highly pigmented. Color pigments are used to minimize color contrast between primer and topcoats. For example, a light gray primer may be used under pastel shades of a colored topcoat; a red oxide may be used under a dark-colored topcoat.

Basecoat   The next layer of paint on a car is the basecoat or colorcoat. This layer provides the color and aesthetics of the finish and represents the "eye appeal" of the finished automobile. The integrity of this layer depends on its ability to resist weather, UV radiation, and acid rain. Most commonly, an acrylic-based polymer comprises the binder system of basecoats. Interestingly, the choice of automotive pigments is dictated by toxic and environmental concerns. Thus, the use of lead, chrome, and other heavy-metal pigments has been abandoned in favor of organic-based pigments. There is also a growing trend toward pearl luster or mica pigments. Mica pigments are coated with layers of metal oxide to generate interference colors. Also, the addition of aluminum flakes to automotive paint imparts a metallic look to the paint's finish.

Clearcoat   An unpigmented clearcoat is applied to improve gloss, durability, and appearance. Most clearcoats are acrylic based, but polyurethane clearcoats are increasing in popularity. These topcoats provide outstanding etch resistance and appearance.

Microscopic Examination of Paint

The microscope has traditionally been and remains the most important instrument for locating and comparing paint specimens. Considering the thousands of paint colors and shades, it is quite understandable that color, more than any other property, gives paint its most distinctive forensic characteristics. Questioned and known specimens are best compared side by side under a stereoscopic microscope for color, surface texture, and color layer sequence (see Figure 13–1).

The importance of layer structure for evaluating the evidential significance of paint evidence cannot be overemphasized. When paint specimens possess colored layers that match in number and sequence of colors, the examiner can begin to relate the paints to a common origin. How many layers must be matched before the criminalist can conclude that the paints come from the same source? There is no one accepted criterion. Much depends on the uniqueness of each layer's color and texture, as well as the frequency with which the particular combination of colors under investigation is observed. Because no books or journals have compiled this type of information, the criminalist is left to his or her own experience and knowledge when making this decision.

Unfortunately, most paint specimens do not have a layer structure of sufficient complexity to allow them to be individualized to a single source, nor is it common to have paint chips that can be physically fitted together to prove common origin, as shown in Figure 13–2. However, the diverse chemical composition of modern paints provides additional points of

FIGURE 13–1 **A stereoscopic microscope comparison of two automotive paints. The questioned paint on the left has a layer structure consistent with the control paint on the right.** *Courtesy Leica Microsystems, Inc., Buffalo, N.Y., www.leica-microsystems.com*

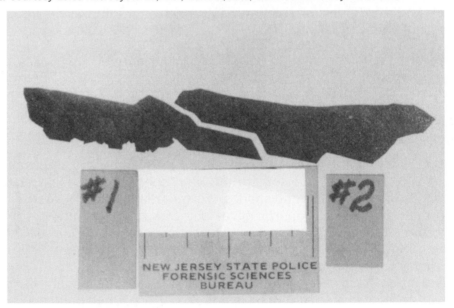

FIGURE 13–2 **Paint chip 1 was recovered from the scene of a hit-and-run. Paint chip 2 was obtained from the suspect vehicle.** *Courtesy New Jersey State Police*

comparison between specimens. Specifically, a thorough comparison of paint must include a chemical analysis of the paint's pigments, its binder composition, or both.

Analytical Techniques Used in Paint Comparison

The wide variation in binder formulations in automobile finishes provides significant information. More important, paint manufacturers make automobile finishes in hundreds of varieties; this knowledge is most helpful to

Closer Analysis

The Stereoscopic Microscope

The details that characterize the structures of many types of physical evidence do not always require examination under very high magnifications. For such specimens, the stereoscopic microscope has proven quite adequate, providing magnifying powers from 10× to 125×. This microscope has the advantage of presenting a distinctive three-dimensional image of an object. Also, whereas the image formed by the compound microscope is inverted and reversed (upside-down and backward), the stereoscopic microscope is more convenient because prisms in its light path create a right-side-up image.

The stereoscopic microscope, shown in Figure 1, is actually two monocular compound microscopes properly spaced and aligned to present a three-dimensional image of a specimen to the viewer, who looks through both eyepiece lenses. The light path of a stereoscopic microscope is shown in Figure 2.

The stereoscopic microscope is undoubtedly the most frequently used and versatile microscope found in the crime laboratory. Its wide field of view and great depth of focus make it an ideal instrument for locating trace evidence in debris, garments, weapons, and tools. Furthermore, its potentially large *working distance* (the distance between the objective lens and the specimen) makes it ideal for microscopic examination of big, bulky items. When fitted with vertical illumination, the stereoscopic microscope becomes the primary tool for characterizing physical evidence as diverse as paint, soil, gunpowder residues, and marijuana.

FIGURE 2 A schematic diagram of a stereoscopic microscope. This microscope is actually two separate monocular microscopes, each with its own set of lenses except for the lowest objective lens, which is common to both microscopes.

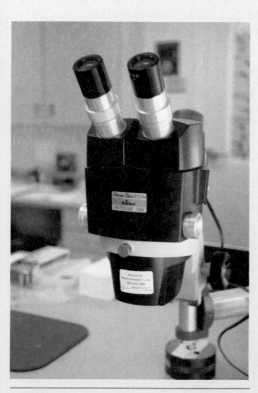

FIGURE 1 A stereoscopic microscope.
Courtesy Mikael Karlsson, Arresting Images

the criminalist who is trying to associate a paint chip with one car as distinguished from the thousands of similar models that have been produced in any one year. For instance, there are more than a hundred automobile production plants in the United States and Canada. Each can use one paint supplier for a particular color or vary suppliers during a model year. Although a paint supplier must maintain strict quality control over a paint's color, the batch formulation of any paint binder can vary, depending on the availability and cost of basic ingredients.

pyrolysis
The decomposition of organic matter by heat.

Characterization of Paint Binders   An important extension of the application of gas chromatography to forensic science is the technique of **pyrolysis** *gas chromatography*. Many solid materials commonly encountered as physical evidence—for example, paint chips, fibers, and plastics—cannot be readily dissolved in a solvent for injection into the gas chromatograph. Thus, under normal conditions these substances cannot be subjected to gas chromatographic analysis. However, materials such as these can be heated, or *pyrolyzed*, to high temperatures (500–1000°C) so that they will decompose into numerous gaseous products. Pyrolyzers permit these gaseous products to enter the carrier gas stream, where they flow into and through the gas chromatography (GC) column. The pyrolyzed material can then be characterized by the pattern produced by its chromatogram, or *pyrogram*.

Pyrolysis gas chromatography is particularly invaluable for distinguishing most paint formulations. In this process, paint chips as small as 20 micrograms are decomposed by heat into numerous gaseous products and are sent through a gas chromatograph.

As shown in Figure 13–3, the polymer chain is decomposed by a heated filament, and the resultant products are swept into and through a gas chromatograph column. The separated decomposition products of the polymer emerge and are recorded. The pattern of this chromatogram or "pyrogram" distinguishes one polymer from another. The result is a pyrogram that is sufficiently detailed to reflect the chemical makeup of the binder.

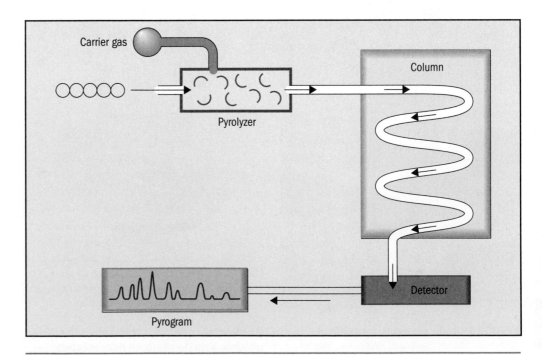

FIGURE 13–3   A schematic diagram of pyrolysis gas chromatography.

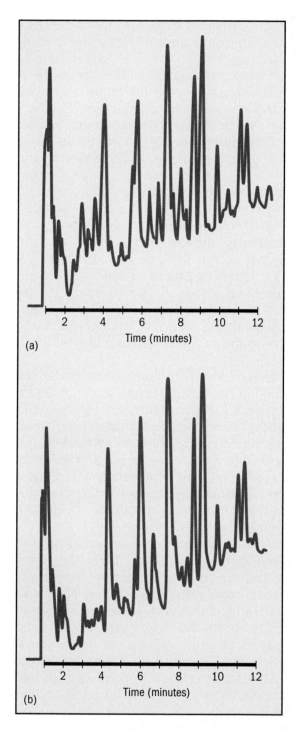

(a)

(b)

FIGURE 13–4   Paint pyrograms of acrylic enamel paints: (a) paint from a Ford model and (b) paint from a Chrysler model. *Courtesy Varian Inc., Palo Alto, Calif.*

Figure 13–4 illustrates how the patterns produced by paint pyrograms can differentiate acrylic enamel paints removed from two automobiles.

Infrared spectrophotometry is still another analytical technique that provides information about the binder composition of paint.[1] Binders selectively absorb infrared radiation to yield a spectrum that is highly characteristic of a paint specimen.

Significance of Paint Evidence

Once a paint comparison is completed, the task of assessing the significance of the finding begins. How certain can one be that two similar paints came from the same surface? For instance, a casual observer sees countless identically colored automobiles on our roads and streets. If this is the case, what value is a comparison of a paint chip from a hit-and-run scene to paint removed from a suspect car?

From previous discussions it should be apparent that far more is involved in paint comparison than matching surface paint colors. Paint layers beneath a surface layer offer valuable points of comparison. Furthermore, forensic analysts can detect subtle differences in paint binder formulations, as well as major or minor differences in the elemental composition of paint. Obviously, these properties cannot be discerned by the naked eye.

The significance of a paint comparison was convincingly demonstrated from data gathered at the Centre of Forensic Science, Toronto, Canada.[2] Paint chips randomly taken from 260 vehicles located in a local wreck yard were compared by color, layer structure, and, when required, infrared spectroscopy. All were distinguishable except for one pair. In statistical terms, these results signify that if a crime-scene paint sample and a paint standard/reference sample removed from a suspect car compare by the previously discussed tests, the odds against the crime-scene paint originating from another randomly chosen vehicle are approximately 33,000 to 1. Obviously, this type of evidence is bound to forge a strong link between the suspect car and the crime scene.

Crime laboratories are often asked to identify the make and model of a car from a very small amount of paint left behind at a crime scene. Such information is frequently of use in a search for an unknown car involved in a hit-and-run incident. Often the questioned paint can be identified when its color is compared to color chips representing the various makes and models of manufactured cars. However, in many cases it is not possible to state the exact make or model of the car in question, because any one paint color can be found on more than one car model. For instance, General Motors may have used the same paint color for several production years on cars in its Cadillac, Buick, Pontiac, and Chevrolet lines.

Color charts for automobile finishes are available from various paint manufacturers and refinishers (see Figure 13–5). Since 1975, the Royal Canadian Mounted Police Forensic Laboratories have been systematically gathering color and chemical information on automotive paints. This computerized database, known as PDQ (Paint Data Query), allows an analyst to obtain information on paints related to automobile make, model, and year. The database contains such parameters as automotive paint layer colors, primer colors, and binder composition (see Figure 13–6). A number of U.S. laboratories have access to PDQ.[3] Also, some crime laboratories maintain an in-house collection of automotive paints associated with various makes and models, as shown in Figure 13–7.

Collection and Preservation of Paint Evidence

As has already been noted, paint chips are most likely to be found on or near people or objects involved in hit-and-run incidents. The recovery of loose paint chips from a garment or from the road surface must be done with the utmost care to keep the paint chip intact. Paint chips may be picked up with a tweezers or scooped up with a piece of paper. Paper druggist folds and glass or plastic vials make excellent containers for paint. If the paint is smeared on or embedded in garments or objects, the investigator should not attempt to remove it; instead, it is best to package the whole item carefully and send it to the laboratory for examination.

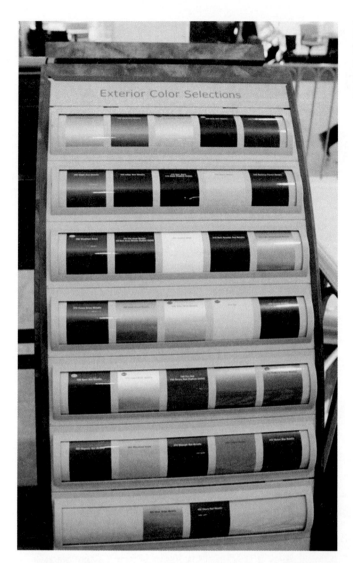

FIGURE 13–5 An automotive color chart of various car models.
Courtesy Damian Dovanganes, AP Wide World Photos

When a transfer of paint occurs in hit-and-run situations (such as to the clothing of a pedestrian victim), uncontaminated standard/reference paint must always be collected from an undamaged area of the vehicle for comparison in the laboratory. The collected paint must be close to the area of the car that is suspected of being in contact with the victim. This is necessary because other portions of the car may have faded or been repainted.

Standard/reference samples are always removed so as to include all the paint layers down to the bare metal. This is best accomplished by removing a painted section with a clean scalpel or knife blade. Samples 1/4 inch square are sufficient for laboratory examination. Each paint sample should be separately packaged and marked with the exact location of its recovery.

When a cross-transfer of paint occurs between two vehicles, again all of the layers, including the foreign as well as the underlying original paints, must be removed from each vehicle. A standard/reference sample from an adjacent undamaged area of each vehicle must also be taken in such cases. An investigator should carefully wipe the blade of any knife or scraping tool used before collecting each sample, to avoid cross-contamination of paints.

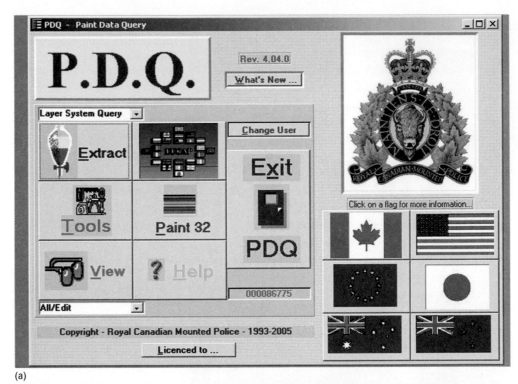

(a)

(b)

FIGURE 13–6 **(a) The home screen for PDQ database. (b) A partial list of auto paints contained in the PDQ database.** *Courtesy Royal Canadian Mounted Police*

FIGURE 13–7   A crime laboratory's automotive paint library. Paints were collected at an automobile impound yard and then cataloged for rapid retrieval and examination. *Courtesy Gavin Edmondstone, Centre for Forensic Sciences, Toronto, Canada*

Case Study

The Predator

September in Arizona is hot and dry, much like the rest of the year—but September 1984 was a little different. Unusually heavy rains fell for two days, which must have seemed fitting for the friends and family of 8-year-old Vicki Lynn Hoskinson. Vicki went missing on September 17 of that year, and her disappearance was investigated as a kidnapping. A school-teacher who knew Vicki remembered a suspicious vehicle loitering near the school that day, and he happened to jot down the license plate number. This crucial tip led police to 28-year-old Frank Atwood, recently paroled from a California prison. Police soon learned that Atwood had been convicted for committing sex offenses and for kidnapping a boy. This galvanized the investigators, who realized Vicki could be at the mercy of a dangerous and perverse man.

The only evidence the police had to work with was Vicki's bike, which was found abandoned in the middle of the street a few blocks from her home. Police found scrapes from her bike pedal on the underside of the gravel pan on Atwood's car, as well as pink paint apparently transferred from Vicki's bike to Atwood's front bumper. The police believed that Atwood deliberately struck Vicki while she was riding her bicycle, knocking her to the ground.

The pink paint on Atwood's bumper was first looked at microscopically and then examined by pyrolysis gas chromatography, which entails heating the paint sample to extremely high temperature to vaporize and fragment the components of the paint. The pyrolyzed sample, in the form of a gas, is then pushed through a gas chromatographic column. By the time the paint

(Continued)

Case Study

The Predator *(Continued)*

components have reached the end of the column, they have separated and each chemical constituent is recorded. This technique provides investigators with a "fingerprint" pattern of the paint sample, enabling them to compare this paint to any other paint evidence. In this case, the pink paint on Atwood's bumper matched the paint from Vicki's bicycle.

Further evidence proving Atwood's involvement in the crime came when a gouge on the surface of Vicki's bicycle was checked for its elemental composition with the aid of a scanning electron microscope (SEM) in combination with an X-ray analyzer. Traces of nickel were found on the gouge's surface. The bumper of Atwood's car was coated with a thin film of nickel, providing solid evidence of the cross-transfer of paint and metal between the bumper of Frank Atwood's car and Vicki Lynn's bicycle.

Vicki's skeletal remains were discovered in the desert, several miles away from her home, in the spring of 1985. Positive identification was made using dental records, but investigators wanted to see if the remains could help them determine how long she had been dead. Atwood was jailed on an unrelated charge three days after Vicki disappeared, so the approximate date of death was very important to proving his guilt.

Investigators found adipocere, a white, fatty residue produced during decomposition, inside Vicki's skull. This provided evidence that moisture was present around Vicki's body after her death, which does not make sense considering she was found in the Arizona desert! A check of the weather revealed that there had been an unusual amount of rainfall at only one time since Vicki was last seen alive: a mere forty-eight hours after her disappearance. This put Vicki's death squarely within Frank Atwood's three-day window of opportunity between her disappearance and his arrest. Frank Atwood was sentenced to death in 1987 for the murder of Vicki Lynn Hoskinson. He remains on death row awaiting execution.

Key Points

- Paint spread onto a surface dries into a hard film that is best described as consisting of pigments and additives suspended in the binder.

- Questioned and known paint specimens are best compared side by side under a stereoscopic microscope for color, surface texture, and color layer sequence.

- Pyrolysis gas chromatography and infrared spectrophotometry are used to distinguish most paint binder formulations.

- PDQ (Paint Data Query) is a computerized database that allows an analyst to obtain information on paints related to automobile make, model, and year.

Forensic Analysis of Glass

Glass that is broken and shattered into fragments and minute particles during the commission of a crime can be used to place a suspect at the crime scene. For example, chips of broken glass from a window may lodge in a suspect's shoes or garments during a burglary; particles of headlight glass found at the scene of a hit-and-run accident may confirm the identity of a suspect vehicle. All of these possibilities require the comparison of glass fragments found on the suspect, whether a person or vehicle, with the shattered glass remaining at the crime scene.

Composition of Glass

Glass is a hard, brittle, amorphous substance composed of sand (silicon oxides) mixed with various metal oxides. When sand is mixed with other metal oxides, melted at high temperatures, and then cooled to a rigid condition without crystallization, the product is glass. Soda (sodium carbonate) is normally added to the sand to lower its melting point and make it easier to work with. Another necessary ingredient is lime (calcium oxide), which is added to prevent the "soda-lime" glass from dissolving in water. The forensic scientist is often asked to analyze soda-lime glass, which is used for manufacturing most window and bottle glass. Usually the molten glass is cooled on top of a bath of molten tin. This manufacturing process produces flat glass typically used for windows. This type of glass is called *float glass*.

The common metal oxides found in soda-lime glass are sodium, calcium, magnesium, and aluminum. In addition, a wide variety of special glasses can be made by substituting in whole or in part other metal oxides for the silica, sodium, and calcium oxides. For example, automobile headlights and heat-resistant glass, such as Pyrex, are manufactured by adding boron oxide to the oxide mix. These glasses are therefore known as *borosilicates*.

Another type of glass that the reader may be familiar with is **tempered glass.** This glass is made stronger than ordinary window glass by introducing stress through rapid heating and cooling of the glass surfaces. When tempered glass breaks, it does not shatter but rather fragments or "dices" into small squares with little splintering (see Figure 13–8). Because of this safety feature, tempered glass is used in the side and rear windows of automobiles sold in the United States. The windshields of all cars manufactured in the United States are constructed from **laminated glass.** This glass derives its strength by sandwiching one layer of plastic between two pieces of ordinary window glass.

Comparing Glass Fragments

For the forensic scientist, comparing glass consists of finding and measuring the properties that will associate one glass fragment with another while minimizing or eliminating the possible existence of other sources. Considering the prevalence of glass in our society, it is easy to appreciate the magnitude of this analytical problem. Obviously, glass possesses its greatest evidential value when it can be individualized to one source. Such a determination, however, can be made only when the suspect and crime-scene fragments are assembled and physically fitted together. Comparisons of this type require piecing together irregular edges of broken glass as well as matching all irregularities and striations on the broken surfaces (see Figure 13–9). The possibility that two pieces of glass originating from different sources will fit together exactly is so unlikely as to exclude all other sources from practical consideration.

Unfortunately, most glass evidence is either too fragmentary or too minute to permit a comparison of this type. In such instances, the search for individual properties has proven fruitless. For example, the general chemical composition of various window glasses within the capability of

tempered glass
Glass to which strength is added by introducing stress through rapid heating and cooling of the glass surface

laminated glass
Two sheets of ordinary glass bonded together with a plastic film.

FIGURE 13–8 **When tempered glass breaks, it usually holds together without splintering.**
Courtesy Robert Ilewellyn, Alamy Images

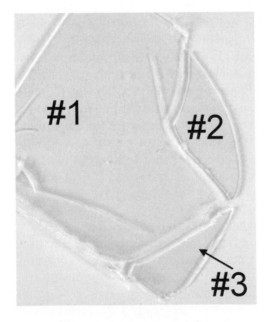

FIGURE 13–9 **A match of broken glass.
Note the physical fit of the edges.** *Courtesy Sirchie Finger Print Laboratories, Inc., Youngsville, N.C., www.sirchie.com*

current analytical methods has so far been found to be relatively uniform among various manufacturers and thus offers no basis for individualization. However, as more sensitive analytical techniques are developed, trace elements present in glass may prove to be distinctive and measurable characteristics.

The physical properties of density and refractive index are used most successfully for characterizing glass particles. However, these properties are class characteristics, which cannot provide the sole criteria for individualizing glass to a common source. They do, however, give the analyst sufficient data to evaluate the significance of a glass comparison, and the absence of comparable density and refractive index values will certainly exclude glass fragments that originate from different sources.

Measuring and Comparing Density

Density is defined as mass per unit volume:

$$\text{Density} = \frac{\text{mass}}{\text{volume}}$$

Density is an **intensive property** of matter—that is, it remains the same regardless of the size of an object; thus, it is a characteristic property of a substance and can be used in identification. Solids tend to be more dense than liquids, and liquids more dense than gases.

A simple procedure for determining the density of a solid is illustrated in Figure 13–10. First, the solid is weighed on a balance against known standard gram weights to determine its mass. The solid's volume is then determined from the volume of water it displaces. This is easily measured by filling a cylinder with a known volume of water (V_1), adding the object, and measuring the new water level (V_2). The difference ($V_2 - V_1$) in milliliters is equal to the volume of the solid. Density can now be calculated from the equation in grams per milliliter.

The fact that a solid object either sinks, floats, or remains suspended when immersed in a liquid can be accounted for by the property of density. For instance, if the density of a solid is greater than that of the liquid in which it is immersed, the object sinks; if the solid's density is less than that of the liquid, it floats; and when the solid and liquid have equal densities,

density
The measurement of mass per unit of volume.

intensive property
A property that is not dependent on the size of an object.

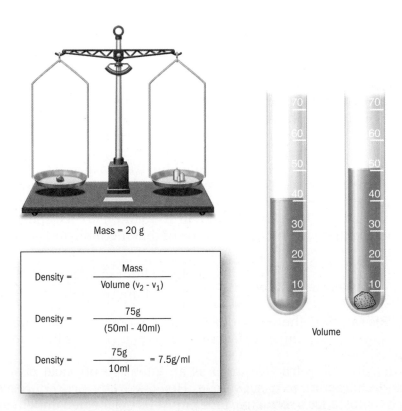

Mass = 20 g

$$\text{Density} = \frac{\text{Mass}}{\text{Volume } (v_2 - v_1)}$$

$$\text{Density} = \frac{75g}{(50ml - 40ml)}$$

$$\text{Density} = \frac{75g}{10ml} = 7.5g/ml$$

Volume

FIGURE 13–10 A simple procedure for determining the density of a solid is to first weigh it and then measure its volume by noting the volume of water it displaces.

the solid remains suspended in the liquid medium. This knowledge gives the criminalist a rather precise and rapid method for comparing densities of glass.

In a method known as *flotation,* a standard/reference glass particle is immersed in a liquid; a mixture of bromoform and bromobenzene may be used. The composition of the liquid is carefully adjusted by adding small amounts of bromoform or bromobenzene until the glass chip remains suspended in the liquid medium. At this point, the standard/ reference glass and liquid each have the same density. Glass chips of approximately the same size and shape as the standard/reference are now added to the liquid for comparison. If both the unknown and the standard/reference particles remain suspended in the liquid, their densities are equal to each other and to that of the liquid.[4] Particles of different densities either sink or float, depending on whether they are more or less dense than the liquid.

The density of a single sheet of window glass is not completely homogeneous throughout. It has a range of values that can differ by as much as 0.0003 g/mL. Therefore, in order to distinguish between the normal internal density variations of a single sheet of glass and those of glasses of different origins, it is advisable to let the comparative density approach but not exceed a sensitivity value of 0.0003 g/mL. The flotation method meets this requirement and can adequately distinguish glass particles that differ in density by 0.001 g/mL.

Determining and Comparing Refractive Index

Once glass has been distinguished by a density determination, different origins are immediately concluded. Comparable density results, however, require the added comparison of refractive indices. The bending of a light wave because of a change in velocity is called refraction. The phenomenon of refraction is apparent when we view an object that is immersed in a transparent medium such as water; because we are accustomed to thinking that light travels in a straight line, we often forget to account for refraction. For instance, suppose a ball is observed at the bottom of a swimming pool; the light rays reflected from the ball travel through the water and into the air to reach the eye. As the rays leave the water and enter the air, their velocity suddenly increases, causing them to be refracted. However, because of our assumption that light travels in a straight line, our eyes deceive us and make us think we see an object lying at a higher point than is actually the case. This phenomenon is illustrated in Figure 13–11.

refractive index
The ratio of the speed of light in a vacuum to its speed in a given medium.

The ratio of the velocity of light in a vacuum to its speed in any medium determines the **refractive index** of that medium and is expressed as follows:

$$\text{Refractive index} = \frac{\text{velocity of light in vacuum}}{\text{velocity of light in medium}}$$

For example, at 25°C the refractive index of water is 1.333. This means that light travels 1.333 times as fast in a vacuum as it does in water at this temperature.

Like density, the refractive index is an intensive physical property of matter and characterizes a substance. However, any procedure used to determine a substance's refractive index must be performed under carefully controlled temperature and lighting conditions, because the refractive index of a substance varies with its temperature and the wavelength of light passing through it. Nearly all tabulated refractive indices are determined at a standard wavelength, usually 589.3 nanometers; this is the predominant

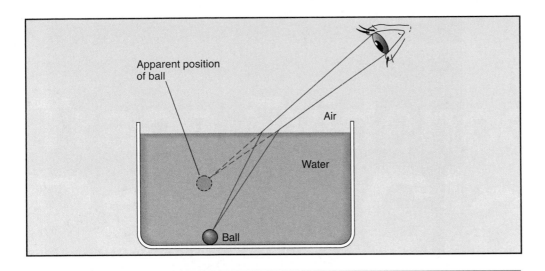

FIGURE 13–11 **Light is refracted when it travels obliquely from one medium to another.**

wavelength emitted by sodium light and is commonly known as the sodium D light.

When a transparent solid is immersed in a liquid with a similar refractive index, light is not refracted as it passes from the liquid into the solid. For this reason, the eye cannot distinguish the liquid–solid boundary, and the solid seems to disappear from view. This observation, as we will see, offers the forensic scientist a rather simple method for comparing the refractive indices of transparent solids.

This determination is best accomplished by the *immersion method*. For this, glass particles are immersed in a liquid medium whose refractive index is adjusted until it equals that of the glass particles. At this point, known as the *match point*, the observer notes the disappearance of the **Becke line**, indicating minimum contrast between the glass and liquid medium. The Becke line is a bright halo observed near the border of a particle that is immersed in a liquid of a different refractive index. This halo disappears when the medium and fragment have similar refractive indices.

The refractive index of an immersion fluid is best adjusted by changing the temperature of the liquid. Temperature control is, of course, critical to the success of the procedure. One approach is to heat the liquid in a special apparatus known as a *hot-stage microscope* (see Figure 13–12). The glass is immersed in a boiling liquid, usually a silicone oil, and heated at the rate of 0.2°C per minute until the match point is reached. The examiner then observes the disappearance of the Becke line on minute glass particles that are illuminated with sodium D light or at other wavelengths of light. If all the glass fragments examined have similar match points, it can be concluded that they have comparable refractive indices (see Figure 13–13). Furthermore, the examiner can determine the refractive index value of the immersion fluid as it changes with temperature. With this information, the exact numerical value of the glass refractive index can be calculated at the match point temperature.[5]

As with density, glass fragments removed from a single sheet of plate glass may not have a uniform refractive index value; instead, their values may vary by as much as 0.0002. Hence, for comparison purposes, the difference in refractive index between a standard/reference and questioned glass must exceed this value. This allows the examiner to differentiate between the normal internal variations present in a sheet of glass and those present in glasses that originated from completely different sources.

Becke line
A bright halo observed near the border of a particle immersed in a liquid of a different refractive index.

FIGURE 13–12 A hot-stage microscope. *Courtesy Chris Palenik, Microtrace, Elgin, IL, www.microtracescientific.com*

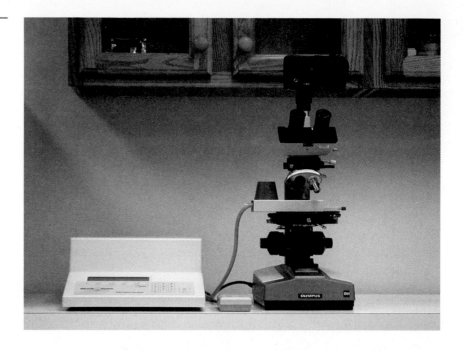

FIGURE 13–13 Determining the refractive index of glass. (a) Glass particles are immersed in a liquid of a much higher refractive index at a temperature of 77°C. (b) At 87°C the liquid still has a higher refractive index than the glass. (c) The refractive index of the liquid is closest to that of the glass at 97°C, as shown by the disappearance of the glass and the Becke lines. (d) At the higher temperature of 117°C, the liquid has a much lower index than the glass, and the glass is plainly visible. *Courtesy Walter C. McCrone*

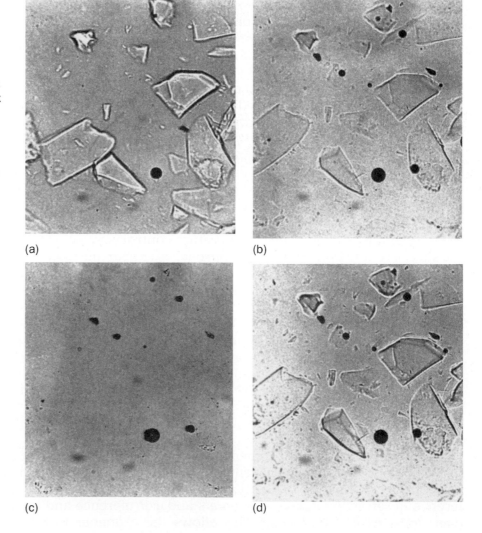

(a)

(b)

(c)

(d)

Closer Analysis

Grim 3

An automated approach for measuring the refractive index of glass fragments by temperature control using the immersion method with a hot-stage microscope is with the instrument known as GRIM 3 (Glass Refractive Index Measurement)* (see Figure 1). The GRIM 3 is a personal computer/video system designed to automate the measurements of the match temperature and refractive index for glass fragments. This instrument uses a video camera to view the glass fragments as they are being heated. As the immersion oil is heated or cooled, the contrast of the video image is measured continually until a minimum, the match point, is detected (see Figure 2). The match point temperature is then converted to a refractive index using stored calibration data.

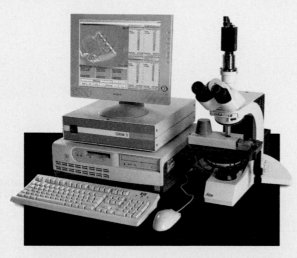

FIGURE 1 An automated system for glass fragment identification. *Courtesy Foster & Freeman Limited, Worcestershire, U.K., www.fosterfreeman.co.uk*

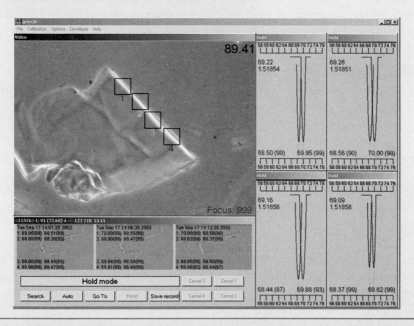

FIGURE 2 GRIM 3 identifies the refraction match point by monitoring a video image of the glass fragment immersed in an oil. As the immersion oil is heated or cooled, the contrast of the image is measured continuously until a minimum, the match point, is detected. *Courtesy Foster & Freeman Limited, Worcestershire, U.K., www.fosterfreeman.co.uk*

*Foster and Freeman Limited, 25 Swan Lane, Evesham, Worcestershire WRII 4PE, U.K.

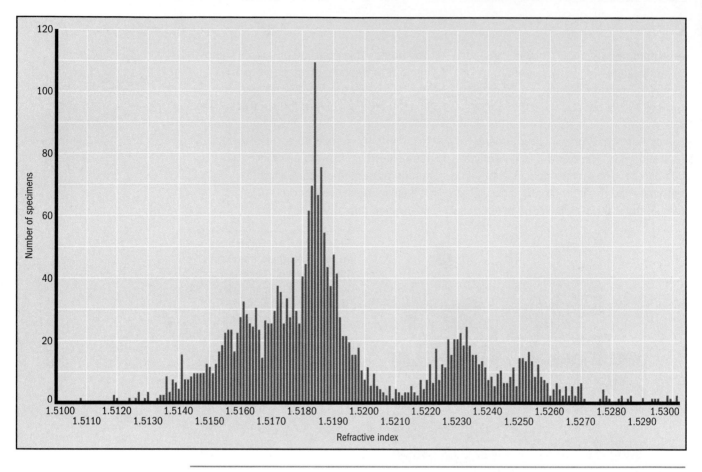

FIGURE 13–14 The frequency of occurrence of refractive index values (measured with sodium D light) for approximately two thousand flat glass specimens by the FBI Laboratory. *Courtesy FBI Laboratory, Washington, D.C.*

Classification of Glass Samples

A significant difference in either density or refractive index proves that the glasses examined do not have a common origin. But what if two pieces of glass exhibit comparable densities and comparable refractive indices? How certain can one be that they did, indeed, come from the same source? After all, there are untold millions of windows and other glass objects in this world.

To provide a reasonable answer to this question, the FBI Laboratory has collected density and refractive indices values from glass submitted to it for examination. What has emerged is a data bank correlating these values to their frequency of occurrence in the glass population of the United States. This collection is available to all forensic laboratories in the United States. This means that once a criminalist has completed a comparison of glass fragments, he or she can correlate their density and refractive index values to their frequency of occurrence and assess the probability that the fragments came from the same source.

Figure 13–14 shows the distribution of refractive index values (measured with sodium D light) for approximately two thousand glass specimens analyzed by the FBI. The wide distribution of values clearly demonstrates that the refractive index is a highly distinctive property of glass and is thus useful for defining its frequency of occurrence and hence its evidential value. For example, a glass fragment with a refractive index value of 1.5290 is found in approximately only 1 out of 2,000 specimens, whereas glass with a value of 1.5180 occurs approximately in 22 specimens out of 2,000.

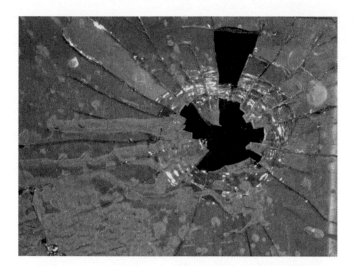

FIGURE 13–15 Radial and concentric fracture lines in a sheet of glass. *Courtesy Sirchie Finger Print Laboratories, Inc., Youngsville, N.C., www.sirchie.com*

The distinction between tempered and nontempered glass particles can be made by slowly heating and then cooling the glass (a process known as *annealing*). The change in the refractive index value for tempered glass upon annealing is significantly greater when compared to nontempered glass and thus serves as a point of distinction.[6]

Glass Fractures

Glass bends in response to any force that is exerted on any one of its surfaces; when the limit of its elasticity is reached, the glass fractures. Frequently, fractured window glass reveals information about the force and direction of an impact; such knowledge may be useful for reconstructing events at a crime-scene investigation.

The penetration of ordinary window glass by a projectile, whether a bullet or a stone, produces a familiar fracture pattern in which cracks both radiate outward and encircle the hole, as shown in Figure 13–15. The radiating lines are appropriately known as **radial fractures**, and the circular lines are termed **concentric fractures**.

Often it is difficult to determine just from the size and shape of a hole in glass whether it was made by a bullet or by some other projectile. For instance, a small stone thrown at a comparatively high speed against a pane of glass often produces a hole very similar to that produced by a bullet. On the other hand, a large stone can completely shatter a pane of glass in a manner closely resembling the result of a close-range shot. However, in the latter instance, the presence of gunpowder deposits on the shattered glass fragments points to damage caused by a firearm.

When it penetrates glass, a high-velocity projectile such as a bullet often leaves a round, crater-shaped hole surrounded by a nearly symmetrical pattern of radial and concentric cracks. The hole is inevitably wider on the exit side (see Figure 13–16), and hence examining it is an important step in determining the direction of impact. However, as the velocity of the penetrating projectile decreases, the irregularity of the shape of the hole and of its surrounding cracks increases, so that at some point the hole shape will not help determine the direction of impact. At this point, examining the radial and concentric fracture lines may help determine the direction of impact.

When a force pushes on one side of a pane of glass, the elasticity of the glass permits it to bend in the direction of the force applied. Once the elastic limit is exceeded, the glass begins to crack. As shown in Figure 13–17, the first fractures form on the surface opposite that of the penetrating force and develop into radial lines. The continued motion of the force places

radial fracture
A crack in a glass that extends outward like a spoke of a wheel from the point at which the glass was struck.

concentric fracture
A crack in a glass that forms a rough circle around the point of impact.

FIGURE 13–16 **A crater-shaped hole made by a pellet passing through glass. The upper surface is the exit side of the projectile.**
Courtesy New Jersey State Police

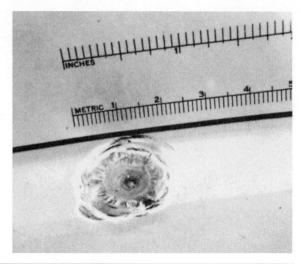

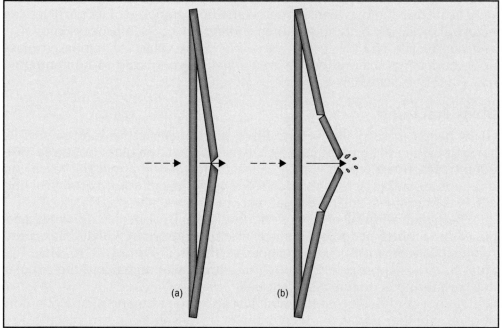

(a)   (b)

FIGURE 13–17   **The production of radial and concentric fractures in glass. (a) Radial cracks are formed first, beginning on the side of the glass opposite the destructive force. (b) Concentric cracks occur outward, starting on the same side of the force.**

tension on the front surface of the glass, resulting in the formation of concentric cracks. An examination of the edges of the radial and concentric cracks frequently reveals stress markings whose shape can be related to the side on which the window first cracked.

Stress marks, shown in Figure 13–18, are shaped like arches that are perpendicular to one glass surface and curved nearly parallel to the opposite surface. The importance of stress marks stems from the observation that the perpendicular edge always faces the surface on which the crack originated. Thus, in examining the stress marks on the edge of a radial crack near the point of impact, the perpendicular end is always found opposite the side from which the force of impact was applied. For a concentric fracture, the perpendicular end always faces the surface on which the force originated. A convenient way for remembering these observations is the 3R rule—*R*adial cracks form a *R*ight angle on the *R*everse side of the force. These facts enable

FIGURE 13–18   Stress marks on the edge of a radial glass fracture. The arrow indicates the direction of force. *Courtesy New Jersey State Police*

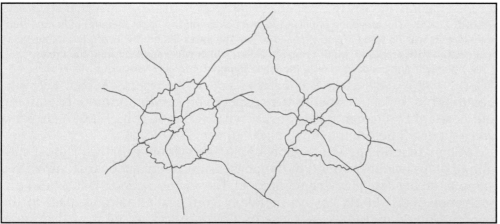

FIGURE 13–19   Two bullet holes in a piece of glass. The left hole preceded the right hole.

the examiner to determine the side on which a window was broken. Unfortunately, the absence of radial or concentric fracture lines prevents these observations from being applied to broken tempered glass.

When there have been successive penetrations of glass, it is frequently possible to determine the sequence of impact by observing the existing fracture lines and their points of termination. A fracture always terminates at an existing line of fracture. In Figure 13–19, the fracture on the left preceded that on the right; we know this because the latter's radial fracture lines terminate at the cracks of the former.

Collection and Preservation of Glass Evidence

The gathering of glass evidence at the crime scene and from the suspect must be thorough if the examiner is to have any chance to individualize the fragments to a common source. If even the remotest possibility exists that fragments may be pieced together, every effort must be made to collect all the glass found. For example, evidence collection at hit-and-run scenes must include all the broken parts of the headlight and reflector lenses. This evidence may ultimately prove invaluable in placing a suspect vehicle at the accident scene by matching the fragments with glass remaining in the

FIGURE 13–20 The presence of black tungsten oxide on the upper filament indicates that the filament was on when it was exposed to air. The lower filament was off, but its surface was coated with a yellow/ white tungsten oxide, which was vaporized from the upper ("on") filament and condensed onto the lower filament *Courtesy New Jersey State Police*

headlight or reflector shell of the suspect vehicle. In addition, examining the headlight's filaments may reveal whether an automobile's headlights were on or off before the impact (see Figure 13–20).

When an individual fit is improbable, the evidence collector must submit all glass evidence found in the possession of the suspect along with a sample of broken glass remaining at the crime scene. This standard/ reference glass should always be taken from any remaining glass in the window or door frames, as close as possible to the point of breakage. About one square inch of sample is usually adequate for this purpose. The glass fragments should be packaged in solid containers to avoid further breakage. If the suspect's shoes and/or clothing are to be examined for the presence of glass fragments, they should be individually wrapped in paper and transmitted to the laboratory. The field investigator should avoid removing such evidence from garments unless absolutely necessary for its preservation.

When a determination of the direction of impact is desired, all broken glass must be recovered and submitted for analysis. Wherever possible, the exterior and interior surfaces of the glass must be indicated. When this is not immediately apparent, the presence of dirt, paint, grease, or putty may indicate the exterior surface of the glass.

Key Points

- To compare glass fragments, a forensic scientist evaluates density and refractive index.

- The immersion method is used to determine a glass fragment's refractive index. It involves immersing a glass particle in a liquid medium whose refractive index is adjusted by varying its temperature. At the refractive index match point, the contrast between the glass and liquid is at a minimum.

- The flotation method is used to determine a glass fragment's density. It involves immersing a glass particle in a liquid whose density is carefully adjusted by adding small amounts of an appropriate liquid until the glass chip remains suspended in the liquid medium.

- By analyzing the radial and concentric fracture patterns in glass, the forensic scientist can determine the direction of impact by applying the 3R rule: *R*adial cracks form a *R*ight angle on the *R*everse side of the force.

Forensic Analysis of Soil

There are many definitions for the term *soil*; however, for forensic purposes, soil may be thought of as any disintegrated surface material, natural or and artificial, that lies on or near the earth's surface. Therefore, forensic examination of soil not only is concerned with the analysis of naturally occurring rocks, minerals, vegetation, and animal matter; it also encompasses the detection of such manufactured objects as glass, paint chips, asphalt, brick fragments, and cinders, whose presence may impart soil with characteristics that make it unique to a particular location. When this material is collected accidentally or deliberately in a manner that associates it with a crime under investigation, it becomes valuable physical evidence.[7]

Significance of Soil Evidence

The value of soil as evidence rests with its prevalence at crime scenes and its transferability between the scene and the criminal. Thus, soil or dried mud found adhering to a suspect's clothing or shoes or to an automobile, when compared to soil samples collected at the crime site, may link a suspect or object to the crime scene. As with most types of physical evidence, forensic soil analysis is comparative in nature; soil found in the possession of the suspect must be carefully collected to be compared to soil samplings from the crime scene and its vicinity.

However, one should not rule out the value of soil even if the site of the crime has not been ascertained. For instance, small amounts of soil may be found on a person or object far from the actual site of a crime. A geologist who knows the local geology may be able to use geological maps to direct police to the general vicinity where the soil was originally picked up and the crime committed.

Forensic Examination of Soil

Most soils can be differentiated by their gross appearance. A side-by-side visual comparison of the color and texture of soil specimens is easy to perform and provides a sensitive property for distinguishing soils that originate from different locations. Soil is darker when it is wet; therefore, color comparisons must always be made when all the samples are dried under identical laboratory conditions. It is estimated that there are nearly 1,100 distinguishable soil colors; hence, color offers a logical first step in a forensic soil comparison.

Low-power microscopic examination of soil reveals the presence of plant and animal materials as well as of artificial debris. Further high-power microscopic examination helps characterize minerals and rocks in earth materials. Although this approach to forensic soil identification requires the expertise of an investigator trained in geology, it can provide the most varied and significant points of comparison between soil samples. Only by carefully examining and comparing the minerals and rocks naturally present in soil can one take advantage of the large number of variations between soils and thus add to the evidential value of a positive comparison.[8]

mineral
A naturally occurring crystalline solid.

A mineral is a naturally occurring crystal, and like any other crystal, its physical properties—for example, color, geometric shape, density, and refractive index—are useful for identification. More than 2,200 minerals exist; however, most are so rare that forensic geologists usually encounter only about twenty of the more common ones. Rocks are composed of a combination of minerals and therefore exist in thousands of varieties on the earth's surface. They are usually identified by characterizing their mineral content and grain size (see Figure 13–21).

Considering the vast variety of minerals and rocks and the possible presence of artificial debris in soil, the forensic geologist is presented with many points of comparison between two or more specimens. The number of comparative points and their frequency of occurrence must be considered before concluding similarity between specimens and judging the probability of common origin.

Rocks and minerals not only are present in earth materials but are also used to manufacture a wide variety of industrial and commercial products. For example, the tools and garments of an individual suspected of breaking into a safe often contain traces of safe insulation. Safe insulation may be made from a wide combination of mineral mixtures that provide significant points of identification. Similarly, building materials such as brick, plaster, and concrete blocks are combinations of minerals and rocks that can easily be recognized and compared microscopically to similar minerals found on the breaking-and-entering suspect.

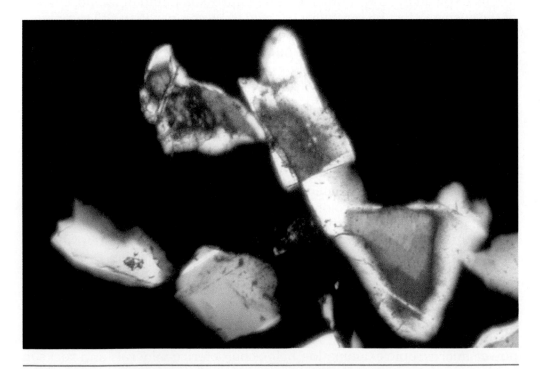

FIGURE 13–21 A mineral viewed under a microscope. *Courtesy Chris Palenik, Ph.D., Microtrace, Elgin, IL., www.microtracescientific.com*

Variations in Soil

The ultimate forensic value of soil evidence depends on its variation at the crime scene. If, for example, soil is indistinguishable for miles surrounding the location of a crime, it will have limited value in associating soil found on the suspect with that particular site. Significant conclusions relating a suspect to a particular location through a soil comparison may be made when variations in soil composition occur every 10 to 100 yards from the crime site. However, even when such variations do exist, the forensic geologist usually cannot individualize soil to any one location unless an unusual combination of rare minerals, rocks, or artificial debris can be located.

No statistically valid forensic studies have examined the variability of soil evidence. A study conducted in southern Ontario, Canada, seems to indicate that soil in that part of Canada shows extensive diversity. It estimated a probability of less than 1 in 50 of finding two soils that are indistinguishable in both color and mineral properties but originate in two different locations separated by a distance of 1,000 feet. Based on these preliminary results, similar diversity may be expected in the northern United States, Canada, northern Europe, and eastern Europe. However, such probability values can only generally indicate the variation of soil within these geographical areas. Each crime scene must be evaluated separately to establish its own soil variation probabilities.

Collection and Preservation of Soil Evidence

When gathering soil specimens, the evidence collector must give primary consideration to establishing the variation of soil at the crime-scene area. For this reason, standard/reference soils should be collected at various intervals within a 100-yard radius of the crime scene, as well as at the site of the crime, for comparison to the questioned soil. Soil specimens also should be collected at all possible alibi locations that the suspect may claim.

All specimens gathered should be representative of the soil that was removed by the suspect. In most cases, only the top layer of soil is picked up during the commission of a crime. Thus, standard/reference specimens must be removed from the surface without digging too deeply into the unrepresentative subsurface layers. Approximately a tablespoon or two of soil is all the laboratory needs for a thorough comparative analysis. All specimens collected should be packaged in individual containers, such as plastic vials. Each vial should be marked to indicate the location at which the sampling was made.

Soil found on a suspect must be carefully preserved for analysis. If it is found adhering to an object, as in the case of soil on a shoe, the investigator must not remove it. Instead, each object should be individually wrapped in paper, with the soil intact, and transmitted to the laboratory. Similarly, loose soil adhering to garments should not be removed; these items should be carefully and individually wrapped in paper bags and sent to the laboratory for analysis. Care must be taken that particles that may accidentally fall off the garment during transportation will remain in the paper bag.

When a lump of soil is found, it should be collected and preserved intact. For example, an automobile tends to collect and build up layers of soil under the fenders, body, and so on. The impact of an automobile with another object may jar some of this soil loose. Once the suspect car has been apprehended, a comparison of the soil left at the scene with soil remaining on the automobile may help establish that the car was present at the accident scene. In these situations, separate samples are collected from under all the fender and frame areas of the vehicle; care is taken to remove the soil in lump form to preserve the order in which the soil adhered to the car. Undoubtedly, during the normal use of an automobile, soil will be picked up from numerous locations over a period of months and years. This layering effect may impart soil with greater variation, and hence greater evidential value, than that normally associated with loose soil.

Key Points

- A side-by-side visual comparison of the color and texture of soil specimens provides a way to distinguish soils that originate from different locations.

- Minerals are naturally occurring crystalline solids found in soil. Their physical properties—for example, color, geometric shape, density, and refractive index—are useful for characterizing soils.

Forensic Brief

Soil: The Silent Witness

Alice Redmond was reported missing by her husband on a Monday night in 1983. Police learned that she had been seen with a co-worker, Mark Miller, after work that evening. When police questioned Miller, he stated that the two just "drove around" after work and then she dropped him off at home. Despite his statement, Miller was the prime suspect because he had a criminal record for burglary and theft.

Alice's car was recovered in town the following morning. The wheel wells were thickly coated in mud, which investigators hoped might provide a good lead. These hopes were dampened when police learned that Alice and her husband had attended a motorcycle race on Sunday, where her car was driven through deep mud.

After careful scrutiny, analysts found two colors of soil on the undercarriage of Alice's car. The thickest soil was brown; on top of the brown layer was a reddish soil that looked unlike anything in the county. Investigators hoped the reddish soil, which had to have been deposited sometime after the Sunday night motorcycle event

and before the vehicle was discovered on Tuesday morning, could link the vehicle to the location of Alice Redmond.

An interview with Mark Miller's sister provided a break in the case. She told police that Mark had visited her on Monday evening. During that visit, he confessed that he had driven Alice in her car across the Alabama state line into Georgia, killed her, and buried her in a remote location. Now that investigators had a better idea where to look for Alice, forensic analysts took soil samples that would prove or disprove Miller's sister's story.

Each field sample was dried and compared for color and texture by eye and stereomicroscopy to the reddish-colored soil gathered from the car. Next, soils that compared to the car were passed through a series of mesh filters, each of a finer gauge than the last. In this way, the components of the soil samples were physically separated by size. Finally, each fraction was analyzed and compared for mineral composition with the aid of a polarizing light microscope.

Only samples collected from areas across the Alabama state line near the suspected dump site were consistent with the topmost reddish soil recovered from Alice's car. This finding supported Miller's sister's story and was instrumental in Mark Miller's being charged with murder and kidnapping. After pleading guilty, the defendant led the authorities to where he had buried the body. The burial site was within a half mile of the location where forensic analysts had collected a soil sample consistent with the soil removed from Alice's vehicle.

Source: T. J. Hopen, "The Value of Soil Evidence," in *Trace Evidence Analysis: More Cases in Mute Witnesses*, M. M. Houck, ed. (Elsevier Academic Press, Burlington, MA: 2004), pp. 105–122.

Chapter Summary

Paint spread onto a surface dries into a hard film consisting of pigments and additives suspended in the binder. One of the most common types of paint examined in the crime laboratory is finishes from automobiles. Automobile manufacturers normally apply a variety of coatings to the body of an automobile. Hence, the wide diversity of automotive paint contributes to the forensic significance of an automobile paint comparison.

Questioned and known paint specimens are best compared side by side under a stereoscopic microscope for color, surface texture, and color layer sequence. Pyrolysis gas chromatography and infrared spectrophotometry are invaluable techniques for distinguishing most paint binder formulations, adding further significance to a forensic paint comparison.

The flotation and immersion methods are best used to determine a glass fragment's density and refractive index, respectively. In the flotation method, a glass particle is immersed in a liquid. The density of the liquid is carefully adjusted by adding small amounts of an appropriate liquid until the glass chip remains suspended in the liquid medium. At this point, the glass has the same density as the liquid medium and can be compared to other relevant pieces of glass. The immersion method involves immersing a glass particle in a liquid medium whose refractive index is adjusted by varying its temperature until it equals that of the glass particle. At this point, minimum contrast between the liquid and particle is observed.

By analyzing the radial and concentric fracture patterns in glass, the forensic scientist can determine the direction of impact. This can be accomplished by applying the 3R rule: *R*adial cracks form a *R*ight angle on the *R*everse side of the force.

The value of soil as evidence rests with its prevalence at crime scenes and its transferability between the scene and the criminal. Most soils can be differentiated by their gross appearance. A side-by-side visual comparison of the color and texture of soil specimens is easy to perform and provides a sensitive property for distinguishing soils that originate from different locations. In many forensic laboratories, forensic geologists characterize and compare the mineral content of soils.

Review Questions

1. The _____ component of paint is commonly a mixture of inorganic and organic compounds and imparts color and hiding (or opacity).

2. The support within paint is provided by the _____ component, which is a polymeric substance.

3. True or False: Layers of paint are applied in the order of primer first, then surfacer, basecoat, and finally clearcoat. _____

4. The questioned and known paint specimens collected from a scene should be compared side by side under a _____ microscope, which shows a three-dimensional image, to look at color, surface texture, and color layer sequence.

5. The most important physical property of paint in a forensic comparison is _____.

6. Paints can be individualized to a single source only when they have a sufficiently detailed _____.

7. True or False: Pyrolysis gas chromatography is a particularly valuable technique for characterizing paint's binder. _____

8. Pyrolysis gas chromatography yields a(n) _____ to reflect the chemical makeup of the binder.

9. The Royal Canadian Mounted Police's computerized database, called _____, allows an analyst to obtain information on paints related to automobile make, model, and year.

10. True or False: Paint samples removed for examination must always include all of the paint layers. _____

11. _____ is defined as a hard, brittle, amorphous substance composed of sand (silicon oxides) mixed with various metal oxides.

12. True or False: Automobile headlights and heat-resistant glass, such as Pyrex, are manufactured by adding lime oxide to the oxide mix. _____

13. _____ glass fragments, or "dices," into small squares with little splintering when broken.

14. _____ glass has added strength from the insertion of one layer of plastic between two pieces of ordinary window glass; it is used in automobile windshields.

15. Glass that can be physically pieced together has _____ characteristics.

16. The two most useful physical properties of glass for forensic comparisons are _____ and _____.

17. Comparing the relative densities of glass fragments is readily accomplished by a method known as _____.

18. When glass is immersed in a liquid of similar refractive index, its _____ disappears and minimum contrast between the glass and liquid is observed.

19. The exact numerical density and refractive indices of glass can be correlated to their _____ in order to assess the evidential value of the comparison.

20. The fracture lines radiating outward from a crack in glass are known as _____ fractures.

21. Glass fracture lines that encircle the hole in the glass are known as _____ fractures.

22. True or False: A crater-shaped hole in glass is wider on the side where the projectile entered the glass. _____

23. True or False: It is easy to determine from the size and shape of a hole in glass whether it was made by a bullet or some other projectile. _____

24. When glass's elastic limit is exceeded, the first fractures develop into radial lines on the surface of the (same, opposite) side to that of the penetrating force.

25. True or False: Stress marks on the edge of a radial crack are always perpendicular to the edge of the surface on which the impact force originated. _____

26. A fracture line from consecutive impacts will always _____ at an existing line fracture.

27. Collected glass fragment evidence should be packaged in _____ containers to avoid further breakage.

28. Glass-containing shoes and/or clothing should be individually wrapped in _____ and transmitted to the laboratory.

29. True or False: Most soils have indistinguishable color and texture. _____

30. Color and texture comparisons cannot be made on samples until they are all _____ with identical laboratory procedures.

31. Naturally occurring crystals commonly found in soils are _____.

32. True or False: The ultimate value of soil as evidence depends on its variation at the crime scene. _____

33. To develop an idea of the soil variation within the crime-scene area, standard/reference soils should be collected at various intervals within a _____-yard radius of the crime scene.

34. True or False: Each object collected at the crime scene that contains soil evidence must be individually wrapped in plastic, with the soil intact, and transmitted to the laboratory. _____

Application and Critical Thinking

1. You are investigating a hit-and-run accident and have identified a suspect vehicle. Describe how you would collect paint to determine whether the suspect vehicle was involved in the accident. Be sure to indicate the tools you would use and the steps you would take to prevent cross-contamination.

2. An accident investigator arrives at the scene of a hit-and-run collision. The driver who remained at the scene reports that the windshield or a side window of the car that struck him shattered on impact. The investigator searches the accident site and collects a large number of fragments of tempered glass.

This is the only type of glass recovered from the scene. How can the glass evidence help the investigator locate the vehicle that fled the scene?

3. Indicate the order in which the bullet holes were made in the glass depicted in the figure at left below. Explain the reason for your answer.

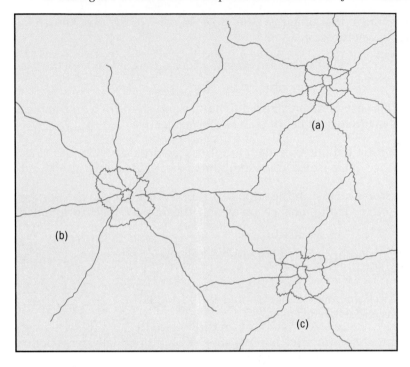

4. The figure at right above depicts stress marks on the edge of a glass fracture caused by the application of force. If this is a radial fracture, from which side of the glass (left or right) was the force applied? From which side was force applied if it is a concentric fracture? Explain the reason for your answers.

5. Criminalist Jared Heath responds to the scene of an assault on an unpaved lane in a rural neighborhood. Rain had fallen steadily the night before, making the area quite muddy. A suspect with very muddy shoes was apprehended nearby, but claimed to have picked up the mud either from his garden or from the unpaved parking lot of a local restaurant. Jared uses a spade to remove several samples of soil, each about 2 inches deep, from the immediate crime scene, and places each in a separate plastic vial. He collects the muddy shoes and wraps them in plastic as well. At the laboratory, he unpackages the soil samples and examines them carefully, one at a time. He then analyzes the soil on the shoes to see whether it matches the soil from the crime scene. What mistakes, if any, did Jared make in his investigation?

Case Analysis

In the case of the missing body, police suspected that the female victim had been moved from the location where she was murdered. Although an eyewitness placed a woman at the scene of the shooting, trace evidence ultimately was the key to solving the case.

1. What was the primary challenge facing the investigators in this case?

2. What items of evidence directly linked the victim to the suspect? Which items indirectly linked the two?

3. How was paint evidence used to show that the female victim was shot at the garage?

Web Resources

Collecting Crime Evidence from Earth (An online article by forensic geologist Raymond C. Murray that includes a discussion of soil analysis)
www.forensicgeology.net/science.htm

Forensic Examination of Soil Evidence (An online report from Interpol about methods and advances in soil examination)
www.interpol.int/Public/Forensic/IFSS/meeting13/Reviews/Soil.pdf

Forensic Paint Analysis and Comparison Guidelines (An article from the July 1999 issue of the online FBI journal *Forensic Science Communications*)
www.fbi.gov/hq/lab/fsc/backissu/july1999/painta.htm

Physical Properties of Glass and Soil (An online slideshow covering important points in this chapter)
www.stfrancis.edu/ns/diab/ForensicCoursePPT/Ch4webGlass&Soil.htm

Endnotes

1. P. G. Rodgers et al., "The Classification of Automobile Paint by Diamond Window Infrared Spectrophotometry, Part I: Binders and Pigments," *Canadian Society of Forensic Science Journal* 9 (1976): 1; T. J. Allen, "Paint Sample Presentation for Fourier Transform Infrared Microscopy," *Vibration Spectroscopy* 3 (1992): 217.
2. G. Edmondstone, J. Hellman, K. Legate, G. L. Vardy, and E. Lindsay, "An Assessment of the Evidential Value of Automotive Paint Comparisons," *Canadian Society of Forensic Science Journal* 37 (2004): 147.
3. J. L. Buckle et al., "PDQ—Paint Data Queries: The History and Technology behind the Development of the Royal Canadian Mounted Police Laboratory Services Automotive Paint Database," *Canadian Society of Forensic Science Journal* 30 (1997): 199. An excellent discussion of the PDQ database is also available in A. Beveridge, T. Fung, and D. MacDougall, "Use of Infrared Spectroscopy for the Characterisation of Paint Fragments," in B. Caddy, ed., *Forensic Examination of Glass and Paint* (New York: Taylor & Francis, 2001), pp. 222–233.
4. As an added step, the analyst can determine the exact numerical density value of the particles of glass by transferring the liquid to a density meter, which will electrically measure and calculate the liquid's density. See A. P. Beveridge and C. Semen, "Glass Density Measurement Using a Calculating Digital Density Meter," *Canadian Society of Forensic Science Journal* 12 (1979): 113.
5. A. R. Cassista and P. M. L. Sandercock, "Precision of Glass Refractive Index Measurements: Temperature Variation and Double Variation Methods, and the Value of Dispersion," *Canadian Society of Forensic Science Journal* 27 (1994): 203.
6. G. Edmondstone, "The Identification of Heat Strengthened Glass in Windshields," *Canadian Society of Forensic Journal* 30 (1997): 181.
7. E. P. Junger, "Assessing the Unique Characteristics of Close-Proximity Soil Samples: Just How Useful Is Soil Evidence?" *Journal of Forensic Sciences* 41 (1996): 27.
8. W. J. Graves, "A Mineralogical Soil Classification Technique for the Forensic Scientist," *Journal of Forensic Sciences* 24 (1979): 323; M. J. McVicar and W. J. Graves, "The Forensic Comparison of Soil by Automated Scanning Electron Microscopy," *Canadian Society of Forensic Science Journal* 30 (1997): 241.

CHAPTER 13

Case Reading

The CBS Murders*

In the early morning hours . . . atop a lonely roof garage on the west side of Manhattan, three men [all employed by CBS-TV] were found murdered. Each man had been shot once in the back of the head. A light-colored van was seen speeding away from the scene. Hours later, in a secluded alley street on the lower east side of Manhattan, the body of a fully clothed woman was found lying face down by two dog walkers. The woman had been killed in the same manner as the men on the roof garage. The condition of the woman's body, and other evidence, made it apparent that she had been shot at the garage, and then transported to the alley.

An eyewitness to the incident stated that he saw a man shoot a woman and place her in a light-colored van. The gunman then chased down the three men who were coming to the woman's aid, and shot each one of them. Days later, the prime suspect to the killings was arrested in Kentucky, in a black-colored van.

Numerous items of evidence (over 100) were collected from the van, and forwarded to the New York City police laboratory for examination. Among the items of evidence forwarded were three sets of vacuum sweepings from the van's interior.

An autopsy of the woman produced several items of trace evidence that were removed from the victim and forwarded to the author for microscopic examination. The woman's clothing was also received by the author for trace analysis.

A prime question that arose during the investigation was: could the woman's body, which had been placed in a

light-colored van at the garage, and later left in an alley on the lower east side, be associated with the black van recovered over 1000 km (600 miles) away from the scene? Microscopic analysis and comparison of the trace evidential materials found on the victim and inside the van made this association possible.

Listed in Table 1 are all the items of similar trace materials that both the victim and the van had in common.

Microscopic comparisons of the questioned human head hair present on the victim's clothing were made with known samples. Ten of the brown-colored and gray-colored Caucasian head hairs from the victim's blazer were consistent in microscopic characteristics to the defendant's known head hair sample. One chemically treated head hair found on the victim was consistent in microscopic characteristics to the known head hair sample obtained from the defendant's wife. One forcibly removed, brown-colored, Caucasian head hair that was found on the rear door of the van's interior by the Kentucky state police was found to be consistent in all characteristics with the decedent's known head hair sample.

Microscopic comparisons of the white- and brown/white-colored dog hair from the victim's clothing, and the van's interior, were made with known samples of dog hair obtained from a dog owned by the defendant's nephew, the van's previous owner. The questioned dog hairs were found to be consistent with the hair from the nephew's dog. The white seed that was recovered from the victim's mouth by the medical examiner, and the white seed that was found in the van's sweepings by the author, were forwarded to an internationally known botanist for

* This case takes its title from the fact that the three victims were employees of CBS-TV.

identification and comparison. During the trial, the botanist testified that the two seeds were identical in all respects, and that although he could not identify the seed, both were either from the same species of plant, if not the same plant, probably a rare wild flower.

Sixteen gray metallic/black-colored paint chips from the victim and her clothing were compared to the gray metallic/black-colored paint removed from the van. Samples from the questioned and known sources were examined and compared by microscopic, chemical, and instrumental means. All of the paint specimens from the van and from the victim were found to be similar in all respects.

The remaining items of trace evidence from the victim and the van were examined and compared microscopically, and where necessary, by chemical and instrumental methods. Each of the remaining types of trace evidence from the victim was found to be similar to its counterpart from the van.

Blue- and black-colored flakes of acrylic paint were found in the van's sweepings, and on the suspect's sneakers. No blue- or black-colored paint flakes were found on the victim and her clothing. During a crime scene search of the defendant's residence in New Jersey, a large quantity of blue- and black-colored acrylic paint was found in the garage. It was apparent from the evidence present in the defendant's garage that a large rectangular shaped object had recently been painted with blue- and black-colored paint. The blue and black paint flakes from all the sources and the known blue (undercoat) and black (topcoat) paint from the van were compared by microscopic, chemical, and instrumental means. All the samples of paint were found to be consistent in every respect.

Table 1	Items of Similar Trace Evidence That Were Recovered from Both the Victim and the Van's Interior	
	Source	
Trace Evidence	**Victim**	**Van**
White seed	mouth	sweepings
Paint chips gray/metallic/black	hair and wool blazer	sweepings and floor
Sawdust	hair, blazer, and sheet	sweepings and misc. items
Glass fragments clear amber green	wool blazer and sheet	sweepings and misc. items
Cellophane	wool blazer	floor
Urethane foam foam mattress	wool blazer	sweepings, misc. items, and foam mattress
Blue olefin plastic	skirt	floor
Dog hair brown/white white	wool blazer	sweepings and misc. items
Human hair brown gray	wool blazer	hairbrush, sweepings, and misc. items

At the trial, extensive testimony concerning the collection, examination, identification, and comparison of the trace evidence from the victim and the van was given by the author, over a two-day period. When questioned about the source of the trace evidence found on the victim and her clothing, the author stated unequivocally that the trace evidence on the victim was from the defendant's van. On the basis of this evidence and other circumstantial evidence, the defendant was found guilty of all charges and sentenced to 100 years in prison.

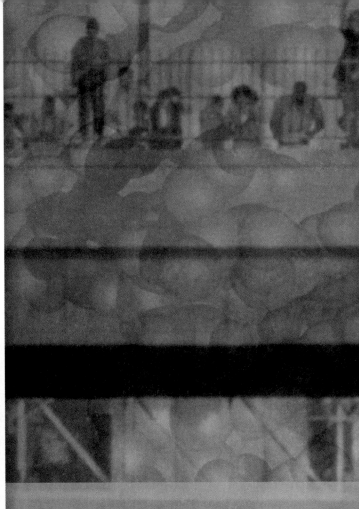

O. J. Simpson: A Mountain of Evidence

On June 12, 1994, police arrived at the home of Nicole Simpson only to view a horrific scene. The bodies of O. J. Simpson's estranged wife and her friend Ron Goldman were found on the path leading to the front door of Nicole's home. Both bodies were covered in blood and had received deep knife wounds. Nicole's head was nearly severed from her body. This was not a well-planned murder. A trail of blood led away from the murder scene. Blood was found in O. J. Simpson's Bronco. Blood drops were on O. J.'s driveway and in the foyer of his home. A blood-soaked sock was located in O. J. Simpson's bedroom, and a bloodstained glove rested outside his residence.

As DNA was extracted and profiled from each bloodstained article, a picture emerged that seemed to irrefutably link Simpson to the murders. A trail of DNA leaving the crime scene was consistent with O. J.'s profile, as was the DNA found entering Simpson's home. Simpson's DNA profile was found in the Bronco along with that of both victims. The glove contained the DNA profiles of Nicole and Ron, and the sock had Nicole's DNA profile. At trial, the defense team valiantly fought back. Miscues in evidence collection were craftily exploited. The defense strategy was to paint a picture of not only an incompetent investigation, but one that was tinged with dishonest police planting evidence. The strategy worked. O. J. Simpson was acquitted of murder.

Biological Stain Analysis:
DNA

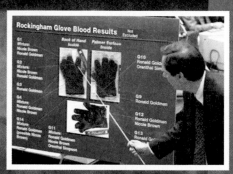

Key Terms

acid phosphatase
agglutination
allele
antibody
antigen
antiserum
aspermia
buccal cells
chromosome
deoxyribonucleic acid (DNA)
egg
gene
heterozygous
homozygous
locus
low copy number
mitochondria
multiplexing
nucleotide
oligospermia
plasma
polymerase chain reaction
(PCR)
serum
short tandem repeat (STR)
sperm
substrate control
X chromosome
Y chromosome
Y-STRs
zygote

Learning Objectives

After studying this chapter, you should be able to:

- List the A-B-O antigens and antibodies found in the blood for each of the four blood types: A, B, AB, and O.

- List and describe forensic tests used to characterize a stain as blood.

- List the laboratory tests necessary to characterize seminal stains.

- Explain how suspect blood and semen stains are to be properly preserved for laboratory examination.

- Contrast chromosomes and genes.

- Name the parts of a nucleotide and explain how they are linked together to form DNA.

- Understand the concept of base pairing as it relates to the double-helix structure of DNA.

- Explain the technology of polymerase chain reaction (PCR) and how it applies to forensic DNA typing

- Understand the DNA-typing technique known as short tandem repeats (STRs).

- Describe the difference between nuclear and mitochondrial DNA.

- Understand the use of DNA computerized databases in criminal investigation.

- List the necessary procedures for the proper preservation of biological evidence for laboratory DNA analysis.

In 1901, Karl Landsteiner announced one of the most significant discoveries of the twentieth century—the typing of blood—a finding that twenty-nine years later earned him a Nobel Prize. For years physicians had attempted to transfuse blood from one individual to another. Their efforts often ended in failure because the transfused blood tended to coagulate, or clot, in the body of the recipient, causing instantaneous death. Landsteiner was the first to recognize that all human blood was not the same; instead, he found that blood is distinguishable by its group or type.

Out of Landsteiner's work came the classification system that we call the *A-B-O system*. Now physicians had the key for properly matching the blood of a donor to that of a recipient. One blood type cannot be mixed with a different blood type without disastrous consequences. This discovery, of course, had important implications for blood transfusion, and millions of lives have since been saved.

Meanwhile, Landsteiner's findings opened a new field of research in the biological sciences. Others began to pursue the identification of additional characteristics that could further differentiate blood. By 1937, the Rh factor in blood had been demonstrated and, shortly thereafter, numerous blood factors or groups were discovered. More than 100 blood factors have been identified. However, the ones in the A-B-O system are still the most important for properly matching a donor and recipient for a transfusion.

Until the early 1990s, forensic scientists focused on blood factors, such as A-B-O, as offering the best means for linking blood to an individual. What made these factors so attractive was that in theory no two individuals, except for identical twins, could be expected to have the same combination of blood factors. In other words, blood factors are controlled genetically and have the potential of being a highly distinctive feature for personal identification. What makes this observation so relevant is the great frequency of bloodstains at crime scenes, especially crimes of the most serious nature—homicides, assaults, and rapes. Consider, for example, a transfer of blood between the victim and assailant during a struggle;

that is, the victim's blood is transferred to the suspect's garment or vice versa. If the criminalist could individualize human blood by identifying all of its known factors, the result would be strong evidence for linking the suspect to the crime.

The advent of DNA technology has dramatically altered the approach of forensic scientists toward the individualization of bloodstains and other biological evidence. The search for genetically controlled blood factors in bloodstains has been abandoned in favor of characterizing biological evidence by select regions of our deoxyribonucleic acid (DNA), which carries the body's genetic information. As a result, the individualization of dried blood and other biological evidence has become a reality and has significantly altered the role that crime laboratories play in criminal investigations. In fact , the high sensitivity of DNA analysis has even altered the types of materials collected from crime scenes in the search for DNA.

deoxyribonucleic acid (DNA)
The molecules that carry the body's genetic information.

The Nature of Blood

The word *blood* refers to a highly complex mixture of cells, enzymes, proteins, and inorganic substances. The fluid portion of blood is called plasma; it is composed principally of water and accounts for 55 percent of blood content. Suspended in the plasma are solid materials consisting chiefly of several types of cells—red blood cells (erythrocytes), white blood cells (leukocytes), and platelets. The solid portion of blood accounts for 45 percent of its content. Blood clots when a protein in the plasma known as *fibrin* traps and enmeshes the red blood cells. If the clotted material were removed, a pale yellowish liquid known as serum would be left.

plasma
The fluid portion of unclotted blood.

serum
The liquid that separates from the blood when a clot is formed.

Obviously, considering the complexity of blood, any discussion of its function and chemistry would have to be extensive, extending beyond the scope of this text. It is certainly far more relevant at this point to concentrate our discussion on the blood components that are directly pertinent to the forensic aspects of blood identification—the red blood cells and the blood serum.

Antigens and Antibodies

Red blood cells transport oxygen from the lungs to the body tissues and remove carbon dioxide from tissues by transporting it back to the lungs, where it is exhaled. However, for reasons unrelated to the red blood cell's transporting mission, on the surface of each cell are millions of characteristic chemical structures called antigens. Antigens impart specific characteristics to the red blood cells. Blood antigens are grouped into systems depending on their relationship to one another. More than fifteen blood antigen systems have been identified to date; of these, the A-B-O and Rh systems are the most important.

antigen
A substance, usually a protein, that stimulates the body to produce antibodies against it.

If an individual is type A, this simply indicates that each red blood cell has A antigens on its surface; similarly, all type B individuals have B antigens, and the red blood cells of type AB individuals contain both A and B antigens. Type O individuals have neither A nor B antigens on their cells. Hence, the presence or absence of A and B antigens on the red blood cells determines a person's blood type in the A-B-O system.

Another important blood antigen has been designated as the *Rh factor*, or D antigen. Those people having the D antigen are said to be *Rh positive*; those without this antigen are *Rh negative*. In routine blood banking, the

antibody
A protein in the blood serum that destroys or inactivates a specific antigen.

antiserum
Blood serum that contains specific antibodies.

agglutination
The clumping together of red blood cells by the action of an antibody.

presence or absence of the three antigens—A, B, and D—must be determined in testing the compatibility of the donor and recipient.

Serum is important because it contains proteins known as **antibodies**. The fundamental principle of blood typing is that for every antigen, there exists a specific antibody. Each antibody symbol contains the prefix *anti-*, followed by the name of the antigen for which it is specific. Hence, anti-A is specific only for A antigen, anti-B for B antigen, and anti-D for D antigen. The serum-containing antibody is referred to as the **antiserum**, meaning a serum that reacts against something (antigens).

An antibody reacts only with its specific antigen and no other. Thus, if serum containing anti-B is added to red blood cells carrying the B antigen, the two will combine, causing the antibody to attach itself to the cell. Antibodies are normally *bivalent*—that is, they have two reactive sites. This means that each antibody can simultaneously be attached to antigens located on two different red blood cells. This creates a vast network of cross-linked cells usually seen as clumping or **agglutination** (see Figure 14–1).

Let's look a little more closely at this phenomenon. In normal blood, shown in Figure 14–2(a), antigens on red blood cells and antibodies coexist

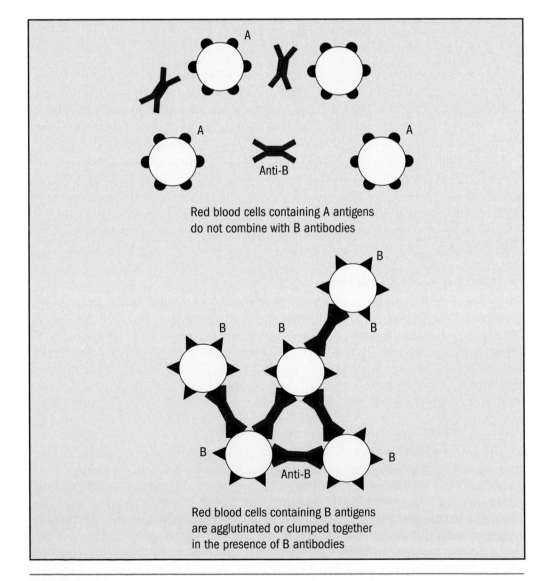

Red blood cells containing A antigens do not combine with B antibodies

Red blood cells containing B antigens are agglutinated or clumped together in the presence of B antibodies

FIGURE 14–1

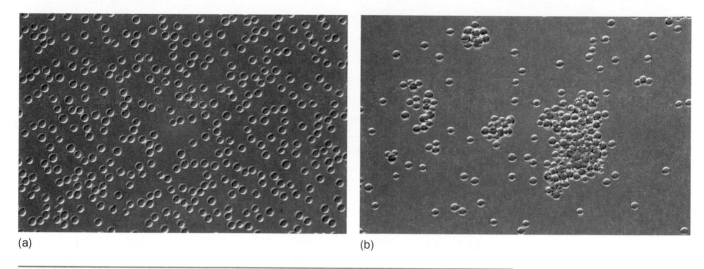

FIGURE 14–2 **(a) A microscopic view of normal red blood cells (500x). (b) A microscopic view of agglutinated red blood cells (500x).** *Courtesy J. C. Revy, Phototake NYC*

without destroying each other because the antibodies present are not specific toward any of the antigens. However, suppose a foreign serum added to the blood introduces a new antibody. This results in a specific antigen–antibody reaction that immediately causes the red blood cells to link together, or agglutinate, as shown in Figure 14–2(b).

Evidently, nature has taken this situation into account, for when we examine the serum of type A blood, we find anti-B and no anti-A. Similarly, type B blood contains only anti-A, type O blood has both anti-A and anti-B, and type AB blood contains neither anti-A nor anti-B. The antigen and antibody components of normal blood are summarized in the following table:

Blood Type	Antigens on Red Blood Cells	Antibodies in Serum
A	A	Anti-B
B	B	Anti-A
AB	AB	Neither anti-A nor anti-B
O	Neither A nor B	Both anti-A and anti-B

The reasons for the fatal consequences of mixing incompatible blood during a transfusion should now be quite obvious. For example, the transfusion of type A blood into a type B patient will cause the natural anti-A in the blood of the type B patient to react promptly with the incoming A antigens, resulting in agglutination. In addition, the incoming anti-B of the donor will react with the B antigens of the patient.

Immunoassay Techniques

The concept of a specific antigen–antibody reaction is finding application in other areas unrelated to blood typing. Most significantly, this approach has been extended to the detection of drugs in blood and urine. Antibodies that react with drugs do not exist naturally; however, they can be produced in animals such as rabbits by first combining the drug with a protein and injecting this combination into the animal. This drug–protein complex

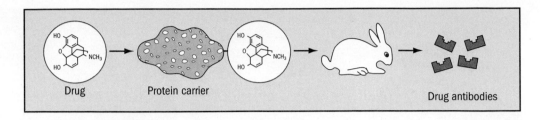

FIGURE 14–3 Stimulating production of drug antibodies.

acts as an antigen stimulating the animal to produce antibodies (see Figure 14–3). The recovered blood serum of the animal now contains antibodies that are specific or nearly specific to the drug.

Currently, each day, thousands of individuals are voluntarily being subjected to urinalysis tests for the presence of drugs-of-abuse. These individuals include military personnel, transportation industry employees, police and corrections personnel, and subjects requiring preemployment drug screening. Immunoassay testing for drugs has proven quite suitable for handling the large volume of specimens that must be rapidly analyzed on a daily basis for drug content. Testing laboratories have available to them a variety of commercially prepared sera arising from animals being injected with any one of a variety of drugs. Once a particular serum is added to a urine specimen, it's designed to interact with either opiates, cannabinoids, cocaine, amphetamines, phencyclidine, barbiturates, methadone, or other drugs. A word of caution: immunoassay is only presumptive in nature and its result must be confirmed by additional testing.

Key Points

- An antibody reacts or agglutinates only with its specific antigen. The concept of specific antigen–antibody reactions has been applied to techniques for the detection of drugs-of-abuse in blood and urine.

- Every red blood cell contains either an A antigen, a B antigen, or no antigen (this is called type O). The type of antigen on one's red blood cells determines one's A-B-O blood type. Persons with type A blood have A antigens on their red blood cells, those with type B blood have B antigens, and those with type O blood have no antigens on their red blood cells.

- To produce antibodies capable of reacting with drugs, one first combines a specific drug with a protein and injects this combination into an animal such as a rabbit. This drug–protein complex acts as an antigen, stimulating the animal to produce antibodies. The recovered blood serum of the animal will now contain antibodies that are specific or nearly specific to the drug.

Forensic Characterization of Bloodstains

The criminalist must answer the following questions when examining dried blood: (1) Is it blood? (2) From what species did the blood originate? (3) If the blood is human, how closely can it be associated with a particular individual?

Color Tests

The determination of blood is best made by means of a preliminary color test. For many years, the most common test was the *benzidine color test*. However, because benzidine has been identified as a known carcinogen, its use has generally been discontinued, and the chemical phenolphthalein is usually substituted in its place (this test is also known as the *Kastle-Meyer color test*).[1]

Both the benzidine and Kastle-Meyer color tests are based on the observation that blood *hemoglobin* possesses peroxidase-like activity. Peroxidases are enzymes that accelerate the oxidation of several classes of organic compounds when combined with peroxides. For example, when a bloodstain, phenolphthalein reagent, and hydrogen peroxide are mixed together, oxidation of the hemoglobin in the blood produces a deep pink color.

The Kastle-Meyer test is not a specific test for blood; some vegetable materials, for instance, may turn Kastle-Meyer pink. These substances include potatoes and horseradish. However, such materials will probably not be encountered in criminal situations, and thus from a practical point of view, a positive Kastle-Meyer test is highly indicative of blood. Field investigators have found Hemastix strips a useful presumptive field test for blood. Designed as a urine dipstick test for blood, the strip can be moistened with distilled water and placed in contact with a suspect bloodstain. The appearance of a green color indicates blood.

WebExtra 14.1

See a Color Test for Blood
www.prenhall.com/saferstein

Luminol and Bluestar®

Another important presumptive identification test for blood is the *luminol* test.[2] Unlike the benzidine and Kastle-Meyer tests, the reaction of luminol with blood produces light rather than color. After spraying luminol reagent onto suspect items, agents darken the room; any bloodstains produce a faint blue glow, known as *luminescence*. Using luminol, investigators can quickly screen large areas for bloodstains. A relatively new product, Bluestar®, is now available to be used in place of luminol (www.bluestar-forensic.com). Bluestar® is easy to mix in the field. Its reaction with blood can be observed readily without having to create complete darkness.

The luminol and Bluestar® tests are extremely sensitive—capable of detecting bloodstains diluted up to 100,000 times. For this reason, spraying large areas such as carpets, walls, flooring, or the interior of a vehicle may reveal blood traces or patterns that would have gone unnoticed under normal lighting conditions (see Figure 14–4). Luminol and Bluestar® will not interfere with any subsequent DNA testing.[3]

Microcrystalline Tests

The identification of blood can be made more specific if microcrystalline tests are performed on the material. Several tests are available; the two most popular ones are the *Takayama* and *Teichmann tests*. Both depend on the addition of specific chemicals to the blood to form characteristic crystals containing hemoglobin derivatives. Crystal tests are far less sensitive than color tests for blood identification and are more susceptible to interference from contaminants that may be present in the stain.

Precipitin Test

Once the stain has been characterized as blood, the serologist determines whether the blood is of human or animal origin. The standard test for this is the *precipitin* test. Precipitin tests are based on the fact that

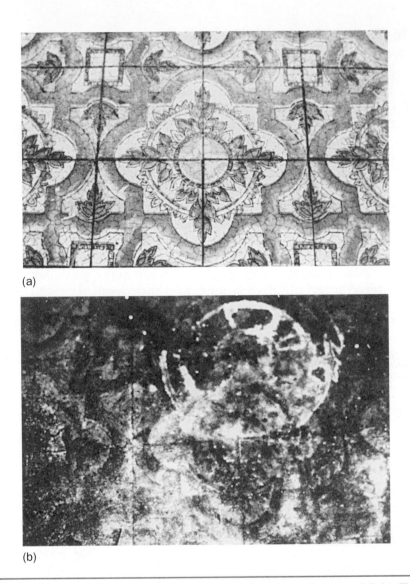

(a)

(b)

FIGURE 14–4 **(a) A section of a linoleum floor photographed under normal light. This floor was located in the residence of a missing person. (b) The same section of the floor shown in (a) after spraying with luminol. A circular pattern was revealed. Investigators concluded that the circular blood pattern was left by the bottom of a bucket carried about during the cleaning up of the blood. A small clump of sponge, blood, and hair was found near where this photograph was taken.** *Courtesy North Carolina State Bureau of Investigation*

when animals (usually rabbits) are injected with human blood, antibodies form that react with the invading human blood to neutralize its presence. The investigator can recover these antibodies by bleeding the animal and isolating the blood serum, which contains antibodies that specifically react with human antigens. For this reason, the serum is known as *human anti-serum.* In the same manner, by injecting rabbits with the blood of other known animals, virtually any kind of animal antiserum can be produced. Antiserums are commercially available for humans and for a variety of commonly encountered animals—for example, dogs, cats, and deer.

Several techniques have been devised for performing precipitin tests on bloodstains. The classic method is to layer an extract of the bloodstain on top of the human antiserum in a capillary tube. Human blood, or for that matter, any protein of human origin in the extract, reacts specifically with

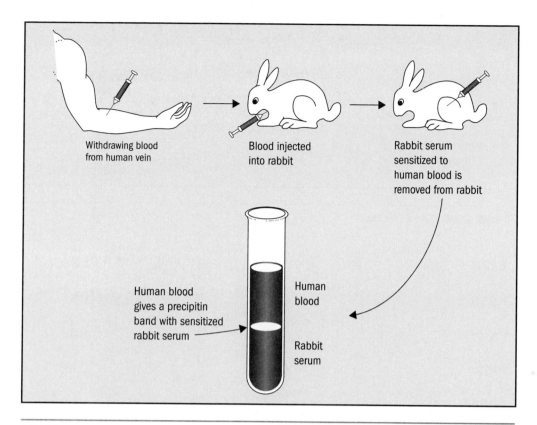

Withdrawing blood from human vein

Blood injected into rabbit

Rabbit serum sensitized to human blood is removed from rabbit

Human blood gives a precipitin band with sensitized rabbit serum

Human blood

Rabbit serum

FIGURE 14–5   The precipitin test.

antibodies present in the antiserum, as indicated by the formation of a cloudy ring or band at the interface of the two liquids (see Figure 14–5).

Gel Diffusion

Another precipitin method, called *gel diffusion,* takes advantage of the fact that antibodies and antigens diffuse or move toward one another on a plate coated with a gel medium made from a natural polymer called agar. The extracted bloodstain and the human antiserum are placed in separate holes opposite each other on the gel. If the blood is human, a line of precipitation forms where the antigens and antibodies meet.

Similarly, the antigens and antibodies can be induced to move toward one another under the influence of an electrical field. In the *electrophoretic method,* an electrical potential is applied to the gel medium; a specific antigen–antibody reaction is denoted by a line of precipitation formed between the hole containing the blood extract and the hole containing the human antiserum (see Figure 14–6).

The precipitin test is very sensitive and requires only a small amount of blood for testing. Human bloodstains dried for ten to fifteen years and longer may still give a positive precipitin reaction. Even extracts of tissue from mummies four to five thousand years old have given positive reactions with this test. Furthermore, human bloodstains diluted by washing in water and left with only a faint color may still yield a positive precipitin reaction (see Figure 14–7).

Once it has been determined that the bloodstain is human, an effort must be made to associate the stain with or disassociate the stain from a particular individual. Until the mid-1990s, routine characterization of

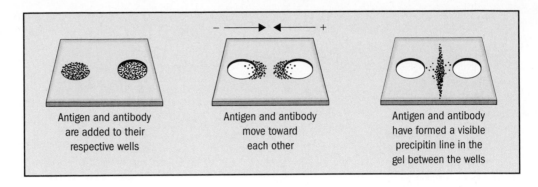

FIGURE 14–6   Gel diffusion.

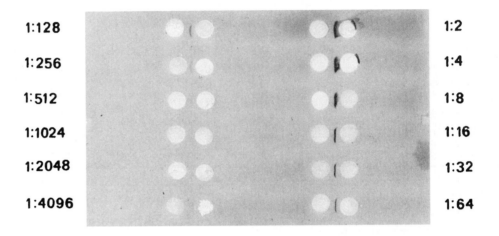

FIGURE 14–7   Results of the precipitin test of dilutions of human serum up to 1 in 4,096 against a human antiserum. A reaction is visible for blood dilutions up to 1 in 256. *Courtesy Millipore Biomedica, Acton, Mass.*

bloodstains included the determination of A-B-O types; however, the widespread use of DNA profiling or typing has relegated this subject to one of historical interest only.

Key Points

- The criminalist must be prepared to answer the following questions when examining dried blood: (1) Is it blood? (2) From what species did the blood originate? (3) If the blood is of human origin, how closely can it be associated to a particular individual?

- The determination of blood is best made by means of a preliminary color test. A positive result from the Kastle-Meyer color test is highly indicative of blood.

- The luminol and Bluestar® tests are used to search out trace amounts of blood located at crime scenes.

- The precipitin test uses antisera normally derived from rabbits that have been injected with the blood of a known animal to determine the species origin of a questioned bloodstain.

Forensic Characterization of Semen

Many cases received in a forensic laboratory involve sexual offenses, making it necessary to examine exhibits for the presence of seminal stains. The forensic examination of articles for seminal stains can actually be considered a two-step process. First, before any tests can be conducted, the stain must be located. Considering the number and soiled condition of outer garments, undergarments, and possible bedclothing submitted for examination, this may prove to be an arduous task. Once located, the stain must be subjected to tests that will prove its identity. It may even be tested for the blood type of the individual from whom it originated.

Testing for Seminal Stains

Often seminal stains are visible on a fabric because they exhibit a stiff, crusty appearance. However, reliance on such appearance for locating the stain is unreliable and is useful only when the stain is in an obvious area. If the fabric has been washed or contains only minute quantities of semen, visual examination offers little chance of detecting the stain. The best way to locate and at the same time characterize a seminal stain is to perform the *acid phosphatase color test*.

Acid Phosphatase Test   Acid phosphatase is an *enzyme* that is secreted by the prostate gland into seminal fluid. Its concentrations in seminal fluid are up to 400 times those found in any other body fluid. Its presence can easily be detected when it comes in contact with an acidic solution of sodium alpha naphthylphosphate and Fast Blue B dye. Also, 4-methyl umbelliferyl phosphate (MUP) will fluoresces (emit light) under UV light when it comes in contact with acid phosphatase.

acid phosphatase
An enzyme found in high concentrations in semen.

The utility of the acid phosphatase test is apparent when it becomes necessary to search many garments or large fabric areas for seminal stains. Simply moistening a filter paper with water and rubbing it lightly over the suspect area transfers any acid phosphatase present to the filter paper. Placing a drop or two of the sodium alpha naphthylphosphate and Fast Blue B solution on the paper produces a purple color that indicates the acid phosphatase enzyme. In this manner, any fabric or surface can be systematically searched for seminal stains.

If it is necessary to search extremely large areas—for example, a bedsheet or carpet—the article can be tested in sections, narrowing the location of the stain with each successive test. Alternatively, the garment can be pressed against a suitably sized piece of moistened filter paper. The paper is then sprayed with MUP solution. Semen stains appear as strongly fluorescent areas under UV light. A negative reaction can be interpreted as an absence of semen. Although some vegetable and fruit juices (such as cauliflower and watermelon), fungi, contraceptive creams, and vaginal secretions give a positive response to the acid phosphatase test, none of these substances normally reacts with the speed of seminal fluid. A reaction time of less than 30 seconds is considered a strong indication of semen.

Microscopic Examination of Semen   Semen can be unequivocally identified by the presence of spermatozoa. When spermatozoa are located through a microscope examination, the stain is definitely identified as having been derived from semen. *Spermatozoa* are slender, elongated structures 50 to

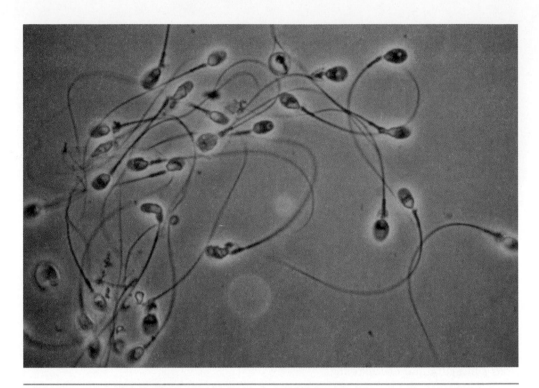

FIGURE 14–8   A photomicrograph of human spermatozoa (300×). *Courtesy John Walsh*

70 microns long, each with a head and a thin flagellate tail (see Figure 14–8). The criminalist can normally locate them by immersing the stained material in a small volume of water. Rapidly stirring the liquid transfers a small percentage of the spermatozoa present into the water. A drop of the water is dried onto a microscope slide, then stained and examined under a compound microscope at a magnification of approximately 400×.[4]

Considering the extremely large number of spermatozoa found in seminal fluid (the normal male releases 250 to 600 million spermatozoa during ejaculation), the chance of locating one should be very good; however, this is not always true. One reason is that spermatozoa bind tightly to cloth materials.[5] Also, spermatozoa are extremely brittle when dry and easily disintegrate if the stain is washed or when the stain is rubbed against another object, as happens frequently in the handling and packaging of this type of evidence. Furthermore, sexual crimes may involve males who have an abnormally low sperm count, a condition known as **oligospermia**, or who have no spermatozoa at all in their seminal fluid (**aspermia**). Significantly, aspermatic individuals are increasing in numbers because of the growing popularity of vasectomies.

oligospermia
An abnormally low sperm count.

aspermia
The absence of sperm; sterility in males.

Prostate-Specific Antigen (PSA)   Analysts often examine stains or swabs that they suspect contain semen (because of the presence of acid phosphatase), but that yield no detectable spermatozoa. How, then, can one unequivocally prove the presence of semen? The solution to this problem came with the discovery in the 1970s of a protein called *p30* or *prostate-specific antigen (PSA)*. Under the analytical conditions employed in forensic laboratories, p30 is unique to seminal plasma.

When p30 is isolated and injected into a rabbit, it stimulates the production of polyclonal antibodies (anti-p30). The serum collected from these immunized rabbits can then be used to test suspected semen stains. As shown in Figure 14–9, the stain extract is placed in one well of an electrophoretic plate and the anti-p30 in an opposite well. When an electric potential is applied, the antigens and antibodies move toward each other. The formation of a visible line midway between the two wells shows the presence of p30 in the stain and proves that the stain was seminal.

A more elegant approach to identifying PSA (p30) is shown in Figure 14–10. First, a monoclonal PSA antibody is attached to a dye and placed on a porous membrane. Monoclonal antibodies are specially designed to attack a single antigen site. Next, an extract from a sample suspected of containing PSA is placed on the membrane. If PSA is present in the extract, it combines with the monoclonal PSA antibody to form a PSA antigen–monoclonal PSA antibody complex. This complex migrates along the membrane, where it interacts with a PSA antibody imbedded in the membrane. The antibody–antigen–antibody "sandwich" that forms is apparent by the presence of a colored line (see Figure 14–10). This monoclonal antibody technique is about 100 times as sensitive as the electrophoretic method for detecting PSA.[6]

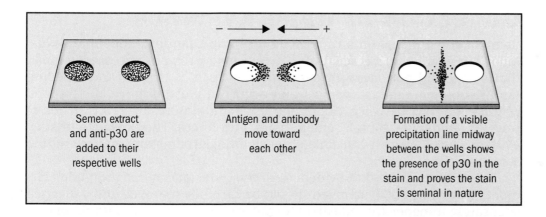

FIGURE 14–9   PSA testing by electrophoresis.

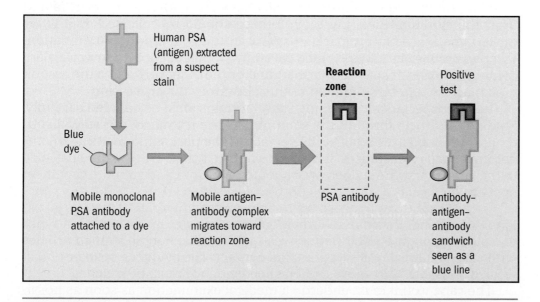

FIGURE 14–10   An antibody–antigen–antibody "sandwich," or complex, is seen as a colored band. This signifies the presence of PSA in the extract of a stain and positively identifies human semen.

Once the material is proven to be semen, the next task is to associate the semen as closely as possible with an individual. As we will learn, forensic scientists can link seminal material to one individual with DNA technology. Just as important is the knowledge that this technology can exonerate many of those wrongfully accused of sexual assault.

Key Points

- The best way to locate and characterize a seminal stain is to perform the acid phosphatase color test.

- The presence of spermatozoa, or of the protein called prostate-specific antigen (PSA), also known as p30, proves that a sample stain contains semen.

- Forensic scientists can link seminal material to an individual by DNA typing.

Collection of Rape Evidence

Seminal constituents on a rape victim are important evidence that sexual intercourse has taken place, but their absence does not necessarily mean that a rape did not occur. Physical injuries such as bruises and bleeding tend to confirm that a violent assault occurred. Furthermore, the forceful physical contact between victim and assailant may result in a transfer of physical evidence—blood, semen, hairs, and fibers. The presence of such evidence helps forge a vital link in the chain of circumstances surrounding a sexual crime.

To protect this kind of evidence, all the outer garments and undergarments from the people involved should be carefully removed and packaged separately in paper (not plastic) bags. A clean bedsheet should be placed on the floor and a clean paper sheet placed over it. The victim must remove her shoes before standing on the paper. The person should disrobe while standing on the paper in order to collect any loose foreign material falling from the clothing. Each piece of clothing should be collected as it is removed and placed in a separate paper bag to avoid cross-contamination. The paper sheet should be folded carefully so that all foreign materials are contained inside. If appropriate, bedding or the object on which the assault took place should be submitted to the laboratory for processing.

Items suspected of containing seminal stains must be handled carefully. Folding an article through the stain may cause it to flake off, as will rubbing the stained area against the surface of the packaging material. If, under unusual circumstances, it is not possible to transport the stained article to the laboratory, the stained area should be cut out and submitted with an unstained piece as a substrate control.

In the laboratory, analysts try to link seminal material to a donor(s) using DNA typing. Because an individual may transfer his or her DNA types to a stain through perspiration, investigators must handle stained articles with care, minimizing direct personal contact. The evidence collector must wear disposable latex gloves when such evidence must be touched.

The rape victim must undergo a medical examination as soon as possible after the assault. At this time, the appropriate items of physical evidence are collected by trained personnel. Evidence collectors should have an evidence-collection kit from the local crime laboratory (see Figure 14–11).

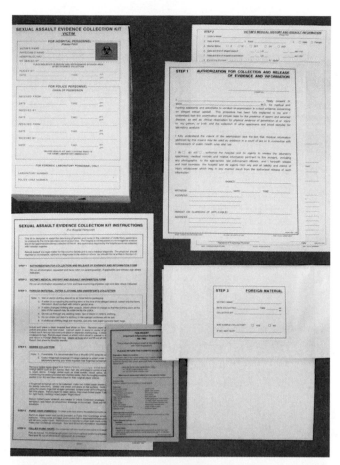

FIGURE 14–11 **(a) A victim rape collection kit showing the kit envelope, kit instructions, medical history and assault information forms, and a foreign materials collection bag.** *Courtesy Tri-Tech, Inc., Southport, N.C., www.tritechusa.com*

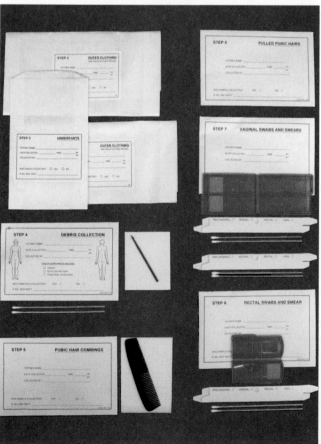

FIGURE 14–11 **(b) A victim rape collection kit showing collection bags for outer clothing, underpants, debris, pubic hair combings, pubic hair standard/reference samples, vaginal swabs, and rectal swabs.** *Courtesy Tri-Tech, Inc., Southport, N.C., www.tritechusa.com*

FIGURE 14–11 **(c) A victim rape collection kit showing collection bags for oral swabs and smear, pulled head hairs standard/ reference, known saliva sample, known blood samples, and anatomical drawings.** *Courtesy Tri-Tech, Inc., Southport, N.C., www.tritechusa.com*

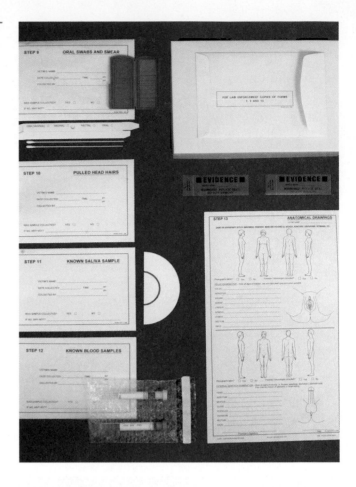

The following items of physical evidence are to be collected:

1. ***Pubic combings.*** Place a paper towel under the buttocks and comb the pubic area for loose or foreign hairs.

2. ***Pubic hair standard/reference samples.*** Cut fifteen to twenty full-length hairs from the pubic area at the skin line.

3. ***External genital dry-skin areas.*** Swab with at least one dry swab and one moistening swab.

4. ***Vaginal swabs and smear.*** Using two swabs simultaneously, carefully swab the vaginal area and let the swabs air-dry before packaging. Using two additional swabs, repeat the swabbing procedure and smear the swabs onto separate microscope slides, allowing them to air-dry before packaging.

5. ***Cervix swabs.*** Using two swabs simultaneously, carefully swab the cervix area and let the swabs air-dry before packaging.

6. ***Rectal swabs and smear.*** To be taken when warranted by case history. Using two swabs simultaneously, swab the rectal canal, smearing one of the swabs onto a microscope slide. Allow both samples to air-dry before packaging.

7. ***Oral swabs and smear.*** To be taken if oral–genital contact occurred. Use two swabs simultaneously to swab the cheek area and gum line. Using both swabs, prepare one smear slide. Allow both swabs and the smear to air-dry before packaging.

8. ***Head hairs***. Cut at the skin line a minimum of ten full-length hairs from each of the following scalp locations: center, front, back, left side, and right side. A total of at least fifty hairs should be cut and submitted to the laboratory.

9. ***Blood sample***. Collect at least 7 milliliters in a vacuum tube containing the preservative EDTA. The blood sample can be used for DNA typing as well as for toxicological analysis if required.

10. ***Fingernail scrapings***. Scrape the undersurface of the nails with a dull object over a piece of clean paper to collect debris. Use separate paper, one for each hand.

11. ***All clothing***. Package as described earlier.

12. ***Urine specimen***. Collect 30 milliliters or more of urine from the victim for analysis for Rohypnol, GHB, and other substances associated with drug-facilitated sexual assaults.

Often during the investigation of a sexual assault, the victim reports that a perpetrator engaged in biting, sucking, or licking areas of the victim's body. As we will learn in the next section, the tremendous sensitivity associated with DNA technology offers investigators the opportunity to identify a perpetuator's DNA types from saliva residues collected off the skin. The most efficient way to recover saliva residues from the skin is to first swab the suspect area with a rotating motion using a cotton swab moistened with distilled water. A second, dry swab is then rotated over the skin to recover the moist remains on the skin's surface from the wet swab. The swabs are air-dried and packaged together as a single sample.[7]

If a suspect is apprehended, the following items are routinely collected:

1. *All clothing* and any other items believed to have been worn at the time of assault.

2. *Pubic hair combings*.

3. *Pulled head and pubic hair standard/reference samples*.

4. A *penile swab* taken within twenty-four hours of the assault, when appropriate to the case history.

5. A *blood sample* or *buccal swab* for DNA typing purposes.

The advent of DNA profiling has forced investigators to rethink what items are evidential in a sexual assault. DNA levels in the range of one-billionth of a gram are now routinely characterized in crime laboratories. In the past, scant attention was paid to the underwear recovered from a male who was suspected of being involved in a sexual assault; seminal constituents on a man's underwear had little or no investigative value. Today, the sensitivity of DNA analysis has created new areas of investigation. It is possible to link a victim and an assailant by analyzing biological material recovered from the interior front surface of a male suspect's underwear. This is especially important when investigations have failed to yield the presence of the suspect's DNA on exhibits recovered from the victim.

The persistence of seminal constituents in the vagina may help determine the time of an alleged sexual attack. Although spermatozoa in the vaginal cavity provide evidence of intercourse, important information regarding the time of sexual activity can be obtained from the knowledge that motile (living) sperm generally survive for up to six hours in the vaginal cavity of a living female. However, a successful search for motile sperm

Forensic Brief

A common mode of DNA transfer occurs when skin cells from the walls of the victim's vagina are transferred onto the suspect during intercourse. Subsequent penile contact with the inner surface of the suspect's underwear often leads to the recovery of the female victim's DNA from the underwear's inner surface. The power of DNA is illustrated in a case in which the female victim of a rape had consensual sexual intercourse with a male partner before being assaulted by a different male. DNA extracted from the inside front area of the suspect's underwear revealed a female DNA profile matching that of the victim. The added bonus in this case was finding male DNA on the same underwear that matched that of the consensual partner.

Source: Gary G. Verret, "Sexual Assault Cases with No Primary Transfer of Biological Material from Suspect to Victim: Evidence of Secondary and Tertiary Transfer of Biological Material from Victim to Suspect's Undergarments," *Proceedings of the Canadian Society of Forensic Science*, Toronto, Ontario, November 2001.

requires a microscopic examination of a vaginal smear immediately after it is taken from the victim.

A more extensive examination of vaginal collections is later made at a forensic laboratory. Nonmotile sperm may be found in a living female for up to three days after intercourse and occasionally up to six days later. However, intact sperm (sperm with tails) are not normally found sixteen hours after intercourse but have been found as late as seventy-two hours after intercourse. The likelihood of finding seminal acid phosphatase in the vaginal cavity markedly decreases with time following intercourse, with little chance of identifying this substance forty-eight hours after intercourse.[8] Hence, with the possibility of prolonged persistence of both spermatozoa and acid phosphatase in the vaginal cavity after intercourse, investigators should determine when and if voluntary sexual activity last occurred before the sexual assault. This information will help in evaluating the significance of finding these seminal constituents in a female victim. Blood or buccal swabs for DNA analysis should be taken from any consensual partner who had sex with the victim within seventy-two hours of the assault.

Another significant indicator of recent sexual activity is p30. This semen marker normally is not detected in the vaginal cavity beyond twenty-four hours following intercourse.[9]

Key Points

- A rape victim must undergo a medical examination as soon as possible after the assault. At that time clothing, hairs, and vaginal and rectal swabs can be collected for subsequent laboratory examination.

- The persistence of seminal constituents in the vagina may help determine the time of an alleged sexual attack.

Understanding DNA

The discovery of deoxyribonucleic acid (DNA), the deciphering of its structure, and the decoding of its genetic information were turning points in our understanding of the underlying concepts of inheritance. Now, with incredible speed, as molecular biologists unravel the basic structure of genes, we can create new products through genetic engineering and develop diagnostic tools and treatments for genetic disorders.

For a number of years, these developments were of seemingly peripheral interest to forensic scientists. All that changed when, in 1985, what started out as a more or less routine investigation into the structure of a human gene led to the discovery that portions of the DNA structure of certain genes are as unique to each individual as fingerprints. Alec Jeffreys and his colleagues at Leicester University, England, who were responsible for these revelations, named the process for isolating and reading these DNA markers *DNA fingerprinting*. As researchers uncovered new approaches and variations to the original Jeffreys technique, the terms *DNA profiling* and *DNA typing* came to be applied to describe this relatively new technology.

This discovery caught the imagination of the forensic science community, for forensic scientists have long searched for ways to definitively link biological evidence such as blood, semen, hair, and tissue to a single individual. Although conventional testing procedures had gone a long way toward narrowing the source of biological materials, individualization remained an elusive goal. DNA typing has allowed forensic scientists to accomplish this goal. Although the technique is still relatively new, DNA typing has become routine in public crime laboratories. It also has been made available to interested parties through the services of a number of skilled private laboratories. In the United States, courts have overwhelmingly admitted DNA evidence and accepted the reliability of its scientific underpinnings.

Genes and Chromosomes

Hereditary material is transmitted via microscopic units called **genes**. The gene is the basic unit of heredity. Each gene by itself or in concert with other genes controls the development of a specific characteristic in the new individual; the genes determine the nature and growth of virtually every body structure.

The genes are positioned on **chromosomes**, threadlike bodies that appear in the nucleus of every body cell (see Figure 14–12). Almost all human cells contain forty-six chromosomes, mated in twenty-three pairs. The only exceptions are the human reproductive cells, the **egg** and **sperm**, which contain twenty-three unmated chromosomes. During fertilization, a sperm and egg combine so that each contributes twenty-three chromosomes to form the new cell (**zygote**). Hence, the new individual begins life properly with twenty-three mated chromosome pairs. Because the genes are positioned on the chromosomes, the new individual inherits genetic material from each parent.

Actually, two dissimilar chromosomes are involved in the determination of sex. The egg cell always contains a long chromosome known as the **X chromosome**; the sperm cell may contain either a long X chromosome or a short **Y chromosome**. When an X-carrying sperm fertilizes an egg, the new cell is XX and develops into a female. A Y-carrying sperm produces an XY fertilized egg and develops into a male. Because the sperm cell determines the nature of the chromosome pair, we can say that the father biologically determines the sex of the child.

Alleles Just as chromosomes come together in pairs, so do the genes they bear. The position a gene occupies on a chromosome is its **locus**. Genes that govern a given characteristic are similarly positioned on the chromosomes inherited from the mother and father. Thus, a gene for eye color on

WebExtra 14.2
Learn About the Chromosomes as Present in Our Cells
www.prenhall.com/saferstein

WebExtra 14.3
Learn About the Structure of Our Genes
www.prenhall.com/saferstein

gene
The basic unit of heredity, consisting of a DNA segment located on a chromosome.

chromosome
A threadlike structure in the cell nucleus composed of DNA, along which the genes are located.

egg
The female reproductive cell.

sperm
The male reproductive cell.

zygote
The cell arising from the union of an egg and a sperm cell.

X chromosome
The female sex chromosome.

Y chromosome
The male sex chromosome.

locus
The physical location of a gene on a chromosome.

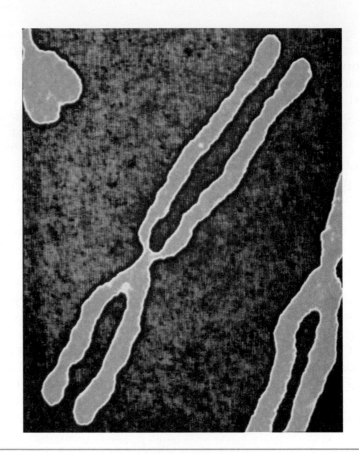

FIGURE 14-12   A computer-enhanced photomicrograph image of human chromosomes.
Courtesy Alfred Pasieka, Science Photo Library

allele
Any of several alternative forms of a gene located at the same point on a particular pair of chromosomes.

homozygous
Having two identical allelic genes on two corresponding positions of a pair of chromosomes.

heterozygous
Having two different allelic genes on two corresponding positions of a pair of chromosomes.

WebExtra 14.4

See How Genes Position Themselves on a Chromosome Pair
www.prenhall.com/saferstein

the mother's chromosome will be aligned with a gene for eye color on the corresponding chromosome inherited from the father. Alternative forms of genes that influence a given characteristic and are aligned with one another on a chromosome pair are known as **alleles**.

Inheritance of blood type offers a simple example of allele genes in humans. An individual's blood type is determined by three genes, designated A, B, and O. A gene pair made up of two similar alleles—for example, AA and BB—is said to be **homozygous**. For example, if the chromosome inherited from the father carries the A gene and the chromosome inherited from the mother carries the same gene, the offspring will have an AA combination. Thus, when an individual inherits two similar genes from his or her parents, there is no problem in determining the blood type of that person. An individual with an AA combination will always be type A, a BB will be type B, and an OO will be type O.

A gene pair made up of two different alleles—AO, for example—is said to be **heterozygous**. For example, if the chromosome from one parent carries the A gene and the chromosome from the other parent carries the O gene, the genetic makeup of the offspring will be AO. When two different genes are inherited, one gene will be *dominant*—that is, the characteristic coded for by that gene is expressed. The other gene will be *recessive*—that is, its characteristics remain hidden. In the case of blood types, A and B genes are dominant, and the O gene is recessive. Thus, with an AO combination, A is always dominant over O, and the individual is typed as A. Similarly, a BO combination is typed as B. In the case of AB, the genes are *codominant*, and the individual's blood type will be AB. The recessive characteristics of O appear only when both recessive genes are present in combination OO, which is typed simply as O.

WebExtra 14.5
See How Genes Define Our Genetic Makeup
www.prenhall.com/saferstein

Key Points

- The gene is the basic unit of heredity. A chromosome is a threadlike structure in the cell nucleus along which the genes are located.

- Most human cells contain 46 chromosomes, arranged in 23 mated pairs. The only exceptions are the human reproductive cells, the egg and sperm, which contain 23 unmated chromosomes.

- During fertilization, a sperm and an egg combine so that each contributes 23 chromosomes to form the new cell, or *zygote*, that develops into the offspring.

- An allele is any of several alternative forms of genes that influence a given characteristic and that are aligned with one another on a chromosome pair.

- A heterozygous gene pair is made up of two different alleles; a homozygous gene pair is made up of two similar alleles.

- When two different genes are inherited, the characteristic coded for by a dominant gene will be expressed. The characteristic coded for by a recessive gene will remain hidden.

What Is DNA?

Inside each of 60 trillion cells in the human body are strands of genetic material—chromosomes. Arranged along the chromosomes, like beads on a thread, are nearly 25,000 genes. The gene is the fundamental unit of heredity. It instructs body cells to make proteins that determine everything from hair color to susceptibility to diseases. Each gene is composed of DNA designed to carry out a single body function.

Although DNA was first discovered in 1868, scientists were slow to understand and appreciate its fundamental role in inheritance. Painstakingly, researchers developed evidence that DNA was probably the substance by which genetic instructions are passed from one generation to the next. However, the first major breakthrough in comprehending how DNA works did not occur until the early 1950s, when two researchers, James Watson and Francis Crick, deduced the structure of DNA. It turns out that DNA is an extraordinary molecule skillfully designed to control the genetic traits of all living cells, plant and animal.

Structure of DNA   Before examining the implications of Watson and Crick's discovery, let's see how DNA is constructed. DNA is a polymer. A polymer is a very large molecule made by linking a series of repeating units, or monomers. In this case, the units are known as **nucleotides**.

Nucleotides   A nucleotide is composed of a sugar molecule, a phosphorus atom surrounded by four oxygen atoms, and a nitrogen-containing molecule called a *base*. Figure 14–13 shows how nucleotides can be strung together to form a DNA strand. In this figure, S designates the sugar

nucleotide
A repeating unit of DNA consisting of one of four bases—adenine, guanine, cytosine, or thymine—attached to a phosphate-sugar group.

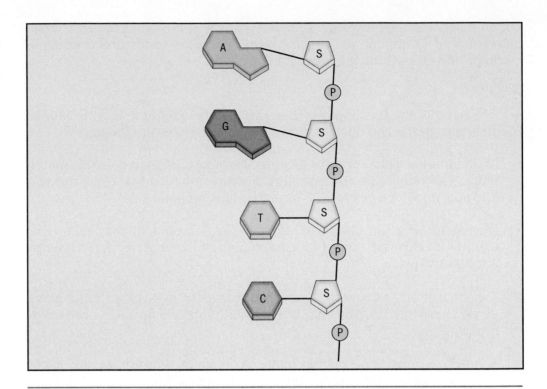

FIGURE 14–13 How nucleotides can be linked to form a DNA strand. S designates the sugar component, which is joined with phosphate groups (P) to form the backbone of DNA. Projecting from the backbone are four bases: *A*, adenine; *G*, guanine; *T*, thymine; and *C*, cytosine.

component, which is joined with a phosphate group to form the backbone of the DNA strand. Projecting from the backbone are the bases.

The key to understanding how DNA works is to appreciate the fact that only four types of bases are associated with DNA: adenine, cytosine, guanine, and thymine. To simplify our discussion of DNA, we will designate each of these bases by the first letter of their names. Hence, *A* will stand for adenine, *C* for cytosine, *G* for guanine, and *T* for thymine.

Again, notice in Figure 14–13 how the bases project from the backbone of DNA. Also, although this figure shows a DNA strand of four bases, keep in mind that in theory there is no limit to the length of the DNA strand; a DNA strand can be composed of a long chain with millions of bases. This information was well known to Watson and Crick by the time they set about to detail the structure of DNA. Their efforts led them to discover that the DNA molecule is composed of two DNA strands coiled into a *double helix*. This can be thought of as resembling two wires twisted around each other.

As Watson and Crick manipulated scale models of DNA strands, they realized that the only way the bases on each strand could be properly aligned with each other in a double-helix configuration was to place base *A* opposite *T* and *G* opposite *C*. Watson and Crick had solved the puzzle of the double helix and presented the world with a simple but elegant picture of DNA (see Figure 14–14).

Complementary Base Pairing The only arrangement possible in the double-helix configuration is the pairing of bases *A* to *T* and *G* to *C*, a concept that has become known as *complementary base pairing*. Although *A–T* and

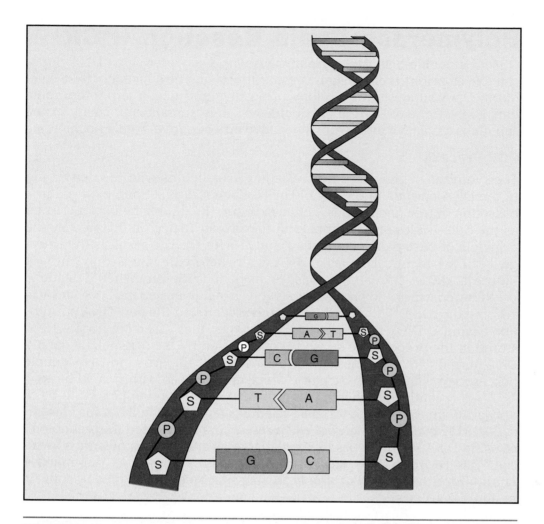

FIGURE 14–14   A representation of a DNA double helix. Notice how bases *G* and *C* pair with each other, as do bases *A* and *T*. This is the only arrangement in which two DNA strands can align with each other in a double-helix configuration.

G–C pairs are always required, there are no restrictions on how the bases are sequenced on a DNA strand. Thus, one can observe the sequences *T–A–T–T* or *G–T–A–A* or *G–T–C–A*. When these sequences are joined with their complements in a double-helix configuration, they pair as follows:

$$
\begin{array}{ccc}
\text{T A T T} & \text{G T A A} & \text{G T C A} \\
| \; | \; | \; | & | \; | \; | \; | & | \; | \; | \; | \\
\text{A T A A} & \text{C A T T} & \text{C A G T}
\end{array}
$$

Any base can follow another on a DNA strand, which means that the number of possible sequence combinations is staggering. Consider that the average human chromosome has DNA containing 100 million base pairs. All of the human chromosomes taken together contain about three billion base pairs. From these numbers, we can begin to appreciate the diversity of DNA and hence the diversity of living organisms. DNA is like a book of instructions. The alphabet used to create the book is simple enough: *A, T, G,* and *C.* The order in which these letters are arranged defines the role and function of a DNA molecule.

WebExtra 14.6

What Is DNA?
www.prenhall.com/saferstein

Polymerase Chain Reaction (PCR)

Once the double-helix structure of DNA was discovered, how DNA duplicated itself prior to cell division became apparent. The concept of base pairing in DNA suggests the analogy of positive and negative photographic film. Each strand of DNA in the double helix has the same information; one can make a positive print from a negative or a negative from a positive.

PCR Process

The synthesis of new DNA from existing DNA begins with the unwinding of the DNA strands in the double helix. Each strand is then exposed to a collection of free nucleotides. Letter by letter, the double helix is recreated as the nucleotides are assembled in the proper order, as dictated by the principle of base pairing (*A* with *T* and *G* with *C*). The result is the emergence of two identical copies of DNA where before there was only one (see Figure 14–15). A cell can now pass on its genetic identity when it divides.

Many enzymes and proteins are involved in unwinding the DNA strands, keeping the two DNA strands apart, and assembling the new DNA strands. For example, DNA *polymerases* are enzymes that assemble a new DNA strand in the proper base sequence determined by the original, or parent, DNA strand. DNA polymerases also "proofread" the growing DNA double helices for mismatched base pairs, which are replaced with correct bases.

Until recently, the phenomenon of DNA replication appeared to be of only academic interest to forensic scientists interested in DNA for identification. However, this changed when researchers perfected the technology of using DNA polymerases to copy a DNA strand located outside a living cell. This relatively new laboratory technique is known as **polymerase chain reaction (PCR)**. Put simply, PCR is a technique designed to copy or multiply DNA strands.

polymerase chain reaction (PCR)

A technique for replicating or copying a portion of a DNA strand outside a living cell.

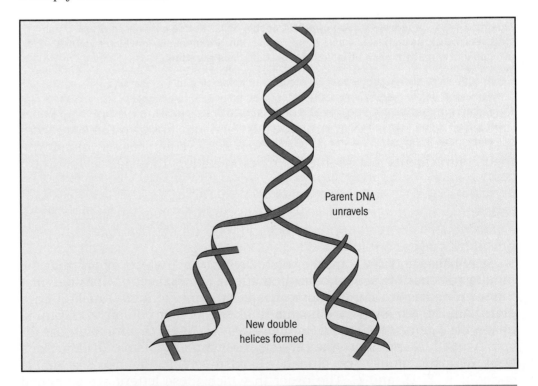

Parent DNA unravels

New double helices formed

FIGURE 14–15 **Replication of DNA. The strands of the original DNA molecule are separated, and two new strands are assembled.**

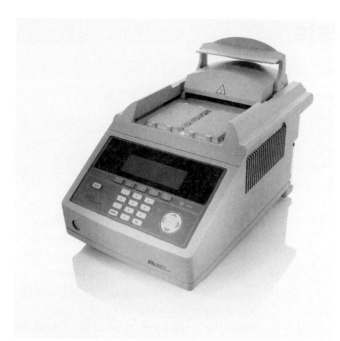

FIGURE 14–16 The DNA Thermal Cycler, an instrument that automates the rapid and precise temperature changes required to copy a DNA strand. Within a matter of hours, DNA can be multiplied a billionfold. *Courtesy Applied Biosystems, Foster City, Calif.*

In PCR, small quantities of DNA or broken pieces of DNA found in crime-scene evidence can be copied with the aid of a DNA polymerase. The copying process is highly temperature dependent and can be accomplished in an automated fashion using a DNA Thermal Cycler (see Figure 14–16). Each cycle of the PCR technique results in a doubling of the DNA, as shown in Figure 14–15. Within a few hours, thirty cycles can multiply DNA a billionfold. Once DNA copies are in hand, they can be analyzed by any of the methods of modern molecular biology. The ability to multiply small bits of DNA opens new and exciting avenues for forensic scientists to explore. It means that sample size is no longer a limitation in characterizing DNA recovered from crime-scene evidence.

Key Points

- The gene is the fundamental unit of heredity. Each gene is composed of DNA specifically designed to control the genetic traits of our cells.

- DNA is constructed as a very large molecule made by linking a series of repeating units called *nucleotides*.

- Four types of bases are associated with the DNA structure: adenine *(A),* guanine *(G),* cytosine *(C),* and thymine *(T)*.

- The bases on each strand of DNA are aligned in a double-helix configuration so that adenine pairs with thymine and guanine pairs with cytosine. The concept is known as *complementary base pairing*.

- The order in which the base pairs are arranged defines the role and function of a DNA molecule.

- DNA replication beigns with the unwinding of the DNA strands in the double helix. The double helix is recreated as the nucleotides are assembled in the proper order (*A* with *T* and *G* with *C*). Two identical copies of DNA emerge from the process.

- PCR (polymerase chain reaction) is a technique for replicating or copying a portion of a DNA strand outside a living cell.

Closer Analysis

Polymerase Chain Reaction

The most important feature of PCR is the knowledge that an enzyme called *DNA polymerase* can be directed to synthesize a specific region of DNA. In a relatively straightforward manner, PCR can be used to repeatedly duplicate or amplify a strand of DNA millions of times. As an example, let's consider a segment of DNA that we want to duplicate by PCR:

–G–T–C–T–C–A–G–C–T–T–**C–C–A–G**–
–**C–A–G–A**–G–T–C–G–A–A–G–G–T–C–

To perform PCR on this DNA segment, short sequences of DNA on each side of the region of interest must be identified. In the example shown here, the short sequences are designated by boldface letters in the DNA segment. These short DNA segments must be available in a pure form known as a *primer* if the PCR technique is going to work.

The first step in PCR is to heat the DNA strands to about 94°C. At this temperature, the double-stranded DNA molecules separate completely:

–G–T–C–T–C–A–G–C–T–T–C–C–A–G–

–C–A–G–A–G–T–C–G–A–A–G–G–T–C–

The second step is to add the primers to the separated strands and allow the primers to combine, or hybridize, with the strands by lowering the test-tube temperature to about 60°C.

–G–T–C–T–C–A–G–C–T–T–C–C–A–G–
C–A–G–A

                              C–C–A–G
–C–A–G–A–G–T–C–G–A–A–G–G–T–C–

The third step is to add the DNA polymerase and a mixture of free nucleotides *(A, C, G, T)* to the separated strands. When the test tube is heated to 72°C, the polymerase enzyme directs the rebuilding of a double-stranded DNA molecule, extending the primers by adding the appropriate bases, one at a time, resulting in the production of two complete pairs of double-stranded DNA segments:

–G–T–C–T–C–A–G–C–T–T–C–C–A–G–
C–A–G–A–G–T–C–G–A–A–G–G–T–C–

–G–T–C–T–C–A–G–C–T–T–C–C–A–G
–C–A–G–A–G–T–C–G–A–A–G–G–T–C–

This completes the first cycle of the PCR technique, which results in a doubling of the number of DNA strands from one to two. The cycle of heating, cooling, and strand rebuilding is then repeated, resulting in a further doubling of the DNA strands. On completion of the second cycle, four double-stranded DNA molecules have been created from the original double-stranded DNA sample. Typically, twenty-eight to thirty-two cycles are carried out to yield more than one billion copies of the original DNA molecule. Each cycle takes less than two minutes.

WebExtra 14.7

Polymerase Chain Reaction
www.prenhall.com/saferstein

DNA Typing with Short Tandem Repeats

Geneticists have discovered that portions of the DNA molecule contain sequences of letters that are repeated numerous times. In fact, more than 30 percent of the human genome is composed of repeating segments of DNA. These repeating sequences, or *tandem repeats,* seem to act as filler or spacers between the coding regions of DNA. Although these repeating segments do not seem to affect our outward appearance or control any other basic genetic function, they are nevertheless part of our genetic makeup, inherited from our parents. The origin and significance of these tandem repeats is a mystery, but to forensic scientists they offer a means of distinguishing one individual from another through DNA typing.

Short Tandem Repeats (STRs)

Currently, short tandem repeat (STR) analysis, has emerged as the most successful and widely used DNA-profiling procedure. STRs are locations (loci) on the chromosome that contain short sequence elements that repeat themselves within the DNA molecule. They serve as helpful markers for identification because they are found in great abundance throughout the human genome.

STRs normally consist of repeating sequences of three to seven bases; the entire strand of an STR is also very short, less than 450 bases long. These strands are significantly shorter than those encountered in other DNA typing procedures. This means that STRs are much less susceptible to degradation and are often recovered from bodies or stains that have been subject to extreme decomposition. Also, because of their shortness, STRs are an ideal candidate for multiplication by PCR, thus overcoming the limited-sample-size problem often associated with crime-scene evidence. Only the equivalent of 18 DNA-containing cells is needed to obtain a DNA profile. For instance, STR has been used to identify the origin of saliva residue on envelopes, stamps, soda cans, and cigarette butts.

To understand the utility of STRs in forensic science, let's look at one commonly used STR known as TH01. This DNA segment contains the repeating sequence *A–A–T–G*. Seven TH01 variants have been identified in the human genome. These variants contain five to eleven repeats of *A–A–T–G*. Figure 14–17 illustrates two such TH01 variants, one containing six repeats and the other containing eight repeats of *A–A–T–G*.

During a forensic examination, TH01 is extracted from biological materials and amplified by PCR as described earlier. The ability to copy an STR means that extremely small amounts of the molecule can be detected and analyzed. Once the STRs have been copied or amplified, they are separated by electrophoresis. Here, the STRs are forced to move across a gel-coated plate under the influence of an electrical potential. Smaller DNA fragments move along the plate faster than do larger DNA fragments. By examining the distance the STR has migrated on the electrophoretic plate, one can determine the number of *A–A–T–G* repeats in the STR. Every person has two STR types for TH01, one inherited from each parent. Thus, for example, one may find in a semen stain TH01 with six repeats and eight repeats. This combination of TH01 is found in approximately 3.5 percent of the population. It is important to understand that all humans have the same type of repeats, but there is tremendous variation in the number of repeats each of us has.

When examining an STR DNA pattern, one merely needs to look for a match between band sets. For example in, Figure 14–18, DNA extracted from a crime-scene stain matches the DNA recovered from one of three suspects. When comparing only one STR, only a limited number of people in a population would have the same STR fragment pattern as the suspect. However, by using additional STRs, a high degree of discrimination or complete individualization can be achieved.

short tandem repeat (STR)
A region of a DNA molecule that contains short segments of three to seven repeating base pairs.

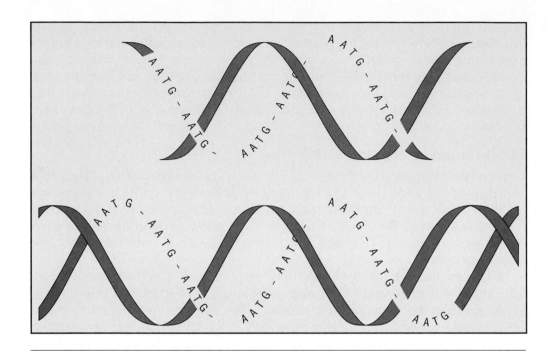

FIGURE 14–17   Variants of the short tandem repeat TH01. The upper DNA strand contains six repeats of the sequence *A–A–T–G;* the lower DNA strand contains eight repeats of the sequence *A–A–T–G.* This DNA type is known as TH01 6, 8.

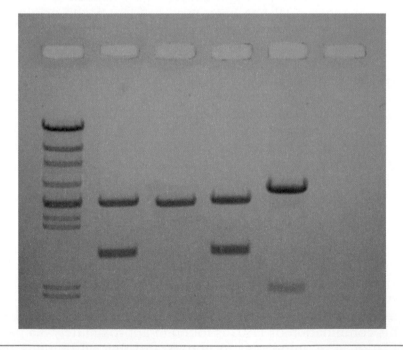

FIGURE 14–18   A DNA profile pattern of a suspect and its match to crime-scene DNA. From left to right, lane 1 is a DNA standard marker; lane 2 is the crime-scene DNA; and lanes 3 to 5 are control samples from suspects 1, 2, and 3, respectively. Crime-scene DNA matches suspect 2.   *Courtesy Edvotek, The Biotechnology Education Company*

Multiplexing

What makes STRs so attractive to forensic scientists is that hundreds of types of STRs are found in human genes. The more STRs one can charac-terize, the smaller the percentage of the population from which these STRs can emanate. This gives rise to the concept of **multiplexing**. Using PCR technology, one can simultaneously extract and amplify a combination of different STRs.

One STR system on the commercial market is the STR Blue Kit.[10] This kit provides the necessary materials for amplifying and detecting three STRs (a process called *triplexing*)—D3S1358, vWA, and FGA. The design of the system ensures that the size of the STRs does not overlap, thereby allowing each marker to be viewed clearly on an electrophoretic gel, as shown in Figure 14–19. In the United States, the forensic science community has standardized on thirteen STRs for entry into a national database known as the Combined DNA Index System (CODIS).

When an STR is selected for analysis, not only must the identity and number of core repeats be defined, but the sequence of bases flanking the repeats must also be known. This knowledge allows commercial manufacturers of STR typing kits to prepare the correct primers to delineate the STR segment to be amplified by PCR. Figure 14–20 illustrates how appropriate primers are used to define the region of DNA to be amplified. Also, a mix of different primers aimed at different STRs will be used to simultaneously amplify a multitude of STRs (multiplexing). In fact, one STR kit on the commercial market can simultaneously make copies of fifteen different STRs.

multiplexing
A technique that simultaneously detects more than one DNA marker in a single analysis.

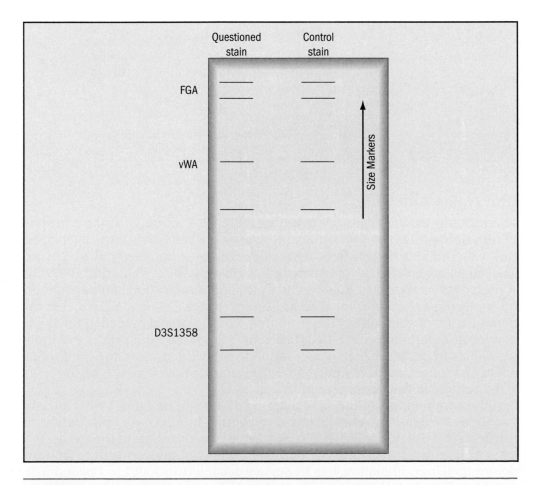

FIGURE 14–19   A triplex system containing three loci: FGA, vWA, and D3S1358, indicating a match between the questioned and the standard/reference stains.

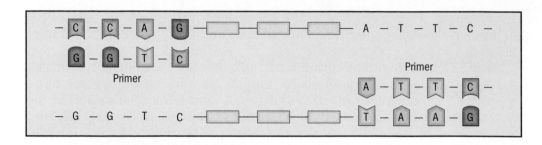

FIGURE 14–20 Appropriate primers flanking the repeat units of a DNA segment must be selected and put in place to initiate the PCR process.

Table 14–1	Thirteen CODIS STRs and Their Probability of Identities	
STR	**African-American**	**U.S. Caucasian**
D3S1358	0.094	0.075
vWA	0.063	0.062
FGA	0.033	0.036
TH01	0.109	0.081
TPOX	0.090	0.195
CSF1PO	0.081	0.112
D5S818	0.112	0.158
D13S317	0.136	0.085
D7S820	0.080	0.065
D8S1179	0.082	0.067
D21S11	0.034	0.039
D18S51	0.029	0.028
D16S539	0.070	0.089

Source: *The Future of Forensic DNA Testing: Predictions of the Research and Development Working Group.* Washington, D.C.: National Institute of Justice, Department of Justice, 2000, p. 41.

DNA Typing with STRs

WebExtra 14.8

See the 13 CODIS STRs and Their Chromosomal Positions
www.prenhall.com/saferstein

The thirteen CODIS STRs are listed in Table 14–1 along with their probabilities of identity. The probability of identity is a measure of the likelihood that two individuals selected at random will have an identical STR type. The smaller the value of this probability, the more discriminating the STR. A high degree of discrimination and even individualization can be attained by analyzing a combination of STRs (multiplexing). Because STRs occur independently of each other, the probability of biological evidence having a particular combination of STR types is determined by the product of their frequency of occurrence in a population. Hence, the greater the number of STRs characterized, the smaller the frequency of occurrence of the analyzed sample in the general population.

The combination of the first three STRs shown in Table 14–1 typically produces a frequency of occurrence of about 1 in 5,000. A combination of the first six STRs typically yields a frequency of occurrence in the range of 1 in 2 million for the Caucasian population, and if the top nine STRs are determined in combination, this frequency declines to about 1 in 1 billion. The combination of all thirteen STRs shown in Table 14–1 typically produces frequencies of occurrence that measure in the range of 1 in 575 trillion for

Caucasian Americans and 1 in 900 trillion for African-Americans. Importantly, several commercially available kits allow forensic scientists to profile STRs in the kinds of combinations cited here.

Sex Identification Using STRs

Manufacturers of commercial STR kits typically used by crime laboratories provide one additional piece of useful information along with STR types: the sex of the DNA contributor. The focus of attention here is the *amelogenin gene* located on both the X and Y chromosomes. This gene, which is actually the gene for tooth pulp, has an interesting characteristic in that it is shorter by six bases in the X chromosome than in the Y chromosome. Hence, when the amelogenin gene is amplified by PCR and separated by electrophoresis, males, who have an X and a Y chromosome, show two bands; females, who have two X chromosomes, have just one band. Typically, these results are obtained in conjunction with STR types.

Another tool in the arsenal of the DNA analyst is the ability to type STRs located on the Y chromosome. The Y chromosome is male specific and is always paired with the X chromosome. More than twenty **Y-STR** markers have been identified, and a commercial kit allows for the characterization of seventeen Y chromosome STRs. When can it be advantageous to seek out Y-STR types? Generally, Y-STRs are useful for analyzing blood, saliva, or a vaginal swab that is a mix originating from more than one male. For example, Y-STRs prove useful when multiple males are involved in a sexual assault.

Keep in mind that STR types derived from the Y chromosome originate only from this single male chromosome. A female subject, or one with an XX chromosome pattern, does not contribute any DNA information. Also, unlike a conventional STR analysis that is derived from two chromosomes and typically shows two bands or peaks, a Y-STR has only one band or peak for each STR type.

For example, the traditional STR DNA pattern may prove to be overly complex in the case of a vaginal swab containing the semen of two males. Each STR type would be expected to show four bands, two from each male. Also complicating the appearance of the DNA profile may be the presence of DNA from skin cells emanating from the walls of the vagina. In this circumstance, homing in on the Y chromosome greatly simplifies

WebExtra 14.9

Calculate the Frequency of Occurrence of a DNA Profile
www.prenhall.com/saferstein

WebExtra 14.10

Understand the Operational Principles of Capillary Electrophoresis
www.prenhall.com/saferstein

WebExtra 14.11

See the Electropherogram Record from One Individual's DNA
www.prenhall.com/saferstein

Y-STRs
Short tandem repeats located on the human Y chromosome.

WebExtra 14.12
An Animation Depicting Y-STRs
www.prenhall.com/saferstein

Closer Analysis

Capillary Electrophoresis

Capillary electrophoresis has emerged as the preferred technology for characterization of STRs. Capillary electrophoresis is carried out in a thin glass column. As illustrated in the figure each end of the column is immersed in a reservoir of buffer liquid that also holds electrodes (coated with platinum) to supply high-voltage energy. The column is coated with a gel polymer, and the DNA-containing sample solution is injected into one end of the column with a syringe. The STR fragments then move through the column under the influence of an electrical potential at a speed that is related to the length of the STR fragments. The other end of the column is connected to a detector that tracks the separated STRs as they emerge from the column. As the DNA peaks pass through the detector, they are recorded on a display known as an *electropherogram*.

(continued)

Closer Analysis

Capillary Electrophoresis (continued)

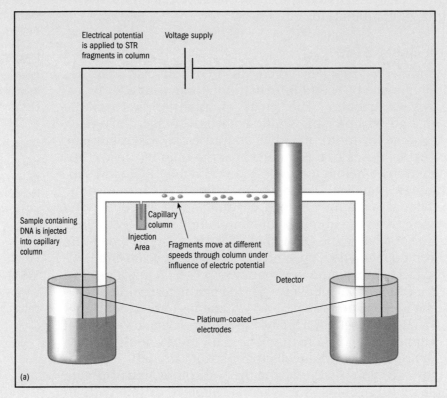

Electrical potential is applied to STR fragments in column

Voltage supply

Capillary column

Injection Area

Sample containing DNA is injected into capillary column

Fragments move at different speeds through column under influence of electric potential

Detector

Platinum-coated electrodes

(a)

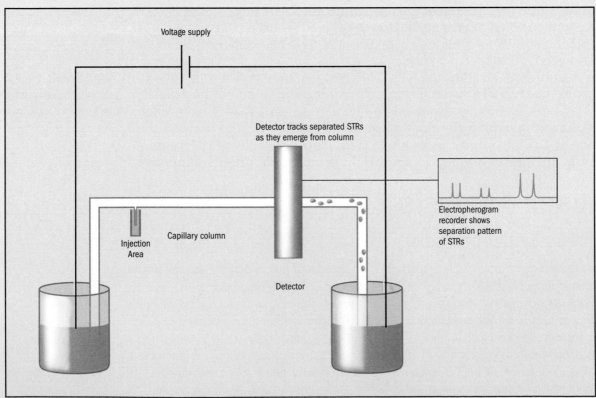

Voltage supply

Detector tracks separated STRs as they emerge from column

Capillary column

Injection Area

Detector

Electropherogram recorder shows separation pattern of STRs

The separation of DNA segments is carried out on the interior wall of a glass capillary tube coated with a gel polymer and kept at a constant voltage. The size of the DNA fragments determines the speed at which they move through the column. This figure illustrates the separation of three sets of STRs (triplexing).

the appearance and interpretation of the DNA profile. Thus, when presented with a DNA mixture of two males and one female, each STR type would be expected to show six bands. However, the same mixture subjected to Y-STR analysis would show only two bands (one band for each male) for each Y-STR type.

Significance of DNA Typing

STR DNA typing has become an essential and basic investigative tool in the law enforcement community. The technology has progressed at a rapid rate and in only a few years has surmounted numerous legal challenges to become vital evidence for resolving violent crimes and sex offenses. DNA evidence is impartial, implicating the guilty and exonerating the innocent.

In a number of well-publicized cases, DNA evidence has exonerated individuals who have been wrongly convicted and imprisoned (see Figure 14–21). The importance of DNA analyses in criminal investigations has also placed added burdens on crime laboratories to improve their quality-assurance procedures and to ensure the correctness of their results. In several well-publicized instances, the accuracy of DNA tests conducted by government-funded laboratories has been called into question.

Key Points

* STRs are locations on the chromosome that contain short sequences that repeat themselves within the DNA molecule. They serve as useful markers for identification because they are found in great abundance throughout the human genome.

* The entire strand of an STR is very short, less than 450 bases long. This makes STRs much less susceptible to degradation, and they are often recovered from bodies or stains that have been subjected to extreme decomposition.

* The more STRs one can characterize, the smaller the percentage of the population from which a particular combination of STRs can emanate. This gives rise to the concept of multiplexing, in which the forensic scientist can simultaneously extract and amplify a combination of STRs.

* With STRs, as little as 18 DNA-containing cells are required for analysis.

Mitochondrial DNA

Typically, when one describes DNA in the context of a criminal investigation, the subject is assumed to be the DNA in the nucleus of a cell. Actually, a human cell contains two types of DNA—nuclear and mitochondrial. The first constitutes the twenty-three pairs of chromosomes in the nuclei of our cells. Each parent contributes to the genetic makeup of these chromosomes. Mitochondrial DNA (mtDNA), on the other hand, is found outside the nucleus of the cell and is inherited solely from the mother.

Mitochondria are cell structures found in all human cells. They are the power plants of the body, providing about 90 percent of the energy that the body needs to function. A single mitochondrion contains several loops of DNA, all of which are involved in energy generation. Further, because each

mitochondria
Small structures outside the nucleus that supply energy to the cell.

After 24 Years in Prison, Man Has a Reason to Smile

By SHAILA DEWAN

MARIETTA, Ga., Dec. 7—It is rare to see a prison inmate with a life sentence who cannot stop grinning. Thus, when presented with a DNA mixture of two males and one female, each STR type would be expected to show six bands. However, the same mixture subjected to Y-STR analysis would show only two bands (one band for each male) for each Y-STR type.

But that was Robert Clark Jr. on Wednesday, the day before his conviction for rape, robbery and kidnapping was expected to be vacated on the strength of a DNA test that showed he was not the rapist.

After 24 years in prison—one of the longest incarcerations served by the 164 people who have been exonerated by DNA testing—Mr. Clark, 45, was buoyant at the prospect of seeing his siblings, children and the five grandchildren he did not have when he was sentenced in 1982.

"I still got a little life in me," he said.

Though wrenching, Mr. Clark's story is not so different from that of others who were wrongfully convicted. What is stunning about it is the fact that the man who the authorities now believe was the real rapist, Floyd Antonio Arnold, was in early reach of the police at the time.

The DNA test that exonerated Mr. Clark started a chain reaction that revealed not just Mr. Clark's innocence, but a series of law-enforcement bungles. Those missteps allowed Mr. Arnold to commit violent crimes repeatedly and, very nearly, to walk out of prison, where he is serving time for cruelty to children, at the end of January, despite the fact that his DNA matches that found in Mr. Clark's case and two other previously unsolved rapes.

"This is the worst case of tunnel vision that we've seen in the history of the Innocence Project," said Peter J. Neufeld, a co-founder of the project, which has been instrumental in DNA exonerations and which is handling Mr. Clark's case.

At 21, Mr. Clark was living with his mother and 5-year-old son in southwestern Atlanta. He worked as a roofer and had no criminal record, save a juvenile burglary charge. One day an acquaintance, Mr. Arnold, lent him a car. Because the car was not hotwired and Mr. Arnold had the keys, Mr. Clark said, he did not think the car was stolen.

But the car had belonged to Patricia J. Tucker, 29, who had been getting into the driver's seat in a Kentucky Fried Chicken parking lot where she was carjacked, kidnapped, taken to the woods and raped three times. At Mr. Clark's trial, the sole defense witness identified Mr. Arnold in the courtroom and testified she had seen him driving the car before Mr. Clark was arrested with it.

But Ms. Tucker testified that Mr. Clark had been her attacker, even though she had initially described him as 5-foot-7 and Mr. Clark was 6-foot-1. The detective in the case told the jury that he never investigated Mr. Arnold because Mr. Clark had initially lied to officers about where he had gotten the car, then switched his story. The judge sentenced Mr. Clark to life.

When Mr. Clark heard that, he interrupted, saying: "Your Honor, they had Tony here. I can't put him on the stand. He'll tell you I didn't do nothing but drive the car two weeks later. Y'all got him right here."

"Mr. Clark, you have had your trial," the jury admonished. "Just remain silent."

Mr. Arnold went on to commit a string of felonies, including burglary, gun possession and sodomy. In 2001, he was charged with multiple counts of child molesting in a case prosecutors say involved a 13-year-old female relative. He pleaded guilty to a lesser charge, cruelty to children, for which he is now serving time.

Meanwhile, Mr. Clark wrote birthday cards to his children and letters to anyone he thought might be able to help with his case.

When his mother came to visit, he would lay his head in her lap and sleep. When her kidneys failed, he asked to be locked up in solitary confinement so he could be alone to grieve. She died last year, before he gained his freedom. "She knew I got the court order I needed," Mr. Clark said, smiling again.

Finally, the Innocence Project took his case, and a DNA test was done on the evidence. In November, the results showed that the attacker was not Mr. Clark. The district attorney in Cobb County, Pat Head, ran the DNA profile against the criminal offender database. A match came back: Mr. Arnold.

But there was more, said Ted Staples, the manager of forensic biology for the Georgia Bureau of Investigation. The printout showed that in 2003, when Mr. Arnold's DNA was first added to the database, it matched that in two other rapes, in Fulton and DeKalb Counties.

No action was taken against Mr. Arnold, who will finish his current sentence on Jan. 31.

Mr. Staples said the police in those jurisdictions were notified at the time by phone and letter. But a spokesman for the Fulton County Police Department said it did not know of the match until last week. It has put a hold on Mr. Arnold so he cannot be released.

In DeKalb, Detective Sgt. K. D. Johnson, of the DeKalb County Police Department's youth and sex crimes unit, acknowledged that the department was notified in 2003, but said that the information had slipped through the cracks. "It had gone through several different detectives who have since been transferred to other departments," Sergeant Johnson said. "We're trying to figure out who had it and when."

For his part, Mr. Clark stands to get some restitution from the state, which has paid $1.5 million to two other exonerated men. But, he said, he is thinking more about his 5-year-old granddaughter, Alexis, than how much he might be owed. "They owe me an apology," he said. "They done messed my life up." And he smiled.

FIGURE 14–21 Copyright © 2005 by The New York Times Company. Reprinted with permission.

cell in our bodies contains hundreds to thousands of mitochondria, there are hundreds to thousands of mtDNA copies in a human cell. This compares to just one set of nuclear DNA located in that same cell.

Forensic scientists rely on mtDNA to identify a subject when nuclear DNA is significantly degraded, such as in charred remains, or when nuclear DNA may be present in only very small quantities (such as in a hair shaft). Interestingly, when authorities cannot obtain a reference sample from an individual who may be long deceased or missing, an mtDNA reference sample can be obtained from any maternally related relative. However, all individuals of the same maternal lineage will be indistinguishable by mtDNA analysis.

Although mtDNA analysis is significantly more sensitive than nuclear DNA profiling, forensic analysis of mtDNA is more rigorous, time consuming, and costly than nuclear DNA profiling. For this reason, only a handful of public and private forensic laboratories receive evidence for mtDNA determination. The FBI Laboratory strictly limits the types of cases in which it will apply mtDNA technology.

WebExtra 14.13

See How We Inherit Our Mitochondrial DNA
www.prenhall.com/saferstein

Closer Analysis

Forensic Aspects of Mitochondrial DNA

As discussed previously, nuclear DNA is composed of a continuous linear strand of nucleotides (A, C, G, and T). By contrast, mtDNA is constructed in a circular or loop configuration. Each loop contains enough A, C, G, and T (approximately 16,569 total nucleotides) to make up thirty-seven genes involved in mitochondrial energy generation.

Two regions of mtDNA have been found to be highly variable in the human population. These two regions have been designated hypervariable region I (HV1) and hypervariable region II (HV2), as shown in the figure. As indicated previously, the process for analyzing HV1 and HV2 is tedious. It involves generating many copies of these DNA hypervariable regions by PCR and then determining the order of the A–T–C–G bases constituting the hypervariable regions. This process is known as *sequencing*. The FBI Laboratory, the Armed Forces DNA Identification Laboratory, and other laboratories have collaborated to compile an mtDNA population database containing the base sequences from HV1 and HV2.

Once the sequences of the hypervariable regions from a case sample are obtained, most laboratories simply report the number of times these sequences appear in the mtDNA database maintained by the FBI. The mtDNA database contains about five thousand sequences. This approach permits an assessment of how common or rare an observed mtDNA sequence is in the database.

Interestingly, many of the sequences that have been determined in case work are unique to the existing database, and many types are present at frequencies of no greater than 1 percent in the database. Thus, it is often possible to demonstrate how uncommon a particular mtDNA sequence is. However, even under the best circumstances, mtDNA typing does not approach STR analysis in its discrimination power. Thus, mtDNA analysis is best reserved for samples for which nuclear DNA typing is simply not possible.

The first time mtDNA was admitted as evidence in a U.S. court was in 1996 in the case of *State of Tennessee* v. *Paul Ware.* Here, mtDNA was used to

(continued)

Closer Analysis *(continued)*

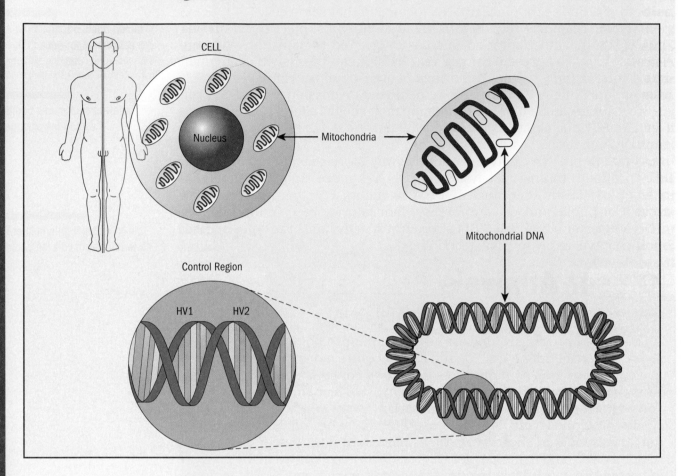

Every cell in the body contains hundreds of mitochondria, which provide energy to the cell. Each mitochondrion contains numerous copies of DNA shaped in the form of a loop. Distinctive differences between individuals in their mitochondrial DNA makeup are found in two specific segments of the control region on the DNA loop known as HV1 and HV2.

link two hairs recovered from the crime scene to the defendant. Interestingly, in this case, blood and semen evidence were absent. Mitochondrial DNA analysis also plays a key role in the identification of human remains. An abundant amount of mtDNA is generally found in skeletal remains. Importantly, mtDNA reference samples are available from family members sharing the same mother, grandmother, great-grandmother, and so on.

WebExtra 14.14

Look into the Structure Mitochondrial DNA and See How It's Used for DNA Typing
www.prenhall.com/saferstein

One of the most publicized cases performed on human remains was the identification of the individual buried in the tomb of the Vietnam War's unknown soldier. The remains lying in the tomb were believed to belong to First Lt. Michael J. Blassie, whose A-37 warplane was shot down near An Loc, South Vietnam, in 1972. In 1984, the U.S. Army Central Identification Laboratory failed to identify the remains by physical characteristics, personal artifacts, or blood-typing results from hairs. The remains were subsequently placed in the tomb. In 1998, at the insistence of the Blassie family, the remains were disinterred for mtDNA analysis and the results were compared to references from seven families

Forensics at Work

Outrage: The O. J. Simpson Verdict

To distill this case down to its irreducible minimum (and temporarily ignoring all the other evidence pointing inexorably to Simpson's guilt), if your blood is found at the murder scene, as Simpson's was conclusively proved to be by DNA tests, that's really the end of the ball game. There is nothing more to say. (And in this case, not only was Simpson's blood found at the murder scene, but the victims' blood was found inside his car and home.) I mean, to deny guilt when your blood is at the murder scene is the equivalent of a man being caught by his wife *in flagrante* with another woman and saying to her (quoting comedian Richard Pryor), "Who are you going to believe? Me or your lying eyes?"

At the crime scene there were five blood drops leading away from the slain bodies of Nicole Brown Simpson and Ronald Goldman toward the rear alley, four of which were immediately to the *left* of bloody size-12 shoe prints (Simpson's shoe size). This indicated, of course, that the killer had been wounded on the left side of his body. And the morning after the murders, Simpson was observed by the police to be wearing a bandage on his left middle finger. When the bandage was removed that afternoon, it was seen that he had a deep cut on the knuckle of the finger.

DNA (deoxyribonucleic acid) is the genetic material found in all human cells that carries the coded messages of heredity unique (with the exception of identical twins) to each individual. DNA, then, is our genetic fingerprint. Each of the approximately 100 trillion cells in a human body contains twenty-three pairs of chromosomes—one of each pair coming from one's father, the other from the mother—which contain DNA molecules. In criminal cases, DNA can be extracted from samples of blood, semen, saliva, skin, or

hair follicles found at a crime scene and then compared to DNA drawn from a suspect to determine if there is a "match." DNA testing is a new forensic science, first used in Great Britain in 1985 and in the United States in 1987.

DNA tests on all five blood drops and on three bloodstains found on the rear gate at the crime scene showed that all of this blood belonged to Simpson. Two DNA tests were used: PCR (polymerase chain reaction) and RFLP (restrictive fragment length polymorphism). The PCR test is less precise than the RFLP, but can be conducted on much smaller blood samples as well as samples that have degenerated ("degraded") because of bacteria and/or exposure to the elements. PCR tests were conducted on four out of the five blood drops. Three showed that only one out of 240,000 people had DNA with the markers found in the sample. (A marker is a gene that makes up one portion of the DNA molecule, and the more markers in the sample, the more comparison tests can be conducted, and hence the greater the exclusion of other humans.) The fourth blood drop had markers which one out of 5,200 people could have. Simpson was one of these people. The fifth blood drop had sufficient markers for an RFLP test, and showed that only one out of 170 million people had DNA with those markers. Again, Simpson's blood did. The richest sample was on the rear gate, and a RFLP test showed that only one out of 57 billion people had those markers. Simpson was one of them. In other words, just on the blood evidence alone, there's only a one out of 57 billion chance that Simpson is innocent. Fifty-seven billion is approximately ten times the current population of the entire world.

Now I realize that Igor in Kiev, Gino in Naples, Colin down Johannesburg way, and

(continued)

Forensics at Work

Outrage: The O. J. Simpson Verdict *(continued)*

Kartac on Pluto might have the same DNA as O. J. Simpson. If you're a skeptic, I wouldn't blame you if you checked to see if Igor, Gino, Colin, or Kartac was in Brentwood on the night of the murders, beat Nicole within an inch of her life, had blood all over his car, driveway, and home on the night of the murders, had no alibi, and, if charged with the murders, would refuse to take the witness stand to defend himself. Who knows—maybe Simpson isn't the murderer after all. Maybe Igor or one of the others is. You should definitely check this out. And while you're checking it out, someone should be checking you into the nearest mental ward.

To elaborate on the irreducible minimum mentioned earlier, there are only three possible explanations other than guilt for one's blood being found at the murder scene, and all three are preposterous on their face. One is that Simpson left his blood there on an earlier occasion. When Simpson was interrogated by LAPD detectives on the afternoon after these murders, he said he had not cut himself the last time he was at the Bundy address a week earlier. But even without that, how can one believe that on some prior occasion Simpson bled, not just on the Bundy premises, but at the precise point on the premises where the murders occurred? In fact, so farfetched is this possibility that even the defense attorneys, whose stock-in-trade during the trial was absurdity, never proffered it to the jury.

And here, not only was Simpson's blood found at the murder scene, but there were the four drops of Simpson's blood found just to the left of the killer's bloody shoe prints leaving the murder scene. If there is someone who isn't satisfied even by this, I would suggest that this book is perhaps not for you, that you think about pursuing more appropriate intellectual pursuits, such as comic strips. When I was a kid,

one of my favorites was *Mandrake the Magician.* You might check to see if Mandrake is still doing his thing.

The second possibility is that Simpson cut himself while killing Ron Goldman and Nicole Brown in self-defense—that is, either Ron or Nicole or both together unleashed a deadly assault on Simpson, and he either took out a knife he had on his own person or wrestled Ron's or Nicole's knife away, and stabbed the two of them to death. This, of course, is just too insane to talk about. Again, even the defense attorneys, who apparently possess the gonads of ten thousand elephants, never suggested this possibility. It should be added parenthetically that if such a situation had occurred, Simpson wouldn't have had any reason to worry, since self-defense is a justifiable homicide, a complete defense to murder.

The third and final possibility is that the LAPD detectives planted Simpson's blood not just at the murder scene but to the left of the bloody shoe prints leaving the scene. This is not as insane a proposition as the first two, but only because there are degrees of everything in life. It is still an insane possibility, and if any reader is silly enough to believe that the LAPD detectives decided to frame someone they believed to be innocent of these murders (Simpson) and actually planted his blood all over the murder scene (and, of course, planted the victims' blood in Simpson's car and home), again, this book is probably not for that reader. This book is for people who are very angry that a brutal murderer is among us—with a smile on his face, no less—and want to know how this terrible miscarriage of justice could have occurred. . . .

Let me point out to those who believe in the "possible" existence of either of the aforementioned three innocent possibilities for Simpson's blood being found at the murder scene, that the prosecution only has the burden of proving guilt beyond a *reasonable* doubt, not beyond all possible doubt. So it isn't necessary to have all possible doubts of guilt removed from one's mind in order to reach a conclusion of guilt. Only reasonable doubts of guilt have to be removed. Of course, in this case, *no* doubt remains of Simpson's guilt. . . .

Source: Vincent Bugliosi, *OUTRAGE: The Five Reasons Why O. J. Simpson Got Away with Murder.* Copyright © 1996 by Vincent Bugliosi. Reprinted by permission of W. W. Norton & Company, Inc.

thought to be associated with the case. The remains in the tomb were subsequently analyzed and confirmed to be consistent with DNA from Lt. Blassie's family.

Key Points

- Mitochondrial DNA is located outside the cell's nucleus and is inherited from the mother.

- Mitochondria are cell structures found in all human cells. They provide most of the energy that the body needs to function.

- Mitochondrial DNA typing does not approach STR analysis in its discrimination power and thus is best reserved for samples, such as hair, for which STR analysis may not be possible.

Combined DNA Index System (CODIS)

Perhaps the most significant investigative tool to arise from a DNA-typing program is CODIS (Combined DNA Index System), a computer software program developed by the FBI that maintains local, state, and national databases of DNA profiles from convicted offenders, unsolved crime-scene evidence, and profiles of missing people. CODIS allows crime laboratories to compare DNA types recovered from crime-scene evidence to those of convicted sex offenders and other convicted criminals.

Thousands of CODIS matches have linked serial crimes to each other and have solved crimes by allowing investigators to match crime-scene evidence to known convicted offenders. This capability is of tremendous value to investigators in cases in which the police have not been able to identify a suspect. The CODIS concept has already had a significant impact on police investigations in various states, as shown in the accompanying "Forensic Brief."

Key Point

- CODIS is a computer software program developed by the FBI that maintains local, state, and national databases of DNA profiles from convicted offenders, unsolved crime-scene evidence, and profiles of missing people.

Forensic Brief

In the fall of 1979, a 61-year-old patient wandered away from a U.S. Department of Veterans Affairs medical facility. Despite an extensive search, authorities never located the missing man. More than ten years later, a dog discovered a human skull in a wooded area near the facility. DNA Analysis Unit II of the FBI Laboratory received the case in the winter of 1999.

The laboratory determined that the mitochondrial DNA profile from the missing patient's brother matched the mitochondrial DNA profile from the recovered skull and provided the information to the local medical examiner. Subsequently, the remains were declared to be those of the missing patient and returned to the family for burial.

Source: *FBI Law Enforcement Bulletin* 78 (2002): 21.

Collection and Preservation of Biological Evidence for DNA Analysis

Since the early 1990s, the advent of DNA profiling has vaulted biological crime-scene evidence to a stature of importance that is eclipsed only by the fingerprint. In fact, the high sensitivity of DNA determinations has even changed the way police investigators define biological evidence.

Just how sensitive is STR profiling? Forensic analysts using currently accepted protocols can reach sensitivity levels as low as 125 *picograms*. Interestingly, a human cell has an estimated 7 picograms of DNA, which means that only eighteen DNA-bearing cells are needed to obtain an STR profile. However, modifications in the technology can readily extend the level of detection down to nine or even fewer cells. A quantity of DNA that is below the normal level of detection is defined as a low copy number. With this technology in hand, the horizon of the criminal investigator extends beyond the traditional dried blood or semen stain to include stamps and envelopes licked with saliva, a cup or can that has touched a person's lips, chewing gum, the sweat band of a hat, or a bedsheet containing dead skin cells. Likewise, skin or *epithelial cells* transferred onto the surface of a weapon, the interior of a glove, or a pen have yielded DNA results.[11]

The ultimate sensitivity goal in forensic DNA analysis is profiling DNA extracted from one human cell. Such an accomplishment seems close to fruition. Researchers have reported obtaining STR profiles from one or two cells and have profiled DNA from single dermal ridge fingerprints.[12] Although it's premature to imply that this technology, or a comparable one, is eligible for admission in criminal trials, one cannot exclude its use in criminal and forensic intelligence investigations. Table 14–2 illustrates the power of DNA as a creator of physical evidence.

low copy number
Fewer than eighteen DNA-bearing cells.

Collection of Biological Evidence

Before investigators become enamored with the wonders of DNA, they should first realize that the crime scene must be treated in the traditional manner. Before the collection of evidence begins, biological evidence

Forensic Brief

In 1990, a series of attacks on elderly victims was committed in Goldsboro, North Carolina, by an unknown individual dubbed the Night Stalker. During one such attack in March, an elderly woman was brutally raped and almost murdered. Her daughter's early arrival home saved the woman's life. The suspect fled, leaving behind materials intended to burn the residence and the victim in an attempt to conceal the crime.

In July 1990, another elderly woman was raped and murdered in her home. Three months later, a third elderly woman was raped and stabbed to death. Her husband was also murdered. Although their house was set alight in an attempt to cover up the crime, fire and rescue personnel pulled the bodies from the house before it was engulfed in flames. DNA analysis of biological evidence collected from vaginal swabs from the three rape victims enabled authorities to conclude that the same perpetrator had committed all three crimes. However, there was no suspect.

More than ten years after these crimes were committed, law enforcement authorities retested the biological evidence from all three cases using newer DNA technology and entered the DNA profiles into North Carolina's DNA database. The DNA profile developed from the crime-scene evidence was compared to thousands of convicted-offender profiles already in the database.

In April 2001, a "cold hit" was made with an individual in the convicted-offender DNA database. The perpetrator had been convicted of shooting into an occupied dwelling, an offense that requires inclusion in the North Carolina DNA database. The suspect was brought into custody for questioning and was served with a search warrant to obtain a sample of his blood. That sample was analyzed and compared to the crime-scene evidence, confirming the DNA database match. When confronted with the DNA evidence, the suspect confessed to all three crimes.

Source: National Institute of Justice, "Using DNA to Solve Cold Cases," NIJ special report, 2002, www.ojp.usdoj.gov/nij/pubs_sum/194197.htm.

---

should be photographed close up and its location relative to the entire crime scene recorded through notes, sketches, and photographs. If the shape and position of bloodstains may provide information about the circumstances of the crime, an expert must immediately evaluate the blood evidence. The significance of the position and shape of bloodstains can best be ascertained when the expert has an on-site overview of the entire crime scene and can better reconstruct the movement of the individuals involved. The blood pattern should not be disturbed before this phase of the investigation is completed.

The evidence collector must handle all body fluids and biologically stained materials with a minimum of personal contact. All body fluids must be assumed to be infectious; hence, wearing disposable latex gloves while handling the evidence is required. Latex gloves also significantly reduce the possibility that the evidence collector will contaminate the evidence. These gloves should be changed frequently during the evidence-collection phase of the investigation. Safety considerations and avoidance of contamination also call for the wearing of face masks, shoe covers, and possibly coveralls.

Table 14–2   Location and Sources of DNA at Crime Scenes

Evidence	Possible Location of DNA on the Evidence	Source of DNA
Baseball bat or similar weapon	Handle, end	Sweat, skin, blood, tissue
Hat, bandanna, or mask	Inside	Sweat, hair, dandruff
Eyeglasses	Nose or ear pieces, lens	Sweat, skin
Facial tissue, cotton swab	Surface area	Mucus, blood, sweat, semen, ear wax
Dirty laundry	Surface area	Blood, sweat, semen
Toothpick	Tips	Saliva
Used cigarette	Cigarette butt	Saliva
Stamp or envelope	Licked area	Saliva
Tape or ligature	Inside/outside surface	Skin, sweat
Bottle, can, or glass	Sides, mouthpiece	Saliva, sweat
Used condom	Inside/outside surface	Semen, vaginal or rectal cells
Blanket, pillow, sheet	Surface area	Sweat, hair, semen, urine, saliva
"Through and through" bullet	Outside surface	Blood, tissue
Bite mark	Person's skin or clothing	Saliva
Fingernail, partial fingernail	Scrapings	Blood, sweat, tissue

Source: National Institute of Justice, U.S. Department of Justice.

Blood has great evidential value when a transfer between a victim and suspect can be demonstrated. For this reason, all clothing from both victim and suspect should be collected and sent to the laboratory for examination. This procedure must be followed even when the presence of blood on a garment does not appear obvious to the investigator. Laboratory search procedures are far more revealing and sensitive than any that can be conducted at the crime scene. In addition, blood should also be searched for in less-than-obvious places. For example, the criminal may have wiped his or her hands on materials not readily apparent to the investigator. Investigators should look for towels, handkerchiefs, or rags that may have been used and then hidden, and should also examine floor cracks or other crevices that may have trapped blood.

Packaging of Biological Evidence

Biological evidence should not be packaged in plastic or airtight containers, because accumulation of residual moisture could contribute to the growth of DNA-destroying bacteria and fungi. Each stained article should be packaged separately in a paper bag or a well-ventilated box. If feasible, the entire stained article should be packaged and submitted for examination. If this is not possible, dried blood is best removed from a surface with a sterile cotton-tipped swab lightly moistened with distilled water from a dropper bottle.

A portion of the unstained surface material near the recovered stain must likewise be removed or swabbed and placed in a separate package. This is known as a substrate control. The forensic examiner might use the substrate swab to confirm that the results of the tests performed were brought about by the stain and not by the material on which it was deposited. However, this practice is normally not necessary when DNA

substrate control
An unstained object adjacent to an area on which biological material has been deposited.

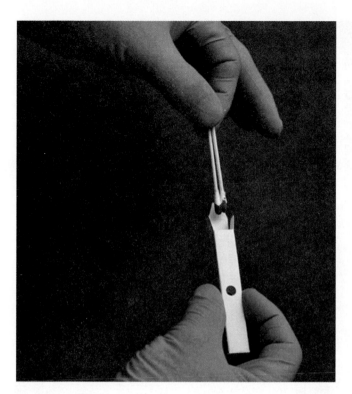

FIGURE 14–22 Air-dried swabs are placed in a swab box for delivery to the forensic laboratory. *Courtesy Tri-Tech, Inc., Southport, N.C., www.tritechusa.com*

determinations are carried out in the laboratory. One point is critical, and that is that the collected swabs must not be packaged in a wet state. After collection, the swab must be air-dried for approximately five to ten minutes. Then it is best to place it in a swab box (see Figure 14–22), which has a circular hole to allow air circulation. The swab box can then be placed in a paper or manila envelope.

All packages containing biological evidence should be refrigerated or stored in a cool location out of direct sunlight until delivery to the laboratory. However, one common exception is blood mixed with soil. Microbes present in soil rapidly degrade DNA. Therefore, blood in soil must be stored in a clean glass or plastic container and immediately frozen.

Obtaining DNA Reference Specimens

Biological evidence attains its full forensic value only when an analyst can compare each of its DNA types to known DNA samples collected from victims and suspects. For this purpose, at least 7 milliliters of whole blood should be drawn from individuals by a qualified medical person. The blood sample should be collected in a sterile vacuum tube containing the preservative EDTA (ethylenediamine tetraacetic acid). In addition to serving as a preservative, EDTA inhibits the activity of enzymes that degrade DNA. The tubes must be kept refrigerated (not frozen) while awaiting transportation to the laboratory.

In addition to blood, other options exist for obtaining standard/reference DNA specimens. The least intrusive method for obtaining a DNA standard/reference, one that nonmedical personnel can readily use, is the *buccal swab*. A cotton swab is placed in the subject's mouth and the inside of the cheek is vigorously swabbed, resulting in the transfer of **buccal cells** onto the swab (see Figure 14–23).

buccal cells
Cells from the inner cheek lining.

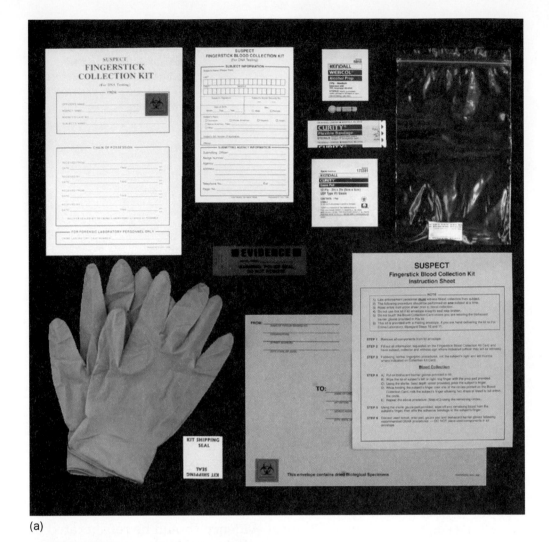

(a)

(b)

(c)

FIGURE 14–23 **A buccal swab collection kit is designed for use by nonmedical personnel. The cotton-tipped swabs are placed in the subject's mouth and the inside of the cheek is vigorously swabbed, resulting in the transfer of buccal cells onto the cotton bulb of the swab. The kit is then delivered to the forensic laboratory.** *Courtesy Tri-Tech, Inc., Southport, N.C., www.tritechusa.com*

If an individual is not available to give a DNA standard/reference sample, some interesting alternatives are available, including a toothbrush, combs and hairbrushes, a razor, soiled laundry, used cigarette butts, and earplugs. Any of these items may contain a sufficient quantity of DNA for typing. Interestingly, as investigators worked to identify the remains of victims of the World Trade Center attack on September 11, 2001, the families of the missing were asked to supply the New York City DNA Laboratory with these types of items in an effort to match recovered DNA with human remains.

Contamination of DNA Evidence

One key concern during the collection of a DNA-containing specimen is contamination. Contamination can occur by introducing foreign DNA through coughing or sneezing onto a stain during the collection process, or there can be a transfer of DNA when items of evidence are incorrectly placed in contact with each other during packaging. Fortunately, an examination of DNA band patterns in the laboratory readily reveals the presence of contamination. For example, with an STR, one will expect to see a two-band pattern. More than two bands suggests a mixture of DNA from more than one source.

Crime-scene investigators can take some relatively simple steps to minimize the contamination of biological evidence:

1. Change gloves before handling each new piece of evidence.

2. Collect a substrate control for possible subsequent laboratory examination.

3. Pick up small items of evidence such as cigarette butts and stamps with clean forceps. Use disposable forceps so that they can be discarded after a single evidence collection.

4. Always package each item of evidence in its own well-ventilated container.

A common occurrence at crime scenes is to suspect the presence of blood, but not be able to observe any with the naked eye. In these situations, the common test of choice is luminol or Bluestar®. Interestingly, luminol and Bluestar® do not inhibit the ability to detect and characterize STRs.[13] Therefore, they can be used to locate traces of blood and areas that have been washed nearly free of blood without compromising the potential for DNA typing.

WebExtra 14.15
DNA Forensics
www.prenhall.com/saferstein

Key Points

- Packaging of bloodstained evidence in plastic or airtight containers must be avoided because the accumulation of residual moisture could contribute to the growth of blood-destroying bacteria and fungi. Each stained article should be packaged separately in a paper bag or in a well-ventilated box.

- The least intrusive method for obtaining a DNA standard/reference is the buccal swab. In this procedure, cotton swabs are placed in the subject's mouth and the inside of the cheek is vigorously swabbed, resulting in the transfer of cells from the inner cheek lining onto the swab.

Forensic Brief

A woman alleged that she had been held against her will and sexually assaulted by a male friend in an apartment. During the course of the assault, a contact lens was knocked from the victim's eye. After the assault, she escaped, but due to fear from threats made by her attacker, she did not report the assault to the police for three days. When the police examined the apartment, they noted that it had been thoroughly cleaned. A vacuum cleaner bag was seized for examination, and several pieces of material resembling fragments of a contact lens were discovered within the bag.

In the laboratory, approximately 20 nanograms of human DNA was recovered from the contact lens fragments. Cells from both the eyeball and the interior of the eyelids are naturally replaced every six to twenty-four hours. As such, both are potential sources for the DNA found. The DNA profile originating from the fragments matched the victim, thus corroborating the victim's account of the crime. The estimated population frequency of occurrence for the nine matching STRs are approximately 1 in 850 million. The suspect subsequently pleaded guilty to the offense.

STR Locus	Victim's DNA Type	Contact Lens
D3S1358	15,18	15,18
FGA	24,25	24,25
vWA	17,17	17,17
THO1	6,7	6,7
F13A1	5,6	5,6
fes/fps	11,12	11,12
D5S818	11,12	11,12
D13S317	11,12	11,12
D7S820	10,12	10,12

Source: R. A. Wickenheiser and R. M. Jobin, "Comparison of DNA Recovered from a Contact Lens Using PCR DNA Typing." *Canadian Society of Forensic Science Journal* 32 (1999): 67.

Chapter Summary

Laboratory tests use specific antigen and serum antibody reactions. An antibody reacts or agglutinates only with its specific antigen. The identity of each of the four A-B-O blood groups can be established by testing the blood with anti-A and anti-B sera.

The concept of specific antigen–antibody reactions has been applied to immunoassay techniques for the detection of drugs-of-abuse in blood and urine. When an animal is injected with an antigen, its body produces a series of antibodies, all of which are designed to attack some particular site on the antigen of interest.

The criminalist must be prepared to answer the following questions when examining dried blood: (1) Is it blood? (2) From what species did the blood originate? (3) If the blood is of human origin, how closely can it be associated to a particular individual? The determination of blood is best made by means of a preliminary color test. A positive result from the Kastle-Meyer color test is highly indicative of blood. Alternatively, the luminol or Bluestar® tests are used to search out trace amounts of blood located at crime scenes. The precipitin test uses antisera normally derived from rabbits that have been injected with the blood of a known animal to determine the species origin of a questioned bloodstain.

Many of the cases sent to a forensic laboratory involve sexual offenses, making it necessary to examine exhibits for the presence of seminal stains. The best way to locate and at the same time characterize a seminal stain is to perform the acid phosphatase color test. Semen can be unequivocally identified by either the presence of spermatozoa or a protein unique to seminal plasma. Forensic scientists can successfully link seminal material to an individual by DNA typing. The rape victim must undergo a medical examination as soon as possible after the assault. At that time clothing, hairs, and vaginal and rectal swabs can be collected for subsequent laboratory examination. If a suspect is apprehended within twenty-four hours of the assault, it may be possible to detect the victim's DNA on the male's underwear or on a penile swab of the suspect.

The gene is the fundamental unit of heredity. Each gene is composed of DNA specifically designed to control the genetic traits of our cells. Portions of the DNA structure are as unique to each individual as fingerprints. DNA is constructed as a very large molecule made by linking a series of repeating units called nucleotides with the four types of bases: adenine *(A)*, guanine *(G)*, cytosine *(C)*, and thymine *(T)*. As a result, adenine pairs with thymine and guanine pairs with cytosine and properly align to form a double helix. This concept is known as base pairing. The order of the bases is what distinguishes DNA strands.

Portions of the DNA molecule contain sequences of bases that are repeated numerous times. To a forensic scientist, these tandem repeats offer a means of distinguishing one individual from another through DNA typing. Length differences associated with relatively short repeating DNA strands are called short tandem repeats (STRs) and form the basis for the current DNA-typing procedure. This procedure incorporates the process of polymerase chain reaction (PCR), in which STR strands are multiplied over a billionfold. PCR is responsible for the ability of STR typing to detect the genetic material of as few as eighteen DNA-bearing cells.

Because STRs are found in great abundance throughout the human genome, they are much less susceptible to degradation and may often be recovered from bodies or stains that have been subjected to extreme decomposition. Also, because of their shortness, STRs are ideal candidates for multiplication by PCR, thus overcoming the limited-sample-size problem often associated with crime-scene evidence.

What makes STRs so attractive to forensic scientists is that hundreds of types of STRs are found in human genes. The more STRs one can characterize, the smaller the percentage of the population from which a particular combination of STRs can emanate. This gives rise to the concept of multiplexing. Using the technology of PCR, one can simultaneously extract and amplify a combination of STRs. Currently, U.S. crime laboratories have standardized on thirteen STRs.

Another type of DNA used for individual characterization is mitochondrial DNA. Mitochondrial DNA is located outside the cell's nucleus and is inherited from the mother. However, mitochondrial DNA typing does not approach STR analysis in its discrimination power and thus is best reserved for samples, such as hair, for which STR analysis may not be possible.

Biological evidence should not be packaged in plastic or airtight containers because accumulation of residual moisture could contribute to the growth of blood-destroying bacteria and fungi. Each stained article should be packaged separately in a paper bag or well-ventilated box.

Review Questions

1. Karl Landsteiner discovered that blood can be classified by its _____.

2. True or False: No two individuals, except for identical twins, can be expected to have the same combination of blood types or antigens. _____

3. _____ is the fluid portion of unclotted blood.

4. The liquid that separates from the blood when a clot is formed is called the _____.

5. _____ transport oxygen from the lungs to the body tissues and carry carbon dioxide back to the lungs.

6. On the surface of red blood cells are chemical substances called _____ that impart blood type characteristics to the cells.

7. Type A individuals have _____ antigens on the surface of their red blood cells.

8. True or False: Type O individuals have both A and B antigens on their red blood cells. _____

9. The presence or absence of the _____ and _____ antigens on the red blood cells determines a person's blood type in the A-B-O system.

10. The D antigen is also known as the _____ antigen.

11. Serum contains proteins known as _____, which destroy or inactivate antigens.

12. True or False: An antibody reacts with any antigen. _____

13. The term _____ describes the clumping together of red blood cells by the action of an antibody.

14. Type B blood contains _____ antigens and anti-_____ antibodies.

15. True or False: Type AB blood has neither anti-A nor anti-B. _____

16. Type B red blood cells agglutinate when added to type _____ blood.

17. Type A red blood cells agglutinate when added to type _____ blood.

18. A drug–protein complex can be injected into an animal to form specific _____ for that drug.

19. For many years, the most commonly used color test for identifying blood was the _____ color test.

20. The reagent in the _____ test will turn pink if oxidation takes place. It is not a specific test for blood as some vegetable materials may turn the reagent pink.

21. _____ reagent reacts with blood, causing it to luminesce.

22. Blood can be characterized as being of human origin by the _____ test.

23. The antigens of a human blood sample will move toward the well containing human antiserum in a process called _____.

24. The concentration of the enzyme _____ secreted by the prostate is up to four hundred times higher in seminal fluid than any other bodily fluid.

25. Semen is unequivocally identified by the microscopic appearance of _____.

26. True or False: Males with a low sperm count have a condition known as oligospermia. _____

27. The protein _____ is useful for the identification of semen.

28. True or False: The collection of rape evidence should include swabs, combings, and fingernail scrapings from the victim and the suspect. _____

29. True or False: Seminal constituents may remain in the vagina for up to six days after intercourse. _____

30. The basic unit of heredity is the _____.

31. Genes are positioned on threadlike bodies called _____.

32. All cells in the human body, except the reproductive cells, have _____ pairs of chromosomes.

33. Genes that influence a given characteristic and are aligned with one another on a chromosome pair are known as _____.

34. When a pair of allelic genes is identical, the genes are said to be _____.

35. A(n) _____ is composed of a sugar molecule, a phosphorus-containing group, and a nitrogen-containing molecule called a base.

36. _____ different bases are associated with the makeup of DNA.

37. Watson and Crick demonstrated that DNA is composed of two strands coiled into the shape of a(n) _____.

38. The base sequence *T–G–C–A* can be paired with the base sequence _____ in a double-helix configuration.

39. True or False: Enzymes known as DNA polymerases assemble new DNA strands into a proper base sequence during replication. _____

40. DNA evidence can be copied using DNA polymerases in a technique known as _____.

41. Used as markers for identification purposes, _____ are locations on the chromosome that contain short sequences that repeat themselves within the DNA molecule and in great abundance throughout the human genome.

42. True or False: The longer the DNA strand, the less susceptible it is to degradation. _____

43. The short length of STRs allows them to be replicated by _____.

44. The concept of _____ involves the simultaneous detection of more than one DNA marker.

45. STR fragments are preferably separated and identified by _____.

46. True or False: Y-STR typing is useful when one is confronted with a DNA mixture containing more than one male contributor. _____

47. Mitochondrial DNA is inherited only from the _____.

48. True or False: Mitochondrial DNA is less plentiful in the human cell than is nuclear DNA. _____

49. (CODIS, AFIS) maintains local, state, and national databases of DNA profiles from convicted offenders, unsolved crime-scene evidence, and profiles of missing people.

50. Amazingly, the sensitivity of STR profiling requires only _____ DNA-bearing cells to obtain an STR profile.

51. During evidence collection, all body fluids must be assumed to be _____ and handled with latex-gloved hands.

52. True or False: Airtight packages make the best containers for blood-containing evidence. _____

53. True or False: Small amounts of blood are best submitted to a crime laboratory in a wet condition. _____

54. Whole blood collected for DNA-typing purposes must be placed in a vacuum container with the preservative _____.

Application and Critical Thinking

1. Police investigating the scene of a sexual assault recover a large blanket that they believe may contain useful physical evidence. They take it to the laboratory of forensic serologist Scott Alden, asking him to test it for the presence of semen. Noticing faint pink stains on the blanket, Scott asks the investigating detective if he is aware of anything that might recently have been spilled on the blanket. The detective reports that an overturned bowl of grapes and watermelon was found at the scene, as well as a broken glass that had contained wine. After the detective departs, Scott chooses and administers what

he considers the best test for analyzing the piece of evidence in his possession. Three minutes after completion of the test, the blanket shows a positive reaction. What test did Scott choose, and what was his conclusion? Explain your answer.

2. Criminalist Cathy Richards is collecting evidence from the victim of a sexual assault. She places a sheet on the floor, asks the victim to disrobe, and places the clothing in a paper bag. After collecting pubic combings and pubic hair samples, she takes two vaginal swabs, which she allows to air-dry before packaging. Finally, Cathy collects blood, urine, and scalp hair samples from the victim. What mistakes, if any, did she make in collecting this evidence?

3. The following sequence of bases is located on one strand of a DNA molecule:

   C–G–A–A–T–C–G–C–A–A–T–C–G–A–C–C–T–G

   List the sequence of bases that will form complementary pairs on the other strand of the DNA molecule.

4. A woman reports being mugged by a masked assailant, whom she scratched on the arm during a brief struggle. The victim gives the police a good description of her attacker, but she is not sure whether the attacker was male or female. Describe the steps and procedures you would use to determine the sex of the attacker.

5. Police discover a badly decomposed body buried in an area where a man disappeared some years before. The case was never solved, nor was the victim's body ever recovered. As the lead investigator, you suspect that the newly discovered body is that of the victim. What is your main challenge in using DNA typing to determine whether your suspicion is correct? How would you go about using DNA technology to test your theory?

6. You are a forensic scientist performing DNA typing on a blood sample sent to your laboratory. While performing an STR analysis on the sample, you notice a four-band pattern. What conclusion should you draw? Why?

Web Resources

Blood Typing Game (An interactive application that teaches about blood types and factors by having the user analyze a patient's blood and determine the right type of blood to give in a transfusion)
http://nobelprize.org/medicine/educational/landsteiner/

Blood Types Tutorial (Offers basic information about blood types and includes a "Blood Type Calculator" to determine the possible blood type of a child based on the blood types of the parents)
www.biology.arizona.edu/human_bio/problem_sets/blood_types/inherited.html

"Convicted by Juries, Exonerated by Science: Case Studies in the Use of DNA Evidence to Establish Innocence After Trial,"
www.ncjrs.gov/pdffiles/dnaevid.pdf

"DNA Evidence: What Law Enforcement Officers Should Know"
www.ncjrs.gov/pdffiles1/jr000249c.pdf

DNA From the Beginning (An animated primer on the basics of DNA, genes, and heredity; features a series of animated flash tutorials on genetics and DNA)
www.dnaftb.org/dnaftb/

DNA Structure (Animated online tutorials about the basics of DNA; includes a lesson plan for instructors teaching about DNA and review questions for students)
http://molvis.sdsc.edu/dna/index.htm

DNA Testing: An Introduction For Non-Scientists: An Illustrated Explanation (An illustrated article that explains in simplified language the theory and process behind various types of DNA testing, including STR and RFLP, and discusses PCR contamination)
www.scientific.org/tutorials/articles/riley/riley.html

DNA Typing and Identification—Lecture Notes
www.apsu.edu/oconnort/3210/3210lect07.htm

DNA Workshop (An overview of the basics of DNA including replication and protein synthesis; features an interactive presentation on replication and synthesis)
www.pbs.org/wgbh/aso/tryit/dna/index.html#

Forensic Serology—Basic Principles
www.apsu.edu/oconnort/3210/3210lect06.htm

How Luminol Works
www.howstuffworks.com/luminol.htm

Human Heredity (An online slideshow covering the basic principles of heredity and gene interactions)
www.bsd405.org/teachers/suttonk/Inheritance/Powerpoint1/humheredity/humanheredity/index.htm

Principles of Forensic DNA for Officers of the Court
www.dna.gov/training/otc/

Short Tandem Repeat DNA Internet Database
www.cstl.nist.gov/biotech/strbase/

"Using DNA to Solve Cold Cases: Special Report"
www.ncjrs.gov/pdffiles1/nij/194197.pdf

Endnotes

1. M. Cox, "A Study of the Sensitivity and Specificity of Four Presumptive Tests for Blood," *Journal of Forensic Sciences* 36 (1991): 1503.
2. The luminol reagent is prepared by mixing 0.1 grans 3-amino-phthalthydrazide and 5.0 grams sodium carbonate in 100 milliliters distilled water. Before use, 0.7 grams sodium perborate is added to the solution.
3. S. H. Tobe et al., "Evaluation of Six Presumptive Tests for Blood: Their Specificity, Sensitivity, and Effect on High Molecular-Weight DNA," *Journal of Forensic Sciences* 52 (2007): 102.
4. J. P. Allery et al., "Cytological Detection of Spermatozoa: Comparison of Three Staining Methods," *Journal of Forensic Sciences* 46 (2001): 349.
5. In one study only a maximum of 4 sperm cells out of 1,000 could be extracted from a cotton patch and observed under the microscope. Edwin Jones (Ventura County Sheriff's Department, Ventura, Calif.), personal communication.
6. J. Kearsey, H. Louie, and H. Poon, "Validation Study of the Onestep ABAcard® PSA Test Kit for RCMP Casework," *Canadian Society of Forensic Science Journal* 34 (2001): 63.
7. D. Sweet et al., "An Improved Method to Recover Saliva from Human Skin: The Double Swab Technique," *Journal of Forensic Sciences* 42 (1997): 320.
8. Anne Davies and Elizabeth Wilson, "The Persistence of Seminal Constituents in the Human Vagina," *Forensic Science* 3 (1974): 45

9. J. Kearsey, H. Louie, and H. Poon, "Validation Study of the Onestep ABAcard® PSA Test Kit for RCMP Casework," *Canadian Society of Forensic Science Journal* 34 (2001): 63.

10. Applied Biosystems, 850 Lincoln Centre Drive, Foster City, California 94404.

11. R. A. Wickenheiser, "Trace DNA: A Review, Discussion of Theory, and Application of the Transfer of Trace Quantities through Skin Contact," *Journal of Forensic Sciences* 47 (2002): 442.

12. E. K. Hanson and J. Ballantyne, "Whole Genome Amplification Strategy for Forensic Genetic Analysis Using Single or Few Cell Equivalents of Genomic DNA," *Analytical Biochemistry* 346 (2005): 246.

13. S. H. Tobe et al., "Evaluation of Six Presumptive Tests for Blood: Their Specificity, Sensitivity, and Effect on High Molecular-Weight DNA," *Journal of Forensic Sciences* 52 (2007): 102.

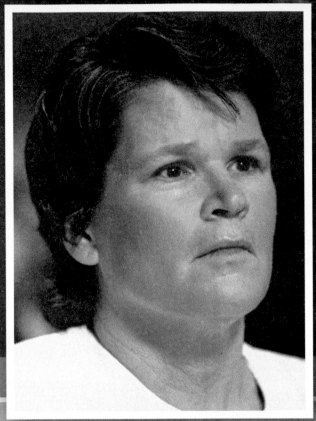

Debora Green—Poisoning the American Dream

On the face of it, the Farrar family had it all. Dr. Debora Green, a nonpracticing oncologist, and her husband, Dr. Michael Farrar, had an opulent home in an exclusive Kansas City suburb. Michael, a cardiologist, had a successful practice that enabled Debora to stay home to raise their three loving children, Tim, Kate, and Kelly.

In late 1995, Michael Farrar was hospitalized for a mysterious illness. Michael entered a revolving door of excruciating stomach pain and recovery, framed in the context of his failing marriage. Unknown to outsiders, Michael had initially asked Debora for a divorce in 1994.

Michael's suspicion of foul play was aroused when he found a large number of castor bean packets in Debora's purse. She had used the castor beans to poison Michael's food; they contain ricin, a deadly poison.

On the night of October 24, 1995, the Green house became engulfed in flames and was destroyed. Michael Farrar was sleeping elsewhere while the couple were beginning a legal separation preceding their divorce. Their daughter Kate, then 10 years old, escaped the fire by exiting her bedroom window, scaling the garage roof, and jumping to safety into the arms of her mother, who was standing outside the house. Their son Tim, 13, and daughter Kelly, 6, were killed in the blaze that consumed their home.

Fire investigators quickly realized that they were confronting a criminal case of arson. Unconnected fires had occurred in various rooms of the house. Throughout the first floor of the house, pour patterns were obvious where someone had spread accelerants—flammable substances used to spread the fire more quickly—on the floors. Heavy soaking of the carpet on the stairways leading to the children's rooms would have created a wall of fire effectively blocking the children's escape route. This arsonist was also a murderer.

Police arrested Debora and charged her with two counts of first-degree murder and aggravated arson. A psychological evaluation of the defendant concluded that she had a schizoid personality that was masked by a high degree of intelligence. Debora Green is currently serving a life sentence in a Missouri prison. Her psychotic behavior became the subject of Ann Rule's novel *Bitter Harvest*.

chapter 15

Forensic Aspects of **Fire Investigation**

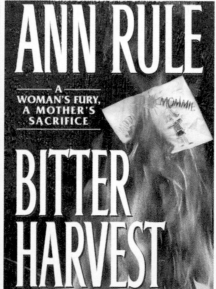

ANN RULE

A WOMAN'S FURY, A MOTHER'S SACRIFICE

BITTER HARVEST

Key Terms

accelerant

combustion

endothermic reaction

energy

exothermic reaction

flammable range

flash point

glowing combustion

heat of combustion

hydrocarbon

ignition temperature

modus operandi

oxidation

pyrolysis

spontaneous combustion

Learning Objectives

After studying this chapter, you should be able to:

- List the conditions necessary to initiate and sustain combustion.

- Understand the three mechanisms of heat transfer.

- Recognize the telltale signs of an accelerant-initiated fire.

- Describe how to collect physical evidence at the scene of a suspected arson.

- Describe laboratory procedures used to detect and identify hydrocarbon residues.

modus operandi
An offender's pattern of operation.

Forensic Investigation of Arson

Arson often presents complex and difficult circumstances to investigate. Normally these incidents are committed at the convenience of a perpetrator who has thoroughly planned the criminal act and has left the crime scene long before any official investigation is launched. Furthermore, proving commission of the offense is more difficult because of the extensive destruction that frequently dominates the crime scene. The contribution of the criminalist is only one aspect of a comprehensive and difficult investigative process that must establish a motive, the **modus operandi**, and a suspect.

The criminalist's function is limited; usually he or she is expected only to detect and identify relevant chemical materials collected at the scene and to reconstruct and identify igniters. Although a chemist can identify trace amounts of gasoline or kerosene in debris, no scientific test can determine whether an arsonist used a pile of rubbish or paper to start a fire. Furthermore, a fire can have many accidental causes, including faulty wiring, overheated electric motors, improperly cleaned and regulated heating systems, and cigarette smoking—which usually leave no chemical traces. Thus, the final determination of the cause of a fire must consider numerous factors and requires an extensive on-site investigation. The ultimate determination must be made by an investigator whose training and knowledge have been augmented by the practical experiences of fire investigation.

Chemistry of Fire

Humankind's early search to explain the physical concepts underlying the behavior of matter always bestowed a central and fundamental role on fire. To ancient Greek philosophers, fire was one of the four basic elements from which all matter was derived. The medieval alchemist thought of fire as an instrument of transformation, capable of changing one element into another. One ancient recipe expresses its mystical power as follows: "Now the substance of cinnabar is such that the more it is heated, the more exquisite are its sublimations. Cinnabar will become mercury, and passing through a series of other sublimations, it is again turned into cinnabar, and thus it enables man to enjoy eternal life."

Today, we know of fire not as an element of matter but as a transformation process during which oxygen is united with some other substance to produce noticeable quantities of heat and light (a flame). Therefore, any insight into why and how a fire is initiated and sustained must begin with the knowledge of the fundamental chemical reaction of fire—oxidation.

Oxidation

In a simple description of oxidation, oxygen combines with other substances to produce new products. Thus, we may write the chemical equation for the burning of methane gas, a major component of natural gas, as follows:

$$CH_4 \quad + \quad 2O_2 \quad \longrightarrow \quad CO_2 \quad + \quad 2H_2O$$

methane   oxygen   yields   carbon dioxide   water

However, not all oxidation proceeds in the manner that one associates with fire. For example, oxygen combines with many metals to form oxides. Thus, iron forms a red-brown iron oxide, or rust, as follows (see Figure 15–1):

$$4Fe \quad + \quad 3O_2 \quad \longrightarrow \quad 2Fe_2O_3$$

iron   oxygen   yields   iron oxide

Yet chemical equations do not give us a complete insight into the oxidation process. We must consider other factors to understand all of the implications of oxidation or, for that matter, any other chemical reaction. Methane burns when it unites with oxygen, but merely mixing methane

oxidation
The combination of oxygen with other substances to produce new substances.

FIGURE 15–1   Rust forming on iron is an example of oxidation. *Courtesy Nichola Gissing—Debut Art, Getty Images—Digital Vision*

and oxygen does not produce a fire. Nor, for example, does gasoline burn when it is simply exposed to air. However, lighting a match in the presence of any one of these fuel–air mixtures (assuming proper proportions) produces an instant fire.

What are the reasons behind these differences? Why do some oxidations proceed with the outward appearances that we associate with a fire while others do not? Why do we need a match to initiate some oxidations while others proceed at room temperature? The explanation lies in a fundamental but abstract concept—energy.

Energy

energy
The ability or potential of a system or material to do work.

Energy can be defined as the ability or potential of a system or material to do work. Energy takes many forms, such as heat energy, electrical energy, mechanical energy, nuclear energy, light energy, and chemical energy. For example, when methane is burned, the stored chemical energy in methane is converted to energy in the form of heat and light. This heat may be used to boil water or to provide high-pressure steam to turn a turbine. This is an example of converting chemical energy to heat energy to mechanical energy. The turbine can then be used to generate electricity, transforming mechanical energy to electrical energy. Electrical energy may then be used to turn a motor. In other words, energy can enable work to be done; heat is energy.

The quantity of heat from a chemical reaction comes from the breaking and formation of chemical bonds. Methane is a molecule composed of one carbon atom bonded with four hydrogen atoms:

$$
\begin{array}{c}
\text{H} \\
| \\
\text{H}-\text{C}-\text{H} \\
| \\
\text{H}
\end{array}
$$

An oxygen molecule forms when two atoms of the element oxygen bond:

$$O = O$$

In chemical changes, atoms are not lost but merely redistributed during the chemical reaction; thus, the products of methane's oxidation will be carbon dioxide:

$$O = C = O$$

and water:

$$H—O—H$$

This rearrangement, however, means that the chemical bonds holding the atoms together must be broken and new bonds formed. We now have arrived at a fundamental observation in our dissection of a chemical reaction—that molecules must absorb energy to break apart their chemical bonds, and that they liberate energy when their bonds are reformed.

The amount of energy needed to break a bond and the amount of energy liberated when a bond is formed are characteristic of the type of chemical bond involved. Hence, a chemical reaction involves a change in energy content; energy is going in and energy is given off. The quantities of energies involved are different for each reaction and are determined by the participants in the chemical reaction.

Combustion

combustion
The rapid combination of oxygen with another substance, accompanied by the production of noticeable heat and light.

All oxidation reactions, including the combustion of methane, are examples of reactions in which more energy is liberated than is required to break the chemical bonds between atoms. Such reactions are said to be **exothermic.** The excess energy is liberated as heat, and often as light, and is known as the **heat of combustion.** Table 15–1 summarizes the heats of combustion of some important fuels in fire investigation.

Although we will not be concerned with them, some reactions require more energy than they eventually liberate. These reactions are known as **endothermic reactions.**

Thus, all reactions require an energy input to start them. We can think of this requirement as an invisible energy barrier between the reactants and the products of a reaction (see Figure 15–2). The higher this barrier, the more energy required to initiate the reaction. Where does this initial energy come from? There are many sources of energy; however, for the purpose of this discussion we need to look at only one—heat.

Heat The energy barrier in the conversion of iron to rust is relatively small, and it can be surmounted with the help of heat energy in the surrounding environment at normal outdoor temperatures. Not so for methane or gasoline; these energy barriers are quite high, and a high temperature must be applied to start the oxidation of these fuels. Hence, before any fire can result, the temperature of these fuels must be raised enough to exceed the energy barrier. Table 15–2 shows that this temperature, known as the **ignition temperature,** is quite high for common fuels.

exothermic reaction
A chemical transformation in which heat energy is liberated.

heat of combustion
The heat liberated during combustion.

endothermic reaction
A chemical transformation in which heat energy is absorbed from the surroundings.

ignition temperature
The minimum temperature at which a fuel spontaneously ignites.

Table 15–1 Heats of Combustion of Fuels	
Fuel	**Heat of Combustion**[a]
Crude oil	19,650 Btu/gal
Diesel fuel	19,550 Btu/lb
Gasoline	19,250 Btu/lb
Methane	995 Btu/cu ft
Natural gas	128–1,868 Btu/cu ft
Octane	121,300 Btu/gal
Wood	7,500 Btu/lb
Coal, bituminous	11,000–14,000 Btu/lb
Anthracite	13,351 Btu/lb

[a]Btu (British thermal unit) is defined as the quantity of heat required to raise the temperature of 1 pound of water 1°F at or near its point of maximum density.

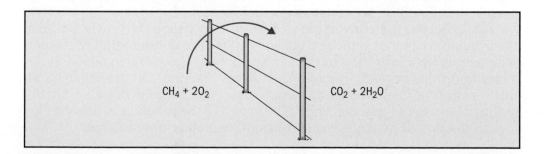

FIGURE 15–2 An energy barrier must be hurdled before reactants such as methane and oxygen can combine with one another to form the products of carbon dioxide and water.

Table 15–2 Ignition Temperatures of Some Common Fuels

Fuel	Ignition Temperature, °F
Acetone	869
Benzene	928
Fuel oil #2	495
Gasoline (low octane)	536
Kerosene (fuel oil #1)	410
n-Octane	428
Petroleum ether	550
Turpentine	488

Once combustion starts, enough heat is liberated to keep the reaction going by itself. In essence, the fire becomes a chain reaction, absorbing a portion of its own liberated heat to generate even more heat. The fire burns until either the oxygen or the fuel is exhausted.

Normally, a lighted match provides a convenient igniter of fuels. However, the fire investigator must also consider other potential sources of ignition—for example, electrical discharges, sparks, and chemicals—while reconstructing the initiation of a fire. All of these sources have temperatures higher than the ignition temperature of most fuels.

Speed of Reaction   Although the liberation of energy explains many important features of oxidation, it does not explain all characteristics of the reaction. Obviously, although all oxidations liberate energy, not all are accompanied by a flame; witness the oxidation of iron to rust. Therefore, one other important consideration will make our understanding of oxidation and fire complete: the rate or speed at which the reaction takes place.

A chemical reaction, such as oxidation, takes place when molecules combine or collide with one another. The faster the molecules move, the greater the number of collisions between them and the faster the rate of reaction. Many factors influence the rate of these collisions. In our description of fire and oxidation, we consider only two: the physical state of the fuel and the temperature.

Physical State of Fuel   A fuel achieves a reaction rate with oxygen sufficient to produce a flame only when it is in the gaseous state, for only in this state can molecules collide frequently enough to support a flaming fire. This remains true whether the fuel is a solid such as wood, paper, cloth, or plastic, or a liquid such as gasoline or kerosene.

For example, the conversion of iron to rust proceeds slowly because the iron atoms cannot achieve a gaseous state. The combination of oxygen with iron is thus restricted to the surface area of the metal exposed to air, a limitation that severely reduces the rate of reaction. On the other hand, the reaction of methane and oxygen proceeds rapidly because all the reactants are in the gaseous state. The speed of the reaction is reflected by the production of noticeable quantities of heat and light (a flame).

Fuel Temperature   How then does a liquid or solid maintain a gaseous reaction? In the case of a liquid fuel, the temperature must be high enough to

Forensic Aspects of Fire Investigation **507**

vaporize the fuel. The vapor that forms burns when it mixes with oxygen and combusts as a flame. The flash point is the *lowest* temperature at which a liquid gives off sufficient vapor to form a mixture with air that will support combustion. Once the flash point is reached, the fuel can be ignited by some outside source of temperature to start a fire. The ignition temperature of a fuel is always considerably higher than the flash point. For example, gasoline has a flash point of –50°F; however, an ignition temperature of 495°F is needed to start a gasoline fire.

With a solid fuel such as wood, the process of generating vapor is more complex. A solid fuel burns only when exposed to heat intense enough to decompose the solid into gaseous products. This chemical breakdown of solid material is known as pyrolysis. The gaseous products of pyrolysis combine with oxygen to produce a fire (see Figure 15–3). Here again, fire can be described as a chain reaction. A match or other source of heat initiates the pyrolysis of the solid fuel, the gaseous products react with oxygen in the air to produce heat and light, and this heat in turn pyrolyzes more solid fuel into volatile gases.

Typically, the rate of a chemical reaction increases when the temperature is raised. The magnitude of the increase varies from one reaction to another and also from one temperature range to another. For most reactions, a 10°C (18°F) rise in temperature doubles or triples the reaction rate. This observation explains in part why burning is so rapid. As the fire spreads, it raises the temperature of the fuel–air mixture, thus increasing the rate of reaction; this in turn generates more heat, again increasing the rate of reaction. Only when the fuel or oxygen is depleted does this vicious cycle come to a halt.

Fuel–Air Mix   As we have seen from our discussion about gaseous fuel, air (oxygen) and sufficient heat are the basic ingredients of a flaming fire.

flash point
The minimum temperature at which a liquid fuel produces enough vapor to burn.

pyrolysis
The decomposition of solid organic matter by heat.

FIGURE 15–3   Intense heat causes solid fuels such as wood to decompose into gaseous products, a process called *pyrolysis.* *Courtesy David Trood/Image Bank/Getty Images*

flammable range
The entire range of possible gas or vapor fuel concentrations in air that are capable of burning.

glowing combustion
Combustion on the surface of a solid fuel in the absence of heat high enough to pyrolyze the fuel.

spontaneous combustion
A fire caused by a natural heat-producing process in the presence of sufficient air and fuel.

There is also one other consideration—the gas fuel–air mix. A mixture of gaseous fuel and air burns only if its composition lies within certain limits. If the fuel concentration is too low (lean) or too great (rich), combustion does not occur. The concentration range between the upper and lower limits is called the flammable range. For example, the flammable range for gasoline is 1.3–6.0 percent. Thus, in order for a gasoline–air mix to burn, gasoline must make up at least 1.3 percent, and no more than 6 percent, of the mixture.

Glowing Combustion   Although a flaming fire can be supported only by a gaseous fuel, in some instances a fuel can burn without a flame. Witness a burning cigarette or the red glow of hot charcoals (see Figure 15–4). These are examples of glowing combustion or *smoldering*. Here combustion occurs on the surface of a solid fuel in the absence of heat high enough to pyrolyze the fuel. Interestingly, this phenomenon generally ensues long after the flames have gone out. Wood, for example, tends to burn with a flame until all of its pyrolyzable components have been expended; however, wood's carbonaceous residue continues to smolder long after the flame has extinguished itself.

Spontaneous Combustion   One interesting phenomenon often invoked by arson suspects as the cause of a fire is spontaneous combustion. Actually, the conditions under which spontaneous combustion can develop are rather limited and rarely account for the cause of a fire. Spontaneous combustion is the result of a natural heat-producing process in poorly ventilated containers or areas. For example, hay stored in barns provides an excellent growing medium for bacteria whose activities generate heat. If the hay is not properly ventilated, the heat builds to a level that supports other types of heat-producing chemical reactions in the hay. Eventually, as the heat rises, the ignition temperature of hay is reached, spontaneously setting off a fire.

FIGURE 15–4   Red-hot charcoals are an example of glowing combustion. *Courtesy Paul Sisul/Stone/Getty Images*

Another example of spontaneous combustion involves the ignition of improperly ventilated containers containing rags soaked with certain types of highly unsaturated oils, such as linseed oil. Heat can build up to the point of ignition as a result of a slow heat-producing chemical oxidation between the air and the oil. Of course, storage conditions must encourage the accumulation of the heat over a prolonged period of time. However, spontaneous combustion does not occur with hydrocarbon lubricating oils, and it is not expected to occur with most household fats and oils.

In summary, three requirements must be satisfied to initiate and sustain combustion:

1. **A fuel must be present.**

2. **Oxygen must be available in sufficient quantity to combine with the fuel.**

3. **Heat must be applied to initiate the combustion, and sufficient heat must be generated to sustain the reaction.**

Heat Transfer

Consider how a structural fire begins. The typical scenario starts with heat ignition at a single location. It may be an arsonist lighting a gasoline-soaked rag, a malfunctioning electric appliance sparking, or an individual falling asleep while smoking a cigarette in bed. How does a flame initially confined to a single location spread to engulf an entire structure? Understanding the anatomy of a fire begins with comprehending how heat travels through a burning structure.

The previous section stressed the importance of the role of heat in generating sufficient fuel vapors to support combustion, as well as the requirement that the heat source be hot enough to ignite the fuel's vapor. Once the fire begins, the heat generated by the fuel's reaction with air is fed back into the fuel–air mix to keep the chemical reaction going.

As a fire progresses, the heat created by the combustion process tends to move from a high-temperature region to one at a lower temperature. Understanding heat transfer from one location to another is important for reconstructing the origin of a fire, as well as for understanding why and how fire spreads through a structure. The three mechanisms of heat transfer are conduction, radiation, and convection.

Conduction Movement of heat through a solid object is caused by a process called *conduction,* in which electrons and atoms within the heated object collide with one another. Heat always travels from hot areas of a solid to cold ones by conduction. Solids whose atoms or molecules have loosely held electrons are good conductors of heat. Metals have the most loosely held electrons and are therefore excellent conductors of heat. Thus, when you insert one end of a metal object into an open flame, the entire object quickly becomes hot to the touch.

Materials that have electrons firmly attached to their molecules are poor conductors of heat. Poor conductors are called insulators. Wood is a good insulator; for that reason, metal objects that are subject to intense heat (such as skillets and saucepans) often have wooden handles (see Figure 15–5).

In reconstructing a fire scene, it's important to keep in mind that heat may be transported through metals such as beams, nails, fasteners, bolts, and other good conductors to a location far from the initial heat source. Any fuel in contact with the conductor may be ignited, creating a new fire

FIGURE 15–5 The wooden handle on this saucepan is a poor conductor of heat. *Courtesy Topham, The Image Works*

location. On the other hand, the conductivity of wood, plastic, and paper are very low, meaning that heat emanating from these surfaces does not spread well and does not cause ignitions far from the initial heat source.

Radiation *Radiation* is the transfer of heat energy from a heated surface to a cooler surface by electromagnetic radiation. A hot surface emits electromagnetic radiation of various wavelengths, and in a fire scene the electromagnetic radiation moves in a straight line from one surface to another. Radiant heat plays a key role in understanding how fire spreads throughout a structure. For example, all surfaces that face the fire are exposed to radiant heat and burst into flames when the surface reaches their ignition temperature. In very large fires, nearby structures and vehicles are often ignited at a distance by radiant heat.

Convection *Convection* is the transfer of heat energy by movement of molecules within a liquid or gas. Water being heated on a stove illustrates the concept of convection. As the water molecules on the bottom of the pot move faster, they spread apart and become less dense, causing them to move upward. Denser, cooler water molecules then migrate to the bottom of the pot. In this way convection currents keep the fluid stirred up as warmer fluid moves away from the heat source and cooler fluid moves toward the heat source. Likewise, warm air expands, becoming less dense and causing it to rise and move toward the cooler surrounding air.

In a structural fire, the gaseous hot products of combustion expand, and convection moves the hot gases to the upper portions of the structure (see Figure 15–6). The convected hot gases become a source of heat, radiating heat energy downward onto all the surfaces below them. The hot surfaces of the exposed objects often pyrolyze or break down, releasing gaseous

FIGURE 15–6 **Convection causes flames to rise to the upper floor of a burning structure.** *Courtesy Dave Frazier, Danita Delimont Photography*

molecules. The phenomenon known as *flashover* occurs when all the combustible fuels simultaneously ignite, engulfing the entire structure in flame.

Key Points

- Oxidation is the combination of oxygen with other substances to produce new substances.

- Combustion is the rapid combination of oxygen with another substance, accompanied by the production of noticeable heat and light.

- In an exothermic reaction, heat energy is liberated. In an endothermic reaction, heat energy is absorbed from the surroundings.

- Pyrolysis is the chemical breakdown of solid organic matter by heat. The gaseous products of pyrolysis combine with oxygen to produce a fire.

- Spontaneous combustion is fire caused by a natural heat-producing process in the presence of sufficient air and fuel.

- To initiate and sustain combustion, (1) a fuel must be present; (2) oxygen must be available in sufficient quantity to combine with the fuel; and (3) heat must be applied to initiate the combustion, and sufficient heat must be generated to sustain the reaction.

• The three mechanisms of heat transfer are conduction, radiation, and convection. Conduction is the movement of heat through a solid object. Radiation is the transfer of heat energy from a heated surface to a cooler surface by electromagnetic radiation. Convection is the transfer of heat energy by the movement of molecules within a liquid or gas.

Searching the Fire Scene

accelerant

Any material used to start or sustain a fire.

The arson investigator should begin examining a fire scene for signs of arson as soon as the fire has been extinguished. Most arsons are started with petroleum-based **accelerants** such as gasoline or kerosene. Thus, the presence of containers capable of holding an accelerant arouse suspicions of arson. Discovery of an ignition device ranging in sophistication from a candle to a time-delay device is another indication of possible arson. A common telltale sign of arson may be an irregularly shaped pattern on a floor or on the ground (see Figure 15–7) resulting from pouring an accelerant onto the surface. In addition to these visual indicators, investigators should look for signs of breaking and entering and theft, and they should begin interviewing any eyewitnesses to the fire.

Timeliness of Investigation

Time constantly works against the arson investigator. Any accelerant residues that remain after a fire is extinguished may evaporate within a few days or even hours. Furthermore, safety and health conditions may necessitate that cleanup and salvage operations begin as quickly as possible. Once this occurs, a meaningful investigation of the fire scene is impossible. Accelerants in soil and vegetation can be rapidly degraded by bacterial action. Freezing samples containing soil or vegetation is an effective way to prevent this degradation.

FIGURE 15–7 An irregularly shaped pattern on the ground resulting from a poured ignitable liquid. *Courtesy Franklin County Crime Scene Unit, North Carolina*

The need to begin an *immediate* investigation of the circumstances surrounding a fire takes precedence even over the requirement to obtain a search warrant to enter and search the premises. The Supreme Court, explaining its position on this issue, stated in part:

> . . . Fire officials are charged not only with extinguishing fires, but with finding their causes. Prompt determination of the fire's origin may be necessary to prevent its recurrence, as through the detection of continuing dangers such as faulty wiring or a defective furnace. Immediate investigation may also be necessary to preserve evidence from intentional or accidental destruction. And, of course, the sooner the officials complete their duties, the less will be their subsequent interference with the privacy and the recovery efforts of the victims. For these reasons, officials need no warrant to remain in a building for a reasonable time to investigate the cause of a blaze after it has been extinguished. And if the warrantless entry to put out the fire and determine its cause is constitutional, the warrantless seizure of evidence while inspecting the premises for these purposes also is constitutional. . . .

In determining what constitutes a reasonable time to investigate, appropriate recognition must be given to the exigencies that confront officials serving under these conditions, as well as to individuals' reasonable expectations of privacy.[1]

Locating the Fire's Origin

A search of the fire scene must focus on finding the fire's origin, which will prove most productive in any search for an accelerant or ignition device. In searching for a fire's specific point of origin, the investigator may uncover telltale signs of arson such as evidence of separate and unconnected fires or the use of "streamers" to spread the fire from one area to another. For example, the arsonist may have spread a trail of gasoline or paper to cause the fire to move rapidly from one room to another.

There are no fast and simple rules for identifying a fire's origin. Normally a fire tends to move upward, and thus the probable origin is most likely closest to the lowest point that shows the most intense characteristics of burning. Sometimes as the fire burns upward, a V-shaped pattern forms

FIGURE 15–8 **Typical V patterns illustrating the upward movement of the fire.** *Courtesy John Lentini*

against a vertical wall, as shown in Figure 15–8. Because flammable liquids always flow to the lowest point, more severe burning found on the floor than on the ceiling may indicate the presence of an accelerant. If a flammable liquid was used, charring is expected to be more intense on the bottom of furniture, shelves, and other items rather than the top.

However, many factors can contribute to the deviation of a fire from normal behavior. Prevailing drafts and winds; secondary fires due to collapsing floors and roofs; the physical arrangement of the burning structure; stairways and elevator shafts; holes in the floor, wall, or roof; and the effects of the firefighter in suppressing the fire are all factors that the fire investigator must consider before determining conclusive findings.

Once located, the point of origin should be protected to permit careful investigation. As at any crime scene, nothing should be touched or moved before notes and photographs are taken and sketches are made. An examination must also be made for possible accidental causes, as well as for evidence of arson. The most common materials used by an arsonist to ensure the rapid spread and intensity of a fire are gasoline and kerosene or, for that matter, any volatile flammable liquid.

Searching for Accelerants

Fortunately, only under the most ideal conditions will combustible liquids be entirely consumed during a fire. When the liquid is poured over a large area, a portion of it will likely seep into a porous surface, such as cracks in the floor, upholstery, rags, plaster, wallboards, or carpet. Enough of the liquid may remain unchanged to permit its detection in the crime laboratory. In addition, when a fire is extinguished with water, the evaporation rate of volatile fluids may be slowed, because water cools and covers materials through which the combustible liquid may have soaked. Fortunately, water does not interfere with laboratory methods used to detect and characterize flammable liquid residues.

The search for traces of flammable liquid residues may be aided by the use of a sensitive portable vapor detector or "sniffer" (see Figure 15–9). This device can rapidly screen suspect materials for volatile residues by sucking in the air surrounding the questioned sample. The air is passed over a heated filament; if a combustible vapor is present, it oxidizes and immediately increases the temperature of the filament. The rise in filament temperature is then registered as a deflection on the detector's meter.

Of course, such a device is not a conclusive test for a flammable vapor, but it is an excellent screening device for checking suspect samples at the fire scene. Another approach is to use dogs that have been trained to recognize the odor of hydrocarbon accelerants.

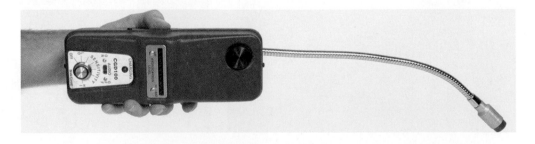

FIGURE 15–9   A portable hydrocarbon detector. *Courtesy Sirchie Finger Print Laboratories, Inc., Youngsville, N.C., www.sirchie.com*

Collection and Preservation of Arson Evidence

Two to three quarts of ash and soot debris must be collected at the point of origin of a fire when arson is suspected. The collection should include all porous materials and all other substances thought likely to contain flammable residues. These include such things as wood flooring, rugs, upholstery, and rags.

Packaging and Preservation of Evidence

Specimens should be packaged immediately in airtight containers so possible residues are not lost through evaporation. New, clean paint cans with friction lids are good containers because they are low cost, airtight, unbreakable, and available in a variety of sizes (see Figure 15–10). Wide-mouthed glass jars are also useful for packaging suspect specimens, provided that they have airtight lids. Cans and jars should be filled one-half to two-thirds full, leaving an air space in the container above the debris.

Large, bulky samples should be cut to size at the scene as needed so that they will fit into available containers. Plastic polyethylene bags are not suitable for packaging specimens because they react with hydrocarbons and permit volatile hydrocarbon vapors to be depleted. Fluids found in open bottles or cans must be collected and sealed. Even when such containers appear empty, the investigator is wise to seal and preserve them in case they contain trace amounts of liquids or vapors.

Substrate Control

The collection of all materials suspected of containing volatile liquids must be accompanied by a thorough sampling of similar but uncontaminated control specimens from another area of the fire scene. This is known as *substrate control.* For example, if an investigator collects carpeting at the point of origin, he or she must sample the same carpet from another part of the room, where it can be reasonably assumed that no flammable substance was placed.

In the laboratory, the criminalist checks the substrate control to be sure that it is free of any flammables. This procedure reduces the possibility (and subsequent argument) that the carpet was exposed to a flammable liquid such as a cleaning solution during normal maintenance. In addition, laboratory tests on the unburned control material may help analyze the

FIGURE 15–10 Various sizes of paint cans suitable for collecting debris at fire scenes. *Courtesy Sirchie Finger Print Laboratories, Inc., Youngsville, N.C., www.sirchie.com*

breakdown products from the material's exposure to intense heat during the fire. Common materials such as plastic floor tiles, carpet, linoleum, and adhesives can produce volatile hydrocarbons when they are burned. These breakdown products can sometimes be mistaken for an accelerant.

Igniters and Other Evidence

The scene should also be thoroughly searched for igniters. The most common igniter is a match. Normally the match is completely consumed during a fire and is impossible to locate. However, there have been cases in which, by force of habit, matches have been extinguished and tossed aside only to be recovered later by the investigator. This evidence may prove valuable if the criminalist can fit the match to a book found in the possession of a suspect, as shown in Figure 15–11.

Arsonists can construct many other types of devices to start a fire. These include burning cigarettes, firearms, ammunition, a mechanical match striker, electrical sparking devices, and a "Molotov cocktail"—a glass bottle containing flammable liquid with a cloth rag stuffed into it and lit as a fuse. Relatively complex mechanical devices are much more likely to survive the fire for later discovery. The broken glass and wick of the Molotov cocktail, if recovered, must be preserved as well.

One important piece of evidence is the clothing of the suspect perpetrator. If this individual is arrested within a few hours of initiating the fire, residual quantities of the accelerant may still be present in the clothing. As we will see in the next section, the forensic laboratory can detect extremely small quantities of accelerants, making the examination of a suspect's clothing a feasible investigative approach. Each item of clothing should be placed in a separate airtight container, preferably a new, clean paint can.

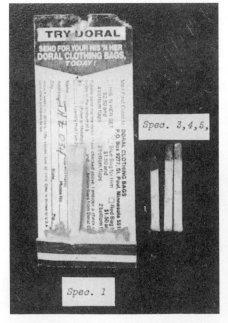

FIGURE 15–11 Three matches (Spec. 3, 4, 5) discarded at the scene of an arson are each shown to fit into a matchbook (Spec. 1) found in the suspect's possession. Such evidence strongly links the crime scene and the suspect. *Courtesy New Jersey State Police*

Key Points

- Telltale signs of arson include evidence of separate and unconnected fires, the use of "streamers" to spread the fire from one area to another, and evidence of severe burning found on the floor as opposed to the ceiling of a structure.

- Other common signs of arson at a fire scene are the presence of accelerants and the discovery of an ignition device.

- Porous materials at the suspected point of origin of a fire should be collected and stored in airtight containers.

Analysis of Flammable Residues

Criminalists are nearly unanimous in judging the gas chromatograph to be the most sensitive and reliable instrument for detecting and characterizing flammable residues. Most arsons are initiated by petroleum distillates, such as gasoline and kerosene, that are composed of a complex mixture of **hydrocarbons.** The gas chromatograph separates the hydrocarbon components of these liquids and produces a chromatographic pattern characteristic of a particular petroleum product.

hydrocarbon
Any compound consisting of only carbon and hydrogen.

Headspace Technique

Before accelerant residues can be analyzed, they first must be recovered from the debris collected at the scene. The easiest way to recover accelerant residues from fire-scene debris is to heat the airtight container in which the sample is sent to the laboratory. When the container is heated, any volatile residue in the debris is driven off and trapped in the container's enclosed airspace. The vapor, or *headspace,* is then removed with a syringe, as shown in Figure 15–12.

FIGURE 15–12 The removal of vapor from an enclosed container for gas chromatographic analysis. *Courtesy New Jersey State Police*

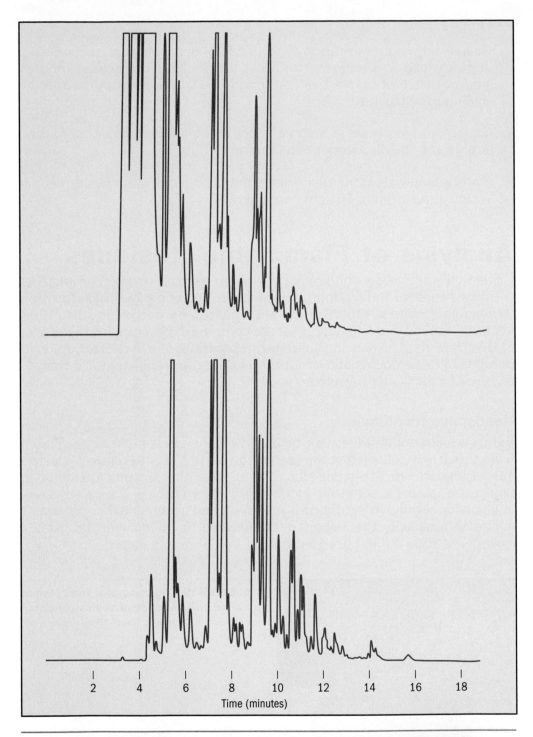

FIGURE 15–13 *(top)* **A gas chromatogram of vapor from a genuine gasoline sample.** *(bottom)* **A gas chromatogram of vapor from debris recovered at a fire site. Note the similarity of the known gasoline to vapor removed from the debris.** *Courtesy New Jersey State Police*

When the vapor is injected into the gas chromatograph, it is separated into its components, and each peak is recorded on the chromatogram. The identity of the volatile residue is determined when the pattern of the resultant chromatogram is compared to patterns produced by known petroleum products. For example, in Figure 15–13, a gas chromatographic analysis of debris recovered from a fire site shows a chromatogram similar to a known gasoline standard, thus proving the presence of gasoline.

In the absence of any recognizable pattern, the individual peaks can be identified when the investigator compares their retention times to known hydrocarbon standards (such as hexane, benzene, toluene, and xylenes). The brand name of a gasoline sample cannot currently be determined by gas chromatography or any other technique. Fluctuating gasoline markets and exchange agreements among the various oil companies preclude this possibility.

Vapor Concentration

One major disadvantage of the headspace technique is that the size of the syringe limits the volume of vapor that can be removed from the container and injected into the gas chromatograph. To overcome this deficiency, many crime laboratories augment the headspace technique with a method called *vapor concentration*. One setup for this analysis is shown in Figure 15–14.

A charcoal-coated strip, similar to that used in environmental monitoring badges, is placed within the container holding the debris that has been collected from the fire scene.[2] The container is then heated to about 60°C for about one hour. At this temperature, a significant quantity of accelerant vaporizes into the container airspace. The charcoal absorbs the accelerant vapor with which it comes into contact. In this manner, over a short period of time a significant quantity of the accelerant will be trapped and concentrated onto the charcoal strip.

Once the heating procedure is complete, the analyst removes the charcoal strip from the container and recovers the accelerant from the strip by washing it with a small volume of solvent (carbon disulfide). The solvent is then injected into the gas chromatograph for analysis. The major advantage of using vapor concentration with gas chromatography is its sensitivity. By absorbing the accelerant into a charcoal strip, the forensic analyst can increase the sensitivity of accelerant detection at least a hundredfold over the conventional headspace technique.

An examination of Figure 15–13 shows that identifying an accelerant such as gasoline by gas chromatography is an exercise in pattern recognition. Typically a forensic analyst compares the pattern generated by the sample to chromatograms from accelerant standards obtained under the same conditions. The pattern of gasoline, as with many other accelerants, can easily be placed in a searchable library.

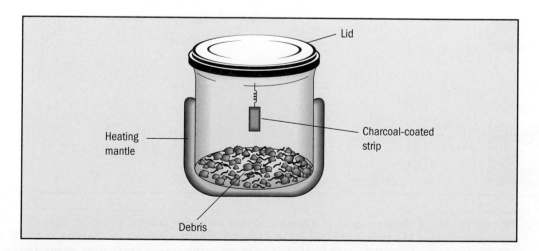

FIGURE 15–14 An apparatus for accelerant recovery by vapor concentration. The vapor in the enclosed container is exposed to charcoal, a chemical absorbent, where it is trapped for later analysis.

Gas Chromatography/Mass Spectrometry

On occasion, discernible patterns are not attainable by gas chromatography. This may be due to a combination of accelerants, or to the mixing of accelerant residue with heat-generated breakdown products of materials burning at the fire scene. Under such conditions, a gas chromatographic pattern can be difficult if not impossible to interpret. In these cases, gas chromatography combined with mass spectrometry (discussed in Chapter 10) has proven valuable for solving difficult problems in the detection of accelerant residues.

Complex chromatographic patterns can be simplified by passing the separated components emerging from the gas chromatographic column through a mass spectrometer. As each component enters the mass spectrometer, it is fragmented into a collection of ions. The analyst can then control which ions will be detected and which will go unnoticed. In essence, the mass spectrometer acts as a filter allowing the analyst to see only the peaks associated with the ions selected for a particular accelerant. In this manner, the chromatographic pattern can be simplified by eliminating extraneous peaks that may obliterate the pattern.[3] The process is illustrated in Figure 15–15.

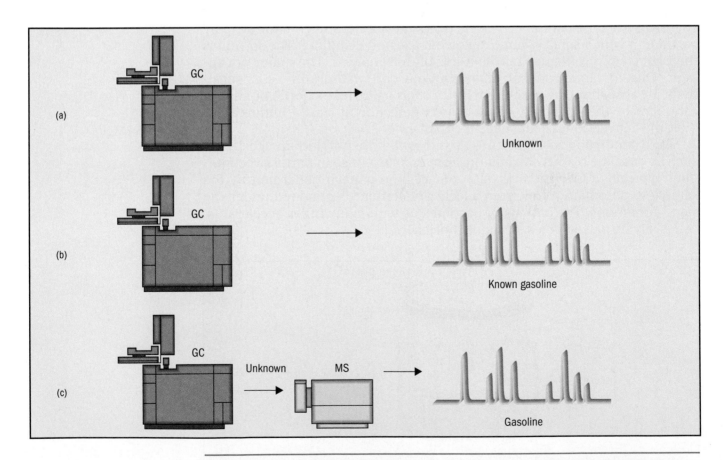

FIGURE 15–15 A chromatogram of a residue sample collected at a fire scene (a) shows a pattern somewhat like that of gasoline (b). However, a definitive conclusion that the unknown contained gasoline could be obtained only after extraneous peaks were eliminated from the unknown by the use of GC/MS (c).

Key Points

* Most arsons are initiated by petroleum distillates such as gasoline and kerosene.

* The gas chromatograph is the most sensitive and reliable instrument for detecting and characterizing flammable residues. A gas chromatograph separates the hydrocarbon components and produces a chromatographic pattern characteristic of a particular petroleum product.

* By comparing select gas chromatographic peaks recovered from fire-scene debris to known flammable liquids, a forensic analyst may be able to identify the accelerant used to initiate the fire.

* Complex chromatographic patterns can be simplified by passing the separated components emerging from the gas chromatographic column through a mass spectrometer.

Chapter Summary

When a fire occurs, oxygen combines with a fuel to produce noticeable quantities of heat and light (flames). Three requirements must be satisfied to initiate and sustain combustion: (1) a fuel must be present; (2) oxygen must be available in sufficient quantity to combine with the fuel; and (3) sufficient heat must be applied to initiate the combustion and generated to sustain the reaction. A fuel achieves a reaction rate with oxygen sufficient to sustain a fire only when it is in the gaseous state.

As a fire progresses, the heat created by the combustion process tends to move from a high-temperature region to one at a lower temperature. Heat transfer during a fire can occur in a number of ways. Conduction is movement of heat through an object caused by electrons and atoms colliding within the heated object. Radiation is the transfer of heat energy from a heated surface to a cooler surface by electromagnetic radiation. Convection is the transfer of heat energy by movement of molecules within a liquid or gas.

The arson investigator must begin examining a fire scene for signs of arson as soon as the fire has been extinguished. Some telltale signs of arson include evidence of separate and unconnected fires, the use of "streamers" to spread the fire from one area to another, and evidence of severe burning found on the floor as opposed to the ceiling of a structure.

The search of the fire scene must focus on finding the fire's origin. There are no fast and simple rules for identifying a fire's origin. Normally a fire tends to move upward, and thus the probable origin is most likely closest to the lowest point that shows the most intense characteristics of burning. Sometimes as the fire burns upward, a V-shaped pattern forms against a vertical wall. At the suspect point of origin of a fire, porous materials should be collected and stored in airtight containers.

In the laboratory, the gas chromatograph is the most sensitive and reliable instrument for detecting and characterizing flammable residues. Most arsons are initiated by petroleum distillates such as gasoline and kerosene. The gas chromatograph separates the hydrocarbon components and produces a chromatographic pattern characteristic of a particular petroleum product. By comparing select gas chromatographic peaks recovered from fire-scene debris to known flammable liquids, a forensic analyst may be able to identify the accelerant used to initiate the fire.

Review Questions

1. The combination of oxygen with other substances to produce new chemical products is called _____.

2. True or False: All oxidation reactions yield carbon dioxide and water as products. _____

3. _____ is the capacity for doing work.

4. Burning methane for the purpose of heating water to produce steam in order to drive a turbine is an example of converting _____ energy to _____ energy to _____ energy.

5. The quantity of heat evolved from a chemical reaction arises out of the _____ and _____ of chemical bonds.

6. Molecules must _____ energy to break their bonds and _____ energy when their bonds are reformed.

7. Reactions that liberate heat are said to be _____.

8. Excess heat energy liberated by an oxidation reaction is called the _____.

9. A chemical reaction in which heat is absorbed from the surroundings is said to be _____.

10. True or False: All reactions require an energy input to start them. _____

11. The minimum temperature at which a fuel burns is known as the _____ temperature.

12. A fuel achieves a sufficient reaction rate with oxygen to produce a flame only in the _____ state.

13. The lowest temperature at which a liquid fuel produces enough vapor to burn is the _____.

14. _____ is the chemical breakdown of a solid material to gaseous products.

15. The _____ defines the upper and lower limits between which a mixture of gaseous fuel and air burns.

16. _____ is a phenomenon in which a fuel burns without the presence of a flame.

17. True or False: The rate of a chemical reaction increases as the temperature rises. _____

18. _____ describes a fire caused by a natural heat-producing process in a poorly ventilated area.

19. A fire moves away from the original point of ignition because the _____ created by the combustion process tends to move from a high-temperature region to one at a lower temperature.

20. Electrons and atoms within a solid object exposed to heat collide with one another, causing movement of heat through the object in a process called _____.

21. In a process known as _____, a heated surface emits electromagnetic radiation of various wavelengths that moves in a straight line from one surface to another, helping the fire to spread throughout a structure.

22. True or False: An immediate search of a fire scene can commence without obtaining a search warrant. _____

23. A search of the fire scene must focus on finding the fire's _____.

24. True or False: The probable origin of a fire is most likely closest to the lowest point that shows the most intense characteristics of burning. _____

25. A portable _____ detector can suck in the air surrounding a questioned sample to rapidly screen for the presence of volatile residues at fire scenes.

26. True or False: The collection of debris at the origin of a fire should include all nonporous materials. _____

27. _____ containers must be used to package all materials suspected of containing hydrocarbon residues.

28. True or False: Substrate controls should be collected at a fire scene from an area where it can be reasonably assumed that no flammable substance was placed. _____

29. A(n) _____ is a mechanism consisting of a glass bottle containing flammable liquid with a cloth rag stuffed into it and lit as a fuse.

30. The simplest way to recover accelerant residues from fire-scene debris for identification is to heat the airtight container in which the sample is packaged and remove the _____ with a syringe.

31. The most sensitive and reliable instrument for detecting and characterizing flammable residues is the _____.

32. True or False: The identity of a volatile petroleum residue is determined by the size of its gas chromatogram. _____

33. True or False: The major advantage of using the vapor concentration technique in combination with gas chromatography is its extreme sensitivity for detecting volatile residues from fire-scene evidence. _____

34. Complex chromatographic patterns can be simplified by passing the components emerging from the gas chromatographic column through a _____.

Application and Critical Thinking

1. Indicate which method of heat transfer is most likely to be responsible for each of the following:
   a) Ignition of papers in the room where a fire starts
   b) Ignition of electrical wiring in a room adjoining the fire's point or origin
   c) Ignition of roof timbers
   d) Ignition of a neighboring house

2. It is late August in Houston, Texas, and you are investigating a fire that occurred at a facility that stores motor oils and other lubricating oils. A witness points out a man who allegedly ran from the structure about the same time that the fire started. You question the man, who turns out to be the owner of the facility. He tells you that he was checking his inventory when barrels of waste motor oil stored in an unventilated back room spontaneously burst into flames. The owner claims that the fire spread so rapidly that he had to flee the building before he could call 911. After speaking with several employees, you learn that the building has no air-conditioning and that the oil had been stored for almost a year in the cramped back room. You also learn from a detective assisting on the case that the owner increased his insurance coverage on the facility within the past three months. Should you believe the owner's story, or should you suspect arson? On what do you base your conclusion?

3. Criminalist Mick Mickelson is collecting evidence from a fire scene. He gathers about a quart of ash and soot debris from several rooms surrounding the point of origin. He stores the debris in a new, clean paint can, filled about three-quarters full. Seeing several pieces of timber that he believes may contain accelerant residues, he cuts them and places them in airtight plastic bags. A short time later, a suspect is arrested and Mick searches him for any signs of an igniter or accelerants. He finds a cigarette lighter on the suspect and seizes it for evidence before turning the suspect over to the police. What mistakes, if any, did Mick make in collecting evidence?

Web Resources

Arson Investigation (An article about the process of arson investigation)
www.crimeandclues.com/arson.htm

Is It an Accidental Fire or Arson?
www.tcforensic.com.au/docs/article3.html

Fire and Arson Scene Evidence: A Guide for Public Safety Personnel
www.ncjrs.gov/pdffiles1/nij/181584.pdf

Endnotes

1. *Michigan* v. *Tyler,* 436 U.S. 499 (1978).
2. R. T. Newman et al., "The Use of Activated Charcoal Strips for Fire Debris Extractions by Passive Diffusion. Part 1: The Effects of Time, Temperature, Strip Size, and Sample Concentration," *Journal of Forensic Sciences* 41 (1996): 361.
3. M. W. Gilbert, "The Use of Individual Extracted Ion Profiles versus Summed Extracted Ion Profiles in Fire Debris Analysis," *Journal of Forensic Sciences* 43 (1998): 871.

The Oklahoma City Bombing

It was the biggest act of mass murder in U.S. history. On a sunny spring morning in April 1995, a Ryder rental truck pulled into the parking area of the Alfred P. Murrah federal building in Oklahoma City. The driver stepped down from the truck's cab and casually walked away. Minutes later, the truck exploded into a fireball, unleashing enough energy to destroy the building and kill 138 people, including 19 children and infants in the building's day care center.

Later that morning, an Oklahoma Highway Patrol officer pulled over a beat-up 1977 Mercury Marquis being driven without a license plate. On further investigation, the driver, Timothy McVeigh, was found to be in possession of a loaded firearm and charged with transporting a firearm. At the explosion site, remnants of the Ryder truck were located and the truck was quickly traced to a renter—Robert Kling, an alias for Timothy McVeigh. Coincidentally, the rental agreement and McVeigh's driver's license both used the address of McVeigh's friend, Terry Nichols.

Investigators later recovered McVeigh's fingerprint on a receipt for 2,000 pounds of ammonium nitrate, a basic explosive ingredient. Forensic analysts also located PETN residues on the clothing McVeigh wore on the day of his arrest. PETN is a component of detonating cord. After three days of deliberation, a jury declared McVeigh guilty of the bombing and sentenced him to die by lethal injection.

Forensic
Investigation of
Explosions

Key Terms

black powder

deflagration

detonating cord

detonation

explosion

high explosive

low explosive

oxidizing agent

primary explosive

safety fuse

secondary explosive

smokeless powder
(double-base)

smokeless powder
(single-base)

Explosions and Explosives

The ready accessibility of potentially explosive laboratory chemicals, dynamite, and, in some countries, an assortment of military explosives has provided the criminal element of society with a lethal weapon. Unfortunately for society, explosives have become an attractive weapon to criminals bent on revenge, destruction of commercial operations, or just plain mischief.

Although politically motivated bombings have received considerable publicity worldwide, in the United States most bombing incidents are perpetrated by isolated individuals rather than by organized terrorists. These incidents typically involve homemade explosives and incendiary devices. The design of such weapons is limited only by the imagination and ingenuity of the bomber.

Like arson investigation, bomb investigation requires close cooperation of a group of highly specialized individuals trained and experienced in bomb disposal, bomb-site investigation, forensic analysis, and criminal investigation. The criminalist must detect and identify explosive chemicals recovered from the crime scene as well as identify the detonating mechanisms. This special responsibility concerns us for the remainder of this chapter.

Chemistry of Explosions

explosion
A chemical or mechanical action caused by combustion, accompanied by the creation of heat and the rapid expansion of gases.

Like fire, an **explosion** is the product of combustion accompanied by the creation of gases and heat. However, the distinguishing characteristic of an explosion is the rapid rate of the reaction. The sudden buildup of expanding gas pressure at the origin of the explosion produces the violent physical disruption of the surrounding environment.

Our previous discussion of the chemistry of fire referred only to oxidation reactions that rely on air as the sole source of oxygen. However, we need not restrict ourselves to this type of situation. For example, explosives are substances that undergo a rapid exothermic oxidation reaction, producing large quantities of gases. This sudden buildup of gas pressure constitutes an explosion. Detonation occurs so rapidly that oxygen in the air cannot participate in the reaction; thus, many explosives must have their own source of oxygen.

oxidizing agent
A substance that supplies oxygen to a chemical reaction.

Chemicals that supply oxygen are known as **oxidizing agents.** One such agent is found in black powder, a *low explosive,* which is composed of a mixture of the following chemical ingredients:

75 percent potassium nitrate (KNO_3)

15 percent charcoal (C)

10 percent sulfur (S)

In this combination, oxygen containing potassium nitrate acts as an oxidizing agent for the charcoal and sulfur fuels. As heat is applied to black powder, oxygen is liberated from potassium nitrate and simultaneously combines with charcoal and sulfur to produce heat and gases (symbolized by ↑), as represented in the following chemical equation:

$$3C \quad + \quad S \quad + \quad 2KNO_3 \quad \rightarrow$$
carbon   sulfur   potassium nitrate   yields

$$3CO_2{\uparrow} \quad + \quad N_2{\uparrow} \quad + \quad K_2S$$
carbon dioxide   nitrogen   potassium sulfide

Some explosives have their oxygen and fuel components combined within one molecule. For example, the chemical structure of nitroglycerin, the major constituent of dynamite, combines carbon, hydrogen, nitrogen, and oxygen:

$$
\begin{array}{ccc}
H & H & H \\
| & | & | \\
H-C-C-C-H \\
| & | & | \\
NO_2 & NO_2 & NO_2 \\
\end{array}
$$

When nitroglycerin detonates, large quantities of energy are released as the molecule decomposes, and the oxygen recombines to produce large volumes of carbon dioxide, nitrogen, and water.

Consider, for example, the effect of confining an explosive charge to a relatively small, closed container. On detonation, the explosive almost instantaneously produces large volumes of gases that exert enormously high pressures on the interior walls of the container. In addition, the heat energy released by the explosion expands the gases, causing them to push on the walls with an even greater force. If we could observe the effects of an exploding lead pipe in slow motion, we would first see the pipe's walls stretch and balloon under pressures as high as several hundred tons per square inch. Finally, the walls would fragment and fly outward in all directions. This flying debris, or shrapnel, constitutes a great danger to life and limb in the immediate vicinity.

On release from confinement, the gaseous products of the explosion suddenly expand and compress layers of surrounding air as they move outward from the origin of the explosion. This blast effect, or outward rush of gases, at a rate that may be as high as 7,000 miles per hour creates an artificial gale that can overthrow walls, collapse roofs, and disturb any object in its path. If a bomb is sufficiently powerful, more serious damage will be inflicted by the blast effect than by fragmentation debris (see Figure 16–1).

Types of Explosives

The speed at which explosives decompose varies greatly from one to another and permits their classification as *high* and *low explosives*. In a low explosive, this speed is called the speed of **deflagration** (burning). It is characterized by very rapid oxidation that produces heat, light, and a subsonic pressure wave. In a high explosive, it is called the speed of detonation. **Detonation** refers to the creation of a supersonic shock wave within the explosive charge. This shock wave breaks the chemical bonds of the explosive charge, leading to the new instantaneous buildup of heat and gases.

deflagration
A very rapid oxidation reaction accompanied by the generation of a low-intensity pressure wave that can disrupt the surroundings.

detonation
An extremely rapid oxidation reaction accompanied by a violent disruptive effect and an intense, high-speed shock wave.

FIGURE 16–1   A violent explosion. © *Stefan Zaklin/ Corbis. All Rights Reserved*

low explosive
An explosive with a velocity of detonation less than 1,000 meters per second.

Low Explosives   Low explosives, such as black and smokeless powders, decompose relatively slowly at rates up to 1,000 meters per second. Because of their slow burning rates, they produce a propelling or throwing action that makes them suitable as propellants for ammunition or sky-rockets. However, the danger of this group of explosives must not be underestimated, because when any one of them is confined to a relatively small container, it can explode with a force as lethal as that of any known explosive.

black powder
Normally, a mixture of potassium nitrate, carbon, and sulfur in the ratio 75/15/10.

safety fuse
A cord containing a core of black powder; used to carry a flame at a uniform rate to an explosive charge.

smokeless powder (single-base)
An explosive consisting of nitrocellulose.

smokeless powder (double-base)
An explosive consisting of a mixture of nitrocellulose and nitroglycerin.

Black Powder and Smokeless Powder   The most widely used explosives in the low-explosive group are black powder and smokeless powder. The popularity of these two explosives is enhanced by their accessibility to the public. Both are available in any gun store, and black powder can easily be made from ingredients purchased at any chemical supply house as well.

Black powder is a relatively stable mixture of potassium nitrate or sodium nitrate, charcoal, and sulfur. Unconfined, it merely burns; thus it commonly is used in safety fuses that carry a flame to an explosive charge. A safety fuse usually consists of black powder wrapped in a fabric or plastic casing. When ignited, a sufficient length of fuse will burn at a rate slow enough to allow a person adequate time to leave the site of the pending explosion. Black powder, like any other low explosive, becomes explosive and lethal only when it is confined.

The safest and most powerful low explosive is smokeless powder. This explosive usually consists of nitrated cotton or nitrocellulose (single-base powder) or nitroglycerin mixed with nitrocellulose (double-base powder). The powder is manufactured in a variety of grain sizes and shapes, depending on the desired application (see Figure 16–2).

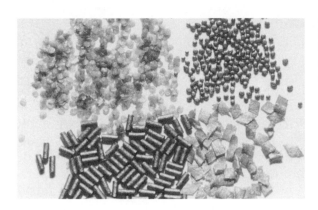

FIGURE 16–2 Samples of smokeless powders. *Courtesy Bureau of Alcohol, Tobacco, Firearms and Explosives*

Chlorate Mixtures The only ingredients required for a low explosive are fuel and a good oxidizing agent. The oxidizing agent potassium chlorate, for example, when mixed with sugar, produces a popular and accessible explosive mix. When confined to a small container—for example, a pipe—and ignited, this mixture can explode with a force equivalent to a stick of 40 percent dynamite.

Some other commonly encountered ingredients that may be combined with chlorate to produce an explosive are carbon, sulfur, starch, phosphorus, and magnesium filings. Chlorate mixtures may also be ignited by the heat generated from a chemical reaction. For instance, sufficient heat can be generated to initiate combustion when concentrated sulfuric acid comes in contact with a sugar–chlorate mix.

Gas–Air Mixtures Another form of low explosive is created when a considerable quantity of natural gas escapes into a confined area and mixes with a sufficient amount of air. If ignited, this mixture results in simultaneous combustion and sudden production of large volumes of gases and heat. In a building, walls are forced outward by the expanding gases, causing the roof to fall into the interiors, and objects are thrown outward and scattered in erratic directions with no semblance of pattern.

Mixtures of air and a gaseous fuel explode or burn only within a limited concentration range. For example, the concentration limits for methane in air range from 5.3 to 13.9 percent. In the presence of too much air, the fuel becomes too diluted and does not ignite. On the other hand, if the fuel becomes too concentrated, ignition is prevented because there is not enough oxygen to support the combustion.

Mixtures at or near the upper concentration limit ("rich" mixtures) explode; however, some gas remains unconsumed because there is not enough oxygen to complete the combustion. As air rushes back into the origin of the explosion, it combines with the residual hot gas, producing a fire that is characterized by a *whoosh* sound. This fire is often more destructive than the explosion that preceded it. Mixtures near the lower end of the limit ("lean" mixtures) generally cause an explosion without accompanying damage due to fire.

High Explosives High explosives include dynamite, TNT, PETN, and RDX. They detonate almost instantaneously at rates of 1,000 to 8,500 meters per second, producing a smashing or shattering effect on their target. High explosives are classified into two groups—primary and secondary explosives—based on their sensitivity to heat, shock, or friction.

Primary explosives are ultrasensitive to heat, shock, or friction, and under normal conditions detonate violently instead of burning. For this

high explosive
An explosive with a velocity of detonation greater than 1,000 meters per second.

primary explosive
A high explosive that is easily detonated by heat, shock, or friction.

reason, they are used to detonate other explosives through a chain reaction and are often referred to as *primers*. Primary explosives provide the major ingredients of blasting caps and include lead azide, lead styphnate, and diazodinitrophenol (see Figure 16–3). Because of their extreme sensitivity, these explosives are rarely used as the main charge of a homemade bomb.

Secondary explosives are relatively insensitive to heat, shock, or friction, and normally burn rather than detonate when ignited in small quantities in open air. This group comprises most high explosives used for commercial and military blasting. Some common examples of secondary explosives are dynamite, TNT (trinitrotoluene), PETN (pentaerythritol tetranitrate), RDX (cyclotrimethylenetrinitramine), and tetryl (2,4,6-trinitrophenylmethylnitramine).

secondary explosive
A high explosive that is relatively insensitive to heat, shock, or friction.

Dynamite   It is an irony of history that the prize most symbolic of humanity's search for peace—the Nobel Peace Prize—should bear the name of the developer of one of our most lethal discoveries—dynamite. In 1867, the Swedish chemist Alfred Nobel, searching for a method to desensitize nitroglycerin, found that when kieselguhr, a variety of diatomaceous earth, absorbed a large portion of nitroglycerin, it became far less sensitive but still retained its explosive force. Nobel later decided to use pulp as an absorbent because kieselguhr was a heat-absorbing material.

This so-called pulp dynamite was the beginning of what is now known as the straight dynamite series. These dynamites are used when a quick

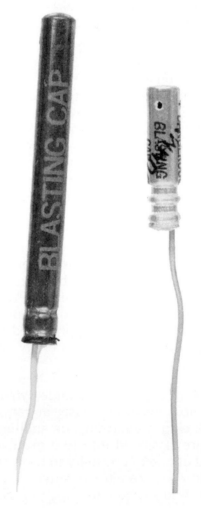

FIGURE 16–3   Blasting caps. The left and center caps are initiated by an electrical current; the right cap is initiated by a safety fuse.

shattering action is desired. In addition to nitroglycerine and pulp, present-day straight dynamites also include sodium nitrate (which furnishes oxygen for complete combustion) and a small percentage of a stabilizer, such as calcium carbonate.

All straight dynamite is rated by strength; the strength rating is determined by the weight percentage of nitroglycerin in the formula. Thus, a 40 percent straight dynamite contains 40 percent nitroglycerin, a 60 percent grade contains 60 percent nitroglycerin, and so forth. However, the relative blasting power of various strengths of dynamite is not directly proportional to their strength ratings. A 60 percent straight dynamite, rather than being three times as strong as a 20 percent, is only one and one-half times as strong (see Figure 16–4).

Ammonium Nitrate Explosives   In recent years, nitroglycerin-based dynamite has all but disappeared from the industrial explosives market. Commercially, these explosives have been replaced mainly by ammonium nitrate–based explosives, that is, water gels, emulsions, and ANFO explosives. These explosives mix oxygen-rich ammonium nitrate with a fuel to form a low-cost and very stable explosive.

Typically, water gels have a consistency resembling that of set gelatin or gel-type toothpaste. They are characterized by their water-resistant nature and are employed for all types of blasting under wet conditions. These explosives are based on formulations of ammonium nitrate and sodium nitrate gelled with a natural polysaccharide such as guar gum. Commonly, a combustible material such as aluminum is mixed into the gel to serve as the explosive's fuel.

Emulsion explosives differ from gels in that they consist of two distinct phases, an oil phase and a water phase. In these emulsions, a droplet of a

FIGURE 16–4   Sticks of dynamite. *Courtesy AP Wide World Photos*

supersaturated solution of ammonium nitrate is surrounded by a hydro-carbon serving as a fuel. A typical emulsion consists of water, one or more inorganic nitrate oxidizers, oil, and emulsifying agents. Commonly, emulsions contain micron-sized glass, resin, or ceramic spheres known as *microspheres* or *microballoons*. The size of these spheres controls the explosive's sensitivity and detonation velocity.

Ammonium nitrate soaked in fuel oil is an explosive known as *ANFO*. Such commercial explosives are inexpensive and safe to handle and have found wide applications in blasting operations in the mining industry. Ammonium nitrate in the form of fertilizer makes a readily obtainable ingredient for homemade explosives. Indeed, in an incident related to the 1993 bombing of New York City's World Trade Center, the FBI arrested five men during a raid on their hideout in New York City, where they were mixing a "witches' brew" of fuel oil and an ammonium nitrate–based fertilizer.

TATP *Triacetone triperoxide* (TATP) is a homemade explosive that has been used as an improvised explosive by terrorist organizations in Israel and other Middle Eastern countries. It is prepared by reacting the common ingredients of acetone and hydrogen peroxide in the presence of an acid catalyst such as hydrochloric acid.

TATP is a friction- and impact-sensitive explosive that is extremely potent when confined in a container such as a pipe. The 2005 London transit bombings were caused by TATP-based explosives and provide ample evidence that terrorist cells have moved TATP outside the Middle East. A London bus destroyed by one of the TATP bombs is shown in Figure 16–5.

A plot to blow up ten international plane flights leaving Britain for the United States with a "liquid explosive" apparently involved plans to smuggle the peroxide-based TATP explosive onto the planes. This plot has prompted authorities to prohibit airline passengers from carrying liquids and gels onto planes.

FIGURE 16–5   A London bus destroyed by a TATP-based bomb. *Courtesy AP Wide World Photos*

Forensics at Work

Liquid Explosives

Of the hundreds of types of explosives, most are solid. Only about a dozen are liquid. But some of those liquid explosives can be readily purchased and others can be made from hundreds of different kinds of chemicals that are not difficult to obtain. A memo issued by federal security officials about the plot to blow up ten international planes highlighted a type of liquid explosive based on peroxide.

The most common peroxide explosive is triacetone triperoxide, or TATP, which is made from two liquids: acetone, the primary ingredient of most nail polish removers, and hydrogen peroxide, commonly used in diluted form as an antiseptic. TATP, which can be used as a detonator or a primary explosive, has been used in Qaeda-related bomb plots and by Palestinian suicide bombers.

TATP itself is a white powder made up of crystals that form when acetone and hydrogen peroxide are mixed together, usually with a catalyst added to speed the chemical reactions. But there is no need to wait for the crystals. Acetone and peroxide form an "exceedingly reactive mixture" that can be easily detonated by an electrical spark, said Neal Langerman, president of Advanced Chemical Safety, a consulting company in San Diego.

Acetone is easy to obtain; hydrogen peroxide is somewhat more difficult to obtain. The hydrogen peroxide solution sold in pharmacies is too dilute—only 3 percent—to be used in an explosive. Stronger hydrogen peroxide of 30 percent concentration can be ordered from chemical supply companies, but concentrations strong enough to generate

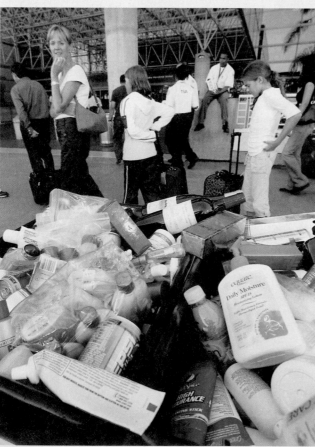

Liquids and gels discarded by airline passengers before boarding. *Stefano Paltera, AP Wide World Photos*

(*continued*)

Forensics at Work

Liquid Explosives (continued)

a powerful explosion—about 70 percent— are not readily available, Dr. Langerman said.

But Dr. Langerman added that acetone mixed with a 30 percent peroxide solution could still set off a fire that might burn through the aluminum skin of an airliner and cause it to crash. "All of them are highly energetic," he said of the various chemical combinations. "It doesn't take much to punch a hole in the side of a plane, and if you punch a hole in the side of a plane, the plane comes down."

In theory, scientists know how to detect peroxide-based explosives. The challenge will be to design machines that can perform the scans quickly and efficiently on thousands of passengers passing through security checks. "It will not be as easy as the swab tests we are using for nitrogen compounds right now," Dr. Langerman said. Other common liquid explosives, such as nitroglycerine and nitromethane (the fuel of dragster race cars) contain nitrogen compounds, so

it may be possible to adjust current scanning machines to detect them.

Robert M. Blitzer, a former FBI terrorism official now at ICF International in Fairfax, Virginia, said the Bureau had worried for more than 15 years about the possibility of liquid explosives on airliners. "We were very concerned about any form of explosive material, including liquids and gels," he said. But after the September 11 attacks, worries about solid explosives became the main concern. It is therefore not surprising that terrorists turned to liquids in this latest plot, said Jimmie C. Oxley, an expert on the chemistry of explosives at the University of Rhode Island who has advised federal officials.

"It was not seen as the threat," she said. "Now that the terrorists have staked out our vulnerabilities, that's where the threat has gone, and we'll have to respond." But, once new equipment gets into airports to reduce the threat of liquid explosives, Dr. Oxley said, terrorists will "look for the next vulnerability."

Source: Kenneth Chang and William J. Broad, "Lethal and Wet: It's Not Hard to Use Fluids to Cause an Explosion on a Plane, Chemists Say." *New York Times*, August 11, 2006. Copyright © 2006 by the New York Times Company. Reprinted by permission.

Military High Explosives No discussion of high explosives would be complete without a mention of military high explosives. In many countries outside the United States, the accessibility of high explosives to terrorist organizations makes them very common constituents of homemade bombs. RDX, the most popular and powerful military explosive, is often encountered in the form of a pliable plastic of doughlike consistency known as *composition C–4* (a U.S. military designation).

TNT was produced and used on an enormous scale during World War II and may be considered the most important military bursting charge explosive. Alone or in combination with other explosives, it has found wide application in shells, bombs, grenades, demolition explosives, and propellant compositions (see Figure 16–6). Interestingly, military "dynamite" contains no nitroglycerin but is actually composed of a mixture of RDX and TNT. Like other military explosives, TNT is rarely encountered in bombings in the United States.

PETN is used by the military in TNT mixtures for small-caliber projectiles and grenades. Commercially, the chemical is used as the explosive

FIGURE 16–6   Military explosives in combat use. *Courtesy Getty Images/Time Life Pictures*

core in a detonating cord or *primacord*. Instead of the slower-burning safety fuse, a detonating cord is often used to connect a series of explosive charges so that they will detonate simultaneously.

Detonators   Unlike low explosives, bombs made of high explosives must be detonated by an initiating explosion. In most cases, detonators are blasting caps composed of copper or aluminum cases filled with lead azide as an initiating charge and PETN or RDX as a detonating charge. Blasting caps can be initiated by means of a burning safety fuse or by an electrical current.

Homemade bombs camouflaged in packages, suitcases, and the like are usually initiated with an electrical blasting cap wired to a battery. An unlimited number of switching-mechanism designs have been devised for setting off these devices; clocks and mercury switches are favored. Bombers sometimes prefer to employ outside electrical sources. For instance, most automobile bombs are detonated when the ignition switch of a car is turned on.

detonating cord
A cordlike explosive containing a core of high-explosive material, usually PETN; also called primacord.

Key Points

- Explosives are substances that undergo a rapid oxidation reaction with the production of large quantities of gases. The sudden buildup of gas pressure leads to the explosion.

- The speed at which an explosive decomposes determines whether it is classified as a high or low explosive.

- The most widely used low explosives are black powder and smokeless powder. Common high explosives include ammonium nitrate–based explosives (water gels, emulsions, and ANFO explosives).

- Among the high explosives, primary explosives are ultrasensitive to heat, shock, or friction and provide the major ingredients found in blasting caps. Secondary explosives normally constitute the main charge of a high explosive.

Collection and Analysis of Evidence of Explosives

The most important step in the detection and analysis of explosive residues is the collection of appropriate samples from the explosion scene. Invariably, undetonated residues of the explosive remain at the site of the explosion. The detection and identification of these explosives in the laboratory depends on the bomb-scene investigator's skill and ability to recognize and sample the areas most likely to contain such materials.

Detecting and Recovering Evidence of Explosives

The most obvious characteristic of a high or contained low explosive is the presence of a crater at the origin of the blast. Once the crater has been located, all loose soil and other debris must immediately be removed from the interior of the hole and preserved for laboratory analysis. Other good sources of explosive residues are objects located near the origin of detonation. Wood, insulation, rubber, and other soft materials that are readily penetrated often collect traces of the explosive. However, nonporous objects near the blast must not be overlooked. For instance, residues can be found on the surfaces of metal objects near the site of an explosion. Material blown away from the blast's origin should also be recovered because it, too, may retain explosive residues.

The entire area must be systematically searched, with great care given to recovering any trace of a detonating mechanism or any other item foreign to the explosion site. Wire-mesh screens are best used for sifting through debris. All personnel involved in searching the bomb scene must take appropriate measures to avoid contaminating the scene, including dressing in disposable gloves, shoe covers, and overalls.

Ion Mobility Spectrometer   In pipe-bomb explosions, particles of the explosive are frequently found adhering to the pipe cap or to the pipe threads, as a result of either being impacted into the metal by the force of the explosion or being deposited in the threads during the construction of the bomb.

One approach for screening objects for the presence of explosive residues in the field or the laboratory is the ion mobility spectrometer (IMS).[1] A portable IMS is shown in Figure 16–7. This handheld detector uses a vacuum to collect explosive residues from suspect surfaces. Alternatively, the surface suspected of containing explosive residues is wiped down with a Teflon-coated fiberglass disc and the collected residues are then drawn into the spectrometer off the disc. Once in the IMS, the explosive residues are vaporized by the application of heat. These vaporized substances are exposed to a beam of electrons or beta rays emitted by radioactive nickel and converted into electrically charged molecules or ions. The ions are then allowed to move through a tube (drift region) under the influence of an electric field. A schematic diagram of an IMS is shown in Figure 16–8.

The preliminary identification of an explosive residue can be made by noting the time it takes the explosive to move through the tube. Because ions move at different speeds depending on their size and structure, they can be characterized by the speed at which they pass through the tube. Used as a screening tool, this method rapidly detects a full range of explosives, even at low detection levels. However, all results need to be verified through confirmatory tests.

FIGURE 16–7   A portable ion mobility spectrometer used to rapidly detect and tentatively identify trace quantities of explosives. *Courtesy GE Ion Track, Wilmington, Mass.*

The IMS can detect plastic explosives as well as commercial and military explosives. More than 10,000 portable and full-size IMS units are currently used at airport security checkpoints, and more than 50,000 handheld IMS analyzers have been deployed for chemical-weapons monitoring in various armed forces.

Collection and Packaging   All materials collected for examination by the laboratory must be placed in airtight sealed containers and labeled with all pertinent information. Soil and other soft loose materials are best stored in metal airtight containers such as clean paint cans. Debris and articles collected from different areas are to be packaged in separate airtight containers. Plastic bags should not be used to store evidence suspected of containing explosive residues. Some explosives can actually escape through the plastic. Sharp-edged objects should not be allowed to pierce the sides of a plastic bag. It is best to place these types of items in metal containers.

Key Points

- The entire bomb site must be systematically searched to recover any trace of a detonating mechanism or any other item foreign to the explosion site. Objects located at or near the origin of the explosion must be collected for laboratory examination.

- The most obvious characteristic of a high or contained low explosive is the presence of a crater at the origin of the blast.

- A device widely used to screen objects for the presence of explosive residues is the ion mobility spectrometer.

- All materials collected at bombing scenes must be placed in airtight containers such as clean paint cans.

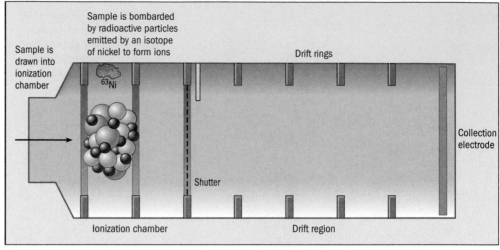

(a)

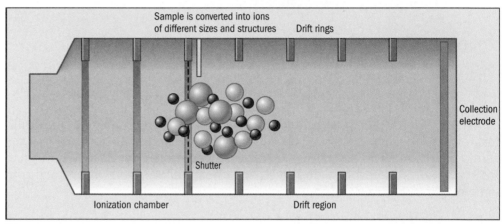

(b)

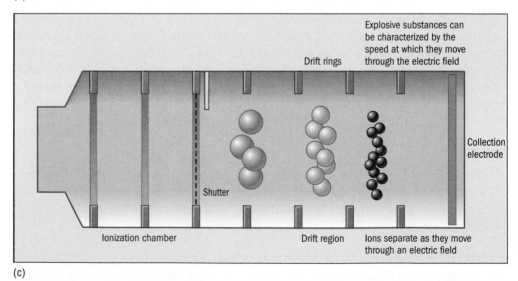

(c)

FIGURE 16–8 A schematic diagram of an ion mobility spectrometer. A sample is introduced into an ionization chamber, where bombardment with radioactive particles emitted by an isotope of nickel converts the sample to ions. The ions move into a drift region where ion separation occurs based on the speed of the ions as they move through an electric field.

Analysis of Evidence of Explosives

When the bomb-scene debris and other materials arrive at the laboratory, everything is first examined microscopically to detect particles of unconsumed explosive. Portions of the recovered debris and detonating mechanism, if found, are carefully viewed under a low-power stereoscopic microscope in a painstaking effort to locate particles of the explosive. Black powder and smokeless powder are relatively easy to locate in debris because of their characteristic shapes and colors (see Figure 16–2). However, dynamite and other high explosives present the microscopist with a much more difficult task and often must be detected by other means.

Following microscopic examination, the recovered debris is thoroughly rinsed with acetone. The high solubility of most explosives in acetone ensures their quick removal from the debris. When a water-gel explosive containing ammonium nitrate or a low explosive is suspected, the debris should be rinsed with water so that water-soluble substances (such as nitrates and chlorates) will be extracted. Table 16–1 lists a number of simple color tests the examiner can perform on the acetone and water extracts to screen for the presence of organic and inorganic explosives, respectively.

Screening and Confirmation Tests   Once collected, the acetone extract is concentrated and analyzed using color spot tests, thin-layer chromatography (TLC), and gas chromatography/mass spectrometry. The presence of an explosive is indicated by a well-defined spot on a TLC plate with an R_f value corresponding to a known explosive—for example, nitroglycerin, RDX, or PETN.

When sufficient quantities of explosives are recoverable, confirmatory tests may be performed by either infrared spectrophotometry or X-ray diffraction. The former produces a unique "fingerprint" pattern for an organic explosive, as shown by the IR spectrum of RDX in Figure 16–9. The latter provides a unique diffraction pattern for inorganic substances such as potassium nitrate and potassium chlorate.

Table 16.1   Color Spot Tests for Common Explosives

	Reagent		
Substance	Griess[a]	Diphenylamine[b]	Alcoholic KOH[c]
Chlorate	No color	Blue	No color
Nitrate	Pink to red	Blue	No color
Nitrocellulose	Pink	Blue-black	No color
Nitroglycerin	Pink to red	Blue	No color
PETN	Pink to red	Blue	No color
RDX	Pink to red	Blue	No color
TNT	No color	No color	Red
Tetryl	Pink to red	Blue	Red-violet

[a]Griess reagent: Solution 1—Dissolve 1 g sulfanilic acid in 100 mL 30% acetic acid. Solution 2—Dissolve 0.5 g N-(1-napthyl) ethylenediamine in 100 mL methyl alcohol. Add solutions 1 and 2 and a few milligrams of zinc dust to the suspect extract.
[b]Diphenylamine reagent: Dissolve 1 g diphenylamine in 100 mL concentrated sulfuric acid.
[c]Alcoholic KOH reagent: Dissolve 10 g of potassium hydroxide in 100 mL absolute alcohol.

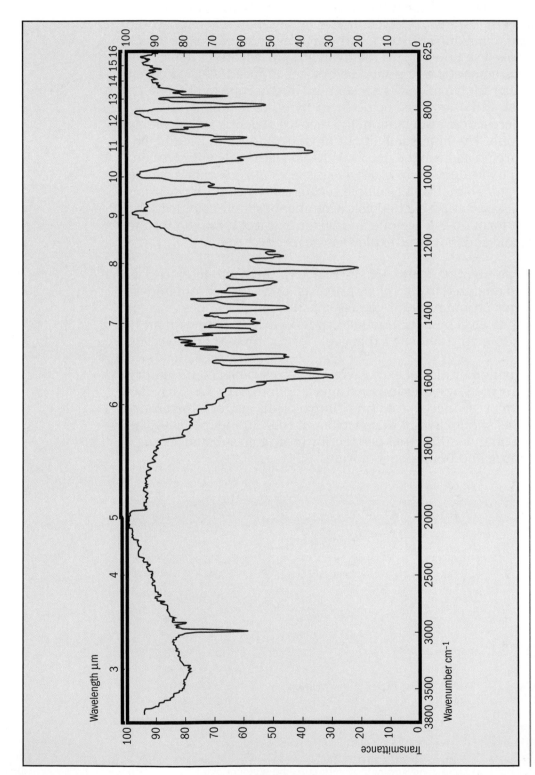

FIGURE 16–9   The infrared spectrum of RDX.

Taggants An explosive "taggant" program has been proposed to further enhance a bomb-scene investigator's chances of recovering useful evidence at a postexplosion scene. Under this proposal, tiny color-coded chips the size of sand grains would be added to commercial explosives during their manufacture. Some of these chips would be expected to survive an explosion and be capable of recovery at explosion scenes. To aid in their recovery, the chips are made both fluorescent and magnetic sensitive. Hence, investigators can search for taggants at the explosion site with magnetic tools and ultraviolet light.

The taggant chip is arranged in a color sequence that indicates where the explosive was made and when it was produced (see Figure 16-10). With this knowledge, the explosive can be traced through its distribution chain to its final legal possessor. The taggant colors are readily observed and are read with the aid of a low-power microscope.

There are no plans to institute a taggant program for commercial explosives in the United States. In Europe, only Switzerland has adopted a taggant program; thus, it is extremely doubtful that taggants will be found in any significant number of bombing incidents in the foreseeable future. Interestingly, the International Civil Aviation Organization has mandated that a volatile taggant be added to plastic explosives during their manufacture in order to facilitate the detection of these explosives. Programs are now under way to tag commercial C–4 with the volatile chemical known as DMNB (2,3-dimethyl-2,3-dinitrobutane).

Key Points

- Debris collected at explosion scenes is examined microscopically for unconsumed explosive particles.

- Recovered debris may be thoroughly rinsed with organic solvents and analyzed by testing procedures that include color spot tests, thin-layer chromatography, and gas chromatography/mass spectrometry.

- Unconsumed explosives are identified by either infrared spectrophotometry or X-ray diffraction.

Closer Analysis

X-Ray Diffraction

One way to elicit information about how elements have combined to constitute the makeup of a particular substance is to aim a beam of X-rays at the material and study how the X-rays interact with the atoms that compose the substance under investigation. This technique is known as *X-ray diffraction*.

X-ray diffraction can be applied only to the study of solid, crystalline materials—that is, solids with a definite and orderly arrangement of atoms. For example, sodium chloride (common table salt) is crystalline. Fortunately, many substances, including 95 percent of all inorganic compounds, are crystalline and are thus identifiable by X-ray diffraction analysis. The atoms in a crystal may be thought of as being composed of a series of parallel planes. As the X-rays penetrate the crystal, a portion of the beam is reflected by each of the atomic planes. As the reflected

(*continued*)

Closer Analysis

X-Ray Diffraction *(continued)*

beams leave the crystal's planes, they combine with one another to form a series of light and dark bands known as a *diffraction pattern*. Every compound produces a unique diffraction pattern, thus giving analysts a means for "fingerprinting" compounds.

Figure 1 illustrates the X-ray diffraction process. Diffraction patterns for potassium nitrate and potassium chlorate, two common constituents of homemade explosives, are shown in Figure 2. Comparing a questioned specimen with a known X-ray pattern is a rapid and specific way to prove chemical identity.

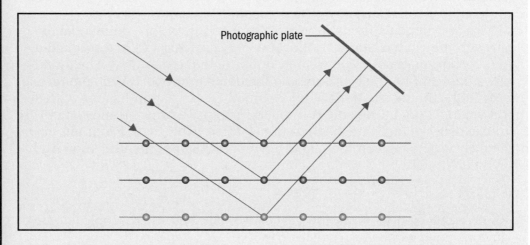

Photographic plate

FIGURE 1   A beam of X-rays being reflected off the atomic planes of a crystal. The diffraction patterns that form are recorded on photographic film. These patterns are unique for each crystalline substance.

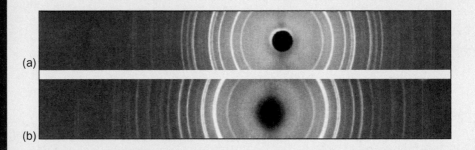

(a)

(b)

FIGURE 2   X-ray diffraction patterns for (a) potassium nitrate and (b) potassium chlorate.

FIGURE 16–10   A cross-section of a taggant. The color sequence of the recovered taggant is observed with the aid of a low-power microscope. The colors are then matched to a color code to yield information about the plant of manufacture, production lot, and purchasers of the explosive material.

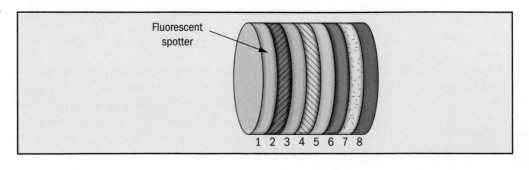

Fluorescent spotter

1 2 3 4 5 6 7 8

Forensics at Work

The Crash of TWA Flight 800

Although the crash of TWA Flight 800 was ultimately not proven to be an act of terrorism, the initial investigation revealed the difficulties investigators can expect to encounter in recovering explosive residues at bombing scenes. For example, in spite of the large quantities of explosive used, investigators encountered extreme difficulties in recovering explosive residues at both the World Trade Center (1993) and Oklahoma federal building bombing sites.

The Search: The TWA Plane Crash

Three weeks after the Atlantic Ocean swallowed a flaming Boeing 747, investigators continue to explore a prevailing theory that the downfall of Trans World Airlines Flight 800 was caused by a bomb. But their complicated mission is made all the more complex by the very water in which much of the plane rests.

Investigators say they are still concerned that the extended submersion in saltwater might have an effect on telltale chemical traces that a bomb would have left on airplane aluminum, plastic containers, luggage—and anything else from the jumbo jet's front end, where, investigators theorize, the explosion that downed the aircraft took place. More than 80 percent of the airplane remains scattered on the ocean floor, 120 feet down.

Their worry has heightened the sense of urgency in recovering debris from the water, said Joseph Cantamessa Jr., an F.B.I. special agent in charge. "It's the reason we have been so impatient about getting the evidence in the lab for testing."

Christopher Ronay, the former head of the Federal Bureau of Investigation's explosives unit and now president of the Institute of Makers of Explosives in Washington, D.C., said investigators have cause for concern. "Your explosive residue," he said, "adheres to all sorts of materials—to carpet fibers and upholstery and plastics, and it can be trapped in the surface material through all sorts of

FBI agents and New York State Police guard the reconstruction of TWA Flight 800. *Courtesy Mark Lennihan, AP World Wide Photos*

(continued)

Forensics at Work

The Crash of TWA Flight 800 *(continued)*

means. And certainly water washes away some kinds of residues."

But the July 17 [1996] explosion of Flight 800, which killed all 230 people on board, remains a puzzle in many pieces. As Mr. Ronay and others point out, the airplane may or may not have been brought down by a bomb. And if a bomb was the cause, the explosive material could have been one of several kinds. And depending on the kind of explosive, ocean water could either wash away the chemical residue or have little effect.

Dr. Jesse L. Beauchamp, a chemistry professor at the California Institute of Technology in Pasadena, said: "It goes without saying that any traces of explosives that were present on wreckage would likely be partially removed—not entirely removed—by continued exposure to saltwater. But it depends on the type of explosives."

Mr. Ronay, who helped coordinate the bureau's successful investigation into the fatal explosion of Pan Am Flight 103 over Lockerbie, Scotland, in 1988, expressed confidence in the F.B.I. laboratory's sophisticated equipment and in Tom Thurman, his successor as chief of the explosives unit and the case agent in the Lockerbie investigation.

Mr. Thurman and his team of forensic specialists have been examining the recovered airplane debris at a hangar in Calverton, Long Island. In general they are concentrating on two avenues of inquiry: finding any explosive's chemical residue, and searching for pockmarks, tearing and other signs found on items that were near the explosion, often called "witness material."

In an explosion, a chemical reaction transforms the explosive material into gas.

But some of that material is merely scattered, albeit in microscopic fragments. And that is what the forensic investigator seeks.

"There's almost always some residue," said Dr. Jimmie Oxley, a professor of chemistry at the University of Rhode Island. "And you look for something abnormal in the chemical analysis, something that shouldn't be there."

Dr. Oxley, who is a consultant to the F.B.I. and the Bureau of Alcohol, Tobacco and Firearms, said that investigators undoubtedly are rinsing airplane parts with an organic solvent to see if there is organic material that would not normally be present. "If you found traces of a military explosive such as RDX, which is not water soluble, it would have no reason for possibly being there," she said. "So now you have positive evidence."

But the ocean presents another variable. "On the other hand, if you never find anything at all, you can't draw any conclusions," Dr. Oxley said. "Now you've got to look at a lot of other things. There are explosive materials that could have been used that are water soluble. There is ammonium nitrate fuel oil, which is water soluble except for the oil. And this stuff has been bathing down there for a long time."

Even in the case of ammonium nitrate fuel oil, or ANFO, the material used in last year's deadly bombing of a federal building in Oklahoma City, the investigators would expect to find traces of insoluble materials used to detonate the mixture.

Investigators in Calverton are using tools such as a gas chromatograph, which separates organic components, and a mass spectrometer, which identifies each component by its molecular weight. But Mr. Ronay said that more in-depth analysis is being done at the F.B.I. laboratory in Washington where, he said, there are specific instruments to use on specific explosives.

"Their equipment is so sensitive that it can track material in parts per trillion," he said. "I don't think a shark can smell blood in the water to that degree."

Still, Mr. Ronay acknowledged the difficulty that his former colleagues face. "It's such a big, big project," he said. "And you might never find the right piece."

That would force investigators to focus on the other avenue of inquiry—the hunt for a specific kind of tear in metal, or the pitting in a piece of luggage that might have been near the source of an explosion.

"If they never find the residue, the experts will probably characterize the damage and make some estimates regarding the kind of explosive that was used," Mr. Ronay said. "But if you find residue, you don't need to guess."

Source: Dan Barry, "Saltwater's Ill Effects Depend on Bomb Type," *New York Times*, August 7, 1996, p. B-5. Copyright © 1996 by the New York Times Company. Reprinted with permission.

Chapter Summary

Explosives are substances that undergo a rapid oxidation reaction with the production of large quantities of gases. This sudden buildup of gas pressure constitutes an explosion. The speed at which explosives decompose permits their classification as high or low explosives.

The most widely used low explosives are black powder and smokeless powder. Among the high explosives, primary explosives are ultrasensitive to heat, shock, or friction and provide the major ingredients found in blasting caps. Secondary explosives normally constitute the main charge of a high explosive.

Among the high explosives, nitroglycerin-based dynamite has all but disappeared from the industrial explosives market and has been replaced by ammonium nitrate–based explosives (such as water gels, emulsions, and ANFO explosives). In many countries outside the United States, the accessibility of military high explosives to terrorist organizations makes them very common constituents of homemade bombs. RDX is the most popular and powerful of the military explosives.

The entire bomb site must be systematically searched with great care given to recovering any trace of a detonating mechanism or any other item foreign to the explosion site. Objects located at or near the origin of the explosion must be collected for laboratory examination.

Typically, in the laboratory, debris collected at explosion scenes is examined microscopically for unconsumed explosive particles. Recovered debris may also be thoroughly rinsed with organic solvents and analyzed by testing procedures that include color spot tests, thin-layer chromatography, high-performance liquid chromatography, and gas chromatography/mass spectrometry.

Review Questions

1. Rapid combustion accompanied by the creation of large volumes of gases describes a(n) _____.

2. True or False: Chemicals that supply oxygen are known as oxidizing agents. _____

3. Explosives that decompose at relatively slow rates are classified as _____ explosives.

4. The speed at which low explosives decompose is called the speed of _____.

5. Three ingredients of black powder are _____, _____, and _____.

6. _____ explosives detonate almost instantaneously to produce a smashing or shattering effect.

7. The most widely used low explosives are _____ and _____.

8. A low explosive becomes explosive and lethal only when it is _____.

9. True or False: Air and a gaseous fuel burn when mixed at any concentration range. _____

10. High explosives can be classified as either _____ or _____ explosives.

11. The blasting power of various dynamite strengths is in direct proportion to the weight percentage of _____ present in it.

12. True or False: The most common commercial explosives incorporate ammonium nitrate. _____

13. The most widely used explosive in the military is _____.

14. The explosive core in detonating cord is _____.

15. A high explosive is normally detonated by a(n) _____ explosive contained within a blasting cap.

16. An obvious characteristic of a high explosive is the presence of a(n) _____ at the origin of the blast.

17. The most important step in detecting explosive residues is the _____ of appropriate samples from the explosion scene.

18. To screen objects for the presence of explosive residues in the field or the laboratory, the investigator may use a handheld _____.

19. Unconsumed explosive residues may be detected in the laboratory through a careful _____ examination of the debris.

20. Debris recovered from the site of an explosion is routinely rinsed with _____ in an attempt to recover most explosive residues.

21. Once collected, the acetone extract is initially analyzed by _____, _____, and _____.

22. True or False: Debris and articles at an explosion scene that are collected from different areas are to be packaged in separate airtight containers.
_____

23. True or False: In the absence of airtight metal containers, plastic bags can be used to store evidence suspected of containing explosive residues.
_____

Application and Critical Thinking

1. The following pieces of evidence were found at separate explosion sites. For each item, indicate whether the explosion was more likely caused by low or high explosives, and explain your answer:
   a) Lead azide residues
   b) Nitrocellulose residues
   c) Ammonium nitrate residues
   d) Scraps of primacord
   e) Potassium chlorate residues

2. Which color test or tests would you run first on a suspect sample to test for evidence of each of the following explosives? Explain your answers.
   a) Tetryl
   b) TNT
   c) Chlorate
   d) Nitrocellulose

3. Criminalist Matt Weir is collecting evidence from the site of an explosion. Arriving on the scene, he immediately proceeds to look for the crater caused by the blast. After finding the crater, he picks through the debris at the site by hand, looking for evidence of detonators or foreign materials. Matt collects loose soil and debris from the immediate area, placing the smaller bits in paper folded into a druggist fold. Larger items he stores in plastic bags for transportation to the laboratory. What mistakes, if any, did Matt make in collecting and storing this evidence?

Web Resources

A Guide for Explosion and Bombing Scene Investigation (An Adobe Acrobat publication from the U.S. Department of Justice outlining federal procedures for the investigation of explosions)
www.bombsecurity.com/downloads2/nij_181869.pdf

Arson and Explosives (An article that discusses principles of combustion, types of explosives, and the investigation of explosion sites; includes a brief list of links to other sites about arson and explosives)
www.apsu.edu/oconnort/3210/3210lect06a.htm

Pyrotechnics, Explosives, & Fireworks (A detailed article on the workings and types of explosives; has good material about low explosives, high explosives, and taggants)
www.faqs.org/docs/air/ttpyro.html

Endnote

1. T. Keller et al., "Application of Ion Mobility Spectrometry in Cases of Forensic Interest," _Forensic Science International,_ 161 (2006): 130.

The Unabomber

In 1978, a parcel addressed to a Northwestern University professor exploded as it was being opened by a campus security officer. This was the start of a series of bomb-containing packages that typically were sent to universities and airlines. Considering the intended victims, the perpetrator was dubbed UN (university) A (airlines) BOM; hence, *the Unabomber*.

The explosives were usually housed in a pipe within a wooden box. The explosive ingredients generally were black powder, smokeless powder, or an ammonium nitrate mix. The box was filled with metal objects to create a shrapnel effect on explosion. The device typically had the initials "FC" punched into it.

The first Unabomber fatality came in 1985, when a computer store owner was killed after picking up a package left outside his business. The Unabomber emerged again in 1993 after a six-year hiatus by mailing bombs to two university professors. Their injuries were not fatal, but his next two attacks did result in fatalities.

In 1995, the case took an unexpected turn when the Unabomber promised to end his mad spree if his 35,000-word typewritten "Manifesto," sent to the *New York Times* and the *Washington Post* were published. The manifesto proved to be a long, rambling rant against technology, but it offered valuable clues that broke the case. David Kaczynski realized that the manifesto's writing style and the philosophy it espoused closely resembled that of his brother, Ted. His suspicions were confirmed by linguistics experts, who carefully pored over the manifesto's content. Ted Kaczynski was arrested in Montana in 1996. Inside his ramshackle cabin were writings similar to the manifesto, three manual typewriters, and bomb-making materials. Forensic document examiners were able to match the typewritten manifesto to one of the typewriters recovered from the cabin.

chapter 17

Document
Examination

Key Terms

charred document

erasure

exemplar

indented writings

infrared luminescence

natural variations

obliteration

questioned document

Learning Objectives

After studying this chapter, you should be able to:

- Define *questioned document.*

- Know what common individual characteristics are associated with handwriting.

- List some important guidelines for collecting known writings for comparison to a questioned document.

- Recognize some of the class and individual characteristics of printers and photocopiers.

- List some of the techniques document examiners use to uncover alterations, erasures, obliterations, and variations in pen inks.

Document Examiner

Ordinarily, the work of the document examiner involves examining handwriting and typescript to ascertain the source or authenticity of a questioned document. However, document examination is not restricted to a mere visual comparison of words and letters. The document examiner must know how to use microscopy, photography, and even such analytical methods as chromatography to uncover all efforts, both brazen and subtle, to change the content or meaning of a document.

Alterations of documents through overwriting, erasures, or the more obvious crossing out of words must be recognized and characterized as efforts to alter or obscure the original meaning of a document. The document examiner identifies such efforts and recovers the original contents of the writing. An examiner may even reconstruct writing on charred or burned papers, or uncover the meaning of indented writings found on a paper pad after the top sheet has been removed.

questioned document
Any document about which some issue has been raised or that is the subject of an investigation.

Any object that contains handwritten or typewritten markings whose source or authenticity is in doubt may be referred to as a questioned document. Such a broad definition covers all of the written and printed materials we normally encounter in our daily activities. Letters, checks, driver's licenses, contracts, wills, voter registrations, passports, petitions, and even lottery tickets are commonly examined in crime laboratories. However, we need not restrict our examples to paper documents. Questioned documents may include writings or other markings found on walls, windows, doors, or any other objects.

Document examiners possess no mystical powers or scientific formulas for identifying the authors of writings. They apply knowledge gathered through years of training and experience to recognize and compare the individual characteristics of questioned and known authentic writings. For this purpose, gathering documents of known authorship or origin is critical to the outcome of the examination. Collecting known writings may entail considerable time and effort and may be further hampered by uncooperative or missing witnesses. However, the uniqueness of handwriting makes this type of physical evidence, like fingerprints, one of few definitive individual characteristics available to the investigator, a fact that certainly justifies an extensive investigative effort.

Handwriting Comparisons

Document experts continually testify that no two individuals write exactly alike. This is not to say that there cannot be marked resemblances between two individuals' handwritings, because many factors make up the total character of a person's writing.

General Style

Perhaps the most obvious feature of handwriting to the layperson is its general style. As children, we all learn to write by attempting to copy letters that match a standard form or style shown to us by our teachers. The style of writing acquired by the learner is that which is fashionable for the particular time and locale. In the United States, for example, the two most widely used systems are the Palmer method, first introduced in 1880, and the Zaner-Bloser method, introduced in about 1895 (see Figure 17–1). To some extent, both of these systems are taught in nearly all fifty states.

The early stages of learning and practicing handwriting are characterized by a conscious effort by the student to copy standard letter forms. Many pupils in a handwriting class tend at first to have writing styles that are similar to one another, with minor differences attributable to skill in copying. However, as initial writing skills improve, a child normally reaches the stage at which the nerve and motor responses associated with the act of writing become subconscious. The individual's writing now begins to take on innumerable habitual shapes and patterns that distinguish it from all others. The document examiner looks for these unique writing traits.

Variations in Handwriting

The unconscious handwriting of two individuals can never be identical. Individual variations associated with mechanical, physical, and mental functions make it extremely unlikely that all of these factors can be exactly reproduced by any two people. Thus, variations are expected in angularity, slope, speed, pressure, letter and word spacings, relative dimensions of letters, connections, pen movement, writing skill, and finger dexterity.

Furthermore, many other factors besides pure handwriting characteristics should be considered. The arrangement of the writing on the paper may be as distinctive as the writing itself. Margins, spacings, crowding, insertions, and alignment are all results of personal habits. Spelling, punctuation, phraseology, and grammar can be personal and, if so, combine to individualize the writer.

In a problem involving the authorship of handwriting, all characteristics of both the known and questioned documents must be considered and compared. Dissimilarities between the two writings strongly indicate two writers, unless these differences can logically be accounted for by the facts surrounding the preparation of the documents. Because any single characteristic, even the most distinctive one, may be found in the handwriting of other individuals, no single handwriting characteristic can by itself be taken as the basis for a positive comparison. The final conclusion must be based on a sufficient number of common characteristics between the known and questioned writings to effectively preclude their having originated from two different sources.

What constitutes a sufficient number of personal characteristics? Here again, there are no hard-and-fast rules for making such a determination. The expert examiner can make this judgment only in the context of each particular case.

Challenges to Handwriting Comparison

When the examiner receives a reasonable amount of known handwriting for comparison, sufficient evidence to determine the source of a questioned document is usually easy to find. Frequently, however, circumstances prevent a positive conclusion or permit only the expression of a qualified opinion. Such situations usually develop when an insufficient number of

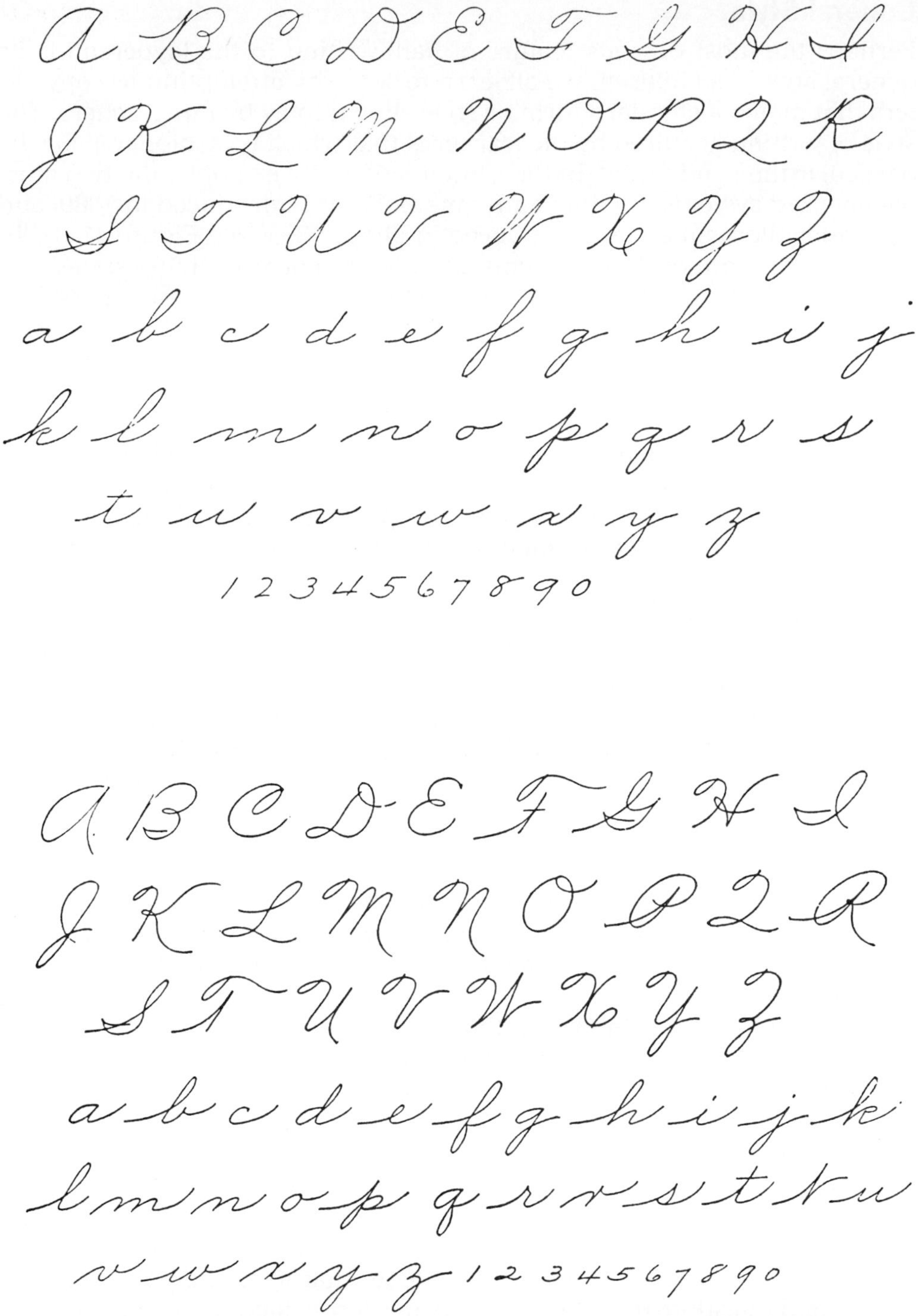

*A B C D E F G H I
J K L M N O P Q R
S T U V W X Y Z
a b c d e f g h i j
k l m n o p q r s
t u v w x y z
1 2 3 4 5 6 7 8 9 0*

*A B C D E F G H I
J K L M N O P Q R
S T U V W X Y Z
a b c d e f g h i j k
l m n o p q r s t u
v w x y z 1 2 3 4 5 6 7 8 9 0*

FIGURE 17–1 **(top) An example of Zaner-Bloser handwriting; (bottom) an example of Palmer handwriting.** *Courtesy Robert J. Phillips, Document Examiner, Audubon, New Jersey*

known writings are available for comparison. Although nothing may be found that definitely points to the questioned and known handwriting being of different origin, not enough personal characteristics may be present in the known writings that are consistent with the questioned materials.

Difficulties may also arise when the examiner receives questioned writings containing only a few words, all deliberately written in a crude, unnatural form or all very carefully written and thought out so as to disguise the writer's natural style—a situation usually encountered with threatening or obscene letters. It is extremely difficult to compare handwriting that has been very carefully prepared to a document written with such little thought for structural details that it contains only the subconscious writing habits of the writer. However, although one's writing habits may be relatively easy to change for a few words or sentences, maintaining such an effort grows more difficult with each additional word.

When an adequate amount of writing is available, the attempt at total disguise may fail. This was illustrated by Clifford Irving's attempt to forge letters in the name of the late industrialist Howard Hughes in order to obtain lucrative publishing contracts for Hughes's life story. Figure 17–2 shows forged signatures of Howard Hughes along with Clifford Irving's known writings. By comparing these signatures, document examiner R. A. Cabbane of the U.S. Postal Inspection Service detected many examples of Irving's personal characteristics in the forged signatures.

For example, note the formation of the letter *r* in the word *Howard* on lines 1 and 3, as compared with the composite on line 6. Observe the manner in which the terminal stroke of the letter *r* tends to terminate with a little curve at the baseline of Irving's writing and the forgery. Notice the way the bridge of the *w* drops in line 1 and also in line 6. Also, observe the similarity in the formation of the letter *g* as it appears on line 1 as compared with the second signature on line 5.

The document examiner must also be aware that writing habits may be altered beyond recognition by the influence of drugs or alcohol. Under these circumstances, it may be impossible to obtain known writings of a suspect written under conditions comparable to those at the time the questioned document was prepared.

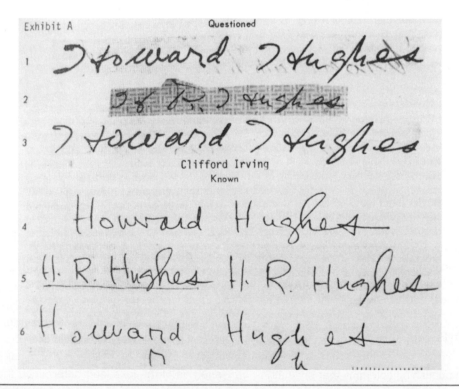

FIGURE 17–2 Forged signatures of Howard Hughes and examples of Clifford Irving's writing. *Reprinted by permission of the American Society for Testing and Materials from the Journal of Forensic Sciences, copyright 1975.*

Collection of Handwriting Exemplars

exemplar
An authentic sample used for comparison purposes, such as handwriting.

The collection of an adequate number of known writings (exemplars) is critical for determining the outcome of a comparison. Generally, known writings of the suspect furnished to the examiner should be as similar as possible to the questioned document. This is especially true with respect to the writing implement and paper. Styles and habits may be somewhat altered if a person switches from a pencil to a ballpoint pen or to a fountain pen. The way the paper is ruled, or the fact that it is unruled, may also affect the handwriting of a person who has become particularly accustomed to one type or the other. Known writings should also contain some of the words and combinations of letters present in the questioned document.

natural variations
Normal deviations found between repeated specimens of an individual's handwriting.

The known writings must be adequate in number to show the examiner the range of natural variations in a suspect's writing characteristics. No two specimens of writing prepared by one person are ever identical in every detail. Variation is an inherent part of natural writing. In fact, a signature forged by tracing an authentic signature can often be detected even if the original and tracing coincide exactly, because no one ever signs two signatures exactly alike (see Figure 17–3).

Many sources are available to the investigator for establishing the authenticity of the writings of a suspect. An important consideration in selecting sample writings is the age of the genuine document relative to the questioned one. It is important to try to find standards that date closely in

Forensics at Work

Hitler's Diaries

In 1981, a spectacular manuscript attributed to Adolf Hitler was disclosed by the brother of an East German general. These documents included Hitler's twenty-seven-volume diary and an unknown third volume of his autobiography, *Mein Kampf.* The existence of these works was both culturally and politically significant to the millions who were affected by World War II.

Authentication of the diaries was undertaken by two world-renowned experts, one Swiss and one American. Both declared that the handwritten manuscripts were identical to the known samples of Adolf Hitler's handwriting that they were given. Bidding wars began for publishing rights, and a major national newspaper in the United States won with a price near $4 million.

The publishing company that originally released the documents to the world market undertook its own investigation, which ultimately revealed a clever but devious plot. The paper on which the diaries were written contained a whitener that didn't exist until 1954, long after Hitler committed suicide. The manuscript binding threads contained viscose and polyester, neither of which was available until after World War II. Further, the inks used in the manuscript were all inconsistent with those in use during the year these pages were allegedly written.

Moreover, the exemplars sent to the Swiss and American experts as purportedly known examples of Hitler's handwriting were actually from the same source as the diaries. Thus, the experts were justified in proclaiming the documents were authentic because they *were* written by the same hand—it just wasn't Hitler's. Chemical analysis of the inks later determined that the "Hitler diaries" were in fact less than one year old—spectacular, but fake!

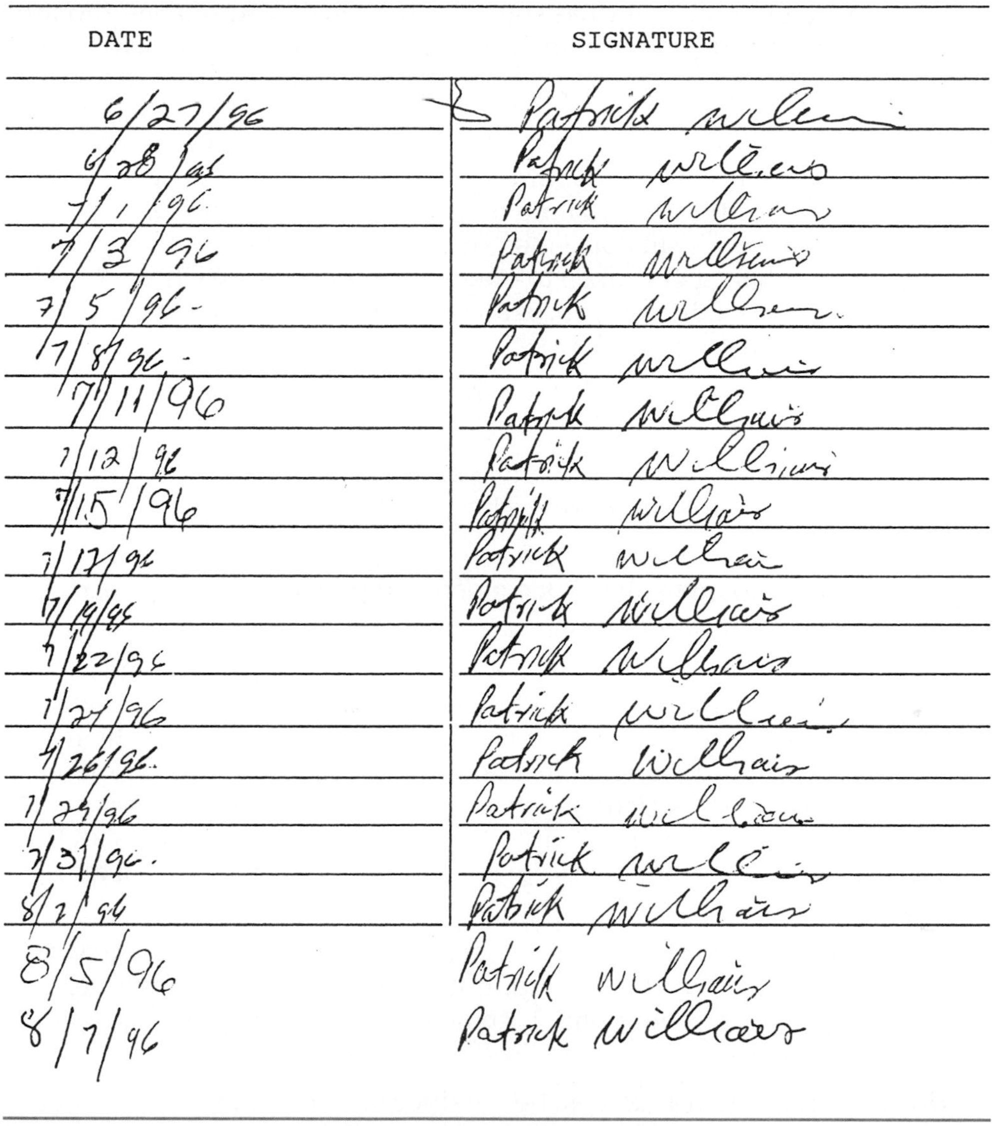

DATE	SIGNATURE

FIGURE 17–3   Examples of handwriting from the same individual over an extended period of time. *Courtesy Robert J. Phillips, Document Examiner, Audubon, New Jersey*

time to the questioned document. For most typical adults, basic writing changes are comparatively slow. Therefore, material written within two or three years of the disputed writing is usually satisfactory for comparison; as the age difference between the genuine and unknown specimens becomes greater, the standard tends to become less representative.

Despite the many potential sources of handwriting exemplars, obtaining an adequate set of collected standards may be difficult or impossible. In these situations, handwriting may have to be obtained voluntarily or under court order from the suspect. Ample case law supports the constitutionality of taking handwriting specimens. In *Gilbert* v. *California*,[1] the Supreme Court upheld the taking of handwriting exemplars before the appointment of counsel. The Court also reasoned that handwriting samples are identifying physical characteristics that lie outside the protection privileges of the Fifth Amendment. Furthermore, in *United States* v. *Mara*,[2] the Supreme Court ruled that taking a handwriting sample did not constitute an unreasonable search and seizure of a person and hence did not violate Fourth Amendment rights.

As opposed to nonrequested specimens (written without the thought that they may someday be used in a police investigation), requested writing samples may be consciously altered by the writer. However, the investigator can take certain steps to minimize attempts at deception. The requirement of several pages of writing normally provides enough material that is free of nervousness or attempts at deliberate disguise for a valid comparison. In addition, the writing of dictation yields exemplars that best represent the suspect's subconscious style and characteristics.

Other steps that can be taken to minimize a conscious writing effort, as well as to ensure conditions approximating those of the questioned writing, can be summarized as follows:

1. The writer should be allowed to write sitting comfortably at a desk or table and without distraction.

2. The suspect should not under any conditions be shown the questioned document or be told how to spell certain words or what punctuation to use.

3. The suspect should be furnished a pen and paper similar to those used in the questioned document.

4. The dictated text should be the same as the contents of the questioned document, or at least should contain many of the same words, phrases, and letter combinations found in the document. In hand-printing cases, the suspect must not be told whether to use uppercase (capital) or lowercase (small) lettering. If, after writing several pages, the writer fails to use the desired type of lettering, he or she can then be instructed to include it. Altogether, the text must be no shorter than a page.

5. Dictation of the text should take place at least three times. If the writer is trying to disguise the writing, noticeable variations should appear among the three repetitions. Discovering this, the investigator must insist on continued repetitive dictation of the text.

6. Signature exemplars can best be obtained when the suspect is required to combine other writings with a signature. For example, instead of compiling a set of signatures alone, the writer might be asked to fill out completely twenty to thirty separate checks or receipts, each of which includes a signature.

7. Before requested exemplars are taken from the suspect, a document examiner should be consulted and shown the questioned specimens.

Key Points

- Any object with handwriting or print whose source or authenticity is in doubt may be referred to as a questioned document.

- Document examiners gather documents of known authorship or origin and compare them to the individual characteristics of questioned writings.

- Collecting an adequate number of known writings is critical for determining the outcome of a handwriting comparison. Known writing should contain some of the words and combinations of letters in the questioned document.

- The unconscious handwriting of two individuals can never be identical. However, the writing style of an individual may be altered beyond recognition by the influence of drugs or alcohol.

Typescript Comparisons

The document examiner analyzes not only handwritten documents, but machine-created ones as well. This includes a wide variety of devices including computer printers, photocopiers, fax machines, and typewriters.

Photocopier, Printer, and Fax Examination

With the emergence of digital technology, document examiners are confronted with a new array of machines capable of creating documents subject to alteration or fraudulent use. Personal computers use daisy wheel, dot-matrix, ink-jet, and laser printers. More and more, the document examiner encounters problems involving these machines, which often produce typed copies that have only inconspicuous defects.

In the cases of photocopiers, fax machines, and computer printers, an examiner may need to identify the make and model of a machine that may have been used in printing a document. Alternatively, the examiner may need to compare a questioned document with test samples printed from a suspect machine. Typically, the examiner generates approximately ten samples through each machine to obtain a sufficient representation of a machine's characteristics. A side-by-side comparison is then made between the questioned document and the printed exemplars to compare markings produced by the machine.

Photocopiers   Transitory defect marks originating from random debris on the glass platen, inner cover, or mechanical portions of a copier produce images. These images are often irregularly shaped and sometimes form distinctive patterns. Thus, they become points of comparison as the document examiner attempts to link the document to suspect copiers. The gradual change, shift, or duplication of these marks may help the examiner date the document.

Fax Machines   Fax machines print a header known as the *transmitting terminal identifier (TTI)* at the top of each fax page. For the document examiner, the TTI is a very important point of comparison (see Figure 17–4). The header and the document's text should have different type styles. TTIs can be fraudulently prepared and placed in the appropriate position on a fax copy. However, a microscopic examination of the TTI's print quickly reveals significant characteristics that distinguish it from a genuine TTI.

In determining the fax machine's model type, the examiner usually begins by analyzing the TTI type style. The fonts of that line are determined by the sending machine. The number of characters, their style, and their position in the header are best evaluated through a collection of TTI fonts organized into a useful database. One such database is maintained by the American Society of Questioned Document Examiners.

Computer Printers   Computer printer model determination requires extensive analysis of the specific printer technology and type of ink used. Visual and microscopic techniques help determine the technology and toner used. Generally printers are categorized as *impact* and *nonimpact* printers by the mechanism of their toner application. Nonimpact printers, such as ink-jet

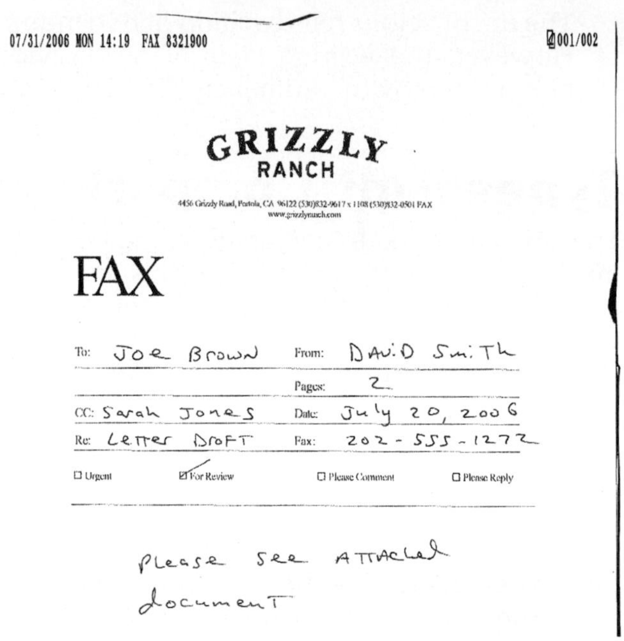

FIGURE 17–4 A fax page showing a transmitting terminal identifier (TTI).

07/31/2006 MON 14:19 FAX 8321900

001/002

GRIZZLY
RANCH

4456 Grizzly Road, Portola, CA 96122 (530)832-9617 x 1108 (530)832-0501 FAX
www.grizzlyranch.com

FAX

To:	JOE BROWN	From:	DAVID SMITH
		Pages:	2
CC:	Sarah Jones	Date:	July 20, 2006
Re:	LETTER DROFT	Fax:	202-555-1272

☐ Urgent   ☑ For Review   ☐ Please Comment   ☐ Please Reply

PLEASE SEE ATTACHED
DOCUMENT

and laser printers, and impact printers, such as thermal and dot-matrix printers, all have characteristic ways of printing documents. Character shapes, toner differentiation, and toner application methods are easily determined with a low-power microscope and help the examiner narrow the possibilities of model type.

In analyzing computer printouts and faxes, examiners use the same approach for comparing the markings on a questioned document to exemplar documents generated by a suspect machine. These markings include all possible transitory patterns arising from debris and other extraneous materials. When the suspect machine is not available, the examiner may need to analyze the document's class characteristics to identify the make and model of the machine. It is important to identify the printing technology, the type of paper, the type of toner or ink used, the chemical composition of the toner, and the type of toner-to-paper fusing method used in producing the document.

Examination of the toner usually involves microscopic analysis to characterize its surface morphology, followed by identification of the inorganic and organic components of the toner. These results separate model types into categories based on their mechanical and printing characteristics. Typically, document examiners access databases to help identify the model type of machine used to prepare a questioned document. The resulting list of possibilities produced by the database hopefully reduces the number of potential machines to a manageable number. Obviously, once a suspect machine is identified, the examiner must perform a side-by-side comparison of questioned and exemplar printouts as described previously.

Typewriters Although typewriters are not used as widely as they were at one time, document examiners still analyze typescripts. Examiners are most often asked the following two questions about typewriters: (1) Can the make and model of the typewriter used to type the questioned document be identified? (2) Can a particular suspect typewriter be identified as having prepared the questioned document?

To answer the first question, the examiner must have access to a complete reference collection of past and present typefaces used by typewriter

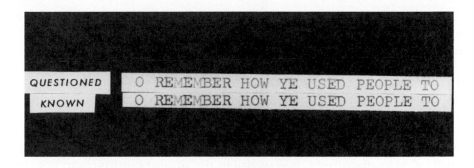

FIGURE 17–5 A portion of a typewriting comparison points to the conclusion that the same machine typed both specimens. Besides the similarity in the design and size of type, note the light impression consistently made by the letter *M*. Also, the letter *E* slants to the right, almost touching *D* in the word *USED* in both specimens. *Courtesy New Jersey State Police*

manufacturers. The two most popular typeface sizes are pica (ten letters to the inch) and elite (twelve letters to the inch). Although a dozen manufacturers may use a pica or an elite typeface, many of these are distinguishable when the individual type character's style, shape, and size are compared.

As is true for any mechanical device, use of a typewriter will result in wear and damage to the machine's moving parts. These changes occur both randomly and irregularly, thereby imparting individual characteristics to the typewriter. Variations in vertical and horizontal alignment (characters are too high or low or too far left or right of their correct position) and perpendicular misalignment of characters (characters leaning to the left or to the right), as well as defects in each typeface, are valuable for proving the identity of a typewriter (see Figure 17–5).

Associating a particular typewriter with a typewritten document requires comparing questioned document to exemplars prepared from the suspect typewriter. As with handwriting, collection of proper standards is the foundation of such comparisons. In this respect, it is best if the document examiner has the questioned typewriter, allowing the examiner to prepare an adequate number of exemplars and examine the machine's typefaces. If the investigator must prepare standards from the questioned machine, a minimum of one copy in full word-for-word order of the questioned typewriting must be obtained.

Another area of investigation relates to the ribbon. An examination of the type impressions left on a ribbon may reveal the portion of the ribbon on which a particular text was typed.

When the suspect typewriter is not available for examination, the investigator must gather known writings that have been typed on the suspect machine. Ideally, material should be selected that contains many of the same combinations of letters and words found on the questioned document. The individual defects that characterize a typewriter develop and change as the machine is used; some may have changed between the preparation of the questioned and standard material. Hence, if many specimens are available, those prepared near the time of the disputed document should be collected.

Key Points

- The examiner compares the individual type character's style, shape, and size to a complete reference collection of past and present typefaces.

- Use of a printing device results in wear and damage to the machine's moving parts in a way that is both random and irregular, thereby imparting individual characteristics to it.

- Transitory defect marks originating from random debris on the glass platen, inner cover, or mechanical portions of a copier produce irregularly shaped images that may serve as points of comparison.

- A TTI, or transmitting terminal identifier, is a header at the top of each page of a fax document. It is useful in document comparison because it serves as a way to distinguish between a real and a fraudulently prepared fax document.

- Variations in vertical and horizontal alignment and perpendicular misalignment of characters, as well as defects in each typeface, are valuable for proving the identity of a typewriter.

Alterations, Erasures, and Obliterations

Documents are often altered or changed after preparation, to hide their original intent or to perpetrate a forgery. Documents can be changed in several ways, and for each way, the application of a special discovery technique is necessary.

One of the most common ways to alter a document is to try to erase parts of it, using an India rubber eraser, sandpaper, a razor blade, or a knife to remove writing or type by abrading or scratching the paper's surface. All such attempts at erasure disturb the upper fibers of the paper. These changes are apparent when the suspect area is examined under a microscope using direct light or by allowing the light to strike the paper obliquely from one side (side lighting). Although microscopy may reveal whether an erasure has been made, it does not necessarily indicate the original letters or words present. Sometimes so much of the paper has been removed that identifying the original contents is impossible.

In addition to abrading the paper, the perpetrator may also obliterate words with chemicals. In this case, strong oxidizing agents are placed over the ink, producing a colorless reaction product. Although such an attempt may not be noticeable to the naked eye, examination under the microscope reveals discoloration on the treated area of the paper. Sometimes examination of the document under ultraviolet or infrared lighting reveals the chemically treated portion of the paper. Interestingly, examination of documents under ultraviolet light may also reveal fluorescent ink markings that go unnoticed in room light, as seen in Figure 17–6.

Some inks, when exposed to blue-green light, absorb the radiation and reradiate infrared light. This phenomenon is known as **infrared luminescence.** Thus, alteration of a document with ink differing from the original can sometimes be detected by illuminating the document with blue-green light and using infrared-sensitive film to record the light emanating from the document's surface. In this fashion, any differences in the luminescent properties of the inks are observed (see Figure 17–7). Infrared luminescence has also revealed writing that has been erased. Such writings may be recorded by invisible residues of the original ink that remain embedded in the paper even after an erasure.

erasure
The removal of writing, typewriting, or printing from a document, normally accomplished by either chemical means or an abrasive instrument.

infrared luminescence
A property exhibited by some dyes that emit infrared light when exposed to blue-green light.

(a)

(b)

FIGURE 17–6 **(a) A $20 bill as it appears under room light. (b) The bill illuminated with ultraviolet light reveals ink writing.** *Courtesy Sirchie Finger Print Laboratories, Inc., Youngsville, N.C., www.sirchie.com*

Another important application of infrared photography arises from the observation that inks differ in their ability to absorb infrared light. Thus, illuminating a document with infrared light and recording the light reflected off the document's surface with infrared-sensitive film enables the examiner to differentiate inks of a dissimilar chemical composition (see Figure 17–8).

Intentional obliteration of writing by overwriting or crossing out is seldom used for fraudulent purposes because of its obviousness. Nevertheless, such cases may be encountered in all types of documents. Success at permanently hiding the original writing depends on the material used to cover the writing. If it is done with the same ink as was used to write the original material, recovery will be difficult if not impossible. However, if the two inks are of a different chemical composition, photography with infrared-sensitive film may reveal the original writing. Infrared radiation may pass through the upper layer of writing while being absorbed by the underlying area (see Figure 17–9).

Close examination of a questioned document sometimes reveals crossing strokes or strokes across folds of perforations in the paper that are not in a sequence that is consistent with the natural preparation of the document. Again, these differences can be shown by microscopic or photographic scrutiny.

obliteration
Blotting out or smearing over writing or printing to make the original unreadable.

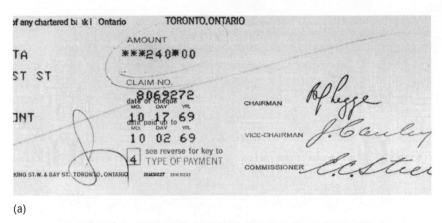

(a)

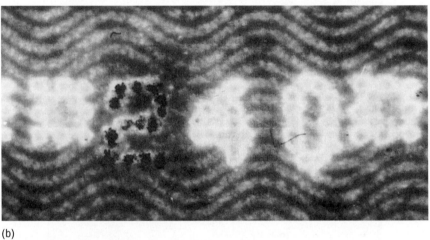

(b)

FIGURE 17–7 **Part of a check stolen from a government agency as it appears to the naked eye is shown in (a). An infrared luminescence photograph was prepared of the amount figures at a magnification of 10× in (b). This clearly shows that the number 2 was added with a different ink. The accused pleaded guilty.** *Courtesy Centre of Forensic Sciences, Toronto, Canada*

(a)

(b)

FIGURE 17–8 **(a) This photograph, taken under normal illumination, shows the owner of an American Express check to be "Freda C. Brightly Jones." Actually, this signature was altered. The check initially bore the signature "Fred C. Brightly Jr." (b) This photograph taken under infrared illumination, using infrared-sensitive film, clearly shows that the check was altered by adding *a* to *Fred* and *ones* to *Jr.* The ink used to commit these changes is distinguishable because it absorbs infrared light, whereas the original ink does not.** *Courtesy New Jersey State Police*

(a)

(b)

FIGURE 17–9 **(a) A photograph showing an area of a document that has been blacked out with a heavy layer of ink overwriting. (b) In this photograph, the covering ink has been penetrated by infrared photography to reveal the original writing.** *Courtesy Centre of Forensic Sciences, Toronto, Canada*

Infrared photography sometimes reveals the contents of a document that has been accidentally or purposely charred in a fire. Another way to decipher **charred documents** involves reflecting light off the paper's surface at different angles in order to contrast the writing against the charred background (see Figure 17–10).

Digital image processing is the method by which the visual quality of digital pictures is improved or enhanced. *Digitizing* is the process by which the image is stored in memory. This is commonly done by scanning an

charred document
Any document that has become darkened and brittle through exposure to fire or excessive heat.

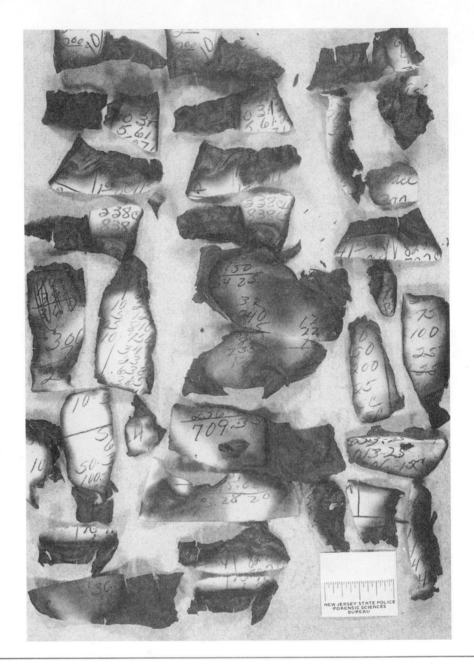

FIGURE 17–10 Decipherment of charred papers seized in the raid of a suspected bookmaking establishment. The charred documents were photographed with reflected light. *Courtesy New Jersey State Police*

image with a flatbed scanner or a digital camera and converting the image by computer into an array of digital intensity values called *pixels,* or picture elements. Once the image has been digitized, an image-editing program such as Adobe Photoshop is used to adjust the image. An image may be enhanced through lightening, darkening, and color and contrast controls. Examples of how the technology is applied to forensic document examination are shown in Figures 17–11 and 17–12.

Other Document Problems

Document examiners encounter other challenges when analyzing questioned documents, including visualizing writing pressed or indented into a surface and analyzing the inks and paper used in suspect documents.

ORIGINAL

EXCLUSION

LEVELS

SCREEN

CURVES

REPLACE COLOR

FIGURE 17–11 This composite demonstrates the various changes that can be applied to a digitized image to reveal information that has been obscured. Using a photo editor (Adobe Photoshop), the original was duplicated and pasted as a second layer. Colors were changed in selected areas of the image using the "screen" and "exclusion" options. "Replace color" allows the user to choose a specific color or range of colors and lighten, darken, or change the hue of the colors selected. "Level" and "curves" tools can adjust the lightest and darkest color ranges and optimize contrast, highlights, and shadow detail of the image for additional clarity. *Courtesy Lt. Robert J. Garrett, Middlesex County Prosecutor's Office, N.J.*

Indented Writings

Indented writings are the partially visible depressions on a sheet of paper underneath the one on which the visible writing was done. Such depressions are due to the application of pressure on the writing instrument and would appear as a carbon copy of a sheet if carbon paper had been inserted between the pages.

Indented writings have proved to be valuable evidence. For example, the top sheet of a bookmaker's records may have been removed and destroyed, but it still may be possible to determine the writing by the impressions left on the pad. These impressions may contain incriminating evidence supporting the charge of illegal gambling activities. When paper

indented writings
Impressions left on paper positioned under a piece of paper that has been written on.

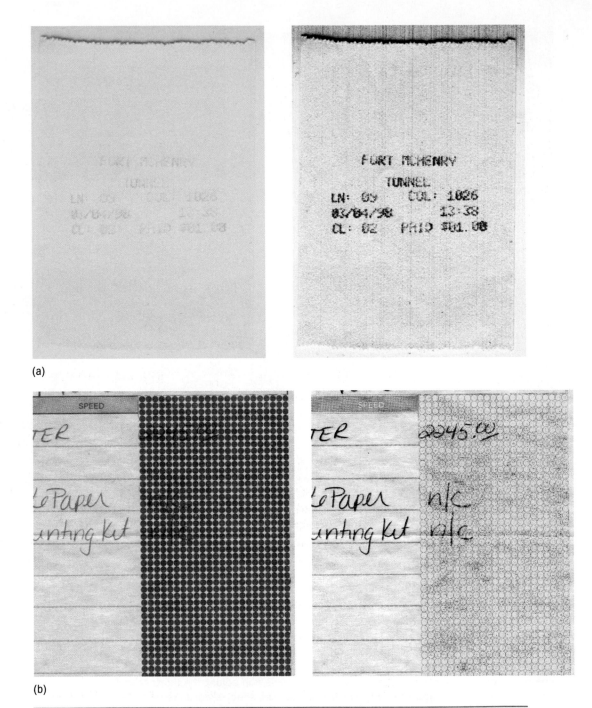

(a)

(b)

FIGURE 17–12 **(a) Receipts have been used in investigations to establish a victim's whereabouts, provide suspects with alibis, and substantiate a host of personal conduct. Unfortunately, due to wear, age, or poor printing at the register, the receipt is often unreadable. This can be corrected using photo-editing software. In this example, the original toll receipt was scanned at the highest color resolution, which allows more than 17 million colors to be reproduced. The image was then manipulated, revealing the printed details, by adjusting the lightest and darkest levels and the color content of the image. (b) Invoices may contain details about a transaction that are important to an investigation. The copy that ships with the merchandise may have that information blocked out. This information may be recovered using digital imaging. The left figure shows the original shipping ticket. The right figure shows the information revealed after replacing the color of the blocking pattern.** *Courtesy Lt. Robert J. Garrett, Middlesex County Prosecutor's Office, N.J.*

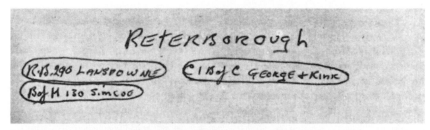

(a)

(b)

FIGURE 17–13 A suspected forger was arrested. In his car, police found written lists of the victims he intended to defraud. Some of these writings are shown in (a). A writing pad found in his house had indentations on the top page of the pad shown in (b). These indentations corresponded to the writings found in the car, further linking the suspect to the writings. *Courtesy Centre of Forensic Sciences, Toronto, Canada*

is studied under oblique or side lighting, its indented impressions are often readable (see Figure 17–13).

An innovative approach to visualizing indented writings has been developed at the London College of Printing in close consultation with the Metropolitan Police Forensic Science Laboratory.[3] The method involves applying an electrostatic charge to the surface of a polymer film that has been placed in contact with a questioned document, as shown in Figure 17–14. Indented impressions on the document are revealed by applying a toner powder to the charged film. For many documents examined by this process, clearly readable images have been produced from impressions that could not be seen or were barely visible under normal illumination. An instrument that develops indented writings by electrostatic detection is commercially available and is routinely used by document examiners.

Ink and Paper Comparisons

A study of the chemical composition of writing ink present on documents may verify whether known and questioned documents were prepared by the same pen. A nondestructive approach to comparing ink lines is accomplished with a visible microspectrophotometer (see page 387).[4] An example of this approach is shown in Figure 17–15, in which the microspectrophotometer is used to distinguish counterfeit and authentic currency by comparing the spectral patterns of inked lines on the paper. Thin-layer chromatography is also suitable for ink comparisons. Most commercial inks, especially ballpoint inks, are actually mixtures of several organic dyes. These dyes can be separated on a properly developed thin-layer chromatographic plate. The separation pattern of the component dyes is distinctly different for inks with different dye compositions and thus provides many points of comparison between a known and a questioned ink.

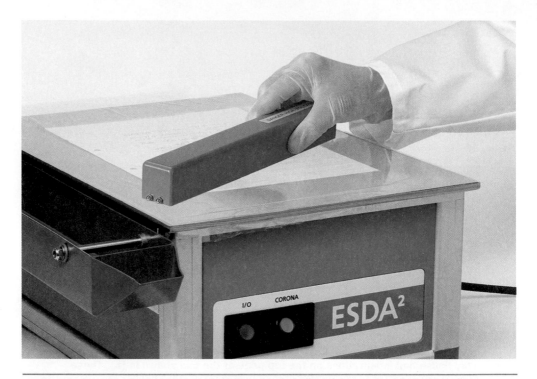

FIGURE 17–14 An electrostatic detection apparatus (ESDA) works by applying an electrostatic charge to a document suspected of containing indented writings. The indentations are then visualized by the application of charge-sensitive toner. *Courtesy Foster & Freeman Limited, Worcestershire, U.K., www.fosterfreeman.co.uk*

Ink can be removed from paper with a hypodermic needle with a blunted point to punch out a small sample from a written line. About ten plugs or microdots of ink are sufficient for chromatographic analysis. The United States Secret Service and the Internal Revenue Service jointly maintain the United States International Ink Library. This collection includes more than 8,500 inks, which date back to the 1920s. Each year new pen and ink formulations are added to the reference collection. These inks have been systematically cataloged according to dye patterns developed by thin-layer chromatography (TLC; see Figure 17–16). On several occasions, this approach has been used to prove that a document has been fraudulently backdated. For example, in one instance, it was possible to establish that a document dated 1958 was backdated because a dye identified in the questioned ink had not been synthesized until 1959.

To further aid forensic chemists in ink-dating matters, several ink manufacturers, at the request of the U.S. Treasury Department, voluntarily tag their inks during the manufacturing process. The tagging program allows inks to be dated to the exact year of manufacture by changing the tags annually.

Another area of inquiry for the document examiner is the paper on which a document is written or printed. Paper is often made from cellulose fibers found in wood and fibers recovered from recycled paper products. The most common features associated with a paper examination are general appearance, color, weight, and watermarks. Other areas of examination include fiber identification and the characterization of additives, fillers, and pigments present in the paper product.

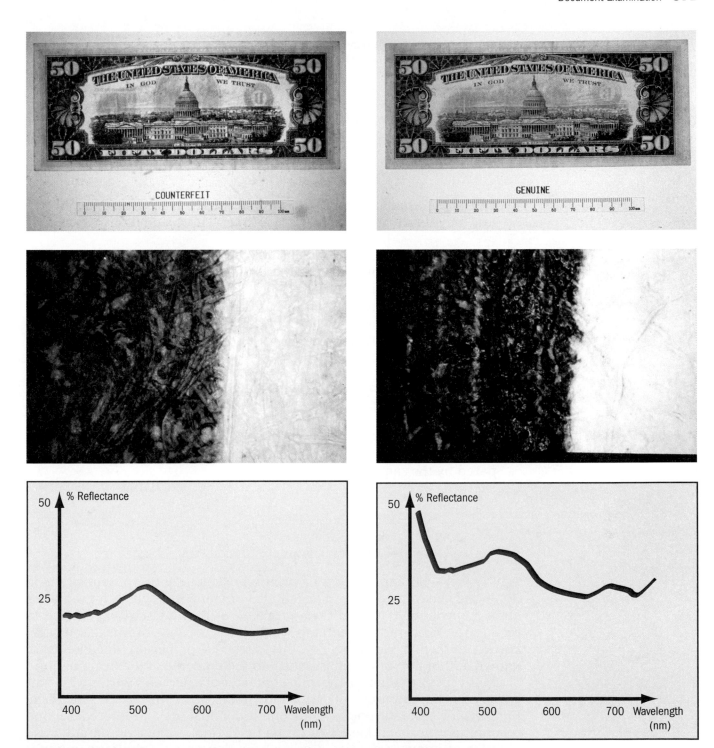

FIGURE 17–15 **Two $50 bills are shown at top; one is genuine and the other is counterfeit. Below each bill is a micrograph of an inked line present on each bill. Each line was examined under a visible-light microspectrophotometer. As shown, the visible light absorption spectrum of each line is readily differentiated, thus allowing the examiner to distinguish a counterfeit bill from genuine currency.** *Courtesy Peter W. Pfefferil, forensic scientist, Lausanne, Switzerland*

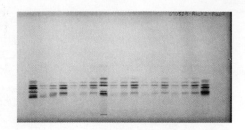

FIGURE 17–16   A chart demonstrating different TLC patterns of blue ballpoint inks. *Courtesy U.S. Secret Service Laboratory.*

Key Points

• Document examiners deal with evidence that has been changed in several ways, such as through alterations, erasures, and obliterations.

• Infrared luminescence can be used to detect alterations to a document made with ink differing from the original. Infrared luminescence can also reveal writing that has been erased.

• A digitized image can be lightened, darkened, and color and contrast adjusted with appropriate software.

• It may be possible to read indented writing—the impressions left on a paper pad—by applying an electrostatic charge to the surface of a polymer film that has been placed in contact with a questioned document.

• Studying the chemical composition of writing ink present on documents may verify whether known and questioned documents were prepared by the same pen.

Chapter Summary

Any object with handwriting or print whose source or authenticity is in doubt may be referred to as a questioned document. Document examiners apply knowledge gathered through years of training and experience to recognize and compare the individual characteristics of questioned and known authentic writings. For this purpose, gathering documents of known authorship or origin is critical to the outcome of the examination.

Many factors compose the total character of a person's writing. The unconscious handwriting of two individuals can never be identical. Furthermore, the writing style of one individual may be altered beyond recognition by the influence of drugs or alcohol. Collecting an adequate number of known writings is critical for determining the outcome of a handwriting comparison. Known writing should contain some of the words and combinations of letters present in the questioned document.

The two requests most often made of the examiner in connection with the examination of typewriters and printing devices are to identify the make and model of the typewriter and printing devices used to prepare the questioned document and to determine whether a particular suspect typewriter or printing device prepared the questioned document. The individual type character's style, shape, and size are compared to a complete reference collection of past and present typefaces. As is true for any mechanical device, use of a printing device results in wear and damage to the machine's moving parts. These changes occur both randomly and irregularly, thereby imparting individual characteristics to the printing device. The document examiner deals with problems involving business and personal computers, which often produce printed copies that have only subtle defects.

Document examiners deal with evidence that has been changed in several ways, such as through alterations, erasures, and obliterations. Indented writings have proved to be valuable evidence. It may be possible to determine what was written by the impressions left on a paper pad. Applying an electrostatic charge to the surface of a polymer film that has been placed in contact with a questioned document visualizes indented writings. A study of the chemical composition of writing ink on documents may verify whether known and questioned documents were prepared by the same pen.

Review Questions

1. Any object that contains handwriting or typescript and whose source or authenticity is in doubt is referred to as a(n)_____.

2. True or False: Our general style of handwriting develops as a result of our attempts in childhood to copy letters that match a standard form or style shown to us by our teachers. _____

3. True or False: Variations in mechanical, physical, and mental functions make it unlikely that the writing of two individuals can be distinguished. _____

4. In a problem involving the authorship of handwriting, all characteristics of both the _____ and _____ documents must be considered and compared.

5. True or False: A single handwriting characteristic can by itself be taken as a basis for a positive comparison. _____

6. Handwriting examples may have a crude, unnatural form or be written very carefully to disguise the writer's natural _____.

7. Known examples of writings, called _____, must be collected in order to determining the outcome of a comparison.

8. As the age difference between genuine and unknown specimens becomes greater, the standard tends to become _____ representative of the unknown.

9. True or False: Two or more specimens of writing prepared by one person are identical in every detail. _____

10. In the Supreme Court case of _____ the court upheld the taking of handwriting exemplars before the appointment of counsel and determined handwriting to be nontestimonial evidence not protected by Fifth Amendment privileges.

11. True or False: Normally, known writings need not contain words and combinations of letters present in the questioned document. _____

12. When requested writing is being given by a suspect, care must be taken to minimize a (n) _____ writing effort.

13. An examiner should generate approximately _____ samples through a questioned photocopier, printer, or fax machine to obtain a sufficient representation of a machine's characteristics.

14. A fax machine prints a kind of header known as a _____ at the top of each page it prints, which can be used for comparison and authentication purposes.

15. Examination of a printer's _____ involves microscopic analysis and the identification of organic and inorganic components.

16. Random wear and damage to a typewriter impart it with _____ characteristics.

17. Examination of a document under _____ or _____ lighting may reveal chemical erasures of words or numbers.

18. Some inks, when exposed to blue-green light, absorb the radiation and emit _____ light.

19. Handwriting containing inks of different chemical compositions may be distinguished by photography with _____ film.

20. True or False: If obliteration of writing is carried out with the same ink as was used to write the original material, recovery will be difficult if not impossible. _____

21. Infrared photography can also be used to visualize writing on paper that has been accidentally or purposely _____ in a fire.

22. _____ writings are partially visible impressions appearing on a sheet of paper underneath the one on which the visible writing was done.

23. When comparing the chemical composition of ink lines on a questioned document, a _____ can be used without destroying the document.

24. Many ink dyes can be separated by the technique of _____ chromatography.

25. True or False: Examination of the paper of a questioned document is based on general appearance, color, weight, and watermarks. _____

Application and Critical Thinking

1. Criminalist Julie Sandel is investigating a series of threatening notes written in pencil and sent to a local politician. A suspect is arrested and Julie directs the suspect to prepare writing samples to compare to the writing on the notes. She has the suspect sit at a desk in an empty office and gives him a pen and a piece of paper. She begins to read one of the notes and asks the suspect to write the words she dictates. After reading about half a page, she stops, then dictates the same part of the note a second time for the suspect. At one point, the suspect indicates that he does not know how to spell one of the words, so Julie spells it for him. After completing the task, Julie takes the original notes and the dictated writing from the suspect to a document examiner. What mistakes, if any, did Julie make?

2. In each of the following situations, indicate how you would go about recovering original writing that is not visible to the naked eye.
   a) The original words have been obliterated with a different ink than was used to compose the original.
   b) The original words have been obliterated by chemical erasure.
   c) The original writing was made with fluorescent ink.
   d) The original documents have been charred or burned.

3. You have been asked to determine whether a handwritten will, supposedly prepared thirty years ago, is authentic or a modern forgery. What aspects of the document would you examine to make this determination? Explain how you would use thin-layer chromatography to help you come to your conclusion.

Web Resources

Emily J. DeWill, Certified Document Examiner (A page with articles on history, theory, and applications of document examination)
www.qdewill.com

Forgery Finder (A site that discusses handwriting identification and offers examples of altered documents, obliterations, ink identification, graffiti, and anonymous letters)
www.forgeryfinder.com

Guidelines for Forensic Document Examination (An article that discusses procedures for collecting, handling, and examining questioned documents)
www.fbi.gov/hq/lab/fsc/backissu/april2000/swgdoc1.htm

Handwriting, Typewriting, Shoeprints, and Tire Treads: FBI Laboratory's Questioned Documents Unit (An article that includes sections on the analysis of questioned handwriting and typewriting samples)
www.fbi.gov/hq/lab/fsc/backissu/april2001/held.htm

Obtaining Handwriting Specimens (An article on sources of and methods for obtaining and submitting handwriting samples)
www.fdeservices.com/Exemplars.htm

Questioned Document Examination (Discusses the history, techniques, and court use of document examination; includes a brief list of links to document examination sites)
www.apsu.edu/oconnort/3210/3210lect08.htm

Endnotes

1. 388 U.S. 263 (1967).
2. 410 U.S. 19 (1973).
3. D. M. Ellen, D. J. Foster, and D. J. Morantz, "The Use of Electrostatic Imaging in the Detection of Indented Impressions," *Forensic Science International* 15 (1980): 53.
4. P. W. Pfefferli, "Application of Microspectrophotometry in Document Examination," *Forensic Science International* 23 (1983): 129.

Bill Thomas Killman
1684 S. Oldmanor
Wichita, KS. 67218

The Wichita Eagle & Beac
Pub. Co. Inc.
825 E. Douglas
Wichita, KS. 67202

The BTK Killer

Dennis Rader was arrested in February 2005 and charged with committing ten murders since 1974 in the Wichita, Kansas, area. The killer, whose nickname stands for "bind, torture, kill," hadn't murdered since 1991, but he resurfaced in early 2004 by sending a letter to a local newspaper taking credit for a 1986 slaying. Included with the letter were a photocopy of the victim's driver's license and three photos of her body. The BTK killer was back to his old habit of taunting the police.

Three months later another letter surfaced. This letter detailed some of the events surrounding BTK's first murder victims. In 1974, he strangled Joseph and Julie Otero along with two of their children.

Shortly after those murders, BTK sent a letter to a local newspaper in which he gave himself the name BTK. In December 2004, a package found in a park contained the driver's license of another BTK victim along with a doll covered with a plastic bag, its hands bound with pantyhose.

The major break in the case came when BTK sent a message on a floppy disk to a local TV station. "Erased" information on the disk was recovered and restored by forensic computer specialists, and the disk was traced to the Christ Lutheran Church in Wichita. The disk was then quickly linked to Dennis Rader, the church council president. The long odyssey of the BTK killer was finally over.

chapter 18

Computer Forensics

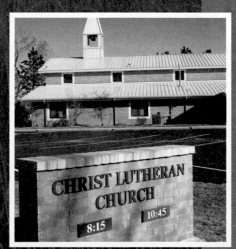

Andrew W. Donofrio

Key Terms

bit

byte

central processing unit (CPU)

cluster

file slack

hard disk drive (HDD)

hardware

latent data

Message Digest 5 (MD5)/Secure Hash Algorithm (SHA)

motherboard

operating system (OS)

partition

RAM slack

random-access memory (RAM)

sector

software

swap file

temporary files

unallocated space

visible data

Learning Objectives

After studying this chapter, you should be able to:

- List and describe the hardware and software components of a computer.

- Understand the difference between read-only memory and random-access memory.

- Describe how a hard disk drive is partitioned.

- Describe the proper procedure for preserving computer evidence at a crime scene.

- Understand the difference between and location of visible and latent data.

- List the areas of the computer that will be examined to retrieve forensic data.

Since the 1990s, few fields have progressed as rapidly as computer technology. Computers are no longer a luxury, nor are they in the hands of just a select few. Technology and electronic data are a part of everyday life and permeate all aspects of society. Consequently, computers have become increasingly important as sources of evidence in an ever-widening spectrum of criminal activities.

Investigators frequently encounter computers and other digital devices in all types of cases. As homicide investigators sift for clues, they may inquire whether the method for a murder was researched on the Internet, whether signs of an extramarital affair can be found in e-mail or remnants of instant messages (which might provide motive for a spouse killing or murder for hire), or whether an obsessed stalker threatened the victim before a murder. Arson investigators want to know whether financial records on a computer might provide a motive in an arson-for-profit fire. A burglary investigation would certainly be aided if law enforcement determined that the proceeds from a theft were being sold online—perhaps through eBay or a similar online auction site.

Accessibility to children and the perception of anonymity have given sexual predators a way to seek out child victims online. The vulnerability of computers to hacker attacks is a constant reminder of security issues surrounding digitally stored data. Finally, the fact that computers control most of our critical infrastructure makes technology an appetizing target for would-be terrorists.

Computer forensics involves preserving, acquiring, extracting, analyzing, and interpreting computer data. Although this is a simple definition, it gets a bit more complicated. Part of this complication arises from technology itself. More and more devices are capable of storing electronic data: cell phones, personal digital assistants (PDAs), iPods, digital cameras, flash memory cards, smart cards, jump drives, and many others. Each method for extracting data from these devices presents unique challenges. However, sound forensic practices apply to all these devices. The most logical place to start to examine these practices is with the most common form of electronic data: the personal computer.

Andrew W. Donofrio is a detective sergeant with the prosecutor's office in Bergen County, New Jersey, and is a leading computer forensics examiner for Bergen County, with more than eighteen years of experience in law enforcement. He has conducted more than five hundred forensic examinations of computer evidence and frequently lectures on the subject throughout the state, as well as teaching multiday courses on computer forensics and investigative topics at police academies and colleges in New Jersey. Detective Sergeant Donofrio writes regularly on Internet-related and computer forensics issues for a number of law enforcement publications and has appeared as a guest expert on Internet-related stories on MSNBC.

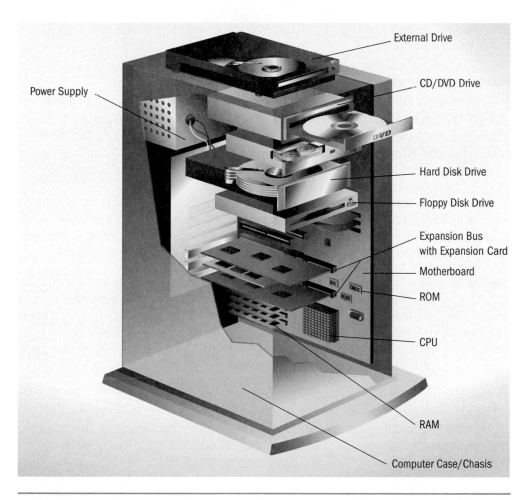

Power Supply

External Drive

CD/DVD Drive

Hard Disk Drive

Floppy Disk Drive

Expansion Bus
with Expansion Card

Motherboard

ROM

CPU

RAM

Computer Case/Chasis

FIGURE 18–1 **A cutaway diagram of a personal computer.** *Courtesy Tim Downs*

From Input to Output: How Does the Computer Work?

Hardware Versus Software

Before we get into the nuts and bolts of computers, we must establish the important distinction between hardware and software. Hardware comprises the physical components of the computer: the computer chassis, monitor, keyboard, mouse, hard disk drive, random-access memory (RAM), central processing unit (CPU), and so on (see Figure 18–1). The list is much more extensive but, generally speaking, if it is a computer component or peripheral that you can see, feel, and touch, it is hardware.

Software, conversely, is a set of instructions compiled into a program that performs a particular task. Software consists of programs and applications that carry out a set of instructions on the hardware. Operating systems (Windows, Mac OS, Linux, Unix), word-processing programs (Microsoft Word, WordPerfect), web-browsing applications (Internet Explorer, Netscape Navigator, Firefox), and accounting applications (Quicken, QuickBooks, Microsoft Money) are all examples of software.

It is important not to confuse software with the physical media that it comes on. When you buy an application such as Microsoft Office, it comes on a compact disc (CD). The CD containing this suite of applications is typically referred to as software, but this is technically wrong. The CD is external computer media that contains the software; it is a container for

hardware
The physical components of a computer: case, keyboard, monitor, motherboard, RAM, HDD, mouse, and so on. Generally speaking, if it is a computer component you can touch, it is hardware.

software
A set of instructions compiled into a program that performs a particular task.

and a medium to load the set of instructions onto the hard disk drive (the hardware).

Hardware Components

Motherboard   The main circuit board in a computer (or other electronic devices) is referred to as the motherboard. Motherboards contain sockets for chips (such as the CPU and ROM, discussed shortly) and slots for add-on cards. Examples of add-on cards are a video card to connect the computer to the monitor, a network card or modem to connect to an internal network or the Internet, and a sound card to connect to speakers.

Sockets on the motherboard typically accept things such as random-access memory (RAM) or the central processing unit (CPU). The keyboard, mouse, CD-ROM drives, floppy disk drives, monitor, and other peripherals or components connect to the motherboard in one way or another.

System Bus   Contained on the motherboard, the system bus is a vast complex network of wires that carries data from one hardware device to another. This network is analogous to a complex highway. Data is sent along the bus in the form of ones and zeros (or, more appropriately stated, as electrical impulses representing an "on" or "off" state—this two-state computing is also known as *binary computing*).

Central Processing Unit (CPU)   The central processing unit (CPU), also referred to as a processor, is the brain of the computer; it is the part of the computer that actually computes. It is the main (and typically the largest) chip that plugs into a socket on the motherboard. Basically, all operations performed by the computer are run through the CPU. The CPU carries out the program steps to perform the requested task. That task can range from opening and working in a Microsoft Word document to performing advanced mathematical algorithms.

Read-Only Memory (ROM)   This rather generic term describes special chips on the motherboard. ROM chips store programs called *firmware,* used to start the boot process (in which the computer starts up before the system is fully functioning) and configure a computer's components. This technology is referred to as the BIOS, for *basic input-output system.* The operation of the BIOS is relevant to several computer forensics procedures, particularly the boot sequence. As will become clear later, it is important not to boot the actual computer under investigation to the original hard disk drive. This would cause changes to the data, thus compromising the integrity of evidence. The BIOS allows investigators to control the boot process to some degree.

Random-Access Memory (RAM)   Random-access memory (RAM) stores software programs and instructions while the computer is turned on; it takes the physical form of chips that plug into the motherboard. Most of the data on a computer is stored on the hard disk drive (HDD). However, if the computer had to access the HDD each time it wanted data, it would run slowly and inefficiently. Instead, the computer, aware that it may need certain data at a moment's notice, stores the data in RAM. This takes the burden off the computer's processor and hard disk drive (HDD). RAM is referred to as *volatile memory* because it is not permanent; its contents undergo constant change and are forever lost once power is taken away from the computer.

Hard Disk Drive (HDD)   Generally speaking, the hard disk drive (HDD) is the primary component of storage in the personal computer (see Figure 18–2).

motherboard
The main system board of a computer (and many other electronic devices) that delivers power, data, and instructions to the computer's components.

central processing unit (CPU)
The main chip within the computer; also referred to as the brain of the computer. This microprocessor chip handles most of the operations (code and instructions) of the computer.

random-access memory (RAM)
The volatile memory of the computer; when power is turned off, its contents are lost. Programs and instructions are loaded into RAM while they are in use.

hard disk drive (HDD)
Typically the main storage location within the computer, consisting of magnetic platters contained in a case.

FIGURE 18–2 An inside view of the platter and read/write head of a hard disk drive.
Courtesy Corbis RF

It typically stores the operating system, programs, and data files created by the user, such as documents, spreadsheets, accounting information, or a company database. Unlike RAM, the HDD is permanent storage and retains its information even after the power is turned off. HDDs work off a controller that is typically part of the motherboard, but sometimes takes the form of an add-on (expansion) card plugged into the motherboard.

Input Devices   Input devices are used to get data into the computer or to give the computer instructions. Input devices constitute part of the "user" side of the computer. Examples include the keyboard, mouse, joystick, and scanner.

Output Devices   Output devices are equipment through which data is obtained from the computer. Output devices are also part of the "user" side of the computer, and provide the results of the user's tasks. They include the monitor, printer, and speakers.

Key Points

- Computer forensics involves preserving, acquiring, extracting, and interpreting computer data.

- Software programs are applications that carry out a set of instructions.

- The central processing unit (CPU) is the brain of the computer—the main chip responsible for doing the actual computing.

- The motherboard is the main circuit board within a computer.

- Read-only memory (ROM) chips store programs that control the boot (startup) process and configure a computer's components.

- Random-access memory (RAM) is volatile memory, which is lost when power is turned off. Programs are loaded into RAM because of its faster read speed.

- The hard disk drive (HDD) is typically the primary location of data storage within the computer.

Storing and Retrieving Data

As mentioned earlier, most of the data in a computer is stored on the hard disk drive (HDD). However, before beginning to understand how data is stored on the HDD, it is first important to understand the role of the operating system (OS). An OS is the bridge between the human user and the computer's electronic components. It provides the user with a working environment and facilitates interaction with the system's components. Each OS supports certain types of file systems that store data in different ways, but some support the methods of others.

Formatting and Partitioning the HDD

Generally speaking, before an OS can store data on a HDD, the HDD must first be formatted, or prepared to accept the data in its current form. Before the HDD can be formatted, a partition must be defined. A partition is nothing more than a contiguous set of blocks (physical areas on the HDD in which data can be stored) that are defined and treated as independent disks. Thus, a hard disk drive can hold several partitions, making a single HDD appear as several disks.

Partitioning a drive can be thought of as dividing a container that begins as nothing more than four sides with empty space on the inside. Imagine that we then cut a hole in the front of the container and place inside two drawers containing the hardware to open and close the drawers. We have just created a two-drawer filing cabinet and defined each drawer as a contiguous block of storage. A partitioning program then defines the partitions that will later hold the data on the HDD. Just as the style, size, and shape of a filing cabinet drawer can vary, so too can partitions.

After a hard drive is partitioned, it is typically formatted. The formatting process *initializes* portions of the HDD, so that they can store data, and creates the structure of the file system. There are various types of file systems—methods for storing and organizing computer files and data so they are easier to locate and access. Each has a different way of storing, retrieving, and allocating data.

At the conclusion of these processes, we say that the drive is *logically defined*. The term *logically* is used because no real divisions are made. If you were to crack open the HDD before or after partitioning and formatting, to the naked eye the platters would look the same.

Mapping the HDD

As shown in Figure 18–3, disks are logically divided into sectors, clusters, tracks, and cylinders. A sector is the smallest unit of data that a hard drive can address; sectors are typically 512 bytes in size (a byte is eight bits; a bit is a single one or zero).[1] A cluster usually is the minimum space allocated to a file. Clusters are groups of sectors; their size is defined by the file system, but they are always in multiples of two. A cluster, therefore, consists of two, four, six, or eight sectors, and so on. (With modern file systems, the user can exercise some control over the number of sectors per cluster.)

---

operating system (OS)
Software that allows the user to interact with the hardware and manages the file system and applications.

partition
A contiguous set of blocks that are defined and treated as independent disks.

sector
The smallest unit of data addressable by a hard disk drive, generally consisting of 512 bytes.

byte
A group of eight bits.

bit
Short for binary digit; taking the form of either a one or a zero, it is the smallest unit of information on a machine.

cluster
A group of sectors in multiples of two; typically the minimum space allocated to a file.

Closer Analysis

Other Common Storage Devices

Although the HDD is the most common storage device for the personal computer, many others exist. Methods for storing data and the layout of that data can vary from device to device. A CD-ROM, for example, uses a different technology and format for writing data than a floppy disk or USB thumb drive. Fortunately, regardless of the differences among devices, the same basic forensic principles apply for acquiring the data. Common storage devices include the following:

CDs and DVDs

Compact discs (CDs) and digital versatile discs (DVDs) are two of the most common forms of storing all sorts of external data, including music, video, and data files. Both types of media consist of plastic discs with an aluminum layer containing the data that is read by a beam of laser light in the CD/DVD reader. Different CDs are encoded in different ways, which makes forensic examination of such discs difficult at times.

Floppy Disks

Although "floppies" are not as common as they once were, forensic examiners still encounter the 3.5-inch floppy disk. Floppy disks can be used to boot an operating system or to store data. They are constructed of hard plastic with a thin plastic disk on the inside. That thin plastic disk is coated with a magnetic iron oxide material. The disk stores data in a similar fashion to the hard disk drive. By today's standards, floppy disks don't hold much data.

Zip Disks

Similar in structure to floppy disks, Zip disks hold a much larger amount of data.

They come in several storage capacities, each with their own drive.

USB Thumb Drives and Smart Media Cards

These devices, which can store a large amount of data, are known as *solid-state storage devices* because they have no moving parts. Smart media cards are typically found in digital cameras and PDAs, whereas USB thumb drives come in many shapes, sizes, and storage capacities.

Tapes

Tapes come in many formats and storage capacities. Each typically comes with its own hardware reader and sometimes a proprietary application to read and write its contents. Tapes are typically used for backup purposes and consequently have great forensic potential.

Network Interface Card (NIC)

Very rarely do we find a computer today that doesn't have a NIC. Whether they are on a local network or the Internet, when computers need to communicate with each other, they typically do so through a NIC. NICs come in many forms: add-on cards that plug into the motherboard, hard-wired devices on the motherboard, add-on cards (PCMCIA) for laptops, and universal serial bus (USB) plug-in cards, to name a few. Some are wired cards, meaning they need a physical wired connection to participate on the network, and others are wireless, meaning they receive their data via radio waves.

Tracks are concentric circles that are defined around the platter. *Cylinders* are groups of tracks that reside directly above and below each other.

Additionally, the HDD has a file system table (map) of the layout of the defined space in that partition. FAT file systems use a *file allocation table* (which is where the acronym *FAT* comes from) to track the location of files and folders (data) on the HDD, while NTFS file systems use, among other things, a *master file table (MFT)*. Each file system table tracks data

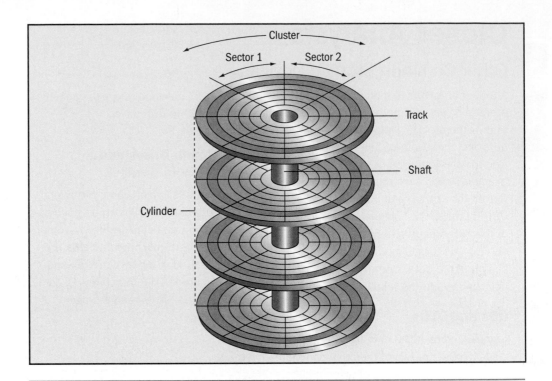

FIGURE 18–3 Partitions of a hard disk drive.

in different ways, and forensic computer examiners should be versed in the technical nuances of the HDDs they examine. It is sufficient for our purposes here, however, to merely visualize the file system table as a map to where the data is located. This map numbers sectors, clusters, tracks, and cylinders to keep track of the data.

One way to envision a partition and file system is as a room full of safe-deposit boxes. The room itself symbolizes the entire partition, and the boxes with their contents represent clusters of data. In order to determine who rented which box, and subsequently where each depositor's property is, a central database is needed. This is especially true if a person rented two boxes located in opposite ends of the room. A similar situation often arises when storing data on a computer, because not all the data in a particular file or program is always stored in contiguous (adjacent) clusters on the HDD. Thus, a database tracking the locations of the safe-deposit boxes is much like a file system table tracking the location of data within the clusters.

This example is also useful to understand the concept of reformatting a HDD, which involves changing the way the disk stores data. If the database managing the locations of the safe-deposit boxes were wiped out, the property in them would still remain; we just wouldn't know what was where. So too with the hard disk drive. If a user were to wipe the file system table clean—for example, by reformatting it—the data itself would not be gone. Both the database tracking the locations of the safe-deposit boxes and the file system table tracking the location of the data in the cluster are maps—not the actual contents.

Key Points

- The computer's operating system (OS) is the bridge between the human user and the computer's electronic components. It provides the user with a working environment and facilitates interaction with the system's components.

- Formatting is the process of preparing a hard disk drive to store and retrieve data in its current form.

- A sector is the smallest unit of data that a hard drive can address. A cluster usually is the minimum space allocated to a file. Clusters are groups of sectors.

- A FAT is a file allocation table. It tracks the location of files and folders on the hard disk drive.

Putting It All Together

Let's now see how all of the parts of a computer come together to allow a user to access and manipulate data. When a person presses the power button, the power supply wakes up and delivers power to the motherboard and all of the hardware connected to the computer. At this point the flash ROM chip on the motherboard (the one that contains the BIOS) conducts a power-on self-test (POST) to make sure everything is working properly.

The flash ROM polls the motherboard to check to see that the hardware that is attached, then reads from itself the boot order, thus determining from what device it should boot. Typically the boot device is the HDD, but it can also be a floppy disk, CD, or USB drive.

If the boot device is the HDD, the HDD is then sent control. It locates the first sector of its disk (known as the *master boot record*), determines its layout (partition[s]), and boots an operating system (Windows, Mac OS, Linux, Unix). The user is then presented with a computer work environment, commonly referred to as a *desktop*.

Now ready to work, the user double-clicks an icon on the desktop, such as a Microsoft Word shortcut, to open the program and begin to type a document. The CPU processes this request, locates the Microsoft Word program on the HDD (using a predefined map of the drive called a *file system table*), and carries out the programming instructions associated with the application. The CPU also loads Microsoft Word into RAM via the system bus and sends the output to the monitor by way of the video controller, which is either located on or attached to the motherboard.

As the user types, data from the keyboard is loaded into RAM. When the user is finished, he or she might print the document or simply save it to the HDD for later retrieval. If printed, the data is copied from RAM, processed by the CPU, placed in a format suitable for printing, and sent through the system bus to a printer. If the document is saved, the data is copied from RAM, processed by the CPU, passed to the HDD controller by way of the system bus, and written to a portion of the HDD. The HDD's file system table is updated so it knows where to retrieve that data later. This is a very simplistic overview of the boot process. Forensic examiners must possess a much more in-depth understanding of the boot process.

The preceding example illustrates how three components of the computer perform most of the work: the CPU, RAM, and system bus. The example can get even more complicated as the user opens more applications and performs multiple tasks simultaneously (multitasking). Several tasks can be loaded into RAM at once, and the CPU is capable of juggling them all. This allows for the multitasking environment and the ability to switch back and forth between applications. (To further enhance this ability, RAM can use a portion of the HDD as virtual memory, which can be very forensically valuable—but more on this later.) All of this is orchestrated by the operating system and is written in the language of the computer—ones and zeros.

Processing the Electronic Crime Scene

Processing the electronic crime scene has a lot in common with processing a traditional crime scene. The investigator must first ensure that the proper legal requirements (search warrant, consent, and so on) have been met so that the scene can be searched and the evidence seized. The investigator should then devise a plan of approach based on the facts of the case and the physical location.

Documenting the Scene

The scene should be documented in as much detail as possible before disturbing any evidence, and before the investigator lays a finger on any computer components. Of course there are circumstances in which an investigator might have to act quickly and pull a plug before documenting the scene, such as when data is in the process of being deleted.

Crime-scene documentation is accomplished through two actions: sketching and photographing. The electronic crime scene is no different. The scene should be sketched in a floor plan fashion (see Figure 18–4), and then overall photographs of the location should be taken. In a case in which several computers are connected together in a network, a technical network sketch should also be included if possible (covered in greater detail in the next chapter).

After investigators photograph the overall layout, close-up photographs should be shot. A close-up photograph of any running computer monitor should be taken. All the connections to the main system unit, such as peripheral devices (keyboard, monitor, speakers, mouse, and so on), should be photographed. If necessary, system units should be moved delicately and carefully to facilitate the connections photograph (see Figure 18–5). Close-up photographs of equipment serial numbers should be taken if practical.

At this point, investigators must decide whether to perform a live acquisition of the data, perform a system shutdown (as in the case of server equipment), pull the plug from the back of the computer,[2] or a combination thereof. Several factors influence this decision. For example, if encryption is being used and pulling the plug will encrypt the data, rendering it unreadable without a password or key, pulling the plug would not be prudent. Similarly, any data that exists in RAM and has not been saved to the HDD will be lost if power to the system is discontinued. Regardless of how investigators decide to proceed, the equipment most likely will be seized. Exceptions exist in the corporate environment, where servers are fundamental to business operations.

After the photographs and sketches are complete, but before disconnecting the peripherals from the computer, a label should be placed on the cord of each peripheral, with a corresponding label placed on the port to which it is connected. A numbering scheme should be devised to identify the system unit if several computers are at the scene (Figure 18–6). The combination of sketching, photographing, and labeling should adequately

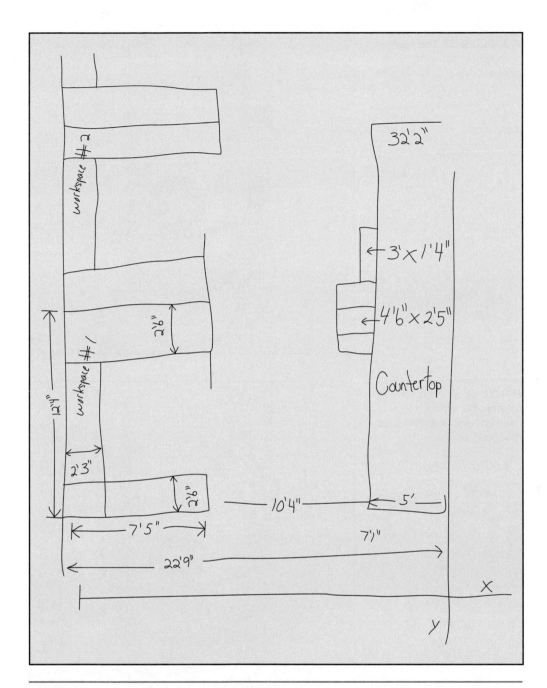

FIGURE 18–4 **A rough sketch made at a crime scene, with necessary measurements included.**

document the scene, prevent confusion of which component went with which system unit, and facilitate reconstruction if necessary for lab or courtroom purposes.

Forensic Image Acquisition

Once a computer has been seized, the data it contains must be obtained for analysis. The number of electronic items that potentially store evidentiary data are too vast to cover in this section. The hard disk drive will be used as an example, but the same "best practices" principles apply for other electronic devices as well.

FIGURE 18–5 The back of a computer showing all connections.

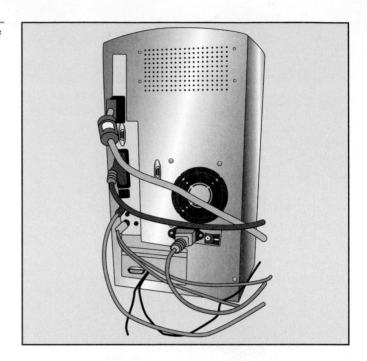

FIGURE 18–6 The back of a computer with each component correlated with its port.

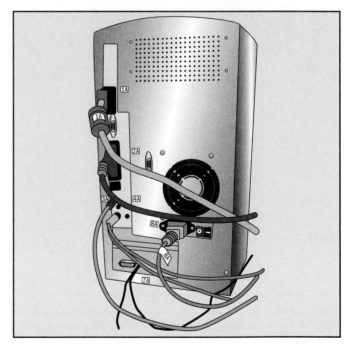

The goal in obtaining data from a HDD is to do so without altering even one bit of data. Thus, throughout the entire process, the forensic computer examiner must use the least intrusive method to retrieve data. Because booting a HDD to its operating system changes many files and could potentially destroy evidentiary data, obtaining data is generally accomplished by removing the HDD from the system and placing it in a laboratory forensic computer so that a *forensic image* can be created. However, the BIOS of the seized computer sometimes interprets the geometry of the HDD differently than the forensic computer does. *Geometry* refers to the functional dimensions of a drive, including the number of heads, cylinders, and sector per track. In these instances, the image of the HDD must be obtained using the seized computer.

Regardless of the computer in which the HDD is placed, the examiner must ensure that, when creating the forensic image, the drive to be analyzed is in a "write-blocked" read-only state in which no new data can be added to the drive. Furthermore, the examiner needs to be able to prove that the forensic image he or she obtained includes every bit of data and caused no changes (writes) to the HDD.

To this end, a sort of fingerprint of the drive is taken before and after imaging through the use of a **Message Digest 5 (MD5)/Secure Hash Algorithm (SHA)**, or similar algorithm. Before imaging the drive, the algorithm is run and a thirty-two-character alphanumeric string is produced based on the drive's contents. The algorithm is then run against the resulting forensic image. If nothing changed, the same alphanumeric string is produced, thus demonstrating that the image is all-inclusive of the original contents and that nothing was altered in the process.

A forensic image of the data on a hard disk drive (or any type of storage medium) is merely an exact duplicate of the entire contents of that medium. In other words, all portions of a hard disk drive—even blank portions—are copied from the first bit (one or zero) to the last. Why would investigators want to copy what appears to be blank or unused portions of the HDD? The answer is simple: to preserve *latent data,* discussed later in the chapter. Data exists in areas of the drive that are, generally speaking, unknown and inaccessible to most end users. This data can be valuable as evidence. Therefore, a forensic image—one that copies every single bit of information on the drive—is necessary.[3] A forensic image differs from a backup or standard copy in that it takes the entire contents, not only data the operating system is aware of.

Many forensic software packages come equipped with a method to obtain a forensic image. The most popular software forensic tools— EnCase, Forensic Toolkit (FTK), Forensic Autopsy (Linux-based freeware), and SMART (Linux-based software by ASR Data)—all include a method to obtain a forensic image. All produce self-contained image files that can then be interpreted and analyzed. They also allow image compression to conserve storage. The fact that self-contained, compressed files are the result of forensic imaging allows many images from different cases to be stored on the same forensic storage drive. This makes case management and storage much easier (see Figure 18–7).

Message Digest 5 (MD5)/Secure Hash Algorithm (SHA)
A software algorithm used to "fingerprint" a file or contents of a disk; used to verify the integrity of data. In forensic analysis it is typically used to verify that an acquired image of suspect data was not altered during the process of imaging.

Key Points

- Aspects of a computer that should be photographed close up at an electronic crime scene include (1) the screen of any running computer monitor; (2) all the connections to the main system unit, such as peripheral devices (keyboard, monitor, speakers, mouse, and so on); and (3) equipment serial numbers.

- Two situations in which an investigator would not unplug a computer at an electronic crime scene are (1) if encryption is being used and pulling the plug will encrypt the data, rendering it unreadable without a password or key, and (2) if data exists in RAM that has not been saved to the HDD, and will thus be lost if power to the system is discontinued.

- The primary goal in obtaining data from a HDD is to do so without altering even one bit of data. To this end, a Message Digest 5 (MD5)/Secure Hash Algorithm (SHA) takes a "fingerprint" of a hard disk drive (HDD) before and after forensic imaging.

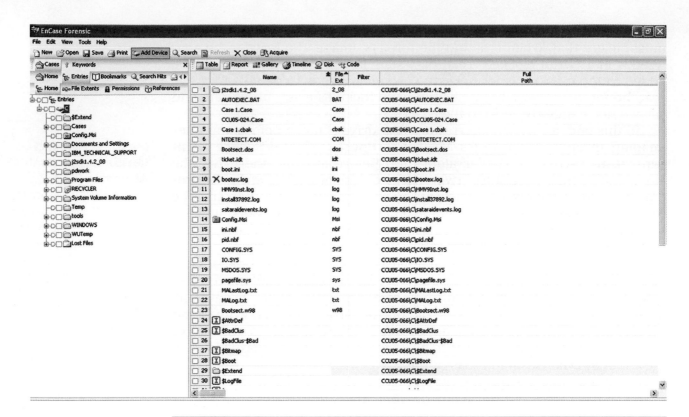

FIGURE 18–7 **A screen shot of EnCase software.** *Courtesy EnCase, www.encase.com*

Analysis of Electronic Data

Analysis of electronic data is virtually limitless and bound only to the level of skill of the examiner. The more familiar an examiner is with computers, operating systems, application software, data storage, and a host of other disciplines, the more prepared he or she will be to look for evidentiary data.

Because computers are vast and complex, discussing each area, file, directory, log, or computer process that could potentially contain evidentiary data is beyond the scope of one chapter—and may be beyond the scope of an entire book. What follows are some of the more common areas of analysis. While reading this section, reflect on your own knowledge of computers and consider what other data might be of evidentiary value and where it might be found.

Visible Data

visible data

All data that the operating system is presently aware of, and thus is readily accessible to the user.

The category of **visible data** includes all information that the operating system is presently aware of, and thus is readily accessible to the user. Here we present several common types of visible data considered in many investigations. This list is by no means exhaustive and can include any information that has value as evidence.

Data/Work Product Files   One place to find evidence is in documents or files produced by the suspect. This category is extremely broad and can include data from just about any software program. Microsoft Word and WordPerfect word-processing programs typically produce text-based files such as typed documents and correspondence. These programs, and a host of other word-processing programs, have replaced the typewriter.

They are common sources of evidence in criminal cases, particularly those involving white-collar crime.

Also relevant in white-collar crime and similar financial investigations are any data related to personal and business finance. Programs such as QuickBooks and Peachtree accounting packages can run the entire financial portion of a small-to-midsize business. Similarly, personal bank account records in the computer are often managed with personal finance software such as Microsoft Money and Quicken. Moreover, criminals sometimes use these programs as well as spreadsheet applications to track bank accounts stolen from unsuspecting victims. Forensic computer examiners should familiarize themselves with these programs, the ways in which they store data, and methods for extracting and reading the data.

Advances in printer technology have made high-quality color printing both affordable and common in many homes. Although this is a huge benefit for home office workers and those interested in graphic arts, the technology has been used for criminal gain. Counterfeiting and check and document fraud are easily perpetrated by home computer users. All that is required is a decent ink-jet printer and a scanner. Including the computer, a criminal could set up a counterfeiting operation for less than $1,500. Examiners must learn the graphics and photo-editing applications used for such nefarious purposes. Being able to recognize the data produced by these applications and knowing how to display the images is key to identifying the evidence.

Swap File Data   When an application is running, the program and the data being accessed are loaded into RAM. A computer's RAM can read data much faster than the hard disk drive, which is why the programs are loaded here. RAM, however, has its limits. Some computers have 256 MB of RAM, others 512 MB, and still others as much as a gigabyte or two. Regardless of the amount, though, most operating systems (Windows, Linux, and so on) are programmed to conserve RAM when possible. This is where the *swap file* comes in. The operating system attempts to keep only data and applications that are presently being used in RAM. Other applications that were started, but are currently waiting for user attention, may be swapped out of RAM and written to the **swap file** on the hard disk drive.[4]

For example, a manager of a retail store may want to type a quarterly report based on sales. The manager starts Microsoft Word and begins his report. Needing to incorporate sales figure data from a particular spreadsheet, he opens Microsoft Excel. Depending on what is running on the computer, the original Word document may be swapped from RAM to the swap space on the HDD to free up space for Excel. As the manager goes back and forth between the programs (and maybe checks his e-mail in between), this swapping continues. Data that is swapped back and forth is sometimes left behind in the swap space. Even as this area is constantly changed, some of the data is orphaned in unallocated space, an area of the HDD discussed later in this chapter.

Swap file can be defined as a particular file or even a separate HDD partition, depending on the operating system and file system type. Data in the swap space can be read by examining the HDD through forensic software or a utility that provides a binary view, such as Norton Disk Editor or Win-Hex (see Figure 18–8).

Temporary Files   Any user who has suffered a sudden loss of power in the middle of typing a document can attest to the value of a **temporary file**. Most programs automatically save a copy of the file being worked on in a temporary file. After typing a document, working on a spreadsheet, or

swap file
A file or defined space on the HDD to which data is written, or swapped, to free RAM for applications that are in use.

temporary files
Files temporarily written by an application to perform a function.

Swapping of data between RAM and the hard drive's swap space or page file

Swap space

RAM module (chip)

FIGURE 18–8 As the user switches between applications and performs multiple tasks, data is swapped back and forth between RAM and the computer's hard drive. This area on the hard drive is referred to as *swap space.*

working on a slide presentation, the user can save the changes, thus promoting the temporary copy to an actual file. This is done as a sort of backup on the fly. If the computer experiences a sudden loss of power or other catastrophic failure, the temporary file can be recovered, limiting the amount of data lost. The loss is limited because the temporary file is not updated in real time. Rather, it is updated periodically (typically defaulted to every ten minutes in most programs), depending on the application's settings.

Temporary files can sometimes be recovered during a forensic examination. Some of the data that may have been orphaned from a previous version may be recoverable, if not the complete file. This is true even when a document has been typed and printed, but never saved. The creation of the temporary file makes it possible for some of this "unsaved" data to be recovered during analysis.

Another type of temporary file valuable to the computer investigator is the *print spool file.* When a print job is sent to the printer, a spooling process delays the sending of the data so the application can continue to work while the printing takes place in the background. To facilitate this, a temporary print spool file is created; this file typically includes the data to be printed and information specific to the printer. There are different methods for accomplishing this, and thus the files created as a result of this process vary. It is sometimes possible to view the data in a readable format from the files created during the spooling process.

Latent Data

latent data
Areas of files and disks that are typically not apparent to the computer user (and often not to the operating system), but contain data nonetheless.

The term **latent data** includes data that are blocked (not necessarily intentionally) from a user's view. It includes areas of files and disks that typically are not apparent to the computer user, but contain data nonetheless. Latent data are one of the reasons a forensic image of the media is created. If a standard copy were all that was produced, only the logical data (that which the operating system is aware of) would be captured. Getting every bit of data ensures that potentially valuable evidence in latent data is not missed.

Once the all-inclusive forensic image is produced, how are the latent data viewed? Utilities that allow a user to examine a hard disk drive on a binary level (ones and zeros) are the answer. Applications such as Norton Disk Editor and WinHex provide this type of access to a hard disk drive or other computer media. Thus these applications, sometimes also referred to as *hex editors* (for the hexadecimal shorthand of computer language), allow all data to be read on the binary level independent of the operating system's file system table. Utilities such as these can write to the media under examination, thus changing data. Consequently, a software or hardware write-blocker should be used.

A more common option in data forensics is to use specialized forensic examination software. EnCase and Forensic Toolkit for Windows and SMART and Forensic Autopsy for Linux are examples of forensic software. Each allows a search for evidence on the binary level and provides automated tools for performing common forensic processing techniques. Examiners should be cautious, however, about relying too heavily on automated tools. Merely using an automated tool without understanding what is happening in the background and why evidentiary data might exist in particular locations would severely impede the ability to testify to the findings.

Slack Space   Slack space is empty space on a hard disk drive created because of the way the HDD stores files. Recall that although the smallest unit of data measure is one bit (either a one or a zero), a HDD cannot address or deal with such a small unit. In fact, not even a byte (eight bits) can be addressed. Rather, the smallest unit of addressable space by a HDD is the sector. HDDs typically group sectors in 512-byte increments, whereas CD-ROMs allocate 2,048 bytes per sector.

If the minimum addressable unit of the HDD is 512 bytes, what happens if the file is only 100 bytes? In this instance there are 412 bytes of slack space. It does not end here, however, because of the minimum cluster requirement. As you may recall, clusters are groups of sectors used to store files and folders. The cluster is the minimum storage unit defined and used by the logical partition. It is because of the minimum addressable sector of the HDD and the minimum unit of storage requirement of the volume that we have slack space.

Minimum cluster allocation must be defined in a sector multiple of two. Thus, a cluster must be a minimum of two, four, six, or eight sectors, and so on. Returning to our initial example of the 100-byte file, suppose an HDD has a two-sector-per-cluster volume requirement. This means that the HDD will isolate a minimum of two 512-byte sectors (a total of 1,024 bytes) of storage space for that 100-byte file. The remaining 924 bytes would be slack space (see Figure 18–9).

To illustrate this point, let us expand on the previous example of safe-deposit boxes. The bank offers safe-deposit boxes of a particular size. This is the equivalent of the HDD's clusters. A person wanting to place only a deed to a house in the box gets the same size box as a person who wants to stuff it full of cash. The former would have empty space should he or she desire to place additional items in the box. This empty space is the equivalent of slack space. But what if the box becomes full and the person needs more space? That person must then get a second box. Similarly, if a file grows to fill one cluster and beyond, a second cluster (and subsequent clusters as needed) is allocated. The remaining space in the second cluster is slack space. This continues as more and more clusters are allocated depending on file size and file growth.

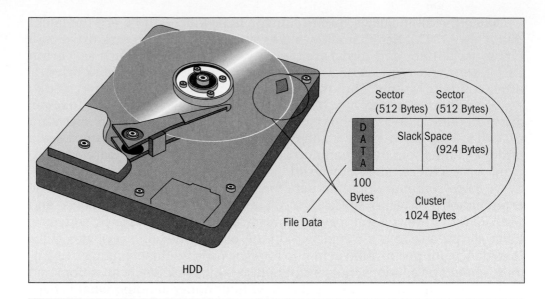

FIGURE 18–9 Slack space illustrated in a two-sector cluster. Cluster sizes are typically greater than two sectors, but two sectors are displayed here for simplicity.

RAM slack
The area beginning at the end of the logical file and terminating at the end of that sector. In some older operating systems this area is padded with information in RAM.

file slack
The area that begins at the end of the last sector that contains logical data and terminates at the end of the cluster.

This example is a bit of an oversimplification because there are actually two types of slack space: RAM slack and file slack. **RAM slack** occupies the space from where the actual (logical) data portion of the file ends to where the first allocated sector in the cluster terminates. **File slack,** therefore, occupies the remaining space of the cluster.

Let us go back to the 100-byte file with the two-sector-per-cluster minimum requirement. Following the end of the logical data (the end of the 100 bytes), the remaining 412 bytes of that sector is RAM slack; the additional 512 bytes completing the cluster is then file slack. See Figure 18–10 for a visual depiction. The question now becomes: What can I expect to find in slack space and why is this important? The answer: junk—valuable junk.

RAM slack is a concept that was more relevant in older operating systems. Remember that the minimum amount of space the HDD can address is the 512-byte sector. Therefore, if the file size is only 100 bytes, the remaining space must be padded. Some operating systems pad this area with data contained in RAM. This could include web pages, passwords, data files, or other data that existed in RAM when the file was written. Modern Windows operating systems pad this space with zeros, but some examinations may still yield valuable data in this area.

File slack, on the other hand, can contain a lot of old, orphaned data. To illustrate this point, let's take the 100-byte file example a bit further. Let's say that prior to the 100-byte file being written to the HDD and occupying one cluster (two sectors totaling 1,024 bytes), a 1,000-byte file occupied this space but was deleted by the user. When a file is "deleted," the data still remains behind, so it is probably a safe bet that data from the original 1,000-byte file remain in the slack space of the new 100-byte file now occupying this cluster. This is just one example of why data exists in file slack and why it might be valuable as evidence.

In one final attempt to illustrate this point, let us again build on our safe-deposit box analogy. Suppose a person rents two safe-deposit boxes, each box representing a sector and the two combined representing a cluster. If that person places the deed to his house in the first box, the remaining space in that box would be analogous to RAM slack. The space in the

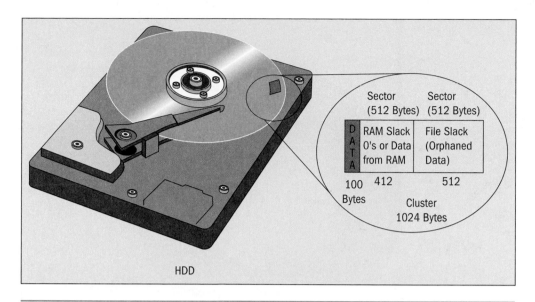

Sector
(512 Bytes)

Sector
(512 Bytes)

| D A T A | RAM Slack 0's or Data from RAM | File Slack (Orphaned Data) |

100
Bytes

412

512

Cluster
1024 Bytes

HDD

FIGURE 18–10 **File slack.**

second box would be the equivalent of file slack. The only difference is that unlike the empty spaces of the safe-deposit box, the slack space of the file most likely contains data that might be valuable as evidence.

The data contained in RAM and file slack is not really the concern of the operating system. As far as the OS is concerned, this space is empty and therefore ready to be used. Until that happens, however, an examination with one of the aforementioned tools will allow a look into these areas, thus revealing the orphaned data. The same is true for unallocated space.

Unallocated Space Latent evidentiary data also resides in **unallocated space**. What is unallocated space, how does data get in there, and what is done to access this space?

If we have an 80-GB hard drive and only half of the hard drive is filled with data, then the other half, or 40 GB, is unallocated space (see Figure 18–11). Returning to our safe-deposit box analogy, if the entire bank of safe-deposit boxes contains 100 boxes, but only 50 are currently in use, then the other 50 would be the equivalent of unallocated space. The HDD's unallocated space typically contains a lot of useful data. The constant shuffling of files on the HDD causes data to become orphaned in unallocated space as the logical portion of the file is rewritten to other places. Some examples of how data is orphaned may help.

Defragmenting Defragmenting a HDD involves moving noncontiguous data back together. Remember that the HDD has minimum space reservation requirements. Again, if a file requires only 100 bytes of space, the operating system might allocate much more than that for use. If the file grows past what has been allocated for it, another cluster is required. If, however, a different file occupies the next cluster in line, then the operating system will have to find another place for that first file on the drive. In this scenario, the file is said to be *fragmented* because data for the same file is contained in noncontiguous clusters. In the case of the HDD, the shuffling of files causes data to be orphaned in unallocated space.

Ultimately, fragmentation of numerous files can degrade the performance of a HDD, causing the read/write heads to have to traverse the platters to locate the data. Defragmenting the HDD takes noncontiguous data

unallocated space
The area of the HDD that the operating system (file system table) sees as empty (containing no logical files) and ready for data. Simply stated, it is the unused portion of the HDD, but is not necessarily empty.

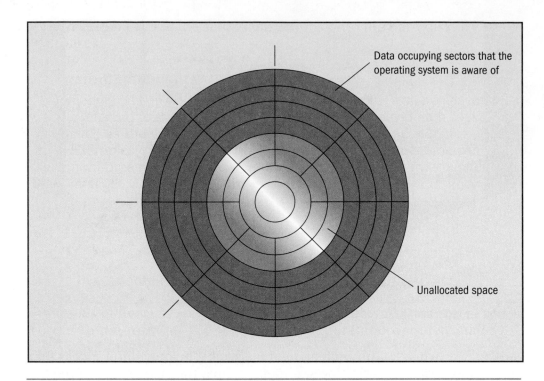

Data occupying sectors that the operating system is aware of

Unallocated space

FIGURE 18–11 **A simplistic view of a hard drive platter demonstrating the concept of unallocated space.**

and rearranges it so it is in contiguous clusters. Building yet again on our safe-deposit box analogy, if a renter eventually needs to store more property than his original box can hold, the bank will rent him a second box. If, however, all the boxes around his are occupied and the only free one is in another section of the room, then his property is "fragmented. " The bank would have to "defrag" the safe-deposit boxes to get the property of users with more than one box into adjacent boxes.

Swap File/Swap Space   Recall that a computer uses the HDD to maximize the amount of RAM by constantly swapping data in and out of RAM to a predetermined location on the HDD, thus freeing valuable RAM. The constant read and write operations of RAM cause a constant change in the swap file or swap space. Data can become orphaned in unallocated space from this constant swapping to and from the HDD.

Deleted Files   The deletion of files is another way that data becomes orphaned in unallocated space. Data from deleted files can manifest itself in different ways during a forensic examination. The actions that occur when a file is deleted vary among file systems. However, generally speaking, the data is not gone. For example, consider what happens when a user or program deletes a file in a Windows operating system with a FAT file system. When a file is deleted, the first character in the file's directory entry (its name) is replaced with the Greek letter sigma. When the sigma replaces the first character, the file is no longer viewable through conventional methods and the operating system views the space previously occupied by the file as available. The data, however, is still there.

This example doesn't account for the actions of the Windows Recycle Bin. When the Windows operating system is set up to merely place the deleted file in the Recycle Bin, the original directory entry is deleted and one is created in the Recycle folder for that particular user. The new Recycle folder entry is linked to another file, the *info* or *info2* file, which includes some additional data, such as the location of the file prior to its deletion should the user wish to restore it to that location. Detailed discussions of the function of the Recycle Bin are beyond the scope of this chapter, but suffice it to say that, even when the Recycle Bin is emptied, the data usually remains behind until overwritten. Moreover, Windows NTFS partitions and Linux EXT partitions handle deleted files differently, but in both cases data typically remains.

What if a new file writes data to the location of the original file? Generally speaking, the data is gone. This is, of course, unless the new file only partially overwrites the original. In this instance we return to the unallocated space orphaned data scenario. If a file that occupied two clusters is deleted, and a new file overwrites one of the clusters, then the data in the second cluster is orphaned in unallocated space. Of course yet a third file can overwrite the second cluster entirely, but until then the data remains in unallocated space.

Let us once again look to our safe-deposit box analogy. If, for example, the owner of two safe-deposit boxes stopped renting them, the bank would list them as available. If the owner didn't clean them out, the contents would remain unchanged. If a new owner rented one of the boxes, the contents from the former owner would be replaced with the new owner's possessions. The second box would therefore still contain orphaned contents from its previous owner. The contents would remain in this "unallocated box" space until another renter occupies it.

Key Points

- The types of computer evidence can be grouped under two major subheadings: visible and latent data.

- Visible data is data that the operating system is aware of, and thus easily accessible to the user. It includes any type of user-created data, such as word-processing documents, spreadsheets, accounting records, databases, and pictures.

- Temporary files created by programs as a sort of backup on the fly can prove valuable as evidence. Data in the swap space (used to conserve the valuable RAM within the computer system) can also yield evidentiary data.

- Latent data is data that the operating system is not aware of. The constant shuffling of data through deletion, defragmentation, swapping, and so on, is one of the ways data is stored in latent areas.

- Latent data can exist in both RAM slack and file slack. RAM slack is the area from the end of the logical file to the end of the sector. File slack is the remaining area from the end of the final sector containing data to the end of the cluster.

- Latent data might be found in unallocated space—space on a HDD that the operating system sees as empty and ready for data.

- When a user deletes files, the data typically remains behind, so deleted files are another source of latent data.

Chapter Summary

Computers have permeated society and are used in countless ways with innumerable applications. Similarly, the role of electronic data in investigative work has realized exponential growth in the last decade. Users of computers and other electronic data storage devices leave footprints and data trails behind. Computer forensics involves preserving, acquiring, extracting, analyzing, and interpreting computer data. In today's world of technology, many devices are capable of storing data and could thus be grouped into the field of computer forensics.

The central processing unit (CPU) is the brain of the computer—the main chip responsible for doing the actual computing. Random-access memory (RAM) is volatile memory containing data that is forever lost when the power is turned off. Programs are loaded into RAM because of its faster read speed. The hard disk drive (HDD) is typically the primary location of data storage within the computer. Different operating systems map out HDDs differently, and examiners must be familiar with the file system they are examining. Evidence exists in many locations and in numerous forms on a HDD. This evidence can be grouped into two major categories: visible and latent data.

Visible data is data that the operating system is aware of, and consequently is easily accessible to the user. From an evidentiary standpoint, it can encompass any type of user-created data, such as word-processing documents, spreadsheets, accounting records, databases, and pictures. Temporary files created by programs as a sort of backup on the fly can also prove valuable as evidence. Finally, data in the swap space (used to conserve the valuable RAM within the computer system) can yield evidentiary visible data.

Latent data, on the other hand, is data that the operating system typically is not aware of. Evidentiary latent data can exist in both RAM slack and file slack. RAM slack is the area from the end of the logical file to the end of the sector. File slack is the remaining area from the end of the final sector containing logical data to the end of the cluster. Another area where latent data might be found is in unallocated space. Unallocated space is space on a HDD that the operating system sees as empty and ready for data. The constant shuffling of data through deletion, defragmentation, and swapping is one of the ways data is orphaned in latent areas. Finally, when a user deletes files, the data typically remains behind. Deleted files are therefore another source of latent data to be examined during forensic analysis.

Computer file systems and data structures are vast and complex. Therefore, areas of forensic analysis are almost limitless and constrained only by the knowledge and skill of the examiner. With a working knowledge of how computers function, how they are used, and how they store data, an examiner is on his or her way to begin to locate the evidentiary data.

Review Questions

1. Computer forensics involves the _____, _____, _____, _____, and _____ of computer data.

2. True or False: Hardware comprises the physical components of the computer. _____

3. _____ is a set of instructions compiled into a program that performs a particular task.

4. The _____ is the main circuit board in a computer and features sockets for chips and slots for add-on cards.

5. The "brain" of the computer is the _____, where the computing actually takes place.

6. _____ chips store programs used to start the boot process, whereas _____ chips store software programs and instructions while the computer is turned on.

7. A _____ within a computer is a contiguous set of areas on the HDD in which data can be stored; these areas are defined and treated as independent disks.

8. The _____ is the primary component of storage in the personal computer.

9. RAM is referred to as volatile memory because it is not _____.

10. A hard drive's partitions are typically divided into _____, _____, _____, and _____.

11. A(n) _____ is a single one or zero in the binary system, and the smallest term in the language of computers.

12. A(n) _____ is a group of eight bits.

13. A group of sectors, always units in multiples of two, is called a(n) _____.

14. _____ data includes all information that the operating system is presently aware of, and thus is readily accessible to the user.

15. True or False: The first thing you should do when you encounter a computer system in a forensic investigation is to connect the power supply and boot the system. _____

16. The existence of _____ data is why a forensic image of the media is created.

17. Most programs automatically save a copy of a file being worked on into a(n) _____ file.

18. The smallest unit of addressable space on a hard disk drive is the _____.

19. The two types of slack space are _____ slack and _____ slack.

20. _____ slack is the area from the end of the logical to the end of the sector.

21. The portion of a disk that does not contain stored data is called _____.

22. True or False: Defragmenting a hard disk drive involves moving noncontiguous data back together. _____

23. True or False: A portion of a "deleted" file may be found in a computer's unallocated space. _____

Application and Critical Thinking

1. If a file system defines a cluster as six sectors, how many bits of information can be stored on each cluster? Explain your answer.

2. Criminalist Tom Parauda is investigating the scene of a crime involving a computer. After he arrives, he photographs the overall scene and takes close-up shots of all the connections to the single computer involved, as well as photos of the serial numbers of the computer and all peripheral devices. Tom then labels the cord to each peripheral device, then disconnects them from the computer. After making sure that all data in RAM has been saved to the hard disk drive, he unplugs the computer from the wall. What mistakes, if any, did Tom make?

3. You are investigating a case in which an accountant is accused of keeping fraudulent books for a firm. Upon examining his computer, you notice that the suspect uses two different accounting programs that are capable of reading the same types of files. Given this information, where would you probably begin to search for latent data on the computer and why?

Case Analysis 1

Suspicious circumstances surrounding the death of Ms. Smith in a home fire led the police to suspect her husband of murder. Evidence later recovered from Mr. Smith's computer proved key in solving the case.

1. What did police hope to prove from examining the Microsoft Word files on Mr. Smith's computer? Why did they believe this would implicate him in his wife's murder?
2. How were the documents titled *insurance1.doc* and *WRL1604.tmp* important to tying Mr. Smith to his wife's death?

Case Analysis 2

When police seized a laptop from a van parked suspiciously outside a local shopping mall, they discovered a cyber counterfeiting ring that employed modern technology to perpetrate this age-old crime.

1. What physical evidence most strongly implicated the driver of the van in a currency counterfeiting operation? What aspect of this evidence confirmed these suspicions?
2. What files located on the suspect's computer indicated that the suspects were producing more than counterfeit currency? What conclusion did the investigators draw from the existence of these files?

Web Resources

Computer Forensics, Cybercrime and Steganography Resources (Links to books, articles, websites, and other resources dealing with computer forensics)
www.forensics.nl

Digital Evidence (Links to articles on computer and Internet forensics)
www.crimeandclues.com/digital.htm

Digital Evidence Collection and Handling (An article about dealing with computer information seized at a crime scene)
www.faculty.ncwc.edu/toconnor/426/426lect06.htm

Computer Forensics World (An online community of computer forensics professionals, with links to articles and other resources on computer forensics)
www.computerforensicsworld.com

The Electronic Evidence Information Center (Links to articles and audio/video presentations on topics in computer forensics)
www.e-evidence.info/biblio.html

Do's and Don'ts of Forensic Computer Investigations (Basic advice on conducting computer forensics)
www.eweek.com/article2/0,1759,1646899,00.asp

Recovering and Examining Computer Forensic Evidence (An article that discusses the process and techniques of computer forensics)
www.fbi.gov/hq/lab/fsc/backissu/oct2000/computer.htm

Endnotes

1. One million bytes is referred to as a megabyte (MB), whereas 1 billion bytes is termed a gigabyte (GB).
2. Pulling the plug should always be done by removing the plug from the back of the computer. If the plug is removed from the wall and a battery backup (UPS) is in place, the UPS might cause an alert to the system and keep the unit powered on.
3. In this instance, *bit* is both metaphorical and literal. Every bit of information is needed, so we must get it all. So too every bit, as in the smallest unit of data storage—a one or a zero—must be imaged.
4. Actually, the more appropriate term is probably *paging* as opposed to *swapping*. This is because entire programs are typically not swapped in and out of memory to the swap space; rather, *pages* of memory are placed there.

Case Reading 1

Computer Forensic Analysis Answers the Question "Arson or Accident?"

Courtesy Peter Arnold, Inc.

Brief

The home of John Smith was destroyed by a fire, which was later determined to be the result of arson. During the fire, Smith's wife, Jane, died. Investigators learned that insurance policies taken against both the home and the life of Jane Smith were recently increased, so Smith stands to receive a very large monetary settlement. This fact, and problems with his purported alibi at the time of the fire, makes him the primary suspect. Smith has steadfastly denied the existence of the insurance policies and offers that his wife must have recently changed the policies.

Further investigation discloses that the couple did not possess a home computer but that Smith uses a computer at work. After applying for and receiving a search warrant for Smith's workplace, the arson investigator seizes the computer system unit from underneath Smith's desk, which he found in a powered-off condition. During execution of the search warrant, the company's computer administrator tells investigators that the computer was used only by Smith. The computer system unit is submitted for forensic analysis.

Analysis Request

Locate any incriminating or exculpatory evidentiary data with respect to Smith's knowledge of changes in his insurance policy. Locate any evidentiary data with respect to a motive for the crimes of arson and/or homicide.

Forensic Image Acquisition

1. The computer system was documented, its chassis was opened, and a single IDE/ATA hard disk drive (HDD) was located and documented. The HDD was removed from the system, and the computer system unit was booted to the BIOS setup program. The system date and time were verified.

2. The HDD was then placed in a forensic workstation, connected to the system using a hardware write-blocking device to ensure that the suspect HDD was not altered in any way.

3. A forensic image of the HDD was acquired using EnCase Version 5. The integrity of this image was verified using the MD5 algorithm inherent in

the EnCase program. A date and time analysis was done on all the files, revealing no dates later than the date of the execution of the search warrant.

Analysis

1. Deleted files were recovered.

2. A file signature analysis was run.

3. All files, including dates and times, logical and physical sizes, and complete location paths, were documented by the EnCase program.

4. User accounts were documented: two default accounts (*Administrator* and *Guest,* SID 500 and 501, respectively) and one user account (*jsmith*).

5. The operating system and file system type were documented: Windows 2000 using an NTFS partition.

6. Keyword text searches, derived from the text of letters received by the insurance company, were conducted.

7. All Microsoft Word documents were examined.

8. All text documents were examined.

9. Print spool files were examined.

Findings

1. A file titled *insurance1.doc* was located in the directory *C:\Documents and Settings\jsmith\ junk.* The directory structure *C:\Documents and Settings\jsmith* coincides with a default directory for the user name *jsmith,* which would have been established with that account. The subdirectory *junk* was then added by a user of the *jsmith* account. The text in this file is the same as the one received by the insurance company requesting an increase in homeowner's insurance.

2. Text found in unallocated space matches sections of text in a second letter received by the insurance company requesting an increase in life insurance for Jane Smith.

3. A file titled *WRL1604.tmp* was found in the directory *C:\Documents and Settings\jsmith\junk*. The file matches that of a temporary Microsoft Word file and contains text matching sections of text in the letter received by the insurance company requesting an increase in life insurance for Jane Smith.

4. A file titled *46127a.SPL* was located in the directory *C:\windows\ system32\spool\printers*. This file appears to be a print spool file. This file, when viewed as an Enhanced Meta File (EMF), reveals a document exact in composition and similar in layout to the letter received by the insurance company requesting an increase in life insurance for Jane Smith. An EMF is a type of spool file created during the printing process and can be viewed as a Windows picture file in the forensic software.

Conclusion

Based on the forensic examination of the computer data submitted in this case, it can be stated within a reasonable degree of scientific certainty that a user of this computer had knowledgeable interaction with letters very similar in content, composition, and structure to the evidentiary letters submitted as reference for analysis.

Case Reading 2

Counterfeiting and Fraud: A Forensic Computer Investigation

Courtesy Getty Images, Inc.

Brief

A detective submits a laptop computer for examination and explains that it was seized in connection with a case of counterfeiting and fraud. According to the detective, patrol officers happened upon a large sport-utility vehicle, occupied by one male driver, parked in the lot of a local mall. According to the officers, the driver and the circumstances appeared suspicious.

After investigating further, the officers located a laptop computer, color printer, and scanner in the rear of the vehicle. All equipment was hooked up and running. Additionally, the officers located gift certificates for one of the stores within the mall, which apparently were printed inside the vehicle. Finally, two $100 bills bearing exactly the same serial number were located in the driver's wallet. In response to questioning, the driver admitted using the system to print bogus gift certificates and counterfeit cash, which he then redeemed inside the mall. Prior to submission at the computer forensics

laboratory, the equipment was processed for fingerprints at the state Bureau of Criminal Identification (BCI).

Analysis Request

Locate any evidentiary data with respect to the crimes of counterfeiting and fraud. Demonstrate any connection between the recovered printed documents and the electronic equipment seized from the vehicle.

Forensic Image Acquisition

1. The computer system was documented, its case was opened, and a single IDE hard disk drive (HDD) was located and documented. The HDD was removed from the system, and the computer system unit was booted to the BIOS setup program. The system date and time were verified.

2. The HDD was then placed in a forensic workstation, connected to the system using a hardware write-blocking device to ensure that the suspect HDD was not altered in any way.

3. A forensic image of the HDD was acquired using EnCase Version 5. The integrity of this image was verified using the MD5 algorithm inherent in the EnCase program. A date and time analysis was done on all the files, revealing no dates later than the date of the execution of the search warrant.

Analysis

1. Deleted files were recovered.

2. A file signature analysis was run.

3. All files, including dates and times, logical and physical sizes, and complete location paths, were documented by the EnCase program.

4. The operating system and file system type were documented: Windows XP using an NTFS file system.

5. All graphics files were viewed, including ones previously deleted.

6. A graphics finder script was run against unallocated space. The script searched this area to locate file signatures of known graphics files.

7. All print spool files were located and examined.

Findings

1. A file titled *100front.jpg* was located in the directory *C:\Documents and Settings\user1\My Documents.* This file is an image of the front of a $100 bill. The serial number on this image matched the serial number of the suspected counterfeit $100 bills found on the suspect.

2. A file titled *100back.jpg* was located in the directory *C:\Documents and Settings\user1\My Documents.* This

file is an image of the back of a $100 bill.

3. A file titled *GapGiftCert1.jpg* was located in the directory *C:\Documents and Settings\user1\My Documents.* This file is an image of the front of a gift certificate for The Gap, a retail store.

4. A file titled *GapGiftCert2.jpg* was located in the directory *C:\Documents and Settings\user1\My Documents.* This file is an image of the back of a gift certificate for The Gap, a retail store.

5. A file titled *thumbs.db.* was located in the directory *C:\Documents and Settings\user1\My Documents.* This file, when viewed as a compound file, displayed several images, namely the images in items 1–4.

6. In the folder *C:\Documents and Settings\User1\My Recent Documents,* link files were found to the following:

    a. *C:\Documents and Settings\user1\My Documents\100front.jpg*

    b. *C:\Documents and Settings\user1\My Documents\100back.jpg*

    c. *C:\Documents and Settings\user1\My Documents\GapGiftCert1.jpg*

    d. *C:\Documents and Settings\user1\My Documents\GapGiftCert2.jpg*

7. The submitted scanner and printer were connected to a laboratory computer system, and the aforementioned evidentiary files were copied onto the HDD of that system.

Several printouts of the images were made. Additionally, test items were scanned and printed. All exemplars produced from the laboratory computer system were submitted to the state Bureau of Criminal Identification. The original counterfeit currency and gift certificates were also submitted to BCI for comparison to the exemplars. BCI was asked to locate any distinguishing characteristics produced by the printer and scanner submitted in this case.

Conclusion

Based on the forensic examination of the computer data submitted in this case, it can be stated within a reasonable degree of scientific certainty that a user of this computer knowingly produced counterfeit currency and counterfeit gift certificates.

Scott Peterson: A Case of Circumstantial Evidence

On the surface, Scott Peterson and his wife, Laci, appeared to live a happy and contented lifestyle in Modesto, California. The 30-year-old Peterson and his 27-year-old former college sweetheart, a substitute teacher, were expecting their first child in about one month when Laci suddenly disappeared. Scott Peterson told investigators that he had last seen his wife on December 24, 2002, at 9:30 A.M. when he left home for a fishing trip off San Francisco Bay.

In April 2003, Laci's decomposed remains washed ashore not far from where Scott said he had gone fishing on the day she vanished. Peterson claimed that Laci was dressed in a white top and black pants when he last saw her, but when her body was found she was wearing khaki pants. Scott's sister recalled that Laci was wearing khaki pants the night before her disappearance.

When questioned, Peterson claimed that he had gone fishing for sturgeon or striped bass. However, the police investigation revealed that he failed to bring the appropriate fishing rod and lines to catch such fish. Further revelations surfaced when it became known that Scott was having an affair with another woman. A search of Scott's warehouse led to the recovery of a black hair on a pair of pliers resting in Scott's boat. A mitochondrial DNA profile of the hair was consistent with Laci's DNA. Scott Peterson was charged with murder and convicted and currently awaits his fate on death row.

Visit WebExtra 19.1 to view the evidence that prosecutors presented to convict Scott Peterson.

chapter 19

Forensic Science and the Internet

Andrew W. Donofrio
Richard Saferstein

Key Terms

bookmark
broadband
browser
cookies
domain
download
e-mail
firewall
hacking
hypertext
Internet cache
Internet history
Internet protocol
Internet service provider (ISP)
mailing list
modem
newsgroups
router
search engine
uniform resource locator (URL)
VoIP (voice over Internet protocol)
Wi-Fi

Today, one cannot read a newspaper or turn on the television without seeing some reference to the Internet. The Internet, often referred to as the "information superhighway," is a medium for people to communicate with others and to access millions of pieces of information on computers located anywhere on the globe. No subject or profession remains untouched by the Internet, including forensic science. Every week many new pages of information are added to the Internet on the subject of forensic science, providing instant access to updated forensic science news and information. The Internet brings together forensic scientists from all parts of the world, linking them into one common electronic community.

What Is the Internet?

WebExtra 19.1

The Scott Peterson Case
www.prenhall.com/saferstein

The Internet can be defined as a "network of networks." A single network consists of two or more computers that are connected in some fashion to share information; the Internet connects thousands of these networks so information can be exchanged worldwide.

Closer Analysis

Building the Internet

The Internet was developed in 1969 by the U.S. Department of Defense to connect computers in different locations. The project, called ARPANET, originated from a group of scientists and engineers funded by the Pentagon's Advanced Research Projects Agency (ARPA). Their idea was based on the premise that the network would still operate even if part of the connection failed.

The first successful link was established between computers housed at UCLA and Stanford Research Institute. Shortly thereafter, USC–Santa Barbara and University of Utah computers were added to the system. In 1972, more than twenty sites were connected on the system when the first electronic mail (e-mail) message was sent.

In the 1980s, this network of interconnected computers grew with the establishment of the National Science Foundation Network (NSFNet), which encompassed five supercomputing centers across the United States. At about the same time, regional networks were formed around the United States for the purpose of accessing NSFNet. By 1989, ARPANET had closed down and NSFNet, along with its regional networks, began to mushroom into a worldwide network known as the Internet.[1]

Connecting to the Internet

Connections are sometimes made through a **modem,** a device that allows computers to exchange and transmit information through telephone lines. A modem passes digital information through a series of steps to convert it to analog signals that can be passed over a telephone line. The process is reversed when the modem converts analog signals coming in from the phone line.

Modems transfer information at a rate measured in bits per second (bps). Recall from the previous chapter that a bit is a single unit of digital data. Obviously, a modem with high-speed capabilities will ensure a faster connection on the Internet. Currently, a modem that transmits at 56,000 bits (or 56 kilobits) per second is recommended for convenience and reasonable connection speed. This speed is roughly equivalent to transmitting one thousand to two thousand words per second.

The trend, however, is to offer Internet users even higher-speed **broadband** connections to websites. Digital subscriber line (DSL) service is available from phone companies in many regions. DSL carries digital information on a regular telephone line without disturbing voice traffic. These lines can carry up to 1.1 megabits per second. Alternatively, one may opt to transmit over a TV cable line. Cable modems offer speeds comparable to DSL.

Once a computer is hooked into a DSL or cable line, the user has an additional option to link other computers in his or her home or office, through either a network wire (typically Ethernet) or high-frequency radio waves via a wireless or **Wi-Fi** connection. A device called a **router** serves as a sort of splitter, designed to link computers and manage traffic between them. The router, whether wired or wireless, allows computers to share a connection to the Internet. The advantage of Wi-Fi technology is that it avoids messy wires. Once a person has positioned a router in a home or office, another option awaits—voice over Internet protocol (**VoIP**). The IP (Internet Protocol) portion of VoIP is the bloodline of the Internet—but more on that later.

A broadband Internet connection can send and receive the human voice in a manner indistinguishable from a traditional telephone line. If it is in the range of a router, a Wi-Fi phone can operate like a traditional cell phone.

It is quite astonishing to think that there is no overriding network controlling the Internet. Rather, various larger, higher-level networks are *connected through network access points.* Many large **Internet service providers (ISPs)** (such as Verizon, AOL, and Yahoo) connect to each other through these network access points. The ISP's customers can then connect to the network by connecting to the bank of modems or the cable/DSL-connected routers located at the Internet service provider location and thus be connected to all the other networks. Because this places many individual computers on the network, an address system is needed so that all the data traveling on the network can get to its intended location.

Internet Addressing

With all of the computer manufacturers and software developers, some rules are necessary for computers to communicate on a global network. Just as any human language needs rules for people to communicate successfully, so does the language of computers. Computers that participate on the Internet, therefore, must be provided with an address known as an **Internet protocol (IP)** address from the Internet service provider to which they connect.

modem
A device that connects a computer to another computer through a phone line.

broadband
Any kind of Internet connection with a download speed of more than 56 kilobits per second.

Wi-Fi
Technology that uses high-frequency radio signals to transmit and receive data over the Internet; allows for a wireless connection to the Internet.

router
A device that manages traffic between computers belonging to a network, enabling them to share a connection to the Internet.

VoIP (voice over Internet protocol)
Transmission of the human voice over the Internet, usually through a telephone.

Internet service provider (ISP)
A company that provides connections to the Internet.

Internet protocol
The set of rules used to transmit packets of data over the Internet and route them to their destinations.

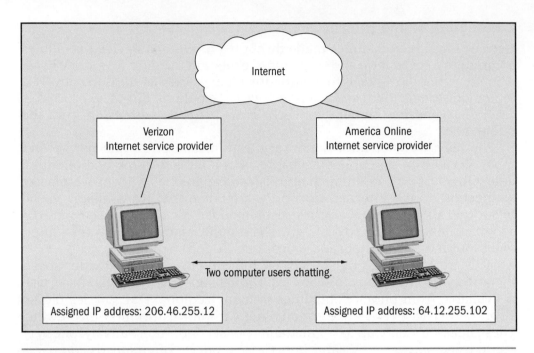

FIGURE 19–1 **Two computers communicating by sending data to each other's IP address via the Internet. An IP address is assigned to each computer by its Internet service provider (ISP).**

IP addresses take the form ###.###.###.###, in which, generally speaking, ### can be any number from 0 to 255. A typical IP address might look like this: 66.94.234.13. Not only do these IP addresses provide the means by which data can be routed to the appropriate location, but they also provide the means by which most Internet investigations are conducted (see Figure 19–1).

Of course, having to remember strings of numbers is a very inefficient and inconvenient way to access sites on the Internet. For this reason, every IP address also is assigned a domain name. **Domains** are human-readable names assigned to IP addresses. A domain name usually consists of two or more labels separated by dots. For example, www.nytimes.com is the registered domain name for the *New York Times.*

The rightmost label in a domain name is the *top-level domain.* Following are the most common abbreviations by which a top-level domain name is identified on the Internet:

domain
A human-readable name and abbreviation for a website.

.gov—government
.mil—military
.edu—educational institution
.com—commercial providers
.org—nonprofit organizations

To the left of the top-level domain is the *subdomain;* thus, nytimes is a subdomain of the .com domain. For the purpose of e-mail, the name of an individual at the *New York Times* may be added before the subdomain, with the @ sign used to separate them. An example of such an e-mail address might be Johndoe@nytimes.com.

At this point you may be wondering: If everything on the Internet uses an IP address to route data to the correct location, how can we use web addresses and e-mail addresses to access web sites and send e-mail? The answer, although technically complex, is quite simple. Understanding the apparent limitations of the human mind to remember numbers, developers created the concept of the domain name system (DNS). *Domain name systems* are essentially large databases distributed over the Internet that relate the names of networks to their actual IP address.

For instance, a person who wants to go to the *New York Times* online needs to know only the domain name. Even if the user is unsure of the actual address, the most logical place to start would obviously be www.newyork times.com or www.nytimes.com (both of which work, by the way). In actuality, however, the address is 199.239.136.245. This can be verified by typing that IP address directly into a web browser where one would normally type the web address. Domain name systems make it much easier to navigate the Web, but for investigative purposes it is important to realize that no names exist on the Internet; rather it's all about the IP address (see Figure 19–2).

Key Points

- A single network consists of two or more computers that are connected to share information. The Internet can be defined as a "network of networks"—it connects thousands of networks so information can be exchanged worldwide.

- Connection to the Internet can be made through a modem, a device that allows computers to exchange and transmit information through telephone lines. Higher-speed broadband connections are available through cable lines or through DSL telephone lines. Computers can be linked or networked through wired or wireless (Wi-Fi) connections.

- Computers that participate in the Internet have a unique numerical Internet protocol (IP) address and usually a name.

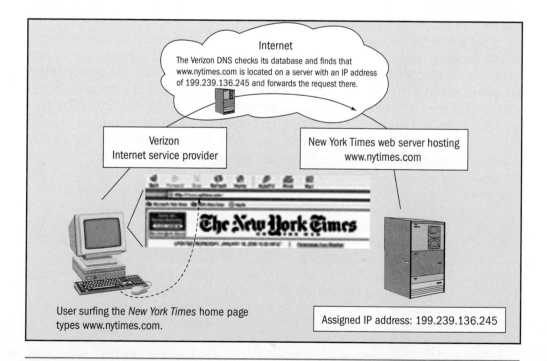

Internet
The Verizon DNS checks its database and finds that www.nytimes.com is located on a server with an IP address of 199.239.136.245 and forwards the request there.

Verizon
Internet service provider

New York Times web server hosting
www.nytimes.com

User surfing the *New York Times* home page types www.nytimes.com.

Assigned IP address: 199.239.136.245

FIGURE 19–2 A user wishing to visit the *New York Times* website types the user-friendly URL (uniform resource locator) www.nytimes.com. Because all traffic on the Internet is routed by IP address, the URL needs to be resolved to the IP address. This is done by the domain name system (DNS) of the user's ISP.

World Wide Web

The most popular area of the Internet is the World Wide Web. Also known as WWW, W3, or the Web, it is a collection of documents called *web pages* that are stored in the computers connected to the Internet throughout the world. Web **browsers**, such as Netscape Navigator and Microsoft Internet Explorer, are programs that allow the user to explore information stored on the Web and to retrieve web pages the viewer wishes to read. Web browsers permit the downloading and capture of documents, as well as printing of selected portions of websites.

Each web page is stored in a specific website that has a unique web address that indicates where the document is actually located. The web address is called the **uniform resource locator (URL)**. The URL designates the site at which information is stored on the Internet. A person can access a page by directly entering the URL into a browser. For example, the FBI has a website that can be accessed by typing in its URL: www.fbi.gov. The URL for the FBI consists of the following components:

> *http://*—Hypertext Transfer Protocol is the programming language the browser uses to locate and read web pages.
>
> *www.*—Denotes the World Wide Web, the place on the Internet where the information is located.
>
> *fbi.*—Designates the subdomain or server in this case, for the Federal Bureau of Investigation.
>
> *gov*—Designates the domain name.

The Internet has made browsing or exploring the Web easy through the existence of **hypertext**. Hypertext is usually easy to find because it is highlighted with a different color within the Web page. When clicked, hypertext enables the user to jump to another Web page related to the subject at hand.

For example, a user interested in examining the FBI's *Law Enforcement Bulletin* web page would merely go to the FBI's home page and search for the term *Law Enforcement Bulletin*. The user is immediately transferred to a hypertext page where, with a click of the mouse, he or she is taken to the website. This website has the URL www.fbi.gov/publications/leb/leb.htm, where leb.htm designates a document on the FBI website. Another FBI publication available online is *Forensic Science Communications*. This quarterly online forensic science journal presents technical articles, technical notes, case reports, and review articles in a paperless format.

The advantage of using hypertext is that the user can quickly switch back and forth between related web pages without having to retype the URL or start over at the beginning of the search. Hypertext makes the Internet user-friendly and has given rise to the expressions *browsing* and *surfing the Net*. Users can navigate from one website to another, browsing at leisure through a succession of documents. Another quick way to reach a site is to designate it as a **bookmark** or favorite place. Most browsers allow the user to customize a list of favorite websites for easy access with one click (see Figure 19–3).

Hundreds of new sites are added every day, providing Internet users with a staggering amount of information. One way to explore popular website locations is to use the list of the Top 100 Classic Websites compiled by *PC Magazine* (www.pcmag.com; see Table 19–1). The PC Magazine Top 100 Classic Websites list includes sites related to business and

browser
A program that allows a computer user to access websites.

uniform resource locator (URL)
A standard method by which Internet sites are addressed.

hypertext
Highlighted text or graphics on a web page that, when clicked, link to other websites.

bookmark
A feature that allows the user to designate favorite websites for fast and easy access.

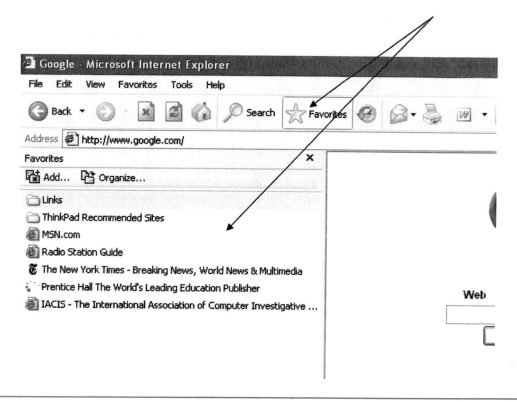

FIGURE 19–3   Bookmarks or favorite places can be saved for quick access in most web browsers.

Table 19–1   PC Magazine's Top 100 Classic Websites

AAPS: PC and Mobile

AvantGo
www.avantgo.com

Homestead
www.homestead.com

Mailblocks
www.mailblocks.com

MSN Hotmail
www.hotmail.com

Shutterfly
www.shutterfly.com

Vindigo
www.vindigo.com

WebEx
www.webex.com

Yahoo! Groups
groups.yahoo.com

Business and Finance

Bloomberg.com
www.bloomberg.com

Internal Revenue Service
www.irs.gov

MSN Money
www.moneycentral.msn.com

SmartMoney.com
www.smartmoney.com

The Motley Fool
www.fool.com

TheStreet.com
www.thestreet.com

U.S. Securities and Exchange
Commission
www.sec.gov

Careers

Dice.com
www.dice.com

Monster.com
www.monster.com

Yahoo! HotJobs
hotjobs.yahoo.com

Computing

Annoyances.org
www.annoyances.org

Answers that Work
www.answersthatwork.com

Digital Photography Review
www.dpreview.com

EarthWeb
www.earthweb.com

eWeek
www.eweek.com

ExtremeTech
www.extremetech.com

Java Technology
www.java.sun.com

PalmGear.com
www.palmgear.com

PC Magazine
www.pcmag.com

Slashdot
slashdot.org

Technology Review
www.technologyreview.com

W3Schools
www.w3schools.com

Webopedia
www.webopedia.com

**Current Events and News
You Can Use**

Electronic Privacy Information
Center
www.epic.org

(continued)

Table 19–1 PC Magazine's Top 100 Classic Websites *(continued)*

IEEE Virtual Museum
www.ieee-virtual-museum.org

NASA
www.nasa.gov

Project Vote Smart
www.vote-smart.org

World Health Organization
www.who.int

Lifestyle and Fun

Citysearch
www.citysearch.com

Discovery Kids
kids.discovery.com

Epicurious
www.epicurious.com

HowStuffWorks
www.howstuffworks.com

ifilm
www.ifilm.com

National Geographic Society
www.nationalgeographic.com

Nickelodeon Online
www.nick.com

Pogo
www.pogo.com

Smithsonian Institution
www.si.edu

Yahoo! Games
games.yahoo.com

News and Entertainment

AMG All Music Guide
www.allmusic.com

BBC News
www.bbc.co.uk

CNN
www.cnn.com

E! Online
www.eonline.com

ESPN.com
www.espn.com

Internet Archive
www.archive.org

Internet Movie Database
(IMDb)
www.imdb.com

Slate
www.slate.com

The New York Times on the Web
www.nytimes.com

NPR
www.npr.org

The Onion
www.theonion.com

RollingStone.com
www.rollingstone.com

Salon.com
www.salon.com

ScienceDaily
www.sciencedaily.com

Television Without Pity
www.televisionwithoutpity.com

Wired News
www.wired.com

Security and the Net

Broadbandreports.com
dslreports.com

CERT Coordination Center
www.cert.org

GetNetWise
www.getnetwise.org

Gibson Research Corp.
www.grc.com

Internet Traffic Report
www.internettrafficreport.com

Netcraft
news.netcraft.com

SecurityFocus
www.securityfocus.com

TrendMicro
www.trendmicro.com

Search, Reference, and Portals

About.com
www.about.com

Centers for Disease
Control and Prevention
www.cdc.gov

Dictionary.com
dictionary.reference.com

Encyclopaedia Britannica
www.britannica.com

FedStats
www.fedstats.gov

FirstGov.gov
www.firstgov.gov

Google
www.google.com

iVillage.com
www.ivillage.com

Librarians' Internet Index
www.lii.org

The Library of Congress
www.loc.gov

MSN Encarta
encarta.msn.com

Nolo.com
www.nolo.com

WebMD
www.webmd.com

Yahoo!
www.yahoo.com

Shopping

Amazon.com
www.amazon.com

CarsDirect.com
www.carsdirect.com

ConsumerReview.com
www.consumerreview.com

eBay
www.ebay.com

Netflix
www.netflix.com

Overstock.com
www.overstock.com

PriceGrabber.com
www.pricegrabber.com

Shopping.com
www.shopping.com

Surprise.com
www.surprise.com

Techbargains.com
www.techbargains.com

Travel

Expedia
www.expedia.com

Fodors
www.fodors.com

Frommers.com
www.frommers.com

Lonely Planet
www.lonelyplanet.com

Orbitz
www.orbitz.com

Travelocity
www.travelocity.com

finance, computing, news, entertainment, online shopping, and reference sources. This list opens a gateway to exploring the diversity of the World Wide Web. For example, through Expedia.com a user can book flights, hotel rooms, and cruises and plan almost any type of vacation. The Amazon.com website provides the largest bookstore on the Internet. Here the user can search by keyword, author, subject, or title to locate or purchase books on any topic imaginable. Users can even ask Amazon .com to send e-mails when books related to their personal interests come in stock.

A favorite site of the author is Switchboard (www.switchboard.com). This site is devoted to helping users locate long-lost friends or relatives. A database of names, phone numbers, addresses, and e-mail addresses can easily be searched with a variety of options. Another interesting website is MapQuest (www.mapquest.com). The user designates a location and the site generates a map, accompanied by written directions. A fun site is Blue-Mountain (www.bluemountain.com), where the user can compose, personalize, and send greeting cards for all sorts of occasions.

Search Engines

Sifting through the enormous amount of information on the World Wide Web can often resemble looking for a needle in a haystack. As the Internet grows, so does the need for automated search tools. Several directories and indexes known as **search engines** help users search the Internet for a particular topic. Through search engines, the user can locate relevant web pages containing a particular piece of information on the Internet. When the user types in keywords and phrases related to the needed information, the search engine searches its database and lists all the pages involving the keyword selection. Most search engines contain tools called *spiders* or *crawlers* that search the Web seeking titles, subjects, and keywords to index the contents of individual web pages.

search engine
A website devoted to searching for information on the Internet using keywords.

The number of search engines continues to change with new technology, as faster, newer tools are adopted and slower, older ones are phased out. Interestingly, search engines have taken on a new look, becoming *portals* offering a wide variety of Internet services in addition to their traditional search functions. Some of the more popular search engines, along with their URLs, are listed here:

Search Engine	URL
Yahoo!	www.yahoo.com
Google	www.google.com
MSN	www.msn.com
Dogpile	www.dogpile.com
Lycos	www.info.com

Users can also find a multitude of search engines at www.easy-searcher.com/index.html. Because each search engine has different capabilities, it is recommended that multiple search engines be used when researching a subject. Automated search tools called *meta-engines* load a query into several of the Net's leading search engines to compile a single list of results. One example of a meta-engine is MetaCrawler (www .metacrawler.com).

Electronic Mail and Mailing Lists

e-mail
Electronic mail.

The service that is most commonly used in conjunction with the Internet is electronic mail. Also called **e-mail,** this communication system can transport messages across the world in a matter of seconds. To use e-mail, a user must acquire an e-mail address, usually through an Internet service provider or a free e-mail server. Like regular postal mail, a user needs an address to receive mail and needs to know a recipient's address to send messages. These messages are stored in an individualized mailbox that can be opened electronically at the user's convenience.

download
The transfer of a file through an Internet connection from a remote computer to a user's computer.

Another interesting feature is that one can attach a file to an e-mail so that the recipient can **download** the attached file. The file can then be saved and stored on the recipient's computer. A file may consist of text, pictures, music, or video. For example, a text file can be viewed and modified by means of a word-processing program.

mailing list
A list of people with a common interest who receive all the e-mails sent to the list.

Also, having an e-mail account provides the opportunity to receive information through **mailing lists.** A mailing list is a discussion group for a selected topic in which related messages are sent directly to a mailbox through e-mail. For example, Forens-L is a mailing list dedicated to the discussion of forensic medicine and forensic science that provides a quick, useful way to exchange ideas or share information about forensics with people with similar interests around the world. To subscribe to the Forens-L mailing list, go to www.geradts.com/mailman/listinfo/forens-geradts.com for instructions.

Newsgroups

newsgroups
Large bulletin board systems that consist of several thousand specialized discussion groups. Messages are posted to a bulletin board for others to read.

Another service much like mailing lists involves **newsgroups.** Like a mailing list, a newsgroup is devoted to a particular topic. Whereas a mailing list, however, is usually managed by a single site, a newsgroup networks many sites that are set up by local Internet service providers. The result is that a newsgroup joins a significantly larger audience compared to a mailing list. A newsgroup is analogous to a bulletin board where subscribers post articles or messages. When a person connects to a newsgroup, he or she can quickly scan through a list of article titles, selecting only those of interest.

To find a newsgroup of interest, users can explore Usenet, an index of the available newsgroups. The index can be located through search engines such as Google. Usenet can be searched through keywords in the same way the World Wide Web is explored. For example, entering the keyword *law enforcement* into Usenet produces a list of articles from any of the newsgroups containing that keyword. The articles are hypertext so that with a click of the mouse, the person can read the article instantaneously. The useful Google Groups website (groups.google.com) lists newsgroups in hypertext so that the newsgroup can be accessed directly from the World Wide Web. Commercial services such as AOL allow the user to subscribe to a newsgroup and provide the program that will keep track of how many articles are available, which ones the person has read, and which ones the person has not read.

Key Points

- Web browsers allow the user to explore information stored on the Web and to retrieve web pages the viewer wishes to read.

- Hypertext is highlighted text or graphics on a web page that, when clicked, links to other websites. Hypertext has given rise to the expressions *browsing* and *surfing the Net.*

- Several directories and indexes on the Internet, known as search engines, help users find information on a particular topic from the hundreds of thousands of websites located on the Internet.

- The service that is most commonly used in conjunction with the Internet is electronic mail (e-mail), a communication system that can transport messages across the world in a matter of seconds.

- Besides web pages, three ways for a computer user to receive information via the Internet are e-mail, mailing lists, and newsgroups.

Exploring Forensic Science on the World Wide Web

There are no limits to the amount or type of information that can be found on the Internet. The fields of law enforcement and forensic science have not been left behind by advancing computer technology. Extensive information about forensic science is available on the Internet. The types of web pages range from simple explanations of the various fields of forensics to intricate details of crime-scene reconstruction. People can also find information on which colleges offer degrees programs in forensics or pages posted by law enforcement agencies that detail their activities, as well as possible employment opportunities.

General Forensics Sites

Reddy's Forensic Home Page (www.forensicpage.com) is a valuable starting point. This site is a collection of forensic web pages listed under categories such as new links in forensics; general forensic information sources; associations, colleges, and societies; literature and journals; forensic laboratories; general web pages; forensic-related mailing lists and newsgroups; universities; conferences; and various forensic fields of expertise.

Another website offering a multitude of information related to forensic science is Zeno's Forensic Science Site (forensic.to/forensic.html). Here users can find links to forensic education and expert consultation, as well as a wealth of information concerning specific fields of forensic science.

A comprehensive and useful website for those interested in law enforcement is Officer.com (www.officer.com). This comprehensive collection of criminal justice resources is organized into easy-to-read subdirectories that relate to topics such as law enforcement agencies, police association and organization sites, criminal justice organizations, law research pages, and police mailing-list directories.

Websites on Specific Topics

An Introduction to Forensic Firearm Identification (www.firearmsid.com) This website contains an extensive collection of information relating to the identification of firearms. An individual can explore in detail how to examine bullets, cartridge cases, and clothing for gunshot residues and suspect shooters' hands for primer residues. Information on the latest technology involving the automated firearms search system IBIS can also be found on this site.

WebExtra 19.2
An Introduction to Forensic Firearms Identification
www.prenhall.com/saferstein

Carpenter's Forensic Science Resources (www.tncrimlaw.com/forensic/) This site provides a bibliography with hypertext references pertaining to various aspects of criminal investigations involving forensic evidence. For example, the user can find references about DNA, fingerprints, hairs, fibers, and questioned documents as they relate to crime scenes and assist investigations. This website is an excellent place to start a research project in forensic science.

Crime Scene Investigation (www.crime-scene-investigator.net/index.html) For those who are interested in learning the process of crime-scene investigation, this site provides detailed guidelines and information regarding crime-scene response and the collection and preservation of evidence. For example, information concerning the packaging and analysis of bloodstains, seminal fluids, hairs, fibers, paint, glass, firearms, documents, and fingerprints can be found through this website. This website explains the importance of inspecting the crime scene and the impact forensic evidence has on the investigation.

Crime and Clues (www.crimeandclues.com) Users interested in learning about the forensic aspects of fingerprinting will find this a useful and informative website. The site covers the history of fingerprints, as well as subjects pertaining to the development of latent fingerprints. The user will also find links to other websites covering a variety of subjects pertaining to crime-scene investigation, documentation of the crime scene, and expert testimony.

Interactive Investigator—Détective Interactif (www.virtualmuseum.ca/Exhibitions/Myst) At this outstanding site, visitors can obtain general information and an introduction to the main aspects of forensic science from a database on the subject. They can also explore actual evidence gathered from notorious crime scenes. Users will be able to employ deductive skills and forensic knowledge while playing an interactive game in which they must help Detective Wilson and Detective Marlow solve a gruesome murder.

The Chemical Detective (http://caligula.bcs.deakin.edu.au/bcs_courses/forensic/Chemical%20Detective/index.htm) This site offers descriptions of relevant forensic science disciplines. Topics such as fingerprints, fire and arson, and DNA analysis are described in informative layperson's terms. Case histories describe the application of forensic evidence to criminal investigations. Emphasis is placed on securing and documenting the crime scene. The site directs the reader to other important forensic links.

Contact a Document Examiner (www.qdewill.com) This basic, informative web page answers frequently asked questions concerning document examination, explains the application of typical document examinations, and details the basic facts and theory of handwriting and signatures. There are also links to noted document examination cases that present the user with real-life applications of forensic document examination.

Table 19–2 lists a number of additional websites available in the forensic science field.

Forensic Analysis of Internet Data

It's important from the investigative standpoint to be familiar with the evidence left behind from a user's Internet activity. A forensic examination of a computer system reveals quite a bit of data about a user's Internet activity.

Table 19.2 Forensic Science Websites

American Academy of Forensic Sciences—A professional society dedicated to the application of science to the law and committed to the promotion of education in the forensic sciences.

American Board of Forensic Entomology—Provides information about the field's history, case studies, and professional status.

American Board of Forensic Toxicology Inc.—Establishes and revises as necessary standards of qualification for those who practice forensic toxicology.

American College of Forensic Examiners (ACFE)—Dedicated to members of the forensic community. Also provides links to help people find expert witnesses in the forensic field.

American Society of Crime Laboratory Directors (ASCLD)—A nonprofit professional society devoted to the improvement of crime laboratory operations through sound management practices.

American Society of Questioned Document Examiners—Online references, technical notes on handwriting identification, and other areas of professional interest to the forensic document analyst.

ASCLD: Laboratory Accreditation Board—Offers the general public and users of laboratory services a means of identifying laboratories that have demonstrated that they meet established standards.

Association for Crime Scene Reconstruction (ACSR)—Members are law enforcement investigators, forensic experts, and educators.

Association of Firearm and Tool Mark Examiners—Defines standards and ethics for individual workers in the field of firearms and toolmark examination.

California Association of Criminalists—Membership is offered to individuals currently employed as laboratory scientists and professionally engaged in one or more fields directly related to the forensic sciences.

Canadian Society of Forensic Science—Includes journal abstracts, history, and meeting information.

European Association for Forensic Entomology—Created in May 2002 in Rosny Sous Bois, France, to promote forensic entomology in Europe.

Forensic Science Service—A source for training, consultancy, and scientific support.

Forensic Science Society—Provides information on careers, conferences, and publications.

International Association for Identification—A professional association for those engaged in forensic identification, investigation, and scientific examination.

International Association of Bloodstain Pattern Analysis—An organization of forensic experts promoting education, establishing training standards, and encouraging research in the field of bloodstain pattern analysis.

(continued)

Table 19.2   Forensic Science Websites *(continued)*

International Association of Forensic Toxicologists—Promotes cooperation and coordination of efforts among members.

International Organisation on Electronic Evidence (IOCE)—Formed to develop international principles for the procedures relating to digital evidence.

National Forensic Science Technology Center—Dedicated to supporting forensic science laboratories to achieve the highest possible quality of operations.

Natural Resources DNA Profiling and Forensic Centre—Undertakes research on natural populations of animals and plants for the purpose of providing information to managers charged with conserving biodiversity and ensuring the sustainable use of Canada's biological resources.

Society of Forensic Toxicologists—Promotes and develops the field of forensic toxicology.

Southern Association of Forensic Scientists—An organization of professional forensic scientists.

Southern California Association of Fingerprint Officers—An association for scientific investigation and identification.

U.S. Department of Justice: National Commission on the Future of DNA Evidence—Working to maximize the value of forensic DNA evidence in the criminal justice system.

Vidocq Society—Forensic experts who meet in the shadow of Independence Hall to investigate and solve unsolved homicides.

Websites are hypertexted at http://dir.yahoo.com/Science/Forensic_science/forensic_science_organizations.

The data described next would be accessed and examined using the forensic techniques outlined in Chapter 18.

Internet Cache

When a user accesses a website, such as the *New York Times* home page, data is transferred from the server at that site to the user's computer. If the user is accessing the Internet via a dial-up connection, the transfer may take a while, because the data transfer rate and capabilities (bandwidth) of the telephone system are limited. Even with the high-speed access of a DSL line or cable connection, conservation of bandwidth is always a consideration.

> **Internet cache**
> Portions of visited web pages placed on the local hard disk drive to facilitate quicker retrieval once revisited.

To expedite web browsing and make it more efficient, most web browsers use an **Internet cache** that stores, or caches, portions of the pages visited on the local hard disk drive. This way, if the page is revisited, portions of it can be reconstructed more quickly from this saved data, rather than having to pull it yet again from the Internet and use precious bandwidth.

The Internet cache is a potential source of evidence for the computer investigator. Portions of (and in some cases, entire) visited web pages can be reconstructed from data in the cache. Even if deleted, these cached files can often be recovered (see the section on deleted data in Chapter 18).

Investigators must know how to search for this data within the particular web browser used by a suspect.

Cookies

Internet **cookies** are another area where potential evidence can be found. Cookies are placed on the local hard disk drive by websites the user has visited, if the user's web browser is set to allow this to happen. The website uses cookies to track certain information about its visitors. This information can be anything from the history of visits and purchasing habits to passwords and personal information used to recognize the user for later visits.

Consider a user who registers for an account at a website and then returns to the same site from the same computer a few days later. The site often displays a banner reading "Welcome, *Your User Name.*" Data about the user is retrieved from the cookie file placed on the user's hard disk drive by the website during the initial visit and registration with the site. It is helpful to think of cookies as a "Caller ID" for websites. The site recognizes visitors and retrieves information about them, just as you recognize the name of a caller when answering a phone equipped with a Caller ID display.

Cookie files can be a valuable source of evidence. In Internet Explorer they take the form of plain text files, which can typically be opened with a standard text viewer or word-processing program, revealing part of the data. The existence of the files themselves, regardless of the information contained within, can be of evidentiary value to show a history of web visits.

A typical cookie may resemble the following: rsaferstein@ forensicscience.txt. From this we can surmise that someone using the local computer login *rsaferstein* accessed the forensic science website. It is possible that the cookie was placed there by an annoying pop-up ad, but considered against other evidence in the computer data, the presence of this cookie may be of corroborative value.

cookies
Files placed on a computer from a visited website; they are used to track visits and usage of that site.

Internet History

Most web browsers track the history of web page visits for the computer user. Like the "recent calls" list on a cell phone, the **Internet history** provides an accounting of sites most recently visited, sometimes storing weeks' worth of visits. Users can go back and access sites they recently visited just by going through the browser's history. Most web browsers store this information in one particular file; Internet Explorer uses the *index.dat* file. On a Windows system, an *index.dat* file is created for each login user name on the computer.

The history file can be located and read with most popular computer forensic software packages. It displays the uniform resource locator (URL) of each website, along with the date and time the site was accessed. An investigation involving Internet use almost always includes an examination of Internet history data.

In some respects, the term *Internet history* is inaccurate because it doesn't encompass all of the functions of this utility. Some browsers store other valuable evidence independent of Internet access. Files accessed over a network are often listed in the history. Similarly, files accessed on external media, such as floppy disks, CDs, or thumb drives, may also appear in the history. Regardless, the Internet history data is a valuable source of evidence worthy of examination (see Figure 19–4).

Internet history
An accounting of websites visited. Different browsers store this information in different ways.

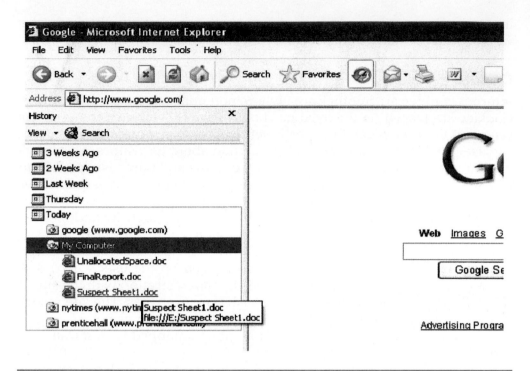

FIGURE 19–4 The Internet history displays more than just web-browsing activity. Here we see Microsoft Word documents and a picture accessed on the current day.

Bookmarks and Favorite Places

Another way users can access websites quickly is to store them in their bookmarks or "favorite places." Like a preset radio station, web browsers allow users to bookmark websites for future visits. Much can be learned from a user's bookmarked sites. You might learn what online news a person is interested in, or what type of hobbies he or she has. You may also see that person's favorite child pornography or computer hacking sites bookmarked.

Key Point

• Places where a forensic computer examiner might look to determine what websites a computer user has visited recently are the Internet cache, cookies, and the Internet history.

Forensic Investigation of Internet Communications

Computer investigations often begin with or are centered on Internet communication. Whether it is a chat conversation among many people, an instant message conversation between two people, or the back-and-forth of an e-mail exchange, human communication has long been a source of evidentiary material. Regardless of the type, investigators are typically interested in communication.

Role of the IP

Recall that in order to communicate on the Internet, a device needs to be assigned an Internet protocol (IP) address. The IP address is provided by the Internet service provider from which the device accesses the Internet.

Thus, the IP address may lead to the identity of a real person. If an IP address is the link to the identity of a real person, then it is quite obviously valuable for identifying someone on the Internet.

To illustrate, let's assume that a user of the Internet, fictitiously named John Smith, connects to the Internet from his home by way of a Verizon DSL connection. Verizon in this case would provide Smith's IP address. Verizon owns a bank of IP addresses to service its customers; these addresses were issued by a regulatory body designed to track the usage of IP addresses, so no two addresses are ever used at the same time.

Suppose that Smith, while connected to the Internet, decides to threaten an ex-girlfriend by sending her an e-mail telling her he is going to kill her. That e-mail must first pass through the computers of Smith's Internet service provider—in this case, Verizon—on its way to its destination, Smith's girlfriend. The e-mail would be stamped by the servers that it passes through, and this stamp would include the IP address given to Smith by Verizon for his session on the Internet.

An investigator tracking the e-mail would locate the originating IP address stamped in the e-mail header. That IP address could be researched using one of many Internet sites (such as www.samspade.org or www.arin.net) to determine which Internet service provider was given this IP as part of a block to service its customers (see Figure 19–5). The investigator then files a subpoena with the Internet service provider (Verizon) asking which of its customers was using that IP address on that date and time.

IP addresses are located in different places for different methods of Internet communications. E-mail has the IP address in the header portion of the mail. This may not be readily apparent and may require a bit of configuration to reveal. Each e-mail client is different and needs to be evaluated on a case-by-case basis. For an instant message or chat session, the service provider making the chat mechanism available would be contacted to provide the user's IP address.

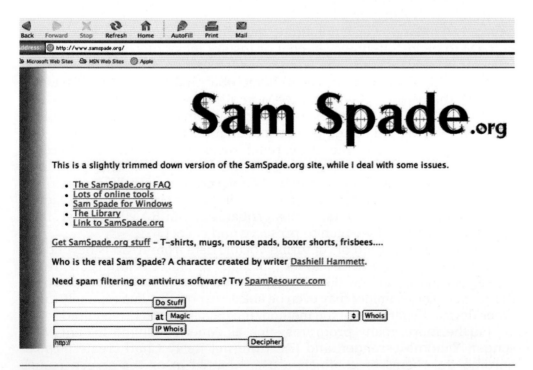

FIGURE 19–5   Sites such as www.samspade.org can be used to track the origins of an IP address. *Courtesy Word to the Wise*

E-Mail, Chat, and Instant Messaging

E-mail can be read by a number of software programs called *clients*. Two of the most popular ways to access, read, and store e-mail in today's Internet environment, however, are Microsoft Outlook and web-based clients. Some people even use a combination of the two.

If an e-mail account is linked through Microsoft Outlook, the e-mail is stored in a compound file (a file with several layers). Typically, a compound file exists for received, sent, and deleted e-mail. Users can also create new categories under which to save e-mail. Most forensic computer software applications can view these compound files so that the e-mail, including any file attachments, can be seen. These files can also be imported into a copy of Microsoft Outlook that is not attached to an e-mail account, and the e-mail can be viewed there. Investigators must also be aware that in a computer network environment, the user's Outlook files may not reside on his or her workstation computer, but rather on a central mail or file server.

Most accounts offer the ability to access e-mail through a web-based interface as well. This way, users can access their e-mail remotely from other computers. For e-mail accessed through a web browser, the information presented earlier on Internet-based evidence applies. The web interface converts the e-mail into a document suitable for reading in a web browser. Consequently, web-based e-mail is often found in the Internet cache. This is particularly true of free Internet e-mail accounts such as Hotmail and Yahoo.

Much of the evidence from Internet communication is also derived from chat and instant message technology. This is particularly true in the world of child sexual exploitation over the Internet. Various technologies provide chat and instant message services. Most chat and instant message conversations are not saved by the parties involved. Although most of the software does allow for conversation archiving, it is typically turned off by default. Therefore, conversations of this nature typically exist in the volatile memory space of random-access memory (RAM).

Recall from Chapter 18 that RAM is termed volatile because it holds data only if it has power. Unplugging the computer causes the data located in RAM to be lost. If, however, chat or instant message conversations are relevant as evidence and the computer was turned off, thus erasing the data in RAM, all might not be lost. Remember that there is an interaction between the computer system's RAM and the hard disk drive. RAM is a commodity, and the computer's operating system conserves it as much as possible by swapping/paging that information back and forth into the swap space/paging file. Therefore, remnants of chat conversations are often found in the swap space/paging file during a forensic examination of the hard disk drive. These remnants, however, are typically fragmented, disconnected, and incomplete. Therefore, if the chat or instant message is still present on the screen (and thus probably still in RAM), the investigator needs a method by which to preserve and collect it.

WebExtra 19.9

Follow the trail of an e-mail as it travels through the Internet
www.prenhall.com/saferstein

A detailed discussion of capturing volatile data from RAM is beyond the scope of this chapter. Suffice it to say that many commercial forensic software packages can capture this data. Similarly, Linux-based tools can accomplish this as well. The examiner may even be able to export the data remotely to another device. Regardless of the method, the data needs to be acquired.

Furthermore, many programs such as America Online Instant Messenger, Yahoo Messenger, and IRC (Internet Relay Chat) create files regarding the rooms or channels a user chatted in or the screen names with which a user exchanged instant messages. Each application needs to be researched and the forensic computer examination guided by an understanding of how it functions.

Hacking

Unauthorized computer intrusion, more commonly referred to as hacking, is the concern of every computer administrator. Hackers penetrate computer systems for a number of reasons. Sometimes the motive is corporate espionage; other times it is merely for bragging rights within the hacker community. Most commonly, though, a rogue or disgruntled employee with some knowledge of the computer network is looking to cause damage. Whatever the motivation, corporate America frequently turns to law enforcement to investigate and prosecute these cases.

Generally speaking, when investigating an unauthorized computer intrusion, investigators concentrate their efforts in three locations: *log files, volatile memory,* and *network traffic.* Log files typically document the IP address of the computer that made the connection. Logs can be located in several locations on a computer network. Most servers on the Internet track connections made to them through the use of logs. Additionally, the router (the device responsible for directing data) may contain log files detailing connections.

Similarly, devices known as firewalls may contain log files listing computers that were allowed access to the network or an individual system. Firewalls are devices (either hardware or software) that permit only requested traffic to enter a computer network. In other words, if a user didn't send out a request for Internet traffic from a specific system, the firewall should block its entry. If the log files captured the IP address of the intruder, then revealing the user behind the IP is the same process as for e-mail. Investigating a computer intrusion, however, gets a bit more complicated than this.

Frequently, in cases of unlawful access to a computer network, the perpetrator attempts to cover the tracks of his or her IP address. In these instances, advanced investigative techniques might be necessary to discover the hacker's true identity. When an intrusion is in progress, the investigator may have to capture volatile data (data in RAM). The data in RAM at the time of an intrusion may provide valuable clues to the identity of the intruder, or at the very least his or her method of attack. As in the case of the instant message or chat conversation, the data in RAM needs to be acquired.

Another standard tactic for investigating intrusion cases is to document all programs installed and running on a system, in order to discover malicious software installed by the perpetrator to facilitate entry. The investigator uses specialized software to document running processes, registry entries, open ports, and any installed files.

Additionally, the investigator may want to capture live network traffic as part of the evidence collection and investigation process. Traffic that travels the network does so in the form of data packets. In addition to data, these packets also contain source and destination IP addresses. If the attack requires two-way communication, as in the case of a hacker stealing data, then data needs to be transmitted back to the hacker's computer using the destination IP address. Once this is learned, the investigation can focus on that system. Moreover, the type of data that is being transmitted on the network may be a clue as to what type of attack is being launched, whether any important data is being stolen, or what types of malicious software, if any, are involved in the attack.

hacking
A slang term for an unauthorized computer or network intrusion.

firewall
Hardware or software designed to protect against intrusions into a computer network.

Key Points

- An investigator tracking the origin of an e-mail seeks out the sender's IP address in the e-mail's header. Chat and instant messages are typically located in a computer's random-access memory (RAM).

- Tracking the origin of unauthorized computer intrusions (hacking) requires investigating a computer's log file, RAM, and network traffic.

- A firewall is a device designed to protect against intrusions into a computer network.

Chapter Summary

The Internet, often referred to as the "information superhighway," is a medium for people to communicate and to access millions of pieces of information from computers located anywhere on the globe. No subject or profession remains untouched by the Internet, including forensic science. The Internet brings together forensic scientists from all parts of the world, linking them into one common electronic community.

The Internet can be defined as a "network of networks." A single network consists of two or more computers that are connected to share information; the Internet connects thousands of these networks so all of the information can be exchanged worldwide. Connections can be made through a modem, a device that allows computers to exchange and transmit information through telephone lines. Higher-speed broadband connections are available through cable lines or through DSL telephone lines. Computers can be linked or networked through wired or wireless (Wi-Fi) connections.

Computers on the Internet have a unique numerical Internet protocol (IP) address and usually a name. Commercial Internet service providers connect computers to the Internet while offering the user an array of options. The most popular area of the Internet is the World Wide Web, a collection of pages stored in computers connected to the Internet throughout the world.

Web browsers allow users to explore information stored on the Web and to retrieve web pages they wish to read. Several directories and indexes on the Internet, known as search engines, help users locate information on a particular topic from the hundreds of thousands of websites on the Internet. A keyword or phrase entered into a search engine locates websites that are relevant to that subject.

The service that is most commonly used in conjunction with the Internet is electronic mail (e-mail). This communication system can transport messages across the world in a matter of seconds. Extensive information relating to forensic science is available on the Internet. The types of web pages range from simple explanations of the various fields of forensics to intricate details of forensic science specialties.

Investigators seeking a history of an Internet user's destinations can take advantage of the fact that computers store or cache portions of web pages visited, and websites often create cookies to track certain information about visitors. An investigator tracking the origin of an e-mail seeks out the sender's IP address in the e-mail's header. Chat and instant messages are typically located in a computer's random-access memory (RAM). Finding the origin of unauthorized computer intrusions (hacking) requires the investigation of a computer's log file, RAM, and network traffic, among other things.

Review Questions

1. A(n) _____ consists of two or more computers that are connected to share information.

2. The device that allows computers to exchange and transmit information through telephone lines is a(n) _____.

3. A _____ is a name assigned to an IP address that can be interpreted or "read" by the user.

4. The most popular area of the Internet from which information can be searched and retrieved is known as the _____.

5. True or False: The URL is a unique electronic address that indicates where a document is actually located. _____

6. True or False: The advantage of using hypertext is to be able to quickly switch back and forth between related web pages without having to retype the URL or to start over at the beginning of the search. _____

7. Typically, a user enters a keyword or phrase into a(n) _____ to locate sites on the Internet that are relevant to a particular subject.

8. True or False: Usenet is a communication system that transports messages across the world in a matter of seconds. _____

9. A(n) _____ takes the form of a series of numbers to route data to an appropriate location on the Internet.

10. A user's hard disk drive will _____ portions of web pages that have been visited.

11. A(n) _____ is placed on a hard disk drive by a website to track certain information about its visitors.

12. E-mails have the _____ address of the sender in the header portion of the mail.

13. True or False: Chat and instant messages conducted over the Internet are typically stored in RAM storage. _____

14. When investigating a hacking incident, investigators concentrate their efforts on three locations: _____, _____, and _____.

15. Devices that permit only requested traffic to enter a computer system are known as _____.

Application and Critical Thinking

1. List the top-level domain most likely to be assigned to each of the following websites:
   a) An online car dealership
   b) The official website of the U.S. Coast Guard
   c) A local humane society
   d) The website of the U.S. Department of Justice
   e) Your school's website

2. You are examining two computers to determine the IP address from which several threatening e-mails were sent. The first computer uses Microsoft Outlook as an e-mail client and the second uses a web-based e-mail client. Where would you probably look first for the IP addresses in each of these computers?

Endnote

1. An excellent history of the Internet is found in Katie Hefner and Matthew Lyon, *Where Wizards Stay Up Late: The Origins of the Internet* (New York: Simon & Schuster, 1996).

Appendixes

Appendix I
Guides to the Collection of Physical Evidence—FBI

| Specimen | Amount Desired | | Send By |
	Standard	Evidence	
Abrasives	Not less than one ounce.	All	Registered mail or equivalent
Ammunition (Live Cartridges)			Live ammunition must be shipped via Federal Express. The following guidelines must be followed to comply with U.S. Department of Transportation regulations. Pack ammunition in a cardboard container. Label invoices FEDERAL EXPRESS. The shipper's certification for restricted articles must be included. The outside of the container must be labeled ORMD AIR, CARTRIDGES SMALL ARMS. The shipping papers must also include the weight in grams.
Anonymous Letters, and Bank Robbery Notes		Documentary evidence It should not be folded, torn, marked, soiled, stamped, written on, or handled unnecessarily. Protect the evidence from inadvertent indented writing. Mark documents unobtrusively by writing the collector's initials, date, and other information with a pencil. Whenever possible, submit the original evidence to the Laboratory. The lack of detail in photocopies makes examinations difficult. Copies are sufficient for reference file searches.	Registered mail or equivalent
Bullets (projector without cartridge) (Live Cartridges)	All found.		Same as Ammunition
Cartridge Cases (shells only)		All	Same as Ammunition

Source: *Courtesy of the Federal Bureau of Investigation, Washington, D.C.*

Identification	Wrapping and Packing	Remarks
Outside container: type of material, date obtained, investigator's name or initials.	Submit abrasives in heat-sealed or resealable plastic bags or paint cans. Avoid using paper or glass containers.	Abrasives settle in oil and fuel. Submit the oil and fuel from the engine sump and/or filters. Abrasives embed in bearings and other parts. Submit the bearings and other parts.
Same as above.	Ammunition components such as bullets, cartridge cases and shotshell casings can be sent via registered mail through the U.S. Postal Service. Evidence should be packaged separately and identified by date, time, location, collector's name, case number, and evidence number.	Unless specific examination of the cartridge is essential, do not submit.
Initial and date each document, if advisable.	Use proper enclosure. Place in envelope and seal with "Evidence" tape or transparent cellophane tape. Flap side of envelope should show: (1) wording "Enclosure(s) to FBI from (name of submitting office)," (2) title of case, (3) brief description of contents, (4) file number, if known. Staple to original letter of transmittal.	Do not handle with bare hands. Advise if evidence should be treated for latent fingerprints. Whenever possible, submit the original evidence to the laboratory. The lack of detail in photocopies makes examinations difficult. Copies are sufficient for reference file searches.
Do not mark bullets, cartridges and cartridge cases, and shotshells and shotshell casings. The date, time, location, collector's name, case number, and evidence number should be on the container.	Pack tightly in cotton or soft paper in pill, match, or powder box. Place in box. Label outside of box as to contents.	Unnecessary handling obliterates marks.
Same as above.	Same as above.	Spent cartridge cases.

Specimen	Amount Desired		Send By
	Standard	**Evidence**	
Casts (Dental or Die Stone Casts of Tire Treads and Shoe Prints)	Send in suspect's shoes and tires. Photographs and sample impressions are usually not suitable for comparison.	All shoe prints and entire circumference of tires.	Registered mail or equivalent
Checks (fraudulent)		See Anonymous Letter (p. 632)	Registered mail or equivalent
Check Protector, Rubber Stamp, and/or Date Stamp Known Standards (if possible, send actual device)	Obtain several copies in full word-for-word order of each questioned check-writer impression. If unable to forward rubber stamps, prepare numerous samples with different degrees of pressure.		Registered mail or equivalent
Clothing		All	Registered mail or equivalent
DNA Examinations (see pp. 644–646)			
Documents (charred or burned)		All	Registered mail or equivalent
Drugs:			
1. Liquids		All	Registered mail or equivalent
2. Powders, Pills, and Solids		All to 30 g.	Registered mail or equivalent
EXPLOSIVES: Detonators, Blasting Caps, Detonating Cord, Black Powder, Smokeless Powder, Explosives, and Accessories: call FBI Laboratory, for shipping instructions.			
Fibers	Entire garment or other cloth item.	All	Registered mail or equivalent
Firearms (unloaded weapons)		Firearms must be packaged and shipped separately from live ammunition. All firearms must be unloaded.	Firearms and ammunition components such as bullets, cartridge cases, and shotshell casings can be sent via registered mail through the U.S. Postal Service. Evidence must be packaged separately and identified by date, time, location, collector's name, case number, and evidence number.

Identification	Wrapping and Packing	Remarks
On back of cast before it hardens, write location and date taken, and investigator's name or initials.	Wrap in paper and cover with suitable packing material to prevent breakage. Label "Fragile." Plaster of Paris is no longer recommended.	For shoeprint and tire tread file searches, submit quality photographs of the impressions. If photographs are not available, submit casts, lifts, or the original evidence. Detailed sketches or photocopies are acceptable.
See Anonymous Letters on p. 632.	See Anonymous Letters on p. 632.	Advise what parts are questioned or known. Furnish physical description of subject.
Place name or initials, date, name of make and model, etc., on sample impressions.	See Anonymous Letters on p. 632.	Do not disturb inking mechanisms on printing devices.
Mark directly on garment or use string tag indicating type of evidence, date obtained, investigator's name or initials.	Wrap each article individually. Place in strong container with identification written on outside of package.	Do not cut out stains, leave clothing whole. If wet, hang in room to dry before packing.
Outside container: indicate if fragile, date obtained, investigator's name or initials.	Pack in rigid container between layers of cotton.	If moisture is added use atomizer, otherwise, not recommended.
Affix label to bottle in which found, including date it was found and investigator's name or initials.	Make sure container does not leak. Seal with tape to prevent any loss.	Mark "Fragile." If possible, use heat-seal plastic bags.
Outside of pillbox: affix label with date found and investigator's name or initials.	Seal with tape to prevent any loss.	If powder, pills, or solids are found in paper bags, place them in plastic bags to prevent any loss. Do not submit used drug field test kits with evidence.
Outside container or on the object fibers are adhering, include date and investigator's name or initials.	Use folder paper or pillbox. Seal edges and openings with tape.	Do not place loose in an envelope.
Do not mark the firearm. Firearms should be identified with a tag containing the caliber, make, model, and serial number. The date, time, owner(s)' name(s), location, collector's name, case number, and evidence number should be on the container.	Wrap in paper and identify contents of packages. Place in cardboard box or wooden box.	The firearm should be handled minimally to avoid loss or destruction of evidence. Do not allow objects to enter or contact the firearm's barrel, chamber, or other operating surface.

Specimen	Amount Desired		Send By
	Standard	Evidence	
Flash Paper	One sheet	All to 5 sheets.	Call FBI Laboratory.
Gasoline	10 ml	All to 10 ml	Call Chemistry-Toxicology Unit for instructions.
General Unknown:			
1. Solids (nonhazardous)	10 gm	All to 10 gm	Registered mail or equivalent
2. Liquids (non-hazardous)	10 ml	All to 10 ml	Registered mail or equivalent
Glass Fractures		All	Registered mail or equivalent
Glass Particles	Submit the victim(s)' and suspect's air-dried clothing. Each item must be packaged separately in a paper bag. Search for particles in the victim(s)' and Suspect(s)' hair, skin, and wounds. Submit particles in leakproof containers such as film canisters or plastic pill bottles. Do not use paper or glass containers. Search for particles in vehicles by vacuuming each section of the vehicle separately. Do not use tape for covering glass particles. Submit vacuum sweepings in leakproof containers. Do not use paper or glass containers.	All	Registered mail or equivalent

Identification	Wrapping and Packing	Remarks
Outside container: label indicating date and investigator's name or initials.	Flash paper is a hazardous material. Do not store flash paper near combustible materials. Seal flash paper in polyethylene envelopes and refrigerate.	
Outside container: label indicating type of material, date, and investigator's name or initials.	Use an all-metal container packed in wooden box.	An all-metal container should be used for its fireproof qualities.
Outside container: label indicating date and investigator's name or initials.	Same as Drugs (see p. 634).	Call Chemistry-Toxicology Unit for instructions.
Same as Liquid Drugs (see p. 634).	Same as Liquid Drugs (see p. 634).	Same as above.
Label the sides of the glass in the frame INSIDE and OUTSIDE. Label the glass where it was removed in the frame such as TOP, BOTTOM, LEFT, and RIGHT.	Wrap each piece separately in cotton. Pack in sturdy container to prevent shifting and breakage. Identify contents.	Submit all glass pieces so that the pieces can be fitted together to identify the radial cracks near and at the point(s) of impact and to increase the probability of matching edges. Pack all glass separately and securely to avoid shifting and breaking during transport.
Outside container: label indicating date and investigator's name or initials.	Place in film canister or plastic vial. Seal and protect against breakage.	Submit samples of glass from each broken window or source in leakproof containers such as film canisters or plastic pill bottles. Avoid using paper or glass containers.

| | Amount Desired | | |
Specimen	Standard	Evidence	Send By
Gunshot Residues The Laboratory provides gunshot residue examinations to assist FBI field office investigations only.		Usually gunshot residue examinations will only be performed when samples are collected from living person's hands. Gunshot residue evidence must be collected within five hours of exposure to the discharge of a firearm.	
On cloth only to determine weapon to target distance.		All	Clothing submitted for gunshot residue examination should be handled carefully, air dried, and wrapped separately in paper. Clothing with blood must be air dried and labeled BIOHAZARD on the inner and outer containers. The date, time, location, collector's name, case number, and evidence number should be on the container.
Hair	Twenty-five full-length hairs from different parts of head and/or pubic region.	All	Registered mail or equivalent
Handwriting and Hand Printing Known Standards			Registered mail or equivalent
Insulation **1.** Glass Wool	1″ mass from each suspect area.	All	Registered mail or equivalent
2. Safe	Sample all damaged areas.	All	Registered mail or equivalent
Matches	One to two books of paper. One full box of wood.	All	Federal Express, UPS, or equivalent
Obliterated, Eradicated, or Indented Writing		Same as Anonymous Letters (see p. 632).	Registered mail or equivalent

Identification	Wrapping and Packing	Remarks
		Collecting gunshot residue samples requires five adhesive lifts suitable for scanning electron microscopic analysis. Dab the adhesive side of the stub against the surface (right palm, back of right hand, left palm, back of left hand). Use one stub per sampling surface. The remaining stub will be used as a control. Label each sampling surface stub (e.g., RIGHT PALM, BACK OF RIGHT HAND). Cap and seal the stubs in separate, resealable plastic bags.
Outside container: Indicate date, obtained from whom, description, name or initials.	Dry and package individually in unused brown wrapping paper or brown grocery bag.	The deposition of gunshot residue on evidence such as clothing varies with the distance from the muzzle of the firearm to the target. Patterns of gunshot residue can be duplicated using a questioned firearm and ammunition combination fired into test materials at known distances. These patterns serve as a basis for estimating muzzle-to-garment distances.
Outside container: Type of material, date, and investigator's name or initials.	Folded paper or pillbox. Seal edges and openings with tape.	Do not place loose in envelope.
Indicate from whom obtained, voluntary statement included in appropriate place, date obtained, and investigator's name or initials.	Same as Anonymous Letters (see p. 632).	Same as Anonymous Letters (see p. 632).
Outside container: type of material, date, name or initials.	Use pillbox or plastic vial. Seal to prevent any loss.	Submit known and questioned debris in leakproof containers such as film canisters or plastic pill bottles. Avoid using paper or glass containers. Pack to keep lumps intact.
Same as above.	Safe insulation can adhere to persons, clothing, tools, bags, and loot and can transfer to vehicles. If possible, submit the evidence to the Laboratory for examiners to remove the debris. Package each item of evidence in a separate paper bag. Do not process tools for latent prints.	
Outside container: label indicating type of material, date, and investigator's name or initials.	Pack in metal container and in larger package to prevent shifting. Pack matches in box or metal container to prevent friction between matches.	Keep and label: "Keep away from fire."
Same as Anonymous Letters (see p. xxx).	Same as Anonymous Letters (see p. 632).	Advise whether bleaching or staining methods may be used. Avoid folding.

	Amount Desired		
Specimen	**Standard**	**Evidence**	**Send By**
Organs of the Body		200 g of each organ.	Call Chemistry-Toxicology Unit for instructions.
Paint:			
1. Liquid	Original unopened container up to 1/4 pint, if possible.	All to 1/4 pint.	Registered mail or equivalent
2. Solid (paint chips or scrapings)	At least 1/2 sq. in. of solid, with all layers represented.	Standard: Control paint chips must be collected from the suspected source of the evidentiary paint. Controls must be taken from an area close to, but not in, any damaged area. If no damage is obvious, controls should be taken from several areas of the suspect substrate. Each layer can be a point of comparison. Controls must have all of the layers of paint to the substrate.	Registered mail or equivalent
Rope, Twine, and Cordage	One yard or amount available.	Submit the entire rope or cord. If the rope or cord must be cut, specify which end was cut during evidence collection. Label the known and questioned samples. Handle the sections of rope or cord carefully to prevent loss of trace material or contamination.	Registered mail or equivalent
Saliva Samples	1.5″ diameter stain in center of filter paper.	All	Registered mail or equivalent
Shoe Print Lifts (impressions on hard surfaces)	Photograph before making lift of dust impression.	For shoeprint and tire tread comparisons, submit original evidence whenever possible (shoes, tires, photographic negatives, casts, lifts).	Registered mail or equivalent
Soils and Minerals	Samples from areas near pertinent spot.	Collect soil samples from the immediate crime scene area and from the logical access and/or escape route(s). Collect soil samples at a depth that is consistent with the depth from which the questioned soil may have originated. If possile, collect soil samples from alibi areas such as the yard or work area of the suspect(s).	Registered mail

Identification	Wrapping and Packing	Remarks
Each biological specimen must be placed in a separate, labeled, sealed glass tube, plastic cup, or heat-sealed or resealable plastic bag. Affix BIOHAZARD labels to the inside and outside containers.	To avoid deterioration, biological specimens must be refrigerated or frozen during storage and shipping. Pack so that no breakage, leakage, or contamination occurs.	Submit a copy of the autopsy or incident report. Describe the symptoms of the suspect(s) or victim(s) at the time of the crime or prior to the death. List any known or questioned drugs consumed by or prescribed for the suspect(s) or victim(s). Describe any known or questioned environmental exposure to toxic substances by the suspect(s) or victim(s).
Outside container: Type of material, origin if known, date, investigator's name or initials. Same as above.	Use friction-top paint can or large-mouth, screw-top jar. If glass, pack to prevent breakage. Use heavy corrugated paper or wooden box. Package paint specimens in leakproof containers such as vials or pillboxes. Do not stick paint particles on adhesive tape. Do not use plastic bags, cotton, or envelopes to package paint specimens.	Protect spray can nozzles to keep them from going off. Avoid contact w/adhesive materials. Wrap to protect paint smears. Do not use envelopes, paper/plastic bags, or glass vials. Avoid contact with adhesive materials. Wrap so as to protect smear. If *small amount:* seal round pillbox, film cannister, or plastic vial to protect against leakage/breakage.
On tag or container: Type of material, date, investigator's name or initials.	Submit in heat-sealed or resealable plastic or paper bags.	
Outside envelope and on filter paper: Type of sample, name of donor, date of collection, and collector's initials or name.	Seal in envelope.	Stain should be circled in pencil for identification. Filter paper available from hospitals and drugstores. Allow to dry.
On lifting tape or paper attached to tape: date, investigator's name or initials.	Prints in dust are easily damaged. Fasten print or lift to bottom of box so that nothing will rub against it.	Always secure crime-scene area until shoe prints or tire treads are located and preserved.
Outside container: Type of material, date, investigator's name or initials.	Do not remove soil adhering to shoes, clothing, and tools. Do not process tools for latent prints. Air-dry the soil and the clothing and package separately in paper bags. Carefully remove soil adhering to vehicles. Air-dry the soil and package separately in paper bags.	Ship known and questioned debris separately to avoid contamination. Submit known and questioned soil in leakproof containers such as film canisters or plastic pill bottles. Do not use paper envelopes or glass containers. Pack to keep lumps intact.

Specimen	Amount Desired		Send By
	Standard	**Evidence**	
Tape (Adhesive Tape)	Recovered roll.	All	Registered mail or equivalent
Tools/Toolmarks	Send in the tool. If impractical, make several impressions on similar materials as evidence using entire marking area of tool.	If it is not possible to submit the tool-marked evidence, submit a cast of the toolmark.	Registered mail or equivalent
Typewriting, known standards	See Anonymous Letters (p. 632).		Registered mail or equivalent
Wire	3 ft. (Do not kink.)	All (Do not kink.)	Registered mail or equivalent
Wood	One foot or amount available.	All	Registered mail or equivalent

Identification	Wrapping and Packing	Remarks
Same as above.	Place on waxed paper, cellophane, or plastic.	Do not cut, wad, distort, or separate tapes that are stuck together.
On object or on tag attached to an opposite end from where toolmarks appear: date recovered and investigator's name or initials.	After marks have been protected with soft paper, wrap in strong wrapping paper, place in strong box, and pack to prevent shifting.	Photographs locate tool-marks but are of no value for identification purposes. Obtain samples of any material deposited on the tools. To avoid contamination, do not place the tool against the toolmarked evidence. Submit the tool rather than making test cuts or impressions. Mark the ends of the evidence and specify which end was cut during evidence collection.
On specimens: serial number, brand, model, etc., date recovered, and investigator's name or initials.	Same as Anonymous Letters (p. 632).	Examine ribbon for evidence of questioned message.
On label or tab: describe type of material, date, investigator's name or initials.	Wrap securely.	Do not kink wire.
Same as above.	Submit wood in heat-sealed or resealable plastic of paper bags.	

DNA Examinations

Deoxyribonucleic acid (DNA) is analyzed in body fluids, stains, and other biological tissues recovered from evidence. The results of DNA analysis of questioned biological samples are compared with the results of DNA analysis of known samples. This analysis can associate victim(s) and/or suspect(s) with each other or with a crime scene.

There are two sources of DNA used in forensic analyses. Nuclear DNA (nDNA) is typically analyzed in evidence containing blood, semen, saliva, body tissues, and hairs that have tissue at their root ends. Mitochondrial DNA (mtDNA) is typically analyzed in evidence containing naturally shed hairs, hair fragments, bones, and teeth.

If DNA evidence is not properly documented, collected, packaged, and preserved, it will not meet the legal and scientific requirements for admissibility in a court of law.

- If it is not properly documented, its origin can be questioned.
- If it is not properly collected, biological activity can be lost.
- If it is not properly packaged, contamination can occur.
- If it is not properly preserved, decomposition and deterioration can occur.

When DNA evidence is transferred by direct or secondary (indirect) means, it remains on surfaces by absorption or adherence. In general, liquid biological evidence is absorbed into surfaces, and solid biological evidence adheres to surfaces. Collecting, packaging, and preserving DNA evidence depends on the liquid or solid state and the condition of the evidence.

The more that evidence retains its original integrity until it reaches the Laboratory, the greater the possibility of conducting useful examinations. It may be necessary to use a variety of techniques to collect suspected body fluid evidence.

Blood Examinations

Examinations can determine the presence or absence of blood in stains. Examinations can also determine whether blood is human or not. Blood examinations cannot determine the age or the race of a person. Conventional serological techniques are not adequately informative to positively identify a person as the source of a stain.

Collecting Known Samples

Blood

- Only qualified medical personnel should collect blood samples from a person.
- Collect at least two 5-ml tubes of blood in purple-top tubes with EDTA as an anticoagulant for DNA analysis. Collect drug- or alcohol-testing samples in gray-top tubes with NaF (sodium fluoride).
- Identify each tube with the date, time, subject's name, location, collector's name, case number, and evidence number.
- Refrigerate, do not freeze blood samples. Use cold packs, not dry ice, during shipping.
- Pack liquid blood tubes individually in Styrofoam or cylindrical tubes with absorbent material surrounding the tubes.
- Label the outer container KEEP IN A COOL DRY PLACE, REFRIGERATE ON ARRIVAL, and BIOHAZARD.
- Submit to the Laboratory as soon as possible.

Blood on a Person

- Absorb suspected **liquid blood** onto a clean cotton cloth or swab. Leave a portion of the cloth or swab unstained as a control. Air-dry the cloth or swab and pack in clean paper or an envelope with sealed corners. Do not use plastic containers.
- Absorb suspected **dried blood** onto a clean cotton cloth or swab moistened with distilled water. Leave a portion of the cloth or swab unstained as a control. Air-dry the cloth or swab and pack in clean paper or an envelope with sealed corners. Do not use plastic containers.

Blood on Surfaces or in Snow or Water

- Absorb suspected **liquid blood or blood clots** onto a clean cotton cloth or swab. Leave a portion of the cloth or swab unstained as a control. Air-dry the cloth or swab and pack in clean paper or an envelope with sealed corners. Do not use plastic containers.

- Collect suspected **blood in snow or water** immediately to avoid further dilution. Eliminate as much snow as possible. Place in a clean airtight container. Freeze the evidence and submit as soon as possible to the Laboratory.

Bloodstains

- Air-dry **wet bloodstained garments.** Wrap **dried bloodstained garments** in clean paper. Do not place wet or dried garments in plastic or airtight containers. Place all debris or residue from the garments in clean paper or an envelope with sealed corners.
- Air-dry small suspected **wet bloodstained objects** and submit the objects to the Laboratory. Preserve bloodstain patterns. Avoid creating additional stain patterns during drying and packaging. Pack to prevent stain removal by abrasive action during shipping. Pack in clean paper. Do not use plastic containers.
- When possible, cut a large sample of suspected **bloodstains from immovable objects** with a clean, sharp instrument. Collect an unstained control sample. Pack to prevent strain removal by abrasive action during shipping. Pack in clean paper. Do not use plastic containers.
- Absorb suspected **dried bloodstains on immovable objects** onto a clean cotton cloth or swab moistened with distilled water. Leave a portion of the cloth or swab unstained as a control. Air-dry the cloth or swab and pack in clean paper or an envelope with sealed corners. Do not use plastic containers.

Blood Examination Request Letter

A blood examination request letter must contain the following information:

- A brief statement of facts relating to the case.
- Claims made by the suspect(s) regarding the source of the blood.
- Whether animal blood is present.
- Whether the stains were laundered or diluted with other body fluids.
- Information regarding the victim(s)' and suspect(s)' health such as AIDS, hepatitis, or tuberculosis.

Semen and Semen Stains

- Absorb suspected **liquid semen** onto a clean cotton cloth or swab. Leave a portion of the cloth or swab unstained as a control. Air-dry the cloth or swab and pack in clean paper or an envelope with sealed corners. Do not use plastic containers.
- Submit small suspected **dry semen-stained objects** to the Laboratory. Pack to prevent stain removal by abrasive action during shipping. Pack in clean paper. Do not use plastic containers.
- When possible, cut a large sample of suspected **semen stains from immovable objects** with a clean, sharp instrument. Collect an unstained control sample. Pack to prevent stain removal by abrasive action during shipping. Pack in clean paper. Do not use plastic containers.
- Absorb suspected **dried semen stains on immovable objects** onto a clean cotton cloth or swab moistened with distilled water. Leave a portion of the cloth or swab unstained as a control. Air-dry the swab or cloth and place in clean paper or an envelope with sealed corners. Do not use plastic containers.

Seminal Evidence from Sexual Assault Victim(s)

- Sexual assault victim(s) must be medically examined in a hospital or a physician's office using a standard sexual assault evidence kit to collect vaginal, oral, and anal evidence.
- Refrigerate and submit the evidence as soon as possible to the Laboratory.

Buccal (Oral) Swabs

- Use clean cotton swabs to collect buccal (oral) samples. Rub the inside surfaces of the cheeks thoroughly.
- Air-dry the swabs and place in clean paper or an envelope with sealed corners. Do not use plastic containers.
- Identify each sample with the date, time subject's name, location, collector's name, case number, and evidence number.
- Buccal samples do not need to be refrigerated.

Saliva and Urine

- Absorb suspected **liquid saliva or urine** onto a clean cotton cloth or swab. Leave a portion of the cloth unstained as a control. Air-dry the cloth or swab and pack in clean paper or an envelope with sealed corners. Do not use plastic containers.

- Submit suspected small, **dry saliva- or urine-stained objects** to the Laboratory. Pack to prevent stain removal by abrasive action during shipping. Pack in clean paper or an envelope with sealed corners. Do not use plastic containers.

- When possible, cut a large sample of suspected **saliva or urine stains from immovable objects** with a clean, sharp instrument. Collect an unstained control sample. Pack to prevent stain removal by abrasive action during shipping. Pack in clean paper. Do not use plastic containers.

- Pick up **cigarette butts** with gloved hands or clean forceps. Do not submit ashes. Air-dry and place the cigarette butts from the same location (e.g., ashtray) in clean paper or an envelope with sealed corners. Do not submit the ashtray unless a latent print examination is requested. Package the ashtray separately. Do not use plastic containers.

- Pick up **chewing gum** with gloved hands or clean forceps. Air-dry and place in clean paper or an envelope with sealed corners. Do not use plastic containers.

- Pick up **envelops and stamps** with gloved hands or clean forceps and place in a clean envelope. Do not use plastic containers.

Hair

- Pick up hair carefully with clean forceps to prevent damaging the root tissue.
- Air-dry hair mixed with suspected body fluids.
- Package each group of hair separately in clean paper or an envelope with sealed corners. Do not use plastic containers.
- Refrigerate and submit as soon as possible to the Laboratory.

Tissues, Bones, and Teeth

- Pick up suspected tissues, bones, and teeth with gloved hands or clean forceps.
- Collect 1–2 cubic inches of red skeletal muscle.
- Collect 3–5 inches of long bone such as the fibula or femur.
- Collect teeth in the following order:
    1. nonrestored molar.
    2. nonrestored premolar.
    3. nonrestored canine.
    4. nonrestored front tooth.
    5. restored molar.
    6. restored premolar.
    7. restored canine.
    8. restored front tooth.
- Place tissue samples in a clean, airtight plastic container without formalin or formaldehyde. Place teeth and bone samples in clean paper or an envelope with sealed corners.
- Freeze the evidence, place in Styrofoam containers, and ship overnight on dry ice.

INSTRUCTIONS FOR COLLECTING GUNSHOT RESIDUE (GSR)
for Scanning Electron Microscopy and Atomic Absorption Analysis

---
NOTE

In control test firings, it has been shown that the concentration of gunshot residue significantly declines on living subjects after approximately 4 hours. In view of these findings, if more than 4 hours have passed since the shooting, it is recommended that you check with your crime laboratory before submitting samples for analysis.

S.E.M. COLLECTION PROCEDURE

(A) When the covering is removed from the metal stubs, the adhesive collecting surface is exposed and care must be used to not drop the stub or contaminate the collecting surface by allowing this exposed surface to come in contact with an object other than the area that is to be sampled. (See Figure 1.)

(B) *Do not* return paper stub cover to stubs after collection. (*Discard stub covers.*)

(C) Heavily soiled or bloody areas should be avoided if possible.

(D) When pressing the stubs on the questioned areas, use enough pressure to cause a mild indentation on the surface of the subject's hand.

STEP 1   Fill out all information requested on the enclosed Gunshot Residue Analysis Information Form.

STEP 2   Put on the disposable plastic gloves provided in this kit. *Do not substitute with other gloves!*

> NOTE: If there is blood on the subject's hands or clothing, the investigating officer should put on latex or other approved barrier gloves to protect him/her from bloodborne pathogens, then put on the plastic gloves provided in this kit.

STEP 3   <u>RIGHT BACK:</u>

(A) Carefully remove the cap from the vial labeled RIGHT BACK, then remove the paper covering from the metal sample stub.

(B) While holding the vial cap, press the collecting surface of the stub onto the back of the subject's right hand until the area shown below in Figure 2 has been covered.

(C) After sampling the back of the subject's right hand, return the cap, with metal stub, to the RIGHT BACK vial. *Do not return paper covering to metal stub!*

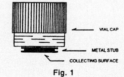

VIAL CAP

METAL STUB

COLLECTING SURFACE

Fig. 1

STEP 4   <u>RIGHT PALM:</u>

Repeat the procedure described in Step 3, using the metal stub in the vial marked RIGHT PALM. Make sure to sample the area shown below in Figure 3.

STEP 5   <u>LEFT BACK and LEFT PALM:</u>

For collection from the left hand, repeat Steps 3 and 4 using the vials labeled LEFT BACK and LEFT PALM.

STEP 6   After sampling all four areas, return capped vials to kit envelope.

Fig. 2   (BACK)

Fig. 3   (PALM)

Source: Tri-Tech, Inc., Southport, N.C., www.tritechusa.com

A.A. COLLECTION PROCEDURE

NOTE: (A) This second part of the GSR collection is *ONLY* to be performed *AFTER* sampling with the SEM stubs.

(B) If you feel that during the SEM collection procedure you have contaminated the gloves, discard contaminated gloves, then thoroughly wash your hands with soap and water and dry with a clean towel. At no time during the collection process should your hands (with or without gloves) come into contact with the cotton tip of the swab.

(C) When dispensing nitric acid, use 2 - 3 drops of 5% nitric acid solution to moisten each swab (do not over-moisten). In order to dispense an appropriate amount of the nitric acid solution, hold the acid dispenser in a horizontal position above and *almost* touching the top of the swab, and squeeze gently.

(D) To swab the subject's hands, the investigator should grasp the subject's arm above the wrist with one hand and swab with the other. The subject's hand should be in a "spread" position. Thorough swabbing of the hands is carried out by using moderate pressure while swabbing. The swab should be rotated during this procedure to insure that all of the surface of the cotton tip is utilized. At least 30 seconds per swab is required.

(E) When placing swabs in tubes, always place cotton tips *FACE DOWN*.

STEP 7 <u>CONTROL SWABS:</u> Remove *two* of the swabs from the unmarked ziplock bag. Moisten both swabs with 2 - 3 drops of the 5% nitric acid solution supplied in kit (do not substitute). Place both swabs in the tube labeled CONTROL. Then recap tube and set it aside.

STEP 8 <u>RIGHT BACK:</u>

(A) Moisten the tip of *ONE* swab with 2 - 3 drops of nitric acid solution, then thoroughly swab the back of the subject's right hand including the back of the fingers and all of the web area which would be exposed while holding a weapon. Fig. 4 illustrates the area of hand for swabbing. Place swab used in the tube labeled RIGHT BACK.

(B) Repeat the above procedure using a *SECOND* swab. Place the second swab used in the RIGHT BACK tube, then recap tube and set it aside.

Fig. 4 (BACK)

STEP 9 <u>RIGHT PALM:</u>

(A) Moisten the tip of *ONE* swab with 2 - 3 drops of nitric acid solution, then thoroughly swab the palm of the subject's right hand as shown in Fig. 5. Place swab used in the tube labeled RIGHT PALM.

(B) Repeat the above procedure using a *SECOND* swab. Place the second swab used in the RIGHT PALM tube, then recap tube and set it aside.

Fig. 5 (PALM)

STEP 10 <u>LEFT BACK/LEFT PALM:</u> Follow the same procedures described in Steps 8 and 9, but swabbing the subject's left hand.

STEP 11 <u>CARTRIDGE CASE:</u>

NOTE: For .22 cal and foreign manufactured ammunition, it is necessary that either Steps A and B described below be completed <u>OR</u> the casings be submitted to the laboratory. If latent prints are required on the expended casing(s), Steps A and B should be omitted and the casings should be submitted for latent print processing. If for any reason the CARTRIDGE CASE swabs are not used, mark the tube "*NOT USED*".

(A) Moisten the tip of *ONE* swab with 2 - 3 drops of nitric acid solution, then thoroughly swab the inside of the cartridge case. Place swab used in the tube labeled CARTRIDGE CASE.

(B) Repeat the above procedure using a *SECOND* swab. Place second swab used in the CARTRIDGE CASE tube, and then recap tube and set it aside.

FINAL INSTRUCTIONS

(A) Fill out all information requested on the front of the kit envelope.

(B) With the exception of the 5% nitric acid dispenser and the disposable gloves, return all other kit components, used or unused, to kit envelope.

(C) Moisten kit envelope flap, then seal envelope. Affix Police Evidence Seal where indicated, then initial seal.

(D) Mail or hand deliver sealed kit to the crime laboratory for analysis. (If mailed, package kit in a cardboard box to prevent damage in transit.)

Appendix III
Chemical Formulas for Latent Fingerprint Development

Iodine Spray Reagent

1. Prepare the following stock solutions:

   Solution A

   Dissolve gram of Iodine in 1 liter of Cyclohexane

   Solution B

   Dissolve 5 grams of a-Naphthoflavone in 40 ml of Methylene Chloride (Dichloramethane)

2. Add 2 ml of Solution B to 100 ml of Solution A. Using a magnetic stirrer, mix thoroughly for 5 minutes.
3. Filter the solution through a facial tissue, paper towel, filter paper, etc., into a beaker. The solution should be lightly sprayed on the specimen using an aerosol spray unit or a mini spray gun powered with compressed air.
4. Lightly spray the suspect area with several applications until latent prints sufficiently develop.

Remarks

- Solution A may be stored at room temperature. Shelf life is in excess of 30 days.
- Solution B must be refrigerated. Shelf life is in excess of 30 days.
- The combined working solution (A and B) should be used within 24 hours after mixing.
- The Iodine Spray solution is effective on most surfaces (porous and non-porous).
- A fine spray mist is the most effective form of application.
- The Cyanocrylate (Super Glue) process cannot be used prior to the Iodine Spray Reagent Process. Cyanoacrylate may be used, however, after the Iodine Spray Reagent.
- On porous surfaces, DFO and/or Ninhydrin may be used after the Iodine Spray.
- Propanol may be used to remove the staining of the Iodine Spray Reagent.
- 1,1,2 Trichlorotrifluoroethane may be substituted for Cyclohexane.

1,8-Diazafluoren-9-one (DFO)

Step 1: Stock solution: Dissolve 1 gram DFO in 200 ml Methanol, 200 ml Ethyl Acetate, and 40 ml Acetic Acid.

Step 2: Working solution (make as needed): Start with stock solution and dilute to 2 liters with Petroleum Ether (40° to 60° boiling point fraction). Pentane can also be used. Solution should be clear.

Source: In part from Processing Guide for Developing Latent Prints, Revised 2000. Washington, D.C.: FBI. http://njiai.org/fbi_2000_lp_guide.pdf

Dip the paper document into the working solution and allow to dry. Dip again and allow to dry. When completely dry, apply heat (200° for 10 to 20 minutes). An oven, hair dryer, or dry iron can be used.

Visualize with an alternate light source at 450, 485, 525, and 530 nm and observe through orange goggles. If the surface paper is yellow, such as legal paper, it may be necessary to visualize the paper at 570 nm and view it through red goggles.

1,2-indanedione
2.0 g 1,2-indanedione
70 ml ethyl acetate
930 ml HFE 7100 (3M Company)

Ninhydrin

20 grams Ninhydrin
3,300 ml Acetone
Shelf life is approximately one month

or

5 grams Ninhydrin
30 ml Methanol
40 ml 2-Propanol
930 ml Petroleum Ether
Shelf life is approximately one year

Dip the paper document in the working solution and allow to dry. Dip again and allow to dry. When completely dry, heat may be applied. A steam iron should be used on the steam setting. Do not touch the iron directly to the paper. Rather, hold the iron above the paper and allow the steam to heat it.

Zinc Chloride Solution (Post-Ninhydrin Treatment)

5 grams of Zinc Chloride crystals
2 ml of Glacial Acetic Acid
100 ml of Methyl Alcohol
Add 400 ml of 1,1,2 Trichlorotrifluoroethane to the mixture and stir.
Add 2 ml of 5 percent Sodium Hypochlorite solution (commercially available liquid bleach such as Clorox, Purex, and others).

Lightly spray the paper with the Zinc solution. Repeat the spraying as needed. Do not overdo the spraying.

The ninhydrin-developed prints treated with this solution may fluoresce at room temperature with an alternate light source. For maximum fluorescence, place the paper in a bath of liquid nitrogen and examine again with an alternate light source.

Physical Developer

When mixing and using these solutions, make sure the glassware, processing trays, stirring rods, and stirring magnets are absolutely clean. Do not use metal trays or tweezer.

Stock Detergent Solution: 3 grams of N-Dodecylamine Acetate are combined with 4 grams of Synperonic-N mixed in 1 liter of distilled water.

Silver Nitrate Solution: 20 grams of Silver Nitrate crystals are mixed in 100 milliliters of distilled water.

Redox Solution: 60 grams of Ferric Nitrate are mixed in 1,800 milliliters of distilled water. After this solution is thoroughly mixed, add 160 grams of Ferrous Ammonium Sulfate, mix thoroughly and add 40 grams of Citric Acid, mix thoroughly.

Maleic Acid Solution: Put 50 grams of Maleic Acid into 2 liters of distilled water.

Physical Developer Working Solution: Begin with 2,125 milliliters of the Redox Solution and add 80 milliliters of the Stock Detergent Solution, mix well, then add 100 milliliters of the Silver Nitrate Solution and mix well. Appropriate divisions can be used if smaller amounts of the working solution are desired.

Immerse specimen in Maleic Acid Solution for 10 minutes

Incubate item in PD working solution for 15–20 minutes

Thoroughly rinse specimen in tap water for 20 minutes

Air-dry and photograph

Cyanoacrylate Fluorescent Enhancement Reagents

Rhodamine 6G

Stock Solution	Working Solution
100 mg Rhodamine 6G 100 ml Methanol (Stir until thoroughly dissolved.)	3 ml Rhodamine 6G Stock Solution 15 ml Acetone 10 ml Acetonitrile 15 ml Methanol 32 ml 2-Propanol 925 ml Petroleum Ether (Combine in order listed.)

Ardrox

2 ml Ardrox P-133D

10 ml Acetone

25 ml Methanol

10 ml 2-Propanol

8 ml Acetonitrile

945 ml Petroleum Ether

MBD

7-(p-methoxybenzylaminol)-4-nitrobenz-2-oxa-1,3-diazole

Stock Solution	Working Solution
100 mg MBD 100 ml Acetone	10 ml MBD Stock Solution 30 ml Methanol 10 ml 2-Propanol 950 ml Petroleum Ether (Combine in order listed.)

Basic Yellow 40

2 grams Basic Yellow 40
1 liter Methanol

RAM Combination Enhancer

3 ml Rhodamine 6G Stock Solution
2 ml Ardrox P-133D
7 ml MBD Stock Solution
20 ml Methanol
10 ml 2-Propanol
8 ml Acetonitrile
950 ml Petroleum Ether
(Combine in order listed.)

RAY Combination Enhancer*

To 940 ml of either isopropyl alcohol or denatured ethyl alcohol add:

1.0 gram of Basic Yellow 40
0.1 gram of Rhodamine 6G
8 ml of Arodrox P-133D
50 ml of Acetonitrile (optional, but dye stain of prints will appear more brilliant)

MRM 10 Combination Enhancer

3 ml Rhodamine 6G Stock Solution
3 ml Basic Yellow 40 Stock Solution
7 ml MBD Stock Solution
20 ml Methanol
10 ml 2-Propanol
8 ml Acetonitrile
950 ml Petroleum Ether
(Combine in order listed.)

The previous solutions are used on evidence that has been treated with cyanoacrylate (Super Glue) fumes. These solutions dye the cyanoacrylate residue adhering to the latent print residue. Wash the dye over the evidence. It may be necessary to rinse the surface with a solvent, such as Petroleum Ether, to remove the excess stain.

CAUTION: These solutions contain solvents that may be respiratory irritants, so they should be mixed and used in a fume hood or while wearing a full-face breathing apparatus. Also, these solvents may damage some plastics, cloth, wood, and painted surfaces.

Because of the respiratory irritation possible and the general inefficiency of spraying, it is not recommended to spray these solutions. To obtain the maximum benefit and coverage, it is recommended that evidence be soaked, submerged, or washed with these types of solutions.

Source of Chemicals

Ardrox P-133D, Basic Yellow 40, and Rhodamine 6G may be obtained from:

Lightning Powder Company, Inc.
Jacksonville, FL 32218
Telephone Number: 1-800-852-0300

MBD may be obtained from:

Sigma Chemical Company
P.O. Box 14508
St. Louis, MO 63178
Telephone Number: 1-800-325-3010

*Source: John H. Olenik, Freemont, Ohio.

Appendix IV
Chemical Formulas for Development of Footwear Impressions in Blood

Amido Black

Staining Solution:
0.2 g Napthalene 12B or Napthol Blue Black
10 ml Glacial Acetic Acid
90 ml Methanol

Rinsing Solution:
90 ml Methanol
10 ml Glacial Acetic Acid

Stain the impression by spraying or immersing the item in the staining solution for approximately one minute. Next, treat with the rinsing solution to remove stain from nonimpression area. Then rinse well with distilled water.

Coomassie Blue

Staining Solution: (Add in this order)
0.44 g Coomassie Brilliant Blue
200 ml Methanol
40 ml Glacial Acetic Acid
200 ml Distilled Water

Rinsing Solution:
40 ml Glacial Acetic Acid
200 ml Methanol
200 ml Distilled Water

Spray object with the staining solution, completely covering the area of interest. Then spray the object with rinsing solution, clearing the background. Then rinse with distilled water.

Crowle's Double Stain

Developer:
2.5 grams Crocein Scarlet 7B
150 mg Coomassie Brilliant Blue R
50 ml Glacial Acetic Acid
30 ml Trichloroacetic Acid

Combine the above ingredients, then dilute into one liter. Place the solution on a stirring device until all the Crocein Scarlet 7B and Coomassie Brillant Blue R are dissolved.

Rinse:
30 ml Glacial Acetic Acid
970 ml Distilled Water

Apply the developer to the item(s) by dipping. Completely cover the target area, leaving the developer on for approximately 30 to 90 seconds, then rinse. Finally, rinse well with distilled water.

Diaminobenzidine (DAB)

Solution A (Fixer solution):
20 g 5-Sulphosalicylic Acid
Dissolved in 1L Distilled Water

Solution B:
100 ml 1M Phosphate Buffer (pH 7.4)
800 ml Distilled Water

Solution C:
1 g Diaminobenzidine
Dissolved in 100 ml Distilled Water

Working Solution (Mix just prior to use):
900 ml solution B
100 ml solution C
5 ml 30% Hydrogen Peroxide

Immerse impression area in fixer solution A for approximately 4 minutes. Remove and rinse in distilled water. Immerse impression area for approximately 4 minutes in the working solution or until print is fully developed. Remove and rinse in distilled water.

Fuchsin Acid

20 g Sulfosalicylic Acid
2 g Fuchsin Acid
Dissolved in 1L Distilled Water

Stain the impression by spraying or immersing the item in the dye solution for approximately one minute. Rinse well with distilled water.

Hungarian Red

This product is available from:

ODV, Inc.
P.O. Box 180
S. Paris, ME 04281

Leucocrystal Violet

10 g 5-Sulfosalicylic Acid
500 ml 3% Hydrogen Peroxide
3.7 g Sodium Acetate
1 g Leucocrystal Violet

If Leucocrystal Violet crystals are yellow instead of white, do not use. This indicates crystals are old and solution will not work.

Spray the object until completely covered. Then allow object to air dry. Development of impressions will occur within 30 seconds. Store the solution in amber glassware and refrigerate.

Leucocrystal Violet Field Kit*

When the reagents are separated in the listed manner below, a "field kit" can be prepared. The field kit separation will allow for an extended shelf life.

Bottle A:
10 grams 5-Sulfosalicylic Acid
500 ml Hydrogen Peroxide 3%

Bottle B:
1.1 grams Leucocrystal Violet
Weigh out reagent and place in an amber 60 ml (2 ounce) bottle.

Bottle C:
4.4 grams Sodium Acetate
Weigh out reagent and place in an amber 60 ml (2 ounce) bottle.

Add approximately 30 ml of Bottle A reagent to Bottle B. Secure cap and shake Bottle B for two (2) to three (3) minutes. Pour contents of Bottle B back into Bottle A.

Add approximately 30 ml of Bottle A reagent to Bottle C. Secure cap and shake Bottle C for approximately two (2) to three (3) minutes. Pour contents of Bottle C into Bottle A. Secure Bottle A's cap and shake thoroughly.

Spray the target area; development will occur within thirty (30) seconds. After spraying, blot the area with a tissue or paper towel. Then allow object to air-dry.

Patent Blue

20 g Sulfosalicylic Acid
2 g Patent Blue V (VF)
Dissolved in 1L Distilled Water

Stain object by spraying or immersing the item in the dye solution for approximately one minute. Rinse well with distilled water.

Tartrazine

20 g Sulfosalicylic Acid
2 g Tartrazine
Dissolved in 1L Distilled Water

Stain object by spraying or immersing the item in the dye solution for approximately one minute. Rinse well with distilled water.

---

*__Source:__ John Fisher, Forensic Research & Supply Corp., Gotha, Fla.

Answers to End-of-Chapter Questions

Chapter 1
Review Questions

1. forensic science
2. Mathieu Orfila
3. Alphonse Bertillion; anthropometry
4. Sherlock Holmes
5. Edmond Locard; Locard's exchange principle
6. Hans Gross
7. True
8. Dr. Leone Lattes
9. Albert S. Osborn
10. Sir Alec Jeffreys
11. True
12. Los Angeles
13. California
14. federal; state; county; municipal
15. regional
16. FBI; Drug Enforcement Administration; Bureau of Alcohol, Tobacco, Firearms, and Explosives; U.S. Postal Inspection Service
17. trace evidence
18. biological
19. firearms
20. document examination unit
21. toxicological
22. crime scene investigation
23. False
24. *Frye* v. *United States*
25. *Daubert* v. *Merrell Dow Pharmaceuticals*
26. False
27. *Coppolino* v. *State*
28. expert witness
29. True
30. True
31. training

Application and Critical Thinking

1. There are a range of possible answers to this question. Under the British fee-for-service model, government budgets might limit the number and type of laboratory tests police and prosecutors may request. On the other hand, if they must pay fees for crime lab services, police and prosecutors may be more careful about the types of evidence they submit. The fact that the U.S. model allows investigators to submit a theoretically unlimited amount of evidence for examination means that it might encourage police to spend more time and resources than necessary to investigate a case. Under a fee-for-service model, police must be more efficient in their investigations. However, this can be a drawback in cases in which initial tests prove inconclusive and more extensive methods of examination are needed.

2. The note would be examined by the document examination unit; the revolver would be examined by both the firearms unit and the latent fingerprint unit; the traces of skin and blood would be examined by the biology unit.

3. Again, this question could have several answers, which might include greater expertise in crime-scene investigation, using the skills of experts in several areas of criminalistics and reducing the workload of patrol officers.

4. On appeal, the defense raised the question of whether a new test that has not been generally accepted by the scientific community is admissible as evidence in court. The court rejected the appeal, arguing that "general acceptance," as stated in *Frye* v. *United States,* is not an absolute prerequisite to the admissibility of scientific evidence.

Chapter 2
Review Questions

1. True
2. first officer
3. medical assistance
4. excluded
5. False
6. log
7. False
8. primary; secondary
9. command center
10. systematic
11. physical evidence
12. False
13. fingerprints
14. True
15. False
16. final survey
17. False

Application and Critical Thinking

1. While waiting for backup, you should summon medical assistance for the victim, take a statement from the victim, detain any suspects at the scene, establish the boundaries of the crime scene, and ensure no unauthorized personnel enter the crime scene.

2. a. grid or line search
   b. quadrant (zone) search
   c. spiral or line search

3. Officer Walter made a mistake by opening the window and airing out the house. He should have kept the window closed until an investigation team arrived. From the lack of blood or evidence of a struggle, he concluded that the murder occurred somewhere else and that the room containing the body was a secondary scene.

Case Analysis

1. The first challenge investigators faced was destruction of evidence. Mexican authorities autopsied the bodies twice before the corpses had been inspected, which likely destroyed potentially helpful evidence. Authorities also prevented forensic scientists from examining the corpses until the bodies had decomposed significantly. Mexican police removed all of the obvious evidence from the residence where the victims were held before allowing the FBI forensic team to enter the scene. Mexican authorities later seized a license plate hidden at the scene and would not allow FBI agents to examine it or to conduct any further searches of the property. In addition, for "health reasons," Mexican authorities destroyed much of the evidence that had been collected from the crime scene.

2. The second challenge was contamination of crime scenes linked to the murders. The location where the bodies were discovered was not sealed by police, thus allowing both police officers and onlookers to contaminate the scene. Also, the residence at 881 Lope De Vega, where the victims were believed to have been killed, was cleaned and painted before forensics experts had an opportunity to examine it. In addition, Mexican federal police officers had been living in the residence since shortly after the time of the murders, further contaminating the scene.

3. Investigators collected reference samples of carpeting from the victims' bodies, as well as bits of the victims' clothing and the sheets in which the bodies were buried. The carpet samples matched samples taken from the residence at 881 Lope De Vega, where investigators suspected the victims were killed. The samples of burial sheet matched pillowcases found at the residence, and bits of clothing matching that worn by the victims were also found at the residence. In addition, hair and blood samples matching those of the victims were found in the residence at 881 Lope De Vega.

4. Investigators found that soil samples from the victims' bodies did not match the soil from the area where the bodies were found. They also found no significant bodily fluids in the area where the bodies were found. This evidence suggested that the bodies had originally been buried elsewhere and later transported to the location where they were found. Investigators later compared soil samples from the victims' bodies to samples taken from a park where the bodies of two Americans killed by drug traffickers had been discovered. Soil samples from the bodies of Camarena and Zavala exactly matched the soil found at the location where the Americans' bodies were found.

Chapter 3
Review Questions

1. notes; photography; sketches
2. True

3. first responding officer
4. False
5. notes
6. False
7. False
8. single lens reflex (SLR)
9. True
10. aperture
11. shutter speed
12. depth of field
13. False
14. electronic strobe flash
15. True
16. large
17. microchip
18. False
19. barrier
20. photography log
21. unaltered
22. True
23. overview; medium range; close-up
24. False
25. 90°
26. painting with light
27. True
28. arson
29. True
30. False
31. False
32. standard operating procedures
33. videotaping
34. rough
35. rectangular; triangulation; baseline; polar coordinates
36. False
37. finished sketch
38. computer-aided drafting

Application and Critical Thinking

1. a. macro lens
   b. normal lens
   c. wide-angle lens
2. a. bypass filter
   b. complementary color filter
   c. barrier filter
3. a. infrared film
   b. tungsten film
   c. low-speed film

Chapter 4
Review Questions

1. physical evidence
2. True

3. mobile crime laboratories
4. carriers
5. True
6. fingernail
7. True
8. False
9. separate
10. False
11. False
12. False
13. druggist fold
14. disposable
15. paper
16. contamination
17. air-dried
18. chain of custody
19. True
20. standard/reference
21. buccal swabs
22. substrate controls
23. True
24. evidence submission
25. infectious
26. biohazard
27. False
28. warrantless
29. arson

Application and Critical Thinking

1. Officer Guajardo should not have removed the scrap of cloth until the photographer had arrived and taken a picture of the evidence. He also should have put on latex gloves or used a forceps or other tool to remove the scrap of cloth. Finally, he should have placed the cloth in a paper bag or other container in which air could circulate, rather than in a sealed plastic bag where moisture could accumulate and cause mold to grow on the cloth.
2. Officer Gurney should have recorded his initials on the original seal, along with the date on which the evidence was sealed. The forensic scientist should have avoided breaking the old seal. The forensic scientist also should not have discarded the old seal.
3. Missing elements are the time, description of the crime, and measurements of the scene.

Chapter 5
Review Questions

1. identification
2. exclude
3. comparative
4. probability
5. individual
6. class

7. True
8. personal experience
9. eyewitness
10. corroborate
11. weight
12. True
13. False
14. False
15. natural variations
16. experience
17. False
18. Combined DNA Index System (CODIS)
19. forensic pathology
20. autopsy
21. victim's clothing; fingernail scrapings; head and pubic hairs; blood; vaginal, anal, and oral swabs; recovered bullets; hand swabs for GSR
22. rigor mortis; livor mortis; algor mortis
23. ocular
24. forensic anthropology
25. pelvic
26. facial reconstruction
27. False
28. True
29. sketch
30. forensic entomology
31. postmortem
32. temperature
33. True

Application and Critical Thinking

1. Determining whether an unknown substance contains heroin would require the least extensive testing because the investigator can select only procedures that are designed to identify the presence of heroin. Determining whether an unknown substance contains an illicit drug would require the next most extensive testing regime because the investigator must select as many procedures as necessary to test for all types of illicit drugs. Determining the composition of an unknown substance would likely require the most extensive testing because of the extremely large number of possible substances to test for.
2. From most common to least common, the order would be a, c, and b.
3. a. class characteristic
   b. individual characteristic
   c. individual characteristic
   d. class characteristic
   e. individual characteristic
   f. class characteristic
   g. individual characteristic
   h. individual characteristic
4. PDQ and SICAR contain information that relates primarily to evidence exhibiting class characteristics. The

paint finishes and sole prints in these databases can identify the manufacturer of a shoe or paint mixture but cannot determine the exact source of evidence that matches the samples stored in the database. CODIS, IAFIS, and NIBIN, on the other hand, contain information that relates primarily to evidence exhibiting individual characteristics. The DNA profiles, fingerprints, and striation markings stored in these databases are unique, and thus can be used to link specific individuals or weapons with a crime scene.

5. An investigator would likely collect standard/reference samples of hair, fibers, and blood because these items are most likely to have been transferred from the perpetrator to the victim, and vice-versa, during a long struggle.

6. Rigor mortis would be an unsuitable method if the victim had been dead longer than 36 hours because the condition disappears after this time. Livor mortis ceases 12 hours after death, so it would be of limited value in estimating time of death after this period had elapsed. Algor mortis would not be an accurate method for estimating time of death if the body was stored in a particularly hot or cold environment because extreme temperatures would affect that rate at which the body lost heat.

7. a. a forensic entymologist
   b. a forensic odontologist
   c. a forensic anthropologist

Case Analysis

1. The primary aspects of the rail noted by Koehler were the presence of nail holes, the general condition of the wood, and the quality of the lumber used to make the rail. The nail holes were not made during the construction of the ladder, which indicates that the wood had been used for another purpose before being made into a ladder rail. The fact that the holes were clean and free of rust suggested that the wood was used inside and not exposed to the elements. The spacing of the nail holes suggested that the wood likely was used in a barn, garage, or attic. The wood itself was also in good shape and not weathered, further confirming that it was used indoors. The lumber was of a poor quality, indicating that it would have been used for rough construction (such as a floor or wall joist) and not finished work (such as a doorframe or decorative trim).

2. Koehler found notches in surfaces and on the edges of the ladder rails that were caused by a defect in the cutting heads of the planer used to finish the wood. By measuring the distance between the notches, Koehler was able to calculate the speed at which the rails passed through the planer. His calculations showed that surfaces and edges of the wood moved through the planer at different speeds. This difference in speed told Koehler that the planer was belt-driven. Information about the speed and type of the planer helped narrow down the number of lumber mills that could possibly have produced the wood.

3. Koehler reasoned that, because the wood was inexpensive, it would not be profitable to ship it very far from where it was milled. Because the ladder was found in New Jersey, Koehler believed it must have been milled somewhere in the Atlantic States region. This information helped narrow the number of possible mills to those along the Atlantic coast. When authorities contacted these mills, they found only a handful that used planers of the type and speed used to mill the ladder rails. When the investigators asked for samples of wood from these mills, they found a sample that had the same notches as found on the ladder rails. This enabled the investigators to pinpoint the mill that produced the wood.

4. Koehler found marks on the wood that were made by a hand planer. He discovered that these marks were comparable to those made by a hand planer found at Hauptmann's house. In addition, investigators found that a section of board had been sawed out of the floor joists in Hauptmann's attic. The nail holes in the ladder rail aligned perfectly with the nail holes in the floor joists. Also, the grain pattern of the wood used in the rail was an exact match with the grain pattern in the remaining portion of the floor joist that had been cut to make the ladder. These facts clearly connected Hauptmann with the ladder used in the kidnapping.

Chapter 6
Review Questions

1. crime scene reconstruction
2. criminalists
3. objectivity
4. False
5. False
6. inductive; deductive
7. circumstantial evidence
8. falsifiability
9. bifurcation
10. False
11. false linkage
12. True
13. physical evidence
14. direct physical evidence
15. testimonial evidence
16. reenactment
17. chain of custody
18. True
19. False
20. theories
21. True
22. event timeline

Application and Critical Thinking

1. a. generalization
   b. false linkage
   c. bifurcation

2. The only direct physical evidence that connects the acquaintance to the crime scene is his fingerprint on the knife. The ticket stub constitutes circumstantial evidence to connect the acquaintance to the scene; there is no proof that it belonged to the acquaintance. Based on direct physical evidence and deductive reasoning only, you can

conclude that the acquaintance had at some time handled the knife found at the crime scene. Using circumstantial evidence and inductive reasoning, you might conclude that there is a probability that the acquaintance murdered the victim with the knife, but there also exists a probability that the acquaintance touched the knife at another time. You also might conclude that there is a probability that the acquaintance bought a ticket to the movie to give himself an alibi for his whereabouts at the time of the crime and dropped the stub at the crime scene. You may also conclude that there is a probability that the victim or another individual purchased the ticket.

Chapter 7
Review Questions

1. Alphonse Bertillion
2. anthropometry
3. Sir Francis Galton
4. Sir Edward Richard Henry
5. True
6. Federal Bureau of Investigation (FBI)
7. 64 billion
8. False
9. ridge characteristics/minutiae
10. fingerprints
11. dermal papillae
12. latent
13. dermal papillae
14. True
15. loops; whorls; arches
16. loop
17. arch
18. radial
19. type lines
20. delta
21. False
22. core
23. two; one
24. plain whorl
25. plain arch
26. False
27. whorl
28. 1/1
29. False
30. True
31. minutiae
32. livescan
33. visible fingerprint
34. plastic
35. powder
36. chemical
37. iodine
38. ninhydrin
39. physical developer
40. False
41. Super Glue fuming
42. fluorescence
43. alternate light sources
44. photography
45. lifting

Application and Critical Thinking

1. a. whorl
   b. arch
   c. loop
   d. whorl
   e. whorl
   f. arch
2. The primary classification for this individual would be as follows:

$$\frac{0 + 8 + 4 + 0 + 1}{16 + 8 + 0 + 2 + 1}$$

Thus, the classification would be 13/27.
3. a. chemicals
   b. powder
   c. powder
   d. chemicals
   e. chemicals
4. a. scaling and resizing
   b. spatial filtering
   c. frequency analysis, or frequency Fourier transform (FFT)

Chapter 8
Review Questions

1. handguns; long
2. single-shot; revolver; semi-automatic
3. revolver
4. shot
5. choke
6. land
7. caliber
8. True
9. individual
10. comparison microscope
11. striations
12. False
13. smooth
14. gauge
15. False
16. True
17. NIBIN
18. True
19. False
20. 12; 18
21. bullet wipe

22. yard
23. infrared
24. True
25. primer
26. barium; antimony
27. False
28. scanning electron microscope
29. True
30. False
31. base; nose
32. False
33. False
34. gunpowder residue
35. tool mark
36. striations
37. cast
38. electrostatic lifting device
39. photography; casting
40. individual

Application and Critical Thinking

1. a. 18–36 inches
   b. more than 36 inches
   c. 12–18 inches or less
   d. 1 inch or less

2. The correct answer is (a), 18 yards. A 12-gauge shotgun with no choke would be expected to produce a spread of about 1 inch for each yard from the shooter to the target. Thus, a spread of 12 inches would represent a distance of about 12 yards. A moderately high choke, however, would narrow the spread of the pattern somewhat. This means that, at a distance of 12 yards, the spread would be less than 12 inches. At a distance of 6 yards, the spread would be much less than 12 inches. Answers (b) and (c), therefore, are incorrect. The distance in answer (d), 30 yards, is probably too far. Although the choke would narrow the spread of the pellets, it would probably not narrow it to such a great extent.

3. Ben made several errors. Before unloading the revolver, Ben should have indicated the chamber position in line with the barrel by scratching a mark on the cylinder. He then should have made a diagram of the gun, designating each chamber with a number. As he removed each cartridge, he should have marked it to correspond to the numbered chambers in the diagram. Ben also should have placed each cartridge in a separate envelope and he should have put the tag on the trigger guard, not the grip. Instead of using pliers to grab the bullet and pull it from the wall, Ben should have carefully broken away the surrounding wall material while avoiding direct contact with the bullet. Finally, he should have wrapped the bullet in tissue paper before placing it in an envelope.

4. a. Photograph the print.
   b. Photograph the tool mark, then make a cast of it.
   c. Photograph the tire marks, then make a cast of them.
   d. Photograph the shoe print, then bring the tile bearing the print to the laboratory.
   e. Photograph the print, then use an electrostatic lifting device to lift it off the surface.

Chapter 9
Review Questions

1. bloodstain patterns
2. control experiments
3. victims; suspects
4. True
5. increases
6. directionality; angle of impact
7. circular
8. width; length
9. impact spatter
10. False
11. low velocity; medium velocity; high velocity
12. False
13. area of convergence
14. area of origin
15. string
16. transfer pattern
17. lightens
18. True
19. True
20. pool
21. skeletonize
22. castoff
23. False
24. arterial spray spatter
25. trail
26. expired blood
27. void
28. True
29. grid method
30. perimeter ruler method
31. True

Application and Critical Thinking

1. a. Drops 1, 5, and 8 struck the surface closest to a 90-degree angle; they are the most nearly circular in shape.
   b. Drops 3, 4, and 9 struck the surface farthest from a 90-degree angle; their shapes are the most elongated.
   c. Drop 2 was traveling right to left and drop was 7 traveling from bottom to top when they struck the surface. The tails of the drops point in the direction of travel.

2. Investigator Wright should conclude that the bullet did not exit the body.

3. The tiny droplets and linear pattern suggest that the weapon used in the assault was likely a small, pointed instrument, such as a knife.

Chapter 10
Review Questions

1. drug
2. True
3. False
4. physical
5. True
6. False
7. regular
8. analgesics; depressive
9. opium
10. heroin
11. OxyContin
12. True
13. hallucinogens
14. hashish
15. THC
16. True
17. liquid hashish
18. lysergic acid
19. clandestine
20. True
21. barbiturates
22. True
23. methaqualone
24. antipsychotic; antianxiety
25. False
26. stimulants
27. cocaine
28. sniffed/snorted
29. False
30. GHB; Rohypnol
31. anabolic
32. five
33. I
34. IV
35. False
36. Marquis
37. marijuana
38. Scott
39. microcrystalline
40. thin layer chromatography
41. False
42. wavelength
43. dispersion
44. True
45. electromagnetic spectrum
46. lower
47. can
48. ultraviolet; visible
49. infrared
50. spectrophotometry; spectrophotometer
51. gas chromatography
52. mass spectrometer
53. mass spectrometry
54. True

Application and Critical Thinking

1. The drug used by the individual was probably amphetamine, cocaine, or phencyclidine. All of these drugs produce psychological dependence, which would explain the individual's behavior, but none are known to produce physical dependence that would cause sickness or physical discomfort.
2. a. depressants; examples include alcohol, barbiturates, and tranquilizers
   b. hallucinogens; examples include marijuana, LSD, PCP, and MDMA (Ecstasy)
   c. stimulants; examples include amphetamines, methamphetamine, and cocaine
   d. narcotics; examples include heroin, morphine, codeine, and synthetic opiates such as OxyContin and methadone
3. a. schedule III
   b. schedule V
   c. schedule II
   d. schedule I
4. A screening test performed for heroin is the Marquis color test. If the powder tests positive for heroin, you would conduct confirmation tests, including mass spectrometry or IR spectrophotometry.
5. a. phenobarbital
   b. butabarbital
   c. three minutes

Chapter 11
Review Questions

1. toxicologist
2. False
3. ethyl alcohol
4. metabolism
5. faster
6. oxidation; excretion
7. liver
8. breath
9. 0.015
10. False
11. True
12. thirty; ninety
13. artery; vein
14. pulmonary
15. alveoli
16. 2,100
17. False
18. False
19. infrared

20. fuel cell
21. fifteen; twenty
22. True
23. gas chromatography
24. nonalcoholic
25. True
26. 0.08
27. four
28. *Schmerber* v. *California*
29. morphine
30. blood; urine
31. acids; bases
32. False
33. pH
34. screening; confirmation
35. thin-layer chromatography; gas chromatography; immunoassay
36. gas chromatography; mass spectrometry
37. hair
38. carbon monoxide
39. False
40. True
41. corroborate
42. drug recognition expert

Application and Critical Thinking

1. a. Randy is four times as likely to have an accident as a sober person.
   b. Marissa's blood-alcohol concentration is approximately 0.13.
   c. Charles is more intoxicated; his blood-alcohol concentration is approximately 0.11.
   d. At the original NHTSA standard of 0.15, an individual is about 25 times more likely to have an accident than is a sober person.

2. John, Gary, Frank, Stephen

3. Bill and Carrie are both legally drunk in Australia and Sweden. Sally is legally drunk in Sweden. Rich is legally drunk in all three countries.

4. Barbiturates are acidic drugs, which means they have a pH less than 7. You can use this knowledge to devise a simple test to determine which blood sample contains barbiturates. First, dissolve blood from each sample into separate containers of water. To each container add an acidic substance such as hydrochloric acid (to make the water more acidic). Then add an organic solvent such as chloroform to the water in each container. The blood sample containing barbiturates will be easily identified because acidic drugs are readily removed from an acidic solution with an organic solvent.

5. To determine whether the victim died before or as the result of the fire, measure the level of carbon monoxide in the victim's blood. High levels of carbon monoxide in the victim's blood indicate that he or she breathed the ombustion products of the fire and was therefore alive when the fire

started. Low levels of carbon monoxide indicate that the victim did not breathe the combustion products of the fire and was therefore dead before the fire started.

Chapter 12
Review Questions

1. hair follicle
2. cuticle; cortex; medulla
3. cuticle
4. cortex
5. medulla
6. medullary index
7. one-third; one-half
8. True
9. True
10. anagen; catagen; telogen
11. True
12. True
13. comparison
14. pubic
15. True
16. False
17. True
18. DNA
19. anagen; catagen
20. 50
21. 24
22. origin
23. natural fibers
24. cotton
25. regenerated
26. synthetic
27. False
28. polymers
29. monomer
30. proteins
31. True
32. visible
33. thin-layer
34. infrared
35. False
36. False
37. carriers

Application and Critical Thinking

1. a. telogen phase
   b. anagen phase
   c. anagen phase
   d. catagen phase

2. Because hair grows at a rate of about 1 centimeter per month, we know that the hair was dyed approximately six weeks earlier.

3. a. Caucasian
    b. Mongoloid
    c. Negroid
    d. Caucasian
4. Pete made several mistakes. First, he should have packaged all items of clothing containing fiber evidence in paper, not plastic. Second, he should have placed each individual piece of fiber evidence in a separate container. Third, he should have carefully folded the sheet before packaging it, rather than simply balling it up. Fourth, he should have used a forceps, rather than his fingers, to collect fibers from the windowsill. Finally, he should have folded the fibers from the windowsill inside a piece of paper and then placed it in another container, not into a regular envelope.

Case Analysis

1. The Williams case was notable for the fact that fiber evidence was used to tie a large number of murder victims to a single suspect. Also, fiber evidence is typically used to support other evidence and testimony in court. In the Williams trial, the fiber evidence was the centerpiece of the state's case and other testimony was used to support the fiber evidence.
2. Investigators hoped to learn the source of the fibers. To do this, they studied the fibers under a microscope and photographed the fibers' cross-sectional shape. The investigators then showed the photographs to chemists and textiles experts to see if they could identify the likely source of the fibers. The investigators learned that a yellowish-green fiber was probably from a carpet but that its shape was not common. The fact that the fiber was relatively rare meant that it probably was not widely used. This significantly reduced the number of possible locations where the murders could have occurred, making it easier for investigators to focus their search for a suspect.
3. Information about the source of the fiber could help investigators determine where the crime might have occurred, which could lead them to a suspect. If investigators know who produced the item from which the fibers came, they can contact the manufacturer and get a list of local stores or individuals who purchased the item before the crime occurred. Interviews with the purchasers may provide investigators with leads to suspects or other information that can help them solve the case.
4. Investigators found that the company produced a carpet using the same rare type of fiber in the same color as that found on Cater's body and in Williams' home. This meant that there was at least a probable connection between Williams and Cater. Investigators also learned that the company used that type of fiber in their carpets for only one year. This significantly narrowed the number of places where such carpeting might be found. During the year the carpet was manufactured using the rare fiber, only a small amount was sold in the southeastern United States. This further narrowed the possible number of rooms in Georgia in which the carpet could have been installed. The extremely small number of possible locations where the carpet could be found in the Atlanta area meant that there could be very few likely suspects besides Williams.

5. The investigators used probability to connect the fibers found on Nathaniel Cater's body and Williams' home. By demonstrating that there was an extremely low probability that the fibers came from any place except Williams' home and car, prosecutors were able to tie Williams to Cater's murder. Investigators also used probability to tie fibers and hairs found on other Atlanta-area murder victims to Williams. Prosecutors showed that each of the victims' bodies contained traces of fibers matching those found in Williams' home and cars and/or hair belonging to Williams' dog. They pointed out that there was an extremely low probability of finding so many matching fibers and hairs on several different individuals. The only reasonable explanation, they argued, was that all the victims had contact with a common source of the fibers and hairs, namely Williams.

Chapter 13
Review Questions

1. pigment
2. binder
3. True
4. stereoscopic
5. layer structure
6. layer structure
7. True
8. pyrogram
9. Paint Data Query (PDQ)
10. True
11. glass
12. False
13. tempered
14. laminated
15. individual
16. density; refractive index
17. floatation
18. Becke line
19. frequency of occurrence
20. radial
21. concentric
22. False
23. False
24. opposite
25. False
26. terminate
27. solid
28. paper
29. False
30. dried
31. minerals
32. True
33. 100
34. False

Application and Critical Thinking

1. In a hit-and-run situation, you would collect from each vehicle standard/reference samples that include all the paint layers down to the bare metal. This is best accomplished by removing a painted section with a clean scalpel or knife blade. Standard/reference samples should be collected from an undamaged area of each vehicle because other portions of the car may have faded or been repainted. To avoid cross-contamination of paints, carefully wipe the blade of any knife or scraping tool used before collecting each sample.

2. Windows on U.S.-built cars use laminated glass in their windshields and tempered glass for all other windows. From this evidence, the investigator knows that the other car involved in the accident has a broken side window, with its windshield intact.

3. Because the cracks from bullet holes A and C both terminate at the cracks from bullet hole B, bullet hole B was made first. Because the cracks from bullet hole C also terminate at the cracks from bullet hole A, bullet hole A was made second. Thus, bullet hole C was the last to be made.

4. If this is a radial fracture, the force was applied from the left side of the glass. If it is a concentric fracture, the force was applied from the right side of the glass. The 3R rule states that *Radial* cracks form a *Right* angle on the *Reverse* side of the force. The cracks in the picture form a right angle on the right side of the glass, so if it is a radial fracture, the force was applied to the reverse (left) side of the glass.

5. Jared made several mistakes. First, the samples he removed from the scene should have included only the top layer of soil. Second, he should have collected soil samples from both alibi locations—the garden and the parking lot. Third, he should have packaged the shoes in paper, not plastic. Finally, he should have dried all of the soil samples under identical laboratory conditions before examining any of them.

Case Analysis

1. The primary challenge facing the investigators in this case was linking the female victim's body to the suspect's van.

2. Items of evidence that directly linked the victim to the suspect included paint chips; Caucasian head hairs from the victim's blazer that were consistent in microscopic characteristics to the defendant's known head hair sample; and a forcibly removed, brown Caucasian head hair that was found to be consistent in all characteristics with the decedent's known head hair sample. Items that indirectly linked the two were the white seeds found in both the victim's mouth and the van, a chemically treated head hair found on the victim that was consistent in microscopic characteristics to the known head hair sample obtained from the defendant's wife, and brown/white-colored dog hair from the victim's clothing and the van's interior that was found to be consistent with the hair from a dog belonging to the suspect's nephew.

3. Blue- and black-colored flakes of acrylic paint found on the victim's clothing matched similar flakes found in the van's sweepings. During a search of the defendant's residence in New Jersey, a large quantity of blue- and black-colored acrylic paint was found in the garage. The blue and black paint flakes from all the sources and the known blue (undercoat) and black (topcoat) paint from the van were compared and found to be consistent in every respect. The presence of matching paint flakes on the victim's clothing showed that she had been inside the van at some time after she was killed. This indicated that she had been shot at the garage at the same time as the other three victims and later transported to the alley where her body was found.

Chapter 14
Review Questions

1. type
2. True
3. plasma
4. serum
5. red blood cells
6. antigens
7. A
8. False
9. A; B
10. Rh
11. antibodies
12. False
13. agglutination
14. B; A
15. True
16. A
17. B
18. antibodies
19. benzidine
20. Kastle-Meyer
21. luminol
22. precipitin
23. gel diffusion
24. acid phosphatase
25. spermatozoa
26. True
27. prostate specific antigen (PSA)/ p30
28. True
29. True
30. gene
31. chromosome
32. 23
33. alleles
34. homozygous
35. nucleotide
36. four
37. double helix
38. A-C-G-T
39. True
40. polymerase chain reaction (PCR)
41. short tandem repeats (STRs)

42. False
43. polymerase chain reaction (PCR)
44. multiplexing
45. capillary electrophoresis
46. True
47. mother
48. False
49. CODIS (Combined DNA Index System)
50. 18
51. infectious
52. False
53. False
54. EDTA

Application and Critical Thinking

1. Scott chose the acid phosphatase test because it is extremely useful in searching for semen on large areas of fabric, such as a blanket. He concluded that the blanket did not contain evidence of semen. First, he knew that certain fruit juices, including watermelon, can generate a positive reaction with acid phosphatase testing. However, these juices react much more slowly to the test than does semen. A reaction time of less than 30 seconds is considered a strong indication of semen. Because it took 3 minutes to obtain a positive reaction, Scott concluded that the positive reaction was caused by the watermelon.

2. Cathy made four mistakes in collecting evidence. First, she should have placed a paper sheet over the sheet on which the victim disrobed in order to collect any loose material that may have fallen from the victim or the clothing. Second, she should have placed each item of clothing in a separate bag instead of placing all of them in the same bag. Third, she should have taken two additional vaginal swabs, smearing them onto microscope slides. Finally, she should have collected fingernail scrapings from the victim.

3. G–C–T–T–A–G–C–G–T–T–A–G–C–T–G–G–A–C

4. You would first collect any blood or skin scrapings under the victim's fingernails because they may contain DNA. You would then amplify the DNA in the sample using PCR and separate the fragments using electrophoresis. Finally, you would look for the bands of separated DNA that correspond to the amelogenin gene. If the sample contains two bands, the attacker is male; if the sample contains only one band, the attacker is female.

5. Investigators use mtDNA to determine whether the body is that of the victim of the unsolved murder. To do so, you would collect mtDNA from one of the victim's maternal relatives and compare it to the mtDNA recovered from the body. If the samples match, the body is that of the victim.

6. With an STR, you should expect to see a two-band pattern. The presence of more than two bands suggests a mixture of DNA from more than one source.

Chapter 15
Review Questions

1. oxidation
2. False
3. energy
4. chemical; heat; mechanical
5. breaking; formation
6. absorb; liberate
7. exothermic
8. heat of combustion
9. endothermic
10. True
11. ignition power
12. gaseous
13. flash point
14. pyrolysis
15. flammable range
16. glowing combustion
17. True
18. spontaneous combustion
19. heat
20. conduction
21. radiation
22. True
23. origin
24. True
25. vapor
26. False
27. airtight
28. True
29. Molotov cocktail
30. headspace
31. gas chromatograph
32. False
33. True
34. mass spectrometer

Application and Critical Thinking

1. a. radiation
   b. conduction
   c. convection
   d. radiation

2. You should suspect arson. Although the conditions in which the oil was stored—high heat and lack of ventilation—may lead to spontaneous combustion with some materials, spontaneous combustion does not occur with hydrocarbon lubricating oils such as motor oil. The owner is lying about the oil igniting spontaneously; he may have deliberately set the fire to collect on the increased insurance.

3. Mick made several mistakes. First, he should have used separate containers for each location where debris was collected. Debris should have come from the point of origin of the fire, not from the surrounding rooms. He should not have placed the timbers in plastic bags, which react with hydrocarbons and permit volatile hydrocarbon vapors to be depleted. Finally, Mick should have collected the suspect's clothes to undergo laboratory analysis for the presence of accelerant residues.

Chapter 16
Review Questions

1. explosion
2. True
3. low
4. deflagration
5. potassium nitrate, charcoal, and sulfur
6. high
7. black powder; smokeless powder
8. confined
9. False
10. primary; secondary
11. nitroglycerin
12. True
13. RDX
14. PETN
15. initiating
16. crater
17. collection
18. ion mobility spectrometer
19. microscopic
20. acetone
21. color spot tests; thin-layer chromatography (TLC); and gas chromatography/mass spectrometry
22. True
23. False

Application and Critical Thinking

1. a. High explosives. Lead azide is a common component of blasting caps, which are used to detonate high explosives.

    b. Low explosives. Nitrocellulose is an ingredient in smokeless powder, one of the most common low explosives.

    c. High explosives. Ammonium nitrate is the primary ingredient in a number of high explosives that have replaced dynamite for industrial uses.

    d. High explosives. Primacord is used to as a detonator to ignite several high-explosive charges simultaneously.

    e. Low explosives. Potassium chlorate mixed with sugar is a popular low explosive.

2. a. Alcoholic KOH. Tetryl is the only explosive that produces a red-violet color in response to this test.

    b. Alcoholic KOH. TNT produces a distinctive red color in response to the alcoholic KOH test.

    c. Diphenylamine produces a blue color. No color is produced in response to the Greiss test or to the alcoholic KOH test.

    d. Diphenylamine. Nitrocellulose produces a distinctive blue-black color in response to this test.

3. Matt made several mistakes. First, to avoid contaminating the scene, Matt should have put on disposable gloves, shoe covers, and overalls before beginning his search.

Second, he should have used a wire mesh screen to sift through the debris instead of picking through it by hand. Third, he should have stored all explosive evidence in airtight metal containers, not plastic or paper bags. Fourth, Matt should have collected material from not only the immediate area of the blast, but also from materials blown away from the blast's origin.

Chapter 17
Review Questions

1. questioned document
2. True
3. False
4. known; questioned
5. False
6. style
7. exemplars
8. less
9. False
10. *Gilbert* v. *California*
11. False
12. conscious
13. ten
14. transmitting terminal identifier (TTI)
15. toner
16. individual
17. ultraviolet; infrared
18. infrared
19. infrared
20. True
21. charred
22. indented
23. microspectrophotometer
24. thin-layer
25. True

Application and Critical Thinking

1. Julie made several mistakes. She should have given the suspect a pencil, not a pen, because the original notes were written in pencil. She should have had the suspect prepare at least a full page of writing, and she should have had him write the material at least three times. Also, she should not have spelled any words for the suspect. Finally, Julie should have shown the original threatening notes to a document examiner before taking exemplars from the suspect, not afterward.

2. a. Photograph the document with infrared-sensitive film.

    b. Examine the document under infrared or ultraviolet lighting.

    c. Examine the document under ultraviolet lighting.

    d. Photograph the document with infrared-sensitive film, or reflect light off the paper's surface at different angles in order to contrast the writing against the charred background.

3. The aspects of the document you would examine to determine whether the document was authentic would be the paper and the ink. You would use thin-layer chromatography to characterize the dye used in the ink to determine whether that particular ink was in use when the original document was prepared.

Chapter 18
Review Questions

1. preserving; acquiring; extracting; analyzing; interpreting
2. True
3. software
4. motherboard
5. central processing unit (CPU)
6. ROM; RAM
7. partition
8. hard disc drive
9. permanent
10. sectors; clusters; tracks; cylinders
11. bit
12. byte
13. cluster
14. visible
15. False
16. latent
17. temporary
18. sector
19. RAM; file
20. RAM
21. unallocated space
22. True
23. True

Application and Critical Thinking

1. Because each sector is 512 bytes, a cluster consisting of 6 sectors would hold 3,072 bytes of data. Because each byte equals 8 bits, each cluster would hold 24,576 bits of data.
2. Tom made several mistakes. When he arrived, he should have sketched the overall layout as well as photographing it. He also should have photographed any running monitors. In addition to labeling the cord of each peripheral, Tom should have placed a corresponding label on the port to which each cord was connected. Before unplugging the computer, he should have checked to ensure that the computer was not using encryption. Finally, he should have removed the plug from the back of the computer, not from the wall.
3. You probably would begin to search for latent data in the swap space on the hard disk drive. If the accountant was keeping fraudulent records, he may have been transferring data from one accounting program to another. Data from those operations will be left behind in the swap space, where it can be retrieved later.

Case Analysis 1

1. By examining Mr. Smith's computer, police hoped to prove that he had changed his wife's insurance policy shortly before the fire in which she died. They believed this would implicate him in his wife's murder because the increased insurance settlement Mr. Smith would receive upon his wife's death would serve as a strong motive for murdering her.
2. The documents titled *insurance1.doc* and *WRL1604.tmp* were important to tying Mr. Smith to his wife's death because they proved that he wrote the letter to his insurance company requesting an increase in his wife's life insurance.

Case Analysis 2

1. The physical evidence that most strongly implicated the driver of the van in a counterfeiting operation was the discovery of two $100 bills in his wallet. These suspicions were confirmed by the fact that both bills had identical serial numbers.
2. The documents titled *GapGiftCert1.jpg* and *GapGiftCert2.jpg* indicated that the suspects were producing more than counterfeit currency. From these files, the investigators concluded that the suspects were also producing counterfeit gift certificates to The Gap.

Chapter 19
Review Questions

1. network
2. modem
3. domain
4. World Wide Web
5. True
6. True
7. search engine
8. False
9. internet protocol address
10. cache
11. cookie
12. IP
13. True
14. log files; volatile memory; network traffic
15. firewalls

Application and Critical Thinking

1. a. .com
   b. .mil
   c. .org
   d. .gov
   e. .edu
2. On the first computer you probably would look first at the compound files created by Microsoft Outlook. On the second computer you probably would look first in the Internet cache.

Index